PERSONALITY THEORIES

FOURTH EDITION

PERSONALITY THEORIES
An Introduction

BARBARA ENGLER
Union County College

Houghton Mifflin Company   **Boston**   **Toronto**
Geneva, Illinois / Palo Alto / Princeton, New Jersey

To my sons, Ted and Bill

Sponsoring Editor: Rebecca J. Dudley
Editorial Assistant: Dana Arnaboldi
Senior Associate Editor: Jane Knetzger
Senior Project Editor: Janet Young
Editorial Assistant: Marybeth Griffin
Senior Manufacturing Coordinator: Marie Barnes

Cover Designer: Harold Burch, Harold Burch Design, New York City

Photo Credits

p. 4: Mickey Ansin; *p. 30:* Courtesy of the Library of Congress; *p. 43:* Elizabeth Crews; *p. 74:* Karsh of Ottawa/Woodfin Camp and Associates; *p. 81:* John Lei/Stock Boston; *p. 98:* Historical Pictures Service, Chicago; *p. 105:* Jerry Berndt/Stock Boston; *p. 118:* Culver Pictures; *p. 120:* Deborah Kahn Kalas/Stock Boston; *p. 136:* Rene Burri/Magnum Photos; *p. 144:* John Blaustein/Woodfin Camp and Associates; *p. 155:* The Bettmann Archive; *p. 156:* Courtesy of

(Continued on page 525)

Printed in the U.S.A.

Library of Congress Catalog Card Number: 94–76501

ISBN: Student Copy 0-395-70835-4
Complimentary Examination Copy 0-395-71710-8

6789-DH-98 97 96

CONTENTS

PART 1: The Psychoanalytic Approach   27

PART 2: The Neopsychoanalytic Approach   71

PART 3: More Recent Trends in Psychoanalysis   151

7 More Recent Psychoanalytic Theorists: Anna Freud, Heinz Hartmann, Erik Erikson, Margaret Mahler, Heinz Kohut, Otto Kernberg, and Nancy Chodorow   152

THINKING CRITICALLY BOXES

PHILOSOPHICAL ASSUMPTIONS BOXES

PREFACE

Personality Theories: An Introduction, Fourth Edition, is designed both to explain the major personality theories and to stimulate critical thinking about them. In developing the Fourth Edition, I have pursued four main objectives.

To present a clear and concise picture of the major features of each important personality theory   I have strived to present the material in an accessible style and, wherever possible, to illustrate theoretical points with concrete examples. I have presented each theory succinctly, to allow for adequate coverage of all the theories. The structure of the text itself is also clear and concise: each chapter focuses on one theory or group of related theories. Brief biographies of the theorists shed light on how they formed their theories.

To focus on significant ideas and themes that structure the content of the different personality theories   I regularly compare the different theories to outline the distinctive characteristics and contributions of each theory and to emphasize significant ideas around which the theories are structured. Because many theories have elaborated on, modified, or refuted psychoanalysis, I have devoted substantial space to Freudian theory, providing the reader with a focal point from which comparisons and contrasts may be made.

To provide criteria to guide the evaluation of each theory   Many of the theories that influence contemporary thought did not develop from strict scientific methods but instead reflect philosophical assumptions. In addition, the application of a theory to a real-life situation such as psychotherapy is a creative act, demonstrating that a personality theory may function as an art. Therefore, the evaluation of a personality theory is best accomplished when the theory is broken down into its component parts — philosophy, science, and art — and judged according to the criteria appropriate to each function. Two features in each chapter — the "Philosophy, Science, and Art" sections and the "Philosophical Assumptions" scale — refer the student back to the basic philosophical assumptions introduced in Chapter 1, relating the parts back to the whole and drawing attention to significant ideas that have generated the structure and content of personality theories. The "Conclusion" at the end of the text wraps up the evaluation discussion.

To present activities, informed by the tenets of each theory, that will provide growth in critical thinking skills   Effective learning is not a passive process; it requires active participation. The fourth objective is accomplished through "Thinking Critically" boxes that provide activities designed to stimulate and foster critical thinking skills. Such boxes, first introduced in the Third Edition, have proven to be very popular. Many of these activities are new; others have been carefully reviewed, revised, and augmented to emphasize more clearly cultural diversity and a postmodern world view.

Features of the Book

Important and effective pedagogical aids continue in the Fourth Edition. To help students read with a sense of purpose and review important points quickly, each chapter begins with a list of "Your Goals for This Chapter" and ends with a "Summary" whose items are keyed to each goal. Key terms and concepts are boldfaced within the text, and a glossary at the back of the book provides definitions. Every chapter includes a list of "Suggestions for Further Reading."

A number of Thinking Critically activities appear in each chapter. These boxes ask the student to return to material that has been presented in the chapter and reconsider it or apply it critically. A list of Thinking Critically activities can be found on pages xvii–xviii.

The discussion of each theorist is accompanied by a Philosophical Assumptions scale, in which students can compare and contrast their own philosophical views with those of the theorist. A list of Philosophical Assumptions boxes can be found on page xix.

New to the Fourth Edition

I have revised the book in response to developments in the field of personality psychology and to feedback from instructors and students who used the previous edition. In addition to updating the text throughout, I have made several significant changes. Every chapter reflects increased coverage of multicultural, feminist, and postmodern concerns. A new Chapter 16 features the cognitive-behavioral theories of Albert Ellis, Aaron Beck, and Arnold Lazarus. A heavily revised Chapter 7 emphasizes the work of object relations theorists, with expanded coverage of Margaret Mahler and Heinz Kohut and the addition of Otto

Kernberg and Nancy Chodorow. In addition, Chapter 11 has been expanded to include Costa and McCrae's Big Five Personality Trait theory and more coverage of Buss and Plomin's temperament theory. Finally, the chapter on Zen Buddhism has been completely reconceived.

Further highlights of the changes in the book, by chapter, include:

Chapter 1

• New emphasis on a postmodern world view, cultural diversity, and narrative thought as a primary form of cognition and understanding.

Chapter 2

• Updating of the bibliographic material and the story of Anna O. in light of more current information.
• Renewed appreciation of Freud's emphasis on biological and cognitive factors as means of understanding development and gender.
• Addition of denial to the defense mechanisms.
• Reference to the dilemmas Freud faced when his observations did not fit his theory.
• Recognition that Freud's work reflects the cultural and social values of Western Europe and North America.

Chapter 3

• Appreciation of Jung's emphasis on the importance of a psychology of cultural difference.

Chapter 4

• Addition of Adler's four primary types of life-style.
• New information on assessment and research in Adler's theory.
• Appreciation of the crosscultural significance of Adler's concept of social interest.
• Recognition of a resurgence of interest in Adler's theory.

Chapter 5

• Addition of Horney's description of American hypercompetitiveness.
• New Thinking Critically box, "Hypercompetitiveness in American Society."
• New Thinking Critically box, "Basic Orientations and Mistaken Life-styles."
• New discussion of and new Thinking Critically box on "The Tyranny of the Should."
• Discussion of four prerequisites for good decision making, followed by a new Thinking Critically box, "Decision Making."

Chapter 6

• New passage on what Fromm might think about the new global economy and the rapid pace of change.

Chapter 7

- A reorganization that covers the following theorists in this order: Anna Freud, Heinz Hartmann, Erik Erikson, Margaret Mahler, Heinz Kohut, Otto Kernberg, and Nancy Chodorow.
- In the Erikson section, extensive revision of the Thinking Critically box "Generativity."
- New discussion of empirical research on Erikson's theory.
- New introduction to the object relations theorists.
- New discussion of research on Mahler's theory.
- Expanded treatment of Kohut.
- Entirely new sections on Otto Kernberg and Nancy Chodorow.
- New Thinking Critically boxes, "Culturally Sanctioned Mutilation" and "Shared Parenting."

Chapter 8

- Recognition that in the last decade, to increase productivity, American businesses have returned to more punitive measures instead of using the type of positive reinforcement that Skinner advocated.
- Recognition that survival of the species may depend on our ability to use scientific forecasts to change cultural practices.

Chapter 9

- In the Bandura section, extensive updating and a new Thinking Critically box, "Filmed Violence."
- In the Rotter section, considerably updated research on locus of control.

Chapter 10

- In the Allport section, brief discussion of what Allport called a "doing" aspect of personality.
- In the Allport section, new discussion and a new Thinking Critically box, "Traits Due to Victimization."
- In the Murray section, new information from Robinson's 1992 biography.
- In the Murray section, discussion of how diverse cultures and eras foster the development of different needs.

Chapter 11

- New material on research on Eysenck's theory.
- Expanded treatment of Buss and Plomin's theory.
- New Thinking Critically box, "Personality Traits That Have Appeared in Families Throughout the Generations."
- New section, "Other Biological and Genetic Research."
- New section, "The Big Five Personality Traits."

Chapter 12

- In reference to Rogers, new information on social cognition and external influences on one's construction of reality.
- New Thinking Critically box, "External Influences on One's Construction of Reality."

Chapter 13

- New material treating possible differences and similarities between Western and Eastern views of how people can realize their potential.
- New Thinking Critically box, "Do We Need a New Concept of Maturity?"

Chapter 14

- Chapter on Rollo May repositioned to follow the humanistic theories of Carl Rogers and Abraham Maslow.
- Brief reference to Victor Frankl and logotherapy.
- New discussion of the importance of myths.
- New Thinking Critically box, "The Myth That Surrounds Your Birth."

Chapter 15

- Chapter on George Kelly moved to group him with the cognitive-behavioral theories of Albert Ellis, Aaron Beck, and Arnold Lazarus.
- Brief mention of how Kelly's theory avoids the limitation of radical individualism and enriches our understanding of sociocultural processes by emphasizing shared social construction of reality.

Chapter 16

- Entirely new chapter on the cognitive-behavioral theories and therapies of Albert Ellis, Aaron Beck, and Arnold Lazarus.

Chapter 17

- Chapter on Zen Buddhism completely rewritten to portray Zen Buddhism more accurately in light of the Fourth Edition's emphasis on cultural diversity.

Conclusion

- New information on signs of change: the emphasis on narrative form, the introduction of values, an emphasis on cultural diversity, and a possible reconceptualization of psychology.

Ancillaries

The text is accompanied by an *Instructor's Resource Manual with Test Items*. The *Instructor's Resource Manual* begins with a transition guide for current users and an essay on teaching methods that foster critical thinking skills, providing some guidelines for both novice and experienced instructors. Then, for each chapter of the text, the *Instructor's Resource Manual* includes 35 multiple-choice questions; 15 fill-in-the-blank questions; 10 to 20 essay questions linked to items in the text's Goals and Summary lists; and two "Challengers," essay questions that encourage students to think critically about topics related to material in the chapter. A computerized version of the manual allows instructors to generate exams and integrate their own test questions with those on disk.

Acknowledgments

Because I teach at a community college where teaching is emphasized over research and writing, and because I recently assumed the role of director of the honors program at Union County College, I was under a great deal of pressure during the past year both to do my job at the college and to complete the Fourth Edition. This edition would not have been possible without the help of two very special people. Yōzan Dirk Mosig, Ph.D., a professor of psychology who has practiced Zen Buddhism for a considerable amount of time, wrote the first draft of the newly conceived chapter on Zen Buddhism. The original draft that Yōzan prepared was considerably longer and had to be cut due to space limitations. Professors using the book can receive a complimentary copy of the full draft by writing to Dr. Mosig, c/o Psychology Department, University of Nebraska at Kearney, Kearney, NE 68849. He has also offered to answer any questions that readers may have on the material. Nancymarie Bride, Ph.D., a certified clinical mental health counselor in private practice in Westfield, New Jersey, and a close personal friend, gave me a great deal of information, some of which I was able to use verbatim, on Albert Ellis, Aaron Beck, and Arnold Lazarus for the new chapter on those theorists.

Once again, I would like to thank my colleagues and students at Union County College for their interest, support, and constructive comments regarding the text and its revision — in particular, Donna Lawless, our reference librarian, who patiently fulfilled my every request for interlibrary loans of books and articles. I am also grateful to the following reviewers who thoughtfully evaluated the manuscript or provided prerevision advice:

Andrew M. Barclay, Michigan State University
Dorothy Bianco, Rhode Island College
C. George Boeree, Shippensburg University
Joan B. Cannon, University of Massachusetts — Lowell
Joseph Horvat, Weber State University
Risetta Jacobs, Union County College
Igor van Krogten, University of Amsterdam
Monte M. Page, University of Nebraska — Lincoln

David R. Peterson, Mount Senario College
Stephen D. Slane, Cleveland State University
Jane Wells, National University

Dr. Mosig would like to acknowledge the helpful suggestions of Hōgen Berman, who read the Zen chapter.

    Finally, I would like to thank the following people at Houghton Mifflin who assisted in the development of the Fourth Edition: Dana Arnaboldi, Mike De-Rocco, Becky Dudley, Fran Gay, Jane Knetzger, LuAnn Belmonte Paladino, and Janet Young.

Barbara Engler

PERSONALITY THEORIES

CHAPTER 1

Introduction: Evaluating Personality Theories

1. Explain why the term *personality* is difficult to define.
2. Define the term *theory*.
3. Discuss the role of personality theory in psychology.
4. Describe three functions of personality theories.
5. Explain how to recognize *philosophical assumptions*.
6. Identify some of the basic philosophical issues on which personality theorists differ.
7. Explain how philosophical assumptions are evaluated.
8. Explain how science has its basis in *philosophy*.
9. Explain the characteristics of *scientific statements*.
10. Explain how scientific statements are evaluated and describe how scientists decide between rival hypotheses.
11. Describe two major techniques of assessing personality and three primary research approaches used in personality.
12. Identify three major goals of *psychotherapy* and indicate the criteria of evaluation suitable for each goal.
13. Explain why it is important to distinguish among the different functions of personality theories.

A definition for the word "personality" would be a good way to begin a book that considers various theories of personality. However, writing a definition is not that simple. A complete search for such a definition takes us back to the early history of the human race, back to the time when the first person asked, "Who am I?" thereby reflecting on his or her identity. The different answers that people have given to that question have found expression throughout history in various cultural constructs such as philosophy, religion, art, politics, and science. Each one of us begins the search anew; as children seeking identity, and later as adults reflecting upon our identity, we wonder who we are and join fellow travelers on the road in search of the self.

What Is Personality?

Although the term **personality** is frequently used, it is not easy to define. In common speech, it usually refers to one's public image. Thus people say, "Becky has a terrific personality!" or "If only Jeff had a more dynamic personality." This common usage reflects the origin of the word "personality" in the Latin *persona,* which referred to the masks that actors wore in ancient Greek plays. In the Greek theatre, there were often more roles in a play than there were actors. Thus an actor would change "masks" to let the audience know a different role was being assumed. Such a concept of social role, however, does not include the complications that are involved in the long search to understand the self.

There is little common agreement among personality theorists on appropriate use of the term personality. Gordon Allport described and classified over fifty different definitions. For Allport, personality was something *real* within an individual that leads to characteristic behavior and thought. For Carl Rogers, another personality theorist, the personality or "self" was an organized, consistent pattern of perception of the "I" or "me" that lies at the heart of an individual's experiences. For B. F. Skinner, possibly the most well known American psychologist, the word "personality" was unnecessary. Skinner did not believe that it was necessary or desirable to use a concept such as self or personality to understand human behavior. For Sigmund Freud, the father of contemporary psychoanalysis, personality was largely unconscious, hidden, and unknown.

Each theorist presents us with his or her own understanding of the term personality. In part, this helps to explain why there are so many different personality theories. Although such a variety of definitions and theories may be confusing, and even disturbing, it does not mean that the theories are not useful. Each offers insight into the question of the self and each can be helpful to us as we develop our own answers.

In the Greek theater, an actor would change masks to let the audience know that a different role was being assumed. Contemporary actors often play very diverse roles representing different personalities.

What Is a Theory?

Since we are referring to theories of personality, the next question is "What is a theory?" Here you may be pleased to see that there is a more definitive answer. The term "theory" comes from the Greek word *theōria*, which refers to the act of viewing, contemplating, or thinking about something. A **theory** is a set of abstract concepts about a group of facts or events to explain them. A theory of personality, therefore, is an organized system of beliefs that helps us to understand human nature.

Describing a theory as a system of beliefs underscores the fact that a theory is something that we create in the process of viewing and thinking about our world. Theories are not given or necessitated by nature; rather, they are constructed by people in their efforts to understand the world. The same data or experiences can be accounted for in many different ways and people of varying cultures and backgrounds construct a wide variety of explanations. As we shall see, there are many theories of personality.

The Role of Personality Theory in Psychology

Because personality addresses that important question "Who am I?", you might imagine that personality is the primary emphasis of psychology. In fact, personality is not the dominant concern in contemporary psychology, it is simply one area of specialization.

The question "What is personality?" takes us back to early human history. Awareness about the self and the world probably existed *before* deliberate reflection, philosophy, and science. In time, as people began to reflect on their ideas, philosophy developed as a mode of understanding and expression. As psychology found expression in the philosophies of Plato and Aristotle, it sought to clarify the essence of a human being and explore what it means to be a person.

By the late nineteenth century the scientific revolution had made great strides in comprehending the physical world and people were eager to apply scientific methods to the study of human beings. Modern-day psychology emerged from a combination of various movements in philosophy and science. In 1879, Wilhelm Wundt (1832–1920) established the first psychological laboratory at the University of Leipzig in Germany to explore the experience of consciousness. By combining careful measurement with *introspection,* or self-examination, Wundt sought to reveal the basic elements and structure of the conscious mind. The psychologist could thereby emulate the natural scientist who had been successful in identifying the basic elements of the physical world.

Wundt was successful in establishing a meticulous, systematic method of study based on the experimental method. However, his emphasis on conscious experience was criticized in the 1920s by John Watson (1878–1958), who came to be known as the father of American behaviorism. Watson recommended that in order to be a science, psychology emphasize the study of overt rather than covert behavior. *Overt* behaviors are those that we can observe directly, such as bodily movements, speaking, and crying. *Covert* behaviors are those that only the individual who experiences them can directly observe, such as thoughts, feelings, and wishes. Watson's recommendation created a curious situation for psychology. Much of what psychologists had traditionally talked about, including Wundt's research, concerned covert phenomena.

Watson pointed out that it is virtually impossible to observe mental processes directly. Therefore, he suggested that the psychologist should act as if mental processes did not exist and simply concentrate on overt behavior. While few psychologists today agree with Watson's extreme view, the behaviorist position that he generated became the dominant movement in American psychology throughout most of the twentieth century. Watson was succeeded as leader of the movement by B. F. Skinner, who took the behaviorist position to its logical extreme. Because of Skinner's influence, students of psychology rapidly discovered that, for the most part, they were not engaged in the study of the person, but in the study of behavior (usually of rats and pigeons). They were encouraged to adopt a rigorous scientific methodology that emphasized extrospective observation, or looking outward. B. F. Skinner's theory will be discussed in greater detail in Chapter 8.

Today, psychologists are very interested in the mental processes shunned by Watson and Skinner. Indeed, one current trend is toward cognitive psychology, which emphasizes how people receive, process, and react to information from their environment. On the other hand, psychology has retained from the behaviorists an emphasis on rigorous methodology emphasizing extrospective observation.

Not all of the personality theorists that we will consider agree that a rigorous scientific method is the best way to understand personality. In fact, the first theories of personality developed outside the mainstream of academic experimental psychology. While Wundt was at work in his laboratory at Leipzig, Sigmund Freud (1856–1939), who was *not* a psychologist but rather a neurologist and physician in private practice in Vienna, was employing introspection somewhat differently in his treatment of patients who were suffering from emotional problems. Instead of using introspection only to examine present phenomena, Freud also taught his patients to employ it retrospectively to examine past experiences. Thus Freud was able to examine phenomena that could not be elicited in a laboratory. Freud found introspection to be a valuable tool for discovering and exploring unconscious processes. On the basis of his clinical observations, Freud developed psychoanalysis and a theory of personality, which will be discussed in Chapter 2. Freud's method was far different from the experimental laboratory research that characterizes much of psychology today.

Some of Freud's followers became dissatisfied with orthodox psychoanalysis and founded their own schools of thought. Although these theorists were all deeply indebted to Freud, they reacted in varying ways against his theory and developed their own positions. Since the study of personality became a formal and systematic area of scientific specialization in American psychology in the mid-1930s, some psychologists have recommended that all research in personality be conducted and evaluated along strict scientific guidelines as defined by mainstream academic psychology. Nevertheless, the study of personality is the heir of two different approaches: academic psychology and clinical practice. These traditions have never fully merged (Boneau, 1992). Examples of each, and other traditions as well, will be found in the theories discussed in this book.

The Evaluation of Personality Theories

As we have seen, personality theory is not simply an expression of psychology as a science. Before the study of personality became a specialization of academic scientific psychology, questions of personality were generally included under the broader umbrella of philosophy. Many of the personality theories we will explore resemble philosophical investigations rather than scientific studies. The methods of science and philosophy are distinguishable but not unrelated. Science is an offspring of philosophy and its methods are the fruit of philosophy's labors. The specific mode of study and investigation characteristic of a modern scientist arose out of an earlier philosophical encounter with the world and retained many of its requirements. Science further demanded that theories be empirically validated, or ultimately based on sensory experience.

If scientific theories of personality have their origin in philosophy, they also lead to some form of art, or practical application. The art of personality theory is much older than the science or even the philosophy of it; from earliest times, much has been spoken and written about how to live a good life and understand people. As science has developed, however, it has provided us with new knowledge, tools, and methods of self-understanding and improvement. Theories of personality are not just armchair speculations, but belief systems that find expression in ways that are designed to help us understand and improve ourselves and the world.

Philosophy, science, and art may be seen as three complementary activities that personality theorists engage in. As scientists, personality theorists hope to develop a workable set of hypotheses that will help us understand human behavior; as philosophers, they seek to explore what it means to be a person; as artists, they seek to apply what is known about people and behavior to foster a better life. Each activity is conducted according to certain rules with its own criteria for success. Just as potential athletes need to become familiar with the rules, equipment, and scoring of whatever sport they wish to engage in, students of personality need to become familiar with the different rules governing the activities of personality theorists. You will have difficulty understanding a personality theory unless you can identify the particular activity that the theorist is engaged in at a particular time and know how to evaluate it. By briefly exploring the activities of philosophy, science, and art, a foundation for understanding personality theories and evaluating them may be created.

Philosophical Assumptions

No psychologist or personality theorist can avoid being a philosopher of sorts. As we have seen, the science of personality theorizing has its origins in philosophy. The very act of theorizing, or thinking about what we see, entails making certain assumptions about the world and human nature. All people — not only personality theorists — hold basic **philosophical assumptions** as they reflect on the world and their own existence. These basic philosophical assumptions profoundly influence the way in which we perceive the world and theorize about it.

The term **philosophy** comes from the Greek *philein,* "to love," and *sophia,* "wisdom"; it means the love or pursuit of wisdom. Each one of us is a philosopher insofar as we think and reflect about the world and ourselves. The search after wisdom, however, involves more than a desire for information to counter our ignorance. Wisdom denotes not merely knowing about something but knowing what ought to be done and how to do it. As philosophers, we make assumptions and judgments about the good life and how to live it.

Traditionally, philosophy has encompassed five types of language and study: logic, aesthetics, ethics, politics, and metaphysics. *Logic* is the study of correct or normative reasoning; it describes the ideal method of making inferences and drawing conclusions. *Aesthetics* is the study of ideal forms and beauty; it deals with the nature of the beautiful and with judgments about beauty. *Ethics* is the study of ideal conduct; it deals with the knowledge of good and evil. *Politics* is the study of ideal social organization; it describes those forms of social and political structures that are most appropriate for human beings. *Metaphysics* is the study of ultimate reality; it attempts to coordinate what is real in the light of what is ideal.

Very few of us have complete and articulate stances on each of these issues. Yet, insofar as our thoughts, statements, and theorizing reflect one or more of these concerns, we can be sure that they are informed by certain basic philosophical assumptions. In the same sense, very few, if any, of the personality theorists whom we will consider aim at developing complete philosophical pictures of ourselves and the world. Most consider themselves psychologists rather than philosophers. Nevertheless, in their psychologizing they raise philosophical issues and, in doing so, reflect philosophical assumptions.

Recognizing Philosophical Assumptions

To introduce the nature and character of philosophical assumptions would take us far afield and belongs more properly in philosophy textbooks. However, it is important to recognize that personality theories do entail philosophical assumptions and to identify them when they occur.

The discourses of philosophy frequently posit a distinction between what is and what ought to be. People do not always think logically, nor do they behave in ideal ways. Philosophical statements suggest that things are not necessarily what they appear to be. *What is* is not necessarily *what should be.* For instance, the fact that many people are aggressive does not necessarily mean that aggression is right or that aggression represents what it means to be human.

Philosophical knowledge is ultimately in the form of an **epiphany** (from the Greek *epiphaneia,* which means "appearance" or "manifestation"), or a sudden perception of essential meaning. The "seeing" of philosophy is a special act of knowing, an extraordinary intuition that transcends everyday experience. Philosophical assumptions, therefore, differ from *empirical statements,* which are based on ordinary observation. The statement "All people seek what is good," for example, does not refer to something that can be seen in everyday observation. This statement refers to some kind of ultimate reality that is perceived in a different way.

Scientific statements also often refer to things that we cannot see in ordinary observation. Many important constructs in science involve imaginary con-

cepts that cannot be seen. However, statements in sc
if indirectly, based on empirical observation and their me
from those of philosophy.

The difference between scientific statements and philo
tions lies in the nature of the observation that gives rise to the
the way in which it is tested. In science, all statements must be op
cation. In fact, science is required to indicate the conditions under
statements might be proven incorrect. If an exception is found to a sc
generalization, that generalization must be qualified. On the other hand, p
osophical assumptions are not tentative hypotheses to be discarded when ev
dence contradicts them. There is no way to construct an empirical test that
would let us falsify a philosophical assumption. If I maintain a philosophy that
"All people seek what is good," I will not permit any ordinary observations to
disprove the assumption. On the contrary, I can account for all exceptions and
seeming contradictions in terms of my assumption itself.

Philosophical assumptions may be *explicit* or *implicit*. It is often difficult to
identify a person's assumptions when they are not stated clearly. Nevertheless, almost everyone takes a stand on certain fundamental philosophical assumptions
that deeply influence one's way of perceiving and understanding the world.

Identifying Basic Philosophical Assumptions

Many of the differences among personality theories can be attributed to fundamental differences in philosophical assumptions. Some of the issues on
which personality theories commonly disagree are described below. Each issue
is presented here as a bipolar dimension. Some theorists may be seen as agreeing
with one or the other extreme. Others are neutral toward the issue or seek a
synthesis.

Freedom versus determinism. Theorists vary as to whether they believe that
people basically have control over their behaviors and understand the motives behind them or whether they believe that the behavior of people is
basically determined by internal or external forces over which they have
little, if any, control.

Hereditary versus environmental. Theorists differ over whether inherited and
inborn characteristics or factors in the environment have the more important influence on a person's behavior.

Uniqueness versus universality. Some theorists believe that each individual is
unique and cannot be compared with others. Others contend that people
are basically very similar in nature.

Proactive versus reactive. Proactive theories view human beings as acting on
their initiative rather than simply reacting. The sources of behavior are perceived as lying within the individual, who does more than just react to
stimuli from the outside world.

Do significant changes in personality and be-
e course of a lifetime? If an individual is moti-
be effected in personality? Can we help others
their environment? Some personality theories
stic and hopeful than others concerning these

Assumptions

ies described in this book represent philosoph-
entific investigations. Some of the theories are
ers, the philosophical assumptions are not
rtheless present. Carl Rogers openly acknowl-
was philosophical and that his primary differ-
h as B. F. Skinner, were philosophical ones.
ed of his work as lacking any philosophy but
many admitted that many of his assumptions functioned philosophically. Because personality theories and our own thoughts involve philosophical assumptions, it is important that we recognize and evaluate them as such.

In empirical science, as we shall see, statements are proven false by the
process of perceptual observation. Philosophical assumptions have criteria that
are suitable to the epiphanic vision that underlies them. In evaluating a person's
assumptions, we cannot set up a crucial test or experiment that will determine
whether or not the hypothesis is justified. Philosophical assumptions have their
own criteria or tests.

We are going to suggest three criteria for evaluating the philosophical assumptions that underlie personality theories. These three criteria add up to a
fourth and final criterion: compellingness.

The first criterion is **coherence.** Are the philosophical assumptions of a personality theory clear, logical, and consistent or are they riddled with contradictions and inconsistencies? A philosophical system may have apparent inconsistencies, perplexing metaphors, or paradoxes and still be coherent, provided that
the contradictions are ironed out within the philosophical stance itself so that
the final position represents a clear, coherent whole. A person's philosophical
system may also be unfinished, that is, open to further growth, but to be coherent it must have a clearly recognizable, consistent thrust.

The second criterion is **relevance.** To be meaningful, a philosophical assumption must have some bearing on our view of reality. If we do not share the
same view of reality we will have considerable difficulty judging the assumption. In our postmodern world, the criterion of relevance further implies the
need to be compatible with empirical reality as best we can ascertain it; thus,
philosophies are invariably reshaped by scientific discoveries.

The third criterion is **comprehensiveness.** Is the philosophical assumption
"deep" enough? In part, this question refers to scope. Does it cover what it
intends to cover? Further, the criterion of comprehensiveness asks whether the
treatment of the subject is profound or superficial. A philosophical assumption

is superficial if it leaves too many questions unanswered or if it refuses to address them.

These three criteria lead to the final criterion, **compellingness.** The final and most important question is "Does the assumption and its underlying philosophy convince you?" A philosophical assumption convinces you if it grabs you in such a way that you find the belief inescapable. It is as if you *have* to believe in it. Actually, it is perfectly possible that a philosophical assumption may strike you as being coherent, relevant, and comprehensive, but in spite of those features it does not compel you to believe it. In such a case, the belief does not move you and you cannot "buy" it. My language here deliberately describes you as passive: "The philosophical assumption grabs you." "You are compelled." This language underscores the fact that philosophical assumptions are not merely subjective opinions that a person has about the world. Rather, philosophical assumptions emerge out of a person's encounter with the world. They entail an active meeting of the person and the world that leads to a position about reality that the person finds inescapable.

The way in which philosophers create their views of the world is similar to, although more formal than, the manner in which each one of us comes up with our own view. We may not have thought as much or written about it, but each one of us, upon reflection, can probably think of a significant incident or period in our lives when we experienced something that led us to think about ourselves and our world in a different way. For example, after an illness or accident an individual often perceives life as having a new mission or purpose that was not present there before. Such experiences constitute the formative insights that shape our lives.

During the second half of the twentieth century, we have moved from a modern view of the world to a postmodern one in which truth is no longer easily attainable and the world is seen as more chaotic (Furedy, 1990; Gergen, 1990; Kvale, 1990; Levin, 1991; Shotter, 1990).

This change in worldview raises a special challenge as we move to develop more globally relevant, multiculturally sensitive explanations appropriate for the twenty-first century. Our reconstructions of the past reveal an ethnocentric Western view of personhood (Hermans, Kempen, & Van Loon, 1992) that cannot be seen as innocent. The postmodern paradigm sees reality not as given to us but as constructed by and among us (Sampson, 1991).

Scientific Statements

As scientists, personality theorists seek to develop a workable set of hypotheses, or tentative assumptions, that will help us understand human behavior. Scientists confirm their hypotheses by testing them according to generally agreed-upon methods. Thus, science, which comes from the Latin *scire,* "to know," is a group of methods of acquiring knowledge that are based on certain principles.

PHILOSOPHICAL ASSUMPTIONS

Examining Your Own Philosophical Assumptions

By looking at your own philosophical assumptions, you can better prepare yourself to recognize them in the theories of others. Each basic issue is presented here as a bipolar dimension along which a person's view can be placed according to the degree of agreement with one or the other extreme. You can rate your own views on a scale from 1 to 5. On each issue, if you completely agree with the first statement, rate the issue with a number 1. If you completely agree with the second statement, rate the issue with a number 5. If you only moderately agree with either statement, a number 2 or 4 would best reflect your view. If you are neutral toward the issue or believe that the best position is a synthesis of the two extremes, rate the issue with a number 3.

The first time you go through the items, rate each issue according to your beliefs. The second time, consider each issue in terms of your actions, the way in which you generally behave.

When you have determined where you stand on each of these major issues, a comparison of your positions can help you assess the importance of these issues to your own understanding of personality. Those assumptions that you feel very strongly about and mark with a 1 or a 5 probably play a very important role in your personal philosophy. If you are not strongly committed to any particular issue, that issue is probably not as important in your thinking about personality.

You should note that even experts differ in their answers to the questions below. The different personality theorists that we shall discuss vary markedly in their position on each of these issues. Each adopts the position that appears most commendable or compelling. Throughout the text, you will be asked to return to these assumptions to consider the stance of specific theorists and to see how your attitudes toward certain theorists are related to your own stance on these five dimensions.

Would strongly agree	Would agree	Is neutral or believes in synthesis of both views	Would agree	Would strongly agree
1	**2**	**3**	**4**	**5**

freedom				**determinism**
People basically have control over their own behavior and understand the motives behind their behavior.				The behavior of people is basically determined by internal or external forces over which they have little, if any, control.

1	2	3	4	5

hereditary
Inherited and inborn
characteristics have the most
important influence on a person's
behavior.

environmental
Factors in the environment have
the most important influence on
a person's behavior.

1	2	3	4	5

uniqueness
Each individual is unique and
cannot be compared with others.

universality
People are basically very similar
in nature.

1	2	3	4	5

proactive
Human beings primarily act on
their own initiative.

reactive
Human beings primarily react to
stimuli from the outside world.

1	2	3	4	5

optimistic
Significant changes in personality
and behavior can occur
throughout the course of a
lifetime.

pessimistic
A person's personality and
behavior are essentially stable and
unchanging.

The Philosophical Basis of Science

Science has its origins in philosophy and, as such, it retains elements of its forebears. Thomas Kuhn, a physicist who has studied the history of science, points this out when he reminds us that the observation on which scientific activity is based is not fixed once and for all by the nature of the world and our sensory apparatus but depends on a prior paradigm (1970). A **paradigm** is a model or concept of the world that is shared by the members of a community and that governs their activities. Everyday observation and perception are shaped through education and subject to change over time. Your view of the world, for example, is very different from that of a person in ancient Greece or a member of an isolated primitive tribe. Indeed, without some sort of paradigm, we could not draw any conclusions from our observations at all.

Scientific statements, therefore, are statements about the world based on observations arising from currently accepted paradigms. The paradigms are not derived from scientific activity but exist prior to it. The scientific viewpoint that one *should* base conclusions on perceptions that can be shared by others rather than on private, intrinsically unique, perceptions is a value statement that is not mandated by our observations but chosen by the community of scientists as more useful.

Recognizing Scientific Statements

The keystone of science is empirical observation and the simplest kinds of statements in science are empirical statements, such as "There is a person in the room." To know whether or not an empirical statement is valid, an individual has to be shown evidence based on sensory data regarding what has been seen, heard, felt, smelled, or tasted.

Empirical statements may be based on objective data or subjective data. If someone reports, "I see a person," we can interpret the statement in two ways. The person may be saying, "I see a *person*" or "I *see* a person." In the first case, we are referring to the object of experience or **objective data.** In the second case, we are referring to an experience of seeing or **subjective data.** Both objective and subjective knowledge refer to empirical data. The difference between them lies in the position of the observer. In objective knowledge, the position is I-it: the self is looking outward on the world as object. In subjective knowledge, the position is I-me: the self is looking inward on its own experience as the object.

Reports that are concerned with the object of experience or extrospective data are relatively simply to verify. We merely indicate the conditions under which the observation may be repeated. If a second observer does not see the reported phenomenon, we suggest that the conditions were not clearly specified; for example, the observer looked for the person in the wrong room. Or we may suspect that the original observer has a distorted sense of perception. Repeated observations of the same phenomenon under specified conditions lead to **consensual validation** or agreement among observers.

Reports that are concerned with introspective or subjective phenomena are much more difficult to validate consensually. A certain piece of art may give one person much joy but fail to move someone else. This is because subjective phenomena often occur under complex conditions and are more difficult to describe than objective information. Repeating such subjective observations may require the second observer to undergo extensive training or other experiences in order to duplicate all of the conditions. Undoubtedly, one's joy on seeing a particular piece of art depends not simply on the art itself, but also on one's culture, mood, personal history, and so forth. Considerable effort is needed to duplicate these observations but it is not impossible (Tart, 1975).

Since reports that are concerned with subjective phenomena are much more difficult to validate, some psychologists have tended to ignore them and invest their efforts in extrospective or objective findings. As we saw, John Watson recommended that inasmuch as our thoughts, feelings, and wishes cannot be directly observed by another person, the psychologist should ignore them and concentrate on overt behaviors. Few psychologists today would agree with this extreme position. Most personality theorists emphasize that we need to be concerned with both subjective and objective data in order to understand behavior.

When a number of different instances of observation coincide, the scientist may make a generalization. A **scientific** (or **empirical**) **generalization** is a conclusion that something is true about many or all of the members of a certain class. Suppose I wanted to test the statement "All aggressive people are controlling." The evidence for this statement could be a number of facts about individual members of the class. I could observe this aggressive person, that aggressive person, and other aggressive persons. If all of them were also controlling, I might conclude that all aggressive people are controlling, even though I have not examined each and every aggressive person.

Because it is impossible for me to examine each and every aggressive person who has existed in the past or might exist in the present or future, I can never know for certain that my empirical generalization is true. Indeed, misleading stereotypes are the result of premature and unwise generalizations. As a scientist, the personality theorist must leave empirical generalizations open to possible falsification.

The scientist also uses **definitions**, statements that are true because of the way in which we have agreed to use words. Some words are easy to define clearly and precisely. Other words are harder to define and subject to more disagreement. To resolve this problem, the social scientist frequently tries to develop operational definitions. An **operational definition** specifies which behaviors are included in the concept. "Stress" might be operationally defined in terms of the rate of one's heartbeat and extent of one's perspiration as measured by polygraph apparatuses, which translate such bodily changes into a printed record. It frequently is difficult to reach agreement on suitable operational definitions, and at times an operational definition distorts or even misses the concept it is trying to describe. For example, "stress" can also be defined as a subjective feeling of intense anxiety. The value of operational definitions lies in giving us a common ground of reference. Nevertheless, some critics have argued that operational definitions as developed by psychologists in the 1930s and 1940s were based on a misunderstanding of an attitude first recommended by Percy Bridgeman, a physicist, in the 1920s. In spite of repeated refutations, including one by Bridgeman himself in the 1950s, current textbooks persist in singing their worth (Green, 1992).

The most important statements in science are based on scientific constructs. A scientist uses **scientific constructs**, which are imaginary or hypothetical and cannot be seen with the naked eye or even with sophisticated optical equipment, in order to explain what we observe. The building blocks of nature, protons, neutrons, and electrons, remain visibly elusive by direct observation, but are indirectly confirmed by their necessary existence in the construct. Today's atomic models require further inference to even smaller unseen particles such as quarks, leptons, and hadrons. The difficulty of not being directly observable does not imply nonexistence; rather it has provided for continual progress toward an understanding of what may be real. Another familiar hypothetical construct is that of IQ or intelligence quotient. The concept of IQ is an imaginary construct that is used to explain certain behaviors, namely, one's likelihood for academic success. Many of our concepts in science, in fact almost all of the important ones, cannot be directly seen; we can only know them through their effects.

Some Basic Scientific Constructs

Constructs such as trait, reinforcement, and self have been created in efforts to understand personality scientifically. The concept of **trait** refers to a determining tendency or predisposition to respond in a certain way. Examples of traits are emotional stability and introversion versus extroversion. Allport, Cattell, Buss, and Plomin make extensive use of trait constructs in their theories. The **self** is another useful construct for understanding personality that is present in many contemporary theories. In Carl Rogers's theory the self refers to those psychological processes that govern an individual's behavior. In Albert Bandura's theory the self is conceived more narrowly in terms of cognitive structures.

Indeed, some personality theorists conceive of the term "personality" itself as a scientific construct. Thus Cattell defines personality as "that which permits a prediction of what a person will do in a given situation." For Cattell, personality is an imaginary construct that permits us to explain and predict behavior. The scientific constructs of a personality theory tie together the empirical findings of that theory and suggest new relationships that will hold true under certain conditions.

Evaluating Scientific Statements

As we have pointed out, there is no one method of validating scientific statements. Personality theorists use a variety of techniques, some of which are very complicated, to evaluate their work. We will be looking at a number of these later in this chapter and in subsequent chapters when we discuss the specific assessment and research procedures used by different personality theorists. However, we can make some general comments about the validating techniques used by scientists.

Even though scientists may build elaborate theories referring to things that they cannot observe directly, they base their theories on perceptions of our sense organs. It is true that I cannot test the statement "John has an IQ of 110" in the same way that I can test the statement "There is a person in the room." I cannot simply look. The statement must be tested indirectly, but the test is still based on empirical observation, such as looking at John's performance on an IQ measuring device. Given the identical conditions, another person could be expected to share the same perceptions and draw the same conclusions. Scientific statements, therefore, are based on *what is* and *what occurs* in our everyday world as it appears to us through our sense organs.

Second, scientific statements must be *open to falsification.* As scientist, the personality theorist is required to indicate the conditions under which theoretical statements might be proven incorrect. If an exception is found to a scientific statement, that statement is considered to be false or in need of qualification. The generalization "All aggressive people are controlling," for example, is disproven by pointing to an aggressive person who is not controlling or qualified by indicating the conditions under which an aggressive person will not seek to control others. This helps us to understand why a scientist never claims that the information produced by scientific methods is ultimately true. Scientific hypotheses are tentative and need to be discarded when evidence contradicts them. Although scientific methods cannot be said to yield ultimate truth, they do provide a wealth of useful information to assist us in living in the everyday world. It is to our advantage, therefore, to act as if the conclusions from our scientific methods are true.

In the process of scientific investigations, the personality theorist frequently develops more than one hypothesis. Each one is examined in turn to rule out those that do not stand up under test conditions. Occasionally, the scientist is left with rival hypotheses. Given that both are sound hypotheses, how does the scientist decide between them? In general, three criteria have been used: compatibility, predictive power, and simplicity. Each of these criteria has advantages and limitations. **Compatibility** refers to the agreement of the hypothesis with previously well-established information. This criterion is a sensible one since it is a lot easier for us to accept a new hypothesis if it is consistent with findings in other areas. However, it should not be too rigidly applied. There are times in science when a new idea completely shatters earlier theories, forcing us to revise or reconsider them.

Predictive power refers to the range or scope of the statement. Scientists seek not only to explain the phenomena that we observe but also to predict and anticipate them. We have seen that, by being testable, a hypothesis is able to generate predictions about experiences that we could have if the hypothesis should turn out to be useful. The more predictions or consequences that we can infer from a hypothesis, the greater its range and usefulness in generating new ideas. On the other hand, too strict a reliance on this criterion may lead to the notion that the only value of a theory lies in the amount of research and predictions it generates. Some theories express their scope by integrating and encompassing ideas rather than by generating specific predictions and research projects.

The last criterion is **simplicity**. Explanations ought to be as simple as possible. If there is too rigid an emphasis on the criterion of simplicity, the hypothesis may fail to account for all of the complexity of human behavior. However, all other things being equal, the simplest explanation is best.

We should note that in its endeavor to be scientific, psychology and its theories of personality has been primarily Western and developed scientific methods under a paradigm informed by the West. Some of the personality theorists that we will cover (such as Jung, Fromm, Horney, Rogers, Maslow, and May), however, have argued that that paradigm frequently fostered *scientism,* or the exclusive reliance on a narrow conception of science, which is inappropriate for understanding human nature. Some of these, most notably Jung and Horney, have suggested that we turn to the East for a more balanced comprehension.

The Application of Personality Theories

If theories of personality have their origin in philosophy and seek to validate their constructs through scientific methods, they also culminate in some form of art or practical application. Personality theories have found application in many areas, such as assessment, research, and psychotherapy.

Assessment

The assessment of personality is a major area in the application of personality theories to everyday life. *Assessment* refers to evaluation or measurement. You have probably been touched by assessment to a greater degree than you realize. In education, for example, assessment is used to measure progress and evaluate learning disabilities. Psychologists in industries and organizations use assessment to assist in job placement. Prior to deciding a course of counseling, a clinician needs to assess the individual in order to evaluate the nature of his or her problem.

The wise and judicious use of appropriate assessment techniques can be invaluable in developing individual and group potential. An accurate understanding of one's limitations and potentialities is important for self-actualization. The point to remember, however, is that there is a distinction between a person's inclination to behave in a certain way and the fact of behaving in such a way. Many personality tests are accurate predictors, but they are not guarantees of certain behaviors. Furthermore, as scientific tools, they must remain open to falsification, and our use of them needs to reflect that fact.

Good techniques of assessment seek to fulfill four primary criteria: standardization, objectivity, reliability, and validity.

Standardization involves assuring uniform conditions and procedures for administering a test. Standardization also informs us of the distribution and variability of scores for a particular test. The process of standardization makes it possible for us to know whether an individual's score is high, low, or average.

Objectivity refers to the avoidance of subjective bias in assessment. If a procedure is objective, qualified administrators and scorers can present it in the same way to any particular subject and obtain the same score as other qualified examiners. Objectivity is easier to obtain if responses are clearly delineated, as in a multiple-choice or true-false test where each response clearly indicates a certain factor. It is more difficult, but nevertheless possible, to develop objective criteria for scoring protracted written or verbal responses. Such criteria provide for objectivity in evaluating interviews, written essays, projective techniques, and so forth.

Reliability refers to the consistency of scores over time. This is similar to an oven thermometer that must register the same degree each time for the same amount of heat in order to be a consistent and useful measuring device. If you were to take an alternative form of the same test on two separate occasions, the two scores should be similar.

Validity asks if an assessment technique measures what it is supposed to measure. Validity is the most important, yet most difficult, criterion of all to meet. Virtually all psychologists agree that certain recognized intelligence tests are valid measures for predicting school performance. They are not all certain, however, that these tests are valid measures of that elusive quality, "intelligence."

The personality theorists discussed in this book have developed specific ways of assessing personality that are informed by and also inform their theories. These procedures range from the interpretation of dreams to statistically sophisticated and elaborately constructed tests. We will discuss each theorist's particular method, but first some general words about two major approaches to assessing personality.

Psychometric Tests   Psychometric tests measure personality characteristics through carefully designed questionnaires developed with theoretical and statistical techniques. Psychometric testing had its origin in the psychological laboratories established at the end of the nineteenth century.

One of the most carefully researched questionnaires is the Minnesota Multiphasic Personality Inventory (MMPI), first published in 1942 and most recently revised in 1989. The MMPI is made up of over 550 self-report items or printed statements to which the subject answers "true," "false," or "cannot say." The MMPI is designed to measure tendencies toward pathology or abnormal behavior. The MMPI is employed as an aid in the diagnosis of psychiatric disorders and is widely used in personality research.

Psychometric measuring devices and techniques have not been used without controversy. Many individuals view such tests as an invasion of personal privacy and are wary of the use to which the test results may be put. Often the validity of the tests is assumed rather than demonstrated. On the basis of a "carefully designed" test, we might imagine a situation in which individuals could be imprisoned for life simply because of the high probability that they might commit murder. Such a situation may seem far-fetched, yet individuals are turned down for jobs or denied educational and other opportunities on the basis of such tests.

Projective Tests   Some psychologists, particularly in a clinical setting, also employ projective techniques. The subject is presented with a deliberately ambiguous stimulus. In responding to the stimulus the subject presumably will project personal attitudes, values, needs, and feelings.

One of the best-known projective techniques is the Thematic Apperception Test, developed by C. D. Morgan and H. A. Murray in 1935 as part of a Harvard Psychological Clinic research program. In this test, the subject is asked to make up stories for a series of ambiguous pictures. The Thematic Apperception Test will be discussed in detail in Chapter 10.

The main advantage of projective techniques is that they disguise the purpose of the test. Because the stimuli are ambiguous and the subject is free to respond in any way, it is difficult for the subject to know what would be an appropriate answer and fake a "correct" response. The difficulty with projective tests is that they are very hard to score in an objective manner that avoids subjective bias and the projection of the scorer.

Research

Personality theorists also differ widely in the type of research methods that they use. Some follow very strict scientific guidelines in their work. Others encourage the use of a wider range of acceptable methodologies, making use of interdisciplinary and eclectic approaches. Indeed, restraints on creative and productive research may occur when the area of personality inquiry is too narrowly demarcated (Duke, 1986). Three primary research approaches used in personality are the clinical approach, the correlational approach, and the experimental approach.

The Clinical Approach   Many of the personality theories that we will be considering originated in the clinical setting. The clinician conducts research through intensive interviews and observation of the subject. Clinical methods of research may also include the analysis of dreams and/or early memories. A clinician may further structure the observations by asking questions or giving one or more tests. Frequently there is considerable overlap between a theorist's methods of research and methods of assessment. A primary tool in the clinical approach to personality is the development of a *case history,* a carefully drawn biography of an individual. Sigmund Freud developed psychoanalytic theory largely on the basis of case histories (including his own).

Unlike most other research methods, the case history entails studying one individual or a small number of individuals in great depth rather than large numbers of subjects. Freud and Erik Erikson also developed case histories of prominent historical figures such as Michelangelo, Leonardo da Vinci, Martin Luther, and Gandhi.

The Correlational Approach In a correlational study, events or variables are carefully and systematically observed as they naturally occur to see the extent to which they covary, or occur together. Events that covary are said to be correlated. A correlation does not imply that one variable caused another; it simply indicates to what extent two events or variables occur together. For example, there is a high correlation between brown hair and brown eyes. This is not to say that brown hair causes brown eyes but rather that a great many people who have brown hair also have brown eyes. Nevertheless, where two variables have a high correlation it is reasonable to hypothesize that one caused the other, or that a third variable caused both.

The Experimental Approach An experimental approach is favored by many psychologists because it permits them to infer a cause and effect relationship between two factors. In its simplest form, a researcher systematically varies the presence of one factor, the *independent variable,* while keeping all other variables constant. The researcher can then determine whether or not the changes in the independent variable have any effect on a particular behavior, the *dependent variable.* If so, it is assumed that the changes in the independent variable caused the changes in the dependent variable. Experiments can be very complex, with several independent and dependent variables.

The experimental method is considered the most precise method of psychological research. It has the advantage of permitting the experimenter to posit a clear cause and effect relationship, but it has limitations. To limit the findings of personality to those that can be demonstrated only within the experimental laboratory would be to circumscribe the study of personality to merely those aspects about the person that can be studied by manipulation. Because of this, many questions about the ultimate meanings, purposes, and goals of human living, questions that traditionally have been and could be included in the study of personality, would be ruled out of inquiry. A wider range of acceptable methodologies is necessary (Atkins, 1990; Henwood & Pidgeon, 1992).

McAdams and Ochberg (1988) note a recent upsurge and focus on psychobiography and life narratives (forms of case histories), which suggests that "once again, it is okay to study the 'whole person.'" Sarbin (1986) suggests that narrative might be considered a root metaphor for understanding human behavior and experience. Narrative thought is emerging as a primary form of cognition and self-understanding that qualitatively varies from abstract proportional or scientific thinking (Mueller & Tingley, 1990) and further enables us to understand moral development (Packer, 1991; Freeman, 1991; Tappan 1991). The search for more effective and sensitive methodologies for studying the person continues (West, 1986). In general, the growing openness of personality theorists to more effective methods contrasts with the perpetuation by some other psychologists of a narrow view of science.

Psychotherapy

The art of **psychotherapy** is the effort to apply the findings of personality theory in ways that will assist individuals and meet human goals. The word *therapy* comes from the Greek *therapeia,* which means "attending" and "healing"; however, psychotherapists are not interested only in healing sick people. They are also interested in understanding "normal" people, learning how they function, and helping them to function more creatively. Although in many respects psychotherapy is the flowering of personality theory, it is also the seed of it, because the desire to help people has fostered and nourished the development of personality theories. The two have gone hand in hand. Many theories of personality cannot be adequately understood without understanding the theory of psychotherapy that led to them.

Goals of Psychotherapy   Joseph Rychlak (1968) points out that psychotherapy has three major motives or goals: the scholarly, the ethical, and the curative.

The *scholarly* motive considers therapy a means of understanding the self and human nature. Psychoanalysis, for example, was seen by Freud as a tool for discovering truths about human nature. His goal was to help the individual acquire self-understanding and to develop a comprehensive theory of human nature. He developed psychoanalysis as a method of research aimed at these ends.

The *ethical* motive considers therapy a means of helping the individual to change, improve, grow, and better the quality of life. Carl Rogers's work is an example of the ethical motive. His emphasis is on an attitude created by the therapist that permits change to occur within the client, rather than on cognitive understanding or the manipulation of behavior.

The *curative* motive aims directly at eliminating troublesome symptoms and substituting more suitable behavior. Most behavior therapists, for example, consider that they have been hired to do a job and seek to do it as effectively and quickly as possible. From this point of view, the therapist is responsible for creating changes, removing symptoms, and controlling behavior.

Most people enter therapy with the expectation that they will be cured or helped to improve. In this respect, the curative motive is most consistent with the popular view of psychotherapy. Because of this expectation, many people have difficulty, particularly at the beginning, in undergoing psychoanalysis or other forms of "insight" therapy. If they stay with it, however, their reasons for being in therapy change, and they begin to appreciate the value of the other motives. Obviously, the reasons for entering, continuing in, and practicing psychotherapy are many and mixed. This is why the evaluation of therapy is a difficult issue.

Evaluating Psychotherapy   How does one go about evaluating psychotherapy? What criteria are appropriate? In 1952, a British psychologist, Hans Eysenck, stunned the therapeutic community with a report on treatment outcomes indicating that the improvement rate for patients in intensive and prolonged psychotherapy was only about 64 percent. The rate was 72 percent for patients who received treatment only from a general practitioner or were in simple custodial care. A second report (1961) did not change the general outlook. However, Eysenck's reports have subsequently been severely criticized, and it is now clear that his results are not the final word on the issue (Smith & Glass, 1977; Landman & Dawes, 1982). It appears likely that Eysenck prejudiced his results. Moreover, Eysenck's criterion for improvement was that of "symptom remission." This criterion, though perhaps appropriate for therapies governed by the curative motive, is not necessarily appropriate for those that are conducted for other purposes.

If the proportion of cures were the only criterion by which psychotherapies were to be judged, psychoanalysis and other insight therapies would have long since disappeared from the scene with the arrival of more efficient and less costly curative techniques. This, however, has not been the case. If one's criterion, on the other hand, rests on scholarly grounds, psychoanalysis emerges a clear winner. No other method of therapy has provided us with such a wealth of information about the complexity and depth of the human personality.

In brief, each method of psychotherapy must be evaluated in terms of its own goals and purposes. Behavior therapists, who aim at curing clients, are particularly interested in discovering the proportion of cures associated with various techniques. Ethical theorists, who aim at creating a suitable climate for therapeutic change and life improvement, have stimulated the study of those conditions that foster personality change and their effects. Freudian psychoanalysis asks to be evaluated in terms of its effectiveness as a method of research aimed at understanding human nature.

The Complexities of Evaluation

We have suggested that science, philosophy, and application/art are three functions that personality theories encompass. Our use of this threefold approach allows us to recognize each activity as it arises and gives us a better idea of how personality theories in general, and any specific personality theory, work. It is important to identify the different aspects of a personality theory because each activity has its own rules and procedures for establishing information and each has its own criteria for judging the worth of its findings.

No theory is simply one or the other: philosophy, science, or application/ art; each theory combines elements of all these activities. Nor are we trying to establish a model that all personality theories must follow. The fact is there is no one scientific method, philosophical approach, or psychotherapeutic strategy that would serve as an adequate model for all others.

Scientific studies of personality rely on paradigms that can only be established philosophically and generally culminate in some form of art or practical application. The desire to be scientific reflects itself in an effort to test constructs by validating evidence rather than by relying on the gut-level feeling of illumination that everyday language calls understanding something (Perrez, 1991).

Some psychologists have attempted to narrow the possible activity of a personality theorist to one function or interpretation of science, such as an objective experimental methodology, and ignored the philosophical assumptions on which all scientific work is based. Others have assumed that the compelling character of philosophical assumptions is sufficient to establish their credibility as scientific findings about personality. Either position is unnecessarily limiting. It is important that we distinguish between the different kinds of functions that personality theories entail so that we can recognize them when they occur and evaluate them accordingly. Part of the current problem in personality theorizing is that the theorists are not always clear about what activity they are engaged in.

As we discuss the major personality theorists in the following chapters, we will try to clarify the function of philosophy, science, and art in each theory. This should enable you to see how the theories fit into the overall framework of personality theories as philosophy, science, and art. As you will see, there is a wide variety and diversity of personality theories providing you with a rich selection from which to choose or develop your own theory of personality.

Summary

1. The term **personality** is difficult to define because there is little common agreement on how the term should be used. In everyday speech it usually refers to one's public image. Different personality theorists present us with their own definitions of the word based on their theoretical positions.

2. A **theory** is a set of abstract concepts that we make about a group of facts or events in order to explain them.

3. Two traditions inform contemporary theories of personality. One stems from psychological laboratories and academic research. The other stems from psychoanalysis and clinical psychology. The study of personality became a formal and systematic area of specialization in American psychology in the mid-1930s, but the two traditions have never fully merged.

4. Personality theories may function as philosophy, science, and art. As scientists, personality theorists develop hypotheses that help us understand human behavior. As philosophers, they explore what it means to be a person. As artists, they seek to apply what is known about human behavior to make a better life.

5. **Philosophical assumptions** suggest that things are not necessarily what they appear to be. They are based on a special **epiphanic** vision, which goes beyond the ordinary perception of our sense organs. Philosophical statements also tend to be global and do not allow for any exceptions. Finally, they often are implicit rather than explicit.

6. Some of the basic issues on which personality theorists differ are *freedom versus determinism, heredity versus environmental* factors, *uniqueness versus universality, proactive versus reactive* theories, and *optimism versus pessimism.*

7. Philosophical assumptions are evaluated by criteria appropriate to the special act of knowing that underlies them. The criteria are **coherence, relevance,** and **comprehensiveness,** all of which add up to a final criterion, **compellingness.**

8. Science has its basis in philosophy because the ordinary observation on which science relies depends upon a prior **paradigm** that is established philosophically. The values and standards of science also function as philosophical commitments.

9. The simplest kinds of **scientific statements** are *empirical,* based directly on observation. The data on which these statements are based may be **objective** or **subjective.** When a number of different observations coincide, a scientist may make a **generalization.** Scientists also use **operational definitions,** which specify the behaviors included in a term, and **scientific constructs,** which use imaginary or hypothetical concepts to explain what we observe.

10. Scientists use a variety of techniques to evaluate their work. All of these techniques are ultimately based on observation, the ordinary perceptions of our sense organs, although some statements can be tested only indirectly. Scientific statements must be open to falsification, that is, a scientist must indicate the conditions under which a statement might be proven false. Scientists do not claim that the information produced by their methods is ultimately true. Scientific statements should be judged for their usefulness rather than their truth. When scientists end up with more than one hypothesis, the criteria they use to decide between rival hypotheses are **compatibility, predictive power,** and **simplicity.**

11. Personality theories have found application in assessment and research. Two major approaches of assessing personality are psychometric and projective techniques. Three primary research approaches used in personality are the clinical approach, the correlational approach, and the experimental approach.

12. The three major goals of **psychotherapy** are the *scholarly, ethical,* and *curative* motives. Scholarly therapies should be evaluated on the basis of their contributions to the understanding of the self and human nature. Ethical therapies should be evaluated in terms of the suitability of the climate they create for fostering change and life improvement. Curative therapies should be evaluated on the basis of symptom remission and number of cures.

13. It is important to distinguish among the different functions of personality theories so that we can recognize each activity when it occurs and therefore evaluate each theory according to the appropriate methods.

Suggestions for Further Reading

Students who are interested in pursuing Gordon Allport's effort to define the word "personality" should see his survey in Chapter 2 of *Personality: A Psychological Interpretation* (Holt, 1937). This chapter provides a compact survey of the origins of the word and the various ways in which it has been defined.

The Story of Philosophy by Will Durant (Pocket Books, 1954) is a lay introduction to philosophy that tells its story by focusing on the lives and ideas of significant philosophers. The introduction, "On the Uses of Philosophy," helps to place the work of these thinkers in perspective. J. B. Conant's *On Understanding Science* (Yale University Press, 1947) gives a concise introduction to the scientific enterprise. A comprehensive history of psychology is provided in the classic work of E. G. Boring, *A History of Experimental Psychology* (Appleton-Century-Crofts, 1929), a detailed but invaluable book for the serious student of psychology.

Books that try to place the study of psychology and personality theory within the general framework of science and philosophy are more difficult reading, but worth the effort of the interested student. The following are especially recommended: M. Turner, *Philosophy and the Science of Behavior* (Appleton-Century-Crofts, 1967); D. Bakan, *On Method: Toward a Reconstruction of Psychological Investigation* (Jossey-Bass, 1969); J. Rychlak, *A Philosophy of Science for Personality Theory* (Houghton Mifflin, 1968); T. S. Kuhn, *The Structure of Scientific Revolutions,* 2nd ed. (University of Chicago Press, 1970); and I. Chein, *The Science of Behavior and the Image of Man* (Basic Books, 1972). These books stress the necessity of developing adequate conceptual structures of science and philosophy within which personality theorizing can flourish as efforts to understand the human being.

A special issue of the *Journal of Personality* (March 1986) was devoted to methodological developments in personality research.

The Psychoanalytic Approach

Of all the giants of intellectual history, Sigmund Freud emerges as an unquestionable leader in helping us to understand human nature. Many of the other theories that we will study were developed as efforts to elaborate on, modify, substitute for, or refute the concepts of Freud. The systematic study of personality may be said to have begun with Freud's development of psychoanalysis at the end of the nineteenth century. Not only did Freud revolutionize psychology, his influence has been felt in all the social sciences, as well as in literature, art, and religion.

CHAPTER 2

Sigmund Freud

YOUR GOALS FOR THIS CHAPTER

1. Describe Freud's early use of the "talking method" and indicate the conclusions he drew about *unconscious processes.*
2. Describe Freud's concept of the role of emotions in human life. Explain why *wishes* are repressed and how they may be dealt with when brought back into consciousness.
3. Cite the instructions for *free association* and explain the premise on which the procedure is based.
4. Indicate the importance of *slips* and *dreams* and explain how they are analyzed.
5. Identify the nature of our repressed wishes and desires and explain how Freud's use of the word *libido* and his concept of *drive* lead to a new understanding of sexuality.
6. Describe the child's sexual activity and outline Freud's *psychosexual stages* of development, explaining the important events of each stage.
7. Describe how the effects of the psychosexual stages may be seen in various adult character traits and disorders.
8. Describe the characteristics and functions of the *id, ego,* and *superego.*
9. Explain how the id, ego, and superego are related in the adjusted and maladjusted personalities.
10. Explain how the id, ego, and superego are related to conscious and unconscious processes.
11. Distinguish among the three forms of anxiety that Freud described.
12. Describe the function of *defense mechanisms* and define and give examples of common defense mechanisms.
13. Describe what happens in psychoanalysis.
14. Discuss efforts to test Freudian concepts.
15. Evaluate Freud's theory in terms of its function as philosophy, science, and art.

The stature and distinguished contributions of Sigmund Freud place him at the forefront of contemporary personality theorists. For over forty years, Freud meticulously studied dimensions of human nature. Developing the technique of free association, he reached far into the depths of his own unconscious life and that of others. In the process, he created psychoanalysis, a unique method of research for understanding the human individual. He discovered psychological processes such as repression, resistance, transference, and infantile sexuality. He developed the first comprehensive method of studying and treating neurotic problems. His position in the history of intellectual thought clearly justifies an extended study of his ideas.

Biographical Background

Sigmund Freud was born in 1856 in Freiburg, Moravia (a small town in what became Czechoslovakia), to a Jewish wool merchant and his young wife. Sigmund was born in a caul; that is, a small portion of the fetal sac covered his head at birth. According to folklore, this was a sign that he would be famous. Freud did not practice religion as an adult, but he remained very conscious of his Jewish origin (cf. Brunner, 1991, and Diller, 1991). His mother, twenty-one at the time of her favored first son's birth, was loving and protective, and the young boy was devoted to her Margolis (1989). Freud's father, Jacob, was forty-one, almost twice as old as his wife. Jacob was stern and authoritarian, but his son respected him. Only later, through his self-analysis, did Freud realize that his feelings toward his parents were mixed: fear and hate, respect and love.

When Sigmund was eleven months old, a brother, Julius, was born, but he died eight months later. A sister, Anna, arrived when Freud was two and a half. Later, four other sisters and a brother completed the family. When Freud was very young, he was very fond of his nanny and impressed by her religious teachings of Catholicism. Nevertheless, shortly after Anna was born, the nanny was suddenly fired for having stolen from the family. Sigmund was also born an uncle. His father, a widower, had two grown sons by his former marriage, and Freud's elder half-brother had a child. Freud and his nephew John, who was one year older than he, were close childhood companions. Freud was to view their early relationship as very significant to his later development. Many have thought that Freud's unusual family constellation set the stage for his later theory of the Oedipus complex.

At the age of four, Sigmund and his family moved to Vienna, where he was to live for almost eighty years. Although he was critical of Vienna, he did not leave the city until it was overwhelmed by Nazis in 1938, the year before he died. In his youth, Freud was a conscientious student. His parents encouraged his studies by giving him special privileges and expecting the other children to make sacrifices in behalf of their older brother. He was the only member of the family who had his own room and he studied by oil lamp while the others had to use candles. A natural student, Freud entered high school a year earlier than normal and stood at the head of the class for most of his days at the Sperl Gymnasium. He was good at languages and was an avid reader, being particularly fond of Shakespeare.

As a child, Freud had dreams of becoming a "mighty warrior" (Warner, 1991) or minister of state, but in reality professional choice was severely restricted for a Jew in Vienna. He thought of becoming a lawyer but instead began medical studies at the University of Vienna in 1873 and graduated eight years later. His studies there took longer than usual because he took his time with those areas that were of particular interest to him. He never intended to practice medicine, being more interested in physiological research; practical considerations, including occupational barriers to Jewish people and the desire to marry, led him to establish a practice as a clinical neurologist in 1881. While still a student, he made substantial and noteworthy contributions to research, publishing his findings on the nervous system of fish and the testes of the eel (cf. Miller & Katz, 1989; Glymour, 1991). He developed a method of staining cells for microscopic study and as a physician explored the anesthetic properties of cocaine. Because he initially had no reason to believe that there were dangers connected with cocaine, he was somewhat indiscriminate in using it himself

Sigmund Freud

and in recommending it to others. After the addictive character of the drug was discovered, Freud said he suffered "grave reproaches." However, he may have continued to use it. Cocaine claimed many physicians as casualties in the 1880s and 1890s.

Because the private practice on which Freud depended for a living brought him patients suffering from primarily neurotic disorders, his attention became focused on the problem and study of neurosis. Neurosis is usually not so severe as to prevent the individual who has it from functioning in normal society. As Freud's goal was a complete theory of humanity, he hoped that his study of neurosis would eventually provide a key to the study of psychological processes in general. He studied in Paris with the French psychiatrist Jean Charcot. On his return from Paris, Freud became influenced by a procedure developed by Joseph Breuer, a Viennese physician and friend, who encouraged his patients to talk freely about their symptoms. Breuer and Freud worked together in writing up some of their cases in *Studies in Hysteria* (1895). Freud's further investigations with Breuer's "talking cure" led to his own development of free association and later psychoanalytic techniques. Eventually they separated, as, according to Freud, Breuer could not agree with Freud's emphasis on the role of sexuality in neurosis.

In 1900 Freud published *The Interpretation of Dreams.* Initially, the book was ignored by all but a few. Nevertheless, Freud's reputation grew, and he began to attract a following. He also encountered a lot of criticism; some accused his work of being pornographic. However, he may have exaggerated the degree of intellectual persecution he received. A psychoanalytic society was founded by Freud and his colleagues, and many of Freud's disciples later became noted psychoanalysts: Ernest Jones (his biographer), A. A. Brill, Sandor Ferenczi, and Karl Abraham. Originally, Carl Jung and Alfred Adler were also close associates, but later they left Freud's psychoanalytic movement to develop and stress other ideas.

In 1909, G. Stanley Hall, noted psychologist and president of Clark University in Worcester, Massachusetts, invited Freud and his associate, Carl Jung, to present a series of lectures. It was Freud's first and only visit to the United States. These lectures contained the basic elements of Freud's theory of personality, and their delivery marked the change of psychoanalysis from a small Viennese movement to one of international scope and recognition.

Freud's work, however, was by no means over. He continued to develop and revise his psychoanalytic theory until his death. At the same time he was very human, among other things superstitious and arrogant. By the end of his life, psychoanalytic concepts had been applied to and were influencing almost every cultural construct of humanity. Freud's published works fill twenty-four volumes in the *Standard English Edition.* He died in London in 1939 at age eighty-three, after many years of suffering from cancer of the jaw, in what would be called today a physician-assisted suicide (Shur, 1972). There remains a considerable quantity of archival material, which will not be released until sometime in the next century. Scholars of Freud are eager to see what additional light this material will shed on such an important figure.

The Origins of Psychoanalysis

Sigmund Freud did not complete a perfected system. *An Outline of Psychoanalysis,* which he began in 1938, the year before he died, had as its aim "to bring together the doctrines of psychoanalysis and to state them . . . in the most concise form." But this book was never finished; in fact much of his work has an unfinished character about it. Ideas appear and are dismissed, only to reappear in a new context. His thought moves in phases, changing and synthesizing what has gone before. The only works that Freud systematically tried to keep up to date were *The Interpretation of Dreams* (first published in 1900) and *Three Essays on Sexuality* (1905). In describing Freud's theories, therefore, it is important to recognize that psychoanalysis does not represent a finished theory, but rather an ongoing process of discovery about the self.

The Discovery of Unconscious Forces

A logical place to begin discussion of the origins of psychoanalysis is Freud's early work with Joseph Breuer. This, in fact, is how Freud began his presentation on the history of psychoanalysis to the American public in his lectures at Clark University. As we have already seen, Freud was deeply influenced by a procedure developed by Breuer, and he frequently credited Breuer with the discovery of the psychoanalytic method. Thus, psychoanalysis may be said to begin with the case history of one of Joseph Breuer's patients, who is known in the literature as Anna O. (Freud, 1910).

Anna O. was a twenty-one-year-old, highly intelligent woman. In the course of a two-year illness beginning in 1880, she had developed a number of physical and mental disturbances. Among her symptoms were a paralysis of the right arm and leg, difficulty in vision, nausea, the inability to drink any liquids, and the inability to speak or understand her mother tongue. Further, she was prone to states of absence, an altered state of consciousness in which there may be considerable personality change, and later amnesia or forgetting of events that occurred during that period.

The medical profession of 1880 was quite puzzled by illnesses such as these and diagnosed them as cases of hysteria, an illness in which there were physical symptoms but no physiological basis for the problem. (Today such disorders are less common and are known as *conversion disorders.*) The cause of hysteria was a mystery. Because they could not understand or effectively treat the problem, many doctors tended to view patients suffering from hysteria with suspicion and to be punitive. Some even went so far as to accuse their patients of faking an illness.

Breuer, however, treated his patients sympathetically. He noticed that during her states of absence, Anna frequently mumbled several words. Once he was able to determine these words, Breuer put her under hypnosis, repeated the words to her, and asked her to verbalize for him any associations that she had to the words. The patient cooperated. She began to tell him stories about herself that seemed to center on one particular event of her life: her father's illness and death.

Before he died, Anna's father had been very sick. She had taken care of him until her own illness prevented her from doing so. After she had related a number of these stories, Anna's symptoms were relieved and eventually disappeared. Anna gratefully called the cure the "talking cure," or referred to it jokingly as "chimney sweeping."

For example, Anna told of a time when she was sitting by her father's bed during his illness and was very worried about him. She was trying to hide her tears so that her father would not see them, when he asked her what time it was. Since she was crying, it was only with difficulty that she could look at her watch and make out the position of the hands on the dial. Recollecting that event and the emotions she had restrained restored her clarity of vision.

Later she recalled another memory. A black snake (common in the area in which she lived) appeared in the room and seemed to go toward her ill father. She tried to drive the reptile away, but it was as if she could not move her arm. She wanted to call for help, but she could not speak. Recalling these events and the emotions they included relieved her paralysis and restored her knowledge of her native tongue.

Breuer concluded that Anna's symptoms were somehow determined by traumatic or stressful events of the past and that the recollection of these events had a cathartic effect. **Catharsis** refers to emotional release. When Anna recalled the events, she did so with a great deal of emotional intensity. This evidently freed her of the symptom to which the emotion had become attached.

By mid-1882, it appeared that Anna was completely and dramatically cured. In any event, according to what may have been a myth initiated by Freud and elaborated on by Jones (1953) (Tolpin, 1993), Breuer was anxious to end the treatment, because Anna's open proclamations of love and strong demands for his services embarrassed him and created domestic problems with his wife. When Breuer announced his wish to end the case, Anna offered a phantom pregnancy as a final symptom. Breuer was very shaken by this turn of events and abruptly dropped the case. He avoided the cathartic method in treating future patients. Anna, whose real name was probably Bertha Pappenheim (Tolpin, 1993), eventually became well known as one of the first social workers, striving to improve the rights and status of children and women. The entire case would probably have gone unnoticed in medical history had Breuer not mentioned it to some of his coworkers, including the young doctor Sigmund Freud, who was deeply interested.

Some time later, Freud recalled the Anna O. episode and began to use the "talking method" with his own patients. He had some measure of success and, after observing his own explorations with the technique, concluded that at the time of the original traumatic event, the patient had to hold back a strong emotion. Perhaps because of the circumstances that surrounded the event, the patient was unable to express the emotion it evoked in a normal way through thought, word, or deed. The emotion, prevented from escaping normally, had found another outlet and was expressing itself through a neurotic symptom. Until they were recalled under hypnosis, the details of the events and the emotions they involved were not a part of the patient's awareness. Thus, the patient was *unconscious* of these memories; but the unconscious memories were influencing the present behavior.

Shortly thereafter, Freud decided to give up hypnosis. In part, it was a practical necessity, since not all of his patients could be hypnotized. He assured his patients that eventually they would be able to remember the traumatic events in a normal waking state. Abandoning hypnosis also proved to be an important step in Freud's discovery of resistances. He had found that assisting his patients to remember was a long process. This led him to think that although the patient consciously wanted to remember those events, some force within prevented the patient from becoming aware of them and kept the memories unconscious. Freud labeled this force "resistance."

Recognizing resistance leads to a dynamic understanding of *unconscious processes,* or forces of which a person is unaware. You may not immediately be able to recall what you did on your last birthday, but with a little effort you probably could remember. Unconscious memories are different. You may recall having been punished as a child but be unable, no matter how hard you try, to remember why you were punished. Such a memory has been rendered unconscious. It can only be recalled, if at all, with considerable difficulty.

What were those ideas or thoughts that would be rendered unconscious? Freud believed that they were **wishes.** During the traumatic event, a wish had been aroused that went against the person's ego-ideal. Because it is hard for people to accept the fact that they are not what they would like to be, such incompatibility causes pain. If it causes too much pain, the wish is repressed.

Underlying Freud's theory is the concept that events and happenings in our lives evoke strong feelings. These emotions help us to evaluate our world, but in some instances the immediate expression of emotion is inappropriate or even disastrous. Ideally, one acknowledges, accepts, and guides an emotion into constructive, or at least harmless, channels of expression.

A certain amount of repression is unavoidable and necessary in order for a civilized society to exist. But the repression is not always successful or constructive. An example Freud gave during his lectures at Clark University illustrates the problems that repressed ideas can create. Suppose, he suggested, that during the course of his lecture a young man in the back of the room interrupts rudely by laughing, talking, and stamping his feet. Other members of the audience, disturbed by his behavior, forcibly eject the young man from the room and station themselves at the door to make sure that he will not reenter the hall. This unpleasant young fellow, however, bangs on the outside of the door, kicks, screams, and, in short, creates a worse ruckus than he made in the first place. A new solution is required: a compromise. Perhaps the audience will agree to permit the young man back into the lecture hall if he will agree to behave a little bit better.

suggests wishes increase intensity when repressed →

Freud admitted that his spatial metaphor was somewhat misleading, but it served to illustrate his primary concepts. We eject painful wishes, not permitting them to enter consciousness, but the repressed wishes refuse to behave agreeably. Instead, they create all sorts of problems, produce neurotic symptoms, and so forth. The need, then, is to restore the wishes to consciousness so that we can deal with them realistically.

The Psychoanalytic Method of Assessment and Research

Our initial discussion of the origin of psychoanalysis presented it as being simple only for the purpose of abbreviation. In fact, the process is much more complicated than the original illustrations suggest. Essentially, several opposing forces are at work. First, there is a conscious effort on the part of the patient to remember the forgotten events. Second, there is resistance, which persists in keeping the memories unconscious. Finally, there are the unexpressed emotions that continue to seek expression. If a wish cannot get out on its own identity, it will seek an outlet in a disguised form. By putting on a mask, it will manage to sneak out and find expression in the person's behavior. Although the trauma cannot be immediately remembered, it may express itself in a hidden manner through the memories and thoughts that are recalled. In order to delve behind these masks and discover the repressed ideas, Freud developed two primary procedures: free association and the interpretation of dreams and slips.

Free Association   In **free association,** a patient is asked to verbalize whatever comes to mind, no matter how insignificant, trivial, or even unpleasant the idea, thought, or picture may seem. Free association is based on the premise that no idea is arbitrary and insignificant. Eventually, these ideas will lead back to the original problem. For example, Anna O. did not immediately remember the scene of her father's death, but her arm was paralyzed, her vision clouded, and she was unable to use her native tongue. Then, what she did talk about hinted at the hidden event. The instructions for free association are deceptively simple, but, in fact, they are very hard to follow. What happens when we try to verbalize everything that comes to mind? We may be flooded with thoughts and find it impossible to put them all into words. At other times, we may go blank and discover that nothing comes to mind. Also, the thoughts that do come may be very painful to discuss. These intruding ideas are like ore, however, for the analysis eventually reduces them from their crude state to a valuable metal. After free association, one *reflects* upon what one has said. In the process, the resistance is analyzed, understood, and weakened so that the wish is able to express itself more directly.

The Interpretation of Dreams and Slips   In the process of free association, particular attention is paid to slips and dreams. **Slips** are bungled acts: a slip of the tongue, a slip of the pen, or a lapse of memory. Many of us dismiss such events as trivial and meaningless, but to Freud slips like these are not without meaning. The Freudian theory assumes that in our psychic life nothing is trifling or lawless; rather, there is a motive for everything.

To understand Freud's view of slips, it is important to distinguish between cause and motive. *Cause* implies the action of a material, impersonal force that brings something about. *Motive* refers to personal agency and implies an emotion or desire operating on the will of a person and leading him or her to act. For Freud, all events are *overdetermined,* that is, they have more than one meaning or explanation. To illustrate: a ball is thrown into the air; after traveling a certain distance, it falls to the ground. A causal explanation of this event would use laws of gravity to account for the ball's fall. A motivational explanation would emphasize that the ball was thrown by someone. This particular ball would not have fallen at this time if someone had not willingly thrown it. Both explanations are correct and they complement each other. Thus, it is not sufficient to argue that we make slips of the tongue because we are tired, although it is true that fatigue may provide the physiological conditions under which a slip may occur. The slip expresses a personal motive as well. Freudian theory is particularly concerned with the explanation in terms of motive.

Here is an example of a slip and its analysis, which Freud reports in *The Psychopathology of Everyday Life* (1904). He recalls how a young student was talking excitedly about the difficulties of his generation and tried to end his comment with a well-known Latin quotation from Virgil, but could not finish the line. Freud recognized the quotation and cited it correctly: *"Exoriare aliquis nostris ex ossibus ultor"* ("Let someone arise from my bones as an avenger"). The forgotten word was *aliquis* ("someone"). The student was embarrassed but, remembering the significance that Freud attached to such slips, indicated that he was curious to learn why he had forgotten the word. Freud took up the challenge and asked the student to tell him honestly and without any censorship whatever came to mind when he directed his attention to the word *aliquis.* The first thought that sprang to his mind was the notion of dividing the word as follows: *a* and *liquis.* Next came the words "relics," "liquify," "fluid." These associations had little meaning for him, but he continued and thought of Simon of Trent and the accusations of ritual blood sacrifices that had often been brought against the Jewish people. Next he thought of an article that he had read recently entitled "What Saint Augustine Said Concerning Women." The next thought appeared to be totally unconnected, but following the cardinal rule he repeated it anyway. He was thinking of a fine old gentleman whose name was Benedict. At this point, Freud noted that he had referred to a group of saints and church fathers: St. Simon, St. Augustine, and St. Benedict. That comment made the student think of St. Januarius and the miracle of blood. Here, Freud observed that both St. Januarius and St. Augustine had something to do with the calendar and asked the student to refresh his memory about the miracle of blood. The blood of St. Januarius is held in a vial in a church in Naples. On a particular holy day it miraculously liquifies. The people attach a great deal of importance to this miracle and become very upset if it is delayed. Once it was delayed and the general in command of the city took the priest aside and made it clear to him that the miracle had better take place very soon. At this point, the student hesitated. The next thought was surely too intimate to pass on and, besides, it had little connection. He had suddenly thought of a lady from whom he might get an awkward piece of news. "Could it be," Freud guessed, "that she missed her period?"

The resolution of the slip was not that difficult. The associations had led the way. The student had mentioned the calendar, the blood that starts to flow on a certain day, the disturbance should that event fail to occur, and the feeling that the miracle must take place. The word *aliquis* and its subsequent allusions to the miracle of St. Januarius revealed a clear concern with a woman's menstrual period. That concern was what was unconsciously occupying the young student when he made the slip. Often a slip is not so obvious and is revealed only after a long chain of associations.

A second area explored by free association is that of dreams (1900). For Freud, the dream is the royal road to the unconscious. It is often easy to understand the dreams of young children, because their defenses have not yet masked their motives. They dream very simply of the fulfillment of unsatisfied wishes from the day before. The child who has not received candy desired during the day may dream of an abundance of it at night.

Adult dreams also express unsatisfied wishes, but, because in the adult many of these wishes have become unacceptable to the self-concept, the dream is in disguise. Therefore, Freud distinguishes between the manifest dream and the latent dream. The **manifest dream** is the dream as it is remembered the next morning. Such a dream frequently appears incoherent and nonsensical, the fantasy of a mad person. Nevertheless, it presents some kind of narrative story (Giora, 1991). The **latent dream** refers to the meaning or motive underlying the manifest dream. Analysis seeks to discover the latent meaning that is expressed within the manifest dream. The dream wish, however, has undergone distortion, and its mask must be removed before it will reveal its meaning.

Dreams provide a particular wealth of information because in sleep a person is more relaxed than when awake, and resistance, so to speak, may be caught off guard. The wishes and desires that are forbidden access in normal conscious states have a chance to slip out. Thus, the manifest dream may be described as a disguised fulfillment of repressed wishes.

It is possible, Freud held, to gain some insight into the process that disguises the unconscious dream wishes and converts them into the manifest dream. This process is called *dream work* and it has many elements. One important element is its use of symbols. Some symbols employed in dreams are unique to the individual dreamer and can be understood only in terms of the individual's particular history and associations. Others are shared by many dreamers. In some instances, symbols have acquired universal meanings; such universal symbols find expression in our myths, legends, and fairy tales, as well as in our dreams (see Bettelheim, 1977).

Freud did not believe that anxiety dreams or nightmares contradicted his concept that dreams fulfill wishes. The meaning of a dream does not lie in its manifest context; thus, a dream that provokes anxiety may still serve to fulfill an unconscious wish. The expression of a forbidden wish also causes anxiety or pain to the conscious self, so an anxiety dream may indicate that the disguise was unsuccessful and permitted too clear expression of the forbidden wish.

An example of a dream that Freud analyzed in the course of his self-analysis and reported in *The Interpretation of Dreams* may help to illustrate the procedure of dream analysis. Freud had this dream when he was seven or eight years old and analyzed it some thirty years later. It was a most vivid dream in which his mother, who was sleeping with a particularly calm expression on her face, was carried into the room and laid on the bed by two or three people with birds' beaks.

Freud indicated that as a child he awoke crying from the dream, but he became calm when he saw his mother. In his subsequent analysis of the dream, the tall figures with beaks reminded Freud of illustrations in Philippson's version of the Bible. The birds appeared to be Egyptian deities such as are carved on tombs. Freud's grandfather had died shortly before the dream. Before his death, he had gone into a coma and worn a calm expression on his face identical to Freud's mother's expression in the dream. At this level of interpretation, the dream appeared to express a young boy's anxiety over the possible death of his mother. Further analysis led deeper. The name "Philippson" reminded Freud of a neighborhood boy named Philip with whom he used to play as a child. Philip introduced Freud to the slang expression *vögeln,* a rather vulgar German phrase for sexual intercourse. The term originates from the German word *Vogel,* which means "bird." Thus, on a deeper level, Freud had to conclude that the wish expressed in the dream was that of sexual (and therefore forbidden) desires toward his mother. This dream led Freud to the discovery of the Oedipus complex, which will be discussed shortly, and assisted Freud in clarifying the nature of repressed wishes and desires.

The Dynamics and Development of Personality

According to Freud, the nature of our repressed wishes and desires is erotic. This emphasis on sexuality is an aspect of Freud's work that many people find problematic. To understand this requires one to understand how Freud redefined the term *sexuality* and how he used it in his work. Still, Freud's theoretical position on the role of sexuality and his insistence on the human being's sexual nature is threatening to some people.

The Importance of Sexuality

In his early work, Freud viewed sexuality as a bodily process that could be totally understood under a model of tension reduction. The goal of human behavior was simply to reduce the tension created by the accumulation of too much en-

THINKING CRITICALLY

Free Association

A simple demonstration suggested by Theodore Reik (1956), one of Freud's followers, can illustrate how difficult, yet potentially valuable, the task of free association is. The exercise is hardly equivalent to the genuine psychoanalytic situation, but it shares some of its elements, has the advantage of being available to anyone, and may show that the value of free association goes beyond its use as a technique in psychoanalysis.

Using a tape recorder, choose a time and place where you can be alone and in relative quiet. Assume a relaxed position and then try to speak into the recorder whatever thoughts come to mind for a period of one half-hour or more. In general, we try to speak logically and develop points in an orderly sequence. Free association requires that we verbalize whatever occurs to us without such order and restriction. You may be surprised, ashamed, and even afraid of the thoughts that emerge. It is difficult to acknowledge hostile and aggressive tendencies, particularly toward those we love. Some of us even have difficulties expressing tender thoughts. Moreover, a petty or trivial thought is often the hardest of all to express. You will be successful if you verbalize and record all of your thoughts, regardless of their significance, importance, pleasantness, or logical order.

When you are finished, put the tape aside. After a reasonable amount of time, perhaps the next day, play the tape back and reflect upon what you have said. You will be listening to a person who reminds you of yourself in many ways, but in other respects will be unknown. You may discover that you have thoughts and impulses that you did not realize before. They may seem minor, but they will surprise you.

You can also use free association to gain greater insight into your own slips and dreams. In dream interpretation, every element of the dream is important. Therefore, you should try to remember small details that arise in dreams, particularly if they are strange or bizarre. Taking each element one by one, you simply verbalize whatever associations come to mind as you ponder it. Later you can replay the tape and reflect on your associations to see whether you can discover aspects of yourself that were expressed in the dream.

ergy and to restore a state of balance. Sexual desires could be compared to a wish to remove an itch. However, as his work developed, Freud began to emphasize the psychological character of mental processes and sexuality. His use of the word **libido** to refer to the emotional and psychic energy derived from the biological drive of sexuality testifies to this shift in his thought.

Freud's desire to emphasize the psychological character of mental processes is also seen in the development of his concept of **drive**. The German word he used was *Trieb,* which has been variously translated as "instinct" or "drive." Since "instinct" refers to an inborn automatic pattern of activity characteristic of animals rather than humans, translation of the word as "drive," or "impulse" (Bettelheim, 1982) seems more appropriate to Freud's intent. Freud used *Trieb* to refer to a psychological or mental representation of an inner bodily source of excitement, a form of energy that cannot be reduced to either a bodily aspect or a mental one because it combines elements of both.

In his concept of drive, Freud abandoned an earlier attempt to reduce psychological processes to physiological ones and also began to resolve a problem inherited from Cartesian philosophy. In the belief that a person is more than a machine, the French philosopher René Descartes (1596–1650) had divided all reality into two separate categories: mind and matter. Matter included all material substances, inorganic and animate, including human bodies. These things, Descartes suggested, could be understood under scientific laws. Mind, which included all conscious states (thinking, willing, feeling, and so forth), was a second kind of substance that Descartes believed could not be explained by scientific laws. For the first time in history, a sharp distinction between mind and matter was made the basis of a systematic philosophy. Descartes's philosophy led people in the West to posit the center of the person in the mind rather than in the entire organism. Freud recognized that a comprehensive view of personality must see body and mind as a unity and his holistic approach began to help repair the Cartesian split.

A drive is characterized by four features: *source,* the bodily stimulus or need; *impetus,* the amount of energy or intensity of the need; *aim,* its goal and purpose (to reduce the excitation); and *object,* the person or object in the environment through which the aim may be satisfied. If Freud had characterized drives simply by source and impetus, he could have continued to think of the sexual drive as just a bodily process. He chose to include also aim and object, which forced him to view sexuality differently and to emphasize its psychological and intentional character. Freud used the German verb *besetzen* (translated as *cathect*) to refer to investing libidinal energy in a mental representation of an object that will satisfy a desire; a person cathects an object that he or she wants. The importance of one's sexual life as a bodily process begins to diminish in favor of one's response to it. For this reason, Freud used the term *psychosexuality* to indicate the totality of elements included in the sexual drive. In Freud's view drives provide a genetic base from which later structures of personality will emerge (Cavell, 1991).

Freud suggested that there are two basic groups of impulsive drives. **Eros** refers to *life impulses* or drives, those forces that maintain life processes and ensure reproduction of the species. The key to these forces is the sexual drive, whose energy force is "libido." **Thanatos,** encompassing *death impulses* or drives, is a biological reality (Badcock, 1992), and the source of aggressiveness, and reflects the ultimate resolution of all of life's tension in death. Although Freud emphasized the importance of the death drive, his discussion of the development of personality centers around the sexual drive.

What is the purpose of sexuality? The traditional answer was reproduction. The medieval theologian Thomas Aquinas (1225–1274) argued in *Summa Theologica* that according to natural law the primary purpose of sexuality was reproduction of the species. Other purposes of sexual activity were secondary. The pleasure that attended sexual activity was permissible, and even encouraged by St. Thomas, but he recommended that it should be submissive to and never prevent the primary purpose of reproduction. If we think that the primary purpose of sexuality is reproduction, what other thoughts about sexuality will logically follow? Sexual behaviors that do not lead to reproduction, such as homosexuality and masturbation, were disapproved of or regarded as perverse.

The nineteenth-century culture in Vienna, from which Freud's theories emerged, reflected such an attitude. It is difficult for us today to appreciate the extent to which sexual impulses and desires were then forcibly repressed, especially by the middle and upper classes. The sexual act was generally viewed as beastly and undignified, but it was tolerated as an outlet for a natural shortcoming of men and for purposes of reproduction. Women were supposed to be above sexual impulses, and children were thought incapable of them.

There was considerable anxiety over what were thought to be inappropriate sexual activities and perversions. Rigid taboos were put upon masturbation and limits were set on the expression of sexuality in adult life. The body's excretory functions were taken care of with embarrassment and prudery was practiced to fanatical extremes.

At the same time Vienna was undergoing a cultural renaissance in philosophy, music, and literature. The intelligentsia was seeking the realities that lay behind the facade of the decaying Austrian empire. One such reality was sex. To a large extent, Freud shared society's puritan attitude; nevertheless, he also relentlessly searched for the reality behind the mask.

Freud suggested that the primary purpose of sexual behavior is pleasure, opening the door to a host of new ideas. Activities that do not focus on the genitals may be seen as key expressions of sexuality to the extent to which they produce pleasure. The young child, who invariably seeks pleasure in the body, may be seen as having a rich sexual life. Activities such as sucking the thumb, previously seen as separate from sexuality, may be viewed as sexual.

Freud, in effect, turned the traditional concept upside down. This reversal permitted him to account for behaviors that were previously inexplicable, such as sexual variations and infantile sexuality. Freud's redefinition of sexuality was twofold. First, he divorced sex from its previous close restriction to the genitals and reproductive activity. Second, he enlarged the concept of sexuality to include activities such as thumb sucking and sublimation that previously were not thought of as sexual.

In Freudian terms, the child, who actively seeks pleasure from many areas of the body, is *polymorphous perverse;* that is, children's activities differ in many respects from reproductive sexual activity. The sexual activity of children is essentially *autoerotic;* they seek pleasure from their own bodies rather than from the body of another person. They find pleasure in sucking their thumbs, exploring their genitals, and so forth. Only in the course of a long history of development do children progress toward reproductive activities.

The Psychosexual Stages of Development

Freud (1905) outlined a path that children travel as they progress from auto-erotic sexual activity to reproductive activity. In this journey, the libido or sexual drive invests itself in various erogenous zones or areas of the body that provide pleasure. Indeed, observations have shown that as children grow, they do focus on different areas of the body; this attentional sequence follows the sequence outlined by Freud. He believed that by passing through a series of **psychosexual stages** in which different erogenous zones are important, children move from autoeroticism to reproductive sexuality and develop their adult personalities.

Oral Stage   The first stage is the **oral stage,** which lasts from birth to approximately age one. During this time, the major source of pleasure and potential conflict is the mouth. From it infants receive nourishment, have their closest contact with the mother (in breast-feeding), and discover information about the world. Infants explore new objects with their mouths. The two main types of oral activity, ingestion and biting, are the first examples of character types and traits that may develop later on. Oral activities are also a source of potential conflict because restraints may be placed on them. A mother may seek to discourage thumb sucking or stop her child from biting the breast. Thus, the focus of greatest pleasure and conflict is located for infants in the mouth.

Anal Stage   Freud's second psychosexual stage is the **anal stage,** which is expected to occur in the second year of life. At this time, the major source of pleasure and potential conflict is activities involving the anus. Generally, toilet training occurs during this period. Toilet training involves converting an involuntary activity, the elimination of bodily wastes, into a voluntary one. It frequently represents the child's first attempt to regulate instinctual impulses. A clash of wills with the caregiver may develop. Children may obtain pain or pleasure in either retaining or expelling their waste products. These two primary modes of anal expression, retention and expulsion, are further models for possible future character traits. In their efforts to train children, parents may forget that control over the sphincter muscles and elimination is an activity that only the child can perform. As early efforts to discipline children begin, the buttocks are frequently selected as a site on which to inflict pain. Since stimulation in the area causes both pleasure and pain, sadistic (pain-inflicting) and/or masochistic (pain-receiving) patterns of behavior may emerge. Subsequent forms of self-control and mastery have their origins in the anal stage.

Phallic Stage   The **phallic stage** of development usually occurs between the ages of three and six. The characteristics of this stage are pleasurable and conflicting feelings associated with the genital organs. The child's interest in the

During the oral stage, each new object an infant meets is immediately placed in the mouth.

genitals is not with their reproductive function, but with their ability to give pleasure in autoerotic activity and their significance as a means of distinguishing between the sexes. At this time, children discover that not all individuals are similarly endowed. They expend considerable energy in examining their genitalia, masturbating, and expressing interest in sexual matters. They are extremely curious, even though their curiosity outstrips their ability to understand sexual matters intellectually. They spin fantasies about the sexual act itself and the birth process, which are frequently inaccurate and misleading. They may believe that a pregnant woman has eaten her baby and that a baby is expelled through the mouth or the anus. Sexual intercourse is frequently viewed as an aggressive act by the father against the mother.

Freud pointed out that for children a fantasy can be as powerful as a literal event in shaping personality, and so in that sense it does not matter whether or not an event really occurred (cf. Juda, 1991). This point is remarkably consistent with contemporary phenomenological and cognitive points of view, which stress that what is important is not an object or event in itself but rather how it is perceived by an individual. This is not to deny that some children do endure real situations of incest or sexual abuse, or that such situations can have a pervasive negative effect on a child's personality development. Recently Freud has been criticized for abandoning his early "seduction theory," which held that adult neurosis was caused by actual incidents of sexual abuse in childhood, in favor of a theory that saw childhood sexual fantasy and immature cognitive structures as primary contributors to neurosis. Moreover, he has been criticized for suppressing the seduction theory for intellectually dishonest reasons (Masson, 1983). However, Freud's point was that the reality of seduction was important only in relation to other factors as well, such as how it is perceived by the child (Paul, 1985; Schimek, 1987; May, 1991).

The pleasures of masturbation and the fantasy life of children set the stage for the **Oedipus complex**, which Freud considered one of his greatest discoveries. Freud's concept was suggested by the Greek tragedy of Sophocles in which King Oedipus unwittingly murders his father and marries his mother. A key point is that Oedipus was unaware, or unconscious, of what he was doing. He did not realize that the man whom he met on the road and killed was his own father, nor did he know that the queen whom he later married was his mother. At the same time, he played an active role in bringing about his fate. On discovering the truth, he blinded himself. Within that Greek myth, Freud perceived a symbolic description of the unconscious psychological conflict that each one of us endures. In brief, the myth symbolizes each child's unconscious desire to possess the opposite-sexed parent and do away with the same-sexed parent.

If the Oedipus complex were to be taken literally, many people would have quickly dismissed Freud's concept as absurd and nonsensical. Incredible as it may seem, Freud suggested that children have incestuous wishes toward the opposite-sexed parent and murderous impulses toward the same-sexed parent. Do children actually desire to perform sexual intercourse and commit murder? Most preschool-age children have no clearly articulated concept of what sexual intercourse is all about. Furthermore, even if they had the will, they would lack the means to perform the act. Finally, for the preschool-age child, the permanence and reality of death are incomprehensible. As a literal depiction, Freud's concept of the Oedipus complex is clearly absurd.

Nevertheless, by this stage in development, the young boy (to tell his side of the story first) has become very fond of his mother, his primary caregiver. He loves her very much and he wants to love her as fully as possible. He senses that Mommy and Daddy have a special kind of relationship, which he wants to imitate. He becomes frustrated because he cannot imagine what the relationship is all about or perform it in a similar manner. At the same time, he wants his mother's love in return, but views love quantitatively as a fixed amount. It is as if his mother's love constitutes an apple. Each kiss or sign of attention that his father receives indicates that a big, juicy chunk has been bitten out of that apple, so that less remains for him. He cannot conceive of love as qualitative or as able to increase to fill a void. Viewing love as a quantity, the child perceives his father as a rival who prevents him from obtaining the full love that he desires from his mother. This perception creates wishes and impulses about getting rid of the father, an activity the child is powerless to carry out.

The child's feelings are very intense and conflicting, besides being too difficult for the child to cope with directly on a conscious level. Furthermore, the feelings create guilt because the child's sentiments toward his father are hostile but also affectionate. The child finds it difficult to cope with ambivalent feelings of love and hostility directed toward the same person. His rivalry culminates in **castration anxiety,** which means that he fears physical retaliation from his father, in particular that he will lose his penis.

The Oedipus complex is resolved by a twofold process. First, the son gives up his abortive attempts to possess his mother and begins to identify with his father in terms of sexual gender. In identifying with the same-sexed parent, he adopts the moral codes and injunctions of his father. This introjection of the parent's standards of good conduct leads to the development of a social conscience, which assists him in dealing with his forbidden impulses. By identifying with his father, the boy can through his imagination vicariously retain his mother as his love object, because he has incorporated those characteristics of his father that his mother loves. Although he may not have his mother in fact, he can wait until he grows up and then look for a girl who reminds him in some ways of Mom.

The little girl undergoes a similar complex. Freud deliberately did not give it a separate name, because he wished to emphasize the universality of the Oedipal situation. Others, however, have referred to the feminine version as the **Electra complex.** The primary love object for girls is also the mother. Yet girls, on discovering the genitals of the opposite sex, abandon the mother and turn to the father instead, making possible the Oedipal situation in reverse. The disappointment and shame that they feel upon viewing the "superior" penis leads to jealousy of the male, **penis envy,** a sense of inferiority, and a feeling of resentment and hatred toward the mother, who is held responsible for the effected castration. Reluctantly, the girl identifies with her mother, incorporates her values, and optimally makes the transition from her inadequate penis, the clitoris, as her chief erogenous zone, to the vagina. Because the female Oedipus complex is secondary, Freud suggests that it is resolved differently from that of the male; thus, the woman's ego-ideal (see page 50) is closer to its emotional origins and she appears to have less capacity for sublimation. The role that the girl adopts for herself is one that has been outlined for her by her society. Doris Bernstein, however, points out that there really is no parallel story for the girl and that Freud's wish to have *one* developmental theory blinded him to clear differences (1991).

Latency Period   After the phallic stage, Freud believed that there is a period of comparative sexual calm from the age of about seven to puberty. During the **latency period,** psychic forces develop that inhibit the sexual drive and narrow its direction. Sexual impulses, which are unacceptable in their direct expression, are channeled and elevated into more culturally accepted levels of activity, such as sports, intellectual interests, and peer relations. Freud was relatively silent about the latency period. He did not consider it a genuine psychosexual stage because nothing dramatically new emerges. Today, the latency period as such is

THINKING CRITICALLY

Freud and the Subject of Women

As you might imagine, Freud's views of the development of women have been the subject of considerable criticism and debate. In particular, many feminists have suggested that Freud's lack of understanding of female psychology reflected a male chauvinistic position.

In his famous dictum "anatomy is destiny," Freud intended to correct Napoleon's earlier motto, "history is destiny," pointing out that history is not the sole component of personality development. In his theory, Freud emphasized the importance of anatomy, in particular one's reproductive organs, as well as history. New research on sexual differences shows that much of Freud's explanation was based on incorrect information (Small, 1989). At the same time, research in ethology, behavior genetics, gender, and moral development (Sayers, 1987) indicates the importance of biology for understanding the individual (also see Neubauer & Neubauer, 1990).

Freud (1937) pointed out that the presence of two sexes is a fact of biology. Our experience of this is a matter for psychology. Biology does not cause our psychic life but our psychic life has to take it into account. The problem is not that Freud's view of women was determined by anatomy, biological determinism, and cultural restraints, but that his understanding of *all* human development was colored by the same interpretation. His discussion of the psychosexual stages of the male, no less than the female, was permeated with the notion of biological determinism and shared the same characteristics of inevitability and cultural bias. As Juliet Mitchell (1974) has pointed out, "psychoanalysis is not a recommendation *for* a patriarchal society but an analysis *of* one" (cf. Toronto, 1991). Jeffrey Okey (1991) suggests that the basic beliefs of contemporary psychoanalytic theory are very relevant to the understanding of the psychology of women. You should note, moreover, that women played a major role in the psychoanalytic movement and that Freud encouraged his daughter Anna and other women to become actively involved.

What do you think? Has Freud been unfairly maligned for his discussion of women? To what extent were his concepts a product of his social and cultural milieu? Gender is a biological division; sexuality is a social and psychological expression (Mitchell, 1991). If the presence of two sexes is a fact of biology, how do psychology and society take it into account? Wilkinson (1989) argues that the limited impact of feminist research in psychology is due to power and politics. In order to have a greater impact, feminists will need to use social processes that establish legitimacy.

questioned by most critics, who suggest it is more correct to observe that children learn to hide their sexuality from disapproving adults.

Genital Stage   With the onset of puberty, the infantile sexual life is transformed into its adult form. The **genital stage** emerges at adolescence when the genital organs mature. There is a rebirth of sexual and aggressive desires, and the sexual drive, which was formerly autoerotic, is redirected to seeking gratification from genuine interaction with others. During the latency period, children prefer the company of same-sexed peers; however, in time the object of the sexual drive shifts to members of the opposite sex. According to Freud, the genital stage is the end point of a long journey, from autoerotic sexual activity to the cultural norm of heterosexual activity. Freud believed that mature individuals seek to satisfy their sexual drives primarily through genital, reproductive activity with members of the opposite sex.

Mature people satisfy their needs in socially approved ways. They accommodate themselves to, function within, and seek to uphold the laws, taboos, and standards of their culture. These implications are clearly spelled out for both males and females. The hallmarks of maturity can be summed up in the German expression *lieben und arbeiten,* "to love and to work." The mature person is able to love in a sexually approved way and also to work productively in society.

The Effects of the Psychosexual Stages

The lingering effects of the psychosexual stages are revealed in various adult character types or traits. Freud believed strongly that events in the past can influence the present. If the libido is prevented from obtaining optimal satisfaction during one or more of the stages because it has been unduly frustrated or overindulged, it may become fixated or arrested at that particular stage. This **fixation** creates excessive needs characteristic of an earlier stage. The fixated libido expresses itself in adult life according to character types or traits that reflect the earlier level of development. Hence, an orally fixated person is likely to be dependent on and easily influenced by others. At the same time, oral personalities are optimistic and trusting to the point of being gullible. Anal personalities tend to be orderly, miserly, and obstinate. Most people, of course, do not reflect a pure type, but these personality traits and their opposites have their origin in the various psychosexual stages.

All of the sexual activities that Freud considered abnormal are at one time normal sexual activities for children. Prototypes of sadistic and masochistic forms of behavior, sexual disorders in which a person obtains pleasure by inflicting pain (sadism) or receiving pain (masochism), are apparent during the toddler years. Voyeurism, obtaining pleasure from seeing sexual organs or sexual acts, is present in the curiosity of the preschool child. Homosexuality, primary attraction to the same sex, is apparent during the latency period and early adolescence when one's primary association is with same-sexed peers. Thus,

Freud believed that sexual deviations may be accounted for in terms of arrested development.

Freud also viewed neurosis as the outcome of an inadequate sexual development, in particular an unsuccessfully resolved Oedipal conflict. Such people are bound to their unhappy past and repond in emotionally immature ways. These unrealistic ways are not helpful to them in the everyday world.

Freud's presentation of the stages of human psychosexual development may appear clumsy, because the gradual change from one stage to another is not as distinct as the outline implies. Therefore, the age references should be seen not as beginning and end points, but rather as focal points, where the stage is at its height. The emergence of the genital stage does not signify the end of the earlier ones; instead it transforms them. Thus, adult behavior is shaped by a complex of earlier conflicts and dynamics.

Freud's discussion of the psychosexual stages of personality was set in the framework of nineteenth-century biological determinism (Richards, 1990) and has been soundly criticized for its failure to appreciate deeply enough the influence of social and cultural factors. Nevertheless, empirical child development research argues against outright rejection of Freud's ideas on psychosexual development (Griffith, 1987; Neubauer & Neubauer, 1990). Moreover, Freud's conclusion overturned almost the entire Western tradition of thought concerning humanity. In Freud's theory, human life is subsumed under a sexual model. The way in which people invest their libido determines their future. Freud used sexuality as a model for a person's style of life: character is built up by responding to one's sexuality; the way in which a person resolves the Oedipus complex is crucial to adult personality; neurosis represents a fixation at an earlier stage of sexual development. The normal or mature individual is one who behaves conventionally, having attained the genital level of sexuality and all its implications. Furthermore, the development of culture and civilization is made possible by sublimated sexuality. Sexuality essentially becomes the model for human understanding.

The Structure of Personality

The familiar Freudian concept of the structure of personality as an id, ego, and superego was a rather late product of his thought. Not until 1923 with the publication of *The Ego and the Id* did Freud's final theory of a threefold structure of personality emerge. In discussing the id, ego, and superego, we must keep in mind that these are not three separate entities with sharply defined boundaries, but rather represent a variety of different processes, functions, and dynamics within the person. The psychoanalytic approach to the study of the mind illuminates processes that cognitive psychologists are studying today from their perspective (Goleman, 1985). Moreover, in his writings Freud used the German personal pronouns, *das Es, das Ich,* and *das uber-Ich.* Literally translated they mean "the it," "the I," and "the above-I." The Strachey translation into Latin pronouns has made them less personal (Bettelheim, 1982), raising the issue of the desirability of attempting a new translation (Likierman, 1990; Cheshire & Thoma, 1991).

The Id, Ego, and Superego

The **id** is the "core of our being," the oldest and original function of the personality and the basis of the other two. We know little of the id, because it does not present itself to our consciousness in naked form. Therefore, we can describe it only by analogies and by comparing it with the ego. Freud referred to it as a "chaos, a cauldron full of seething excitations." The id includes the instincts and drives that motivate us as well as our genetic inheritance and our reflexes and capacities to respond. It represents our basic drives, needs, and wishes. Further, it is the reservoir of psychic energy that provides the power for all psychological functioning.

The impersonal and uncontrollable character of the id is more readily expressed in the German language than in English. For example, the German idiom for "I am hungry" ("*Es hungert mich*") translates literally as "It hungers me," implying that I am a recipient of actions initiated *in* me, not *by* me.

The id operates according to the pleasure principle and employs primary processes. The **pleasure principle** refers to seeking immediate tension reduction. When libido (psychic energy) builds up, it reaches an uncomfortable level of tension. The id seeks to discharge the tension and return to a more comfortable level of energy. In seeking to avoid painful tension and obtain pleasure, the id takes no precautions but acts immediately in an impulsive, nonrational way. It pays no heed to the consequences of its actions and therefore frequently behaves in a manner that may be harmful to the self or others.

The id seeks to satisfy its needs partly through reflex action. Inborn automatic responses like sneezing, yawning, and blinking are spontaneous and unlearned, and operate without any conscious thought or effort. Many of our reflexes are protective in that they help us to ward off dangers in our environment. Others are adaptive and enable us to adjust to the conditions of our environment. Newborn infants have several reflexes that help to ensure their survival. For instance, they turn their heads toward the source of tactile stimulation. This "rooting reflex" assists them in locating the nipple. Sucking is also an automatic reflex enabling infants to take in nourishment.

The id also seeks to reduce tension through **primary processes**, hallucinating or forming an image of the object that would satisfy its needs. Freud thought that visualizing a forthcoming hamburger or sirloin steak momentarily relieves our hunger pangs; such activity is also called **wish fulfillment**. It is present in newborns, in our dreams, and in the hallucinations of psychotics. Visualizing a bottle or the breast partly pacifies the infant, but it does not satisfy its hunger. Since the primary process does not distinguish between its wish-fulfilling images and real objects in the external world that would satisfy needs, it is not very effective in reducing tension. A second structure must develop if the organism is to survive.

The **ego** ("I") emerges in order to realistically meet the wishes and demands of the id in accordance with the outside world. People who are hungry have to be effective in securing food for themselves from the environment in order to meet their needs and survive. The ego evolves out of the id and acts as an intermediary between the id and the external world. It draws on the id's energy, acquires its structures and functions from the id, and endeavors to serve the id by realistically meeting its demands. Thus, the ego is the executor of the personality, curbing the id and maintaining transactions with the external world in the interests of the fuller personality.

Whereas the id obeys the pleasure principle, the ego follows the **reality principle**, satisfying the id's impulses in an appropriate manner in the external world. The ego postpones the discharge of tension until the appropriate object that will satisfy the need has been found. Although the ego does not prevent the satisfaction of the id, it may suspend or redirect the id's wishes in accordance with the demands of reality. The id employs the fantasies and wishes of the primary process; the ego uses realistic thinking characteristic of **secondary processes**, the cognitive and perceptual skills that help an individual distinguish between fact and fantasy. They include the higher intellectual functions of problem solving, which let the ego establish suitable courses of action and test them for their effectiveness. Actually, there is no natural enmity between the ego and the id. The ego is a "faithful servant" of the id and tries to fulfill its needs realistically.

Harbored within the ego as "its innermost core" is the **superego** ("above-I"). Heir to the Oedipus complex, it represents internalized values, ideals, and moral standards. The superego is the last function of the personality to develop and may be seen as an outcome of the interactions with one's parents during the long period of childhood dependency. Rewards and punishments originally placed on us from without become self-administered as we internalize the teachings of our parents and society. As a result of the activity of the superego we experience guilt when we disobey acceptable moral standards.

The superego consists of two subsystems: the conscience and the ego-ideal. The **conscience** refers to the capacity for self-evaluation, criticism, and reproach. It scolds the ego and creates feelings of guilt when moral codes are violated. The **ego-ideal** is an ideal self-image consisting of approved and rewarded behaviors. It is the source of pride and a concept of who we think we should be.

The superego strives for perfection. It seeks moralistic rather than realistic solutions. Practically speaking, the development of the superego is a necessity. The id's demands are too strong, and young children's egos are too weak to prevent them from acting on their impulses. For a period of time, strong introjected moral injunctions — "Thou shalt nots" — are required to curb behavior. But the superego may also be relentless and cruel in its insistence on perfection. Its moralistic demands may resemble those of the id in their intensity, blindness, and irrationality. In its uncompromising manner, the superego may inhibit the needs of the id, rather than permit their ultimate necessary and appropriate satisfaction.

In the well-adjusted adult personality, the ego is the primary executor. It controls and governs both id and superego, mediating between their demands and the external world. In ideal functioning, the ego maintains a balanced, harmonious relationship among the various elements with which it has to deal, setting values (Treurniet, 1989) and assuming responsibility (Wallwork, 1991). Development, though, does not always proceed optimally. The ego frequently ends up harassed by two harsh masters. One demands instant satisfaction and release. The other places rigid prescriptions on that release. Drawing on Plato's analogy, Freud described the ego as a charioteer trying to control two strong horses, each of which is trying to run in the opposite direction from the other.

Freud's final picture of personality is that of a self divided. The specific roles played by the id, ego, and superego are not always clear; they mingle at too many levels. The self is seen to consist of many diverse forces in inevitable conflict. Freud's picture of the person is not optimistic, but it is an attempt to account for the fact that as human beings we are not always able to cope with certain situations.

Although the trifold division of personality appears to be a finished structure, essentially the person is understood as a product of development. The ego and superego have evolved historically in response to specific personal situations. In the case of the superego, that situation is also interpersonal since it involves other people. It would be wrong to freeze the id, ego, and superego into systems; instead, the personality is created by a dynamic of forces that can be divided against themselves at many levels. Thus, in his mature formulation, Freud holds in tension the biological ground of the self and its historical development.

The Relationship of the Id, Ego, and Superego to Consciousness

There is no easy correlation between the words "id," "ego," and "superego" and the qualities of "conscious" and "unconscious." At times, Freud tended to make the easy equation of ego with consciousness and id with unconsciousness. His discoveries, reflected in *The Ego and the Id,* that aspects of the ego and the superego are unconscious, as is the id, forced him to revise his theory. "Conscious" and "unconscious" could be used only as adjectives describing qualities that psychological processes may or may not have (cf. Stolorow & Atwood, 1989).

If one were to diagram Freud's picture of the psyche, perhaps the best image would be Freud's own: an iceberg, nine-tenths of which is submerged under water (Figure 2.1). The surface of the water represents the boundary between conscious and unconscious. Its line intersects, or potentially intersects, all three functions of id, ego, and superego. But any spatial metaphor is ultimately misleading. "Id," "ego," and "superego" are best understood as dynamic functions

THINKING CRITICALLY

Are We Better Off?

Freud (1933) wrote, "Where id is, there shall ego be." He might also have written, "Where superego is, there shall ego be." What kind of balance between the forces of id, ego, and superego do you think best fosters a healthy personality? Which human responses do we need to inhibit and which do we need to encourage for a healthy society?

Different cultures and social conditions foster different patterns of defense. Because Victorian society placed rigid taboos on the expression of sexual impulses, Freud believed that many of his patients developed neuroses as a result of rigid and unrelenting superegos.

Our culture, on the other hand, is characterized by far less repression of sexual and aggressive impulses. Indeed, the media actually seem to foster the explicit expression of sexual behavior. Graphic portrayals of murder and violence in the media have desensitized many young people to life's tragedies. They sometimes react with laughter (rather than fear or empathy) at bizarre forms of horror depicted on the screen and are less able to give help to other people in a genuine emergency. The laughter may serve as protection from the feelings of anxiety and depersonalization generated by a high-technology society.

One might say that a shift has occurred from an overactive superego to an unrepressed id. But are we better off because of this change? What do you think? During the 1970s American psychologists found fewer anxiety disorders, such as Freud observed in his patients, and more personality disorders involving maladaptive personality patterns such as the antisocial or narcissistic personality (Lasch, 1978), which disrupt society rather than the individual. However the 1990s is seeing a renewed increase in stress and anxiety disorders in part due to the increased pace and economic recession of the past decade.

This is not to say that we are a totally unrepressed society. An increase in sexual behaviors does not mean that sexual feelings are not repressed. There is reason to suspect that the so-called sexual liberation has not been very liberating (especially for women). The average person still seems to have trouble with aggressive feelings. Our competitive society may be inhibiting the development of nourishing impulses or empathetic responses. If the id is unrepressed, the ego is repressed.

Freud advocated more social opportunities for the sublimation of both sexual and aggressive impulses. You may be able to think of other human responses that our society and other cultures either repress or encourage.

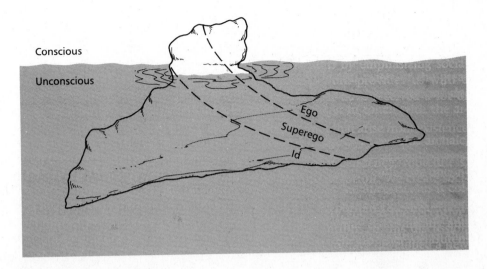

Figure 2.1   *The Psyche as an Iceberg*
Freud described the psyche as an iceberg, nine-tenths of which is submerged under water.

of personality, while "conscious" and "unconscious" are adjectives that describe qualities that these functions may have.

The dynamic forces within the self are many. The self is not simply divided against itself by id, ego, and superego but divided against itself and the world at many levels. Conflict is the keynote of Freud's final understanding of the self. The world, Freud once wrote, is *anake* (the Greek word for "a lack"), too poor to meet all of our needs. As the id's demands increase, the ego becomes overwhelmed with excessive stimulation that it cannot control and becomes flooded with anxiety.

The Ego's Defense Mechanisms

Freud made a distinction among three kinds of anxiety. *Reality anxiety* refers to fear of a real danger in the external world. *Neurotic anxiety* refers to fear that one's inner impulses cannot be controlled. *Moral anxiety* is a fear of the retributions of one's own conscience. All have their basis in reality anxiety. In order for an individual to cope with anxiety, the ego develops **defense mechanisms,** procedures that ward off anxiety and prevent our conscious perception of it. Defense mechanisms share two features: they occur on an unconscious level so that we are not aware of what we are doing, and they deny or distort reality so as to make it less threatening. Defense mechanisms are not necessarily maladaptive; indeed, we cannot survive without them. They must be created to assist the developing ego in carrying out its functions. However, should their distortion of reality become too extreme or should they be used to the exclusion of other, more effective means of dealing with reality, defense mechanisms may become maladaptive and destructive, preventing further personal and social growth. Some of the more common defense mechanisms follow.

Repression involves blocking a wish or desire from expression so that it cannot be experienced consciously or expressed directly in behavior. It is an involuntary act, which prevents us from being aware of many of our own anxiety-producing conflicts or remembering certain traumatic emotional events from our past. The repressed emotion seeks an alternative outlet, and resistance is required to prevent its emergence into consciousness. Nevertheless, once formed, repressions are difficult to eliminate.

Denial entails refusing to believe a reality or fact of life. Many people who indulge in substance abuse deny that the alcohol, nicotine, crack, or other substance could ever really hurt them. They may see it affect other people, but "that's not going to happen to me."

Projection refers to the unconscious attribution of an impulse, attitude, or behavior onto someone or something else in the environment. An individual who unconsciously feels hostile toward someone may project the hostility onto the other person. Such a defense reduces anxiety by placing its source in the external world, which makes it seem easier to handle. Further, it permits us to defend ourselves aggressively against our opponent and thereby indirectly express our impulses.

Reaction formation expresses an impulse by its opposite. Hostility, for example, may be replaced by friendship. Frequently, however, the substitution is exaggerated, thereby calling into question the genuineness of the feeling.

In **regression** the person moves backward in time to a stage that was less anxious and had fewer responsibilities. Regression frequently occurs following a traumatic experience. The child who begins bedwetting again when frightened by the prospect of going to school may be showing signs of regression.

Rationalization involves dealing with an emotion or impulse analytically and intellectually in order to avoid feeling it. As the term implies, it involves faulty reasoning, since the problem remains unresolved on the emotional level. Aesop's fable about the fox who could not reach the grapes and concluded that they were probably sour is a classic example of rationalization.

In **identification** we reduce anxiety by modeling our behavior on that of someone else. By assuming the characteristics of a model who appears more successful in gratifying needs, we can believe that we also possess those attributes. We may also identify with an authority figure who is resented and feared. Such identification may assist us in avoiding punishment. As we have already seen, identification with the same-sexed parent plays an important role in development of the superego and subsequent personality.

If an object that would satisfy an impulse of the id is unavailable, we may shift our impulse onto another object. Such substitution is called **displacement.** A child who has been scolded may hit a younger sibling or kick the dog. The substitute object, however, is rarely as satisfying as the original object. Thus,

THINKING CRITICALLY

Identifying Defense Mechanisms

You can familiarize yourself with the various defenses by trying to identify each of the mechanisms in Table 2.1 as you have seen them occur in someone else, and then trying to recognize instances in which you may have used them yourself. It is much easier, of course, to observe defense processes at work in someone else; however, some of the following hints may help you to spot them. Have you ever ''forgotten'' an important event, such as an assigned test or a dentist appointment? You may also recall momentarily forgetting the name of someone you know quite well. Such occasions indicate the tendency we all have to repress. Memory gaps on childhood events, in which you can recall only part of an event but not what preceded or followed, may indicate that the event involved certain traumatic elements that make it hard for you to remember it completely. Have your parents ever told you about an experience that you had as a child but cannot remember? Have you ever found yourself laughing at an inappropriate moment? You may have compensated for an impulse you are ashamed of by reaction formation. Have you ever provided an alibi for something you did or did not do? Could it have been an attempt to rationalize your behavior? Can you recall ever taking out your anger on someone who was helpless, such as a child or pet? Use of scapegoats is a common form of displacement. What kinds of leisure activities, sports, or creative and artistic activities do you enjoy? Through sublimation you may have been able to redirect certain antisocial impulses into socially approved and constructive behaviors. Sublimation is one of the more productive defense mechanisms available to us. In short, we all have and need defenses. Recognizing the use of a defense mechanism is not an occasion for finding fault with ourselves; rather, it is an opportunity for further exploration of our use of defense mechanisms so that they can be employed to foster instead of hinder growth.

displacement does not bring complete satisfaction but leads to a buildup of undischarged tension.

Sublimation rechannels an unacceptable impulse into a more socially desirable outlet. It is a form of displacement that redirects the impulse itself rather than the object. For example, sexual curiosity may be redirected into intellectual research; sexual activity into athletics. Freud suggested that sublimation was crucial to the development of culture and civilization. It is clear from biographical studies that sublimation was a defense commonly used by Freud.

Defense mechanisms, in and of themselves, are not harmful. No one is free of defenses; we need them in order to survive. Although defenses can block personal and social growth if they become predominant, they do protect us from excessive anxiety and frequently represent creative solutions to our

Table 2.1 *Defense Mechanisms*

Repression

characteristics: blocking a wish or desire from conscious expression
example: being unaware of deep-seated hostilities toward one's parents

Denial

characteristics: refusing to believe a reality
example: refusing to believe that one has AIDS or a terminal cancer

Projection

characteristics: attributing an unconscious impulse, attitude, or behavior to another
example: blaming another for your act or thinking that someone is out to get you

Reaction formation

characteristics: expressing an impulse by its opposite
example: treating someone whom you intensely dislike in a friendly manner

Regression

characteristics: returning to an earlier form of expressing an impulse
example: resuming bedwetting after one has long since stopped

Rationalization

characteristics: dealing with an emotion intellectually to avoid emotional concern
example: arguing that "Everybody else does it, so I don't have to feel guilty."

Identification

characteristics: modeling behavior after someone else
example: imitating one's mother or father

Displacement

characteristics: satisfying an impulse with a substitute object
example: scapegoating

Sublimation

characteristics: rechanneling an impulse into a more socially desirable outlet
example: satisfying sexual curiosity by researching sexual behaviors

problems. In recent years new research has begun to emerge on the develop-ment, measurement, and future potential of Freud's concepts of defense mech-anisms and ego processes. Some of this work has been summarized by Cooper (1989), Grzegolowska-Klarkowska (1988), Schibuk, Bond, & Bouffard (1989), and Vaillant (1992a, 1992b).

Psychoanalysis

We have seen that for Freud neurosis emerges from an unsatisfactory or arrested libidinal development, when the realistic satisfaction of erotic needs is denied. The person turns to neurosis as a surrogate satisfaction and creates a partially satisfying world of fantasy. Neurotics have no peculiar psychic content or func-tioning of their own that is not also found in healthy people. The neurotic is one who falls ill from the same conflicts and complexes with which normal people struggle. There are no clearly defined boundaries between illness and health. The primary question is not "Am I normal or neurotic?" but rather "To what degree is my neurosis debilitating?"

Transference

Early in his work, Freud realized that the relationship between patient and phy-sician was important in determining the outcome of the therapy. Nevertheless, it was with considerable embarrassment that he discovered one of his patients had fallen in love with him. We recall that a similar episode with his patient Anna O. had led Dr. Breuer to abandon the cathartic technique. Only after con-siderable reservations and initial attempts to discourage similar occurrences did Freud begin to appreciate the dynamics of what was happening. He discovered that the feelings that were expressed toward him as a doctor were not directed at him as a person but rather were repetitions of earlier feelings of love and affection that the patient had for significant persons in her life. Thus, Freud was forced to recognize the value of the **transference,** a process whereby the patient transfers to the analyst emotional attitudes felt as a child toward important per-sons. By deliberately cultivating and analyzing the transference, Freud and his patients were able to learn a great deal.

Freud distinguished between *positive transference,* friendly, affectionate feel-ings toward the physician, and *negative transference,* characterized by the expres-sion of hostile, angry feelings. By studying the transference, Freud learned that his patients were relating to him in the same unsatisfactory and inefficient ways in which they had related to other important people in their lives. However, in the security of analysis, the patient could rework these earlier unsatisfactory relation-ships through the current relationship to a satisfactory resolution.

It is difficult to know if Freud himself ever fully recognized the implications of the transference, but its cultivation and interpretation have become crucial to the psychoanalytic technique he fathered. Transference offers the patient an opportunity to relive the emotional conflicts and cognitive structures that led to repressions and provides the analyst with a deeper understanding of the patient's characteristic ways of perceiving and reacting. The major point here is that in analysis the patient experiences conflicts under a different set of circumstances. The analyst does not respond to the patient with disapproval or rejection as earlier individuals may have done. Rather, the analyst reacts with insight and understanding, which permits the patient to gain insight into experiences and feelings and allows for change.

Freud's solution is one of *insight,* but the insight that psychoanalysis provides is a special kind of knowing that is not intellectual but existential. It touches the heart as well as the head. The solution does not lie in the realm of knowing but in the realm of doing: working through earlier conflicts. Discovering one's self is not only an intellectual act, but also an emotional experience. To use the Socratic expression: "To know is to do." Thus, therapy provides a more effective resolution of the situation that provoked the neurosis.

The Analytic Process

In classical analysis, the patient lies on a couch and the analyst sits behind, out of view. The patient is instructed to verbalize whatever comes to mind regardless of how irrelevant, absurd, or unpleasant it may seem. During free association the patient may make a slip of the tongue or refer to a dream, both of which may be interpreted and utilized to assist the patient to acquire a deeper understanding of the problem.

In the initial phase of analysis, the patient obtains considerable relief just by being able to unburden certain thoughts and feelings to a sympathetic listener. A positive transference is developed, and the patient frequently believes that the analysis has reached a successful conclusion, even though the work of analysis has barely begun. There are as yet undisclosed and conflicting feelings. During the next phase, the analyst gently assists the patient in exploring these emotion-laden areas by pointing out and interpreting the resistance in an effort to weaken the patient's defenses and bring repressed conflicts into the open. The analyst's efforts leave the patient angry, anxious, or depressed; the analyst is now perceived as rejecting and unhelpful. Thoughts of prematurely concluding the analysis may again arise. Eventually the negative transference begins to cohere around specific areas. The patient reconstructs and re-experiences crucial episodes from childhood. The unremediated situation of the past includes not simply insufficiently resolved traumatic events but, more important, inadequately resolved interpersonal relationships and fantasies. The analyst maintains a neutral stance, interpreting the transference and encouraging the patient to re-examine those circumstances in the light of increased maturity. The analyst's stance enables the patient to work through these situations to a more satisfactory conclusion. Last, the analyst assists the patient in converting newly won insights into everyday existence and behavior. This emotional re-education enables the new insights to become a permanent part of the patient's personality.

In its traditional form, analysis is a protracted and expensive procedure. The patient meets with the analyst for fifty-minute sessions an average of five times a week for a period of several years. This requires a considerable commitment in terms of time, effort, and money. Contemporary analysts have refined the process further, realizing the importance of such issues as overcoming resistance, recognizing the danger of countertransference (which proceeds from the analyst to the patient; see Ornstein, 1983; Goleman, 1993a), and working through issues on an emotional level. The goal of psychoanalysis is an ambitious one — a full understanding, reorganization, and basic change of the personality structure. Such goals cannot be accomplished quickly or easily. And, as Freud (1917) once wrote, "A neurotic who has been cured has really become a different person . . . he has become his best self, what he would have been under the most favorable conditions."

Empirical Validation of Psychoanalytic Concepts

Freud's theory generated a great deal of empirical research and attempts to test his concepts. A large body of literature (for example, Sears, 1943, Kline, 1972, and Fisher & Greenberg, 1977; Geisler, 1985) deals with attempts to test in a laboratory or other setting hypotheses derived from Freud's ideas to see whether they function usefully as science.

As we have seen (in Chapter 1), an experimental method is favored by many psychologists because it permits us to infer a cause-and-effect relationship between two factors. Thus, for example, Lloyd Silverman (1976) designed an experiment to test the hypothesis that depression arises from aggressive feelings that have been turned inward against the self. He tried to activate unconscious aggressive wishes to see whether or not they would result in an intensification of depressed feelings. In one session, he showed a group of subjects pictures and verbal messages that were designed to elicit unconscious aggressive wishes. The images included pictures such as a fierce man with a knife and the message "Cannibal eats person." In another session, Silverman showed the same group neutral images of people reading or walking. These two sets of images constituted the independent variable. The subjects were exposed to the images for only 4/1000 of a second, so that their perception was assumed to be subliminal. Before and after the sessions, the subjects were asked to rate their feelings. Their self-ratings represented the dependent variable. As expected, the subjects reported more depressive feelings after seeing the aggressive images than after seeing the neutral ones.

In yet another study, Hall and Van de Castle (1965) investigated whether or not male dreamers reported more dreams expressive of castration anxiety and fewer dreams expressive of penis envy than women. They did. Of course, Hall and Van de Castle had to carefully develop a scoring manual that spelled out specific criteria for interpreting various dream themes as indicative of castration anxiety and penis envy. They also had to show that there was agreement among different scorers. As you can see, some of these efforts to test Freud's theory have demonstrated much ingenuity and sophistication.

Not all Freudian concepts have held up well under scrutiny. For example, it has become untenable in light of modern research in embryology, biology, and female psychosexual development to view the female as a castrated male whose less-developed superego and negative view of her body is due to penis

PHILOSOPHICAL ASSUMPTIONS

Examining Freud

How would you rate Freud on each of the basic philosophical assumptions described in Chapter 1? Each basic issue was presented as a bipolar dimension along which a person's view can be placed according to the degree of agreement with one or the other extreme. Rate Freud's views on these issues.

When you have determined where you think Freud stands, compare your responses with those of your classmates and your instructor. You should be willing to defend your ratings, but also be prepared to change them in light of others' compelling arguments. Afterward, compare your rating of Freud with your own position on each issue and with those of other theorists. Does this comparison help you to understand why his theory does or does not appeal to you?

Would strongly agree	Would agree	Is neutral or believes in synthesis of both views	Would agree	Would strongly agree
1	2	3	4	(5)

freedom	**determinism**
People basically have control over their own behavior and understand the motives behind their behavior.	The behavior of people is basically determined by internal or external forces over which they have little, if any, control.

envy (Small, 1989). Wolberg (1989) suggests Freud's views on female sexuality are more illuminating about the dilemmas Freud faced when his observations did not fit his theory. Similar comments have been made about some of his case studies (Magid, 1993). Nor has it been substantiated that the male resolves the Oedipus complex by identifying with the father and accepting his superego standards out of fear (Schultz, 1990). Studies have supported Freud's idea that dreams may express in a disguised or symbolic manner an individual's emotional concerns (Breger, Hunter, & Lane, 1971) but do not confirm that they fulfill unconscious wishes (Demont & Wolper, 1958).

Other Freudian concepts, however, appear to stand up under scrutiny.

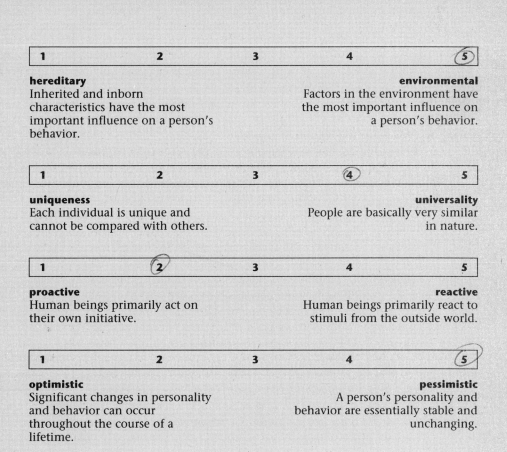

| 1 | 2 | 3 | 4 | ⑤ |

hereditary
Inherited and inborn characteristics have the most important influence on a person's behavior.

environmental
Factors in the environment have the most important influence on a person's behavior.

| 1 | 2 | 3 | ④ | 5 |

uniqueness
Each individual is unique and cannot be compared with others.

universality
People are basically very similar in nature.

| 1 | ② | 3 | 4 | 5 |

proactive
Human beings primarily act on their own initiative.

reactive
Human beings primarily react to stimuli from the outside world.

| 1 | 2 | 3 | 4 | ⑤ |

optimistic
Significant changes in personality and behavior can occur throughout the course of a lifetime.

pessimistic
A person's personality and behavior are essentially stable and unchanging.

These include aspects of Freud's oral and anal personality types (Masling, Rabie, & Blondheim, 1967; Tribich & Messer, 1974; Kline, 1972). Studies in both normal and psychiatric populations seem to confirm that psychopathology results from unconscious, conflicting aggressive or sexual wishes. Brain research has supported concepts such as unconscious processes, primary process cognition, conversion disorders, and the conflictual nature of the mind (Ducat, 1985). The concept of repression has been operationally defined as a stronger tendency to forget events identified with unpleasant or fearful associations than with neutral or pleasant events (Glucksberg & King, 1967; Davis, 1987). Defining unconscious as *unable to be verbalized* enables such processes to be subjected to experimental study (Kline, 1987). Experimental test of these and other psychoanalytically oriented hypotheses indicates their usefulness (Shurcliff, 1968; Hammer, 1970; Silverman, 1976).

It is often difficult to translate Freud's concepts into operational procedures that allow for unequivocal test. The operational translation of many of Freud's concepts may misinterpret and oversimplify his ideas. The Freudian theory of repression does not simply imply experiences associated with unpleasant thoughts; thus, studies on repression may deal with phenomena that are essentially different from the kind of phenomena that concerned Freud. At this time, there is no direct evidence that will substantiate concepts such as the id, ego, superego, libido, death wish, and anxiety. Moreover, if the concepts are distorted and minimized, they will not truly represent the constructs in Freud's thought. Freud's own investigations and those of other psychoanalysts hardly allow for replication because they were carried out under conditions of privacy and confidentiality.

Some critics believe that the scientific pretension of psychoanalytic theory rests on very shaky ground (MacIntyre, 1958; Fingarette 1963; Grünbaum, 1979, 1980, 1984; Rinaldi, 1990). Others are very optimistic about achieving a merger of experimental operations and clinical observations in the study of psychoanalytic phenomena. Some suggest that there may be a possible convergence of psychoanalysis and recent neuroscientific information (Edelson, 1986). Erdelyi (1985), Power & Brewin (1991), Shevrin (1992), Stein (1992), and Wakefield (1992) suggest that the emerging cognitive psychology, which is based on generative linguistics and information science, may provide the cognitive framework with which to assimilate psychoanalysis. They point out that psychoanalysis is essentially a cognitive psychology concerned with problems of consciousness, structure, representation, meaning, storage and retrieval, transformation, and bias in thinking. There is a wealth of information in modern psychology that was not available to Freud: the findings of anthropology regarding the cultural nature of humanity, empirical studies of mother-infant interaction and of the competence of infants, the discovery of REM (rapid eye movement) sleep, the role of emotions in individual arousal and social communication, the growth of the psychology of sex differences, and studies in cognitive style (Lewis, 1988). Given the information that was not available to him, the visionary nature of many of Freud's ideas and the fact that his concepts continue to engender such lively research and debate is all the more impressive.

Freud's Theory: Philosophy, Science, and Art

Educated in the precise methods of nineteenth-century science, Freud established a reputation as a medical researcher before he developed the theory of psychoanalysis. In his writings he clearly defined and described the scientific enterprise. He asserted that knowledge is based on empirical observation and dogmatically maintained that his own theories were so based. His concepts, he claimed, were merely tentative constructs to be discarded if later observation failed to confirm them. He frequently revised his theories because new data had emerged that could not be accounted for by those theories.

Freud made careful observations of his patients in the therapeutic setting and garnered considerable information from the techniques of free association and dream analysis. He made interpretations and viewed the subsequent behavior of his patients as confirmation or disproof of his hypotheses. And he also conducted his own self-analysis, beginning in 1897 and continuing throughout his life. Data collected through self-analysis may properly be called empirical, as it is based on observation. The fact that the observer is looking in ("introspection") rather than out ("extrospection") does not make the data any less empirical, although information gathered through introspection may be more difficult to test.

Nevertheless, in determining how Freud's theory functions, we have to look not only at the data on which it was initially based, but also at the method he used to test the data. Although he claimed that he was merely extending scientific knowledge by placing the psychic life of human beings under scientific observation, Freud permitted many of his concepts to function philosophically. We have seen that an important criterion of scientific constructs is the requirement that they be open to falsification; the desire to be scientific reflects itself in an effort to test constructs by validating evidence rather than by simply relying on the compelling character of a philosophical assumption. Freud, however, defined many of his concepts as all-controlling factors in everything we do, think, and are. It is impossible to conceive of any activity in Freud's theory that does not reflect unconscious motives as well as conscious ones. The doctrine of unconscious processes is thus lifted out of an immediate empirical construct and made applicable to all possible human behavior. Even objections to the concept can be explained in terms of resistance or other unconscious processes. Sexuality is a philosophical concept insofar as Freud asserted that all human behavior can be considered in its light.

And so we see that Freud drew conclusions from careful self-observation and the observation of his patients in a clinical setting and projected those conclusions into philosophical assumptions. Although Freud invested his theories with an aura of science, in evaluating them he made primary use of philosophical criteria, relying on their compelling power rather than validating evidence. The kind of knowing on which psychoanalysis is ultimately based is epiphanic, a form of knowing that does not rely on everyday experiences but transcends them.

It is inaccurate to portray Freud as a scientific medical doctor. To do so distorts much of the humanism present in his writings and blunts the challenge of psychoanalysis, which is to know oneself with the constant obligation to change oneself (Bettelheim, 1982).

In evaluating Freud's work, therefore, it is most appropriate to use the criteria that apply to philosophical positions and ask if it is coherent, relevant, comprehensive, and compelling.

Although Freud changed and revised his theory, in the end it presented a coherent pattern with a clearly recognizable consistent thrust. To be sure, his theory is not a finished whole. Not only did he continually modify it, but it has been revised, modified, and updated by others working within the Freudian tradition. Freud was frequently unsympathetic to efforts to modify his theory and claimed the ultimate right to declare what should and should not be called psychoanalysis, but he was not unreceptive to changes that reflected the spirit of psychoanalysis as an evolving movement of a particular form of thought and investigation.

MacIntyre (1958) suggested that Freud's theoretical work denoted a "kind of creative untidiness." His thought was characterized by illuminating insights followed by efforts at sterile systematization, yet "he never presents us with a finished structure but with the far more exciting prospect of working through a number of possible ways of talking and thinking." This may be taken as the essential character of Freud's work. He seems to be saying, "You don't have to talk that way"; that personality can be illuminated by a different picture. If you take one image and isolate it, you tend toward being either reductionistic or projectionistic. Thus Freud himself would talk several different ways at once, often flagrantly contradicting himself in order to illumine his subject. Freud depicted a person as simultaneously an economic machine, a personal history, a case, comprehended totally by sexuality, socially and historically constructed.

For Freud's ideas to be relevant in the twentieth and twenty-first centuries, they must be reworked and reformulated in contemporary terms. Many of Freud's arguments, informed by nineteenth-century culture, science, and philosophy, are clearly dated. Critiques of Freud that focus on the analysis of language and meaning (for example, Ricoeur, 1970, and Lacan, 1981) have been helpful in assimilating Freud's work into the greater body of philosophy. Doi (1990) suggests that the Japanese concept of *amae,* an interpersonal process and important organizing principle for understanding emotions, may complement psychoanalysis. Today several of Freud's concepts are seen as foreshadowing current views on the importance of both nature and nurture by evolutionary biologistic and developmental psychologists (Koch, 1991). Freud's theory does not constitute a finished structure; it is an open one capable of continued growth.

The relevance of Freud's theory is evidenced by its impact on the Western world. Freud's faults were his virtues in that they enabled him to break through the rational optimism of the enlightenment and make possible a new view. Freud changed, perhaps irrevocably, humanity's image of itself. Since Aristotle, the essence of humanity had been located in our ability to think. This image found ultimate expression in Descartes's phrase "I think, therefore I am." In this post-Freudian world, our self-image has changed. We no longer conceive of ourselves as primarily rational animals; rather, we are pleasure-seeking, sexual, and aggressive creatures driven by our emotions. In a sense Freud begins his philosophy with "I love (or crave), therefore I am." For many, the gospel of psychoanalysis is not "good news" because it forces us to consider aspects of ourselves that we would prefer to ignore. Still, it is virtually impossible to deny Freud his influence.

The impact of Freud's accomplishments has been favorably compared with the impact of Copernicus, Darwin, and Einstein. Freud's name is a household word. Errors of the pen or tongue are commonly known as "Freudian slips," and many people cannot make one without wondering what the unconscious reason is. He grappled with ideas that were, are, and will continue to be of primary concern to us. Because of that his theories interest, allure, and excite people.

Freud's aim was to develop a comprehensive theory of humanity. He consistently maintained that his study of neurosis would eventually provide a key to the study of psychological processes in general. Freud's quest for the truth was unrelenting; no question was too small for his consideration; no probe was too trivial; no psychological process was too insignificant for his attention. To look for meaning on the surface was, for him, to settle for appearances and superficiality. Only by risking a plunge into the depths of the unconscious could one discover the truth about oneself and others. Any contradiction or opposition to his theory was to be met by analysis of the resistance, for only through such analysis could true insight emerge.

Some (see, for example, Ellenberger, 1970) have suggested that Freud founded a school comparable to the philosophical schools of ancient Greece and Rome. With the creation of psychoanalysis, Freud developed a movement characterized by its own rules, rituals, and doctrine of membership. As an art, Freudian psychoanalysis is an excellent example of the scholarly approach to psychotherapy (cf. Magid, 1993).

It is possible that after studying Freud, one may agree that his concepts are coherent, relevant, and comprehensive, yet remain uncompelled. Freud would counter that the insight required for a full appreciation of his theory is of a particular kind, one that can be acquired only through the kind of analytic self-investigation practiced by him and his followers. Freud's theory is by no means universally accepted. Indeed, few other positions in the history of philosophical thought have been subject to as much attack, ridicule, and criticism (see, for example, Torrey, 1992). In modern science, only the theory of Charles Darwin has been met with equal scorn and resistance. Nevertheless, Freud's picture of personality is one that compels many people. His picture of the personality as beset by anxieties, governed by forces of which we are largely unaware, living in a world marked by external and internal conflicts, resolving problems by solutions informed by fantasy or reality, is a concept of personality that some people find irresistible. Nevertheless, Freud's work reflects the cultural and social values of Western Europe and North America. The concept of ego is rooted in a culture that cultivates and emphasizes the individual. Such a concept may not be as fundamental to the development of personality in collectivist societies such as Latin America, Africa, and Asia (Markus & Kitayama, 1991; Landrine & Klonoff, 1992).

Summary

1. The case of Anna O. may be seen as the beginning of psychoanalysis. Anna O. suffered from a conversion disorder in which her right arm and leg were paralyzed, she had difficulty seeing, was nauseous, and was unable to drink any liquids or to speak and understand her mother tongue. She was also prone to states of absence. Dr. Joseph Breuer hypnotized her and asked her to verbalize associations she might have to words she mumbled during her absences. She began to tell him stories about her father's illness and death. After she had told a number of these stories, her symptoms went away.

    Freud began to use the "talking method" with his own patients and he concluded that at the time of the original trauma the patient had had to hold back a strong emotion. The patient had forgotten the event and was unconscious or unaware of it. Freud's concept of unconscious processes is a dynamic one in which certain forces repress undesirable thoughts and then actively resist their becoming conscious.

2. An emotion, prevented from expressing itself normally, may be expressed through a neurotic symptom. **Wishes** are repressed because they go against a person's self-concept. Underlying Freud's concept is the idea that emotions that accompany events must ultimately be expressed. If they cannot find direct expression, they will find indirect ones, such as neurotic symptoms. Ideally, the expression of emotions is nondestructive.

3. Freud developed the technique of **free association** in order to help his patients recover repressed ideas. The patient is asked to verbalize whatever comes to mind no matter how insignificant, trivial, or even unpleasant the idea might be. Later he or she *reflects* upon those associations.

4. Freud considered **slips** and dreams to be "the royal road" to the unconscious. They are analyzed by free associating to the slip itself or to the various elements of the dream. The analysis helps us to distinguish between the **manifest dream** and the **latent dream** that underlies it.

5. The nature of our repressed wishes and desires is sexual. Freud redefined the concept of sexuality as pleasure seeking. In doing so, he reversed many traditional concepts and was able to account for previously unexplained behaviors. As his work developed, he emphasized the psychological aspects of mental processes and sexuality, an emphasis apparent in his use of the terms **drive** and **libido**.

6. Freud outlined a set of **psychosexual stages** that children travel as they progress from **autoerotic** sexual activity to mature, reproductive activity. The libido invests itself in various **erogenous zones**. During the **oral stage**, the major source of pleasure and pain is the mouth. The **anal stage** follows; libidinal energy is focused on the anus and the buttocks. During the **phallic stage** the genital organs become important and children experience the **Oedipus complex**, whose resolution leads to the development of a **superego** and sexual identification. The **latency period** is one of rest, and the **genital stage** begins at puberty when the sexual organs mature and the individual is able to assume the sexual role outlined by his or her culture.

7. The effects of the psychosexual stages can be seen in various adult character traits and disorders. If the libido is unduly frustrated or overindulged at an early stage, it may become **fixated**. Many adult behaviors reflect early patterns that are characteristic of the different stages.

8. The **id, ego,** and **superego** represent different functions of the personality. The id is the oldest and original function. It includes our genetic inheritance, reflexes, and instincts and drives that motivate us. It operates according to the **pleasure principle** and uses **primary processes**. The ego develops in order to realistically meet the wishes of the id. It follows the **reality principle** and operates according to **secondary processes**. The superego consists of a **conscience** and the **ego-ideal**. It strives for perfection.

9. In the mature and well-adjusted personality, the ego is the executor controlling and governing the id and superego and mediating between their demands and the external world. In the maladjusted personality, the id or the superego gains control.

10. There is no easy correlation between the id, ego, and superego and consciousness or unconsciousness. The terms conscious and unconscious are best seen as adjectives describing qualities that the id, ego, and superego may or may not have.

11. Freud distinguished reality anxiety, neurotic anxiety, and moral anxiety.

12. In order to protect us against anxiety, the ego develops **defense mechanisms** that occur on an unconscious level and deny or distort reality so as to make it less threatening. Some of the more common defense mechanisms are **repression, denial, projection, reaction formation, regression, rationalization, identification, displacement,** and **sublimation**. Freud believed that by strengthening the ego we can become more aware of our impulses and deal with them more effectively.

13. Freud's psychoanalysis emphasizes the importance of the **transference** in which the patient transfers to the analyst emotional attitudes felt as a child toward significant persons. The patient repeats with the analyst infantile and ineffective ways of relating to other people. The analysis permits the patient to re-experience and rework these relationships to a more satisfactory resolution.

14. Efforts to test Freud's concepts have been made and the results are mixed. It is difficult to translate many of his concepts into operational procedures that allow for unequivocal test.

15. Although Freud frequently suggested that his theory functioned as science, he permitted many of his concepts to function philosophically. Thus, in the final analysis, Freud's theory needs to be evaluated in terms of a philosophy according to its coherence, relevance, comprehensiveness, and compellingness.

Suggestions for Further Reading

Freud's published works fill twenty-four volumes in *The Complete Psychological Works of Sigmund Freud: Standard Edition,* published by Hogarth Press of London, beginning in 1953. The lay reader will find the following most useful as a further introduction to the development of Freud's thought and theory. The *Five Lectures on Psychoanalysis* (1910), which were delivered at Clark University in Worcester, Massachusetts, represent a concise introduction by Freud to his own work. They are included in Vol. 11, 1957, of the complete works. More extensive presentations by Freud on his general theory are provided in *Introductory Lectures on Psychoanalysis* (1917), Vols. 15–16, 1963, and *New Introductory Lectures on Psychoanalysis* (1933), Vol. 22, 1964. Freud's classic writings on dreams, slips, and sexuality are *The Interpretation of Dreams* (1900), Vols. 4–5, 1953; *The Psychopathology of Everyday Life* (1901), Vol. 6, 1960; and *Three Essays on Sexuality* (1905), Vol. 7, 1953.

Freud's final theory of a threefold dynamic of personality was presented in *The Ego and the Id* (1923), Vol. 19, 1961. His re-evaluation of the problem of anxiety and the defense mechanisms is included in *Inhibitions, Symptoms and Anxiety* (1926), Vol. 20, 1959. The various introductory lectures provide useful information on the development of psychoanalysis as a therapeutic technique. The reader may also enjoy two later essays on the subject: "Analysis Terminable and Interminable" and "Constructions in Analysis" (both written in 1937), included in Vol. 23, 1964, in which Freud tries to assess realistically the benefits and limitations of psychoanalysis. Portions of the Standard Edition are also available in paperback editions published by Norton.

Secondary sources that provide a comprehensive picture of Freudian theory are C. Brenner, *An Elementary Textbook on Psychoanalysis* (Doubleday, 1955) and C. S. Hall, *A Primer of Freudian Psychology* (World, 1954).

R. Appignanesi and O. Zarate, *Freud for Beginners* (Pantheon, 1979) uses a comic book format to introduce readers to Freud.

The serious student of Freud will also be interested in the three-volume biography, *The Life and Work of Sigmund Freud* (Basic Books, 1953–1957), written by a close friend and follower, Ernest Jones. Briefer, more popular introductions to Freud's life and work are Irving Stone, *Passions of the Mind* (Doubleday, 1971),

P. Roazen, *Freud and His Followers* (Knopf, 1975), and P. Gay, *Freud: A Life for Our Time* (Norton, 1988). Bruno Bettelheim in his *Freud and Man's Soul* (Knopf, 1982) helps to clarify the essential humanism of Freud's work.

Eleanor Schuker and Nadine Levinson have edited an encyclopedic text summarizing psychoanalytic views of female psychology from Freud to the present in *Female Psychology: An Annotated Psychoanalytic Bibliography* (Analytic Press, Inc., 1991).

PART 2

The Neopsychoanalytic Approach

Although he always had a group of loyal followers, it was no doubt inevitable that a dynamic figure like Freud would both attract and repel. Some of his original followers became dissatisfied with orthodox psychoanalysis, defected from the movement, and founded their own schools of thought. Carl Jung, Alfred Adler, Karen Horney, and Erich Fromm were all deeply indebted to Freud and psychoanalysis, which provided a major impetus for their work. At the same time, each reacted in varying ways against Freud's psychoanalytic theory and developed his or her own position. In many instances, certain developments in these theories have been identified as valuable elaborations or adjuncts to classical psychoanalysis. Nevertheless, each theorist presented his or her theory as one that could stand by itself.

CHAPTER 3

Carl Jung

Carl Jung is recognized as one of the greatest and most controversial psychological thinkers of the twentieth century. It would be unfair to consider Jung only as a defector from the psychoanalytic movement. He was a mature scholar, with his own developing ideas, before he encountered Freud. Although he was closely associated with Freud for a period of time, he went on to develop an independent school of thought that contrasts markedly with orthodox psychoanalysis. He is indebted to Freud but is a personality theorist in his own right. His concept of the collective unconscious vastly enlarges an aspect of personality that was barely explored by Freud.

Biographical Background

Carl Gustav Jung was born in 1875 in Switzerland, where he lived all his life. He was the only surviving son of a poor country pastor and scholar of the Reformed church. Jung described his father as conventional and kind, but weak. He respected his father even though he had difficulty communicating with him, especially in matters of religion, which concerned Jung throughout his life. Skeptical of the orthodox faith in which he was reared, he searched relentlessly for adequate answers. This search is reflected in his psychology, with its interest in religion, mythology, and the occult.

His mother was a powerful person. Jung felt that she was a good mother but that she suffered from emotional disturbances. He was later to describe her as possessing two personalities, one kind and loving, the other harsh and aloof.

Jung described his childhood as lonely and his personality as introverted. Two brothers had died in infancy before Jung was born and his sister was not born until he was nine. The young boy frequently played by himself, inventing games and carving a small companion out of wood to console himself. These long periods of solitude were later to find expression in his self-analysis. His psychology also reflected his predilection for being alone. Maturity for Jung is defined not in terms of interpersonal relations, as it is for Freud, but in terms of integration or balance within the self.

As a child, he not only had several close contacts and brushes with death but he was also familiar with illness. When he was a young child his mother had to be hospitalized for several months, leaving him in the care of an elderly aunt and a family maid. During his youth a series of fainting spells caused him to miss over six months of school. The boy enjoyed the freedom from formal studies that his illness afforded him and the opportunity to explore other areas that interested him but were not in the traditional academic curriculum. However, shortly after he overheard his father's anguished comment to a friend, "What will become of the boy if he cannot earn his living?" his health was restored and he returned to school.

Jung originally wanted to be an archaeologist, but for financial reasons he could only afford to attend the University of Basel, which did not offer courses in that area. Therefore, he chose to study medicine. He was planning to

Carl Jung

specialize in surgery when he came across a textbook by Krafft-Ebing, a German neurologist (1840–1902), that described psychiatry as invariably subjective. The description provoked Jung's interest. Here was a field that might provide the key to some of the dreams, mysteries, and obscure happenings that he had been trying to understand.

His first professional appointment was as an assistant in a mental hospital in Zurich, where he worked with Eugen Bleuler, a well-known psychiatrist who coined the term "schizophrenia." Later, he became a lecturer at the University of Zurich. He established a private practice and developed a word-association test in order to study emotional reactions.

Jung first met Sigmund Freud in 1907 after having corresponded with him about their mutual interest for a short period. The two men were highly impressed with each other and with each other's work. That meeting began an intense personal and professional relationship. For some time Freud regarded Jung as his heir apparent and he looked on him with all of the affection that a father has for his son. When the International Psychoanalytic Society was founded, Jung, with Freud's endorsement, became its first president. They traveled together to Clark University where both had been invited to lecture.

On several occasions when Jung disagreed with Freud, Freud became very upset and in a few instances actually fainted. In 1913, Jung broke away from Freud and his school. Freud described the break as "a great loss" and it was also shattering for Jung, who entered a period of extensive inner disorientation in which he could not read or write and which eventually led to his self-analysis. Many reasons underlay the break with Freud; the most pronounced point of disagreement was Jung's rejection of Freud's emphasis on sexuality. Whereas for Freud all higher intellectual processes and emotionally significant experiences are ultimately substitutes for sexuality and can be understood thereby, for Jung sexuality itself must be seen as symbolic. Sexuality and the creativity it represents have a mysterious quality and cannot be fully analyzed or completely depicted.

Thereafter, Jung developed his own school of thought, which eventually came to be known as **analytical psychology.** He wrote extensively and his unique theories were informed by a vast array of concerns including Eastern religions, mythology, and alchemy. Although such subjects are frequently considered scientifically suspect, Jung felt that they were essential to the psychologist and indispensable in understanding the mysterious forces of the unconscious. Some critics argue that Jung's theories foster racism, that Jung was psychotic, anti-Semitic, and pro-Nazi. Other critics argue that although Jung was at times a troubled individual, he was a sensitive historian with unique and insightful ideas, that his peculiarities were the signs of genius rather than madness, and that the allegations of anti-Semitism and pro-Nazism have no basis in fact. A recent re-evaluation of Jung's emphasis on the importance of a psychology of cultural difference suggests his ideas can make a powerful contribution to those who are concerned about processes of political and social transformation (Samuels, 1992). Jung died in 1961 at the age of eighty-five after a long and fruitful life.

The Nature and Structure of Personality

Whereas Freud described the structure of personality in terms of three forces that are in conflict — the id, the ego, and the superego — Carl Jung conceived of the structure of personality as a complex network of interacting systems that strive toward eventual harmony. The primary ones are the ego; the personal unconscious with its complexes; and the collective unconscious and its archetypes. Jung also described two primary attitudes toward reality and four basic functions, which together constitute separate but related aspects of the **psyche,** or total personality.

The psyche refers to all psychological processes: thoughts, feelings, sensations, wishes, and so forth. Jung used the terms "psyche" and "psychic," rather than "mind" and "mental," to avoid the implications of consciousness in the latter and to emphasize that the psyche embraces both conscious and unconscious processes.

Jung and Freud differed in their approaches to the unconscious. Freud tended to view the unconscious essentially as materials that have been re-pressed, whereas Jung emphasized a concept of the unconscious as the source of consciousness and the matrix of new possibilities of life.

Psychic Energy

Different theorists often use the same words, such as *psyche, unconscious, libido,* and *ego,* to define processes and characteristics of human beings that they feel are well rendered by the term. These concepts are not interchangeable and must be understood in terms of each theory as a whole.

For Freud, the motive force of personality consists of libido, the sexual drive. Jung also used "libido" to refer to psychic energy, but his use should not be confused with Freud's definition. Jung used the term in a more generalized fashion as an undifferentiated life energy (1948b). **Libido** is an appetite that may refer to sexuality and to other hungers as well. It reflects itself as striving, desiring, and willing. Psychic energy operates according to the principles of equivalence and entropy; it seeks a balance and moves the person forward in a process of self-realization.

Although Jung did not reject an instinctual basis of personality, he criticized Freud's emphasis on sexuality, suggesting that it is ultimately reductive or sim-plistic, as it reduces any and all activities to sexual ones. For example, the phal-lus represents *mana* or power as well as sexuality. Jung believed that sexuality itself must be seen as symbolic, having a mysterious quality of otherness that cannot be fully described.

The Ego

For Freud, the ego is ideally the executor of the personality. Although Freud initially thought that the ego is primarily conscious, he later considered that a large portion of the ego is unconscious and beyond conscious control or awareness.

For Jung, the **ego** is one's conscious mind, the part of the psyche that selects perceptions, thoughts, feelings, and memories that may enter consciousness. The ego is responsible for our feelings of identity and continuity. It is through our ego that we establish a sense of stability in the way we perceive ourselves. The ego, however, is not the true center of personality for Jung. This runs counter to our everyday point of view. Most of us identify ourselves or our center as that awareness or consciousness that we have of ourselves, but for Jung, as we shall shortly see, the true center of personality is centered else-where.

Psychological Types

One of Jung's contributions to the psychology of the conscious psyche is his explanation and description of psychological types. Jung distinguished between two basic **attitudes** (1933a), and four **functions,** or ways of perceiving the environment and orienting experiences.

The Attitudes   *Extraversion* is an attitude in which the psyche is oriented outward to the objective world. The extravert tends to be more comfortable with the outer world of people and things. *Introversion* is an attitude in which the psyche is oriented inward to the subjective world. The introvert is more comfortable with the inner world of concepts and ideas. These words have become so commonplace in today's vocabulary that many of us readily identify ourselves as introverted or extraverted. Jung labeled himself an introvert and Freud an extravert. Yet in describing people as introverted or extraverted, Jung dealt primarily with the psychology of consciousness. An individual's habitual conscious attitude is either introverted or extraverted, but the other attitude is also present, although it may be undeveloped and mostly unconscious.

The Functions   Jung's four functions are grouped into opposite pairs. The functions of *sensation* and *intuition* refer to how we gather data and information. The sensor is more comfortable using the five senses and dealing with facts and reality. The intuitor looks for relationships and meanings or possibilities about past or future events. *Thinking* and *feeling* refer to how we come to conclusions or make judgments. The thinker prefers to use logic and impersonal analysis. The feeler is more concerned with personal values, attitudes, and beliefs. Jung suggested that one of these functions tends to be dominant in each individual and its opposite inferior. The other two functions play an auxiliary role. A professor, for example, may have so cultivated intellectual and cognitive powers that the feeling aspect of personality is submerged. Though primitive and undeveloped, feelings may nevertheless invade the professor's life in the form of strange moods, symptoms, or projections.

The two attitudes and four functions may be combined to form eight psychological types.

The Extraverted Types   Four of the types are extraverted. These include

Thinking: Such individuals tend to live according to fixed rules. They repress feelings and try to be objective but are sometimes dogmatic in their thinking.

Feeling: Such individuals are sociable people who seek harmony with the world and respect tradition and authority. They tend to be rather emotional, since thinking is repressed.

Sensing: Such individuals seek pleasure and enjoy new sensory experiences. They are strongly oriented toward reality and repress intuition.

Intuitive: Such individuals are very creative and find new ideas appealing. They tend to make decisions based on hunches rather than facts and are in touch with their unconscious wisdom. Sensation is repressed.

The Introverted Types   The other four psychological types are introverted.

Thinking: Such individuals have a strong need for privacy. They tend to be theoretical, intellectual, and somewhat impractical. The individual represses feelings and may have trouble getting along with other people.

Feeling: Such individuals tend to be quiet, thoughtful, and hypersensitive. Thinking is repressed and the individual may appear mysterious and indifferent to others.

Sensing: Such individuals tend to be passive, calm, and artistic. They focus on objective sensory events and repress intuition.

Intuition: Jung described himself as an introverted intuitor. Such individuals tend to be mystic dreamers who come up with unusual new ideas and are seldom understood by others. Sensing is repressed.

Jung cautioned that the types as described rarely occur in a pure form. There is a wide range of variation within each type, and people of a specific type may change (though not to another type) as their personal and collective unconscious changes. No one type is better than another type. Each has its own strengths and weaknesses.

The Personal Unconscious

Jung compared the conscious aspect of the psyche to an island that rises from the sea. We notice only the part above water, even though a much greater land mass, the unconscious, lies below (Fordham, 1953). The **personal unconscious** is a land that is not always covered by sea and thus can be reclaimed. Here reside those perceptions, thoughts, feelings, and memories that have been put aside (for our consciousness can only hold a few items at a time), and they may be easily retrieved. The personal unconscious also includes those experiences of an individual's life history that have been repressed or forgotten. This is an aspect of the unconscious that, as we have seen, Freud also emphasized. These forgotten experiences are accessible to consciousness even though becoming aware of some of them may be an arduous process.

Experiences are grouped in the personal unconscious into clusters, which Jung calls complexes. A **complex** is an organized group of thoughts, feelings, and memories about a particular concept (1934). A complex is said to have a **constellating power**, which means that the complex has the ability to draw new ideas into it and interpret them accordingly. It can be compared to a magnet that attracts related experiences. The more constellating power a complex has, the more powerful it may become. Complexes have important implications for our interpersonal relationships, specifically influencing how we react toward others.

A complex may be organized around a particular person or object. One of Jung's examples concerns motherhood (1954). A mother complex refers to the cluster of ideas, feelings, and memories that have arisen from our own particular experience of having been mothered. It also draws into it other experiences of mothering to which we have been exposed. Each new instance of mothering that we encounter is drawn into our mother complex and understood and interpreted by it.

A complex, however, may make it difficult for us to disengage ourselves from a situation. Jung described a man who believed that he was suffering from a real cancer, even though he knew that his cancer was imaginary. The complex, Jung wrote, is "a spontaneous growth, originating in that part of the psyche which is not identical with consciousness. It appears to be an autonomous development intruding upon consciousness" (1938). A complex may act like an independent person, behaving independently of our conscious self and intentions.

A complex may be conscious, partly conscious, or unconscious. Certain elements of it may extend into the collective unconscious. Some complexes appear to dominate an entire personality. Napoleon is frequently described as being driven by inner forces to obtain power.

Jung's concept of complex may be seen as an effort to overcome the traditional categories of mind versus body and conscious versus unconscious (Brooke, 1991).

The Collective Unconscious

Whereas the personal unconscious is unique for each individual, the **collective unconscious** is shared. Jung referred to the collective unconscious as "transpersonal"; that is to say, it extends across persons. It consists of certain potentialities that we all share because we are human (1936). Many critics believe that Jung made a unique contribution to depth psychology in his concept of the collective unconscious. Freud's concept of unconscious forces was mostly limited to personal experiences that have been repressed or forgotten. Whereas other dissenters from Freud tended to minimize the power of unconscious forces, Jung placed a greater emphasis on them and stressed the qualities that we share with other people.

All people, because they are human beings, have certain things in common. All human beings live in groups and develop some form of family life or society in which roles are assigned to various members. These roles may vary from society to society but they exist in all human groups. All human beings share certain emotions such as joy, grief, or anger. The ways of expressing these emotions may vary, but the emotions themselves are shared. All human beings develop some form of language and symbolization. The particular words may vary, but the concepts and symbols are shared. Thus, certain archetypes and symbols reappear again and again from society to society and they may be seen to have a common meaning.

Jung considered the collective unconscious an empirical concept whose existence can be demonstrated through dreams, mythology, and cross-cultural data. The workings of the collective unconscious are seen in experiences we have all had, such as falling in love with a "perfect other," feeling overwhelmed by a piece of art or music, or being drawn to the sea, and it expresses itself in shared symbols that have universal meaning.

Archetypes   Within the collective unconscious lie the archetypes or primordial images. An **archetype** is a universal thought form or predisposition to respond to the world in certain ways (1936). The word "predisposition" is crucial to Jung's concept of the collective unconscious and its archetypes. It emphasizes potentialities, for the archetypes represent different potential ways in which we may express our humanness.

The archetypes can never be fully known or described because they never fully enter consciousness. They appear to us in personified or symbolized pictorial form and may penetrate into consciousness by means of myths, dreams, art, ritual, and symptoms. It is helpful for us to get in touch with them because they represent the latent potentiality of the psyche. In doing so, we go beyond developing our individual potentialities and become incorporated in the eternal cosmic process.

Jung wrote, "The archetype is a kind of readiness to produce over and over again the same or similar mythical ideas. Hence it seems as though what is impressed upon the unconscious were exclusively the subjective fantasy — ideas aroused by the physical process. We may therefore assume that the archetypes are recurrent impressions made by subjective reasons" (1954).

Persona   The **persona** refers to the social role that one assumes in society and one's understanding of it. As mentioned in Chapter 1, the Latin word *persona* refers to the masks that actors wore in ancient Greek plays. Thus, one's persona is the mask that one wears in order to adjust to the demands of society. Each one of us chooses or is assigned particular roles in our society. The persona represents a compromise between one's true identity and social identity. To neglect the development of a persona is to run the risk of becoming asocial. On the other hand, one may identify too completely with the persona at the expense of one's true identity and not permit other aspects of one's personality to develop.

Shadow   The **shadow** encompasses those *unsocial* thoughts, feelings, and behaviors that we potentially possess and other characteristics that we do not accept. It is the opposite side of the persona, in that it refers to those desires and emotions that are incompatible with our social standards and ideal personality. It could be described as the devil within. Jung's choice of the word "shadow" is deliberate and designed to emphasize its necessity. There can be no sun that does not leave a shadow. The shadow cannot be avoided and one is incomplete without it (cf. Johnson, 1991). Jung agreed with Freud that such base and unsocial impulses may be sublimated and channeled to good ends. The shadow can also be projected onto others, with important interpersonal and social consequences such as prejudice.

*Your persona represents a compromise
between your true self and the
expectations of society.*

To neglect or try to deny the shadow involves us in hypocrisy and deceit. Angels are not suited for existence on earth. Jung suggested a need to come to know our baser side and recognize our animalistic impulses. To do so adds dimension and credibility to personality as well as increased zest for life.

Anima and Animus   Each one of us is assigned a sex gender, male or female, based on our overt sexual characteristics. Yet none of us is purely male or purely female. Each of us has qualities of the opposite sex in terms of biology and also in terms of psychological attitudes and feelings. Thus, the **anima** archetype is the feminine side of the male psyche and the **animus** archetype is the masculine side of the female psyche. One's anima or animus reflects collective and individual human experiences throughout the ages pertaining to one's opposite sex. It assists us in relating to and understanding the opposite sex. For Jung, there was a distinct difference between the psychology of men and women. Jung believed that it was important that one express these opposite-sex characteristics in order to avoid an unbalanced or one-sided personality. If one exhibits only the traits of one's assigned sex, the other traits remain unconscious, undeveloped, and primitive. Those of us who have difficulty in understanding the opposite sex probably are not in tune with our anima or animus.

Jung has usually been considered friendly to women because of his assertion of the need to get in touch with one's opposite-sex archetype. However, his writings have also been criticized for including stereotypes of women as well as potentially racist comments about other groups such as blacks and primitive people. Jung stoutly maintained that the psyche of women is different from that of men and he tended to be rigid in his discussion of those behaviors that would or would not overstep the boundaries of appropriate expression of one's assigned gender role and one's opposite-sex archetype. He warned of the dangers of pushing one's capacity to behave like the opposite sex too far, so that a man loses his masculinity or a woman her femininity.

Jung believed that women's consciousness is characterized by the ability to enter into relationships, whereas men's consciousness is characterized by the ability to engage in rational and analytic thought. The persona, or social mask, differs for men and women because of the various roles that society and culture have assigned to them. The anima and the animus function in ways that compensate for the outer personality and show the qualities that are missing in outward conscious expression. Because psychological development involves integrating one's persona and one's anima or animus, Jung believed it will progress differently for the male and for the female.

A woman may react to her animus in various ways. Traditionally, women have repressed their masculine qualities and striven to fulfill their feminine role. Jung thought this might lead to an imbalance in the personality and unconscious efforts on the part of the animus to intrude upon the woman's life; he pointed out that both the anima and the animus may behave as if they are laws unto themselves and have disruptive influences. Another way to react to the animus is to identify with it, but this usually makes it more difficult for a woman to fulfill her assigned role.

However, a woman's animus need not be thought of as acting in opposition to femininity. In ideal development, the animus will lead a woman to transform her femininity into a renewed form of consciousness that overcomes the traditional dualities. The same would be true of ideal development in the male.

While Jung's theory may be interpreted as sexist, a feminist analysis of his work may be warranted (Romaniello, 1992). His comments about the anima and the animus led to the now very popular concept of an androgynous ideal. *Androgyny* refers to the presence of both masculine and feminine qualities in an individual and the ability to realize both potentialities. Considerable research has been done in the area of androgyny (see, for example, Singer, 1991).

Self   The central archetype in Jung's understanding is that of the self. Jung's use of the term "self" differed from the usual use of the term. The **self** represents the striving for unity of all parts of the personality. It is the organizing principle of the psyche that draws unto itself and harmonizes all the archetypes and their expressions. The self directs an orderly allotment of psychic energy so that different parts of the personality are expressed appropriately. Depending upon the occasion and our personal needs, the self allows us to be socially acceptable at work (persona), outrageous at a Halloween party (shadow), emotional at a concert (shadow), and so forth. The self, rather than the ego, is the true midpoint of personality. Thus, the center of one's personality

THINKING CRITICALLY

Active Imagination

Jung developed *active imagination* as a way of getting in touch with the archetypes, such as the anima or the animus. You are invited to imagine your anima or animus. Place yourself in a comfortable position, relax, and close your eyes. You might imagine what the fantasized archetype would say to you and enter into a dialogue with it. If a scene becomes too difficult or produces anxiety, you should discontinue it.

Because the archetypes also appear in dreams in the form of people, animals, or symbols, you may try to understand them by placing yourself in the role of one of the figures in your dreams. In dreams, the anima variously appears as a virgin, a mother, or a witch. The animus often takes on the appearance of a Prince Charming, a savior, or a sorcerer. However, they may take other forms as well. When you place yourself in the role of one of your dream figures, speak as if you were that individual. Describe yourself, indicate what you wanted to express in the dream, and relate to other figures in the dream.

Getting in touch with the anima or animus may permit us to feel and experience opposite-sex characteristics. Historically, the male has been associated with aggressiveness, analytic and instrumental thought, emotional control, and self-concern, while the female has been identified with passivity, intuitive and expressive thought, emotionality, and concern for others. In active imagination, a male might permit himself to feel vulnerable and hurt, and to cry. A woman might be able to express her aggression. According to Jung, each of us shares the components of our sexual opposite. If we do not get in touch with the other side of our personality, we run the risk of being one-sided and missing a valuable dimension of our experience.

Can you think of aspects of your anima or animus that you tend to ignore? In our culture at large are there ways in which women have had trouble expressing their latent masculinity and men their latent femininity?

is not to be found in rational ego consciousness. For Jung, the true self lay on the boundary between conscious and unconscious, reason and unreason. The development of the self is life's goal, but the self archetype cannot begin to emerge until the other personality systems have been fully developed. Thus, it usually does not begin to emerge until one has reached middle age. Jung spoke of the realization of the self as a goal that lies in the future. It is something to be striven for but rarely achieved.

A symbol of the self is the **mandala** (1955), a concentrically arranged figure such as the circle, the wheel, or the cross, which Jung saw appearing again and again in his patients' dreams and in all the artwork of all cultures (see Figure 3.1). The mandala represents the self striving toward wholeness.

Figure 3.1 *Mandalas*
Mandalas appear in the symbolism of both East and West, in nature, and in our doodles.

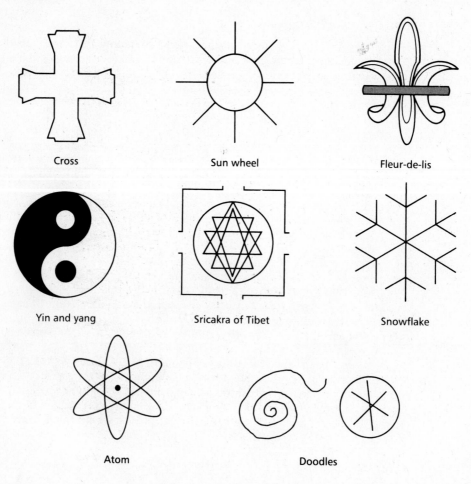

Cross   Sun wheel   Fleur-de-lis

Yin and yang   Sricakra of Tibet   Snowflake

Atom   Doodles

Jung described numerous other archetypes of the collective unconscious: birth, death, rebirth, power, magic, the child, the hero, God, the demon, the great mother, and the wise old man. The point is that one cannot deny or destroy these archetypes.

For example, Western culture's denial of the dreadful facets of the great mother culminated in a patriarchal society that oppressed women and destroyed nature (Myyra, 1992). Therefore, we need to get in touch with the archetypes and their healing power.

At the deepest levels, Jung believed that our unconscious remains archaic, despite our scientific technology and the development of our rational powers. Freud disclaimed Jung's plea for originality in articulating the collective unconscious, stating that he (Freud) had known all along that the unconscious is collective. And, of course, there are certain archetypal patterns in Freud's understanding of the unconscious. The psychosexual stages involve predispositions toward acting out the human drama in certain ways. The Oedipal situation that we experience is a collective archetypal myth. Symbols in dreams may be unique to the individual, but also shared. Thus, a concept of collected unconscious forces is implied in Freud's theory although certainly not clearly articulated. And whereas Freud emphasized the unique unfolding of unconscious forces in the individual's life history and personal unconscious (it is not enough to know that one has gone through the Oedipal situation — one must fully experience its particular unfolding within one's distinct family constellation), Jung emphasized the shared and collective aspects. As you might imagine, Jung's concept is an important and controversial one in personality theorizing.

Self-Realization

Jung suggests that the self is in the process of **self-realization**. He did not outline stages in the development of personality nor did he consider the early childhood years to be the most important ones, as Freud did. The "psychic birth" of an individual does not really occur until adolescence, when the psyche starts to show a definite form and content. Personality development continues throughout life, and the middle years (35 to 40) mark the beginning of major changes.

Although the concept of self-realization was fully described by Jung, it cannot be said to be new with his thought. The origin of the principle takes us back to the Greek philosopher Aristotle (384–322 B.C.). Aristotle held that everything has a *telos,* a purpose or goal, that constitutes its essence and indicates its potentiality. Thus, every acorn has the essence of treeness and the potential to become a mighty oak. In the same way, each one of us has the potential to develop into a self, that is, to realize, fulfill, and enhance our maximum human potentialities. This viewpoint is essentially *teleological,* or purposeful. It explains the present in terms of the future with reference to a goal that guides and directs our destiny. Whereas Freud's view was primarily a causal one, comprehending personality in terms of antecedent conditions of the past, Jung maintained that both causality and teleology are necessary for a full understanding of personality.

While development is largely forward moving, regression may occur under conditions of frustration. Jung did not view such regression negatively. Rather, it may, in the end, facilitate the forward movement of progression. By exploring the unconscious, both personal and collective, the ego may learn from past experiences and resolve the problem that led to the regression. Whereas for Freud a neurosis represents the return of the repressed, for Jung it is the insistence of the undeveloped part of the personality on being heard and realized.

Self-realization involves individuation and transcendence (1916, 1939). In **individuation,** the systems of the individual psyche achieve their fullest degree of differentiation, expression, and development. **Transcendence** refers to integration of the diverse systems of the self toward the goal of wholeness and identity with all of humanity. Jung's concepts of individuation and transcendence are difficult for the average Westerner to understand. In Western psychology, we generally think of personality in terms of an individual's uniqueness. People who do not appear to be unique are often said to "lack personality."

For Jung, individuation does not mean individualism in that narrow sense, but rather fulfilling one's own specific nature and realizing one's uniqueness in one's place within the whole. In the process of transcendence, a deeper self or essence emerges to unite a person with all of humanity and the universe at large.

Individuation and transcendence are both ongoing processes. However, the first half of life is often more concerned with the cultivation of consciousness and gender-specific behavior, while the second half of life may be more concerned with coming into closer contact with self and expressing our collective unconscious and oneness with humanity as a whole. Mary Loomis (1991) has made a comparison to a process that Native Americans refer to as the Red Road.

Thus, as the self realizes, a stormy process that may never be fully completed, it perpetually rises to a greater enhancement and realization of itself and humanity. If we view the psyche as a wheel, the hub of which is the archetype of the self, we can suggest that the true self emerges when the opposites coincide (Figure 3.2). The true person does not consist of the conscious or the unconscious, mind or body, persona or shadow, overt sexual characteristics or complements, but of all of these. Neurosis results from a one-sided personality development. The coincidence of opposites is the ultimate goal of personality development in the Jungian view. Although both Freud and Jung emphasized the dynamic opposition of portions of the personality, they differed in the implications of this conflict. For Freud, the person is inescapably in conflict; for Jung, the person ultimately seeks harmony. Mansfield and Spiegelman (1991) have employed quantum mechanical models and symbols to deepen our understanding of the coincidence of opposites, Van Eenwyk (1991) has further suggested that chaos theory, which attempts to describe complicated systems

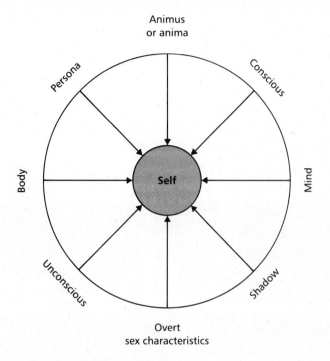

Figure 3.2 *The Coincidence of Opposites*
If we were to view the psyche as a wheel, the hub of which is the archetype of the self, the true self emerges when the opposites coincide. The resulting image is, of course, a mandala.

formerly outside the range of classical mathematics and physics, illumines Jung's theory.

Jungian Psychotherapy

Jung viewed neurosis as a person's attempt to reconcile the contradictory aspects of personality. One side of the psyche, such as the conscious, adaptive, social persona, may be exaggerated at the expense of the darker, unconscious aspects. It is difficult to describe Jung's method of psychotherapy specifically because he did not clearly outline his procedures as Freud did. Further, Jung maintained that no one approach is suitable for everyone. The individual who has had difficulty in accepting the sexual and aggressive urges of life may well require a Freudian interpretation. But for others, or at different stages in development, the Freudian understanding may not be sufficiently comprehensive.

In classical Freudian psychoanalysis, the analyst remains detached and reveals few personal feelings and reactions in order to facilitate the transference, whereas the Jungian analyst is more self-disclosing, foreshadowing Rogerian and other contemporary therapies. Therapy is a "dialectical procedure," a dialogue between doctor and patient, conscious and unconscious. Although the couch may be used to facilitate procedures such as active imagination, for the most part analyst and patient sit facing each other. The Jungian analyst also sees patients far less frequently than the Freudian. The frequency of visits depends on the stage that the patient has reached.

PHILOSOPHICAL ASSUMPTIONS

Examining Jung

How would you rate Jung on each of the basic philosophical assumptions described in Chapter 1? Each basic issue was presented as a bipolar dimension along which a person's view can be placed according to the degree of agreement with one or the other extreme. Rate Jung's views on these issues.

When you have determined where you think Jung stands, compare your responses with those of your classmates and your instructor. You should be willing to defend your ratings, but also be prepared to change them in light of others' compelling arguments. Afterward, compare your rating of Jung with your own position on each issue and with those of other theorists. Does this comparison help you to understand why his theory does or does not appeal to you?

Would strongly agree	Would agree	Is neutral or believes in synthesis of both views	Would agree	Would strongly agree
1	2	3	4	5

freedom	determinism
People basically have control over their own behavior and understand the motives behind their behavior.	The behavior of people is basically determined by internal or external forces over which they have little, if any, control.

During the early stages of treatment, there is a need for *confession*. Such confession is generally accompanied by emotional release, and Jung viewed it as the aim of the cathartic method originated by Breuer and Freud. But Jung pointed out that emotional release, in itself, is not therapeutic any more than temper tantrums or other emotional outbursts are curative in and of themselves. For Freud, conscious intellectual understanding and insight renders the catharsis effective. Jung emphasized that the presence of the other, the therapist who supports the patient morally and spiritually as well as intellectually, makes the confession curative.

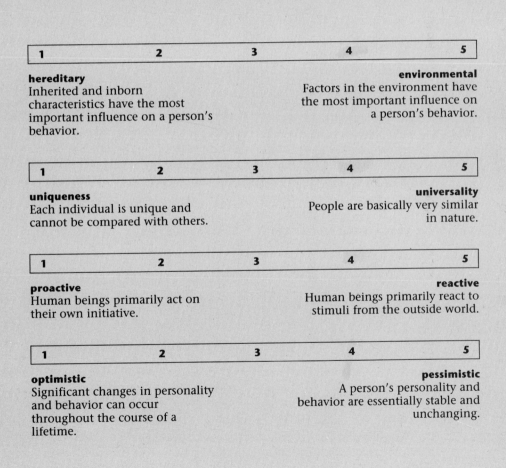

| 1 | 2 | 3 | 4 | 5 |

hereditary
Inherited and inborn characteristics have the most important influence on a person's behavior.

environmental
Factors in the environment have the most important influence on a person's behavior.

| 1 | 2 | 3 | 4 | 5 |

uniqueness
Each individual is unique and cannot be compared with others.

universality
People are basically very similar in nature.

| 1 | 2 | 3 | 4 | 5 |

proactive
Human beings primarily act on their own initiative.

reactive
Human beings primarily react to stimuli from the outside world.

| 1 | 2 | 3 | 4 | 5 |

optimistic
Significant changes in personality and behavior can occur throughout the course of a lifetime.

pessimistic
A person's personality and behavior are essentially stable and unchanging.

Projection and transference play an important role in Jungian analysis, though Jung added to Freud's concept of transference the recognition that not only significant persons from the patient's past but also archetypal images are projected onto the analyst. Jung also viewed the sexual components of the transference as symbolic efforts on the patient's part to reach a higher integration of personality. In contrast to Freud, Jung did not think that transference was a necessary precondition for therapy.

Whereas Freud treated dreams as the expression of unconscious wishes, Jung gave them a prospective function as well as a retrospective one. By prospective function Jung meant that the dream represents an effort by the person to prepare for future events. Dreams also have a **compensatory function**; they are efforts to complement the patient's conscious side and speak for the unconscious.

In interpreting dreams, Jung used the method of **amplification** (1951) rather than the method of free association. In free association, each dream element is the starting place for a chain of association that may lead far afield from the original element. In amplification, one focuses repeatedly on the element and gives multiple associations to it. The dream is taken exactly as it is with no precise effort to distinguish between manifest and latent contents. The therapist joins the patient in efforts to interpret the dream, adding personal associations and frequently referring to mythology, fairy tales, and the like in order to extend the dream's meaning. Whereas Freud tended to deal with dreams singly, Jung concentrated on series of dreams. Analysis of a series of dreams unfolds the inner life of the patient, which is taken as a guide to true-life meanings for the patient.

As a therapist, Jung also valued the use of active imagination as a means of facilitating self-understanding and the use of artistic production by the patient. He encouraged his patients to draw, sculpt, paint, or develop some other art form as a means to listening to their inner depths. In all of this, he emphasized obedience to the unfolding inner life as the appropriate, ethical fulfillment of one's humanity.

Assessment and Research in Jung's Theory

Jung's ideas have had a significant but frequently unacknowledged impact on assessment and research in personality. Jung developed the *word-association test,* which provided the first experimental data on unconscious processes and is widely used in current laboratory research and clinical practice. The subject responds to a list of stimulus words designed to elicit emotions. An unusual response, a long pause before responding, the same response to very different words, and other factors may indicate a complex. Jung's word-association test may be termed the forerunner of later projective techniques and attempts to assess personality by techniques such as free association, sentence completion, and psychophysiological monitoring, including the polygraph, or lie detector. Indeed, Jung is credited with identifying at least two thieves through the technique of word association (Ellenberger, 1970).

A Swiss psychiatrist, Hermann Rorschach, developed the Rorschach Inkblot Test, which is heavily influenced by Jungian concepts such as introversion and extraversion. Henry Murray also was deeply influenced by Jung when he developed the Thematic Apperception Test.

Jung's typology has also led to the development of assessment and research on psychological type. The Myers-Briggs Type Indicator (MBTI) is one of the most popular tools for nonpsychiatric populations in the area of clinical, counseling, and personality assessment. The instrument, developed primarily by Katherine Briggs and her daughter Isabel Briggs Myers, is designed to implement Jung's theory of type by sorting people into groups on the basis of four separate dichotomies or indices: Extraversion-Introversion (EI), Sensing-Intuition (SI), Thinking-Feeling (TF), and Judgment-Perception (JP). You will recognize the first polarity as the two attitudes identified by Jung and the second and third polarities as the four ego functions. The last polarity indicates a preference for judgment or perception (JP): J's prefer a great deal of structure and closure in their lives and P's prefer more spontaneity and openness. The J pole refers to the two judging functions (thinking and feeling) and the P pole refers to the two perceiving functions (sensing or intuition). The preference for J or P tells which mode — J (decision making) or P (information gathering) — is shown to the outside world.

Given the four dichotomies, sixteen different four-letter types are possible. An ESFJ, for example, is an extravert who is sensing, feeling, and judging. The assessment manual provides descriptions that distinguish each type from the others. One of the distinct advantages of the MBTI is its face validity: individuals invariably recognize themselves in their types (cf. Furnham, 1990). As in Jung's original typology, no one type is preferred over other types. Each type has its own strengths and weaknesses.

The MBTI generated considerable research, some of which was summarized by Myers and McCaulley (1985). There may be a correlation of type and changes in the temporal lobes of the brain (Huot, Makarec, & Persinger, 1989). The MBTI has enormous potential for helping people to understand learning styles and leadership styles in order to help motivate students and workers by recognizing that not everyone dances to the same drummer (Keirsey & Bates, 1984). More research needs to be done on whether or not the findings of the MBTI apply across cultures.

Jung's techniques of research and assessment drew upon not only empirical and scientific methods, but also nonscientific and mystical approaches. Thus Jung studied a variety of cultures and periods, exploring their myths, symbols, religions, and rituals. He was interested in subjects such as alchemy and astrology. This "unorthodox blend of opposites" (Schultz, 1990) does not always sit well with more scientifically oriented psychologists who, in spite of the widespread use of the MBTI, tend to ignore Jungian concepts.

Jung's Theory: Philosophy, Science, and Art

Many of Jung's discoveries, like Freud's, took place in the clinical setting. He also obtained information from sources outside the treatment room. Observations of other cultures and studies of comparative religion and mythology, symbolism, alchemy, and the occult afforded him a wealth of information. Jung considered these sources secondary but legitimate ones for psychologists seeking to uncover the mysteries of the human psyche. He believed that a comparative method of study, often used in history and anthropology, was a valuable approach in science as well.

Jung did not believe that psychologists should be bound to an experimental, scientific approach. He did believe, however, that conclusions should be based on empirical data. Jung criticized the contemporary scientific atmosphere for limiting its concepts to those of causality and emphasized the concept of teleology. After all, he pointed out, the concepts of *cause* and *goal* are not themselves found in nature but are imaginary constructs imposed by scientists. Jung urged scientists to work within a broader scope and conceptual design.

Jung's concepts are particularly difficult to study in the laboratory. As with Freud, it is virtually impossible to define many of his terms operationally or to develop a test that would disprove them. Further, Jung's interest in the occult has led many critics to dismiss him as a mystic. Consequently, scientific psychology has until recently largely ignored Jung's analytical psychology. Nevertheless, Jung has influenced developments in psychology and other disciplines.

Jung indicated that he was more interested in discovering facts than in developing a philosophy. Because his concepts were based on empirical data, in the broadest sense of the word he operated as a "scientist." However, his theory falls short of rigorous standards of compatibility, predictive power, and simplicity. Fundamentally, the Jungian quest may be viewed as a philosophical or religious one. Jung explicitly raised philosophical questions and suggested philosophical answers. For example, asserting that questions about human nature should be answered empirically is in itself a philosophical position that distinguishes science from philosophy. For Jung, the power of self-understanding stems from an appropriate philosophy of life. It should not be surprising that although Jung has been largely ignored by experimentally oriented psychologists, theologians have found his work very fruitful. His concept of God's revealing himself through the collective unconscious is particularly attractive to theologians who seek a more relevant articulation of traditional theistic concepts. Although it is complex, his theory is coherent; its relevance is attested to by the resurgence of interest in it today; and the comprehensive features of his theory are remarkable for their profundity.

As an art, Jungian therapy emphasizes a scholarly goal. With the resurgence of interest in Jung, training in Jungian analysis has become available in major American cities, and several new and controversial books about Jung's ideas have appeared in the past decade. Jung influenced the development of trans-personal psychology (Guest, 1989).

Jung's emphasis on inborn qualities, the duality of human nature, symbol-ism, androgyny, and the importance of inner experiences — factors that at one time led psychologists to neglect his work — are now seen as important, if not indispensable, for understanding personality. In particular, Jung's interest in the developmental process with his attention to the second half of the human life span has proved valuable to social scientists who are concerned about the needs and growth of our older population. In particular Jung helps us deal with the reality of death (Busick, 1989, and Mogenson, 1990).

In this postmodern era, Jung's concepts can further help us to understand the place of the self in our talk about different cultures (Thrasher, 1991) and helps us forge a new holistic paradigm (Clarke, 1992). Many of Jung's archetypal images tell an ecological tale of the profound dialogue between the earth and the soul (Noel, 1991).

Drawing upon Jung, Sliker (1992) explores how politics, culture, and eth-nicity can be understood. She believes her model can foster discussion for re-solving conflicts among various cultures.

Jung's thinking poses a significant challenge to Western thought and psychol-ogy with its emphasis on an extrospective methodology based on experimen-tation and causal rather than teleological explanations. His ideas are compatible with thinking in the East (cf. Coward, 1989), which emphasizes self-understand-ing through introspection and experience. It is unfortunate that many psychol-ogists in America have been quick to dismiss the concepts of Jung. They merit more serious consideration.

Summary

1. Jung uses the term **psyche** to refer to all psychological processes, emphasiz-ing that it embraces both conscious and unconscious processes.

2. For Freud the **libido** consists of the sexual drive, whereas Jung used the term in a more generalized fashion as an undifferentiated energy that moves the person forward.

3. Whereas for Freud the ego is the executor of the personality, for Jung it is one's conscious perception of self.

4. Jung described two basic **attitudes** (introversion and extraversion) and four **functions** (sensation, thinking, feeling, and intuition). In each person, one of the attitudes and functions is dominant and its opposite is weaker. The other two functions play an auxiliary role.

5. The **personal unconscious** includes experiences of an individual's history that have been repressed or forgotten. These are organized into **complexes**.

6. Freud's concept of unconscious forces is mostly limited to a personal unconscious; Jung's **collective unconscious** consists of potential ways of being that all humans share.

7. **Archetypes** are universal thought forms of the collective unconscious and predispositions to perceive the world in certain ways. Some widely recognized archetypes are the **persona**, the **shadow**, the **anima**, and the **animus**. The **self** is the central archetype and true midpoint of the personality. Active imagination is a method of getting in touch with the archetypes.

8. **Self-realization** is a teleological process of development that involves **individuation** and **transcendence.** In the process, the systems of the psyche achieve their fullest degree of differentiation and are then integrated in identity with all of humanity.

9. In his psychotherapy, Jung sought to reconcile unbalanced aspects of the personality. It is a dialectical procedure and initially entails confession. Jung considered dreams to have a prospective function as well as a **compensatory** one; in interpreting them he used the method of **amplification.**

10. Jung's word-association test was the forerunner of projective techniques. The MBTI was developed to implement Jung's typology and is widely used in a variety of settings.

11. Although Jung's concepts were based on empirical data, he raised philosophical questions and suggested philosophical answers. His theory may therefore be seen as largely philosophical.

Suggestions for Further Reading

Carl Jung was a voluminous writer. His *Collected Works* have been published in this country by Princeton University Press, beginning in 1953. Statements about his theory are scattered throughout these works, but Volumes 7, 8, and 9 present the major features. Because Jung is a difficult writer to follow, the lay person would be best advised to begin with books that are more directed to the general public. *Man and His Symbols* (Doubleday, 1964) is probably the best introduction to Jungian psychology. It was written by Jung and several of his disciples. Jung's autobiography, describing the spiritual journey that led to his position, is *Memories, Dreams, and Reflections* (Random House, 1961). A statement of the major principles of analytic psychology as well as the theory of types and functions is included in *Psychological Types* (Harcourt, Brace, 1933a). Several of Jung's lectures were also collected in a basic introduction entitled *Modern Man in Search of a Soul* (Harcourt, Brace, 1933b).

Also recommended are the *Freud/Jung Letters* (Princeton University Press, 1974). The best secondary sources introducing Jung's ideas are F. Fordham, *An Introduction to Jung's Psychology* (Penguin, 1953); J. Jacobi, *The Psychology of C. G. Jung* (Routledge and Kegan Paul, 1942); I. Progoff, *Jung's Psychology and Its Social Meaning* (Grove, 1953); J. Singer, *Boundaries of the Soul* (Doubleday, 1973);

and C. S. Hall and V. J. Nordby, *A Primer of Jungian Psychology* (Mentor, 1973). More recent re-evaluations of Jung's work are J. Clarke, *In Search of Jung: Historical and Philosophical Enquiries* (Routledge, 1992) and P. Young-Eisendrath and J. A. Hall, *Jung's Self Psychology: A Constructivist Perspective* (Guilford Press, 1991). C. Downing has recently edited *Mirrors of the Self: Archetypal Images that Shape Your Life,* (Jeremy P. Tarcher, Inc., 1991) in which several prominent psychologists show readers how to identify those archetypes and tap into their power.

CHAPTER 4

Alfred Adler

1. Explain the difference between an *intrapsychic* and an *interpsychic* emphasis in personality theorizing.
2. Define what is meant by *social interest* and explain why it must be cultivated.
3. Explain what Adler meant by *finalism* and describe some *fictional finalisms.*
4. Identify the ultimate goal of the psyche.
5. Describe how *inferiority feelings* shape one's personality.
6. Tell what is meant by an individual's *style of life,* distinguish four primary types of style, and describe how *family constellation* and *family atmosphere* may shape it.
7. Discuss Adler's concept of the *creative self* and show how it restores consciousness to the center of personality.
8. Describe some of the major features of Adlerian psychotherapy, assessment, and research.
9. Evaluate Adler's theory in terms of its function as philosophy, science, and art.

Alfred Adler chose the term **individual psychology** for his conception of personality because he was interested in investigating the uniqueness of the person. He maintained that the individual was indivisible and must be studied as a whole. His emphasis shifted from a stress on **intrapsychic** ("within the psyche") phenomena such as Freud and Jung dealt with to an appreciation of **interpsychic** ("interpersonal") relations. Adler's theory holds that understanding a particular individual entails comprehending his or her attitude in relation to the world. Thus, for Adler, the human person emerged as a social and cultural creature rather than a sexual creature. According to Adler, we are motivated by social interests and our primary life problems are social ones.

Biographical Background

Alfred Adler, second of six children born to a successful merchant, was born in 1870 and reared in a suburb of Vienna. He described his childhood as difficult and unhappy. He suffered from rickets, a deficiency disease of childhood that affected the bones and made him clumsy and awkward. Initially, his parents pampered him, but when his younger brother was born he sensed that his mother transferred her attention to him. He felt dethroned and turned to his father, who favored him and expected great things from him.

When he was three, he saw his younger brother die in the next bed. Twice during his early childhood Adler was run over in the streets. He began to be afraid of death, and his fear was further increased by a bout of pneumonia at the age of four. Later, he traced his interest in becoming a doctor to that near-fatal illness.

At school he was an average student. At one point his teacher suggested that his father take him out of school and apprentice him to a shoemaker. Nevertheless, he rose to a superior position in school, especially in mathematics, which he originally had had the greatest difficulty in mastering. In spite of his physical handicaps, he developed courage, social interest, and a feeling of being accepted in his play with other children. His interest and joy in the company of others remained throughout his life.

His weak physique and feelings of inferiority during childhood were later to find expression in his concepts of organic inferiority and the striving for superiority. His sensitivity about being the second son was reflected in his interest in the family constellation and ordinal position of birth. His efforts to get along with others found expression in his conviction that the human being is a social and cultural animal and in the Adlerian concept of social interest.

Adler studied medicine at the University of Vienna, where Freud had received his medical training. Although he trained as an eye specialist, he became a general practitioner and later established himself as a practicing neurologist and psychiatrist. In 1902 he was invited by Freud to join a group for weekly

Alfred Adler

discussions on psychoanalysis. This group eventually grew into the Vienna Psychoanalytic Society, of which Adler was the first president, and later became the International Psychoanalytic Association.

There are many stories concerning Adler's association with Freud and their subsequent split. Adler was never a student of Freud nor was he ever psychoanalyzed. He joined the discussions because he was interested in psychoanalysis, but from the beginning he discovered points of disagreement. By 1911 these differences appeared crucial. Adler was invited to state his position to the society, and he did, but his views were denounced, he resigned, and about one-third of the members left with him.

Adler founded his own group and attracted many followers. He served in the Austrian army during World War I. Afterward he assisted the government in establishing child guidance clinics in Vienna. Although he and Freud both practiced in Vienna during the 1920s and early 1930s, they did not associate with each other.

Adler visited the United States frequently and came here to live in 1935. He continued his private practice, accepted a position as professor of medical psychology at the Long Island College of Medicine, and lectured widely. He died suddenly in 1937 of a heart attack while on a lecture tour in Scotland; he was sixty-seven.

Social Interest

A leading concept of Adler's individual psychology is his emphasis on the importance of human culture and society. Human society is crucial not simply for the development of an individual personality, but also for the orientation of each and every behavior and emotion in a person's life.

Human beings, like all living creatures, are driven by certain innate instincts, drives, or needs. All living organisms feel an impulse to maintain life, which causes them to seek nourishment. They have a compulsion to reproduce, which finds its expression in sex. Although much of the behavior of lower animals appears to be regulated by instincts, this is not true of human behavior. Human beings have tamed their instincts and subordinated them to their attitudes toward the environment. At times, human beings deny or disobey their natural instincts because of their social relations. A prisoner may die rather than betray her country. A young child may refuse food if he believes that such a tactic gives him an advantage in a power struggle with his parents.

This shaping of instinctual expression in terms of one's attitude toward the environment suggests that underlying all other instincts and needs is the innate characteristic of social interest (1939). **Social interest** refers to that urge in human nature to adapt oneself to the conditions of the social environment. Social interest expresses itself subjectively in one's consciousness of having something in common with other people and of being one of them. It expresses itself objectively in cooperation with others toward the betterment of human society. This innate social characteristic, while common to all, does not automatically emerge, nor does it invariably find constructive expression. It must be nurtured and cultivated if young children are to achieve adequate fulfillment of the complex demands of society and work toward its perfection (Lewis, 1991).

Finalism

The personality and characteristics of an individual are developed by the attitudes that she or he adopts toward the social environment in early childhood. This occurs through the goal-oriented activity of the human psyche. Adler stressed the fact that the movement of all living things is governed by goals. We cannot think, feel, will, or act, except with the perception of some goal (1927). To try to understand human behavior in terms of external causes is to fail to understand psychic phenomena. If I know a person's goal, I begin to understand in a general way the individual's behavior.

When an individual behaves in a certain way we naturally ask why. Past efforts to answer that question had emphasized material and mechanical explanations. Freud maintained that it is not enough to look for physiological causes;

we must also try to understand the psychological motives underlying behavioral events. However, Freud was misled by the principle of causality into regarding these motives as past and looking to the past for the explanation of all human behavior. Adler emphasized the purposefulness of human behavior by recognizing that the motivational force of every human action is the goal or future orientation of that action. This means that for Adler the human psyche is teleologically oriented. You will recall from our discussion of Jung that the term "telos" means a purpose or goal. Adler agreed with Jung that teleology is necessary for a full understanding of personality. For Adler, the goal that the individual pursues is the decisive factor and he called this concept of goal orientation the principle of **finalism** (1930).

Adler suggested that many of our guiding goals are fictions. His use of the term "fiction" may be puzzling. Adler did not equate fiction with falseness; rather he indicated that we cannot know whether or not our goals are true or false because there is no way to scientifically test them. "Fiction" comes from the Latin root *fictio,* which means "to invent," "fashion," or "construct." We are unable to have a complete understanding of things as they really are, so we structure our own idea of reality. "Fictions" are an individual's or group's interpretations of the events of the world. They are philosophical assumptions. We may assume that it is best to tell the truth, that all people are basically good, or that hard work will eventually pay off. In Adlerian vocabulary, such basic concepts are **fictional finalisms.** Adler was indebted to an earlier philosopher, Hans Vaihinger, for his concept of fictional finalisms. Vaihinger wrote a book, *The Philosophy of "As-if,"* in which he suggested that people create ideas that guide their behavior. Under the influence of a fiction, people behave "as if" their goals were true. If people believe that it is to their best advantage to be honest, they will strive to be so, even though there is no way in which they can ultimately test that belief as a hypothesis. It is important to note that psychologists also often pose fictional finalisms in their discussion of the good life. Concepts such as the "healthy personality" and "self-realization" function as fictional finalisms and cannot be empirically tested.

A fiction may be healthy or unhealthy. Adler maintained that it is inappropriate to judge a fiction as true or false, right or wrong; rather, the goal should be judged according to its usefulness. (Adler's concept of the **usefulness** of fictional finalisms should not be confused with the concept of usefulness in reference to scientific hypotheses, which was discussed in the introductory chapter. The scientific hypothesis is useful if it can generate predictions about experiences that we might observe.) Belief in a deity and the desire to serve it have proved to be a valuable fiction for many individuals. For others, however, belief in God and the desire to please God have had deleterious effects. Whether or not God really exists is beside the point; the point is that belief in God has a demonstrable effect, positive or negative, on the behavior and life of an individual. Healthy individuals continually examine the effectiveness of their fictions and alter their goals when they are no longer useful. They maintain their fictions in a state of flux in order to meet the demands of reality.

Striving for Superiority

Adler suggested that the psyche has as its primary objective the **goal of superiority.** This is the ultimate fictional finalism for which all human beings strive, and it gives unity and coherence to the personality. Initially, Adler conceived of the primary motivating force as aggression. Later, he identified the primary drive as a "will to power." Then, he refined the concept of a drive toward power and suggested that the essential dynamic of human nature lies in its striving for superiority (1930). Finally, he changed from striving for individual superiority to striving for a superior society.

Adler's concept of the striving for superiority does not entail the everyday meaning of the word "superiority." He did not mean that we innately seek to surpass one another in rank or position, nor did he mean that we seek to maintain an attitude of exaggerated importance over our peers. Rather, the drive for superiority involves the desire to be competent and effective in whatever one strives to do. The concept is similar to Jung's idea of self-realization. Adler frequently used the term *perfection* as a synonym for the word "superiority." This term can also be misleading unless we recognize its origin in the Latin *perfectus,* which means "completed" or "made whole."

The striving for superiority may take the form of an exaggerated lust for power. An individual may seek to exercise control over objects and people and to play god. The goal may introduce a hostile tendency into our lives, in which we play games of "dog eat dog." But such expressions of the goal for superiority are abortive and do not reflect its constructive nature.

The striving for superiority is innate and part of the struggle for survival that human beings share with other species in the process of evolution. According to Adler, life is not motivated by the need to reduce tension or restore equilibrium, as Freud tended to think; instead, life is encouraged by the desire to move from below to above, from minus to plus, from inferior to superior. This movement entails adapting oneself to and mastering the environment. The particular ways in which individuals undertake this quest are determined by their culture, their own unique history, and style of life.

Inferiority Feelings

The striving for superiority arises because as human beings we feel inferior. **Inferiority feelings** have their origin in our encounter as infants with the environment. As human infants, unlike other animals, we are born immature, incomplete, and incompetent to satisfy even our basic needs. There is a protracted period during which we are almost totally dependent on other people for our survival. Feelings of inferiority thus reflect a fact of existence. Such feelings are inescapable, but also invaluable, as they provide the major motivating force that leads to growth. Our efforts and success at growth and development may be seen as attempts to compensate for and overcome our imagined or real inferiorities and weaknesses. Thus, feelings of inferiority are not deviant but are the basis for all forms of human accomplishment and improvement in life (1927).

The concept of human nature as driven by feelings of inferiority first came to Adler during his practice of general medicine. He observed that many of his patients localized their complaints in specific body organs. He hypothesized that in many cases an individual is born with a potentially weak organ that may not respond adequately to external demands (1917). This "organ inferiority" can have profound effects on both the body and the psyche. It may have a harmful effect and lead to neurotic disorders, but it can also be compensated for and lead to optimal achievements. A classic historical example of compensation is found in the story of the ancient Greek, Demosthenes, who suffered as a child from a speech impediment. He learned to overcome his stuttering and became a great orator by forcing himself to shout in front of the ocean with pebbles in his mouth. Later, Adler broadened the concept of organ inferiority to include any feelings of inferiority, whether actual or imagined.

In his early writings, Adler termed the compensation for one's inferiorities the **masculine protest.** At the time, he associated inferiority with femininity. This concept finds common expression in references to "the weaker" or "the stronger" sex. Adler himself soon became dissatisfied with this shortsighted view. Women and men are different biologically, but neither sex is inferior. Later, Adler emphasized that inferiority is a condition of existence that affects males and females alike. In that sense, Adler became an early proponent of women's liberation. Basically, he recognized that the alleged inferiority of women was a cultural assignment rather than a biological one.

Adler's views were no doubt fostered by his marriage to Raissa Epstein, a member of the intelligentsia, who expected equality between them and helped him to overcome his earlier concepts of male dominance. Adler came to appreciate fully the role that culture and society has played in perpetuating male dominance and privilege. Indeed, he went so far as to suggest that psychological differences between women and men are entirely the result of cultural attitudes. Adler pointed out the devastating effect of these attitudes on the lives of children and the development of their self-confidence. He described how such biases disturb the psychological development of women and have led some of them to a pervasive dissatisfaction with their role. The "excessive pre-eminence of manliness" in our culture leads women into unhealthy forms of compensation or resignation and encourages men to unwisely depreciate and flee from women (Ansbacher and Ansbacher, 1956). Adler felt that exaggerated masculinity has a negative impact on men and women alike. He recommended the cultivation of comradeship and education for cooperation between the sexes. His ideas are confirmed today by research on sex roles and the influence of education.

Style of Life

Each individual seeks to cope with the environment and develop superiority in a unique way. This principle is embodied in Adler's concept of the **style of life,** which was a primary theme in his later writings (1929a, 1931). Each of us shares the common goal of striving for superiority, even though there are many different ways by which we may achieve this goal. One individual may try to develop competence and superiority through intellectual skills. Another may seek self-perfection by capitalizing on physical strengths. Style of life acts in part as a perceptual filter, influencing the ways in which we view the world. These different life-styles develop early in childhood. Adler suggested that the life-style is pretty clearly established by the time a child is five years old. Thereafter it remains relatively constant. It can be changed, but only through hard work and self-examination.

The style of life results from a combination of two factors: the inner goal orientation of the individual with its particular fictional finalisms and the forces of the environment that assist, impede, or alter the direction of the individual. Each individual's style of life is unique because of the different influences of our inner self and its constructs. Adler suggested that no two individuals ever had or could have the very same style of life. Even identical twins respond to their environment in different ways.

Nevertheless, Adler (1927) felt that he could distinguish four primary types of style, three of which he termed "mistaken styles." These include *the ruling type:* aggressive, dominating people who have little social interest or cultural perception; *the getting type:* dependent people who take rather than give; and *the avoiding type:* people who try to escape life's problems and engage in little socially constructive activity. The fourth primary life-style Adler termed *the socially useful type:* people who have a great deal of social interest and activity.

Birth Order

Among the factors that lead to different life-styles are the ordinal position of birth and different experiences in childhood. Adler did not postulate any stages of development as Freud did, but he emphasized the importance of the atmosphere of the family and the family constellation. **Family constellation** refers to one's position within the family in terms of birth order among siblings and the presence or absence of parents and other caregivers. Adler hypothesized that the personalities of oldest, middle, and youngest children in a family are apt to be quite dissimilar simply by virtue of the different experiences that each child has as that particular member of the family group.

Oldest children tend to be more intelligent, achievement oriented, conforming, and affiliative. They often try to regain the glory that was theirs before they were dethroned by younger siblings. Thus, they are frequently oriented toward the past and show a high degree of concern with power, which may

Birth Order and Personality

Read through the following lists and check those items that apply to you in comparison with your brothers and sisters. If you are an only child, check those items that apply to you in comparison with your peers.

List A
You tend to

1. be more conforming
2. be less hostile
3. have more motivation
4. be a better student
5. achieve more recognition
6. assume more leadership roles
7. be closer to your parents
8. like nurturing professions
9. consult others when making a decision
10. be less aggressive
11. associate more with others
12. receive high expectations from your parents
13. have similar values to your parents
14. seek help or nurturance from others
15. be more anxious
16. have more worries

    Total _____

List B
You tend to

1. be more aggressive
2. be more democratic
3. be more independent
4. be more popular
5. value parents' opinions less
6. like solitary professions
7. fight, "get into trouble" more
8. be a better mixer
9. like more dangerous activities
10. be less verbal
11. be less likely to seek help from others
12. be less conforming
13. "slide by" more
14. have been brought up less strictly by your parents
15. be more of a "loner"
16. have been given less attention by your parents

    Total _____

Add up your totals in each list. If you are an only or a firstborn child, the research indicates that more of the items on List A will apply to you. If you are a laterborn (but not the youngest in a large family), more of the items on List B will apply. If you are the youngest child in a large family, your pattern will be closer to that of a firstborn. If you are a middle child, you will show a combination of the characteristics of both lists. How do your findings compare with the research predictions? Can you think of other factors in your family constellation that have helped to shape your personality? Today, many students live in families other than the traditional nuclear family. They may live with a single parent or have stepparents and step- or half siblings. How might these constellations further influence personality?

express itself as a desire to exercise authority, lead, or protect and help others. Adler described Freud as a "typical eldest son."

The second child may feel the need to accelerate and catch up with the first child. While oldest children often dream of falling from places (dethronement), second children often dream of running to catch things. Second children are apt to be competitive and ambitious and often surpass the firstborn in achievement and motivation. However, they are not as concerned with power. Adler was a second child.

Lastborn children are more sociable and dependent, having been the "baby" of the family. At the same time they may also strive for excellence and superiority in an effort to surpass their older siblings. Adler pointed out that many fairy tales, myths, and legends (for example, the biblical story of Joseph) describe the youngest child as surpassing his or her older rivals. (It was Adler who fully developed the concept of *sibling rivalry,* in which the children within a family compete with one another.) The lastborn child who is spoiled and pampered may continue a helpless and dependent style of life into adulthood.

Only children tend to be more like older children in that they enjoy being the center of attention. Because they spend more time in the company of adults,

The personalities of oldest, middle, and youngest child in a family often differ greatly.

rather than siblings, they tend to mature sooner and to adopt adultlike behaviors earlier in life. However, only children are also the most likely to be pampered, in which case, Adler wrote, "the only child has difficulties with every independent activity and sooner or later they become useless in life" (Lieberman, Shaffer, & Reynolds, 1985). Adler considered pampering the "greatest curse of childhood."

Middle children show a combination of the characteristics of oldest and youngest. If children are spaced several years apart, they have more of the characteristics of only children. The family constellation becomes further complicated when one considers all the additional possibilities such as the only brother among sisters, twins, and so forth. In recent years a considerable amount of research has been done in the area of birth order and family constellation. One of the interesting findings suggests that longer marriages may occur among partners whose birth orders are complementary. Thus, an oldest brother of sisters will probably be happier with a younger sister to a brother than with an only child, because each of them is used to that familial pattern and mode of relating.

Family Atmosphere

The quality of emotional relationships among members of the family reflects the **family atmosphere,** which assists in determining whether or not the child will react actively or passively, constructively or destructively, in the quest toward superiority. Adler thought children who are pampered or neglected are particularly predisposed to a faulty style of life. The pampered child is one who is excessively spoiled and protected from life's inevitable frustrations. Such a child is being deprived of the right to become independent and learn the requirements of living within a social order. Parents who pamper a child make it difficult for the child to develop social feelings and become a useful member of society and culture. The child grows to dislike order and develops a hostile attitude toward it. The neglected child is one who feels unwanted and rejected. Such a child is virtually denied the right to a place in the social order. Rejection arouses resistance in the child, feelings of inferiority, and a tendency to withdraw from the implications of social life. Adler pointed out that child-rearing practices frequently consist of a continuing alternation between indulgence and rejection. The pampered child often demands undue attention and regard, which eventually leads to parental anger and punishment that are often interpreted by the child as rejection. Though few parents actually reject their children, many children feel humiliated and defeated.

Although parental "rejection" is overcome when parents learn alternative ways of handling their children that avoid pampering or neglect, Adler stressed that the individual is fully responsible for the meaning attached to parental behavior and action. Many of us harbor deep feelings of having been rejected by our parents when they actually gave us their best efforts. Thus, in the end, only the person can assume responsibility for his or her style of life.

The Creative Self

Adler considered the concept of **creative self** the climax of his theory (1964). It is the self in its creative aspects that interprets and makes meaningful the experiences of the organism and that searches for experiences to fulfill the person's unique style of life. In other words, the creative self establishes, maintains, and pursues the goals of the individual. Adler's concept of the creative self underscored his belief that human nature is essentially active, creative, and purposeful in shaping its response to the environment.

The concept of the creative self also reinforces Adler's affirmation that individuals make their own personalities from the raw materials of their heredity and environment. In his concept of the creative self, Adler restored consciousness to the center of personality. Adler believed that we are aware of everything we do and that, through self-examination, we can understand why we behaved in a certain way. The forces of which we are unaware are simply unnoticed; they are not buried in a sea of repression.

Adler's position regarding consciousness was in such direct contrast to that of Freud that it is no wonder the two could not work together. Adler did not deny unconscious forces, but he minimized them by reducing unconsciousness to simple temporary unawareness. He opposed Freud's determinism by emphasizing the vast extent to which people can achieve conscious control over their behavior. People, Adler argued, may become largely aware of their deepest impulses and fictional finalisms, and with conscious intent create their own personalities and life-styles that will achieve their highest goals. In the end, Adler's position was almost the complete opposite of Freud's, which emphasized that our behavior is largely determined by forces of which we are unaware. Freud offered his followers the hope of being able to endure or live without crippling fear of one's unconscious conflicts, but he never offered freedom from them. By restoring consciousness to the center of personality, by again crowning the king Freud had struggled so valiantly to dethrone, Adler aroused Freud's anger. To Freud, Adler was encouraging the very illusion that Freud had sought to destroy.

For many people, Adler's optimistic view provides a welcome contrast to the pessimistic and conflict-ridden picture of human nature shown in Freudian psychoanalysis and reinstates hope to the human condition. In his optimism, Adler foreshadowed the humanistic school of personality, which will be discussed later in Chapters 12 and 13.

Adlerian Psychotherapy

Neuroses, according to Adler (1929b), entail unrealistic life goals or fictional finalisms. Goals are not realistic unless they take into account our capacities, limitations, and social environment. A person who felt extremely inferior or rejected as a child may set goals that are too high and unattainable. A person of average intelligence cannot expect to perform at a consistently outstanding level in academic work. Some individuals adopt goals that are unrealistically low. Having felt defeated and unable to cope with certain situations, such as school, people may seek to avoid situations in which they could develop and perfect those skills that would enable them to perform effectively.

Neurotics also choose inappropriate life-styles as a means of attaining their goals. In their efforts to offset feelings of weakness, neurotics tend to overcompensate. **Compensation** entails making up for or overcoming a weakness. For example, blind people learn to depend more on auditory senses. **Overcompensation** refers to an exaggerated effort to cover up a weakness that entails a denial rather than an acceptance of the real situation (1954). The bully who persists in using force may be overcompensating for a difficulty in working cooperatively with others.

Adler's terms "inferiority complex" and "superiority complex," phrases that have become commonplace in our vocabulary, also describe neurotic patterns. Individuals who feel highly inadequate may be suffering from an **inferiority complex.** In Adlerian terms, there is a gulf between the real person and excessively high life goals. Individuals who exaggerate their own importance may be suffering from a **superiority complex.** In Adlerian terms, such individuals have overcompensated for feelings of weakness. Both complexes originate in a person's responses to real or imagined feelings of inferiority.

Adler suggests that neurotics actually live a **mistaken style of life,** or **life lie.** Neurotics strive for personal aggrandizement. Their style of life belies their actual capacities and strengths. They act "as if" they were weak, "as if" they were doomed to be losers, when in fact they could create a constructive existence for themselves. They capitalize on imagined or real weaknesses and use them as an excuse rather than a challenge to deal constructively with life. They employ **safeguarding tendencies,** compensatory devices that ward off feelings of inferiority in a maladaptive rather than adaptive fashion. To be sure, we all use such protective defense mechanisms at times, but neurotics employ them in an exaggerated manner and degree.

Adlerian therapy aims at restoring the patient's sense of reality, examining and disclosing the errors in goals and life-style, and cultivating social interest. Adler did not establish strict rules or methods for treatment; he believed that the patient's life-style should determine the procedure. On the whole, Adler's approach was somewhat more informal than Freud's. He abandoned the use of the couch, suggested that the patient sit facing the therapist, and reduced the frequency of contact between patient and doctor to once or twice a week.

The first goal of the Adlerian therapist is to establish contact with and win the confidence of the patient (1929b). Such confidence is won by approaching the patient as a peer, rather than an authority, and thereby eliciting cooperation. Whereas Freud viewed the transference, in which a patient works through earlier unsatisfactory relations by projecting them onto the doctor, as essential

THINKING CRITICALLY

First Memories

Your early memories probably refer to experiences that are in line with your basic goals. You may use these memories to justify your present stance. It is unimportant whether or not the remembered events really happened. Even imagined memories may be revealing. Jot down your earliest memories. When you have finished, pretend that you are an observer studying someone else's actions and behavior. Ask yourself, "What goal might a person be trying to accomplish by acting in this manner?" Then, on the basis of your memories, complete these sentences: "I am _____ . Others are _____ . Life is _____ . Therefore, I must _____ ." Compare the goals expressed in your early memories with those that are currently present in your dreams. In our dreams, we are not bound by realistic or commonsense solutions to our problems. Our dreams reveal how we would like to cope with issues in our lives. Running away from a dream monster may be indicative of the desire to run away from a current problem. Being paralyzed in a dream may suggest a style of acting helpless in the face of pressing demands. Look for consistencies and similar postures in your early memories and current dreams. If the goals therein appear unattainable, or the style of life ineffective, you may wish to examine their usefulness further.

to the effectiveness of treatment, Adler suggested that therapy is effective because healthy features of the physician-patient relationship are transferred, or carried over, into the patient's life. Such transference need not have regressive features and is really another name for the cultivation of social interest.

Second, the therapist seeks to disclose the errors in the patient's life-style and provide insight into the present condition. The patient is led gently and gradually to recognize the errors in personal goals, life-style, and attitude toward life.

Adlerian therapy seeks to encourage the patient to face present problems and to develop constructive means of dealing with them. The therapist hopes to instill (or promote) the courage to act "as if" the old limiting fictions and mistaken life-styles weren't true. The therapist who does not make decisions or assume responsibilities for the patient may structure or suggest situations that will assist in cultivating the patient's own skills. Such deliberate attempts at encouragement enable the patient to become more courageous and to accept new tasks and responsibilities. In this sense, the therapist plays the role of an educator who re-educates the neurotic in the art of constructive living. Additionally, Adler sought to minimize latent feelings of rejection and resentment and to cultivate feelings of social interest and good will. Adler believed that only by subordinating our private gain to public welfare can we attain true superiority. The true and inevitable compensation for all the natural weaknesses of individual human beings is that of social justice for all.

Adler had a tremendous influence on psychiatrist Harry Stack Sullivan, who developed the very important concept of *participant observation,* referring to the fact that an observer of an interpersonal relationship is also a participant in it. Sullivan also coined one of today's latest buzzwords—*co-dependence*—which is used frequently in Al-Anon, an organization for relatives of alcoholics, to refer to individuals who, usually unwittingly, help the alcoholic remain dependent on alcohol.

Many of Adler's concepts have been used to develop more effective methods of child rearing and education (Dreifurs, 1952–1953; Bitter, 1991). Adler would most definitely encourage prospective parents to engage in parental training. As creative selves, we construct the primary forces that shape our existence: our goals and life-styles. We can change these, should they become inappropriate, through insight into our errors. Through education, Adler believed, our innate and shared concept of social interest and justice could be made to flower and to provide the final and most appropriate form of compensation for our individual weaknesses. Adler was active in child guidance clinics and involved in penal reform. He was attracted to the political movement of socialism and many hours of his later years were devoted to specifying ways of educating for social justice. Adler "was radically opposed to the kind of therapy which overemphasized independence and egocentricity" (May, 1991).

Assessment and Research in Adler's Theory

Adler's theory, like that of many others, stemmed from clinical observations. Like Freud, Adler paid close attention to patients' nonverbal behavior as well as to what they said. He noted how they stood, walked, sat, or shook hands. He believed that nonverbal communication or behavior is indicative of a person's life-style. Adler himself conducted little systematic empirical research to validate his ideas. Instead, he viewed the importance of these data in terms of their relevance as clinical observations. Adler referred to the study of birth order, early memories, and dreams as the "three entrance gates to mental life"; these three tools constituted Adler's primary techniques of assessment.

Many early researchers attempted to test Adler's birth-order theory. Not all of the research supports Adler's findings, but it is easy to see that his theory has been valuable in stimulating further thought and research.

Zajonc and Marcus (1975) believe firstborns are more intelligent and theorize that is because the intellectual climate of a family decreases as the number of children increases. This has led to a rather blustery argument with Steelman (1985 and 1986), who says the educational, occupational, and income levels of the parents were not adequately controlled in the studies specified by Zajonc and Markus and could have been the primary reason (see also Zajonc, 1986).

Modern research has illustrated relationships between birth order and factors such as vocational preferences (Bryant, 1987); achievement motivation (Shell, Hargrove, & Falbo, 1986); divergent thinking (Runco & Bahleda, 1987); machiavellianism (Gupta, 1987); introversion and extraversion (Klein, 1984); self-esteem (Kidwell, 1982); humanitarian concerns (Lieberman, Shaffer, & Reynolds, 1985); fear of success (Ishiyama, Munson, & Chabassol, 1990), health (Elliot, 1992), and perception of parental favoritism (Kiracofe & Kiracofe, 1990). Some studies discover that gender may make a difference as well on factors such as psychological health (Lester, Eleftheriou, & Peterson, 1992; Fullerton, Ursano, Harry, & Slusarcick, 1989), narcissism (Narayan, 1990), perceptions of responsibility and dominance (Harris & Morrow, 1992), and toughmindedness (Singh, 1990). Eisenman (1992) discusses causes of some of these differences in terms of parental anxieties and available time for children of different birth orders.

Research about life-style continues to be limited but research in early memories, birth order, and social interest continues. A Social Interest Index has been cross-validated as a valid empirical measure of social interest (Hjelle, 1991).

Adler believed that early memories frequently summarized the essential characteristics of one's stance toward life. For example, Adler observed from a study of over one hundred physicians that their first memories often entailed the recollection of an illness or death. In the course of successful therapy, Adler also discovered that patients frequently recall previously overlooked memories that are more consistent with their new life-styles. Reichlin and Niederehe (1980) conducted research that confirms Adler's belief that early memories reflect personality traits.

New research on memory, which ties it to the development of language and the ability to shape events into a story, seemingly challenges Freud's theory of infantile amnesia and may support Adler's view that our earliest memories are full of symbolic meanings (Goleman, 1993b).

In Adler's theory, dreams are goal oriented rather than reflections of the past. They reveal the mood that we want to feel and suggest how we might deal with a future problem or task. Taking note of the options we choose to follow in our dream life gives us further insight into our style of life. Research by Greisers, Greenberg, and Harrison (1972) provided evidence that dreaming may assist individuals in dealing with ego-threatening situations and their analysis may suggest alternative options.

Adler preferred the use of clinical observations rather than psychological tests in the assessment of personality (Rattner, 1983). However, a Social Interest Index (SII) and a Social Interest Scale (SIS) have been developed by other psychologists to measure Adler's concept of social interest and test related hypotheses (Greever, Tseng, & Friedland, 1973; Crandall, 1981; Mullis, Kern, & Curlette, 1987). Measurements of inferiority need to be developed. Most available today focus on the self-concept (Dixon & Strano, 1989). Thus Adler's theory has been helpful in generating additional assessment tools.

Adler's Theory: Philosophy, Science, and Art

Adler's commitment to a philosophical viewpoint is clear in his discussion of fictional finalisms. Human beings, he asserted, are goal-oriented organisms, and all human behavior may be understood in terms of its contribution and adherence to a goal. Difficulties in living result from an inappropriate philosophy and the inappropriate style of life that accompanies it. By recognizing and cultivating the need for social justice, a person fulfills her or his ultimate potential.

Adler added *usefulness* to the criteria for judging philosophical assumptions: a philosophy is useful if it fosters productive living and enhances our lives. In

PHILOSOPHICAL ASSUMPTIONS

Examining Adler

How would you rate Adler on each of the basic philosophical assumptions described in Chapter 1? Each basic issue was presented as a bipolar dimension along which a person's view can be placed according to the degree of agreement with one or the other extreme. Rate Adler's views on these issues.

When you have determined where you think Adler stands, compare your responses with those of your classmates and your instructor. You should be willing to defend your ratings, but also be prepared to change them in light of others' compelling arguments. Afterward, compare your rating of Adler with your own position on each issue and with those of other theorists. Does this comparison help you to understand why his theory does or does not appeal to you?

Would strongly agree	Would agree	Is neutral or believes in synthesis of both views	Would agree	Would strongly agree
1	2	3	4	5

freedom
People basically have control over their own behavior and understand the motives behind their behavior.

determinism
The behavior of people is basically determined by internal or external forces over which they have little, if any, control.

doing so, he followed the pragmatic philosophy of William James (1842–1910), who argued that the meaning of a statement lies in the particular enriching consequences it has for our future experiences and the quality of our lives. Adler's emphasis on the importance of the usefulness of our goals has become very popular among psychologists and personality theorists.

Although Adler emphasized the factors in society that contribute to the shaping of personality, he did not adopt a radical environmentalist position and suggest that personality is *entirely* shaped by society. There are forces within the self, such as the drive for superiority and the creative self, that assist in shaping personality. Thus the individual plays an important, responsible role.

Adler was much more optimistic than Freud about human and societal potentialities. He saw human nature as flexible and changeable. The forward-moving

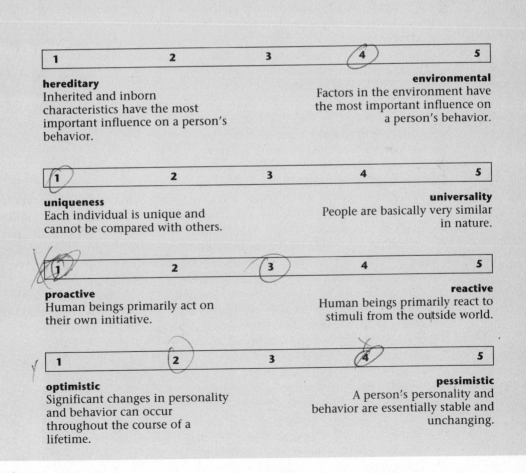

| 1 | 2 | 3 | 4 | 5 |

hereditary
Inherited and inborn characteristics have the most important influence on a person's behavior.

environmental
Factors in the environment have the most important influence on a person's behavior.

| 1 | 2 | 3 | 4 | 5 |

uniqueness
Each individual is unique and cannot be compared with others.

universality
People are basically very similar in nature.

| 1 | 2 | 3 | 4 | 5 |

proactive
Human beings primarily act on their own initiative.

reactive
Human beings primarily react to stimuli from the outside world.

| 1 | 2 | 3 | 4 | 5 |

optimistic
Significant changes in personality and behavior can occur throughout the course of a lifetime.

pessimistic
A person's personality and behavior are essentially stable and unchanging.

tendency within the self, the drive for superiority, implies that many obstacles to growth are imposed by society rather than by human nature itself. However, through the creative self, human beings largely create their own personalities. Ultimately, Adler envisioned the possibility of creating a better society through the cultivation of our social interest. He stressed the application of personality theory through the art of psychotherapy, believing that through self-understanding and education we can construct a better world.

Critics, however, have found Adler optimistic and naive, suggesting that he may have exaggerated the potentialities of the creative self in being aware of and creating the personality that will best fulfill the individual's goals and the possibilities of change at any point in one's lifetime. Although initially Adler adhered to the notion of determinism, in the end he was a strong advocate of free will. At times, it appears that the creative self is exempt from or able to overcome causal laws, an idea that both Freudians and later behaviorists would have trouble with.

Adler's emphasis on the social forces that play a part in shaping personality influenced subsequent social psychoanalytic theorists like Karen Horney and Erich Fromm. Adler's optimistic constructs also influenced the humanistic school of thought in psychology (see Ansbacher, 1990). Moreover, many of Adler's concepts, particularly that of the creative self, are congruent with the contemporary cognitive emphasis in psychology. There is a whole new resurgence of Adler in the counseling and education communities (see Dinkmeyer, 1989). Albert Ellis's system of rational-emotive therapy (1973), which holds that behaviors are a function of beliefs, draws on Adler's psychology as does the cognitive social learning theory of Julian Rotter, who studied with Adler in New York City. Thus, Adler's ideas and their application have become widespread even though they are sometimes not recognized as Adlerian, possibly because Adler does not mesh with America's "intoxication with narcissism and the ego-centered self" (May, 1991).

Adler's concept of social interest is extremely significant cross-culturally. Both Christian and Buddhist concepts of religious maturity include ideas similar to Adler's social interest. Adler tried to bring understanding to a significant part of our heritage as individuals. The extreme convergence with major religions indicates he was successful (Leak, Gardner, & Pounds, 1992). Adler saw the individual as concerned not only with the self but with the entire world (Lazarsfeld, 1991). One of Adler's goals for his individual psychology was to demonstrate that it was "heir to all great movements whose aim is the welfare of mankind" (Weiss-Rosmarin, 1990). Evans and Meredith (1991) ponder whether Adlerian psychology was in advance of its time.

Summary

1. Adler's **individual psychology** marks a shift from an emphasis on **intra-psychic** ("within the psyche") phenomena to an emphasis on **interpsychic** ("interpersonal") phenomena.

2. Adler believed that human beings have an innate urge to adapt themselves to the conditions of the environment. He named this urge **social interest** but stressed that it is not automatic and must be cultivated.

3. The principle of **finalism** means that individuals are oriented toward goals that guide their behavior. However, these individual interpretations of the world cannot be proven and are therefore called **fictional finalisms.** Adler suggested that they be judged by their **usefulness.**

4. The primary objective of the psyche is the **goal of superiority,** the desire to be competent and effective in what one does. This striving may take on the form of an exaggerated lust for power, if not properly directed.

5. As young children, we normally feel inferior, and these **inferiority feelings** lead us to seek ways in which we can compensate for our weaknesses.

6. Each individual develops a unique way of striving for superiority that is called a **style of life.** The four primary ones are *ruling, getting, avoiding,* and *socially useful.* The style of life is influenced by factors such as **family constellation** and **family atmosphere.**

7. Adler considered the concept of the **creative self** to be the climax of his theory. The creative self interprets the experiences of the organism and establishes a person's style of life. Adler's position was that the creative self is essentially conscious; he restored consciousness to the center of personality (in direct opposition to Freud's view).

8. Adlerian therapy aims at restoring the patient's sense of reality, examining and disclosing the errors in goals and style of life, and cultivating social interest. He believed the study of birth order, early memories, and dreams were the best tools for assessing personality.

9. Adler's theory emphasizes a philosophical point of view rather than an effort to study personality empirically. He also made substantial contributions to psychotherapy, education, and child rearing.

Suggestions for Further Reading

Alfred Adler wrote a number of books and articles. Since his writings were often intended for a lay audience, they are relatively easy to understand. The classic introduction to Adlerian thought is *The Practice and Theory of Individual Psychology* (Harcourt, Brace, 1927). A shorter summary, "Individual Psychology," appears in C. Murchison (Ed.), *Psychologies of 1930* (Clark University Press, 1930). Selections of Adler's writings have also been edited and presented by H. L. and Rowena R. Ansbacher (Basic Books, 1956, 1964).

For biographical data and an assessment of Adler's contemporary influence, the reader is referred to H. Orgler, *Alfred Adler: The Man and His Work* (New American Library, 1973); H. Musak (Ed.), *Alfred Adler: His Influence on Psychology Today* (Noyes, 1973); M. Sperber, *Masks of Loneliness: Alfred Adler in Perspective* (Macmillan, 1974); H. L. Ansbacher, *Alfred Adler Revisited* (Praeger, 1984); and K. Leman, *The Birth Order Book* (Revell, 1985).

CHAPTER 5

Karen Horney

1. Explain what Horney means by *hypercompetitiveness* and explain its effects.
2. Describe Horney's concept of *basic anxiety* and explain how it differs from Freud's concept of anxiety.
3. Explain how ten *neurotic needs* or *trends* can be summarized in terms of three ways of relating to others and three *basic orientations* toward life.
4. Distinguish between the *real self* and the *idealized self* and explain what is meant by the tyranny of the should.
5. Explain the relationship of the real self and the idealized self in normal, neurotic, and alienated individuals.
6. Compare and contrast Freud's and Horney's views of women.
7. Describe the processes of *self-analysis* and decision making.
8. Evaluate Horney's theory in terms of its function as philosophy, science, and art.

Karen Horney concentrated on the neurotic aspects of behavior in order to help us understand why we behave as we do. She subscribed to much of Freud's work but sought to overcome what she perceived as his limitations by emphasizing social and cultural factors and minimizing biological ones. Her work provides us with a number of fascinating insights and provocative concepts that have received a lot of attention.

Biographical Background

Karen Danielson Horney (pronounced "horn-eye") was born in 1885 near Hamburg, Germany, into an upper-middle-class family that was economically and socially secure. Her father was of Norwegian descent and her mother was Dutch. As a child, Horney sometimes traveled with her father, a sea captain. Although Horney admired her father, he was frequently stern and sullen. His intense gazes frightened her and he was often critical of her intelligence, interests, and appearance. Because of her father's long absences from home, Horney spent considerably more time with her mother, a younger, dynamic, freethinking woman who greatly influenced her daughter. Karen was devoted to her mother even though at times she felt that she favored her older brother. An experience with a kind doctor when she was twelve years old made her want to become a physician. Mrs. Danielson encouraged her daughter to study medicine at a time when it was unusual for women to enter that profession and in spite of rigid opposition from her husband. It was not the first time that the differences of temperament in Horney's parents led to discord. Eventually they separated and Horney's mother moved near Freiburg, where her daughter was pursuing her studies at the university. Later, Horney emphasized in her writings the role that a stressful environment plays in nurturing basic anxiety. Lack of love and encouragement, quarrelsome parents, and other stressful environmental factors lead to feelings of rejection, worthlessness, and hostility. She acknowledged these feelings in herself and worked hard to overcome them.

Horney received her degree in medicine from the University of Berlin. Thereafter she was associated with the Berlin Psychoanalytic Institute. She was analyzed by Karl Abraham and Hans Sachs, loyal disciples of Freud, who were two of the foremost training analysts of the day.

In 1909 she married Oscar Horney, a Berlin lawyer. They had three daughters. As a result of their different interests and her increased involvement in the psychoanalytic movement, they were divorced in 1937. The challenges of being a career woman and a mother, and of dissolving a marriage that was no longer viable, gave her considerable insight into the problems of women. We will see that she was one of the first to speak directly to the issue of feminine psychology.

Horney spent most of her life in Berlin, but in 1932 she was invited to come to the United States and assume the position of associate director of the Chicago

Karen Horney

Psychoanalytic Institute. Two years later, she moved to New York City, opened a private practice, and taught at the New York Psychoanalytic Institute.

Coming to America during the Great Depression, she began to appreciate more and more the role of environmental factors in neurosis. Her patients were not troubled primarily by sexual problems but with keeping a job and paying bills. Economic, educational, occupational, and social pressures seemed to be foremost in inducing neurotic behavior. Although earlier she had had disagreements with the Freudian point of view, orthodox psychoanalysis with its stress on genetic and instinctual causes of behavior appeared increasingly one-sided. Eventually her dissatisfaction and the refusal of orthodox psychoanalysis to integrate or even acknowledge her ideas led her to leave the New York Psychoanalytic Society. In April 1941 she walked out singing "Go Down Moses." Horney founded the Association for the Advancement of Psychoanalysis and the American Institute of Psychoanalysis and was dean of the Institute until her death, of cancer, in 1952.

American Hypercompetitiveness

Horney (1937) believed that a primary characteristic of American society and culture is **hypercompetitiveness**, a sweeping desire to compete and win in order to keep or heighten beliefs that one is worthy. Trying to avoid defeat at any price, individuals are willing to cheat, manipulate, speak out against, abuse, and behave aggressively toward other people. Relatively early in the twentieth century, Horney began to see a trend in America that has become even more pervasive as we come to the end of the century. She stated that this stance had a negative effect on the growth and development of children and adults.

"Our modern culture," she wrote, "is based on the principle of individual competition." "The . . . individual has to fight with other individuals of the same group, has to surpass them, and frequently, thrust them aside." Horney believed that the consequence of this "is a diffuse hostile tension between individuals" that "pervades all human relationships. Competitive stimuli are active from the cradle to the grave . . . [making] a fertile ground for the development of neurosis" (1937, pp. 284–287).

People who are hypercompetitive view others as evil and feel that the best way to survive is not to trust other people before they can confirm that they are trustworthy. In their sexual relations, they have a need to dominate and embarrass their partners (1937). In Adlerian terms, they have a neurotic need to prove that they are superior.

Horney disagreed with Freud's concept of a death instinct. "Human aggression was not innate, she argued, but was produced by individual anxiety. This anxiety, she said, was fostered by a faulty social and economic structure that oppressed the masses and by a patriarchal culture that derogated the females who shaped the children of the world" (Garrison, 1981).

THINKING CRITICALLY

Hypercompetitiveness in American Society

Can you think of examples of hypercompetitiveness in American society? Think about the business world, jobs that you might have had, your own experiences in school, and your relationships with members of the opposite sex. Do you ever find yourself acting competitively in circumstances that do not require competition? You might wish to talk to people who have come to America from other cultures to learn their perceptions about competitiveness in American society. Perhaps some of those people will be able to share with you ways in which their culture and society have been able to foster a spirit of cooperation rather than competitiveness.

Basic Anxiety

Social forces, such as hypercompetitiveness, foster anxiety and lead to neurosis. Unlike Freud, Horney did not see anxiety as an inevitable part of the human condition.

As human beings, our essential challenge is to be able to relate effectively to other people. **Basic anxiety**, an insidiously increasing, all-pervading feeling of being lonely and helpless in a hostile world (1945), results from feelings of insecurity in these relations. According to Horney's concept of basic anxiety, the environment as a whole is dreaded because it is seen as unrealistic, dangerous, unappreciative, and unfair. Children are not simply afraid of their own inner impulses or of punishment because of their impulses, as Freud postulated in his

When children are threatened by a hostile environment, it is important that they be made to feel safe and secure.

concepts of neurotic and moral anxiety; they also feel at times that the environment itself is a threat to their development and innermost wishes. Children are dependent on their parents or caregivers for the satisfaction of many of their needs. Some parents and caregivers, however, are unable to meet children's needs satisfactorily. A variety of negative conditions in the environment can produce the lack of security entailed in basic anxiety: domination, isolation, overprotection, hostility, indifference, inconsistent behavior, disparagement, parental discord, lack of respect and guidance, or the lack of encouragement and warmth. Children's fears may be objectively unrealistic, but for them they are real. In a hostile environment, children's ability to use their energies and develop self-esteem and reliance is, in fact, thwarted. Children may be rendered powerless in the face of these encroachments on their environment. Their biological dependency and the failure of parents to foster adaptive self-assertive behavior may leave them helpless. Although children may endure a certain amount of frustration and trauma, it is essential for healthy personality development that they feel safe and secure.

Research on parenting styles by Baumrind (1972) and Maccoby and Martin (1983) underscores Horney's conviction that parenting patterns have a strong impact on children and that children respond positively to parents who are both affectionate and firm. Research on attachment between parents and children shows that three essentials that impact and are impacted by attachments are biological fitness, psychological well-being, and cultural norms and values. In all cultures the likelihood that children will be insecurely attached increases where there is poverty, abuse, or maternal depression (Spieker & Booth, 1988). However, children can endure considerable stress provided they have a warm and affectionate relationship with at least one caring adult.

Neurotic Needs or Trends

In the face of basic anxiety, children develop certain defense attitudes or strategies that permit them to cope with the world and afford a certain measure of gratification (1937). Many of these strategies continue into adulthood. Specifically, we use them to deal with or minimize feelings of anxiety and to assist us in effectively relating to others. Where they become exaggerated or inappropriate, these strivings may be referred to as **neurotic needs** or **trends**. Neurotic trends are the result of the formative experiences that create basic anxiety. The trends are not instinctual in nature but highly dependent on the individual's formative experiences of being either safe or insecure in the world. Horney criticized Freud for his image of neurotic needs as instinctual or derived from the instincts. She placed environmental factors at the center of personality development.

Horney outlined ten different neurotic needs or trends (see Table 5.1). What makes a need neurotic? For the neurotic, the need is too intense, too unrealistic,

Table 5.1 *Horney's Ten Neurotic Trends*

Neurotic trends	Primary modes of relating to others	Basic orientations toward life
1. Exaggerated need for affection and approval	Moving toward: accepting one's helplessness and becoming compliant	Self-effacing solution: an appeal to be loved
2. Need for a dominant partner		
3. Exaggerated need for power	Moving against: rebelling and resisting others to protect one's self from a threatening environment	Self-expansive solution: a striving for mastery
4. Need to exploit others		
5. Exaggerated need for social recognition or prestige		
6. Exaggerated need for personal admiration		
7. Exaggerated ambition for personal achievement		
8. Need to restrict one's life within narrow boundaries	Moving away: isolating one's self to avoid involvement with others	Resignation solution: the desire to be free of others
9. Exaggerated need for self-sufficiency and independence		
10. Need for perfection and unassailability		

SOURCE: Based on information in K. Horney, *Self-Analysis.* New York: Norton, 1942; K. Horney, *Our Inner Conflicts,* New York: Norton, 1945; and K. Horney, *Neurosis and Human Growth,* New York: Norton, 1950. Used by permission of W. W. Norton & Co.

too indiscriminate, too anxiety laden. These trends lead to three types of coping strategies or primary modes of relating to other people: **moving toward** (compliance), **moving against** (hostility), and **moving away** (detachment). These types of behavior lead, in turn, to three **basic orientations** toward life: the **self-effacing solution,** an appeal to be loved; the **self-expansive solution,** an attempt at mastery; and the **resignation solution,** a desire to be free of others (1950). These orientations are interpersonal in nature, as opposed to the Freudian and Jungian character types, which are intrapsychic. Research on attachment patterns in infants suggests a distinct similarity between Horney's three

THINKING CRITICALLY

Basic Orientations and Mistaken Life-styles

Compare and contrast Adler's three mistaken styles of life (described in Chapter 4) with Karen Horney's basic orientations (summarized in Table 5.1). Do you see any parallels here? Remember that when you compare and contrast, you need to tell first how the concepts are alike and then how they are different. Adler considered his fourth primary life-style, the socially useful type, a healthy life-style, whereas Karen Horney believed that health involved balancing the three basic orientations. Which of these views best commends itself to you? Explain your position.

basic orientations and young children's behavior (Ainsworth, Bleihav, Waters, & Wall, 1978).

Normal or mature individuals resolve their conflicts by integrating and balancing the three orientations, which are present in all human relations. They are able to express each mode at the appropriate time. Neurotics express one mode at the expense of other aspects of their personality. They actively, although unconsciously, repress tendencies to react according to the other orientations. This repression, however, is not successful; the repressed tendencies continue to seek expression and increase the neurotic's anxiety. As the neurotic continues to emphasize one need or mode and overlook the others, a "vicious circle" develops and the anxiety is never adequately resolved. Thus neurotics transform normal strivings into pathological ones. Table 5.1 summarizes the ten neurotic trends, three modes of relating to others, and three basic orientations toward life.

The Idealized Self

Karen Horney (1950) also distinguished between the real self and the idealized self. The **real self** represents what we are; those things that are true about us. The **idealized self** represents what we think we should be and is used as a model to assist us in developing our potential and achieving self-actualization. The dynamic of creating an idealized self in order to facilitate self-realization is universal and characteristic of each of us. An individual who seeks to be a competent doctor posits an ideal of what an effective doctor is like. In the normal individual, the idealized self and the real self largely coincide because the idealized self is based on a realistic assessment of one's abilities and potentials. But in the neurotic, the real self and the idealized self are discrepant or separated. A doctor who believes that an ideal doctor never loses a patient to death is being unrealistic. This situation can be represented diagrammatically by circles as is shown in Figure 5.1.

A person is able to recognize and develop only those aspects of the real self that coincide with the idealized self. Thus, as neurosis becomes more severe, an increasing amount of the powers and potentialities of the real self may be rendered unavailable for cultivation. In an extreme neurosis, the individual may completely abandon the real self for the sake of an idealized *glorified self.* Horney referred to this situation as one of **alienation** (or *the devil's pact*). In a state of alienation, a person identifies with the ideal self and thereby loses the true source of strength, since our only source of strength comes from who we really are.

Horney (1950) suggests that neurotics' lives are governed by "the tyranny of the should." Instead of meeting genuine needs, those individuals create false

Figure 5.1 *The Normal and Neurotic Self*
Circles can be used to represent the real and idealized self in Horney's theory of personality: In the normal individual, the circles largely coincide. In the neurotic individual, the circles are increasingly distinct.

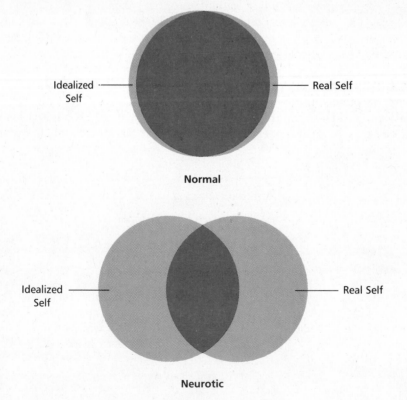

THINKING CRITICALLY

The Tyranny of the Should

Can you name some significant "shoulds" that you have devised to safeguard your image of self? Can you identify the origin of your "shoulds," for example, your parents, or your culture? Can you think of different types of "shoulds" that diverse cultures foster? What might happen if you were to give up one of the "shoulds" that is giving you problems?

ones. For example, some people have the idea that in order to be good they must never feel jealous, and so they posit an idealized self that does not permit feelings of jealousy. Therefore, the part of the real self that does experience feelings of jealousy is denied. The individual becomes estranged from a part of the self.

A classic illustration clarifies Horney's point: normal individuals, by and large, are happy with and function within the everyday world. Neurotics are unhappy with the everyday world. To the extent that they are dreaming about castles in the sky, they do not function as effectively as they might. Alienated individuals try to escape to their castles in the air. Such total identification with the idealized self renders these people virtually unable to cope.

Horney's concept of the idealized self may be seen as a constructive revision or correction of Freud's concept of the ego-ideal. Freud's concept of the super-ego includes two aspects: an introjected social conscience and an ego-ideal that is an idealized image consisting of approved and rewarded behaviors. The ego-ideal is the source of pride and provides a concept of who we think we should be. In her elaboration, Horney emphasized social factors that influence the development of an idealized self. Furthermore, Horney did not view the idealized self as a special agency within the ego but as a special need of the individual to keep up appearances of perfection. She also pointed out that the need to maintain an unrealistic idealized self does not involve simply repression of "bad" feelings and forces within the self. It also entails repression of valuable and legitimate feelings that are repressed because they might endanger the mask.

Feminine Psychology

Karen Horney's interest in feminine psychology was stimulated by the fact that certain clinical observations appeared to contradict Freud's theory of the libido. In his concept of libidinal development, sexual activities and attitudes appear to be instinctual, inevitable processes unaffected by culture or society.

Freud had suggested that penis envy was largely responsible for a woman's development, that women view themselves as castrated males. Horney pointed out that both men and women develop fantasies in their efforts to cope with the Oedipal situation. She also emphasized that many men and boys express jealousy over women's ability to bear and nurse children, a phenomenon that has since been clearly seen in primitive puberty rites as well as in clinical settings. Horney termed this phenomenon **womb envy.** Her work suggests that womb envy and penis envy are complements (1967). The appearance of these attitudes does not necessarily reflect unsatisfactory development or harmful emotions but rather shows the mutual attraction and envy that the sexes have for each other.

Horney believed that the essence of sexual life lies in its biological creative powers. It follows that a greater role in sexual life belongs to the female because she is the one who is able to bear and nurse children. The woman's capacity for motherhood demonstrates her "indisputable superiority." This superiority is recognized by the male and is the source of intense envy.

Womb envy, rather than being openly acknowledged by most males, has often taken subtle and indirect forms, such as the rituals of taboo, isolation, and cleansing that have frequently been associated with menstruation and childbirth, the need to disparage women, accuse them of witchcraft, belittle their achievements, and deny them equal rights. Similar attempts to deal with these feelings have led men to equate the term "feminine" with passiveness and to conceive of activity as the prerogative of the male.

Erik Erikson (1975) and Bruno Bettelheim also commented on observations of womb envy in their practices. For example, in the fairy tale *Little Red Riding Hood,* the wolf devoured both the grandmother and Little Red Riding Hood, who were subsequently rescued by a hunter who performed a kind of cesarean operation on the wolf, evoking the idea of the male being pregnant and giving birth. The wolf's belly was then filled with stones so that when he woke and tried to jump away, the weight of the stones dragged him to his death (Bettelheim, 1977). In the past three decades ethnographic accounts from many cultures have found male envy and its denial of female menses and reproductive ability (Paul, 1992).

Both men and women have an impulse to be creative and productive. Women can satisfy this need naturally and internally, through becoming pregnant and giving birth, as well as in the external world. Men can satisfy their need only externally, through accomplishments in the external world. Thus, Horney suggested that the impressive achievements of men in work or other creative fields may be seen as compensations for their inability to bear children.

The woman's sense of inferiority is not constitutional but acquired. In a patriarchal society, the attitude of the male has predominated and succeeded in convincing women of their supposed inadequacies. But these are cultural and social factors that shape development (Eckardt, 1991; Symonds, 1991), not biological ones.

During her practice in the 1920s, Karen Horney believed a "flight from womanhood" could be observed in society, in which many women inhibited their femininity and became frigid. While distrusting men and rebuffing their advances, these women wished that they were male. Such a flight from womanhood was due not to instinctual developments but to the experience of real social and cultural disadvantages that women have had to deal with. Sexual unresponsiveness, Horney pointed out, is not the normal attitude of women. It is the result of cultural factors. Our society, as has been well acknowledged, is a male society, and therefore for the most part it is not amenable to the unfolding of a woman's individuality.

Although Horney's psychology of women, which is almost a direct inversion of Freud's theory, has met with criticism because she maintained that the essence of being a woman lies in motherhood, her contributions to feminine psychology have been very valuable. In breaking away from orthodox psychoanalysis, Alfred Adler and Erich Fromm were also especially concerned about female development.

In her own life Horney struggled to resolve many of the problems that face women in contemporary culture, combining the difficulties of motherhood with an active career. Much of Horney's work in feminist psychology and her challenge to male authority was ground breaking for the important field of psychology of women. In many ways, she was prophetic. As early as the 1920s, she observed that it was men who had written human history and men who had shaped the psychoanalytic movement. Thus these enterprises reflected male need and biases. She insisted that men should "let women speak, and hear *their* 'interpretations', even 'biases', if you will" (Coles, 1974).

Not long ago, the dependency needs of men were cared for routinely by women. As women change and become more involved outside the home, they are not as able to meet all those needs and this has provoked a great deal of anxiety and frequently negative behavior in men. Feminine "values of closeness, love, intimacy, and sensitivity to relationships . . . as contrasted with achievement, success, power, mastery, and repression of feelings assigned to men in our culture can be readily understood in Horneyan terms." In her later writings, Horney developed a theory "that was not gender-specific, but applied to all humans. Perhaps, because Horney was a woman who saw the distortion that developed by overlooking women's identity, she was able to encompass a broader spectrum of human behavior." As such, her theory can be very helpful in "illuminating gender issues and the conflicts that women [and men] struggle with" (Symonds, 1991, pp. 301, 304).

Assessment and Research in Horney's Theory

In her assessment of personality, Karen Horney primarily employed the techniques of free association and dream analysis. She also suggested (1942) that **self-analysis** can assist normal personality development. By analyzing one's self, significant gains may be made in self-understanding and in reaching freedom from inner bondages that hinder developing one's best potentialities.

Although Horney acknowledged that self-analysis can be difficult and painful, she believed that it is possible. While it is true that many of us have become estranged from parts of our world and desire not to see them, the fact remains that knowledge about our world is available to us. By observing and then examining our observations, we can gain access to those aspects of our world that we have neglected.

To those critics who were concerned that self-analysis might be dangerous, Horney pointed out that the advantages that might accrue from self-analysis outweigh any possible dangers. The likelihood of danger is minimized because an individual who is attempting self-analysis will simply fail to make observations that might be intolerable and lead to further personality disorientation. While self-analysis can never be considered a totally adequate substitute for professional analysis of neurosis, its possible benefits for enhancing individual development merit its use.

Each one of us engages in self-analysis when we try to account for the motives behind our behaviors. A student who fails a test that she thought was unfair might ask whether she had properly prepared for it. An individual who yields to another in a disagreement might ask if he gave in because he was convinced that the other's point of view was superior or because he was afraid of a possible argument. Such analyses are common in normal living.

Systematic self-analysis differs from occasional self-analysis in degree rather than kind, entailing a serious and protracted effort for self-understanding undertaken on a regular basis. Systematic self-analysis employs the tool of free association, followed by reflection on what one has thought and an analysis of the resistance that aims to maintain the status quo. When one obtains insight into one's personality, energies that were previously engaged in perpetuating neurotic trends are freed and can be used for making constructive changes.

Compared with Freudian psychoanalysis, Horney's theory recommends a more interpersonal understanding of the patient's issues. Like Freud, however, she felt that tracing the genetic sources in repetition of early patterns is critical, as is the analysis of transference.

Horney (1945) discussed four prerequisites for good decision making. First, she said, we need to be cognizant of our real feelings and wishes. Second, we need to have created our own set of values (not merely accepted those of our parents or society). Third, we have to make a deliberate choice between two opposite possibilities. Finally, we have to take responsibility for the decision that we make.

Van den Daele (1987) has suggested that Horney's theory of personality can be operationally defined and is essentially compatible with the requirements of psychological measurement. Some parallels have been noted between her concepts of "movement against others" and the idealized self and research on coronary-prone Type A behavior (Hamon, 1987). Other research that fails to support some of Freud's ideas concerning women (Fisher & Greenberg, 1977) can be seen as supportive of Horney's views (Schultz, 1990).

Ryckman, Hammer, Kaczor, and Gold (1990) developed a Hypercompetitive Attitude Scale to evaluate the soundness of Horney's concept of hypercompeti-

THINKING CRITICALLY

Decision Making

Think about a significant decision that you have made in your life. Discuss the manner in which you made the decision. Taking into account Horney's four prerequisites, which gave you the most trouble? Next think of an important decision that you face now or expect to make shortly. Try to analyze that decision in terms of Horney's prerequisites. For example, what are your real feelings and wishes? What do you value, and how do these values affect this particular decision? Does this analysis help you to make a choice? How hard will it be for you to take responsibility for your decision?

tiveness and found empirical backing for the concept. College men and women scoring higher in hypercompetitiveness had less self-esteem and were not as healthy psychologically as those who scored lower. Moreover, men with higher scores were more macho and thought of women as sexual objects. Kaczor, Ryckman, Thornton, and Kuelnel (1991) forecast and found that hypercompetitive men were more likely to charge rape victims as being responsible for having been raped and to view them as losers in a fierce physical fight for supremacy.

Horney's Theory: Philosophy, Science, and Art

Horney was an astute observer and talented clinician. She frequently tested, revised, and discarded her theories in the light of new observations. She asserted that certain therapeutic approaches bring forth desired and predictable changes in behavior, changes that can be observed during the course of therapy if not in a rigorous laboratory experiment. She was clearly engaged in scientific activity and believed that her method and therapy must be open to scientific investigation and research.

Horney was not greatly interested in abstract thinking, but her theory does reflect deep philosophical commitments, such as a belief in the process of growth and forward movement (akin to Jung's concept of self-realization) and an optimistic view of human nature. Toward the end of her life she became interested in Zen Buddhist writings and practices (see DeMartino, 1991). The underlying philosophical assumptions that support her work are both profound and compelling.

Horney's contributions to the art of psychotherapy have been particularly valuable. Her theory and therapeutic techniques have been adopted by many clinicians. Several aspects of her technique are discussed in current Freudian literature as useful additions to psychoanalysis.

Horney has been criticized for simply elaborating on concepts that were implied but not clearly expressed in Freud's writings; however, these elaborations contain valuable, original contributions. Horney clarified the ego-ideal; her concept of neurotic trends clarified Freudian defense mechanisms; and she

PHILOSOPHICAL ASSUMPTIONS

Examining Horney

How would you rate Horney on each of the basic philosophical assumptions described in Chapter 1? Each basic issue was presented as a bipolar dimension along which a person's view can be placed according to the degree of agreement with one or the other extreme. Rate Horney's views on these issues.

When you have determined where you think Horney stands, compare your responses with those of your classmates and your instructor. You should be willing to defend your ratings, but also be prepared to change them in light of others' compelling arguments. Afterward, compare your rating of Horney with your own position on each issue and with those of other theorists. Does this comparison help you to understand why her theory does or does not appeal to you?

Would strongly agree	Would agree	Is neutral or believes in synthesis of both views	Would agree	Would strongly agree
1	2	3	4	5

freedom	**determinism**
People basically have control over their own behavior and understand the motives behind their behavior.	The behavior of people is basically determined by internal or external forces over which they have little, if any, control.

provided significantly more insight into the psychology of women. Moreover, "her disagreements with Freud were profound" (Garrison, 1981), as she emphasized that "everything depended upon the interaction of culture and personality." Her work foreshadowed that of object relations theorists who emphasize interpersonal relations (Ingram & Lerner, 1992; and Cassel, 1990) and Heinz Kohut's ideas about grandiosity as a major developmental trend. These represent substantial contributions to psychoanalysis.

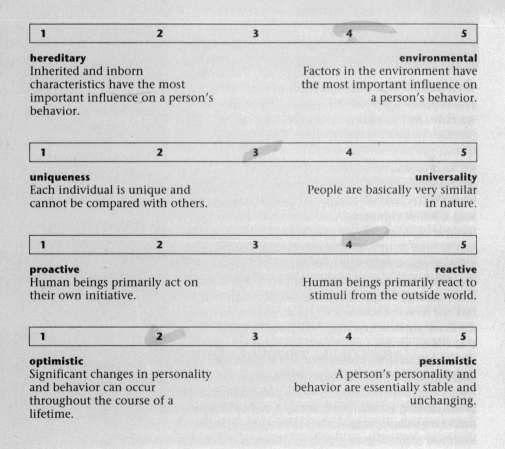

| 1 | 2 | 3 | 4 | 5 |

hereditary
Inherited and inborn characteristics have the most important influence on a person's behavior.

environmental
Factors in the environment have the most important influence on a person's behavior.

| 1 | 2 | 3 | 4 | 5 |

uniqueness
Each individual is unique and cannot be compared with others.

universality
People are basically very similar in nature.

| 1 | 2 | 3 | 4 | 5 |

proactive
Human beings primarily act on their own initiative.

reactive
Human beings primarily react to stimuli from the outside world.

| 1 | 2 | 3 | 4 | 5 |

optimistic
Significant changes in personality and behavior can occur throughout the course of a lifetime.

pessimistic
A person's personality and behavior are essentially stable and unchanging.

Summary

1. Horney believed *hypercompetitiveness,* a sweeping desire to compete and win in order to believe one is worthy, is rife in American culture. It leads to anxiety and neurosis and has a negative effect on growth and development.

2. Horney described **basic anxiety** as anxiety that results from feelings of insecurity in interpersonal relations. Unlike Freud, she did not believe that anxiety is an inevitable part of the human condition. It results from cultural forces. Research on parenting styles and attachment emphasize the importance of an affectionate and warm relationship between children and parents.

3. Basic anxiety is reflected in ten **neurotic needs** or **trends**, which lead to three ways of relating to others (**moving toward, moving against,** and **moving away**) and to three **basic orientations** toward life: the **self-effacing solution,** the **self-expansive solution,** and the **resignation solution.**

4. The **real self** represents that which a person actually is; the **idealized self** represents that which a person thinks he or she should be.

5. In a normal individual the real self and the idealized self closely coincide, but in a neurotic individual they are more separate. In extreme cases of **alienation,** a person may completely abandon the real self for the sake of the idealized self. Horney suggests that neurotics are governed by "the tyranny of the should."

6. Horney's view of women is almost a direct inversion of Freud's. Whereas Freud suggested the phenomenon of penis envy in women, Horney pointed out the phenomenon of **womb envy** in men. She emphasized the superiority of women as reflected in their capacity for motherhood and stressed that a woman's sense of inferiority is not constitutional but acquired. In her later writings Horney developed a theory that was not gender specific but applied to all humans.

7. **Self-analysis** is difficult but not impossible. It entails a serious and protracted effort for self-understanding undertaken on a regular basis. Horney identified four prerequisites for decision making.

8. Horney's greatest contributions have been to the art of psychotherapy and her formulations regarding women and psychoanalysis.

Suggestions for Further Reading

Karen Horney's writings, clear and easy to read, have attracted a large lay audience. *New Ways in Psychoanalysis* (Norton, 1939) describes Horney's disagreement with Freudian theory: her belief that its stress on instinctual determinants is one-sided and needs to be rounded out by the consideration of cultural and social elements. *The Neurotic Personality of Our Time* (Norton, 1937), *Our Inner Conflicts* (Norton, 1945), and *Neurosis and Human Growth* (Norton, 1950) outline Horney's theory of neurosis. Identifying ten neurotic trends in the earliest book, Horney's thought developed through the concept of three modes of relating to others and, later, three basic orientations to life. In the last book, Horney introduced the concept of the idealized self. Her writings on the psychology of women have been brought together in *Feminine Psychology* (Norton, 1967). *Self-Analysis* (Norton, 1942) familiarizes the lay person with the methods and techniques of psychoanalysis. It is an invaluable work for any individual who is interested in pursuing his or her own self-understanding through analysis.

A good biography of Karen Horney is S. Quinn, *A Mind of Her Own: The Life of Karen Horney* (Summit Books, 1987). A volume of papers and commentaries honoring Karen Horney's work is M. M. Berger (ed.), *Women Beyond Freud: New Concepts of Feminine Psychology* (Brunner-Mazel, 1993).

CHAPTER 6

Erich Fromm

YOUR GOALS FOR THIS CHAPTER

1. Explain why Fromm's approach is described as humanistic social analysis.
2. Describe three common mechanisms of escape from freedom.
3. Distinguish between *existential* and *historical dichotomies* and give an example of each.
4. Describe Fromm's five basic needs and explain how they are related to the development of society.
5. Discuss the character orientations that Fromm identified.
6. Describe three basic types of relationship between persons.
7. Distinguish between Fromm's concept of *self-love* and narcissism.
8. Describe Fromm's concept of the role of society in structuring personality and tell how he studied the influence of society on personality.
9. Evaluate Fromm's theory in terms of its function as philosophy, science, and art.

The early 1920s were a time of vibrant excitement in the academic community. Nineteenth-century scholars such as Freud, Comte, Spencer, and Marx had opened the door to the analytical study of human behavior and social institutions. New disciplines of psychology, sociology, and anthropology were emerging and efforts were being made to build interdisciplinary foundations for understanding social institutions and human behavior. Erich Fromm was particularly impressed with the writings of Freud and Marx and he attempted a synthesis of their ideas. Fromm's approach is best described, then, as humanistic social analysis.

Biographical Background

Erich Fromm was born in Frankfurt, Germany, in 1900, the only child of a deeply orthodox Jewish family. At the age of thirteen, Fromm began to study the Talmud, beginning an interest in religious literature and an admiration of the German mystic "Meister" Eckhart (1260?–1327?) that remained throughout his life. In his later years, Fromm did not formally practice religion but he referred to himself as an "atheistic mystic," and it is clear that Fromm's early religious experiences left a distinct mark on his personality and work. The moral and committed tone of his writings has a quality that has been described as reminiscent of the Old Testament prophets. He was deeply interested in religion and both his earlier and later writings reflect this concern.

Fromm wrote little about his early childhood. In his few comments, he described his early family life as tense and acknowledged that his parents were probably neurotic. His mother was "depression-prone," and his father, an independent businessman, "moody" and "overanxious." Fromm was fourteen years old when World War I broke out. He was impressed, almost to the point of being overwhelmed, by the irrationality of human behavior as it showed itself in the brutalities of war. By 1919 he had identified his political attitude as socialist and began to pursue formal studies in sociology and psychology at the University of Heidelberg. He received the Ph.D. in 1922.

Erich Fromm was trained in analysis in Munich and at the Institute of Berlin. He was one of the early *lay analysts;* that is, he had no formal medical training. The desirability of a medical background for the practice of psychoanalysis is still debated. Many psychoanalysts in America view psychoanalysis as primarily a medical method of treatment for neurotic disorders and therefore consider a medical background indispensable. Freud, however, had argued against medical training as the optimal background for an analyst and had advocated the training of lay people. He felt that analysis should be viewed as more than simply a method for the treatment of neurosis and suggested that it should also be seen as a wide cultural force offering insight into such areas as sociology, philosophy, art, and literature. Fromm's own broad understanding of the social

Erich Fromm

sciences and philosophy was to enrich his understanding of psychoanalytic theory and its applications. At the same time, these interests eventually led to his severance from orthodox psychoanalysis and his criticism of Freud for his unwillingness to acknowledge the importance of social and economic forces in shaping personality.

In 1933, during the Depression, Fromm came to the United States. He helped found the William Alanson White Institute for Psychiatry, Psychoanalysis, and Psychology and was a trustee and teacher for many years. He taught at other universities, such as Yale and the New School for Social Research, and maintained an active private practice. In 1949 he was appointed professor of psychiatry at the National University in Mexico. After his retirement in 1965, he continued teaching and consulting activities. He moved in 1976 to Switzerland, where he died of a heart attack in 1980. He was almost eighty years old.

Basic Human Conditions and Needs

Erich Fromm began with the thesis (1941) that *freedom* is a basic human condition that posits a "psychological problem." As the human race has gained more freedom by transcending nature and other animals, people have become increasingly characterized by feelings of separation and isolation. Thus, a major theme of Fromm's writings is the concept of loneliness. To be human is to be isolated and lonely, because one is distinct from nature and others. Loneliness also represents a basic human condition, and it is this characteristic that radically separates human nature from animal nature. The condition of loneliness finds its ultimate expression in the problem of death. Unlike other animals, we know we are going to die. This knowledge leads to a feeling of despair. Most of us find death incomprehensible and unjust — the ultimate expression of our loneliness.

In response to the basic condition of freedom, human beings have two ways to resolve the problem. They can work with one another in a spirit of love to create a society that will optimally fulfill their needs, or they can "escape from the burden" of freedom into "new dependencies and submission" (1941). Such escape may alleviate feelings of isolation but it does not creatively meet the needs of humanity or lead to optimum personality development.

Escape Mechanisms

Fromm (1941) identified three common mechanisms of escape from freedom: authoritarianism, destructiveness, and automaton conformity. These mechanisms do not resolve the underlying problem of loneliness but merely mask it.

In **authoritarianism**, one seeks to escape the problem of freedom by adhering to a new form of submission or domination. Authoritarianism may assume either a masochistic or sadistic form. In its *masochistic* form, individuals who feel inferior or powerless permit others to dominate them. In its *sadistic* form, individuals seek to dominate and control the behavior of others. In either case, the root of the tendency comes from an inability to bear the isolation of being an individual self. The individual seeks a solution through *symbiosis,* the union of one's self with another or with an outside power. A common feature of authoritarianism is the belief that one's life is determined by forces outside one's self, one's interests, or one's wishes, and that the only way to be happy is to submit to those forces.

Destructiveness seeks to resolve the problem of freedom, not by symbiotic union with other people or forces but by the elimination of others and/or the outside world. "The destruction of the world is the last, almost desperate attempt to save myself from being crushed by it" (1941). Fromm believed that signs of destructiveness are pervasive in the world, although it is frequently rationalized or masked as love, duty, conscience, or patriotism.

The majority of individuals seek to escape the problem of freedom through **automaton conformity.** They cease to be themselves and adopt the type of personality proffered by their culture. Like the chameleon who changes its color to match its surroundings, they become indistinguishable from the millions of other conforming automatons in their world. Such individuals may no longer feel alone and anxious, but they have paid a high price — "the loss of the self."

Fromm perceived similarities between his mechanisms of escape and Karen Horney's neurotic trends. The differences between them are that Horney's emphasis was on anxiety whereas Fromm's was on isolation. Also, Horney's neurotic trends are the force behind individual neurosis whereas the mechanisms of escape are forces in normal people. The mechanisms of escape are not satisfactory solutions. They do not lead to happiness and positive freedom. By relating spontaneously to love and work and by genuinely expressing our emotional, sensual, and intellectual abilities, we can become one again with other human beings, nature, and ourselves without forgoing the independence and integrity of our individual selves.

Existential and Historical Dichotomies

Fromm (1947) posited a number of existential dichotomies that arise simply from the fact that one exists. Loneliness is one of these. An **existential dichotomy,** as Fromm used the term, is a problem that has no solution because none of the alternatives it presents is entirely satisfactory. We desire immortality, but we face death; we would like to be at one with nature, but we transcend it. In short, we desire a certain kind of world, but we find the world into which we were born unsatisfactory.

Finding the given world unsuitable and unsatisfactory, we as humans attempt to create a more satisfying environment. In doing so, we may further create **historical dichotomies**, which are problems that arise out of our history because of the various societies and cultures that we have formed. The inequitable distribution of wealth is a historical dichotomy, as is the long history of war.

It is important not to confuse or mislabel the two types of dichotomies. Historical dichotomies are created by people and thus they are not inescapable, as existential dichotomies are. They are products of history and therefore open to change. Together, existential and historical dichotomies structure our limitations and potentialities. They are the basis for our aspirations and hopes but at the same time they generate our frustrations.

Fromm's concern with existential dichotomies led him to focus on the "having" and "being" orientations to life. He pointed out that these two modes of existence are competing for the spirit of humanity (1976). The **having mode,** which relies on the possessions that a person *has,* is the source of the lust for power and leads to isolation and fear. The **being mode,** which depends solely on the fact of existence, is the source of productive love and activity and leads to solidarity and joy. People whose being depends solely on the fact that they *are* respond spontaneously and productively and have the courage to let go in order to give birth to new ideas. Fromm believed that everyone is capable of both the having and being modes, but that society determines which of the modes will prevail (1976).

Basic Needs

The existential dichotomies that characterize the human condition give rise to five basic needs (1955). These needs stem from our existence and they must be met in order for a person to develop fully. Our primary drive is toward the affirmation of life, but unless we can structure our existence in such a way that it fulfills our basic needs, we either die or become insane.

The five basic needs are

Relatedness The ability to relate to other people and love productively is not innate or instinctive in human beings. As people, we have to create our own relationships. We may seek to relate to others by submission or dominance, but these ultimately prove defeating. Only productive love, which involves care, responsibility, respect, and knowledge, prevents self-isolation.

Transcendence Human beings need to rise above the accidental and passive creatureliness of their existence by becoming active creators. If we cannot solve the problem of transcendence by creativity, we turn to destructiveness, which is an abortive method of fulfilling this drive.

Rootedness Rootedness refers to the need to feel that one belongs. Initially we find such belonging in our natural tie to our mother, but only insofar as we find new roots in a feeling of universal comradeship with all people can we feel at home in the world as a responsible adult.

Sense of Identity Human beings need to become aware of themselves as unique individuals. This sense of "I" requires experiencing oneself as distinct from others and as the center and active subject of one's powers. Failure to develop a sense of identity leads us to develop a sense of identification by unquestioning conformity to a group or whole.

The Need for a Frame of Orientation and Object of Devotion Each of us needs a stable and consistent frame of reference by which we can organize our perceptions and make sense of our environment. Such a thought system may be rational or irrational, true or false, but it is mandated by the very character of being human and leads to our devotion to a particular world view.

Human beings create society in order to fulfill these basic needs that arise independently of the development of any particular culture. But the type of society and culture that humans create structures and limits the way in which the basic needs may be fulfilled. For example, in a capitalistic society, acquiring money is a means of establishing a sense of identity. In an authoritarian society, identifying with the leader or the state provides a sense of identity. Thus, one's final personality represents a compromise between his or her inner needs and the demands of the society.

Character Orientations and Love Relationships

Fromm identified five character types that are common in Western societies (1947). The primary difference between Fromm's theory of character types and orientations and that of Freud is that Freud envisioned the fixation of libido in certain body zones as the basis for future character types, whereas Fromm set the fundamental basis of character in the different ways in which a person deals with basic dichotomies. A person's character is determined in large measure by the culture and its objectives; thus, it is possible to speak of social character as qualities that are frequently shared by the people of a particular culture.

1. The **receptive orientation.** Receptive people feel that the source of all good things is outside themselves; therefore, they believe that the only way to obtain something they want is to receive it from an outside source. They react passively, waiting to be loved.

2. The **exploitative orientation.** Exploitative people, like receptive ones, feel that the source of all good things is outside, but they do not expect to receive anything good from others. Therefore, they take the things they want by force or cunning. They exploit others for their own ends.

3. The **hoarding orientation.** Whereas receptive and exploitative types both expect to get things from the outside world, hoarding personalities are convinced that nothing significantly new is available from others. Therefore, they seek to hoard and save what they already have. They surround themselves with a wall and are miserly in their relations to others.

4. The **marketing orientation.** The modern marketplace is the model for Fromm's fourth character orientation. The concept of supply and demand, which judges an article of commerce in terms of its exchange worth rather than its use, is the underlying value. Marketing personalities experience themselves as commodities on the market. They may be described as opportunistic chameleons, changing their colors and values as they perceive the forces of the market to change.

5. The **productive orientation.** Fromm's description of the productive orientation tries to go beyond Freud's definition of the genital character, which suggested that the mature individual is capable of adequate functioning sexually and socially. Fromm sought to describe an ideal of humanistic development and moral stance that characterizes the normal, mature, healthy personality. These individuals value themselves and others for who they are. In using their powers productively, they relate to the world by accurately perceiving it and by enriching it through their own creative powers.

A further characteristic of the productive orientation is the use of humanistic rather than authoritarian ethics (1947). Whereas **authoritarian ethics** have their source in a conscience that is rooted outside the individual, **humanistic ethics** represent true virtue in the sense of the unfolding of a person's powers in accordance with the law of one's own human nature and the assumption of full responsibility for one's existence.

The traits that arise from each of Fromm's character orientations have both positive and negative qualities, but on the whole Fromm saw the first four types as largely unproductive. A person may exhibit a combination of types. The first three types are reminiscent of Freud's oral and anal character types, and parallels can be drawn between Freud's and Fromm's typologies. However, in his discussion of the marketing orientation, Fromm is generally thought to have gone further and developed a new character type.

Fromm (1964, 1973) also distinguished between biophilous character orientations that seek to live life and a necrophilous character, which is attracted to what is dead and decaying and seeks to destroy life. The biophilous character is largely synonymous with the productive orientation. The desire to destroy emerges when life forces are frustrated.

A classic example of the necrophilous character is Adolf Hitler, who was fascinated and obsessed with death and destruction. In Fromm's descriptive case study (1973), Hitler emerges as a narcissistic and withdrawn personality who, because he could not change reality, falsified and denied it and engaged in fantasy. Hitler's coldness, apathy, and self-indulgence led to failures early in life and humiliations that resulted in a wish to destroy. This wish could not be recognized; instead, it was denied and rationalized as defensive maneuvers and actions undertaken on behalf of the glorious emerging German nation. What is unique is not the personality of Hitler, but the sociopolitical and historical situation that permitted a Hitler to rise to a position of great power. Fromm believed that malignant forms of aggression can be substantially reduced when socioeconomic conditions that favor the fulfillment of human needs and potential are developed in a particular society.

Parent-Child Relationships

The various character orientations come into being, in part, because of the particular love relationship that a child has experienced with primary caregivers. As children grow, they become increasingly independent, thus repeating the pattern of development of the species. This freedom brings with it insecurity, and the child will seek to re-establish the earlier security. Fromm described three basic kinds of parent-child relationships (1956).

In **symbiotic relationships,** two persons are related in such a way that one of the parties loses or never attains independence. One person is swallowed by the other person, the *masochistic* form of the symbiotic relationship. One person may swallow the other person, the *sadistic* form. The **withdrawal-destructiveness relationship** is characterized by distance rather than closeness.

The relationship is one of apathy and withdrawal or direct expressions of hostility and aggression. **Love** is the productive relationship to others and the self. It is marked by mutual respect and the fostering of independence for each party.

The receptive character originates in a masochistic response to a symbiotic relationship. The exploitative type emanates from a sadistic pattern developed by the child who reacts destructively to parental withdrawal. The marketing orientation is the behavior pattern of a child who reacts to parental destructiveness by withdrawal. The productive orientation has its roots in the relationship of love.

Productive, biophilous people comprehend the world through love, which enables them to break down the walls that separate people. Productive love, Fromm asserted, is an art. We can master its theory and practice only if we make love a matter of ultimate concern. Productive love is the true creative answer to human loneliness, whereas symbiotic relationships are immature or pseudo forms of love.

Self-Love

Fromm (1956) distinguished among various types of love, such as brotherly love, motherly love, erotic love, love of God, and self-love. Of particular interest are his comments on **self-love,** which he saw as a prerequisite for loving others. It is important that we distinguish Fromm's concept of self-love and affirmation from the narcissistic self-indulgence that appears to be so prevalent in our day and that excludes the love of others. Today many people use "self-love" as a substitute for the more difficult task of loving others. Fromm insisted that the ability to love requires the overcoming of *narcissism* (experiencing as real only that which exists within ourselves). We must strive to see other people and things objectively and to recognize those times when we are limited by our subjective feelings. Fromm's concept of self-love foreshadows Rogers's emphasis on congruence and Maslow's discussion of self-esteem.

The Analysis of Culture and Society

Fromm emphasized the role that society plays in structuring, shaping, and limiting personality. He synthesized the insights of Freud and Karl Marx, a nineteenth-century German political philosopher and socialist, in his analysis of different social and cultural situations and their effects on human nature (1947, 1955).

Human beings are predisposed to develop some form of social organization. We create society in order to fulfill our needs, but the type of society that we create, in turn, structures and limits the way in which our needs may be fulfilled. Furthermore, for a particular society to function adequately, it is absolutely necessary that the people within the society be shaped to satisfy its de-

THINKING CRITICALLY

Relationships

Fromm suggested that there are specific standards by which a relationship may be judged healthy or unhealthy. Consider some of the relationships that you have had or observed and evaluate them according to Fromm's characteristics.

For example, can you identify some relationships that you have observed that were *symbiotic,* characterized by the dominance of one individual and the loss of independence of the other? Can you give examples of relationships characterized by *withdrawal* or *destructiveness* in which the relationship is marked by apathy and withdrawal or hostility and aggression? Are you aware of ever having been involved in such relationships yourself? Fromm would suggest that these types of relationships are unhealthy ones.

Productive love, on the other hand, is characterized by care (feeling concern for the life and growth of the other); responsibility (responding to the needs of the other); respect (seeing and accepting the other as is); and knowledge (experiencing unity with the other yet permitting the other to remain a mystery). These are the marks of a healthy relationship. Can you identify relationships that you have observed or had that fulfill these characteristics? Share your discoveries with classmates.

mands. Otherwise, that system of society cannot be maintained. Nevertheless, if a particular society makes demands on its members that are contrary to their nature, that society warps and frustrates their human potential. In fact, Fromm believed that no society yet developed has been able to meet all of the basic human needs constructively. He outlined specifically how both capitalism and communism have failed in their efforts to satisfy basic human needs productively.

Although Fromm did not imply that personality is shaped entirely by society, he believed that obstacles to growth are imposed by society rather than by human nature itself. Since human beings create the societies in which they live, Fromm (1955) could envision the creation of a utopian society, which he labeled *humanistic communitarian socialism,* that would more adequately meet human needs and fulfill human potentialities. He was optimistic about the possibility of a society in which individuals would relate to one another lovingly, transcend nature creatively, and respond productively. Each individual would experience himself or herself as the source of power and would relate realistically to the world. Taking Fromm's discussion of love seriously and attempting to implement it in our society would require rather drastic changes in our social relations.

*We create society in order to fulfill our
needs. Conversely, the type of society we
create structures and limits the way in
which our needs may be filled.*

Three and a half centuries ago, Fromm reminded us, we developed a new
science that attracted the most brilliant minds and led to a highly technical
society such as had only been dreamed of before. What we need now is a new
social science. The goal this time "is not control over nature but control over
technique and over irrational social forces and institutions that threaten the
survival of Western society, if not of the human race" (1976). Fromm believed
that there is a common human nature transcending race or color that explains
how people can understand distant cultures, their art, myths, and dramas (Bian-
coli, 1992). In his later writing, Fromm was sobered by our failure to achieve
some of his goals, but he remained optimistic, believing that as long as life exists
there is hope.

Assessment and Research in Fromm's Theory

Fromm described the psychoanalytic method of investigation as genuinely scientific, its essence being the observation of facts. Over the protracted period of an analysis, the analyst observes many facts about the patient. The analyst draws inferences from these observations, forms hypotheses, considers these hypotheses in the light of additional facts that emerge, and eventually arrives at a conclusion regarding the possible validity of the hypotheses. The theoretical models of the psychoanalyst do not lend themselves to scientific falsification by means of experiment, but they are based on many hours of careful empirical observation within the clinical setting. Thus, although the method of verification is different from that of the natural sciences, Fromm believed that it is a reliable method.

Fromm did not write much about his precise methods of assessment. He did write about good science as productive relationship. He appears to have combined free association and dream analysis with insights from and scholarly knowledge of religion, philosophy, psychology, sociology, and anthropology, as well as new findings in other areas.

An example of the way in which Fromm assessed and researched culture and society was published in 1970 (Fromm & Maccoby). Psychologists, anthropologists, historians, and other experts joined together in an interdisciplinary field study of a Mexican village. With the advent of technology and industrialization, these villagers had been lured away from their traditional values and life-style. Movies and television took the place of festivals and local bands. Mass-produced utensils, furniture, and clothing took the place of hand-crafted items. Trained Mexican interviewers administered an in-depth questionnaire that was interpreted and scored for characterological and motivational factors. The Rorschach Ink Blot Test, which purports to indicate repressed feelings, attitudes, and motives, was also given. These data showed that the three main classes in the village also represented three social character types: the landowners, productive–hoarding; the poor workers, unproductive–receptive; and the business group, productive–exploitative. The findings about the village's history, economic and social structure, belief systems, and fantasies illustrated and appeared to confirm Fromm's theory that character is affected by social structure and change.

Michael Maccoby, who coauthored the Mexican village study, has done two more studies based on Fromm's character types. In the first, interviews of 250 managers in large corporations led to the identification of the "company man," a character type similar to the marketing orientation (1976). Company men seem to be marketing themselves as if they are commodities. Rather than emphasize actual job skills and knowledge, they focus on superficial packaging of themselves, which they can adapt as one might change clothes to fit various situations. A potentially new character type, *self-orientation*, which is highly narcissistic and reflects social changes that have occurred in America since the 1960s, emerged in the second study of corporate leaders (1981). This type tends to be cynical and rebellious, reflecting a breakdown in respect for authority and other traditional values. Self-indulgent and undisciplined, the self-oriented individual tends to lack loyalty and commitment to a work ethic. Maccoby's research supports Fromm's concept that historical and cultural forces shape the development of character types.

If he were alive today, Fromm might well agree with Nina Tassi (1991), who believes that young people coming of age today need to learn how to live in a new global economy and time. There are no longer long-term guarantees of employment. Corporations are downsizing, encouraging employees

PHILOSOPHICAL ASSUMPTIONS

Examining Fromm

How would you rate Fromm on each of the basic philosophical assumptions described in Chapter 1? Each basic issue was presented as a bipolar dimension along which a person's view can be placed according to the degree of agreement with one or the other extreme. Rate Fromm's views on these issues.

When you have determined where you think Fromm stands, compare your responses with those of your classmates and your instructor. You should be willing to defend your ratings, but also be prepared to change them in light of others' compelling arguments. Afterward, compare your rating of Fromm with your own position on each issue and with those of other theorists. Does this comparison help you to understand why his theory does or does not appeal to you?

Would strongly agree	Would agree	Is neutral or believes in synthesis of both views	Would agree	Would strongly agree
1	2	3	4	5

freedom	determinism
People basically have control over their own behavior and understand the motives behind their behavior.	The behavior of people is basically determined by internal or external forces over which they have little, if any, control.

to work increasingly long hours and weekends at the expense of family and health. The "career ladder" is gone. The rapid pace of change in the world will certainly continue into the twenty-first century. "The global economy and global time are both here to stay." Survivors will best draw on "five rings" of power drawn from both the East and West: self-reliance, mutualism (building a group with the capacity for growth of like-minded people), playfulness (which fosters creativity), knowledge (useful information rather than data), and the empty bag or void into which one can place excess baggage and negative emotions.

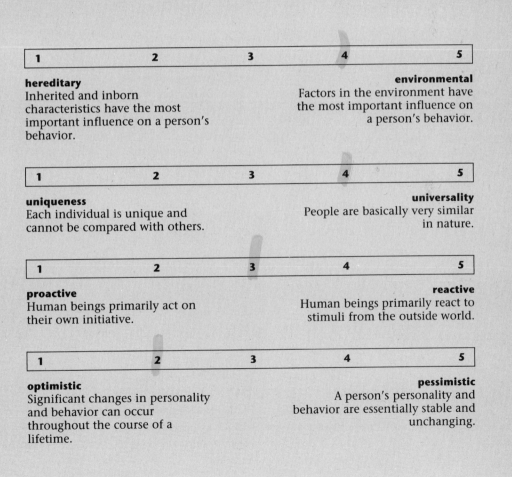

| 1 | 2 | 3 | 4 | 5 |

hereditary
Inherited and inborn characteristics have the most important influence on a person's behavior.

environmental
Factors in the environment have the most important influence on a person's behavior.

| 1 | 2 | 3 | 4 | 5 |

uniqueness
Each individual is unique and cannot be compared with others.

universality
People are basically very similar in nature.

| 1 | 2 | 3 | 4 | 5 |

proactive
Human beings primarily act on their own initiative.

reactive
Human beings primarily react to stimuli from the outside world.

| 1 | 2 | 3 | 4 | 5 |

optimistic
Significant changes in personality and behavior can occur throughout the course of a lifetime.

pessimistic
A person's personality and behavior are essentially stable and unchanging.

Fromm's Theory: Philosophy, Science, and Art

Fromm rejected *scientism,* or the exclusive reliance on a narrow conception of science, deeming it inadequate for the full comprehension of human nature. He was critical of a narrow scientific approach because it tends to be reductive and it does not permit the final nuances of personality to emerge. He realized, perhaps more clearly than many, that the process of scientific activity begins with an epiphanic vision that is informed by the scientist's philosophy. Fromm's theory is a speculative and transcendental one, incorporating several vantage points that initially may appear contradictory.

We have seen how Freud's theory was a product of nineteenth-century thought, rooted and cast in the framework of a currently outdated biological determinism. Although Freud's concepts helped to shatter the nineteenth-century understanding of human nature, they require revision to meet the demands of the twentieth century. Fromm took advantage of the emerging disciplines of psychology, sociology, and anthropology, as well as new findings in other areas, to revise Freud's theory and develop his own point of view.

Although Fromm's methods of research are empirical, based on observation, they could not be described as rigorous or precise scientific techniques. In the final analysis, Fromm, like many other followers of Freud, was philosophical in his emphasis. He considered that proof grows out of the internal coherence of a theory and the theory's ability to shed light on the human condition. This "coherence theory of truth" is characteristic of the philosopher (Rychlak, 1973).

Fromm wrote little about his technique of therapy. He indicated that he was a more active therapist than Freud and employed the term "activating" to describe the therapist's interventions to facilitate progress. Fromm emphasized that the therapist must *feel* what the patient is talking about and recognize the common humanity that both of them share. That element of empathy permits the patient to realize that inner feelings are shared by others.

There are clear ethical themes in the writings of Fromm. He tried to develop a norm or an ethic that presents the best answers to the problems we all face. He considered the behaviors that are most appropriate in unifying, harmonizing, and strengthening the individual to be ethical behaviors. Fromm's theory enlarges our concept of the application of personality theory to include efforts to inform and restructure society. His goals for the art of personality theory uniquely combine the scholarly and the ethical motives.

Although some of his writings may seem somewhat dated because they refer specifically to conditions surrounding the mid-twentieth century, his central ideas remain relevant. Many of Fromm's themes have been picked up by the humanist movement in psychology. His theory is coherent and sophisticated in its depth. A commitment to Fromm's point of view represents a commitment to the way of life espoused by his theory.

Summary

1. Fromm's approach is termed humanistic social analysis; he attempted a synthesis of Freud and Marx.

2. Three common mechanisms of escape from freedom are **authoritarianism**, **destructiveness**, and **automaton conformity.**

3. He distinguished between **existential dichotomies** that arise from existence itself and **historical dichotomies** that are created by society.

4. Fromm posited five basic needs: **relatedness, transcendence, rootedness, sense of identity,** and **frame of orientation and devotion.** We create society in order to fulfill these needs.

5. Fromm identified character types in Western society, such as the **receptive, exploitative, hoarding,** and necrophilous **orientations.** In his discussion of the **marketing orientation,** Fromm is thought to have developed a new type. The **productive orientation** depicts the mature individual, who is biophilous, is able to love and work in the broadest sense, and uses **humanistic** rather than **authoritarian ethics.**

6. Fromm described three basic kinds of relationship: **symbiotic, withdrawal-destructiveness,** and **love.**

7. Fromm believed that **self-love** is a prerequisite for loving others. Self-love requires overcoming narcissism and self-indulgence.

8. Human beings create society in order to fulfill their needs, but the society they create then structures how the needs are fulfilled. Fromm believed that no society developed to date is able to meet all of the basic human needs constructively. Radical changes are needed. Fromm recommended an interdisciplinary approach to the study of society such as in his study of a Mexican village.

9. Fromm described the psychoanalytic method of investigation as genuinely scientific and empirical, but he recognized that a scientific approach is informed by philosophy. In the final analysis, his approach represents a deep commitment to an underlying philosophy of life.

Suggestions for Further Reading

Erich Fromm's writings have had a vast appeal. He is one of the theorists most likely to be read by the lay person, for whom he wrote expressly. Fromm's first and, in the eyes of many, most important book is *Escape from Freedom* (Holt, Rinehart, 1941). In it he explored the problem of human freedom and our tendency to submit to tyranny or authority. *Man for Himself* (Holt, Rinehart, & Winston, 1947) discusses the problem of authoritarian versus humanistic ethics and outlines his five character orientations. *The Sane Society* (Holt, Rinehart, & Winston, 1955) describes the five basic human needs and considers the effects of capitalism and other social forms on character development. Fromm's most popular work is *The Art of Loving* (Harper & Row, 1956), which outlines his theory of love. The distinction between the necrophilous and biophilous orientation and Fromm's case study of Adolf Hitler are included in *The Anatomy of Human Destructiveness* (Holt, Rinehart, & Winston, 1973). Fromm's last work, *To Have or To Be* (Harper & Row, 1976), offers us a choice of two primary modes, one of which offers the potential for growth.

PART 3

More Recent Trends in Psychoanalysis

In many respects Freud's theory was a product of nineteenth-century thought, cast in the framework of a now-outdated biological determinism. Yet it was Freud who shattered the nineteenth-century image of human nature and opened the door to a new point of view. Many of his concepts moved us forward into the twentieth century, but they require revision if they are to continue to meet the demands of our time and remain abreast of modern intellectual ideas. The thought of the analysts in Part 3 moves considerably beyond Freud, yet remains consistent with basic psychoanalytic doctrine. In updating and revising Freud, they have been largely responsible for the continued relevance of his theory.

For the most part, these theorists believe that the changes they have made are consistent with basic psychoanalytic doctrine. The biological grounding of human existence remains, as does the power of sexuality. Repression and transference, keynotes of psychoanalysis, remain fast in their thought. More recent analysts, however, reformed and revised psychoanalysis so that it reflects the modern world and contemporary self-understanding.

CHAPTER 7

More Recent Psychoanalytic Theorists: Anna Freud, Heinz Hartmann, Erik Erikson, Margaret Mahler, Heinz Kohut, Otto Kernberg, and Nancy Chodorow

YOUR GOALS FOR THIS CHAPTER

1. Describe the contributions the ego psychologists, Anna Freud and Heinz Hartmann, have made to psychoanalysis.
2. Identify four ways in which Erikson extended Freudian psychoanalysis.
3. Explain how Erikson's theory enlarged our understanding of the ego.
4. Discuss the general characteristics of Erikson's *psychosocial stages* of development.
5. Discuss each one of Erikson's stages in terms of the Freudian psychosexual stage it reflects, the emotional duality that it involves, and the particular ego strength that emerges from it.
6. Describe how Erikson explored the role of culture and history in shaping personality.
7. Discuss Erikson's findings in the area of sex differences.
8. Discuss Erikson's methods of research and empirical research on Erikson's theory.
9. Describe the contributions of Margaret Mahler.
10. Explain how Heinz Kohut clarifies **narcissism.**
11. Describe how Otto Kernberg accounts for borderline individuals and discuss his method of treatment.
12. Tell how Nancy Chodorow's work differs from traditional psychoanalytic theory.
13. Explain what Chodorow means by *the reproduction of mothering.*
14. Explain how Chodorow believes family structures need to be transformed.
15. Evaluate more recent psychoanalytic theories in terms of their function as philosophy, science, and art.

As we have seen, Freud's theory sparked a great deal of controversy and some of his original followers sought to develop separate theories. In doing so, Jung, Adler, Horney, and Fromm discarded a number of Freudian concepts that were considered crucial to psychoanalysis. Others, however, have worked within the mainstream of psychoanalysis to refine and update Freud's ideas. The thought of the analysts discussed in this chapter moves considerably beyond Freud without abandoning his key concepts and principles. The focus has changed from the study of the adult to the study of the child. The emphasis has shifted from the id to the ego. There has been an expansion of psychoanalysis as a therapeutic tool and a greater appreciation of the role of society and culture in the development of personality.

This chapter will consider some contributions to psychoanalytic theory made by ego psychologists Anna Freud, Heinz Hartmann, and Erik Erikson, who accepted Freud's three-part division of the personality but emphasized the role of the ego, in some cases giving it a greater degree of autonomy. It will also consider some object relations theorists—Margaret Mahler, Heinz Kohut, Otto Kernberg, and Nancy Chodorow—who looked at how people develop patterns of living from their early relationships with significant others.

The Ego Psychologists

Sigmund Freud believed that in optimal personality development the ego acts as an executor, effectively juggling the demands of the id and superego to meet their needs realistically. He emphasized the influence of the id, believing that the ego acts only out of borrowed energy and is at best a harassed, if not overwhelmed, commander. In his later years, Freud conjectured that the ego might have some psychological energy of its own, a position that his daughter Anna endorsed (1946). Subsequent practitioners of psychoanalysis focused on the ego and began to consider it an independent force with a larger role.

Anna Freud tended to restrict the ego's function to warding off drives, whereas Heinz Hartmann explored the ego's adaptive responses to its environment. Even though Anna Freud had been his training analyst, Erik Erikson found himself attracted to Hartmann's approach. As an educator, Erikson was interested in how one might strengthen and enrich the ego of young children.

Anna Freud (1895–1982)

Anna, Freud's youngest daughter, was her father's intellectual heir, the only member of his family to follow in his profession. After her analysis by her own father, she worked closely with him, as a highly skilled and respected colleague. After his death, she became an eminent lay psychoanalyst and international authority in her own right. Until her death in 1982, she was recognized as the guardian and elucidator of her father's revolutionary doctrine. She also extended the interest of psychoanalysis to the study of the child and the exploration of the ego.

In her efforts to clarify psychoanalytic theory, she introduced some genuinely new and creative ideas. Her observations of children extended beyond normal or disturbed children growing up in average homes and included children who had met with extraordinary circumstances such as war, physical handicaps, and parentless homes. Her research opened the way to a new era of research in psychoanalytic child psychology under the auspices of the Hampstead clinic, with applications to a wide area of concerns associated with child rearing.

Some of Anna Freud's observations concerning children overturned previous notions of their reactions. For example, it had been widely assumed that children have an instinctive horror of combat, blood, and destruction and that war has a devastating effect on young children. However, her case studies of the effects of World War II bombings on British children, written in collaboration with Dorothy Burlingham, a long-time friend and colleague (see Burlingham, 1990, and Jackson, 1991), revealed that the world of the child pivots on the mother. Her findings led her to be a strong advocate of the need to protect the natural rights and interests of the child.

Anna Freud considered infancy and childhood as prologues to greater maturity. Her therapy stressed protective, supportive, and educational attitudes. She suggested how the classic features of adult psychoanalysis could be utilized with children four years old and upward. In working with children, she recognized that child analysis could not be conducted like the analysis of an adult. Classical techniques such as free association, the interpretation of dreams, and analysis of the transference had to be changed to correspond with the child's level of maturity. She saw the need for a long preparatory period in which the analyst is established as a trusted and indispensable figure in the child's life. She also recognized that neurotic symptoms do not necessarily have the same meaning in the life of a child that they do in the life of an adult. Her system of diagnosis, which conceives of personality as arising out of a developmental sequence, permitted her to distinguish between less serious manifestations of childhood and important threats to optimal personality growth. She produced a classification system of childhood symptoms that reflects developmental issues and a formal assessment procedure known as a **diagnostic profile.** Such profiles have since been developed for infants, children, adolescents, and adults. In each profile, different aspects of psychoanalytic theory are used to organize and integrate the data acquired during a diagnostic assessment into a complete picture of the various functionings of the patient's personality and an indication of their developmental appropriateness.

Anna Freud used the term **developmental line** to refer to a series of id-ego interactions in which children decrease their dependence on external controls and increase ego mastery of themselves and their world (1965). Her six developmental lines stress the ego's ability to cope with various internal, environmental, and interpersonal situations and complement her father's discussion of psychosexual development. As children grow they progress from (1) dependency to emotional self-reliance, (2) sucking to rational eating, (3) wetting and soiling to bladder and bowel

Anna Freud

control, (4) irresponsibility to responsibility in body management, (5) play to work, and (6) egocentricity to companionship.

In addition, Anna Freud learned from her work with children that there are realistic limits to analysis. Certain constitutional or environmental factors may not be open to real change through analysis, though their effects may be reduced. While recognizing the greater importance of environmental factors over internal ones in childhood disturbances, she was also impressed by the efforts of children to cope with and master extremely devastating situations.

Finally, Anna Freud systematized and elaborated on Freud's discussion of the *ego's defenses.* Whereas Freud concentrated on exploring the unconscious drives of the id, his daughter realized that in order for these to emerge in an analysis, the ego must become aware of the defenses that it is using to prevent the material from re-emerging into consciousness. The ego's defenses may be inferred from observable behavior. Analysis of the defenses permits one to understand the child's life history and instinctual development. Anna Freud elaborated on the ego defenses outlined by her father and suggested some additional ones of her own (1946). She clarified the process of identification with the aggressor, in which a victim begins to react to his or her captor with gratitude and admiration. This phenomenon has since been recognized in prisoners of war and hostages. Anna Freud's graphic case descriptions illustrating these processes have become classic. Thus, a schoolboy's involuntary grimace caricatures the angry face of his teacher and testifies to his identification with the aggressor. Anna Freud points out that the intensity of adolescence and the extremes of acting out are not pathological but are normative and functional.

Heinz Hartmann (1894–1970).

In Anna Freud's view, the ego remains inescapably bound to the id and necessarily regulated by the superego. Heinz Hartmann suggested that the ego is an important autonomous force (1958, 1964). Its energy is not necessarily derived from the id (as Freud thought), but both ego and id originate in inherited predispositions that follow independent courses of development. Thus, the ego's functions are not limited to the avoidance of pain and the service of instinctual gratification. Hartmann paid considerable attention to the synthesizing and in-

Heinz Hartmann

tegrative functions of the ego. He described its processes of perception, attention, memory, rational thought, and action and showed increased interest in accounting for normal behavior. Hartmann also suggested that certain spheres of ego activity may be "conflict free," that is, the ego is not perpetually in conflict with the id, external world, and superego. Through experience and adaptation, many of the ego's functions may become increasingly distinct from original instinctive and defensive maneuvers.

In Hartmann's view, memory, learning, and other ego functions are *prerequisites* for the ego's interactions with the id, rather than arising out of it. They emerge independently and are then brought into service. Moreover, the ego has the capacity to neutralize sexual and aggressive energy so that they function in ways other than simple drive reduction. A defense, such as regression, may be employed in the service of the ego. Thus, a college student may be able to concentrate and study better after a weekend of play. Ego functions may be autonomous from the id and practiced for their own sake.

Hartmann's emphasis on the cognitive functions of the ego is consonant with the current interest in the role of cognition in personality formation and development (see Sampson, 1990). He conceived of adaptation as a reciprocal relationship between the organism and the environment. The organism changes the environment in order to make it more agreeable and then changes itself in order to adapt to the changes it has created. Adaptation is a continual process entailing ever more complex levels of mastery, molding, and synthesis. In its synthesizing function, the ego integrates and reconciles not only conflicts between itself, the id, the superego, and the external world, but also conflicts within itself.

Erik Erikson (1902–1994)

Erik H. Erikson was born on June 15, 1902, near Frankfurt, Germany, the product of an extramarital relationship. He never knew his mother's first husband or his birth father. His mother subsequently married a pediatrician, Theodore Homburger, who adopted Erik and gave him a last name. In an act that Erikson later called "loving deceit," his parents concealed the fact of his adoption from him for several years. Thus, the man who is famous for coining the term "identity crisis" did himself experience a significant identity crisis. Not only did he have to struggle with the usual quest for psychological identity, he was also unsure of his biological identity. His resolution of that problem became apparent in 1939; in the process of becoming an American citizen, he added the surname by which we know him, assuming the identity of Erik Homburger Erikson.

Erikson was able to find his professional identity in Vienna, where he and Peter Blos, a theorist and researcher on adolescence, established a progressive, nongraded school, providing children optimal freedom within an appropriate structure. After a short time, Anna Freud asked Erikson if he would be interested

Erik H. Erikson

in beginning analysis with her and becoming a child analyst. Over the next few years, Erikson established himself as a key figure in psychoanalysis, publishing articles on education and psychoanalysis. These articles reflect the precision of the Montessori philosophy, a method of education that Erikson was studying at the time. The two complementary forms of training enabled Erikson to make a unique contribution to our understanding of child development.

Erikson left Vienna in 1933 and settled with his wife and family in Boston, where he became the city's first child psychoanalyst. In 1936 Erikson accepted a position in the Yale University Institute of Human Relations to teach at the medical school. In 1938, he learned of a unique opportunity to study child-rearing methods among the Sioux in South Dakota. Here he observed first-hand how childhood events are shaped by society and its customs, a theme he was to stress again and again in his later writings.

Between 1939 and 1960 Erikson held various positions in California and Massachusetts. In 1960 Harvard University offered him the position of professor in spite of the fact that he had never received a university or college degree. Erikson was a popular speaker at colleges and universities throughout the United States. He died on May 12, 1994, following a brief illness.

Erikson extended Freudian analysis in four main ways. First, he increased our understanding of the ego, showing how it is a creative problem solver that emerges out of the genetic, cultural, and historical context of each individual. Second, he elaborated on Freud's stages of development, making explicit a social dimension that was implied in Freud's theory but never clearly stated. Third, he extended our concept of development to embrace the entire life span from infancy to old age. Fourth, he explored the impact of culture, society, and history on the developing personality and illustrated this in psychohistorical studies of famous people.

An Enhanced Understanding of the Ego

In Erikson's theory, the ego is the part of the mind that gives coherence to experiences, conscious or unconscious. Erikson agreed with Freud that many aspects of ego functioning are unconscious, but he believed the ego has an overall unifying purpose that leads to consistent behavior and conduct. The ego has the positive role of maintaining effective performance, rather than just a negative role of avoiding anxiety. Its defenses are adaptive as well as maladaptive (1974).

Erikson did *not* believe that we can best reconstruct the ego's functions from an understanding of its dysfunctions. He elaborated on its adaptive capacities, its ability to deal with stress, to resolve vital conflict, to recuperate, and to contribute to identity formation. In the final analysis, Erikson defined the ego as a strong, vital, and positive force: an organizing capacity of the individual that leads to "that strength which can reconcile discontinuities and ambiguities" (1975).

The development of the ego was clearly outlined in Erikson's psychosocial stages of the life cycle. Ideally, at each stage the ego develops certain strengths or basic virtues that enable it to move forward. These ego strengths lay the foundation for a set of ethical rules based on ideals that we can strive for, as Erikson also conceived of the superego and human consciousness in terms of an evolutionary process.

The Psychosocial Stages of Development

In his discussion of the psychosexual stages of development, Freud concentrated on their biological character and tended to neglect the social dimension. Nevertheless, Freud's stages reflect more than simply a psychosexual progress in which children come to terms with their sexuality. For Erikson they are definitely a psychosocial development, in which children try to understand and relate to the world and others. In effect, Erikson made explicit the social dimension implied in Freud's work.

Each of Erikson's **psychosocial stages** centers on an emotional polarity or conflict that children encounter at certain critical periods. New environmental demands introject positive and negative emotional components into the development of personality. Both emotional components are to some extent incorporated into the emerging person, but if the conflict is resolved satisfactorily, the positive component is reflected to a higher degree. If the conflict persists, or is not adequately resolved, the negative component predominates. Erikson's first four stages correspond to Freud's psychosexual stages (oral through latency). Erikson then subdivided the genital stage into four phases that represent growth and development throughout maturity.

Erikson's stages are *epigenetic* (from the Greek words *epi,* "upon," and *genesis,* "emergence"): one stage develops on top of another in a sequential and hierarchical pattern. At each successive level the human personality becomes more complex. Erikson stressed the prospective features of the life cycle and amended the logic of psychoanalysis so that early events are seen not only in terms of their contributions to later development, but as themselves directed by potentials that do not flower until later.

Erikson's psychosocial stages do not occur within a strict chronological framework. Each child has a personal timetable. However, as in fetal development, each aspect of psychosocial development has a critical period of readiness during which, if it does not flourish, it is likely to flounder. In addition, the stages progress in a cumulative rather than a linear fashion. The behaviors of one stage do not disappear with the successive stage (1969).

Erikson made psychoanalytic concepts more consistent with contemporary scientific findings. His psychosocial stages are a gradual series of decisive encounters with the environment; interactions between biological development, psychological abilities, cognitive capacities, and social influences. Erikson saw the person as a way of being in the world. Thus the first stage, rather than a cathexis of libido onto an oral zone, is a complex of experiences centered in the mouth.

Each of the eight stages entails its own **life crisis**, a crucial period in which the individual cannot avoid a decisive turn one way or the other. Each stage also provides new opportunities for particular ego strengths or basic *virtues* to develop. These psychosocial gains result from the ego's successful adaption to its environment and must be nurtured and reaffirmed continuously.

Trust versus Mistrust: Hope   The emotional duality of **trust versus mistrust** is the key consideration of the first stage, which corresponds to Freud's oral, sensory, and kinesthetic one (1963). The basic psychosocial attitude to be learned at this stage is whether or not you can trust the world. For a protracted period of time children are highly dependent on others for their care. Certain frustrations are inevitable and socially meaningful, but too much of either frustration or indulgence may have negative effects. Basic trust implies a perceived correlation between one's needs and one's world. If infants receive unreliable, inadequate, or rejecting care, they will perceive their world as indifferent or hostile and they will develop a high degree of mistrust. Granted, it is important that infants develop some sense of how much to trust and when to be ready for danger and discomfort. The danger lies in the extremes of trust and mistrust. This crisis is not permanently resolved during the first year or two of life, but a foundation is laid that influences the subsequent course of development.

An appropriate balance of trust and mistrust leads to the development of the ego strength *hope,* a basic human virtue without which we are unable to survive. Hope represents a persistent conviction that our wishes can be satisfied in spite of disappointment and failures (1964). Hope is the basis of faith, reflected in mature commitments.

Autonomy versus Shame and Doubt: Will   Erikson's second psychosocial stage, **autonomy versus shame and doubt,** arises during the second and third years of life and corresponds to the anal-muscular stage in Freud's psychosexual scheme (1963). The primary emotional duality here is that of control over the body and bodily activities as opposed to a tendency for shame and doubt. "Just when a child has learned to trust his mother and to trust the world, he must become self-willed and must take chances with his trust in order to see what he, as a trustworthy individual, can will" (Erikson, as cited in Evans, 1967). The struggle for autonomy is not limited to sessions on the toilet, but extends to many other areas of life as the ego begins to establish psychosocial independence. Toddlers, who are making rapid gains in neuromuscular maturation, verbalization, and social discrimination, begin to explore independently and interact with their environment. The negativism of the two-year-old whose favorite word is "no" is evidence of the child's struggling attempt at autonomy. A temper tantrum is simply a momentary loss of self-control. Cultures have different ways of cultivating or breaking the child's will, either reinforcing or rejecting the tentative explorations of the child. Doubts about their ability for self-control may give children feelings of inadequacy or shame.

Will, the virtue corresponding to this stage, is a natural outgrowth of autonomy. Clearly in the toddler years only rudiments emerge, but these will build into a mature sense of will power. Will is an unbroken determination to exercise freedom of choice and self-restraint (1964) and forms the basis for our subsequent acceptance of social laws.

Initiative versus Guilt: Purpose   The emotional duality that Erikson envisioned for the phallic or genital-locomotor stage of psychosexuality (three to five years) is **initiative versus guilt** (1963). At this period, children are active in their environment, mastering new skills and tasks. Their dominant social modality is the *intrusive* mode: their bodies vigorously intrude into space and onto other people. Preschoolers direct their activities toward specific goals and achievements. Their intrusion and curiosity extends not only to sexual matters but to many other concerns of life as well. The characteristic word of preschoolers is "why?" Parental responses to children's self-initiated activities determine the successful or unsuccessful outcome of this stage. If initiative is reinforced, a child's behavior will become increasingly goal oriented. Excessive punishment or discouragement may lead to feelings of guilt, resignation, and the belief that it is wrong to be curious about the world and ill-advised to be active in it.

Immense new faculties develop in children at this time as they begin to imagine goals for which their locomotive and cognitive skills have prepared them. Their use of language becomes more polished. Children begin to envision themselves as growing up and identify with people whose work and personalities they can understand and admire. Earlier fantasies are repressed or redirected and the play of preschoolers becomes more realistic and purposeful. They begin to engage in projects. Children are at no time more open to learning than during these years. They are able to work cooperatively and to profit from teachers. Their learning is vigorous, leading away from their own limitations and into later possibilities.

Erikson believed that the Oedipus complex is both more and less than Freud made of it. He preferred to call it an early generational complex. From the point of view of evolution, it is the child's first experience with the unrelenting sequence of generations, growth, and death. The same-sexed parent becomes "naturally" involved in the child's early genital fantasies at a time when the child's initiative is ready to turn away from the present situation to new goals. At the same time, the child's strong imagination and powerful locomotive skills produce gigantic, terrifying fantasies that awaken a sense of guilt and lead to the development of conscience (Evans, 1967). Thus the Oedipal stage results in a moral sense that establishes permissible limits and begins to attach childhood dreams realistically to the various possible goals of one's technology and culture.

The virtue that emerges out of the duality of initiative versus guilt is *purpose,* a view of the future giving direction and focus to our mutual efforts. Purposefulness slowly enables one to develop a sense of reality that is defined by what is attainable (1964).

Industry versus Inferiority: Competence   The next stage in the child's life loosely parallels Freud's latency period. Freud gave few clues as to what was happening to personality development during this period apart from suggesting that latency involves a move from premature sexual expression to a nonactive sexual phase. Erikson agreed that during latency certain passionate and imaginative qualities of earlier years calm down so that the child is free to concentrate on learning. However, he pointed out that learning involves more than just suppressed or displaced sexual curiosity. Learning contains its own energy; it is a basic form of striving that takes place throughout the life cycle and undergoes a special crisis during the school years. The focus moves sharply from the id to the ego as the child applies to specific and approved goals the drives that earlier motivated dreams and play. Yet the ego can remain strong only through interaction with cultural institutions. At this time society intervenes in a more formal manner to develop the child's capacities and potentials.

During the school years (six to eleven), the primary emotional duality is **industry versus inferiority** (1963). The term "industriousness" might be better than "industry" as it implies being busy with something, learning to make something and to make it well. Children in all cultures receive some form of systematic instruction at this time to teach them skills that will be needed in their society and to help them attain a sense of mastery.

New demands are placed upon children at this time. They are no longer loved simply for who they are; they are expected to master the technology of their culture in order to earn the respect of their teachers and peers. Their ability to conform and master the tasks of this level depends in large measure on how successfully they have traveled the preceding stages. If children emerge from the preceding stages with a basic sense of trust, autonomy, and initiative, they are ready for the industrious labor that "school" presupposes. But if their development has left heavy residues of mistrust, doubt, and guilt, they may have difficulty performing at an optimal level. From a psychoanalytic point of view, the child who has not adequately resolved his or her Oedipal complex may not be ready to fulfill the other demands of his or her society. If potentialities have been permitted to develop fully in the earlier stages, the child is in less danger.

The peril during this period is that feelings of inadequacy and inferiority will develop. Children begin to make comparisons between themselves and others and to perceive themselves in a more or less favorable light. The avoidance of group labels that differentiate children's performances may minimize but can in no way erase a child's consciousness of doing superior or inferior work. Children know, or think they know, where they stand.

Children at this age are ready to learn to work and need to develop a sense of *competence,* the ego strength or virtue associated with this stage. Competence entails the ability to use one's intelligence and skill to complete tasks that are of value in one's society (1964).

Ego Identity versus Role Confusion: Fidelity   For Freud, the hallmarks of the genital stage were *lieben und arbeiten,* "to love and to work." Erikson agreed with the importance of these accomplishments, but he further divided Freud's final stage into four substages to underscore the point that "genitality is not a goal to be pursued in isolation" (Evans, 1967). In so doing, Erikson greatly enriched our understanding of adolescence and the adult years.

The primary duality during adolescence (twelve to eighteen) is **ego identity versus role confusion.** The process of forming an ego identity requires that one compare how one sees oneself with how significant others appear to expect one to be. "Ego identity, then, in its subjective aspect, is the awareness of the fact that there is a self-sameness and continuity to the ego's synthesizing methods and a continuity of one's meaning for others" (1963). Ego identity results in a sense of coherent individuality that enables one to resolve one's conflicts adaptively. Adolescents must answer the question "Who am I?" satisfactorily. If they fail to do so, they will suffer role confusion.

Erikson suggested that adolescence is a particularly crucial period. Along with rapid physical growth and changes, new psychological challenges occur. Previous continuities are called into question as young people begin to reconnect the roles and skills that they have developed into a maturer sense of identity. This integration is more than the sum total of previous accomplishments. Erikson often spoke of adolescence as a moratorium between childhood and adulthood and considered such a moratorium particularly important in a complex society.

The greatest danger at this stage is role confusion, the inability to conceive of oneself as a productive member of one's society. Erikson pointed out that "a sound ego identity is the only safeguard against the anarchy of drives as well as the autocracy of conscience" (1958). Role confusion frequently arises out of the adolescent's difficulty in finding an occupational identity but it may also express a general inability to find a meaningful place in one's culture. The development of a positive identity depends on support from significant groups. The adolescent who cannot find a meaningful adult role runs the risk of an **identity crisis**, a transitory failure to establish a stable identity. Some young people may drop out of mainstream society for a short period, as Erikson himself did. Others may adopt a **negative identity**, one that is opposed to the dominant values of their upbringing. Where support has not been forthcoming and the climate has not been favorable to the development of inner resources, a negative identity may provide the only way of demonstrating mastery and free choice in one's culture. Negative identifications may result in unfortunate consequences — social pathology, crime, or expressions of prejudice. However, Erikson wanted us to recognize that such developments are an important testimony to the adolescent's readiness for ideological involvement. It is vitally important that a society present its young people with ideals they can share enthusiastically. The conspicuous absence of a sense of promise in any society, due to economic conditions, population trends, high unemployment, or other problems that thwart the occupational aspirations of young people, means that those adolescents will have a difficult time establishing a clear and positive ego identity.

The virtue or ego strength developed as this time is *fidelity;* the adolescent is ready to learn to be faithful to an ideological point of view. Fidelity consists of "the ability to sustain loyalties freely pledged in spite of the inevitable contradictions of value systems" (1964). Without fidelity, the young person will either have a weak ego and suffer a "confusion of values" or search for a deviant group to be loyal to.

Intimacy versus Isolation: Love   Young adulthood (eighteen to twenty-four) is marked by the emotional duality of **intimacy versus isolation** (1963). Intimacy refers to the ability to develop a close and meaningful relationship with another person. Erikson here applied Freud's dictum "to love and to work" as the model orientation. Isolation entails self-absorption and an inability to develop deep, committed relationships. Having grown beyond the beginnings of establishing an identity, the young adult is able to overcome the fear of ego loss and form a close affiliation with another individual. The task of young adulthood is to couple genitality with general work productiveness. Clearly, genitality is an inadequate definition of health. On the other hand, an individual's dedication to work should not be such that she or he loses the capacity to love.

Thus, it is at this point that the virtue of *love* emerges as an ego strength (1964). This is not to deny the involvement of love in previous stages, but in young adulthood the individual is able to transform the love received as a child and begin to care for others. Love further represents a mutual devotion that is able to overcome the natural antagonism involved in any relationship between the sexes. Erikson acknowledged that there are different functions of the sexes, particularly with regard to procreation; however, the capacities of the mature ego can transcend these so that male and female cooperate.

Generativity versus Stagnation: Care   The middle years (twenty-five to sixty-four) are characterized by the conflict of **generativity versus stagnation (1963)**. Generativity entails more than parenthood; it is the ability to be productive and creative in many areas of life, particularly those showing a concern for the welfare of ensuing generations. The adult actively participates in those elements of culture that will ensure its maintenance and enhancement. Failure to do so leads to feelings of stagnation, boredom, and interpersonal impoverishment. An individual who does not have children can fulfill generativity by working with other people's children or helping to create a better world for them. Thus, while the idea of generativity includes the concepts of productivity and creativity, it is much broader. A person is generative when making a contribution appropriate to her or his particular potential, be it children, products, ideas, or works of art.

Erikson suggested that because Freud stressed early inhibition of the expression of the libido or sexual drive, he underestimated the importance of the procreative desires of human beings. Erikson considered a procreative drive to be instinctual and saw generativity as a further psychosexual stage whose frustration leads to symptoms of self-absorption and indulgence.

The ego strength that emerges during the middle years is *care*. The adult needs to be needed. *Care* implies doing something for somebody. Care is also able to overcome the inevitable ambivalent feelings that are involved in the parent-child relationship. Once again, when the mature ego is able to transcend these emotions, the adult can fulfill obligations to youth.

Ego Integrity versus Despair: Wisdom   Maturity, the final stage of life (sixty-five to death), is marked by **ego integrity versus despair (1963)**. Ego integrity entails the ability to reflect on one's life with satisfaction even if all dreams are not fulfilled. Death is not feared but accepted as one among many facets of one's existence. Despair refers to regret over missed and unfulfilled opportunities at a time when it is too late to begin again. Ego integrity represents the fruit of the seven stages that have preceded. The virtue of this stage is *wisdom*. Wisdom enables an individual to bring life to an appropriate closure. It is the ability to stand back and reflect on one's life in the face of impending death (1964).

Table 7.1 summarizes Erikson's psychosocial stages, indicates their relationship to Freud's psychosexual stages, and lists their respective ego strengths.

Table 7.1   *The Life Cycle*

Psychosexual stage	Psychosocial stage	Ego strength or virtue
Oral sensory and kinesthetic (Infancy)	Trust versus mistrust	Hope
Anal-muscular (toddler years)	Autonomy versus shame and doubt	Will
Phallic or genital-locomotor (preschool years)	Initiative versus guilt	Purpose
Latency period (school years)	Industry versus inferiority	Competence
Genital (Adolescence)	Ego identity versus role confusion	Fidelity
(Young adulthood)	Intimacy versus isolation	Love
(Adulthood)	Generativity versus stagnation	Care
(Maturity)	Ego integrity versus despair	Wisdom

SOURCE: Life Cycle Chart, based on material from CHILDHOOD AND SOCIETY by Erik H. Erikson, Copyright 1950, © 1963 by W. W. Norton & Company, Inc.; INSIGHT AND RESPONSIBILITY by Erik H. Erikson, Copyright © 1964 by Erik H. Erikson. Additional rights for material from CHILDHOOD AND SOCIETY obtained from Chatto and Windus Ltd.

Assessment and Research in Erikson's Theory

Erikson used cultural studies, psychohistories, and inquiries into sex differences in his development of unique methods of assessment and research based on direct observation of a particular (configurational) kind followed by theoretical formulation (Coles, 1970).

The Study of Two Native American Tribes   In 1938 Erikson went to the Pine Ridge Reservation in South Dakota to observe the children of the Sioux. He had become increasingly interested in the work of anthropologists and welcomed an opportunity to observe how the events of an individual's life are shaped by societal practices. Because he traveled with an old friend of the Sioux, Erikson was able to establish a close relationship with the Native Americans and to observe them and speak with them freely. Later, he traveled to northern California to observe a very different tribe, the Yurok. Ultimately he undertook other unique forms of investigation to study the impact of society, culture, and history on personality development.

The Sioux had originally been buffalo hunters. When the white settlers came, both the buffalo and the traditional Sioux way of life vanished amid bloody massacres. Defeated, the Sioux had become withdrawn and apathetic. In part the present behavior of the Sioux was undoubtedly due to their painful history, but Erikson found additional reasons in the Sioux child-rearing practices. Unlike most American middle-class parents who impose firm structures on their children at an early age in the belief that this will help them to become productive adults, the Sioux actively encouraged their children to be free and delayed imposing restrictions on them. The Sioux mother was at ease with her tasks of mothering and liberally breast-fed her infants. Sioux toddlers were allowed extensive liberties. Generosity was encouraged, property disregarded, and competition avoided. Boys were trained to be self-confident, boastful, spirited hunters of game and women. Girls were taught to be the wives and mothers of hunters. These child-rearing practices, probably well suited to the earlier lifestyle of the buffalo hunter, had continued even though the historical situation of the Sioux had changed radically. The traditional practices now could not cultivate or sustain a more adaptive system of social roles. The adult Sioux, who had been given considerable freedom as a child but whose life was now severely restricted, could cope with the dilemma only by looking back to the glorious past. The future of the Sioux tribe seemed "empty except for dreams of restoration."

The Yurok, on the other hand, showed "folkways of stinginess, suspicion, and anger" and an emphasis on acquiring and retaining possessions. Infants were weaned promptly at about six months and encouraged to be independent. Self-restraint was urged and the child was swiftly taught to subordinate all instinctual drives to economic considerations. The Yurok, who fished along a salmon river, learned to live more easily with the white settlers because their values were similar in many ways and their present work (farming, lumbering, and fishing) was both useful and familiar to them.

In describing the behavior of these two Native American tribes, Erikson deliberately avoided talking about basic character traits even though he was aware that traditional psychoanalysts would perceive "oral" and "anal" character structures in the Sioux and the Yurok, respectively. Erikson preferred to "concentrate on the configurations with which these two tribes try to synthesize their concepts and their ideals in a coherent design for living." He pointed out that each society uses childhood in a number of ways: to give meaning to the child's early experiences of its body and other people, to channel the child's energies in socially constructive ways, and to provide an overall framework of meaning for the anxieties that social living provokes (1963).

Psychohistories   Erikson also explored the contribution of culture and history to personality by examining the lives of significant historical figures. **Psychohistory** is "the study of individual and collective life with the combined methods of psychoanalysis and history" (1974). Freud too had examined the lives of various famous people, but Erikson refined the method of psychohistory and it is his name that is typically associated with the term.

In studying historical figures, Erikson explored how the ego strength of certain individuals is able to transform the conflicts that inhibit others so that they become leaders who make an impression on their era. Thus, in studying Martin Luther, an influential leader of the Protestant Reformation, Erikson did not focus on the pathological features of Luther's behavior as other psychiatric biographers had done. He concentrated on how Luther was able to overcome some of his limitations.

Erikson conceived of a seizure, which Luther is said to have experienced in the choir of his monastery, as a turning point in Luther's struggle for identity. Young Luther's exclamation, "It isn't me!" expressed his need to repudiate certain roles in order to break through to what he intended to be.

The focus on a key episode is apparent in Erikson's effort to understand what led Gandhi to a position of militant nonviolence. Erikson saw Gandhi's decision to put his life on the line by fasting during a local labor dispute (which culminated in a strike in Ahmedabad in 1918) as a crisis through which Gandhi was able to transform a negative Indian identity of weakness into a positive and active political technique.

THINKING CRITICALLY

Generativity

Erikson believed that the dominant task of the adult years for both men and women is generativity. Parenthood is one way of expressing generativity. Social and economic considerations, however, may make it necessary to restructure the ways in which people express this form of generativity. In America today, small rather than large families are the norm. Most households need two incomes to meet expenses.

While Erikson's age limits have always been approximations, some teenagers today have children at much earlier ages than his theory predicts; other young adults delay marriage and child bearing. Many people in their sixties and seventies and even eighties continue to be very generative. Are we out of synch with Erikson's stages? Is it morally advisable or necessary for a parent to be married or in a relationship before having a child? What do you think about homosexual couples raising children? Some speak of women as having a biological clock. Do men have such a clock, biological or psychological?

Some critics suggest that Erikson's life stages, emotional polarities, and ego strengths bear the hallmarks of a white Western patriarchal society that would not apply well to other cultures. Does the task of generativity apply with the same force to civilizations with large populations? Try to speak with someone from a non-Western culture in order to identify what might be some more appropriate emotional challenges during the life span in that culture.

Erikson's approach has been applied by other writers to the lives of significant figures, such as Robert Hogan's analysis of Malcolm X (1976). Malcolm X was a well-adjusted, superior student, yet an English teacher criticized his choice of a law career as unrealistic and suggested that he consider carpentry instead. Malcolm knew he was smarter than most of his white classmates, but society refused him the identity he wished to choose because he was an African American. Therefore, he turned to a negative identity, becoming a "hoodlum, thief, dope peddler, pimp," before assuming the role of the militant African-American leader of the 1950s and 1960s. The interdisciplinary approach of psychohistory provides a deeper exploration of the past than what is offered by separate disciplines (Lawton, 1990; Rousselle, 1990).

Sex Differences   In *Childhood and Society* (1963), Erikson reported on an investigation he had undertaken with a large number of children between the ages of ten and twelve in order to explore how their inner lives might be reflected in their play. He set up a table with a random selection of toys and invited each child individually to construct "an exciting scene out of an imaginary movie" and then tell the plot. The resulting constructions accurately reflected each child's inner development when compared with other sources. However, Erikson also noticed distinct sex differences in the children's configurations (see Figure 7.1). Girls were apt to represent the interior of a room with a circle of furniture. Occasionally they included an intruder who was accommodated in the room. Boys, on the other hand, made towers and other

Figure 7.1 *Sex Differences in Children's Play Constructions*
In his observation of children's play constructions, Erikson noted that boys tended to erect structures and towers whereas girls used the play area as the interior of a house.

Reprinted from CHILDHOOD AND SOCIETY, by Erik H. Erikson, with the permission of W. W. Norton & Company, Inc. Copyright 1950, © 1963 by W. W. Norton & Company, Inc.

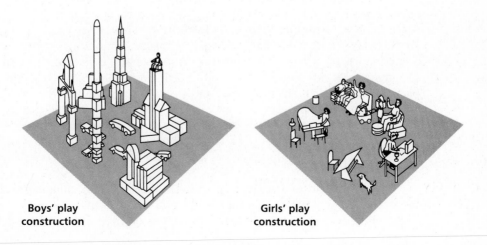

Boys' play
construction

Girls' play
construction

high structures, some of which were in a state of collapse. Erikson concluded that in order to understand a child's play construction, he had to realize that girls and boys use space differently. Girls emphasized *inner space* and qualities of openness versus closedness. Boys concentrated on *outer space* and qualities of highness and lowness. These particular tendencies reminded him of the respective structures of the female and male genitals. This discovery led him to hypothesize that "one's experience is anchored in the ground plan of the body" and that there may be a "profound difference in the sense of space in the two sexes."

It is important to point out that Erikson's study, given the age of the children (ten to twelve), does not prove that the differences are inherent. Indeed, an effort to replicate Erikson's study found no significant sex differences (McKay, Pyke, & Goranson, 1984). Thus Erikson may have been incorrect in his judgment about the data, or changes in sex-role socialization since his original study may account for the different findings.

Erikson concluded, however, that the development of women is influenced by their awareness of their reproductive capacity and identified a woman's maternal potential as a key determinant of her personality. Unlike Freud, Erikson's clinical observations did not support the idea that a girl's awareness of her sex focused on a missing penis. Rather, in normative development, the focus is on a sense of vital inner potential. A woman's productive inner space is an inescapable factor in her development whether social, historical, and other conditions lead her to build her life around it or not.

Erikson, like Freud, employed a male paradigm in his theory. The "eight ages of man" are, in fact, for men. While Erikson believed women could make significant contributions in the political and work world, he did not believe they find identity in work. Subsequent research has shown that Erikson's stages of development are more satisfactory in accounting for the development of males than of females (Forisha-Kovach, 1983).

Comments on Erikson's Research Methods   Erikson did not hesitate to develop techniques of study appropriate to his subject. Thus, as a child psychoanalyst he used the media of children's play and their positioning of objects in space in order to explore their inner lives. In the clinical setting, it quickly became apparent to Erikson that "basic psychological insight cannot emerge without some involvement of the observer's impulses and defenses, and that such insights cannot be communicated without the ambivalent involvement of the participants" (1975). His anthropological field work gave him further insight into how an observer necessarily participates in the lives of subjects and limits and structures the research. This finding was termed *participant observation* by Sullivan (1954); consistent with a twentieth-century understanding of science, it recognizes that we cannot speak of the observed without also speaking of the observer.

There are distinct parallels between the clinical evidence obtained and used by psychoanalysts in formulating their hypotheses and that used in the study of historical events. The discipline of psychohistory permits psychoanalysts to become aware of their own historical determinants and the historian to realize that in seeking to understand history we are also making history. The analyst asks the patient to free-associate and then reflect on those associations in order to perceive patterns and themes by which past experiences can be reconstructed. The study of a historical figure takes into account the coherence of statements, life, and time. Each event is considered in terms of its meaning for the individual at that particular stage of life and also in terms of its meaning for the life history as a whole. This means that early events need to be compatible with the developmental stage at which they occur and that there has to be a plausible continuity in the life history as a whole, just as the pieces of the developmental puzzle of an individual's life need to fall into place.

In psychoanalysis the significance of an episode, life period, or life trend is made clear by subsequent therapeutic crises that lead to decisive advances or setbacks. In biography, the validity of any relevant theme lies in its crucial recurrence in the person's development. Psychohistory permits us to see how universal phenomena (such as the complex of emotions termed Oedipal) are re-enacted in different ways by different people in different periods of history. Psychohistory seeks to clarify the personal aims of an individual in terms of the goals of the times and the relation of both of these to the psychohistorian's values (1974).

Some critics have suggested that the difficulty in distinguishing between historical fact and legend jeopardizes the conclusions of a psychohistorical study. Erikson was not distressed by such comments: "If some of it is legend, so be it; the making of a legend is as much of the scholarly re-writing of history as it is a part of the original facts used in the work of scholars" (1958). Such critics ask whether or not a theory corresponds to what we can observe: the empirical data. That criterion is characteristic of the scientist but it is inappropriate for the historian or psychoanalyst engaged in a retrospective activity. The reconstruction of the past in these instances can be based only on present clues, which may or may not correspond with the actual past. After all, the historical data that survive, even the most well established, survive thanks to "a previous generation's sense of the momentous" (1969).

A given world image needs to be anchored "in facts and figures cognitively perceived and logically arranged, in experiences emotionally confirmed, and in a social life cooperatively affirmed," "to provide a reality that seems self evident" (1974). Thus, Erikson considered proof to be a matter of the internal coherence or consistency of a theory and its ability to illumine the human condition.

Empirical Research in Erikson's Theory

Adequate research on Erikson's stages of development would require extensive and costly longitudinal studies. Thus they have not been conducted. However, Marcia (1966, 1980) described four statuses implied in Erikson's concept of identity formation in adolescence by focusing on Erikson's belief that there are two components to identity formation: crisis (the struggle to re-examine old values) and commitment (making a decision and following its implications). In addition, Marcia developed an intricate interview formula to assess his statuses. Research with his instrument by Papini, Micka, and Barnett (1989) shows correlations between different parenting styles and patterns of family communication and statuses. Additional research by Waterman (1982) suggests that if a young person undergoes an identity crisis it usually happens later than Erikson first suggested. Moreover, approximately one-third of young people do not experience a crisis but simply follow a predictable pattern. Archer (1989) proposes that the identity development pattern for both sexes is comparable. However, women's identity is more likely to be based on a number of factors (occupation, marriage, mothering) whereas men focus primarily on their profession (see also Patterson, Sochting, & Marcia, 1992). Research has also included the importance of ethnicity in the development of identity of African Americans (Aries & Moorehead, 1989) and Mexican Americans (Bernal et al., 1990) as well as other groups (Markstrom-Adams, 1992).

Orlofsky (1976) has described six different statuses related to the intimacy challenge facing young adults. He believes that men who achieve identity are also able to achieve a high level of intimacy. Some individuals known as *mergers* commit themselves to a relationship at the price of their own independence. Women who are mergers, for example, tend to be overly dependent on their husbands and are more likely to experience depression (Levitz-Jones & Orlofsky, 1985).

Van de Water and McAdams (1989) asked adults to describe three creative projects they were working on to assess their level of generativity. Generativity was defined broadly and by no means limited to biological parenting. Highly generative individuals were more likely to be focused on altruistic endeavors.

Finally, Whitbourne, Zuschlag, Elliot, and Waterman (1992) suggest that the last decade has seen less favorable resolution of ego integrity versus despair. Hamacheck (1990) has suggested behavioral criteria that can be used to assess the level of development in Erikson's last three psychosocial stages.

The Object Relations Theorists

In the 1950s and 1960s, American psychoanalysis was dominated by ego psychology. It emphasized conflict between internal structures and their defense in the individual psyche. Meanwhile, in Britain, Melanie Klein (1932) initiated object relations theory, and thereafter Ronald Fairbairn (1952) revised it. A distinction needs to be made between *object relationships,* one's external contemporary relationships with others, which were discussed by Anna Freud (Dyer, 1983), and *object relations,* the intrapsychic experience of early relationships with others. Object relations theory recognizes that from birth onward individuals relate to other people and form attachments. Object relations theorists seek to understand the interaction between intrapsychic dynamics and interpersonal relationships.

Klein and Fairbairn were more interested in the reality of the "inner world" than that of the "outer world." One result of their preference has been that object relations theory is more satisfactory for understanding psychopathology than normality (Dyer, 1983), and the interest in object relations has become particularly important as a framework for understanding some of the syndromes that have become a part of our popular clinical literature these days, such as borderline and narcissistic personality disorders and various forms of abuse (see also Grotstein, 1991).

Margaret Mahler, Heinz Kohut, and Otto Kernberg explored the roots of ego development by further emphasizing the interaction between the infant and primary caregiver. Nancy Chodorow discusses the impact of women's mothering and women's roles.

Margaret Mahler (1897–1985)

Margaret Mahler (1975) explored the processes of separation and individuation by which the child emerges from a symbiotic, or intimate, fusion with the mother and assumes individual characteristics. Her findings confirm that the biological birth of an infant and the psychological birth of an individual are not the same. The former is a distinct event, whereas the latter is a gradual unfolding process.

By studying and comparing severely disturbed and normal children, Mahler constructed a sequence of stages through which the ego passes in the process of becoming an individual. The **separation-individuation process** optimally begins about the fourth month and leads to the formation of a stable self-concept near the end of the third year. Separation implies physical differentiation and separateness from primary caregiver, while individuation suggests psychological growth away from one's primary caregiver and toward one's unique identity. Thus, in Mahler's view the roots of identity, ego strength, and conflict resolution precede the Oedipus complex.

Prior to separation-individuation, there are two "forerunner phases," *normal autism* and *normal symbiosis,* in which the infant's ego develops from a state of absolutely primary narcissism to a recognition of an external world. At this time there is no real separation of self from mother, but developments may occur that promote or impede the subsequent individuation process. The separation-individuation process itself is composed of four stages: *differentiation,* the development of a body image separate from that of mother (five to nine months); *practicing,* perfecting motor abilities and developing physical independence (ten to fourteen months); *rapprochement,* increased awareness of separateness from mother, with an accompanying sensitivity to her absence that expresses a conflict between the urge to separate and the fear of loss, and a recognition that mothers have both good and bad aspects (fourteen to twenty-four months); *consolidation,* unification of the good and bad in mother with the image of her as a separate entity in the external world and the beginnings of the child's own individuality and separate personhood as seen in the development of a self-concept based on a stable sense of "me" (two to three years). Mahler's concept expresses her belief that normal, healthy infants show

Margaret Mahler

a "drive for and towards individuation" that is demonstrated in the separation-individuation process. Mahler's theory is receiving attention currently because her concept of a separation-individuation process is so helpful.

Jessica Benjamin (1988) observes that Mahler's research on separation-individuation was a "landmark in the theory of self" that deeply altered psychoanalytic theory and practice. It acknowledged *two* realities, both of which need to be understood: the importance of interpersonal dynamics and unconscious reality. She points out, however, that during the last twenty years, infancy research (e.g., Stern, 1985) has emphasized reciprocity and criticizes Mahler for emphasizing the separation of the child while neglecting to recognize the mother as a separate person as well.

Weingberg (1991) sees points of convergence between Mahler's theory and Stern's research into infants' development of self. However, Stern argues that infants are born with far more "hardwiring" than Mahler gives them credit for, and Stern emphasizes the role of mutuality, reciprocity, and the "holding" environment as critical to an infant's development.

Neubauer and Neubauer (1990, p. 80) noted that "identical twins reared apart share *the same timing* of their developmental phases, and with a strikingly similar progression." This underscores, once again, the fact that both the environment and heredity need to be taken into account in order to understand personality.

Heinz Kohut

Heinz Kohut (1913–1981)

Heinz Kohut developed a new dimension in psychoanalysis that he called self-theory (1971, 1977). Extending Margaret Mahler's observations on the beginnings of individuality and the importance of the mother-child relationship, Kohut focused on narcissism and narcissistic character disorders that occur when an individual fails to develop an independent sense of self. He assumed a narcissistic line of development distinct from and before ego and psychosexual development.

The term **narcissism** comes from the ancient Greek myth of Narcissus, who "unwittingly" fell in love with his own reflection in a pool of water. He talked to it and tried to embrace it, but all in vain as it fled at his touch. The passion with which he burned was self-consuming.

The narcissistic personality is characterized by an exaggerated sense of self-importance and self-involvement, behaviors that hide a fragile sense of self-worth. Freud believed that narcissistic and borderline disorders could not be treated by psychoanalysis because they originated before the patient was able to talk and thus were not amenable to verbal analysis. Because the libido is withdrawn from external objects, resistance is insuperable and it is difficult to cultivate a transference. However, disruptions in family relationships and in society have led to an increase in these disorders and to more efforts to deal with them psychoanalytically. Kohut and others (such as Giovacchini, Kernberg, and Spotnitz) have expanded the psychoanalytic repertoire to include techniques designed to work through transferences and resistances that stem from preoedipal phases of development.

Kohut (1971, 1977) conceived of narcissistic feelings not as qualities of a certain stage of development but as an aspect of personality that gradually unfolds, permeates the entire life span, and leads to a distorted sense of self. He believed that disorders of the self arise from a failure in parental empathy. Children need an adequate response to their infantile needs. To be specific, they need to be **mirrored** — to have their talk and their accomplishments acknowledged, accepted, and praised. Little children believe that they are omnipotent and they also **idealize** their parents. Such idealization enables them to develop goals. In time, most children learn that their idealized notions are incorrect and they substitute a more realistic assessment of both themselves and their parents. In part, this learning depends on parents responding positively to their children's unique, lovable, and commendable characteristics. If parents fail to respond in appropriate ways, children may be unable to develop a good sense of self-worth and may spend the rest of their lives looking without success for such acceptance. In short, narcissistic individuals are looking for an idealized parent substitute that can never be found.

With a well-developed self, one is aware of who one is and that awareness gives significance and purpose to one's behavior. In ideal development, *the nuclear self* emerges in the second year. Kohut believed that the nuclear self is bipolar. The two poles, archaic nuclear ambitions and subsequent goals, create a tension arc that fosters the development of early skills and talents. The ideal **autonomous self** has qualities of *self-esteem* and *self-confidence,* establishes both general ambition and precise goals, and develops talents and skills in order to meet them. Furthermore, the autonomous self shows a lack of dependence on other people.

Kohut believed that narcissistic disorders are characterized by recurrent self-absorption, low self-esteem, unimportant physical complaints, and a chronic sense of emptiness. He pointed out that psychoanalysis cannot be useful unless the therapist deals first with the narcissistic disorder. Suggesting that therapists imagine themselves "into the client's skin," Kohut believed that therapists can cultivate feelings of being understood and appreciated in the patient so that the arrested growth of the patient's self can begin again. Thus, Kohut stressed empathy and introspection over the conventional psychoanalytic blend of free association and evenly suspended attention (Balter & Spencer, 1991). In the course of treatment, Kohut discovered that narcissistic patients develop idealizing or mirroring transferences to their analysts that reflect their early and troubled parent-child relationships. Therapy permits them to rework these relationships through to a better resolution.

Kohut (1977) reminded us that the "presence of a firm self is a precondition for the experience of the Oedipus complex." Kohut found that at the end of their analysis some of his patients who had primary self disorders acquired an Oedipal constellation. "This he considered to be the positive result of the consolidations of the self the patient had never achieved before" (Ornstein, 1993). Moreover, this development was associated with positive emotions leading Kohut to believe that when children develop normally, the Oedipus complex may be a "joyful" experience. An Oedipus complex that is filled with conflict may be a sign that narcissistic parents have been unable to respond with empathy to their preschool age child and may lead their child to turn to a fantasy life. Kohut (1977, 1984) pointed out that the necessity for children to have nurturing and affectionate parents was just currently being given genuine notice by psychoanalysts although it was well understood much earlier by neo-Freudians and humanists. Watson, Little, and Biderman (1992) found correlations between Baumrind's parenting styles and Kohut's theory suggesting that an authoritative (rather than permissive or authoritarian) parenting style is less likely to foster narcissistic maladjustment.

Kohut (1984) pointed out that some parts of Freud's theory are "time-bound" whereas other parts have a more "enduring validity." Eagle (1984) suggests that "if, as Kohut argues, forms of pathology are shifting more in the directions of narcissistic disorders; and if it is true and self psychology is uniquely appropriate to these phenomena; and if . . . the traditional theory of intrapsychic conflict is *inappropriate* to these phenomena, it follows that . . . the validity and applicability of traditional psychoanalytic theory [and I might add contemporary psychoanalytic theory] are culture — and era — bound . . . rather than . . . timeless and universal." Moreover, the increase in self disorders may be due to cultural forces such as an absence of stable beliefs and values and an attitude of cynicism that negatively affects teenagers and young adults.

Kohut's self-theory has resulted in some fruitful reinterpretations of Freud's classic case studies (see Magid, 1993) and has helped to revitalize psychoanalytic theory.

Otto Kernberg (1928–   )

Otto Kernberg (1975) agrees with Freud and Kohut that many people who suffer from narcissistic disorders have parents who were indifferent, cold, and also subtly hostile and vengeful toward them. Kernberg further underscores the atypical and high amount of self-reference in narcissistic individuals' interpersonal relationships and the dissimilarity between their seemingly exaggerated self-images and their insatiable need for approval from other people. While their craving for admiration and approval may lead others to think that narcissists are dependent, Kernberg believes that they are actually unable to trust other people and are, therefore, powerless to depend on others.

Otto Kernberg

Kernberg has also focused on what are called "borderline" personality disorders. It was in the 1950s that analysts and therapists started to portray a type of patient who was unable to engage in introspection, develop insight, and work through problems. Such patients frequently had strong mood swings and were inclined to see significant others in their lives as all good or all bad. These patients displayed oral tendencies such as dependency needs or an incorporative style but also powerful aggressive tendencies, particularly with reference to their Oedipal struggles (1989).

The psychoanalytic models of that time found such patients puzzling. The term "borderline" initially meant a person who was on the border between functioning adequately (if not neurotically) some of the time and lapsing over into psychotic episodes at other times. In time, the definition was narrowed and in the DSM-IV criteria of 1994, a person is considered to have a borderline personality disorder if he or she displays five or more specific clinical features. Kernberg would prefer, however, a diagnosis and explanation of borderline based on a causal description of early, historical relationships.

Kernberg introduced the notion of **splitting** — failing to consolidate positive and negative experiences between oneself and other people — to account for the intense changes that are apparent in a borderline individual's interpersonal relationships. Borderline people swing back and forth between conflicting images, seeing one and the same person as both loving and hateful rather than being able to see one loving person who at times accepts and at other times rejects. Kernberg portrays this behavior:

In one session, the patient may experience me as the most helpful, loving, understanding human being and feel totally relieved and happy, and all the problems solved. Three sessions later, she may berate me as the most ruthless, indifferent, and manipulative person she has ever met. Total unhappiness about the treatment, ready to drop it and never come back. (Sass, 1982)

Kernberg prefers to treat borderline patients face to face in intensive sessions three or more times a week. The therapist plays a more active role than is typical of classical psychoanalysis. Initially the stress is placed on current behavior rather than past events. Kernberg's method of treatment, which he calls **expressive psychoanalytically oriented psychotherapy,** differs from classical psychoanalysis in that a complete transference neurosis is not permitted to develop, nor is transference resolved through interpretation alone." Instead, the therapist clearly depicts and discusses the patient's seeming distortions of reality, such as a distorted view of the therapist.

Kernberg, Selzer, Koenigsberg, Carr, and Appelbaum (1989) suggest that interpretation has three stages: clarification by the patient of his or her problem, confronting the patient with unconscious internal contradictions, and interpreting the meaning of the repressions in the here-and-now and in the there-and-then.

Kernberg (1990) has suggested that libido and aggression, the two drives proposed by Freud, should be seen as a hierarchy made up by the structure of feelings that constitute the "building block" of these drives. He suggests that rather than view erogenous zones as the source of libido, we conceive of the source as a peak emotional state of sexual excitement that embraces all physiologically activated functions and body zones mixed up in a parent-child relationship of erotic arousal. Rage, on the other hand, makes up the necessary emotion around which assembles the feeling of aggression as a drive.

The differences between Kohut and Kernberg provide an interesting counterpoint. Kohut believes that narcissistic personality disorders are the result of empathic failures, while Kernberg believes that personality disorders are the result of unneutralized drives. Thus, Kohut focuses much more on the interpersonal domain while Kernberg emphasizes the intrapsychic dimension.

For Kernberg, aggression is a major motivation force. In this respect he believes that Kohut fails to recognize the importance of analyzing negative transferences. Further he suggests that a therapist needs to emphasize with what patients have split off from as well as their subjective experiences. At the same time, he is careful not to let patients feel that their cure is essential to his own well-being because that feeds into a patient's omnipotence. Kernberg also believes that self-psychology is missing a serious consideration of the cultural determinants of sexual excitement as well as the intrapsychic and biological ones.

If you live in an Arab country where women are all covered except for the eyes, the wind lifts the veil, and it is a primal scene! If you go to beaches in Western Europe where everybody goes topless, then you have a different attitude towards erotic stimulation than if you were brought up in the Puritan atmosphere in the American mid-West 30 years ago. (1987)

More recently, Kernberg (1992) has suggested changing but not giving up Freud's drive theory. His change acknowledges the basic role of affects in the structure of drives and unites the neuropsychological causes of primitive affects with the first interpersonal experiences of babies and children as causes of personality formation. He also seeks to shed light on the associations of aggression, rage, and hatred. He is convinced that personality disturbances are caused by the psychic structures built under the influence of early emotional events with significant others. In this latest work, he updates his theory, emphasizing distortions due to aggression in the transference and countertransference, and applies his theory to the full range of personality disorders.

Nancy J. Chodorow (1944–   )

Chodorow's work differs from traditional psychoanalytic theory because she sees a strong relationship between gender identity and the organization of work and the family in capitalist societies in the West.

Chodorow (1978) points out that in the last two centuries, mothering by women has become increasingly separate from other work that had traditionally been done in the home (such as weaving). Industrialization eliminated many people who previously lived in the same household and limited men's role in family life. At the same time, social scientists were emphasizing the significance of the mother-child relationship. Chodorow argues that "the contemporary reproduction of mothering occurs through social structurally induced psychological processes. It is neither a product of biology nor of intentional role-training." She believes that "women's mothering reproduces itself cyclically. Women as mothers, produce daughters with mothering capability and the desire to mother. These capacities and needs are built into and grow out of the mother-daughter relationship itself." On the other hand, boys' nurturing abilities are methodically limited and repressed as they are prepared to work outside the family.

Explanations of mothering rooted on biology or role socialization are not enough. There is nothing in a pregnant woman's physical or instinctual makeup that makes her especially fit to care for children past the first few months of infancy when she may choose to breast-feed. Psychoanalytic object relations theory offers a better explanation. The early relationship between mothers and infants establishes a basis for parenting in children of both sexes and "expectations that women will mother." Mothering meets a woman's psychological need for reciprocal intimacy initiated during her own infancy when she and her mother saw one another as extensions of themselves. Mothers are also close to their baby sons, but they see their sons as dissimilar and do not experience the same feeling of "oneness" they have with their daughters. Women's separation from their mothers results in their inability to recapture mother (if they establish a heterosexual relationship), whereas men may separate and still recapture mother via a relationship with an adult woman. Hence, there is pressure for women to remain "tied" or connected while there is no threat of a loss for men in separating.

Nancy J. Chodorow

Imbalances in family events stemming from women's mothering leads to a different development of the psyche in men and women. The establishment of gender identity occurs in the preoedipal period and there are sex differences in the Oedipal experience due to this awareness and parental involvement. Women's personality develops in a way that emphasizes ongoing interpersonal relations but men grow to see themselves as distinct and separate. This prepares the two sexes for different roles: nonrelationship activities for men and relational activities for women. The different development of women and men further recreates women's mothering by preparing them to take "adult gender roles which situate women primarily within the sphere of reproduction in a sexually unequal society." Grown men, unused to a psychologically intimate relation, are satisfied with letting women mother.

Women and children's primary place in the home and men's involvement in the public sphere "defines society itself as masculine. It gives men power to create and enforce institutions of social and political control, important among these to control marriage as an institution that both expresses men's rights in women's sexual and reproductive capacities and reinforces these rights."

Differential feminine and masculine development leads to discrepancies in the present structure of parenting. Women's mothering assures that parenting is done. However, the process creates stresses and pressures that subvert the sex-gender system. Women who are isolated at home are more at risk for over-investing in their children and looking for their children to meet their unmet emotional needs. Where women are permitted to do significant constructive work and have continuous good adult relationships while parenting, they are not as apt to overinvest in their children. When women are solely responsible for parenting, it is more difficult for men to develop "a stable sense of masculine self." If we want to be free of this inequality, we will have to restructure parenting "so that primary parenting is shared between men and women."

In Chodorow's *Feminism and Psychoanalytic Theory* (1989) we can see the development of her thought during a career change from feminist social scientist to psychoanalyst. Believing that object relations theory has not generated a sufficient description of gender or an acknowledgment of the mother's subjectivity. Chodorow extends and improves the theory via a feminist contribution. She states that object relations is in error in thinking of mothers primarily as objects for their children.

The fact that women are the fundamental caregivers is experienced very differently by boys and girls. Girls feel connected to their mothers while boys experience a feeling of threat because they have to depend on someone of another sex and later turn away from her. Girls' early development, therefore, is

THINKING CRITICALLY

Shared Parenting

Recent years have seen fathers taking a greater role in parenting their children. When his wife was pregnant my nephew announced, "We're pregnant!" — an indication that he intended to take an active role as coach during pregnancy and childbirth and that he would share parenting responsibilities for his children.

What do you think? If you are a woman, would you like for your husband to assume a more active role in parenting? If you are a man, are you or do you plan on assuming a more active role than your father did?

Are there some ways in which our society could encourage more shared parenting, such as providing paternity leaves as well as maternity leaves, more flexible work hours, job-sharing, or daycare centers closer to the workplace? Is it realistic to think that some of these things will occur, given current economic conditions? (See also Kinkead, 1994.)

What are some of the implications of shared parenting for the personality development processes described by the theorists in this chapter?

optimistic and positive while boys' development is pessimistic and negative, entailing repression of "affect," "relational needs" and "a sense of connection."

However, when children become three or four years old, power changes to male dominance. The behaviors connected with diverse sex roles are given a new interpretation. Men have caused this new interpretation via their power and cultural supremacy, which is based on their fear and resentment of strong women due to their mother's power over them.

Chodorow believes that it is "crucial" for us to recognize that "the ideologies of difference, which define us as women and as men, as well as inequality itself, are produced, socially, psychologically, and culturally, by people living in and creating their social, psychological, and cultural worlds" (1989).

Chodorow (1989) points out that Freud's theory does not simply subjugate women. "Freud tells us how nature becomes culture and how this culture comes to appear as and be experienced as 'second nature.'" Moreover, "Freud suggests that these processes do not happen so smoothly, that this reproduction of gender and sexuality is rife with contradiction and strains" (1989).

Chodorow (1991) observes that while Freud indicated that his understanding of feminine psychology was "shadowy and incomplete," he developed a theory

THINKING CRITICALLY

Culturally Sanctioned Mutilation

In many parts of the world, most notably in Africa and places in the Near East, clitoridectomy, or even removal of the entire vulva, is practiced with full religious and cultural sanctions. These practices are thought to ensure that the woman will be a virgin and pure when she is married. Women who have not had these procedures done are thought to be prostitutes. Therefore, mothers regularly subject their daughters to the painful and embarrassing practice even at a very young age. Such mutilation, however, effectively denies these women their sexuality and ability to fully satisfy their sexual drives (Walker and Parmar, 1993; see also Ugwu-Oju, 1993).

On the other hand, in the United States and in other parts of the world as well, many male babies are routinely circumcised. In some cases this is for religious reasons; in other cases it is done for "health purposes." While a circumcised penis is easier to keep clean, circumcision does desensitize the tip of the penis, making it less amenable to intense sexual sensation. While such action certainly cannot compare to the destruction of women's genitals, could it be called a form of "mutilation?"

What do you think? Are these practices a sign of our continuing struggle as human beings to come to terms with our sexuality, gender fears, and power? Because these practices are culturally, and in some cases religiously, sanctioned they could be very difficult to change.

and treated many women. She appreciates "his clinical accounts, his forthright defense of hysterical women, and his condemnation of the conditions leading to repression and hysteria in women . . . [as well as] his toleration and understanding of variations in sexual object-choice and sexual subjectivity."

She further notes that "by contrast, Freud's understandings about male attitudes towards women and femininity do not seem to be shadowy and incomplete at all. They are specific, informative, persuasive, precise, and clear."

Freud made it clear that his Oedipal theory stemmed from his own self-analysis. Biographical literature on early psychoanalysts is becoming more avail-

PHILOSOPHICAL ASSUMPTIONS

Examining More Recent Psychoanalytic Theorists

How would you rate the more recent psychoanalytical theorists on each of the basic philosophical assumptions described in Chapter 1? Each basic issue was presented as a bipolar dimension along which a person's view can be placed according to the degree of agreement with one or the other extreme. Rate the views of Anna Freud, Hartmann, Erikson, Mahler, Kohut, Kernberg, and Chodorow on these issues.

When you have determined where you think the theorists stand, compare your responses with those of your classmates and your instructor. You should be willing to defend your ratings, but also be prepared to change them in light of others' compelling arguments. Afterward, compare your ratings with your own position on each issue and with those of other theorists. Does this comparison help you to understand why their theories do or do not appeal to you?

Would strongly agree	Would agree	Is neutral or believes in synthesis of both views	Would agree	Would strongly agree
1	2	3	4	5

freedom	**determinism**
People basically have control over their own behavior and understand the motives behind their behavior.	The behavior of people is basically determined by internal or external forces over which they have little, if any, control.

able. In some of these writings, Anna Freud asserted her animosity and envy of totally evil mothers and her glorification of fathers who are totally good.

   Chodorow's speculation may be limited to families rooted in a conventional separation of labor. Some suggest that her speculation "holds only for white, middle-class nuclear families. Still it is useful in explaining how gendered personalities are recreated through the social structure of the family." Also "an important test of her theory would involve the study of boys and girls who are raised by men or in cultures where women are not devalued and parenthood is more equally shared" (Anderson, 1991).

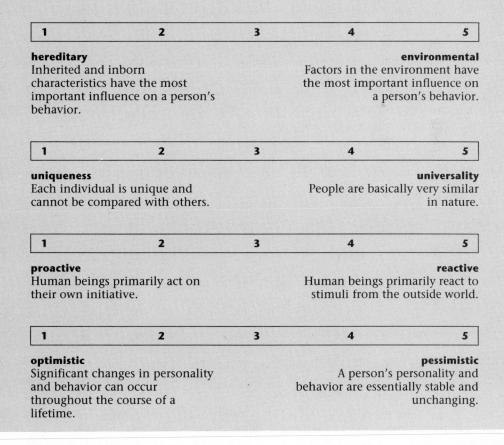

| 1 | 2 | 3 | 4 | 5 |

hereditary
Inherited and inborn characteristics have the most important influence on a person's behavior.

environmental
Factors in the environment have the most important influence on a person's behavior.

| 1 | 2 | 3 | 4 | 5 |

uniqueness
Each individual is unique and cannot be compared with others.

universality
People are basically very similar in nature.

| 1 | 2 | 3 | 4 | 5 |

proactive
Human beings primarily act on their own initiative.

reactive
Human beings primarily react to stimuli from the outside world.

| 1 | 2 | 3 | 4 | 5 |

optimistic
Significant changes in personality and behavior can occur throughout the course of a lifetime.

pessimistic
A person's personality and behavior are essentially stable and unchanging.

Chodorow is not the only important contributor to feminist psychoanalytic thought. Others include Naomi Wolf, Carol Gilligan, Anne Shaeff, and Juliet Mitchell.

Chodorow describes herself as a "self-defined 'interpretive,' or even 'humanist,' psychoanalytic sociologist and psychoanalytic feminist" (1989). Her unique interdisciplinary combination and sweeping view make her technique controversial. At sociology meetings she hears papers on how "absurd" her work is. She finds she is "taken more seriously by literary critics who need a formal way to think about how an individual life works" (Goleman, 1991).

More Recent Psychoanalytic Theories: Philosophy, Science, and Art

The more recent psychoanalytic theorists do not insist on a simply scientific pretense for their work. As clinicians, their work is based on empirical observation. At the same time, many of them, most notably Erikson and Chodorow, emphasize the need for an interdisciplinary perspective.

Erikson, like Erich Fromm, emphasized that important moral commitments lie within the psychoanalytic framework. Thus the ego strengths that he outlined may be seen as ethical values toward which the human race can strive. Ultimately he aimed for a universally applied ethical standard, a contemporary version of the Golden Rule, which he translated as "What is hateful to yourself, do not do to your fellow man" (1964). Unlike Freud, Erikson's philosophical statements were explicit. His theory was highly comprehensive.

Some of these theories include many variables, such as biological, cognitive, cultural, sociological, and historical factors. The theories also speak to issues that concern us today, such as personality disorders that have become more pervasive and the need to rethink the issues of gender and parenting. The theories have a heuristic value, stimulating thinking among historians, sociologists, literary people, and philosophers as well as psychoanalysts. Psychoanalysis is a good example of a science that has resisted the tenets of natural science and maintained aspects of the literary and descriptive language of everyday life (Jager, 1989).

This is not to say that these theorists ignore empirical data or shun verification of their concepts. However, they believe that a narrow scientific methodology is not appropriate for the study of personality and they urge a broader approach for the social scientist.

Their theories have not generated much laboratory research because of their lack of specificity and operational definitions. Complex concepts such as *identity* and *splitting* do not readily lend themselves to precise measurement. Longitudinal studies could provide us with information on the validity of some of their ideas, such as Erikson's concept of the developmental process and Chodorow's notion of the reproduction of mothering, but such studies are expensive and lengthy. Researchers have largely focused on other personality constructs that are easier to translate into operational terms.

Much of this work has had an enormous impact in the clinical area. As the median age of our population rises, gerontologists turn to Erikson's work for insight into the needs of our senior citizens. Further progress may be made by forging theoretical links with neurology, cognitive and developmental psychology, evolutionary theory, literature, linguistics, information and systems theory, and philosophy (Paul, 1989; Krystal, 1990). In addition, links could be forged with the Russian psychologist Vygotsky, who focused on issues such as the social origins of the intrapsychological level of functioning, the interfunctional nature of consciousness, and the need to take into account mediational needs. These ideas are very different from the individualistic underpinning of Western psychology, especially in the United States. Vygotsky believes the boundaries between individuals are much more permeable and the boundaries between individuals and the sociocultural tools they use are more difficult to preserve (Wertsch, 1990).

The current work in psychoanalysis is imaginative and creative. These theorists have helped to maintain the viability and relevance of Freudian psychoanalytic theory in the contemporary world. For all the criticism of psychoanalytically oriented theories that declares the lack of "'scientifically demonstrated' hypotheses — it is also a commonly overlooked fact that none of the modern competitive theories (cognitive, behavioral, or humanistic) have withstood similar rigid scientific tests to validate their claims to legitimacy as acceptable theories underlying the conceptualization and application of psychotherapy" (W. L. Kelly, 1991). These theorists clearly demonstrate that psychoanalysis is far from dead.

Summary

1. Ego psychologists emphasize the role of the ego, giving it a greater degree of autonomy. Anna Freud also extended the interest of psychoanalysis to the study of the child. Heinz Hartmann explored the synthesizing and integrative functions of the ego.

2. Erikson extended Freudian psychoanalysis in four ways: he increased our understanding of the ego; he elaborated on Freud's stages of development; he extended the concept of development to include the entire life span; and he explored the impact of culture, society, and history on the developing personality.

3. Erikson emphasized the adaptive qualities of the ego whereas Freud tended to emphasize defensiveness. He also described the social and historical forces that influence the ego's strengths and weaknesses, stressing its constructive rather than its repressive effects on development. He suggested that ego development reaches a climax during adolescence.

4. Erikson's **psychosocial stages** made explicit the social dimension that was implied in Freud's work. Each of Erikson's stages was established around an emotional conflict that people encounter at certain critical periods. His stages were **epigenetic,** progressing in a cumulative fashion. Each stage provided opportunities for a basic ego strength, or **virtue,** to grow.

5. **Trust versus mistrust** is the emotional duality that corresponds to Freud's oral stage. It leads to the development of *hope.* **Autonomy versus shame and doubt** marks the anal-muscular stage and culminates in *will.* The phallic stage is characterized by **initiative versus guilt.** The ego strength that emerges at this time is *purpose.* **Industry versus inferiority** is the hallmark of the latency period, whose ego strength is *competence.* Erikson subdivided the genital stage into four stages. The primary duality during adolescence is **ego identity versus role confusion.** The virtue developed at this time is *fidelity.* **Intimacy versus isolation** is characteristic of young adulthood and leads to the emergence of *love.* The middle years are characterized by a conflict of **generativity versus stagnation;** the ego strength that emerges is *care.* The final stage is marked by **ego integrity versus despair** and the ego strength is *wisdom.*

6. Erikson engaged in several studies that show how culture and history shape personality. He compared the child-rearing practices of two Native American groups, the Sioux and the Yurok. He undertook a number of biographical studies on important historical figures such as Luther and Gandhi.

7. In his discussion of sex differences, Erikson explored boys' and girls' concepts of **inner** and **outer space.**

8. Erikson developed techniques of study appropriate to his subject. There are parallels between the evidence used by a psychoanalyst and that used in a **psychohistorical** study. Each event is considered in terms of its coherence with the individual's life. Empirical research on Erikson's theory stems from Marcia's theory of adolescence, research on ethnicity and identity. Orlofsky's description of young adulthood, and research on generativity and the final years of the life span.

9. Object relations theorists look at how people develop patterns of living from their early relationships with significant others, particularly the mother. Margaret Mahler explored the processes of **separation** and **individuation** by which the child emerges from a symbiotic fusion with the mother and develops individual characteristics. She constructed a sequence of stages through which the ego passes in the process of becoming an individual.

10. Heinz Kohut accounted for **narcissism** and narcissistic character disorders that occur when an individual fails to develop an independent sense of self. He has developed psychoanalytic techniques designed to work through transferences and resistances stemming from pre-oedipal phases of development.

11. Otto Kernberg introduces the notion of **splitting** to account for *borderline* individuals' interpersonal relationships and has developed a method of treat-

ment, **expressive psychoanalytically oriented psychotherapy.** More recently he has focused on aggression and suggested change to Freud's drive theory.

12. Chodorow's work differs from traditional psychoanalytic theory because she places gender identity explicitly in the framework of the divergence of labor by sex in the workplace and the family.

13. Chodorow believes that mothering by women reproduces cyclically, producing daughters with the desire and capacity to mother but sons whose nurturing abilities are limited and repressed.

14. Chodorow believes that the family structure needs to be transformed so that primary parenting is shared between men and women.

15. More recent psychoanalytic theorists do not insist on a simply scientific pretense for their work. Some have explicit philosophical assumptions. They include many variables in their discussion, believing that a narrow scientific methodology is not appropriate for the study of personality. Their work has had an enormous impact in the clinical area.

Suggestions for Further Reading

Anna Freud's significant books and papers have been collected into a seven-volume set, *The Writings of Anna Freud* (International Universities Press, 1965–1974). Heinz Hartmann's classic work is *Ego Psychology and the Problems of Adaption* (International Universities Press, 1958). His later papers are found in *Essays in Ego Psychology* (International Universities Press, 1964).

Erik H. Erikson's books are very readable. His first and most important book is *Childhood and Society* (Norton, 1950; 2nd ed. revised and enlarged, 1963). It describes different forms of child rearing among the Sioux and Yurok, introduces his eight psychosocial stages of development, and discusses the growth of the ego and evolution of identity. *Insight and Responsibility* (Norton, 1964) discusses Erikson's concept of the ethical implications of psychoanalysis and introduces his idea of ego strengths. The term "identity crisis" is most associated with *Identity, Youth, and Crisis* (Norton, 1968) in which he re-evaluated his theory of identity in the light of historical change. Erikson's well-known psycho-historical studies are *Young Man Luther* and *Gandhi's Truth* (Norton, 1958 and 1969), a method of research that he clarified in *Life History and the Historical Moment* (Norton, 1975). Comments on sexual differences can be found in essays throughout his writings. In particular, "The Inner Space" in *Childhood and Society* and "The Inner Space Revisited" in *Life History and the Historical Moment* are recommended.

Many of the writings of object relations theorists, especially Otto Kernberg, are difficult reading, but they are well worth study by the serious student. The best introduction to Margaret Mahler's work is *The Psychological Birth of the Human Infant* (Basic Books, 1975). Heinz Kohut's position is stated in *The*

Restoration of the Self (International Universities Press, 1977). Kohut also wrote *How Does Analysis Cure?* (University of Chicago Press, 1984).

Otto Kernberg's titles are quite forthright descriptions of the contents. He has written *Borderline Conditions and Pathological Narcissism* (Jason Aronson, 1975), *Internal World and External Reality* (Jason Aronson, 1980), *Psychodynamic Psychotherapy of Borderline Patients* (Basic Books, 1989), and *Aggression in Personality Disorders and Perversions* (Yale University Press, 1992). Perhaps most readable is his article " 'Mythological Encounters' in the Psychoanalytic Situation," published in Hartocollis and Graham, eds., *The Personal Myth in Psychoanalytic Theory.*

Nancy Chodorow's doctoral dissertation became *The Reproduction of Mothering* (University of California Press, 1978). She has also written *Feminism and Psychoanalytic Theory* (Yale University Press, 1989).

PART 4

Behavior and Learning Theories

One of the most puzzling questions in personality theorizing has been the dichotomy between internal and external determinants of behavior. Is behavior caused by inner predispositions or tendencies that lead a person to act in a certain way or is it caused by the situation in which one finds oneself? A dominant trend in American psychology has been the behaviorist movement with its emphasis on learning and experience as the primary forces that shape behavior. Rather than postulate complex personality structures and dynamics within the individual, behavior and learning theories focus on those factors in the environment that determine an individual's conduct. However the either/or nature of this debate has been mitigated in light of more recent trait and temperament positions in which a combination of both biology and society, as well as other factors, is involved.

Most behavior and learning theories begin in the psychological laboratory where infrahuman (lower-than-human) species, such as rats or pigeons, are studied. Theoretical speculation is avoided in favor of careful observation and experimentation. Behavior theorists have been increasingly committed to a rigorous methodology, trying to perfect the techniques of psychology and raise them to the sophistication of the natural sciences. This has permitted precision and economy in theory construction as well as clear empirical foundations for the major concepts of their theories. Part 4 presents major contributions to the behavior and learning approach to personality theory and shows their outstanding influence.

C H A P T E R   8

John Dollard, Neal Miller, and B. F. Skinner

1. Describe how behavior and learning theorists study personality experimentally.
2. Identify the early contributions of Pavlov, Watson, Thorndike, and Hull.
3. Define and give examples of *habits, drives,* and *reinforcers.*
4. Describe the four main conceptual parts of the learning process.
5. Discuss findings from research into the learning process.
6. Explain how Dollard and Miller have integrated learning theory and psychoanalysis.
7. Describe Dollard and Miller's practice of psychotherapy.
8. Evaluate Dollard and Miller's theory in terms of its function as philosophy, science, and art.
9. Explain why Skinner emphasizes overt behavior and avoids developing a theory of personality.
10. Describe the process of operant conditioning, and compare it with classical conditioning.
11. Distinguish among different schedules and types of *reinforcement* and indicate their effectiveness.
12. Discuss Skinner's concept of *behavior modification* and explain how it has been successfully employed.
13. Describe Skinner's concept of a utopian society.
14. Show how Skinner's position includes philosophical assumptions as well as scientific statements.
15. Evaluate Skinner's theory in terms of its function as philosophy, science, and art.

John Dollard, Neal Miller, and Burrhus Frederick Skinner are behavior and learning theorists who emphasize experience and learning as the primary forces that shape human behavior. Dollard and Miller's orientation has been called *psychoanalytic learning theory* because it is a creative attempt to bring together the basic concepts of Freudian psychoanalytic theory with the ideas, language, methods, and results of experimental laboratory research on learning and behavior. Skinner espouses a point of view now known as *radical behaviorism*. Believing that a stimulus-response theory of psychology can account for all of the overt behaviors that psychologists seek to explain, Skinner omits the psychoanalytic underpinnings and simply relies on behaviorist principles. In doing so, he suggests that the term "personality" and personality theories are superfluous. However, his work includes points of interest to students of personality and has had an impact on subsequent developments in the field. Thus, Skinner is typically included in books on personality theories.

Dollard and Miller's and Skinner's views on personality stem from experimental and laboratory procedures rather than clinical investigations. However, the principles that they have developed have been widely applied in areas such as education, psychotherapy, industry, and corrections.

John Dollard and Neal Miller: Biographical Background

John Dollard and Neal Miller were both born in Wisconsin. They taught and worked together at the Institute of Human Relations at Yale University, which was founded in 1933 in an effort to explore the interdisciplinary relationships among psychology, psychiatry, sociology, and anthropology. Dollard and Miller's joint efforts resulted in a personality theory based on Clark Hull's reinforcement theory of learning and Freud's psychoanalytic theory. This integration resulted in a behaviorist theory that became representative of the mainstream of American psychology throughout most of the twentieth century.

John Dollard, born in 1900, was granted the A.B. from the University of Wisconsin and the M.A. and Ph.D. from the University of Chicago. His primary interests were in sociology and anthropology and he was a strong advocate of interdisciplinary studies. Neal Miller, born in 1909, was granted the B.S. from the University of Washington, the M.A. from Stanford, and the Ph.D. from Yale. His primary interests lay in experimental psychology. Both men underwent psychoanalytic training, each held a number of significant positions, and each authored several books or articles, in addition to their affiliation and collaboration at the Institute of Human Relations.

John Dollard died in New Haven, Connecticut, in 1980. Neal Miller spent more than twenty years at Rockefeller University, and since 1985, has been a research affiliate in the psychology department at Yale University.

John Dollard   *Neal Miller*

The Experimental Analysis of Behavior

Before discussing the work of Dollard and Miller, it will be useful to take a brief look at some of the origins of the experimental analysis of behavior.

Behavior and learning theories have their roots in a philosophical point of view known as **empiricism**, which suggests that all knowledge originates in experience. John Locke (1632–1704), one of the first empiricist philosophers, suggested that at birth the mind is a blank slate on which sensory experience writes in a number of different ways. Locke's phrase "blank slate" (or tabula rasa) expressed the philosophical view of empiricism in its classic form just as Descartes's "I think, therefore I am" expressed the essence of rationalism.

Behavior and learning theories hold that valid knowledge arises out of experience and needs to be continually checked against it. Thus, behavior and learning theories are largely based on the experimental analysis of behavior. The behavior of individual organisms is carefully studied in controlled laboratory settings and the relationship between the behavior and factors in that environment is articulated.

Although behavioral theory is singularly American, the historical background of the approach begins in Russia where Ivan Pavlov (1849–1936) demonstrated and articulated a form of learning known as *classical conditioning.* In a classic laboratory situation, Pavlov took a hungry dog and presented it with food, an *unconditioned stimulus* that normally elicits salivation, an *unconditioned,* or *automatic, response.* Then he simultaneously paired the food with the sound of a bell, a *neutral stimulus* that does not normally elicit salivation. The dog salivated to the paired food and sound of the bell. After several presentations of both food and bell, Pavlov was able simply to present the sound of the bell, and the dog salivated. The sound of the bell had become a *conditioned stimulus* that elicited a *conditioned response.* In other words, Pavlov showed that by pairing an unconditioned stimulus with a neutral stimulus, he could elicit a response that previously would have been elicited only by the original stimulus.

John Watson (1878–1958), the father of American behaviorism, expanded classical conditioning into a theory of behaviorism in which he recommended that psychology emphasize the study of overt rather than covert behavior. Watson's point of view was quickly adopted by many American psychologists. The behaviorist movement became the dominant movement in psychology in America. Even today, the distinctive methodology of American psychology reflects Watson's emphasis on objectivity and extrospection.

Another figure in the history of learning theory is Edwin Thorndike (1874–1949). Thorndike conducted several experiments with animals in order to gain further understanding of the learning process. He formulated many important laws of learning. The law that is particularly important for our purposes is the **law of effect**, which states that when a behavior or performance is accompanied by satisfaction, it tends to happen again. If the performance is accompanied by frustration, it tends to decrease. We now recognize that the law of effect is not necessarily universal. Sometimes frustration leads to increased efforts to perform. Still, most psychologists believe that the law of effect is generally true.

A final figure to consider is Clark Hull (1884–1952), whose systematic theory of learning based on the concept of drive reduction will be discussed shortly, as it directly influenced the development of Dollard and Miller's theory of personality.

Habits, Drives, and the Learning Process

Dollard and Miller emphasize the role of learning in personality and place less stress on personality structure. They suggest (1950) that the structure of personality can be defined very simply as habits.

Habits refer to some kind of learned association between a stimulus and response that makes them occur together frequently. Habits represent a temporary structure because they can appear and disappear; because they are learned, they can also be unlearned. This is a much simpler concept of the structure of personality than we have encountered before. The primary concern of Dollard and Miller's theory is to specify those conditions in the environment that encourage the acquisition of habits.

The primary dynamic underlying personality development and the acquisition of habits is **drive reduction** (1950). Dollard and Miller drew heavily on Clark Hull's systematic theory of learning based on the concept of drive reduction. A **drive** is a strong stimulation that produces discomfort, such as hunger. Hull believed that learning occurs only if a response of an organism is followed by the reduction of some need or drive. The infant learns to suck the breast or a bottle of milk in order to relieve hunger. If sucking the breast or bottle did not result in some drive or need reduction, the infant would not continue to perform that activity. Dollard and Miller point out that reducing a drive is reinforcing to an individual, and thus an individual will behave in ways that relieve the tension created by strong drives.

Primary drives are those associated with physiological processes that are necessary for an organism's survival, such as the drives of hunger, thirst, and the need for sleep. We rarely observe primary drives in a direct form because society has developed some means of reducing the drive before it becomes overwhelming. Thus, primary drives, by and large, are satisfied through secondary drives. **Secondary drives** are learned on the basis of primary ones. Dollard and Miller consider them to be elaborations of the primary drives. An example of a secondary drive is being motivated to eat at 6:30 P.M., or one's usual dinner hour. Other secondary drives are wanting to earn money in order to buy food, and satisfying other drives of physical comfort in the normal mode of one's culture.

Dollard and Miller also distinguish between primary and secondary reinforcers. A **reinforcer** is any event that increases the likelihood of a particular response. **Primary reinforcers** are those that reduce primary drives, such as food, water, or need for sleep. **Secondary reinforcers** are originally neutral but they acquire reward value on the basis of having been associated with primary reinforcers. Money is a secondary reinforcer because you can use it to buy food. A mother's smile or a word of praise is also a secondary reinforcer, associated with a state of physical well-being.

We acquire habits and develop specific behavioral responses through the process of learning. As infants each of us begins life with the basic equipment needed to reduce our primary drives: reflex responses and an innate hierarchy of response. **Reflex** responses are automatic responses to specific stimuli. All of us blink automatically to avoid an irritant to the eye or sneeze to eliminate an irritant to the nose. Such reflexes are important for our survival. **Hierarchy of response** refers to a tendency for certain responses to occur before others. For example, an animal runs to avoid a shock rather than cringe and bear it in pain. If a response is unsuccessful, however, an organism will try the next response in the hierarchy. Learning, in part, involves reinforcing and/or rearranging the response hierarchy.

Dollard and Miller (1950) suggest that the learning process can be broken down into four main conceptual parts (see Figure 8.1):

A **drive**, as we have already seen, is a stimulus impelling a person to act, but in no way does the drive direct or specify behavior. It simply impels.

A **cue** refers to a specific stimulus that tells the organism when, where, and how to respond. The yellow arches of McDonalds may act as a cue directing us to stop and get something to eat. The ringing of a bell or the time on a clock is a cue to students to enter or leave the classroom.

A **response** is one's reaction to the cue. Because these responses occur in a hierarchy, we can rank a response according to its probability of occurring. But this innate hierarchy can be changed through learning.

Reinforcement refers to the effect of the response. Effective reinforcement consists of drive reduction. If a response is not reinforced by satisfying a drive, it will undergo extinction. Extinction does not eliminate a response but merely inhibits it, enabling another response to grow stronger and supersede it in the response hierarchy. If present responses are not reinforcing, the individual is placed in a **learning dilemma** and will try different responses until one is developed that satisfies the drive.

Dollard and Miller suggest that all human behavior can be comprehended in terms of the learning process. It is through the learning process that one acquires secondary drives. These drives may form a very complex system, but the underlying process by which they are developed is essentially the same: drive,

Figure 8.1   *A Simple Diagram of the Learning Process*
The circular nature of learning is illustrated below, whereby one *wants* something (DRIVE), *notices* something (CUE), *does* something (RESPONSE), and *gets* something (REINFORCEMENT).

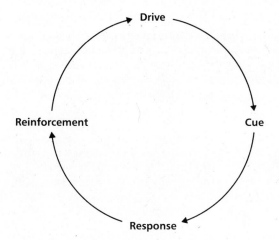

cue, response, reinforcement. Even our higher mental processes can be understood in terms of the learning process. A chain of thought simply involves an internalized process of drive, cue, response, reinforcement, in which one thought serves as a cue for the next thought and so forth.

Frustration and Conflict

Dollard and Miller have conducted extensive experimental studies on different aspects of the learning process. A number of these studies have been in the area of responses to frustration and conflict (Miller, 1944, 1951, 1959). **Frustration** occurs when one is unable to reduce a drive because the response that would satisfy it has been blocked. For example, the child who is not permitted to take a cookie from the cookie jar is frustrated. If the frustration arises from a situation in which incompatible responses are occurring at the same time, the situation is described as one of **conflict.** Dollard and Miller used Kurt Lewin's (1890–1947) concept of approach and avoidance tendencies to distinguish among several different types of conflict in which an individual seeks to approach or avoid one or more goals. They developed ways of graphically presenting different types of conflict and of plotting the strengths of various forces

THINKING CRITICALLY

The Learning Process

The four steps in the learning process as outlined by Dollard and Miller can be fruitfully used to help us understand some of our own habits and frequent responses. Choose a habit that you engage in frequently. Remember that "habit" simply means a learned association between a stimulus and a response. The habit may be positive, such as locking your car when it is parked in a questionable neighborhood, or negative, such as overeating. What are the basic underlying primary and subsequent secondary drives that your behavior seeks to fulfill? What are the specific cues that trigger your response? What are the consequences of your behavior that reinforce the habit? Such an analysis may assist you in discriminating between cues that trigger specific behaviors and reinforcements that strengthen them.

You might also wish to discuss the four steps in the learning process with someone from another culture or background to see if it applies equally as well.

involved in them. Thus, the child who is required to choose between two attractive objects, a toy and a bar of candy, can be diagrammed as follows:

with a circle representing the child and plus signs representing each desired goal. (An undesired goal would be represented by a minus sign.) The arrows indicate that there are forces moving the child in the direction of the goals (or away from them). The intensity of the force varies as the child moves closer to or further from each goal.

The value of these graphic presentations lies in the fact that if we could measure the complex forces that impel human behavior and if we could develop formulas that encompass all of the variables involved, we could also predict a person's actions in reference to a particular goal. Human situations are so complex that such prediction is not possible at present. But Dollard and Miller's experiments with infrahuman species have shown that we can be quite successful in predicting the behavior of simple laboratory animals under controlled conditions.

Conflicts, in brief, result from some sort of opposition between our tendencies to approach or avoid certain objects and goals. Dollard and Miller

Figure 8.2 *Diagramming Conflicts*
The conflicts that Dollard and Miller describe may be diagrammed simply as shown here.

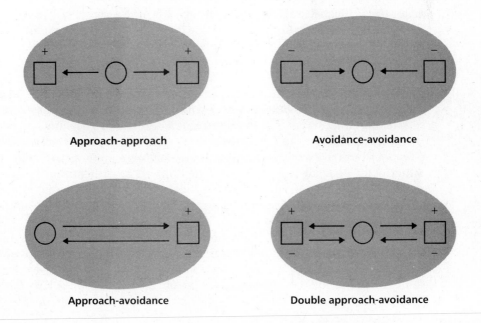

distinguish among several different types of conflict. In an *approach-approach conflict,* the individual is simultaneously attracted to two goals that have positive value but are incompatible. (You are in love with two people at once and are forced to make a choice.) In an *avoidance-avoidance conflict,* a person faces two undesirable alternatives. (The hot plate is burning your hands but if you drop it you will spill the food.) In an *approach-avoidance conflict,* one goal both attracts and repels the individual. (Your date is both attractive and obnoxious.) These conflicts may be diagrammed simply, as is shown in Figure 8.2. In everyday life, of course, the situation is seldom so simple. Therefore, it is often necessary to consider compounded situations of conflict, such as a *double approach-avoidance conflict,* in which an individual must deal simultaneously with multiple goals that both attract and repel.

The Integration of Learning Theory and Psychoanalysis

In their attempt to integrate learning theory and psychoanalysis, Dollard and Miller adapted many Freudian concepts and reconceived them in learning theory terms. They appreciate the importance of unconscious forces underlying human behavior but they redefine the concept of *unconscious processes* in terms of their own theory.

There are two main determinants of unconscious processes. First, we are unaware of certain drives or cues because they are *unlabeled.* These drives and cues may have occurred before we learned to speak and therefore we were unable to label them. Other cues may be unconscious, because a society has not given them adequate labels. In our society, we have essentially one word for snow, although we might further describe it as dry or slushy. In certain Eskimo cultures, there are thirty or more different words for the various textures of snow. Such a society is certainly much more aware of the different variations in snow than we are. Distortions in labeling may also affect one's conscious perception. Through distorted labeling, an emotion such as fear may become confused with another emotion, such as guilt. Thus, an individual may react in frightening situations as if guilty because of a distortion in labeling.

Second, unconscious processes refer to cues or responses that once were conscious but have been repressed because they were ineffective. Dollard and Miller point out that repression is learned like all other behaviors. When we repress, we do not think about certain thoughts or label them because they are unpleasant. Avoiding these thoughts reduces the drive by reducing the unpleasant experience.

Dollard and Miller also articulate many of the other defense mechanisms that Freud outlined: projection, identification, reaction formation, rationalization, and displacement. In each case, however, they are seen as learned responses or behaviors and they are articulated in terms of learning. For example, identification entails imitating the behavior that one has learned from another.

Displacement is explained in terms of generalization and the inability to make proper discriminations.

Dollard and Miller posit four critical training stages in child development: the feeding situation in infancy, cleanliness training, early sex training, and the training for control of anger and aggression. These are critical training stages in the child's development in which social conditions of learning imposed by the parents may have enormous consequences for future development. The parallel to Freud's stages is obvious. The conflict situation of feeding in infancy is reminiscent of Freud's oral stage, cleanliness training is reminiscent of Freud's anal stage, and early sex training as well as the effort to control anger and aggression are elements of Freud's phallic stage. Dollard and Miller agree with Freud that events in early childhood are vitally important in shaping later behavior. Further, they suggest that the logic of these events may be comprehended within the learning process as they have outlined it. Whereas Freud's stages unfold biologically, the outcomes of Dollard and Miller's stages are controlled by learning. Thus, the infant whose cry when hungry brings immediate relief in the sense of being fed learns that self-generated activity is effective in reducing drives. The infant left to "cry it out," may learn that there is nothing self-generated that can be done to reduce the drive and begin to develop a passive attitude toward drive reduction. Thus, in their incorporation of Freud's theories, Dollard and Miller reconsidered and elaborated his ideas in the light of learning theory principles.

It was easy to merge Freud's and Hull's theories because both of them are based on drive reduction and share the common feature of determinism. Dollard and Miller's work helps us to appreciate the role of learning in the development of defenses and other psychoanalytic structures. However, there are significant differences between Freud's concepts and Dollard and Miller's articulation of them, so that the translation is not exact. For example, whereas for Freud anxiety, conflict, and repression are inevitable aspects of the human condition, for Dollard and Miller they are simply learned responses. Nevertheless, by transforming Freud's concepts into the terms of learning theory and experimental psychology, Dollard and Miller rendered Freud more palatable to a large number of people. It is less threatening to believe that unconscious processes and defense mechanisms are learned and may therefore be unlearned than to conceive of them as largely universal and inescapable. In Freud's view, one could merely try to recognize them in order to cope with them more effectively. In addition, Dollard and Miller's work stimulated a great deal of scientific research and experimental testing of Freud's concepts.

Psychotherapy

We have seen that for Dollard and Miller behavior is learned in the process of seeking to reduce drives. Deviant behavior is also learned, but in the neurotic the behaviors that have been learned are frequently self-defeating and unproductive. Dollard and Miller (1950) refer to neurosis as a **stupidity-misery syndrome.** The patient has strong, unconscious, and unlabeled emotional conflicts. The neurotic has not labeled the problem and therefore does not discriminate effectively, generalizing and applying old, ineffective solutions to current problems and situations. A young man whose father was a tyrant may have learned in early childhood that he had to react meekly in order to avoid his father's wrath. Unable to discriminate between his father's attitude and the attitude of other authority figures in his life, the young man may generalize his response to his father to later authority figures who in fact are not tyrants. In such situations, his meek response may not be the most appropriate one. Dollard and Miller (1950) suggest that "neurotic conflicts are taught by parents and learned by children."

Therapy involves unlearning old, ineffective, unproductive habits and substituting new, more adaptive, and productive responses. Dollard and Miller (1950) refer to two phases in therapy. In the **talking phase,** neurotic habits are studied, examined, and identified so the patient may unlearn them. Essentially, this procedure entails providing appropriate labels for the patient's responses. When we label a repression appropriately, the repression is lifted because we have erased the distortion. You may recall the fairy tale of Rumpelstiltskin, who loses his demonic powers once he is confronted with his name. When the repressions are correctly identified and labeled for what they are, their power to harm the individual disappears.

The second phase of therapy is the **performance phase.** During this phase, the patient acquires new, more adaptive and productive responses and habits and is encouraged to apply them. Training in *suppression* (the conscious, deliberate stopping of a thought or an action) can be helpful. The patient can be trained to suppress, rather than repress, thoughts or actions that reinforce old habits and at the same time, be deliberately exposed to new cues that will evoke different responses.

Dollard and Miller's theory of therapy represents a bridge to the more directive and active therapies of other learning theories such as Skinner's. It is pragmatic and action oriented. Whereas Freud thought it necessary to work through past problems for an analysis to be successful, Dollard and Miller believe that historical recollection is effective only if it is instrumental in creating change. If historical recollection is unnecessary for change to occur, it is only a short step to exclude that emphasis on the past and concentrate on the behaviors of the present as Skinner and other subsequent learning and behavioral cognitive theorists do.

Dollard and Miller's Theory: Philosophy, Science, and Art

Dollard and Miller developed their theory of personality through laboratory studies and experimentation. They try to base their statements on empirical evidence and submit theoretical differences to observational tests. They recognize, perhaps more than many other theorists, that a theory is useful according to its effectiveness in leading to predictions that can be tested. As a scientific theory, therefore, Dollard and Miller's work has been very attractive to many psychologists because of its use in validating evidence.

Empirical evidence, however, has not always given as much support to Dollard and Miller's theory as the theorists imply. What an organism can learn is limited by *species specific behavior* — complex, rather than reflex, behaviors that occur in all members of a species. Some stimuli are more relevant to a particular species than others; responses also differ. Pigeons peck, chickens scratch, and pigs root. It is difficult, if not impossible, to alter these behaviors. One cannot easily generalize from a rat to a human being.

As we have seen, Dollard and Miller have rendered many psychoanalytic concepts into the constructs of a scientific theory. Many consider this a substantial contribution to the viability of Freud's ideas. Whether psychoanalysis has gained or lost in the process, however, is a matter of considerable debate (Rapaport, 1953). Some would point out that in the process of translation Freudian concepts have lost considerable dynamism and have been emptied of their original intent. Others suggest that Freud's in-depth clinical study of humans illuminates the dynamics of human personality far more than Dollard and Miller's research with rats does.

Ideally, if we could measure forces that impel human behavior and develop sophisticated formulas that encompass all of the variables involved, we could predict complex human behavior; the applications of such a science would be mind-boggling indeed. Dollard and Miller's theory has been quite successful in predicting the behavior of simple laboratory animals under controlled conditions. Their views have been central to the field of personality since they first published their major work, *Personality and Psychotherapy,* in 1950. They were among the first to seek to emulate a purely scientific model in understanding personality.

Dollard and Miller combine the insights of Freud's psychoanalysis with the principles of learning theory. Skinner, however, believes that the principles of learning theory can account for all of the behaviors psychologists wish to explain and relies entirely on behaviorist principles.

B. F. Skinner: Biographical Background

B. F. Skinner was born in 1904 in Susquehanna, Pennsylvania. His father was an ambitious lawyer; his mother was bright and of high moral standards. A younger brother, of whom he was fond, died suddenly at the age of sixteen. Skinner was reared in a warm, comfortable, and stable home, permeated with the virtues and ethics of small-town, middle-class America at the turn of the century. His parents did not employ physical punishments but their admonitions succeeded in teaching their son "to fear God, the police, and what people

B. F. Skinner

would think." His parents and grandparents, to whom he was close, taught him to be faithful to the puritan work imperative, to try to please God, and to look for evidence of God's favor through "success." Later, Skinner (1983b) suggested that childhood reinforcements shaped his own adult behavior.

As a child, Skinner was fascinated with machines and interested in knowing how things work. He developed a mechanical device to remind himself to hang up his pajamas, a gadget that enabled him to blow smoke rings without violating his parents' prohibition against smoking, and a flotation system to separate ripe from green elderberries. For many years he tried to design a perpetual motion machine, but it did not work.

Skinner was also interested in animal behavior. He caught and brought home the small wildlife of the woodlands in central Pennsylvania, such as snakes, lizards, and chipmunks. This interest in biology was later reflected in his training of animals.

Skinner was an excellent student. Majoring in English at Hamilton College, a small liberal arts school in upstate New York, he thought seriously of becoming a writer. He sent a few short stories to the poet Robert Frost, who encouraged him to write. He decided to take a year or two off to write, but he quickly became discouraged and decided he could not write as he "had nothing important to say." During this interlude, he read books by Ivan Pavlov and John Watson, whose work impressed him, and he decided to begin graduate studies in psychology at Harvard. He received the Ph.D. in 1931.

He taught at the University of Minnesota for nine years and was chairman of the department of psychology at Indiana University before he returned to Harvard in 1948, having established a reputation as a major experimental psychologist and having written an influential book *Walden II*, which describes a utopian society based on psychological principles.

Skinner died in 1990 after a battle with leukemia. He was 86.

A Theory of Personality Without Personality

Skinner, the leading heir of the behaviorist position, took the beliefs and concepts of Watson's behaviorist theory to their logical extreme. He concurred with Watson that it is unproductive and foolish to refer to structures of the personality that cannot be directly observed. Thus, Skinner, developed a psychology that concentrates not on the person but solely on those variables and forces in the environment that influence a person and that may be directly observed, presenting behaviorism and learning theory in its purest and most extreme form.

For Skinner the term "personality" was ultimately superfluous, as overt behavior can be completely comprehended in terms of responses to factors in the environment. The effort to understand or explain behavior in terms of internal structures such as a personality or an ego is to speak in terms of "fictions," because the terms are not very helpful. First, they are presented in such a way that they cannot be directly observed; second, it is very difficult to deduce operational definitions from them; and, last, it is virtually impossible to develop systematic and empirical means of testing them (1953; see also Moore, 1992). Instead, Skinner suggested that we concentrate on the environmental consequences that determine and maintain an individual's behavior. One can consider the person as if empty and observe how changes in the environment affect the individual's behavior.

It is also unnecessary to posit internal forces or motivational states within a person as causal factors of behavior. Skinner did not deny that such states occur: they are important by-products of behavior. He simply saw no point in using them as causal variables because they cannot be operationally defined and their intensity cannot be measured.

Rather than try to determine how hungry someone was, Skinner tried to determine what variables or forces in the environment affect an individual's eating behavior. What is the effect of the time period that has elapsed since the last meal was eaten? What are the consequences of the amount of food consumed? Such factors in the environment can be specifically defined, measured, and dealt with empirically.

Skinner also differed from other researchers in that he emphasized individual subjects. Typically, he studied each animal separately and reported his results in the form of individual records. Whereas other experimenters draw their conclusions on the basis of the performance of comparison groups as a whole, Skinner believed that the laws of behavior must apply to each and every individual subject when it is observed under the appropriate conditions. He encouraged psychology to remain within the dimensional system of natural science, suggesting that to move away from that model makes it difficult to continue to call psychology a science (1983a).

The Development of Behavior Through Learning

At birth, the human infant is simply a bundle of innate capacities but consequent behaviors can be comprehended in terms of learning. Thorndike's law of effect stated that when a behavior or performance is accompanied by satisfaction it tends to be stamped in or increased. If the performance is accompanied by frustration, it tends to decrease. Omitting Thorndike's reference to internal states, Skinner derived a very simple definition of reinforcement. A **reinforcement** is anything that increases the likelihood of a response. It is the effect of one's behavior that determines the likelihood of its occurring again. If a young child cries or whines, perhaps parental attention will follow. If the behavior results in reinforcement, chances are the child will repeat that behavior pattern. If the behavior does not result in reinforcement, that is, if the child is ignored and does not receive attention, then it is likely that the behavioral response will cease and the child will behave in alternative ways to find patterns of behavior that are reinforced.

Operant Conditioning

Skinner (1938) distinguished between two types of behavior: respondent and operant. **Respondent behavior** refers to reflexes or automatic responses that are elicited by stimuli. A beam of light causes the pupil of one's eye to contract. Tapping the knee on the right spot makes the leg jerk forward. When our fingers touch hot metal, we reflexively pull our hand away. Such behaviors are unlearned: they occur involuntarily and automatically.

Respondent behaviors may, however, be conditioned or changed through learning. Respondent behaviors were involved in Pavlov's demonstration of classical conditioning. Pavlov's dog learned to salivate to the tone of a bell. An infant learns to suck at a nipple. These are reflexes or automatic responses that have come to be performed in the presence of the previously neutral stimulus through the process of association.

Operant behaviors are responses emitted without a stimulus necessarily being present. They occur spontaneously. Not all of a newborn's movements are reflex responses. Some of them are operant behaviors in which the infant acts on the environment. An infant swings an arm or moves a leg and certain consequences follow. These consequences determine whether or not the response will be repeated. Skinner believed that the process of *operant conditioning* is of far greater significance than simple classical conditioning. Many of our behaviors cannot be accounted for in terms of classical conditioning. Rather, they are originally spontaneous behaviors whose consequences determine their subsequent frequency.

There is a clear distinction between the nature of a respondent behavior and an operant behavior. A respondent behavior is evoked or elicited by a stimulus. Operant behavior is emitted or freely made by the organism. The nature of reinforcement also differs. In classical conditioning, the stimulus is the reinforcement and it precedes the behavior. In operant conditioning, the effect of the behavior is the reinforcement. Thus, in operant conditioning the reinforcement follows the behavior.

Operant conditioning can be systematically described by depicting the behavior of a rat in an operant conditioning apparatus, a piece of laboratory equipment that Skinner designed in order to train animals and conduct research. Commonly known as a "Skinner box," the apparatus makes possible controlled and precise study of animal behavior.

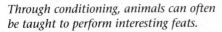

Through conditioning, animals can often be taught to perform interesting feats.

When a food-deprived rat is first placed within the box, it may behave in a variety of random ways. The rat may first walk around the box and explore it. Later, it may scratch itself or urinate. In the course of its activity the rat may at some point press a bar on the wall of the box. The bar pressing causes a food pellet to drop into a trough under the bar. The rat's behavior has had an effect on the environment. The food acts as a reinforcement, increasing the likelihood of that behavior occurring again. When it occurs again it is reinforced. Eventually, the rat begins to press the bar in rapid succession, pausing only long enough to eat the food.

When a food-deprived rat is conditioned in a Skinner box to press a bar and is reinforced for that behavior with food, we can predict pretty accurately what the rat is going to do in subsequent sessions in the Skinner box. Furthermore, we can control the rat's behavior by changing the reinforcement. When the desired behavior occurs, it is reinforced. Appropriate reinforcement increases the likelihood of that behavior occurring again.

Shaping

Frequently the behavior that one wishes to train an organism to perform is a complex, sophisticated one that the organism would not naturally be expected to do shortly after entering the box. Suppose you wished to train a pigeon to peck at a small black dot inside a white circle. If you were to wait until that behavior spontaneously occurred, you might wait a very long time. Therefore, Skinner employed a procedure termed **shaping**, in which he deliberately shaped or molded the organism's behavior in order to achieve the desired behavior.

Initially, the pigeon moves randomly about the box. When it moves in the direction of the circle, it is reinforced by a pellet of food in the trough below the circle. The next time it approaches the circle, it is again reinforced. Later, it is required to approach the circle more closely before it is reinforced. Later still, it is not reinforced until it pecks the white circle. Finally, the pigeon is reinforced only for pecking at the small black dot within the circle.

Through shaping, Skinner was able to induce animals to perform unique and remarkable feats; he taught pigeons how to play Ping-Pong and to guide missiles to their target. His pigeons never actually were put to work guiding missiles, but Skinner showed that it was possible for them to do so. Using behavioral-shaping methods, other animal trainers have been able to produce unusual tricks and feats.

Skinner believed that most animal and human behavior is learned through operant conditioning. The process of learning to speak one's native tongue involves reinforcing and shaping of operant behavior. The young infant emits certain spontaneous sounds. These are not limited to the sounds of its native tongue but represent all possible languages. Initially, the infant is reinforced for simply babbling. Later, the child is reinforced for making sounds that approximate meaningful words. Eventually the child is reinforced only for meaningful

THINKING CRITICALLY

Classical and Operant Conditioning in Your Life

You have learned many things through classical and operant conditioning. Through the process of association you have probably learned to pair a wide variety of objects with events that give meaning to your life and influence your behavior. Can you identify some incidents of classical conditioning in your life? For example, one of my students is claustrophobic, afraid of being in small, enclosed places. As a young child she made the mistake of playing in a discarded refrigerator. Fortunately, she was rescued in time, but the incident had a lasting impact on her life. Similarly, many of us have distinct preferences for or aversions to certain things. As a young child, I enjoyed sitting next to my father as he played the piano and we sang together. To this day, I find particular enjoyment in a song fest around a piano.

Operant conditioning is even more important in our lives than simple classical conditioning. Many of our behaviors involve complex shaped responses such as tying our shoes, rolling up a back pack, or playing a musical instrument. Think of the relationship between a parent and a child. Describe some ways in which a parent might reward a child for appropriate behaviors. What are some of the ways in which parents encourage children to learn to walk, talk, and perform well in school? Consider some of the behaviors that you perform because you find them reinforcing and identify those that you have learned through operant conditioning. Can you also identify ways in which people from other cultures and societies shape their children? These deliberations should help you to recognize the pervasive importance of classical and operant conditioning in our lives.

speech. Skinner (1986) suggested that verbal behavior evolved from signaling, imitating, and other nonverbal behaviors, following the rules of contingencies of reinforcement. Thus, the process of shaping is involved in learning to speak, as well as many other human behaviors.

Schedules and Types of Reinforcement

A practical necessity led Skinner to explore the effect of different *schedules of reinforcement*. In the 1930s, commercially made food pellets were not available. Skinner and his students found that it was a laborious, time-consuming process to make the eight hundred or more food pellets a day that were necessary to sustain his research. Skinner wondered what the effect would be if the animal was not reinforced every time it performed the desired behavior. This question led to the investigation of various schedules of reinforcement.

Skinner (1969) described three schedules of reinforcement and indicates their effectiveness. In **continuous reinforcement**, the desired behavior is reinforced each time that it occurs. A continuous schedule of reinforcement is extremely effective in initially developing and strengthening a behavior. However, if the reinforcement is stopped, the response quickly disappears or undergoes extinction.

In **interval reinforcement**, the organism is reinforced after a certain time period has elapsed, regardless of the response rate. Interval reinforcement may be given on a fixed or a variable basis. If it is *fixed,* the same time period elapses each time (such as five minutes). If it is *variable,* the time periods may differ in length. This type of reinforcement schedule occurs frequently in the everyday world. Employees are paid at the end of each week. Students are given grades at certain intervals within the year. In each of these cases, the reinforcement is independent of the rate of the individual organism's performance. Interval reinforcement produces a level of response that is more difficult to extinguish than responses that have been continuously reinforced. However, the level of response tends to be lower than the level produced by other kinds of schedule.

In **ratio reinforcement**, reinforcement is determined by the number of appropriate responses that the organism emits. A factory worker may be paid according to the number of pieces that he or she completes. Ratio schedules of reinforcement may also be fixed or variable. If they are *fixed,* the number of responses required prior to reinforcement is stable and the same each time. If they are *variable,* the number of appropriate operant behaviors that must occur prior to reinforcement changes from time to time. Whereas a continuous schedule of reinforcement is most effective for initially developing and strengthening a behavior, a variable ratio schedule is most effective thereafter in maintaining it. Responses maintained under the conditions of variable ratio reinforcement are highly resistant to extinction and less likely to disappear. Gambling casinos have learned this lesson well. Their use of the principle of variable ratio schedules keeps many a gambler at the table long after the money allotted for gambling has disappeared.

Where reinforcement is haphazard or accidental, the behavior that immediately preceded the reinforcement may be increased even if it is not the desired behavior. Athletes often engage in personal rituals before positioning themselves for play because of an earlier fortuitous connection between that behavior and success. Such behaviors are *superstitious,* yet many ineffective habits and common superstitions have their origin in chance reinforcement. Some of these behaviors are culturally transmitted and reinforced. Now that research has confirmed the effects of various types of reinforcement, we can systematically apply effective schedules of reinforcement to shape desired behavior.

In addition to primary and secondary reinforcers, Skinner (1953) described the effects of **generalized conditioned reinforcers** such as praise and affection, which are learned and have the power to reinforce a great number of different behaviors. Moreover, they can be self-given. As we grow older, we move from primary reinforcers to more generalized types. Initially, young children will respond to food or something that meets their basic needs. Later, they respond to an allowance. At the same time, they associate these reinforcers with the praise and affection that accompany them. Eventually, children will work primarily for the reinforcement of praise, which can be self-given.

Skinner (1972) distinguished positive reinforcement, punishment, and negative reinforcement. *Positive reinforcement* occurs when a behavior is followed by a situation that increases the likelihood of that behavior occurring in the future. *Negative reinforcement* comes about when a behavior is followed by the *termination of an unpleasant situation,* increasing the likelihood of that behavior in similar situations. Taking an aspirin is negatively reinforcing because it relieves a headache. *Punishment* occurs when a behavior is followed by an unpleasant situation designed to *eliminate* it.

Skinner (1953) observed that punishment is the most common technique of behavioral control in our society. Children are spanked if they misbehave and lawbreakers are fined or imprisoned. Punishment may stop or block a behavior but it does not necessarily eliminate it. The organism may seek other means of acquiring the same ends. Punishment creates fear but, if the fear is diminished, the behavior will recur. It can also lead to undesired side effects: anger, hatred, or helplessness.

Skinner (1953, 1971) suggested the use of methods other than those based on aversive stimuli to eliminate behaviors that are not desired. One may ignore the behavior until it undergoes extinction or one may permit satiation to occur. **Satiation** entails permitting the behavior to occur until the individual tires of it. A child may be allowed to turn a light switch on and off until she becomes bored. One may also change the environment that provokes the behavior. Fragile objects may be placed out of a young child's reach. Finally, one can promote behaviors that counteract and inhibit the undesirable behaviors through positive reinforcement.

Skinner emphasized that positive reinforcement is most effective in initiating and maintaining desired behaviors. All too often we do not recognize how we inadvertently give positive reinforcement to a behavior that is not desirable. The child who is seeking attention may be *positively* reinforced by a parental scolding because the scolding affords the child attention. By identifying our reinforcement patterns, we can strengthen those that are most effective and develop more efficient means of controlling behavior.

Psychotherapy and Behavioral Change

Skinner explained maladaptive or neurotic behavior in terms of environmental contingencies that sustain and maintain it. The neurotic or psychotic has been conditioned by the environment to behave in inappropriate ways. If we wish to change an individual's behavior, we can restructure the environment in such a way that it will no longer sustain maladaptive behavior and it will reinforce desirable behavior. Thus, in describing neurosis, Skinner did not find it necessary to refer to explanatory fictions, such as repression or conflict because maladaptive behavior can simply be reduced to the variables in the environment that reinforce and sustain it.

The role of therapy is to identify the behaviors that are maladaptive, remove them, and substitute more adaptive and appropriate behaviors through the process of operant conditioning. Skinner concurred with Dollard and Miller that there is no need to review the individual's past or encourage reliving it. Therapy is not dependent on self-understanding or insight. Some insight may occur, but such self-understanding is not necessary for behavioral change.

The contrast between Freud and Skinner emerges clearly in their attitudes toward therapy. As we have seen, Freud's intent was primarily scholarly. He sought to increase an individual's self-understanding, and psychoanalysis is relatively uninterested in specific behavioral change. Skinner's interest, on the other hand, was totally pragmatic and curative. **Behavior modification** seeks to eliminate undesired behaviors by changing the environment within which they occur.

Skinner's approach to behavior modification has been notably successful in areas where traditional insight therapy has failed or is inappropriate. One of its more spectacular successes has been with mute individuals, who for obvious reasons are not amenable to traditional therapies, which are largely based on talking. Dr. O. I. Lovaas (1966) has used a systematic program of shaping to teach autistic and mute children to speak. First, he identifies something that is reinforcing to the child. Since food is generally reinforcing for children, it is commonly employed. Initially, Lovaas reinforces the child with a small piece of food every time he or she makes a sound. Gradually he shapes these sounds until they approximate words. Eventually, he reinforces the child only for communicating in full sentences, and so forth. The reinforcement of food is coupled with praise and affection so that the type of reinforcement grows from primary and secondary reinforcers to generalized conditioned reinforcers that can be self-applied. These methods are also generalized to include training in other desired behaviors.

Since sustaining the newly learned behavior depends on maintaining a supportive environment, Lovaas includes parents and other significant figures in his program of behavior modification. Parents and other influential figures such as teachers are taught to systematically apply the same reinforcers to similar situations in the home or school. In this way the circle of the environment is widened to permit greater control.

Skinner's influence has also extended into many areas. With Sidney Presley, Skinner developed the *teaching machine*, a device whereby students may be taught without the need for an ever-present human instructor. Skinnerian principles also underlie numerous systems of individualized and programmed instruction. In such programs, the work is broken down into small units, each of which must be mastered before a student is permitted to proceed to the following unit. The student is virtually being shaped while mastering the material. There is immediate reinforcement in the sense of feedback to the student on correct and incorrect answers. Some computer-assisted instruction programs are based on Skinnerian principles and many suggest the need for a more systematic application of his ideas in our schools.

His methods have been employed in schools for the mentally retarded, mental institutions, and rehabilitation centers. In many of these institutions, a **token economy** has been established. The person is reinforced for appropriate behaviors by being given tokens of some kind that may subsequently be exchanged for special privileges or things. Making one's bed, getting dressed, talking to other patients, and other desirable behaviors are reinforced by tokens that can be exchanged for candy, watching TV, and other amenities that would not normally be provided. Last, Skinner's concepts and principles have been applied systematically in industrial and business settings to encourage greater productivity through a performance-improvement system based on accurate feedback and positive reinforcement. However, in the last decade in America, perhaps due to the economic recession and also the feeling that we need to be harder on crime, there has been less use of methods relying on the insights of psychological findings in all of these areas and a return to more punitive measures. That is unfortunate.

Social Utopias

Skinner's interest in the environment that shapes the individual and his bent toward a technological and reformist orientation (Smith, 1992) led quite naturally to his interest in the design of an ideal environment or a utopian society. In 1948 Skinner wrote *Walden II,* a book that described his concept of a utopia. **Walden II** was a behaviorally engineered society designed by a benevolent psychologist who employed a program of positive reinforcements. Because positive rather than aversive means were used to shape behavior, residents sought those reinforcers and willingly behaved in socially responsible and productive ways.

In 1971 Skinner wrote *Beyond Freedom and Dignity* and again argued for the creation of a behaviorally engineered society, pointing out that most major problems today — war, overpopulation, unemployment, inflation, and so forth — are caused by human behavior. What we need is a behavior technology that will enable us to cope with them. Such a technology cannot be established, however, unless we give up several cherished "fictions," such as the notions that people are responsible for their own behavior and that human beings are autonomous. For Skinner, human behavior is controlled by forces in the environment and the concept of free will is a superstition. We feel free when we are abundantly reinforced and have learned effective behaviors. The clue to our behaviors and emotional states lies within the environment rather than the individual.

In Skinner's view (1984), operant conditioning is to the origin of behavior what natural selection is to the origin of the species in Darwin's theory. Skinner's emphasis on the environment did not negate the impact of heredity, but it did stand in sharp contrast with the position taken by cognitive psychologists who suggest that certain learned behaviors are due to cognition rather than environmental variables (Smith, 1983).

In his utopian speculation, Skinner shifted from scientist to social philosopher. Presenting us with a form of social Darwinism, he suggested that "survival is the only value according to which a culture is eventually to be judged" (1971). Further, his concepts were informed by the philosophical assumption that a human being is nothing more than an organism, a bundle of behavior, shaped by his or her environment. During evolution, the environment shaped the behavior that survives in our genes. After birth, environmental conditioning shapes each one of us in this life. We need more, not less, control, Skinner argued. To his critics, he pointed out that human beings are already controlling and being controlled. The process of controlling should not be denied but rather studied and understood so that we can implement it effectively in developing the society that we want. We have the power to develop a behavioral technology. To ignore this is to run the risk not of no control but rather of continued ineffective or deleterious control.

Skinner mellowed with age and conceded that psychologists and other people do not possess the means or the motivation to implement his utopian schemes (1981). In the end, the very reasoning of behaviorism explains its lack of success. If, as behaviorism maintains, people do not initiate actions on their own but simply act in ways in which they have been conditioned, they cannot change on the basis of predictions. Problems such as pollution, energy depletion, nuclear contamination, and other environmental issues have not been dealt with effectively because they have not yet happened in sufficient extremes to reinforce behavioral change. Survival of the species may depend on our ability to use scientific forecasts to change cultural practices (1990). By then, however, it may be too late.

Skinner's Theory: Philosophy, Science, and Art

Skinner provided a great deal of experimental data and research to support his ideas. More than any other contemporary theorist, he stimulated research, undertaken to validate the concepts of behaviorism. His own work was character-

ized by the intensive study of individual subjects, primarily drawn from infrahuman species, the careful control of laboratory conditions through automated
apparatus, and an emphasis on variables easily modified by manipulating the
environment.

Skinner's concepts clearly evolved from experimental laboratory investigations and he showed tremendous respect for well-controlled data. His constructs
have been empirically tested and have held up well under the scrutiny of the
scientific method. His theory is elegant in its simplicity. It is also admirable in
its ability to predict and control behavior, particularly in infrahuman species.
Although he set out to avoid theorizing, he presented a theory of human behavior, if not a theory of personality, and even played the role of a social
philosopher.

But Skinner did not always recognize the kinds of evidence on which his
various statements are based. He frequently presented his social philosophy as
if it were an empirical science with all the appropriate validating evidence. For
example, Skinner observed that an individual may be controlled by the manipulation of the environment. This is an empirical statement that holds up under
test. However, one cannot jump from that empirical observation to the conclusion that human beings are *nothing but* organisms controlled by their environment and claim that the conclusion is simply based on validating evidence. The
conclusion entails a philosophical commitment that Skinner acknowledged
(1972).

Skinner himself went beyond the development of a scientific theory. In
designing his utopia he invoked ethical commitments. He suggested, for instance, that the value of a society lies in its ability to survive, that human beings
should give up the conceits of freedom and dignity. These are ethical considerations, not empirical ones. As such, they need to be evaluated in terms of their
adequacy as philosophy.

Skinner regretted that psychology persisted in its search for internal determinants of behaviors, suggesting that humanist psychology, the helping professions, and the recent emphasis on cognitive psychology represent three obstacles in the continued development of psychology as a science of behavior (1987,
1988). He continued to argue for psychology as an experimental science and
analysis of behavior in spite of controversy over the possible decline in the popularity of behaviorism (see Lambert, 1988; Place, 1988; Power, 1988).

Skinner's theory, as we have noted, works well in predicting and controlling
behavior, particularly the behavior of infrahuman species. It also deals effectively with human behavior when that behavior occurs under situations of
positive or negative reinforcement; in everyday terms we would say that it is
effective in dealing with human situations that are surrounded by reward
or punishment.

Skinner's theory is less successful, however, in accounting for other areas
of human behavior. For example, although there can be no question that operant conditioning, reinforcement, and shaping play a large role in the child's
acquisition of language, these concepts alone do not fully explain how the child

learns to speak (Chomsky, 1959; Hayes & Hayes, 1988). Skinner's theory does not account for the child's creative use of language. He did not tell us how it is possible for the child to come up with a new sentence never heard before. Nor do Skinner's concepts account for the meaningful errors that the child makes in learning to speak. The child who says, "I branged it home," may have never heard the verb *branged*. The error shows us that the child understands the use of the suffix *-ed* in expressing the past tense without the assistance of formal lessons in grammar.

Nor can Skinner's own behavior be comprehended solely in stimulus-response terms. Skinner asserted that all behavior is determined by the environ-

PHILOSOPHICAL ASSUMPTIONS

Examining Dollard, Miller, and Skinner

How would you rate Dollard and Miller and Skinner on each of the basic philosophical assumptions described in Chapter 1? Each basic issue was presented as a bipolar dimension along which a person's view can be placed according to the degree of agreement with one or the other extreme. Rate Dollard and Miller's views and then Skinner's views on these issues.

When you have determined where you think the theorists stand, compare your responses with those of your classmates and your instructor. You should be willing to defend your ratings, but also be prepared to change them in light of others' compelling arguments. Afterward, compare your ratings with your own position on each issue and with those of other theorists. Does this comparison help you to understand why their theories do or do not appeal to you?

Would strongly agree	Would agree	Is neutral or believes in synthesis of both views	Would agree	Would strongly agree
1	2	3	4	5

freedom
People basically have control over their own behavior and understand the motives behind their behavior.

determinism
The behavior of people is basically determined by internal or external forces over which they have little, if any, control.

ment. If that statement is true, then it must logically follow that Skinner's own statements were determined by his environment. Thus, his behavior as a theorist would have been equally open to change by manipulation of the environment, a position with which Skinner concurred.

Of all the theorists discussed in this book, Skinner and Freud have generated the most controversy and criticism. Both theories offend us because they attack our illusion that we are in full control of our behaviors. Yet their responses to the concept of our lack of self-control differ widely because of the very different philosophical assumptions that undergird their work. Freud, a pessimist, offers us hope of gaining a small margin of control over the

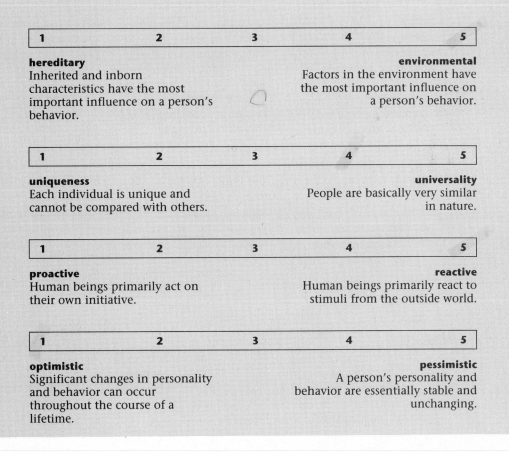

| 1 | 2 | 3 | 4 | 5 |

hereditary
Inherited and inborn characteristics have the most important influence on a person's behavior.

environmental
Factors in the environment have the most important influence on a person's behavior.

| 1 | 2 | 3 | 4 | 5 |

uniqueness
Each individual is unique and cannot be compared with others.

universality
People are basically very similar in nature.

| 1 | 2 | 3 | 4 | 5 |

proactive
Human beings primarily act on their own initiative.

reactive
Human beings primarily react to stimuli from the outside world.

| 1 | 2 | 3 | 4 | 5 |

optimistic
Significant changes in personality and behavior can occur throughout the course of a lifetime.

pessimistic
A person's personality and behavior are essentially stable and unchanging.

unconscious forces of which we have been unaware through the painful process of self-understanding. Skinner, an optimist, believes that the answer lies in recognizing our lack of control, renouncing our ambitions for inner control, and committing ourselves to being more effectively controlled by a behaviorally designed technology.

Conclusions

We have seen that Dollard and Miller developed a psychoanalytically oriented behavioral theory in which they combined the insights of Freud's psychoanalytic position with the principles of learning theory. Skinner took what he saw as the logical step that follows from Dollard and Miller's approach. If a stimulus-response theory of psychology can account for all of the overt behaviors that psychologists seek to explain, why not omit the psychoanalytic underpinnings and simply rely on behaviorist principles (Rychlak, 1973)?

The learning and behavior theories of Dollard and Miller and Skinner have strongly influenced American psychology. Throughout much of the twentieth century, the behaviorist movement was a dominant trend. Their emphasis on a rigorous scientific approach set the model for subsequent psychological investigations. However, while their theories seem to be able to account for the learned behavior of animal species and for the learned habits and simple behaviors of human beings, they are less able to explain complex human behaviors. Blackman (1991) sees contacts between Skinner's emphasis on behavior as a biological phenomenon and Mead's social behaviorism and Vgotsky's general genetic law of cultural development. Miles (1988) suggests that there are two Skinners (the pioneer who revolutionized psychology and the naive controversialist who diverts attention from the original contributions). It is not surprising that the radical nature of Skinner's theory, which took the learning and behavior theory of Dollard and Miller to a logical extreme, led to the development of an alternative approach to learning and behavior (discussed in Chapter 9), which, while emphasizing situational factors, also reintroduces covert factors such as cognition.

Summary

1. Behavior and learning theories explore personality experimentally by studying behavior in laboratory settings. Their precise methods reflect an **empirical** point of view and the careful manipulation of variables under specified controlled conditions.

2. Early behaviorists include Pavlov, who explained the process of classical conditioning, Watson, whose theory recommended an emphasis on overt behavior, Thorndike, who formulated the **law of effect,** and Hull, who clarified the concept of **drive reduction.**

3. Dollard and Miller describe the structure of personality in terms of **habits** that may be learned and unlearned. They distinguish between **primary** and **secondary drives** and **reinforcers** as the primary motivating forces of personality.

4. Human behavior can be understood in terms of the learning process, which is broken down into four main conceptual parts: **drive, cue, response,** and **reinforcement.**

5. A number of experiments have been conducted on the learning process, especially in the area of **frustration** and **conflict.** Experiments with infrahuman species have been quite successful in predicting the behavior of simple laboratory animals under controlled conditions.

6. Dollard and Miller have adapted many Freudian concepts and integrated them into learning theory terms. Unconscious processes are reconceived as unlabeled drives and cues. The defense mechanisms and critical stages of development are also reconceived in terms of the learning process. The translation, though inexact, has helped to popularize Freud and stimulate experimental study of his ideas.

7. Dollard and Miller's therapy represents a bridge to the more directive and active therapies of other learning theories. Behavior therapy involves unlearning ineffective habits and substituting more adaptive responses. During a **talking phase,** the patient learns to label responses accurately. In the **performance phase,** deliberate training in suppression is carried out.

8. Dollard and Miller's theory of personality seeks to emulate a scientific model and places a great deal of emphasis on empirical research.

9. Skinner chooses to describe variables and forces in the environment that shape overt behavior rather than to develop a theory of personality because he believes that the term "personality" and concepts of internal structure are ultimately superfluous. Behavior is best understood in terms of responses to the environment.

10. **Operant conditioning** involves reinforcing and **shaping** spontaneous responses. It differs from *classical conditioning* in terms of the nature of the behavior (which is freely made rather than elicited by a stimulus) and the nature of the **reinforcement** (which follows rather than precedes the behavior).

11. Skinner distinguishes three different schedules of reinforcement — **continuous, interval,** and **ratio reinforcement** — and describes their effectiveness. A continuous schedule is more effective for initially developing a behavior but a variable ratio schedule is more effective for maintaining it. Skinner also describes the effects of **generalized conditioned reinforcers**

and distinguishes among positive reinforcement, negative reinforcement, and punishment.

12. **Behavior modification** therapy consists of restructuring the environment so that undesired behaviors are eliminated and more desired ones substituted. Skinner's approach has been successful in situations where traditional insight methods are inapplicable. His methods have also been used in therapeutic communities, education, and industry.

13. Skinner has advocated the development of a social utopia, a behaviorally engineered society that employs a program of positive reinforcers to shape behavior.

14. In his utopian speculations, Skinner's statements reflect philosophical assumptions as well as scientific generalizations by not allowing for any exceptions and by invoking values and ethical commitments.

15. Skinner's theory clearly evolved from experimental laboratory investigations and emulates a strict scientific approach. However, Skinner has acknowledged the philosophical assumptions that underlie his theory.

Suggestions for Further Reading

For students who are interested in a historical introduction to the experimental movement in psychology, E. G. Boring, *A History of Experimental Psychology* (Appleton-Century-Crofts, 1929) is an encyclopedic survey. A classic statement of John Watson's behaviorism may be found in his book *Behaviorism* (Norton, 1925).

Dollard and Miller have jointly written two books that describe their effort to develop a theory of personality. Of primary interest is *Personality and Psychotherapy: An Analysis in Terms of Learning, Thinking, and Culture* (McGraw-Hill, 1950). In this work, the authors outline how they have applied the concepts of learning theory to reconsider many of the insights and observations of Freudian psychoanalysis. They translate Freud's theory of personality, therapeutic concepts, and procedures into learning theory terms. The book is an outstanding introduction to the learning and behavior approach to personality.

Social Learning and Imitation (Yale University Press, 1941) represents an early attempt to apply Hull's principles of learning to the study of personality. It is a good introduction to an effort to use learning theory to understand personality. Dollard and Miller have also written several articles. Some of these are cited in the References.

B. F. Skinner's most influential work is *The Behavior of Organisms* (Appleton-Century-Crofts, 1938), in which he formulates a theory of behavior in terms of the principles of conditioning. However, the lay person will probably be more interested in *About Behaviorism* (Random House, 1974), in which Skinner clarifies his position in a highly readable way. Also of interest are his utopian speculations in *Walden II* (Macmillan, 1948) and *Beyond Freedom and Dignity* (Knopf, 1971). Skinner is in the habit of writing down ideas as they occur. In twenty-five years he has filled over one hundred spiral-bound notebooks. A selection of these have been published in *Notebooks* (Prentice-Hall, 1982).

Students may also be interested in part two of Skinner's autobiography, *The Shaping of a Behaviorist* (New York University Press, 1985). An even-handed evaluation of Skinner's work is provided by Robert Nye's *The Legacy of B. F. Skinner: Concepts and Perspectives, Controversies and Misunderstandings* (Brooks/Cole, 1992).

CHAPTER 9

Albert Bandura and Julian Rotter

YOUR GOALS FOR THIS CHAPTER

1. Explain what Bandura means by *reciprocal determinism* and identify the three factors that enter into it.
2. Explain what is meant by *observational learning.*
3. Identify three factors that influence modeling.
4. Describe the four processes that enter into observational learning.
5. Discuss the role of reinforcement in observational learning and compare Bandura's concept of reinforcement with that of Skinner.
6. Discuss the controversies surrounding television film and aggression.
7. Describe Bandura's contributions to behavioral modification.
8. Evaluate Bandura's theory in terms of its function as philosophy, science, and art.
9. Identify the two major trends in personality research that Rotter's theory integrates.
10. Describe the *I-E Scale* and discuss the construct it measures and the findings to which it has led.
11. Describe the four variables that Rotter includes in his formula for predicting behavior.
12. Discuss Rotter's concepts of *need* and *minimum goal level.*
13. Discuss applications of cognitive social learning theory in the area of psychotherapy.
14. Evaluate Rotter's theory in terms of its function as philosophy, science, and art.
15. Discuss some current trends in cognitive personality theory.

nterest in a cognitive and social behavior and learning approach has grown rapidly. The theories of Albert Bandura and Julian Rotter emerged out of the behavior and learning tradition but they seek to correct some of the shortcomings of radical behaviorism. Cognitive and social behavior and learning theories reflect the careful scientific procedures and methodology that characterize the behaviorist approach. At the same time, they have broadened many original learning theory concepts and integrated them with other current movements in psychology.

These theories have also moved from very simple laboratory situations to more complex ones and have increasingly used human rather than animal subjects. Laboratory conditions have been made more similar to the everyday life of people. Some of the contingencies under investigation are very complex, but laboratory procedures have become increasingly sophisticated in order to deal with them.

Albert Bandura believes that human behavior can be explained by a reciprocal determinism that involves behavioral, cognitive, and environmental factors. His theory reflects the behavior and learning tradition's emphasis on extrospection. Nevertheless, Bandura believes that it is desirable to reintroduce internal variables, such as *self-efficacy,* a person's perception of his or her effectiveness. Julian Rotter stresses that it is the subjective meaning and interpretation of the environment that actually regulates our lives. The effectiveness of reinforcement and the decision as to what we will learn depend on internal cognitive factors. The result is two theories that seek to correct some of the flaws of earlier behavior and learning theory and combine its insights with newer findings in the area of cognition and social psychology.

Albert Bandura: Biographical Background

A small town in Alberta, Canada, was the childhood home of Albert Bandura, who was born on December 4, 1925, to wheat farmers of Polish descent. He has written little of his early years. We know that he attended a high school where there were only twenty students and two teachers. The students had largely to educate themselves, yet almost all of them went on to professional careers.

Bandura received his B.A. from the University of British Columbia in Vancouver in 1949 and his M.A. and Ph.D. from the University of Iowa in 1951 and 1952. There was a strong Hullian emphasis at Iowa, yet Bandura felt that the psychology department was very forward looking. He spent a year as a clinical intern at the Wichita (Kansas) Guidance Center and then accepted a position at Stanford University, where he has been ever since. He became a full professor in 1964 and in 1974 was awarded an endowed chair.

Bandura has been an active scholar and writer, publishing several important books and a great many articles. His first research was in collaboration with Richard Walters (1918–1967), his first Ph.D. student at Stanford. Together they authored many of the early books and articles that laid the foundation for his theory.

Albert Bandura

Bandura has received many awards for his contributions to psychology and has been a consultant to several organizations. He was elected president of the American Psychological Association in 1973. At the present time, he teaches two undergraduate seminars at Stanford on the psychology of aggression and personal and social change.

Reciprocal Determinism and the Self-System

Bandura criticizes Skinner for being too extreme in his primary emphasis on external factors. The Skinnerian explanation is incomplete and leads to a truncated view of human nature because it does not take into account internal processes that also guide behavior. On the other hand, Bandura criticizes psychoanalytic theories for using circular reasoning in attributing behavior to underlying unconscious forces. To say that hostile behavior is due to underlying aggressive impulses or domineering behavior to unconscious power motives does not tell us anything new above and beyond the fact that the behavior exists. Bandura feels that in a science of behavior such constructs are not very helpful. They do not permit us to predict how a person will behave in a given situation, nor do they account for the wide variation of behavior in different circumstances (1977).

According to Bandura (1978), human behavior is due to a **reciprocal determinism** that involves behavioral, cognitive, and environmental factors. All three factors operate as "interlocking determinants" of one another. If we were

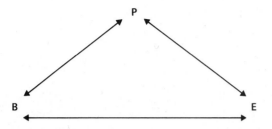

Figure 9.1   *A Diagram of Reciprocal Determinism*
In this diagram, *B* signifies behavior, *P* the person, and *E* the environment.

to diagram the process, each factor would have arrows pointing toward it and toward the other two (Figure 9.1) to show their reciprocal interaction.

In Bandura's concept of reciprocal determinism, although environmental stimuli influence our behavior, individual personal factors such as beliefs and expectations also influence how we behave. The selection of a tuna fish sandwich for lunch is not simply determined by the menu and other environmental stimuli but also by one's attitude toward tuna fish and an expectation as to how it will taste. Further, the outcomes of our behavior serve to change the environment. A rush on any particular item will cause a restaurant or household to run out of it and perhaps subsequently to order an extra supply.

Many psychologists have agreed with Bandura that behavior arises from the interactions of a person and the environment rather than from either factor alone. However, earlier conceptualizations have either seen the person and situation as separate agents that combine to produce behavior or considered the behavior that they produce a by-product that does not enter into the causal process. Bandura believes that his concept is significant because it emphasizes the reciprocal nature of the interaction among all three factors (1989, 1991a).

Although actions are regulated by their consequences, external stimuli affect behavior through intervening cognitive processes. While they are behaving, people are also thinking about what they are doing. Their thoughts influence how their behavior is affected by the environment. Cognitive processes determine which stimuli we will recognize, how we will perceive them, and how we will act upon them. Cognitive processes also permit us to use symbols and to engage in the type of thinking that enables us to anticipate different courses of action and their consequences. Because we act reflectively rather than automatically, we are able to change our immediate environment. In so doing, we arrange reinforcements for ourselves and influence our own behavior.

Processes relating to the self play a major role in Bandura's theory, but he does not conceive of the self as a psychic agent controlling behavior. Instead he uses the term **self-system** to refer to "cognitive structures that provide reference mechanisms," a "set of subfunctions for the perception, evaluation, and regulation of behavior" (1978). Thus the *self* in social learning theory is a group of cognitive processes and structures by which people relate to their environment and that help to shape their behavior.

Television viewing is a good example of the way in which behavioral, cognitive, and environmental factors may be interlocked. Bandura points out that

> personal preferences influence when and which programs, from among the available alternatives, individuals choose to watch on television. Although the potential televised environment is identical for all viewers, the actual televised environment that impinges on given individuals depends on what they select to watch. Through their viewing behavior, they partly shape the nature of the future televised environment. Because production costs and commercial requirements also determine what people are shown, the options provided in the televised environment partly shape the viewers' preferences. Here all three factors — viewer preferences, viewing behavior, and televised offerings — reciprocally affect each other (1978).

The relative influence of the three interlocking factors varies in different individuals and in different situations. In a reciprocal interaction process, one and the same event can be a stimulus, a response, or an environmental reinforcer, depending on where in the sequence we begin our analysis. Thus, it is useless to search for an ultimate environmental cause of behavior. Moreover, chance encounters frequently play a role in shaping the course of a human life. In a chance encounter, each separate chain of events has its own causal determinants but their occurrence together arises fortuitously (1986). The science of psychology cannot predict the likelihood of chance encounters but it can clarify the factors that influence their impact (1986).

Learning Through Observation

Bandura is best known for his emphasis on the process of learning through observation or by example. Bandura points out that most human behavior is learned by following a model rather than through the processes of classical and operant conditioning.

Bandura suggests that behavior is learned through observation either intentionally or accidentally. This is how children learn to play with their toys, to perform household chores, and to develop other skills such as riding a bicycle. The young child learns to speak by hearing the speech of others and imitating it. If learning a language were totally dependent on classical or operant conditioning, it could not be accomplished so readily, since the child would not be reinforced until after spontaneously uttering a sound that approximated a real word. In practice, parents repeat meaningful words over and over again to their children, who mimic those words as they learn to speak.

In many cases the behavior that is being learned must follow the same form as the modeled activity. Driving an automobile, for example, requires us to follow a prescribed method of action. However, learning through observation can

*Young children learn how to perform cer-
tain tasks by watching others do them and
then repeating the tasks for themselves.*

also encompass new behaviors. Observers have been able to solve problems correctly even after the model has failed to solve the same problem. Thus observational learning exceeds mere imitation: the observer learns from the model's
mistakes and successes. Learning through observation can account for innovative and creative behaviors. Bandura suggests that observers draw similar features from different responses and create rules of behavior that permit them to
go beyond what they have seen or heard. Through this type of synthesis, they
are able to develop new patterns of conduct that may be quite different from
those they have actually observed (1974).

Experimental Analysis of the Influence of Modeling

Bandura's theory of **observational learning** is largely based on experimental
analysis of the influence of modeling on behavior. In a typical modeling experiment, the subject observes another person performing a behavior or sequence
of behaviors. Afterward the subject is observed to see whether or not the model's
behavior is imitated. The subject's behavior is compared with that of a control

group who did not observe the model to see if there are any significant differences.

Bandura's most famous study involved the use of a Bobo doll, a large inflated plastic figure about four feet tall (Bandura and Walters, 1963). Young preschool-aged children observed an adult playing with the doll in an aggressive fashion. The adult vigorously attacked the doll, hitting and kicking it while shouting things like "Sock him in the nose!" "Throw him in the air!" Other children did not see the adult playing with the doll aggressively. Later, when the experimental group was given the opportunity to play with the Bobo doll themselves, their behavior was similar to that of the model. It was twice as aggressive as that of the control group.

Through manipulating various independent variables in this kind of experiment, Bandura and his colleagues (1977) have demonstrated three factors that influence modeling.

First, the *characteristics of the model* affect imitation. We are more likely to be influenced by someone who we believe is similar to ourselves than by someone who is different. Simpler behaviors are more readily imitated than complex ones and certain kinds of behavior seem more prone to imitation than others. Hostile and aggressive behaviors are readily copied, especially by young children.

The *attributes of the observer* also influence modeling. People who are lacking in self-esteem or who are incompetent are especially prone to imitate a model. So too are highly dependent individuals and those who have been rewarded previously for conforming behavior. A highly motivated individual will also emulate a model in order to master a desired behavior.

Last, the *reward consequences associated with a behavior* influence the effectiveness of the modeling. Subjects are more likely to imitate a behavior if they believe that such actions will lead to positive short- or long-term results. Bandura believes that this variable is stronger than the other ones.

Processes of Observational Learning

Bandura believes that models influence learning primarily through their informative function. Learning through observation is not a simple matter of imitation. It is an active judgmental and constructive process. Through exposure, observers acquire symbolic representations of different ways of doing things and these ideas serve as guides for their own behavior. Observational learning is governed by four interrelated processes: attentional processes, retention processes, motor reproduction processes, and motivational processes (1977).

A number of variables influence *attentional processes*. Some of these have to do with the characteristics of the model, others with the nature of the activity, and still others with the subject. Some models are more noticeable than others and thus more readily copied. Charismatic models command considerable attention, whereas persons low in interpersonal attractiveness tend to be ignored.

Bandura points out that certain associations determine the types of activities we will be exposed to. The people with whom one regularly associates limit and structure the kinds of behaviors that one will observe. For example, those who live in an inner city where hostile gangs stalk the streets are more likely to learn aggressive modes of response than those who are reared in a pacifist commune.

Television has greatly enlarged the range of models that are available to people today, whereas our great-grandparents were pretty much limited to modeling sources within their own family and community. Personal qualities, such as our own interests, needs, wants, and wishes, also determine what we attend to.

A second system involved in observational learning is the *retention process.* When you observe someone's behavior without immediately performing the response, you have to represent it in some way in order to use it as a guide for action on later occasions.

There are two basic forms of symbols or representational systems that facilitate observational learning: *imaginal* and *verbal.* If you are trying to remember "Big Mac" you can do it either by remembering the words *BIG MAC* or by developing a visual image of two all-beef patties, special sauce, lettuce, cheese, pickles, onion, on a sesame-seed bun. These symbols may then be present to us when the actual stimulus is not.

The third mechanism of modeling involves *motor reproduction processes.* In order to imitate a model, an individual has to convert the symbolic representation of the behavior into the appropriate actions. The response has to be carried out in space and time in the same way that the original behavior was. Motor reproduction processes involve four substages: cognitive organization of the response, initiation of the response, monitoring of the response, and refinement of the response.

The skills that we learn through observational learning are perfected slowly through a process of trial and error. We follow the behavior of a model and then seek to improve our approximations through adjustment and feedback.

The final system involved in observational learning is made up of *motivational processes.* Social learning theory distinguishes between *acquisition,* what a person has learned and can do, and *performance,* what a person actually does. People do not enact everything that they learn. Most of us have the theoretical know-how to rob a store. We have seen robberies in real life or on television and we are acquainted with the behaviors that are entailed in committing that crime. However, this does not mean that we will go out and do it.

We are more likely to engage in a modeled behavior if it leads to consequences that we value and less likely to engage in it if the results are punitive. We also learn from observing the consequences of others' behavior. Finally, we can engage in self-reinforcement. We generate evaluative responses toward our own behavior and this leads us to continue to engage in behaviors that we find self-satisfying and to reject those of which we disapprove or that feel uncomfortable.

No behavior occurs without sufficient incentive. Proper motivation not only brings about the actual performance of the behavior but it also influences the other processes involved in observational learning. When we are not motivated to learn something, we do not pay attention and so there is little we select to retain. Moreover, we are not willing to practice hard or to engage in the kind of trial-and-error activities necessary for the successful reproduction of a task. Thus, motivation emerges as a primary component in learning through observation.

Bandura notes that many imitative behaviors occur so rapidly that it is easy to overlook the processes underlying observational learning. However, it is important to postulate them in order to understand the phenomenon and to predict the circumstances under which learning will occur. In early development, children's modeling consists largely of instantaneous imitation. With age, children develop symbol and motor skills that enable them to follow more complex behaviors. Positing these processes helps us to specify the different variables that are involved in observational learning, develop hypotheses concerning them, and find ways of testing these hypotheses experimentally. In short, they enable us to make more accurate predictions. These constructs also help us to understand those instances in which an individual does not appear to learn from observation. Failure to reproduce a modeled behavior arises from insufficient attention, inadequate symbolization or retention, lack of physical capacities, skill, or practice, inadequate motivation, or any combination of these.

Reinforcement in Observational Learning

Bandura suggests that almost any behavior can be learned by an individual without the direct experience of reinforcement. We do not have to be reinforced to pay attention to vivid images or loud sounds: the impact of the stimulus itself commands our attention. Nor do we have to be directly rewarded in order to learn something. Driving home from work each day, I pass a gas station along the route. One day, when I am out of gas, I drive directly to the station, demonstrating that I had learned where it was even though I was not directly reinforced for doing so. Observational learning is often seen to occur where neither the model nor the observer is directly reinforced and there is a delay between the original behavior being modeled and the later response.

Bandura believes that observational learning occurs through symbolic processes *while* one is being exposed to the modeled activity and *before* any response has been made. Therefore, it does not depend on external reinforcement. Where such reinforcement plays a role in observational learning, it acts as a facilitator rather than a necessary condition. Its role precedes rather than follows a response. It serves an informative and incentive function. The individual's anticipation of a reward or punishment influences how he or she behaves.

Social learning theory considers a broad range of reinforcements including extrinsic, intrinsic, vicarious, and self-generated consequences.

Extrinsic reinforcement is external. Its relationship to the behavior is arbitrary or socially arranged rather than the natural outcome of the behavior. Being spanked for touching a hot stove is an extrinsic reinforcement. Being burnt by touching the stove is not. External reinforcement is clearly effective in creating behavioral change and has an important role to play in early development.

Many of the activities we need to learn are difficult and tedious to perform initially. They do not become rewarding until we have become proficient in them. If we did not receive positive encouragements in the early stages of learning such behaviors, we would quickly become discouraged and stop learning them.

Depending on the activities involved and the way in which rewards are used, extrinsic incentives can increase interest in activities, reduce interest, or have no effect. It is what people make of incentives rather than the incentives themselves that determines how extrinsic rewards affect motivation.

Intrinsic reinforcement comes in three different forms. Some intrinsic reinforcement arises from without but is naturally related to the behavior by its sensory effects. Being burnt while touching a hot stove is an example of this. Other behaviors produce a natural physiological effect; for example, relaxation exercises relieve muscle fatigue. In other instances it is not the behavior itself or the feedback that is rewarding, but how we feel about it. Playing a difficult piece of music well leads to a feeling of accomplishment. The self-satisfaction sustains the practice of the behavior.

Vicarious reinforcement occurs when we learn appropriate behavior from the successes and mistakes of others. It can take the form of either a reward or a punishment. A child who sees a sibling being spanked for a misdemeanor quickly learns not to do the same thing.

Self-reinforcement refers to the fact that people have self-reactive capacities that permit them to control their own thoughts, feelings, and actions. People do not behave like weathervanes that shift in different directions according to the external pressures that are placed upon them. Instead, they regulate their own behavior by setting standards of conduct for themselves and responding to their own actions in self-rewarding or self-punishing ways.

Self-reinforcement increases performance primarily through its motivational function. One runner might be satisfied by completing a mile in five minutes; another would want to finish it in less time. The standards that govern self-reinforcing responses are established by teaching or by example. High standards are frequently emulated because they are actively cultivated through social rewards.

After individuals learn to set standards for themselves, they can influence their behaviors through self-produced consequences. Bandura believes that most of our behavior as adults is regulated by the continuing process of self-reinforcement (1992).

Television and Aggression

Some of Bandura's experiments were specifically designed to investigate the influence of television viewing on the development of aggressive responses. In many different variations on his classic Bobo doll studies, Bandura studied the impact of a live model as opposed to a filmed model and a cartoon model. The aggressive film model was just as effective in teaching aggressive forms of be-havior as the live model. The cartoon character was somewhat less influential but nevertheless successful. In each study, children who observed an aggressive model (live, film, or cartoon) performed more aggressive responses than did children who observed a nonaggressive model or no model at all (1973).

Bandura has concluded that frequent exposure to aggression and violence on television encourages children to behave aggressively and he has been very concerned about the aggressive models that our culture provides.

Bandura's demonstrations led to considerable attention to the possible re-lationship between violence in society and violence on television. It was sug-gested that several real-life instances of aggression and risk taking had actually been triggered by similar episodes on television or in the movies. For example, death was the result when teenagers copied a stunt from the movie *The Program* in which the "tough" hero lies down at night in the middle of a busy highway (Hinds, 1993). Concern over behaviors such as this led to a number of studies throughout the 1960s and 1970s. With the increased popularity of video games, attention turned to the effects of these on aggression as well (Cooper & Mackie, 1986; Silvern & Williamson, 1987).

The results have been mixed. Much of the early research suggested a causal relationship between observing violence on television and aggressive behavior (Berkowitz & Powers, 1979). On the other hand Comstock and Strasburger (1990) suggest that the initial research suggesting a link was based on earlier (and, perhaps, too simplified) concepts. They also point out that the cumulative effects of watching television over a long period has not yet been evaluated. Moreover, other factors such as personality characteristics of the viewer may make a difference (Russell, 1992). Duhs and Gunton (1988) discuss methodo-logical and definitional problems in the research and conclude that on the basis of it, no particular policy advice is sustainable. They also express the concern that policymakers may be misled by present empirical findings to propose meaningless and even counterproductive restrictions.

In the past decade, the major television networks' new programs have been less violent (although still replete with sex and strong language), but violence, often seemingly pointless, on cable and in films has increased. However, legis-lation controlling violent content may just be an easy way of avoiding the more difficult root issues of crime, poverty, and gun control. As the debate escalates, "the movie and television industries say they face a difficult, if not unsolvable, problem: how [as art forms] to reflect the violence in the United States without exploiting it" (Weinraub, 1993). Comstock and Strasburger (1990) believe that the negative effects of television viewing can be alleviated by increasing the undesirability of aggressive behavior and increasing knowledge and skepticism about the medium, leading children and parents to be more critical watchers.

Our society is most definitely a violent one. Many children no longer feel safe either at school or in their own home. However, one of the factors that we frequently overlook is that most parents employ corporal punishment as a means of disciplining their children. Corporal punishment has deeply embedded roots in many religious and cultural traditions. But parents who hit are sending their children clear messages of anger and rejection. They are also modeling aggressive behavior as a viable solution to problems, thus influencing their children to act out aggression. Bandura (1973) reminds us that children whose parents employ a lot of corporal punishment are often very aggressive. They are also less obedient (Power & Chapeski, 1986). We need to raise the question: Is the violence of society and culture also fostered by physical abuse of children in the name of discipline? And we must recognize that the answer is, Yes! And we also need to recognize that children born in poverty are more likely to have parents who are authoritarian or neglecting and who employ corporal punishment (Farran, Haskins, & Galligher, 1980; Dornbusch, Gross, Duncan, & Ritter, 1987).

Psychotherapy and Behavior Modification

Since observation is central in the learning of behaviors, it also has a useful place in modifying undesirable behaviors. Bandura has added to the techniques of behavior modification the systematic use of *modeling* as an aid in changing

THINKING CRITICALLY

Filmed Violence

What are your thoughts concerning the increased violence we are seeing in American society and in the television and film industry that reflects it? Do you believe that government intervention would be a good thing?

In order to think carefully about this question, it would be helpful if you formulate the strongest possible argument that you can muster both for and against the position. Once you have synthesized the main pros and cons of the issue, state your own opinion and support it with reasons and examples.

In may be of interest for you to know that one reason behind the increase in violence in American films "is that violence, which needs no translation, sells well abroad." In 1980 about 30 percent of film income came from abroad. By 1993 it had increased to nearly 50 percent. Another factor to consider is that Hollywood's rating system is far more disturbed by sex than by violence (Weinraub, 1993).

What are some other factors that play a role in fostering aggressive behavior, such as influences in the home and culture and society at large, individual dispositions, and situational factors?

behaviors. Modeling has been used to reduce fears in children and adults, to teach domineering and hyperaggressive children to be more cooperative, to teach language skills to autistic children, to increase communication facility in asocial psychiatric patients, to lessen anxiety and improve performance in college students, and to facilitate many other behavior changes. In each case, a model or models illustrate or explain an appropriate way of handling a situation and the patient is encouraged to emulate the model. Thus, in order to eliminate a strong animal phobia, a subject might watch filmed and live models progressively interact with the animal in question and then be encouraged to engage in increasingly intimate interactions with the animal along with the model. Results have shown that modeling procedures are clearly instrumental in reducing and sustaining a reduction in fears and in making other behavioral changes.

Bandura (1977) points out that people who behave in abnormal ways generally have a poor sense of **self-efficacy.** They do not believe that they can successfully perform the behaviors that will enable them to cope with everyday life. Their lowered expectations lead them to avoid situations that are threatening and in which they do not believe they could perform well. Where situations cannot be avoided, they try only a little and give up quickly. As a result, they do not engage in activities that might demonstrate their abilities and serve to change their sense of self-efficacy.

The concept of self-efficacy has been the subject of a great deal of research. A high degree of self-efficacy has been shown to be positively related to health, behavior change, perceived control, and other desirable behaviors (Holden, 1991; Gist & Mitchell, 1992; Schwarzer, 1992; Walker & Bates 1992). Convergent evidence from the research on self-efficacy suggests that it is a useful explanatory and predictive concept (Bandura, 1986; 1991a; 1991b).

Bandura's therapeutic strategies are designed to help patients improve their perception of their own effectiveness. He recommends that therapists use a variety of techniques in order to enhance their patients' self-confidence. Thus, in treating a group of *agoraphobics* (people who are afraid of public places), Bandura used a number of different procedures. Initially, Bandura met with the agoraphobics in small groups where he or cotherapists helped them to identify and rank those situations that aroused fear in them. He also taught them how to use relaxation techniques and how to substitute positive thoughts for self-debilitating ones. Then, through graduated field experiences, he encouraged them to engage in successful interactions with their feared objects and settings. Appropriate responses and behaviors were modeled by therapists and ex-agoraphobics. Exposure to feared situations was taken gradually, one step at a time, in order not to overwhelm or discourage the client. Through successful experiences, the subjects were able to improve their sense of self-efficacy and to increase the length of time they spent in intimidating situations. Gradually, the field therapists lessened their guided participation and support. Thus, through a variety of techniques, Bandura and his associates were able to increase self-efficacy and modify behaviors (1980).

THINKING CRITICALLY

Developing Self-Control

Techniques informed by social learning theory can be used to develop ways of changing your behavior. By carefully observing your behavior and the factors that lead to it, you can begin to see how to influence an undesired activity and change it. The environment can often be varied so that either the stimuli that precede the activity or the consequences that follow it are changed. Through a strategy of behavioral programming, a person can gradually eliminate inappropriate behaviors and substitute more desirable ones.

In developing a program of self-control, the first step is to decide on a particular behavior pattern that you would like to modify. Carefully monitor and observe that behavior so that you can determine the conditions under which it is likely to occur. Your observation should be very specific. You need to count, chart, and evaluate each instance. It is helpful to keep a behavioral diary or chart. This is one way in which social learning theorists assess behavior. Next, make a list of graduated objectives that would shape you in developing a more appropriate behavior. Do not be overambitious. Select only one problem area and break it down into small, manageable steps. Consider the techniques that would help you achieve your objectives. Are there any factors in your environment that you could change in order to facilitate the development of more appropriate behaviors? A student who has difficulty studying might consider the time and place where studying normally occurs. Is it an area and time that is free from distractions and interruptions? Perhaps you would study more effectively in the library. Leaving the phone off the hook during study hours can eliminate intruding phone calls. Are there any models whose behavior you could emulate? Finally, you should develop a systematic schedule of reinforcements for appropriate behaviors that lead toward your objectives. Make sure that the reward is something that you value and are willing to work for. And then be sure that you employ it as a means of reinforcement.

Corcoran (1991) suggests that in his concept of self-efficacy Bandura may be shifting "from a cognitive-behavioral model to a largely cognitively based approach to motivation and behavior."

In those cases where behavior modification has stressed a change in the environment, Bandura points out that it usually has had only a short-term effect. As long as the person is under the control of the therapist or in a carefully monitored environment, the behavior is controlled; once that external control and support is gone, the behavior regresses. Reciprocal determinism assumes that behavior is controlled by both the person and the environment. It is possible, therefore, to indicate the conditions under which behavior will generalize and hold up over time and the conditions under which it will not. The conditions under which change is maintained are

— when the new behavior has functional value for the individual
— when there are strong social and environmental supports for the behavior
— when an individual's own self-evaluation becomes an important reinforcer.

Many inappropriate behavior patterns are immediately rewarding but have long-range negative effects. Examples are overeating, smoking, and alcohol and substance abuse. In such cases, the task of the therapist is to help the individual acquire some capacity to control her or his own behavior. There are several different elements involved in *self-control,* but one that Bandura has explored carefully is delay of gratification. *Delay of gratification* involves the self-imposed postponement of an immediate reward in favor of a more significant reward in the future. The student who decides not to cut class may forgo the fun in the coffee shop over the next hour but stands a greater chance of getting a good grade in the course. Bandura's studies have shown that modeling can influence the ability to delay gratification (Bandura and Mischel, 1965). In our achievement-oriented society, the ability to delay gratification is a desired, if not necessary, skill. Bandura believes that most individuals who are able to delay gratification were reared in homes where parents modeled the delay of reward and emphasized its importance. However, adults can also be taught to delay gratification. Bandura believes that research on self-control is our most promising approach to the management of detrimental behavior (Evans, 1976).

Bandura (1991d) suggests that a similar self-regulation system is entailed in moral conduct. However, "compared to the achievement domain, in the moral domain evaluative standards are more stable, judgement factors more varied and complex, and affective self-reactions more intense."

Bandura has responded sharply to charges that behavior modification entails manipulation of human beings and denial of their freedom. He points out that procedures used to create a behavior pattern that is convenient to the reinforcer but of little value to the subject usually do not produce lasting results. Bandura does not see this as a regrettable state of affairs because otherwise it would be too easy to develop procedures that would enslave people (Evans, 1976). A client comes to a therapist with a request for help in changing behavior. The relationship is not that of a controller (however benevolent) and an unwitting subject: it is a contractual relationship between two consenting individuals. Behavior modification increases rather than limits an individual's freedoms. For example, the individual with a strong fear is not really free but crippled by limiting behavioral responses.

Bandura's Theory: Philosophy, Science, and Art

Heir to the behavior and learning tradition in American psychology, Bandura's theory is rapidly becoming one of the most popular approaches to the study of personality. It is particularly appealing to academic psychologists because it lies within the mainstream of American psychology. It strongly emphasizes experimental research and clearly emulates a scientific model.

Bandura's reintroduction of internal variables, his emphasis on reciprocal determinism, and his investigation of human subjects allow his theory to deal with complex social responses more adequately than radical behavior and learning theories. B. F. Skinner's learning theory can account for the learned behavior of animals and very simple learned habits and behaviors of human beings; it does not explain complex human behaviors like decision making and creativity well. Bandura's account clearly includes those kinds of complex activities, permitting scientific analysis of a wide range of human behaviors. Bandura's work has helped to overcome the earlier behaviorist view of human nature as a machine whose output depends upon the input provided. Indeed, Bandura's theory underscores the vast differences between a human being and a computer.

Bandura's theory is clearly grounded in empirical research and amenable to precise laboratory methods of investigation. It has stimulated research in other areas. It economically states major constructs in relatively simple terms. And it is compatible with our existing concept of the world.

Bandura's work has been criticized, however, for its emphasis on overt behaviors, in spite of his reintroduction of covert factors, and for its excessive bias against psychoanalysis, which leads him to ignore distinctly human problems such as conflict and unconscious motivation.

We have also seen that learning and behavior theorists have sometimes failed to appreciate that scientific work is based on philosophical assumptions. Skinner, for example, for many years did not acknowledge the philosophical commitments that inform his work. Although Bandura does not explicitly discuss his philosophical assumptions, with the exception of reciprocal determinism, he is more sophisticated than Skinner in his recognition that scientific efforts rest on philosophical assumptions. He also avoids elevating his empirical conclusions into philosophical ones.

In spite of their desire to limit their activities to empirical science, learning and behavior theorists invariably raise philosophical issues and ethical questions (Rottschaefer, 1991). This is particularly evident in their efforts to apply their theories toward the improvement of human behavior and society. Bandura has developed significant new forms of psychotherapy, like modeling. He has spoken candidly about the dangers of aggressive models. Other findings from observational learning theory have been taken from the laboratory and applied to problems in the everyday world, clearly demonstrating the practicality of Bandura's approach but implying an underlying philosophy as well.

Bandura has helped to revitalize the learning and behavior approach by infusing it with a cognitive dimension and by acknowledging some of its philosophical underpinnings. The scientific emphasis makes his approach an extremely popular one. His influence will undoubtedly continue to be substantial.

Like Bandura, Julian Rotter's theory also seeks to correct some of the shortcomings of earlier behavior and learning theory and to incorporate new findings in or from cognitive psychology.

Julian Rotter: Biographical Background

Julian Rotter was born in Brooklyn, New York, in 1916. He has not yet written about his early life or indicated how it might have influenced his theory other than to say that throughout his school years he was an avid reader. In his junior year in high school, unable to find any new fiction to read in one of his frequent visits to the Avenue J Library in Brooklyn, he browsed in the philosophy and psychology section and came across some books by Alfred Adler and Sigmund Freud. By his senior year he was seriously interested in psychology and was interpreting his friend's dreams. He also wrote a paper on "Why we make mistakes" (1982).

Rotter would have liked to major in psychology but because he was unaware of any professional opportunities in psychology and because of the financial pressures of the Great Depression, he selected chemistry. However, he took electives in psychology, and when he graduated he actually had more credits in that discipline than in chemistry. He also met and studied with Alfred Adler, from whose theory he came to appreciate the unity of personality and the goal-directedness of behavior.

Rotter graduated from Brooklyn College in 1937. Adler's sudden death that very summer and the encouragement of professors led him to go to the University of Iowa to study with Kurt Lewin. He arrived in Iowa with enough money to survive only a few weeks, but was able to find a job as a part-time research assistant. From Kurt Lewin's field theory, he came to appreciate the interrelatedness of behavior and the fact that many factors are responsible for any single behavior. His writings show the influence of Adler and Lewin as well as of learning theorists such as E. L. Thorndike and Clark Hull. Rotter received his M.A. in 1938 and the Ph.D. in psychology from Indiana University in 1941.

During World War II, Rotter served as a psychologist and personnel consultant to the U.S. Army. Following the war, he took a position at Ohio State University, where George Kelly was the director of the clinical psychology program. At Ohio State, he developed his social learning theory of personality and first described it in a book entitled *Social Learning and Clinical Psychology* (1954). He also conducted a great deal of research based on his theory.

Rotter went to the University of Connecticut in 1963, where he was a professor in the department of psychology, director of the Clinical Psychology

Julian Rotter

Training Program, and a diplomate in clinical psychology of the American Board of Examiners in Professional Psychology. In 1976–1977, he was president of the Eastern Psychological Association. Currently an emeritus professor at the University of Connecticut, he continues to teach courses in psychodynamics and the construction and validation of personality measures. Rotter's view has come to significantly influence thinking about personality in contemporary psychology.

Internal versus External Control of Reinforcement

In his early years, Rotter conducted a series of experimental studies designed to tell whether or not people learn tasks and perform differently when they see reinforcements as related or unrelated to their own behaviors. The results of these experiments led him to develop the **I-E Scale**, a significant assessment tool that measures an individual's perception of *locus of control* (1966). An individual may come to believe on the basis of past experiences that the reinforcements received depend on certain behaviors or, conversely, may come to believe that reinforcements are controlled by outside forces (1966). Internally controlled individuals assume that their own behaviors and actions are responsible for the consequences that happen to them. Externally controlled people believe that the locus of control is out of their hands and that they are subject to the whims of fate, luck, or other people. Internal versus external control of reinforcement refers to a continuum of belief of which we have cited the two extremes. Competence, mastery, helplessness, powerlessness, or alienation are but a few of the terms used to describe whether or not people believe they can control their own lives. Rotter believes that his construct has an advantage over others because it is an integral part of a formal theory from which predictions can be made.

Although various measuring devices have been developed to assess locus of control as a stable personality characteristic, Rotter's scale remains one of the most widely used. The I-E Scale consists of twenty-three forced-choice items and six filler items. The subject indicates which of each pair of items applies best. The final score can range from zero to twenty-three, with higher scores indicating greater externality. Rotter does not indicate any cutoff score that separates internals from externals, but norms have been published for various groups to facilitate comparisons. On a national sample of high school students, the mean score was 8.50. The lowest mean score reported by Rotter was 5.94 among a group of Peace Corps trainees (1966).

The I-E Scale has been widely used in research and has led to a number of significant findings: internality increases with age; as children grow older, their locus of control tends to become more internal; internality becomes stable in middle age and does not diminish in old age, contrary to popular views of the elderly as dependent. Certain parental practices help to foster a belief in internal control: warm, responsible, supportive conditions and the encouragement of independence (Lefcourt, 1976; de Mann Leduc, & Labrèche-Gauthier, 1992).

Several studies have shown that internals are more perceptive and ready to learn about their surroundings. They ask more questions and process information more efficiently than externals. They have greater mastery tendencies, better problem-solving abilities, and more likelihood of achievement (Agarwal & Misra, 1986). Thus, internal prison inmates know more about the institution and conditions affecting their parole and are more likely to be paroled (Rotter, 1966). Internals are better versed about critical political events that may influence their lives (Ryckman & Malikiosi, 1975).

Internal locus of control appears to protect one against unquestioning submission to authority. Internals are more resistant to influences from other people. They make more independent judgments and try harder to control the behavior of others (Lefcourt, 1976). They tend to assume more responsibility for their own behavior and attribute responsibility to others. As a result, they are more likely to be punitive and less sympathetic than externals.

Internals are more likely to know about the conditions that lead to good physical and emotional health and to take positive steps to improve their health such as quitting smoking, avoiding substance abuse, and engaging in regular

THINKING CRITICALLY

Internal-External Locus of Control

You can assess your own belief in locus of control by selecting the one statement from each pair that best describes your belief. The following are sample items taken from an earlier version of the I-E Scale but not used in the final version. You can discover whether you are inclined toward internal control or external control by adding up the choices you make on each side. Items on the left indicate internality and items on the right indicate externality.

I more strongly believe that:	*Or:*
Promotions are earned through hard work and persistence.	Making a lot of money is largely a matter of getting the right breaks.
In my experience I have noticed that there is usually a direct connection between how hard I study and the grades I get.	Many times the reactions of teachers seem haphazard to me.
The number of divorces indicates that more and more people are not trying to make their marriages work.	Marriage is largely a gamble.
When I am right I can convince others.	It is silly to think that one can really change another person's basic attitudes.
In our society a man's future earning power is dependent upon his ability.	Getting promoted is really a matter of being a little luckier than the next guy.
If one knows how to deal with people they are really quite easily led.	I have little influence over the way other people behave.
In my case the grades I make are the results of my own efforts; luck has little or nothing to do with it.	Sometimes I feel that I have little to do with the grades I get.
People like me can change the course of world affairs if we make ourselves heard.	It is only wishful thinking to believe that one can really influence what happens in society at large.
I am the master of my fate.	A great deal that happens to me is probably a matter of chance.
Getting along with people is a skill that must be practiced.	It is almost impossible to figure out how to please some people.

Do you concur with Rotter that an internal locus of control is more conducive to positive social adjustment and functioning?

Reprinted from Julian B. Rotter, ''External Control and Internal Control,'' PSYCHOLOGY TODAY MAGAZINE, June 1971, 5, 42. Copyright © 1971.

exercise (Powell, 1992; Rosolack & Hampson, 1991; Bezjak & Lee, 1990). They suffer less from hypertension and are less likely to have heart attacks. When they do become ill, they cope with the illness more adequately than externals (Strickland, 1978, 1979). Internals also derive more benefit from social support (Lefcourt, Martin, & Saleh, 1984) and are more likely to use contraception (Visher, 1986).

Externals are more likely to conform (Singh, 1984) and prefer not to have to make a choice (Harrison, Lewis, & Straka, 1984). Externals tend to be more anxious and depressed, as well as more vulnerable to stress. They develop defensive strategies that invite failure in coping with a task and use defensive strategies afterward to explain their failures. They attribute their lack of success to bad luck or to the difficulties of the task (Drwal & Wiechnik, 1984; Lester, 1992).

Some research has shown sex differences in locus of control, with females tending to be external (de Brabander & Boone, 1990). The increase in external scores for women in the seventies may reflect greater awareness of external constraints on their ability to meet their goals at work and in other settings (Doherty & Baldwin, 1985). However, family socioeconomic status is an even stronger correlate of locus of control (Young & Shorr, 1986), as well as not being a member of a vulnerable population, "such as children, medical patients, lower level employers, and the elderly" (Thompson & Spacapan, 1991).

Rotter believes that extreme belief in either internal or external locus of control is unrealistic and unhealthy. He has hypothesized a curvilinear relationship between locus of control measures and assessments of maladjustment (Rotter & Hochreich, 1975). However, it is clear that many favorable characteristics have been associated with internal locus of control and it has been proposed that an internal orientation is more conducive to positive social adjustment and functioning. The locus of control construct is durable and has had a major impact (Lefcourt, 1992). Some of the more recent research is cross-cultural (e.g., Banks, Ward, McQuater & De Britlo, 1991; Murk & Addleman, 1992; Saeeduzzafar & Sharma, 1991).

Basic Concepts

Rotter's empirical observations about individual differences led to a more general motivational theory in which behavior potential, expectancy, reinforcement value, and the psychological situation are seen as four variables that can be measured and related in a specific formula that enables us to predict a person's behavior in any given situation (Rotter & Hochreich, 1975). The concepts of need and minimum goal level also play an important role in Rotter's theory.

Behavioral Potential

The **behavioral potential** refers to the likelihood that a particular behavior will occur in a given situation. Rotter uses the term "behavior" broadly to refer to a wide class of responses that include overt movements, verbal expressions, and cognitive and emotional reactions. In any given situation, an individual could react in a number of different ways. The behavior potential is specific both for the particular behavior and for the related reinforcement. Thus, we must know what goal the behavior is related to before we can tell how likely it is to occur.

Covert, as well as overt, behaviors can be observed and measured and their likelihood predicted. They can be inferred from overt behaviors. An individual who takes a longer time to answer one question than another may be considered to be evaluating alternative solutions. Rotter believes that the principles that govern covert behaviors are the same as those that might apply to any observable behavior (Rotter, Chance, & Phares, 1972). The objective study of internal cognitive responses is difficult but necessary for a complete understanding of behavior.

Expectancy

Expectancy refers to individuals' subjective expectations about the outcome of their behavior. It is an estimation of the probability that a particular reinforcement will occur if one behaves in a certain way in a given situation. What does Johnny expect will be the outcome of his temper tantrum? The answer to that question will influence the likelihood of a tantrum occurring.

Expectancies are based on previous experience. An individual who has performed consistently well in mathematics will expect to do well in subsequent math courses. The expectancy is a subjective estimate; it tends to reflect the way a person feels about a subject. Therefore, it is not necessarily based on all of the pertinent objective data nor is it necessarily a true estimate.

Reinforcement Value

Reinforcement value refers to the importance or preference of a particular reinforcement for an individual. In a given situation, Mary may refuse to wash Dad's car if she thinks that the only reward for the task is a verbal thank-you. On the other hand, she might be anxious to wash the car if she believes that she will receive ten dollars for the chore. The reinforcement value of a particular reward differs from individual to individual. Some children are more eager to please their parents than others. People also engage in activities for different reasons. One individual might go to a party in order to meet new friends; another might seek to get high. Some rewards are compatible and others are incompatible. A child might be asked to choose between a toy and a box of candy as a prize for winning a game. Where a choice must be made, the relative reinforcement value of each reward becomes clear.

Rotter suggests that individuals tend to be consistent in the value they place on different reinforcements. Each one of us has a characteristic set of preferences that we bring to situations. Like expectancies, the values associated with different reinforcers are based on past experiences. Out of these associations, we also form expectations for the future. Thus, there is a relationship between the expectancy construct and the reinforcement value.

The Psychological Situation

The **psychological situation** refers to the psychological context in which the individual responds. It is the situation as defined from the perspective of the person. Any given situation has different meanings for different individuals and these meanings affect the response. Rotter's concept of the psychological situation takes into account the importance of both dispositional and situational influences. It recognizes that an individual may have a strong need for aggression but may or may not behave aggressively in a particular situation depending on reinforcement expectancies. Rotter believes that the complex cues of each situation arouse in individuals expectations for behavior reinforcement outcomes and for reinforcement sequences.

Rotter has used a number of different techniques in his efforts to measure the variables that enter into his formula. Some of these rely on self-reports of the individual. Ranking methods in which individuals are asked to rank verbal descriptions of reinforcements from the most to the least reinforcing have been used to measure reinforcement value. Verbal questionnaires in which subjects are asked to predict the likelihood of success in various tasks have been used to measure expectancy. Behavior potential can be measured by asking people what they think they will do in certain situations. Behavioral observations have also been used to indicate the strength of these constructs. Individuals may be observed actually behaving in ways so as to receive one reinforcement over another. A subject choosing one alternative over another is thought to be indicating a higher level of expectancy for the chosen alternative. Observations of an individual's behavior over a long period of time give us an indication of how frequently certain behaviors tend to occur. The development of precise measuring techniques for these constructs, however, is only at a very early stage.

The Concepts of Need and Minimum Goal Level

Rotter believes that human behavior is always directional and determined by needs that may be inferred from the ways in which an individual interacts with the environment. A **need** is "a group of behaviors which are related in the sense that they lead to the same or similar reinforcements" (Rotter & Hochreich, 1975). Rotter makes a distinction between unlearned, biologically based needs and psychological needs, internal cognitive conditions that are the result of experience rather than instinct. Psychological needs come into being through the association of experiences with the reinforcement of reflexes and basic needs such as hunger, thirst, freedom from pain, and sensory stimulation. As we develop, our psychological needs become less dependent on physiological needs and increasingly related to cues in the environment. Since as infants and children we are largely dependent upon other people for the satisfaction of our needs, many of our learned goals, such as the need for love, affection, recogni-

The need for recognition and status is the need to be seen as competent in valued activities.

tion, and dependency, are social in origin. Human needs also vary in terms of their generalness and predictability. Some of our motives and needs are very specific, and thus, behaviors that they include are easily predicted. Other motives are broader and more inclusive, making it difficult to predict specific behaviors that they entail.

Through empirical research, Rotter and Hochreich (1975) have established six broad categories of psychological needs:

recognition-status: the need to be seen as competent in socially valued activities

dominance: the need to control the actions of others

independence: the need to make one's own decisions and rely on oneself

protection-dependency: the need to have others prevent frustration or help obtain goals

love and affection: the need for acceptance and liking by others

physical comfort: learned needs for physical satisfactions associated with security

A need has three basic components. The first component is the **need potential**, the likelihood that a set of behaviors directed toward the same goal will be used in a given situation. The second component is **freedom of movement**, the degree of expectation a person has that a particular set of responses will lead to a desired reinforcement. A high expectancy or freedom of movement leads to the anticipation of success in meeting one's goals. A low expectancy or lack of freedom is associated with the anticipation of failure or punishment. The third basic component of needs is the **need value**, the importance attached to the goals themselves or the extent to which an individual prefers one goal over another. It is an average of reinforcement values taken over a number of similar reinforcing circumstances. The advantage to computing these components is that they facilitate the prediction of behaviors that are likely to occur in new situations in which similar reinforcements are obtainable. Whereas the constructs of behavior potential, expectancy, and reinforcement value are useful for prediction in specific situations or in the laboratory, the constructs of need potential, freedom of movement, and need value help us to deal with broader situations and behaviors that occur in everyday life.

The concept of **minimum goal level** refers to the lowest level of potential reinforcement that is perceived as satisfactory in a particular situation (1954). Reinforcements may be seen as existing on a continuum. Individuals vary as to their minimum goal levels or the point on the continuum that divides positively rewarding reinforcements from negative ones.

The concept of minimum goal level together with the concept of freedom of movement can be useful for predicting behavior and understanding personality adjustment. An individual who is adjusted in a particular sphere has a high freedom of movement in that area and realistic goal levels. Thus, an individual who is well adjusted in school is one who establishes academic goals that are commensurate with her or his abilities and engages in a wide variety of behaviors designed to meet those goals. The individual who is maladjusted sets unrealistic goals, such as the need always to obtain A's, and engages in unproductive behaviors that reflect a low expectation of success. There are distinct parallels between Rotter's concept of the maladjusted person as one who experiences low freedom of movement yet sets unrealistic minimal goals and Adler's concept of the neurotic as one who sets unattainable fictional goals and experiences feelings of inferiority.

Psychotherapy

Rotter's concepts have found application in the field of clinical psychology. In general, Rotter (1975) suggests that maladjusted individuals are characterized by low freedom of movement and high need value. They believe that they are unable to get the gratifications they desire through their own efforts. Instead of working toward their goals realistically, they seek to obtain them through fantasy or they behave in ways that avoid or defend against failure. Problem behaviors, such as substance abuse and delinquency, have been shown to be associated with a discrepancy between an individual's need values for recognition and his or her freedom of movement for getting it.

Low freedom of movement may result from a lack of knowledge or ability to develop the behaviors that are necessary to reach one's goals. An individual who is mentally retarded may have low expectancies because of an inability to learn basic skills. Low freedom of movement may arise from the nature of the goal itself. If a goal is antisocial, behaving in ways that fulfill the goal invites punishment. An expectancy for failure can also arise from the mistaken generalization of experiences of frustration from one area to another. A child whose paralyzed leg prevents participation in sports may erroneously generalize to assume being disliked by others. Individuals who were severely punished as children may generalize from those experiences to the present. Maladjusted individuals often apply expectations and behaviors from one situation to another inappropriately. They tend to seek immediate rewards and deny the long-term consequences of their behaviors and they emphasize the gratification of one need to the exclusion of others.

Maladjusted individuals are frequently unaware of the self-defeating character of their own behaviors and of their actual potential for success. Rotter makes use of the defense mechanisms developed by the psychoanalysts, but he reconceives them as avoidance or escape behaviors. Thus, projection entails blaming others for one's own mistakes to avoid punishment and rationalization entails making excuses in order to avoid punishment. According to social learning theory, all of the defenses and symptoms of psychopathology and mental illness may be seen as avoidance or fantasy behaviors (1975).

A social learning therapist would seek to help a maladjusted person by reducing the discrepancy between need value and freedom of movement. Rotter points out that it is essential that the therapist be flexible. In time, he hopes that patients can be systematically matched to therapists, since therapists vary in their effectiveness with different methods and patients. In general, cognitive learning theory emphasizes a problem-solving orientation to therapy and the development of problem-solving skills such as looking for alternative means of reaching a goal, analyzing the consequences of one's behavior, and discriminating among situations. The therapist assumes a highly active and directive role.

Rotter frequently advocates use of environmental change in order to effect personality change. He may try to alter the attitude of those who live with the patient or recommend a change in school or job. His work on the importance of an appropriate environment for change has led to a new conception of the mental hospital as a therapeutic community in itself. In other instances, Rotter employs various behavior strategies such as systematic desensitization, aversive conditioning or covert sensitization (the association of undesired behaviors with aversive stimuli in one's imagination), assertiveness training, and behavioral training in specific skills.

With its cognitive emphasis, Rotter's social learning theory also emphasizes the need to cultivate insight into one's own motives as they have developed from past experiences, insight into the motives of others, and insight into the long-term consequences of one's behavior. Rotter points out, however, that it is not enough for clients to understand the origins of their problems; they must also be taught new behaviors that will overcome them. Social learning theory conceives of psychotherapy broadly in the context of social interaction. The therapist's role is to help the patient develop a more satisfactory relationship with his or her social environment.

The cognitive approach to personality promises to be a very fruitful one. Cognitive factors may provide the link that will help us to transcend the traditional dichotomy between dispositional and situational factors in behavior. Distinctive cognitive and behavior patterns determine the unique meaning that

PHILOSOPHICAL ASSUMPTIONS

Examining Bandura and Rotter

How would you rate Bandura and Rotter on each of the basic philosophical assumptions described in Chapter 1? Each basic issue was presented as a bipolar dimension along which a person's view can be placed according to the degree of agreement with one or the other extreme. Rate Bandura's and Rotter's views on these issues.

When you have determined where you think the theorists stand, compare your responses to those of your classmates and your instructor. You should be willing to defend your ratings but also be prepared to change them in light of others' compelling arguments. Afterward, compare your ratings of Bandura and Rotter with your own position on each issue and with those of other theorists. Does this comparison help you to understand why their theories do or do not appeal to you?

Would strongly agree	Would agree	Is neutral or believes in synthesis of both views	Would agree	Would strongly agree
1	2	3	4	5

freedom
People basically have control over their own behavior and understand the motives behind their behavior.

determinism
The behavior of people is basically determined by internal or external forces over which they have little, if any, control.

stimuli and reinforcers have for different individuals. An individual's cognitive style influences adaption to the world and interpersonal competence. Recently, there have been efforts to construct complex information-processing models that might eventually simulate a wide variety of human mental activity. In addition, there has been increased contact between cognitive psychology and neurophysiology based upon the belief that cognitive systems might be tied to underlying neural systems. Most of the research in personality today involves cognitive elements at some point. There is little doubt that the emphasis on cognition has grown and will continue as an important factor in the discussion of personality.

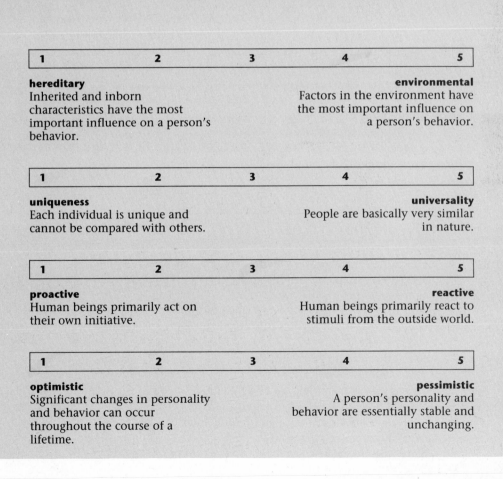

| 1 | 2 | 3 | 4 | 5 |

hereditary
Inherited and inborn characteristics have the most important influence on a person's behavior.

environmental
Factors in the environment have the most important influence on a person's behavior.

| 1 | 2 | 3 | 4 | 5 |

uniqueness
Each individual is unique and cannot be compared with others.

universality
People are basically very similar in nature.

| 1 | 2 | 3 | 4 | 5 |

proactive
Human beings primarily act on their own initiative.

reactive
Human beings primarily react to stimuli from the outside world.

| 1 | 2 | 3 | 4 | 5 |

optimistic
Significant changes in personality and behavior can occur throughout the course of a lifetime.

pessimistic
A person's personality and behavior are essentially stable and unchanging.

Rotter's Theory: Philosophy, Science, and Art

Rotter's cognitive social learning theory creatively combines traditional learning theory with an interest in cognition. Rotter's position represents a significant departure from B. F. Skinner's radical behaviorism but retains the important emphasis on a strict methodology and the classical features of the learning tradition. Thus, his theory is very appealing to experimentally oriented researchers. It also appeals to those who are attuned to advances being made in cognitive studies. His emphasis on cognitive factors is greater than Albert Bandura's. In brief, his theory is very much in line with current trends in academic psychology.

Rotter's research is rigorous and well controlled even though he permits introspective methods in addition to the objective observation of behavior. Indeed, he has fostered a new appreciation of introspection as a methodological technique and in doing so has made a valid correction of the rigid narrowness that characterizes radical behavior and learning theory.

As a science, Rotter's theory excels. His terms are operationally defined and measurable, and lend themselves to empirical test. His theory readily meets the criterion of verifiability. Empirical support for his theory has been strong, particularly regarding his concept of locus of control. His work has considerable heuristic value and may eventually enable us to predict behavior. Rotter's theory has stimulated research and has found wide application in the clinical setting, where the I-E scale has proved very useful. Because his concepts are stated as simply as possible, his theory compares well with more complex rival theories.

Rotter's theory has been criticized, however, for its lack of depth (Cartwright, 1979). It takes few risks in hypothesizing and does little more than summarize existing, generally well known knowledge.

Other Trends in Cognitive Theory

The work of Walter Mischel and research based on information processing theories exemplifies some of the current thinking related to Bandura's and Rotter's contemporary scientific approaches to personality. This research also reflects psychologists' renewed interest in cognition.

Walter Mischel, who studied with George Kelly and Julian Rotter and worked with Henry Murray, has emphasized behavioral specificity in his discussion of human behavior. *Behavioral specificity* (1968) means that an individual's behavior is determined by the specific situation. We behave consistently or in the same manner in different situations only to the extent that these situations lead to similar consequences. When the consequences are different we learn to discriminate among different situations and behave accordingly.

Which reaction we show at any particular moment depends on discriminative stimuli: where we are, whom we are with, and so forth. Thus Mischel and other social learning theorists emphasize behavioral specificity rather than trait consistency.

Much of the research on cognition is influenced by information processing models of cognition (Simon, 1979). Such models employ concepts such as schemas and scripts (Cantor & Kihlstrom, 1982). *Schemas* are cognitive structures by which people organize and understand the world. Similar to Adler's fictional finalisms, schemas influence attention, perception, and memory of an event. They account for individual biases and preconceptions (Nisbett & Ross, 1980).

The concept of schemas can be traced to Piaget and Kelly. However, the effort to operationally define and experiment with such concepts is characteristic of recent research in cognition (Hollon & Kriss, 1984; Singer & Kolligian, 1987). Schemas are seen as basic underlying cognitive structures that provide a general overall framework for guiding information processing.

Scripts are expectations about a series of events. Some scripts involve everyday events, such as eating a meal; others concern the life span — identifying by what age it is appropriate to marry, achieve financial independence, have children, and so forth. Scripts are major tools of social interaction and are often socially shared (Abelson, 1981). Individual differences in schemas and scripts are in part a function of individual cognitive style (Kreitler & Kreitler, 1982).

Research in cognition has led to a renewed appreciation of introspection and self-reports (Singer & Kolligian, 1987). By asking questions about a person's conscious beliefs and expectations, psychologists have been able to increase their accuracy in predicting overt behavior (McGuire, 1984). There has also been a renewed interest in autobiographical materials, case studies, and other idiographic methods of research that focus on the individual rather than on the normative behavior of groups. Contemporary uses of self-report inventories and idiographic methods are different from earlier uses because they seek to operationally define and measure variables and to test conclusions within the framework of a scientific conception of psychology.

Pervin (1985) has pointed out several significant differences between current information processing approaches to personality and traditional theories. Traditional personality theories have tended to emphasize stability and consistency in personality, tried to make generalized predictions about people, and focused on dispositions and needs, motivation and dynamics, and the self as unitary causal agent. Current cognitive theories of personality emphasize discrimination and flexibility, make predictions specific to situations, focus on particular rather than global cognitive processes, and employ an experimental methodology.

In reference to computer models, Bandura has written:

> If computer models are to be fully instructive for understanding human cognitive functioning, they must include capabilities to learn and create one's own competencies, to organize and categorize knowledge, to make sense of imprecise and incomplete information by enlisting a frame of reference, to imagine and originate things, and to appraise one's own knowledge and capabilities. It should also have consciousness of its own states and sense of self. A machinelike existence without any consciousness of

one's thoughts, feelings and what is happening around one, and with no sense of selfhood would be devoid of meaning or excitement. Moreover, a comprehensive psychological theory must explain not only how the mind works, but also how people construct, motivate, and regulate their actions (1991a).

A final trend has been efforts to integrate the many facets of self in psychoanalytic and social-cognitive thinking about the self (Westen, 1992). Some of these discussions review cross-cultural concepts of the self and show significant differences between the West and the East (e.g., Landrine, 1992).

Conclusions

Bandura's and Rotter's theories are good examples of contemporary scientific approaches to personality. Cognitive and social behavior and learning theorists appreciate that we cannot understand an individual's behavior or personality without also asking what is going on in his or her mind. Moreover, they realize that the mind and its processes can be investigated scientifically. Bandura and Rotter have combined the insights of earlier behavior and learning theories with contemporary findings in the area of cognition and social psychology.

As we have seen, learning and behavior theories tend to limit the kinds of phenomena psychologists can study and the ways in which they can investigate the phenomena. Their preoccupation with objective methodology and overt behaviors may constrain psychological investigation and prevent a more holistic understanding of human nature.

The validating evidence of the scientist is seldom as insightful or compelling as the epiphanic vision of the philosopher. This may be the price that Bandura and Rotter pay for the precision, power, and predictability of their work. Nevertheless, it has been their deliberate choice to restrict their assumptions and mechanisms to those that can be embraced by an exact scientific methodology. Thus, although they do not evoke deep insight or new philosophical understanding, they do provide precise, accurate, and measurable constructs.

Summary

1. According to Albert Bandura, human behavior is due to a **reciprocal determinism** that involves behavioral, cognitive, and environmental factors. Their relative influence varies in different individuals and in different situations.
2. Bandura believes that most human behavior is learned through the process of **observational learning,** by following a model.

3. Three factors influence modeling: *characteristics of the model, attributes of the observer,* and *reward consequences associated with the behavior.*

4. Bandura has described four processes that enter into observational learning: *attentional processes, retention processes, motor reproduction processes,* and *motivational processes.*

5. *Extrinsic, intrinsic,* and *vicarious reinforcement* and *self-reinforcement* all play a role in observational learning. Unlike Skinner, Bandura does not believe that direct reinforcement is necessary for learning to occur.

6. Bandura believes that frequent exposure to aggression and violence on television encourages children to behave aggressively. Research on the question has been mixed.

7. Bandura has added the systematic use of *modeling* as a therapeutic technique of behavior modification and developed strategies designed to help people improve their sense of **self-efficacy.** He has also conducted research in the area of self-control.

8. Bandura's theory clearly emulates a scientific model.

9. Julian Rotter's theory integrates two major trends in personality research: learning theory and cognitive theory.

10. Rotter developed the **I-E Scale** to measure internal versus external control of reinforcement. The scale has been widely used in research and has led to a number of significant findings.

11. There are four main concepts in Rotter's cognitive social learning approach: **behavior potential, expectancy, reinforcement value,** and the **psychological situation.** These four variables can be measured and related in a specific formula that enables us to predict a person's behavior in any given situation.

12. The concepts of **need** and **minimum goal level** also help us to predict behavior and understand personality adjustment.

13. Rotter's concepts have been applied in the field of clinical psychology and therapy to account for maladjustment and develop strategies of change.

14. Rotter's theory excels as a scientific theory but he and Bandura have been criticized for a lack of depth.

15. Recent trends in cognitive theory emphasize behavioral specificity and employ concepts, such as schemas and scripts, borrowed from information processing models.

Suggestions for Further Reading

Albert Bandura's writings are quite difficult and highly technical. The most comprehensive statement of his position is *Social Learning Theory* (Prentice-Hall, 1977). His concept of personality also emerged in two articles written for the

American Psychologist: "Behavior Theory and the Models of Man" (1974, *29,* 859–869) and "The Self System in Reciprocal Determinism" (1978, *33,* 344–358). Also significant is *Aggression: A Social Learning Analysis* (Prentice-Hall, 1973).

The best introduction to Julian Rotter's theory is *Personality,* co-authored with D. J. Hochreich (Scott Foresman, 1975). Students who are interested in his point of view will also want to consult J. B. Rotter, J. E. Chance, and E. J. Phares, *Applications of a Social Learning Theory of Personality* (Holt, Rinehart, & Winston, 1972) and H. M. Lefcourt, *Locus of Control: Current Trends in Theory and Research* (Erlbaum, 1976).

Dispositional Theories

The oldest and most persistent approach to personality is the dispositional. People have always described one another by talking about their differences and putting them into general categories. People have been described as hot-tempered or placid, shy or aggressive, masculine or feminine, intelligent or dull, and so forth. Even though our specific actions may vary according to the situation we are in, we conceive of ourselves as the same person and recognize a certain regularity or pattern in our behavior. These qualities appear to be long-term dispositions or traits that can be used to characterize our personality.

Part 5 concentrates on the contributions of dispositional theorists who emphasize the importance of long-term characteristics in personality. At the same time, any classification system, by its very nature, tends to be arbitrary. Many of the theorists included in this part could also be given other "labels." For example, Allport could well be called a humanist. Increasingly we are becoming impressed with the fact that emerging theories influence other developing neighboring theories so that it is rather difficult to expressly pinpoint many theories as belonging to just one category.

CHAPTER 10

Gordon Allport and Henry A. Murray

YOUR GOALS FOR THIS CHAPTER

1. Discuss Allport's final definition of personality.
2. Distinguish between continuity and discontinuity theories of personality.
3. Explain how *common traits* differ from *personal dispositions*.
4. Distinguish among three levels of personal dispositions.
5. Explain why Allport coined the term *proprium* and identify his seven *propriate functions*.
6. Discuss the concept of *functional autonomy*.
7. Describe Allport's concept of maturity.
8. Distinguish between *nomothetic* and *idiographic* approaches to the study of personality and give examples of each.
9. Evaluate Allport's theory in terms of its function as philosophy, science, and art.
10. Describe the study of personology.
11. Identify the units by which Murray suggests behavior can be studied.
12. Explain how Murray studied human *needs,* and identify Murray's twenty basic human needs.
13. Explain what Murray means by *press* and give examples.
14. Discuss assessment and research in Murray's theory and describe the *Thematic Apperception Test.*
15. Evaluate Murray's theory in terms of its function as philosophy, science, and art.

Gordon Allport and Henry Murray were dispositional theorists who emphasized the complexity of personality and the need for an interdisciplinary approach to its study. Critical of narrow conceptions of personality and research, they believed that new methods of study were required to capture the richness and fullness of an individual's personality. Gordon Allport's theory emphasized the uniqueness of the individual, the contemporaneity of motives, and a holistic view of the person. Allport paved the way for the humanistic approach, which we will consider in Part 6. Indeed, he was the first to coin the term "humanistic psychology" in 1930 (DeCarvalho, 1991b). Henry Murray's theory was distinguished by its explicit discussion of motivation and the careful construction of a list of needs that characterize and direct human behavior.

Gordon Allport: Biographical Background

Gordon Allport was born in 1897 in Indiana and grew up near Cleveland, Ohio. He was the son of a country doctor, and he described his practical but humanitarian home life as one characterized by "plain Protestant piety and hard work." Allport has written little about his childhood; he has indicated that he spent much of it alone. He was adept at language, but poor at sports and games.

After he graduated from high school, his brother Floyd, who also became a distinguished psychologist, encouraged him to apply to Harvard, where Floyd had gone. As an undergraduate, Allport concentrated on both psychology and social ethics and in his spare time engaged in social service activities. He ran a boys' club in Boston's West End, served as a volunteer probation officer for the Family Society, and assisted other groups.

Upon graduation, he accepted an opportunity to teach English and sociology at Robert College in Istanbul, Turkey, in a venture that was an early forerunner of the Peace Corps. He enjoyed teaching and accepted a fellowship from Harvard for graduate study in psychology. He received his Ph.D. only two years later, in 1922. His dissertation, "An Experimental Study of the Traits of Personality," was also the first American study on personality traits.

Another fellowship for travel abroad gave an opportunity for Allport to meet Freud. Allport described their meeting as follows. When he arrived, Freud sat silent, apparently waiting for Allport to state the reason for his visit. Allport was simply curious. Then, an incident came to mind that he thought might interest Freud, because it concerned a small boy who had a phobia that appeared to be set very early in life. He told him about an event that had happened on the streetcar on the way to Freud's office. A small boy who was obviously afraid of dirt kept saying to his mother that he didn't want to sit on a dirty seat or next to a dirty man. When Allport finished, Freud looked at him and said, "And was that little boy you?" Allport was surprised, but he regained his

Gordon Allport

composure and changed the subject. Still, he was shaken and he never forgot the incident. He began to feel that Freud's ascription of most behaviors to unconscious motives was incorrect and that an alternative theory of motivation was necessary. In his own theory, Allport did not probe into the dark side of personality; he did not concur with Freud's emphasis on sexuality and unconscious motivations.

On his return from Europe, Allport became an instructor in social ethics at Harvard, where he developed and taught what was probably the first course offered in personality in this country. In 1926 he left to take up an assistant professorship in psychology at Dartmouth, but in 1930 he returned to Harvard, this time to stay. His contributions to Harvard were many. Most notably, he was an early advocate of interdisciplinary studies and a leader in the creation of the department of social relations, which combined degree programs in psychology, sociology, and anthropology. His professional honors were manifold and he was a popular and respected teacher. He died in 1967, one month before his seventieth birthday.

The Nature of Personality

As we mentioned in Chapter 1, Allport described and classified over fifty definitions of personality before he developed his own in 1937. After working with this definition for many years, he revised it in 1961. His final definition is: "Personality is the dynamic organization within the individual of those psychophysical systems that determine his characteristic behavior and thought." Each word in this definition is carefully chosen. Personality is *dynamic* (moving and changing), *organized* (structured), *psychophysical* (involving both the mind and the body), *determined* (structured by the past and predisposing of the future), and *characteristic* (unique for each individual).

For Allport, personality is not a mere fiction or imaginary concept but a real entity. He wanted to suggest that one's personality is really *there*. He referred to the concept of personality as a hypothetical construct, which is currently unobservable because it cannot be measured empirically. However, Allport suggested that personality is an inference that may someday be demonstrated directly as a real existence within the person, involving neural or physiological components. At one time the planet Pluto was a hypothetical construct, postulated long before any telescope could observe it. In time, science was able to point directly to it. Allport also hoped that neurophysiological and psychological research will in time show us the way to directly locate our present hypothetical construct of personality. In this connection, Allport was rather prophetic in recognizing that in the future much of psychology's research would focus on the brain.

Allport (1960b) distinguished among continuity and discontinuity theories of personality and argued for a discontinuity theory. A **continuity theory** suggests that the development of personality is essentially the accumulation of skills, habits, and discriminations, without anything really new appearing in the person's makeup. Changes are merely quantitative relative to the amount of inputs. Such continuity theories are closed systems.

A **discontinuity theory** suggests that in the course of development, an organism experiences genuine transformations or changes so that it reaches successively higher levels of organization. Here growth is conceived as qualitatively different. Walking is considered very different from crawling, talking is viewed as discontinuous with babbling, and so forth, even though these behaviors emerge out of the earlier ones. If we picture personality as an organism into which inputs are introduced, a continuity theory merely sees the inputs accumulating, whereas a discontinuity theory suggests that at times during its development, the organism reorganizes, regroups, and reshapes these inputs so that the structure of personality changes radically. Such theories view the person as open and active in consolidating and integrating experience. Change is qualitative rather than merely quantitative. Theories that posit stages of development of personality have the potential to imply discontinuity, because each stage entails a different organization of personality from the stage before it.

Allport believed that Freud's psychoanalytic theory, though outlining stages of development, did not fully realize this potential because of its primary emphasis on the individual and intrapsychic factors. Elements within Freud's theory pointed toward discontinuity, but it remained semiclosed.

Traits

With the possible exception of Raymond Cattell, Allport has explored the concept of **trait** more fully than any other personality theorist. Allport proposed a biophysical conception of traits as neuropsychic structures (1937). He emphasized that traits are bona fide structures within a person that influence behavior; they are not simply labels we use to describe or classify behaviors.

Allport defined a trait as a determining tendency or predisposition to respond to the world in certain ways. Traits are consistent and enduring; they account for consistency in human behavior. Allport suggested that traits may be considered the ultimate reality of psychological organization. The trait, like personality, is not in principle unobservable. In time, trait theorists may be able to measure traits empirically.

Allport distinguished between individual traits and common traits (1937). In his later writings, to clarify his position, he used the terms "common traits" and "personal dispositions."

Common Traits

A **common trait** is a hypothetical construct that permits us to compare individuals within a given culture. Although no two people can be said to possess identical traits, we can discover roughly comparable traits that allow us to compare the predispositions that are held in common with other persons. Normal people in any given culture tend to develop along similar modes or lines of adjustment. In a competitive society, most individuals develop a level of assertiveness or ascendance that can be compared with the level of assertiveness in others. There are several aspects of personality in respect of which all people in a given culture may be compared.

Personal Dispositions

Comparisons may be made among individuals but in the last analysis no two individuals are exactly alike. A **personal disposition** is, like a trait, a general determining characteristic, but it is unique to the individual who has it. Although comparisons cannot be made among personal dispositions, personal dispositions are necessary if one is to reflect accurately the personality structure of a particular individual. Whereas common traits place individuals into comparable categories, personal dispositions, if correctly diagnosed, more accurately describe the individual's uniqueness.

THINKING CRITICALLY

Central Dispositions

Think of a close friend or someone whom you know well. On a blank sheet of paper, try to describe your friend's personality by jotting down those words or phrases that express his or her essential characteristics. Include those qualities that you consider of major importance in an accurate description. Then do the same thing for yourself. Count the number of words or phrases necessary to describe your friend or yourself. Chances are the number falls between five and ten. Allport suggests that the number of highly characteristic central dispositions along which a personality is organized generally falls within that range. In his own research the average was seven. Does your evidence support his hypothesis?

Each one of us has personal dispositions that are of greater or lesser importance. If a personal disposition is so pervasive that almost every behavior of the individual appears to be influenced by it, it is called a **cardinal disposition.** An example would be an extreme lust for power, so intense that virtually every act of the individual can be seen to be governed by that desire. Allport believed that cardinal dispositions are quite rare. Nevertheless, some historical figures, such as Napoleon, have been described as possessed of a cardinal disposition like the lust for power.

Central dispositions refer to highly characteristic tendencies of an individual. They provide the adjectives or phrases a person might use in describing the essential characteristics of another individual in a letter of recommendation (e.g., intelligent, responsible, independent, sensitive, caring). Allport suggests that the number of central dispositions necessary to describe the essential characteristics of an individual normally varies between five and ten. **Secondary dispositions** are more specific, focused tendencies that are often situational in character and less crucial to the personality structure. A person may have a large number of these. A man might be domineering and aggressive at home in his role as father but behave submissively when confronted by a police officer who is giving him a ticket.

Cantor (1990) points out that the concept of personal dispositions can be complemented by a cognitive view providing what Allport (1937) called a "doing" aspect of personality, by centering on how dispositions are cognitively symbolized and kept in social interaction. This view shows how people understand life tasks in terms of their most available schemas (or primary patterns of understanding the world), by imagining different future selves and developing cognitive methods to shape their behavior. This view asks the question, How do people change their schemas and tasks because of their experience? An accent on the doing side can also help us understand the changeability of personality.

An important distinction between common traits and personal dispositions is the way in which each is established and assessed. The concept of common traits lends itself to traditional psychometric research (rating scales, testing instruments, and so on). The concept of personal dispositions requires new methodologies that permit the unique individuality of the person to emerge. We will explore this further in the section on assessment and research.

The Proprium

Allport's humanistic orientation can be seen most clearly in his concept of the proprium. Allport coined the term "proprium" in order to avoid the terms "ego" or "self," which he believed are often used as catchall phrases for those elements of personality that cannot be accounted for in any other way. Allport's **proprium** refers to the central experiences of self-awareness that people have as they grow and move forward. Allport purposely chose a term with the prefix "pro" to connote forward movement.

The proprium is defined in terms of its functions or the things that it does. Allport described seven **propriate functions** (1961). None of them is innate; rather, they develop gradually over time as an individual grows from infancy to adulthood. Together, the activities of the proprium constitute an evolving sense of self as known and felt.

The first propriate function to emerge is the sense of **bodily self.** It consists of sensations in the body and entails coming to know one's body limits. Certain parts of the body are emphasized as more important than others. Thus, young children, when instructed to wash their faces and hands, wash the palms and the front of the face but invariably overlook the back of their hands and behind their ears. Most of us, even as adults, tend to locate the self in the head region. This bodily sense, which is learned, remains the foundation of our self-awareness.

The second propriate function, the sense of **self-identity,** refers to the awareness of inner sameness and continuity. Infants are not aware of themselves as individuals and cannot distinguish themselves from other objects. Gradually, out of an undifferentiated whole, the infant comes to distinguish between inner and outer. The external world is developed first; later, the child discovers a sense of "I." These first two propriate functions begin to emerge from eighteen months onward. The development of self-awareness also depends on maturation of the central nervous system. However it cannot be reduced to simple maturation (Kagan, 1991).

Between the ages of two and three the third propriate function, **self-esteem,** develops. Self-esteem refers to the feelings of pride as the child develops the ability to do things. It is comparable to Erikson's stage of autonomy, which reflects the child's need to feel control over the self and other objects. Two-year-olds are eager to do things for themselves and usually do not want others to help them. One mark of the child's emerging sense of self-esteem is negativism. The child employs the word "no" to assert freedom from adult control. A certain amount of negativism is necessary for the development of self-esteem.

Between the ages of four and six, two other propriate functions emerge: self-extension and self-image. **Self-extension** refers to a sense of possession. Children recognize that certain toys and certain people belong to them and identify them as "my ball," "my daddy." Self-extension leads into a valuing of others because of their relationship to oneself. In the adult years one's children are perceived as extensions of one's self. **Self-image** refers to a sense of the expectation of others and its comparison with one's own behavior. Children come to understand parental expectations and to see themselves as fulfilling or not fulfilling those desired roles. This early self-image lays the foundation for development of conscience and, later, intentions and goals.

Between the ages of six and twelve, the propriate function of self as rational coper develops as children discover that they can use their intellectual capacities to solve problems. This boy is demonstrating a home recycling system.

Between the ages of six and twelve, the propriate function of **self as rational coper** develops. Children discover that they can use their own rational capacities to solve problems. They begin to perceive of themselves as active, problem-solving agents, who can develop a sense of competence in what they do. Allport compared the self as coper with Freud's concept of the ego as the executor of the personality.

Last, during adolescence, the function of propriate striving emerges. **Propriate striving** refers to the projection of long-term purposes and goals and the development of a plan to attain them. Such efforts are essential for the development of self-identity, which Erikson had pinpointed as the primary feature of adolescence.

Allport believed that there is a marked difference between the infant and the adult. The infant is a dependent, impatient, pleasure-seeking, "unsocialized horror," largely governed by unlearned biological drives, who can tolerate little delay in the fulfillment of those drives and reflexes. The infant has the potentialities for personality, but "can scarcely be said to have personality" (1961). Given the appropriate security and affection, the child will grow in the direction of developing a proprium. The child will be transformed from a biologically dominated organism to a psychologically mature adult. The adult person is discontinuous from the child. The adult emerges from the child but is no longer governed by the child's needs.

Not only is there a radical discontinuity between the child and the mature adult; Allport also suggests that there is a radical discontinuity between healthy adults and neurotics. The life of neurotics is marked by cognitive crippling. In their efforts to find security, neurotics react in rigid, inflexible ways. Such individuals continue to behave as children, dominated by infantile drives and conflicts. Their propriums are undeveloped and their motives remain tied to original needs.

Functional Autonomy

Closely related to Allport's concepts of the proprium and discontinuity is his concept of **functional autonomy**, which implies that adult motivation is not necessarily tied to the past. A given behavior may become a goal in itself regardless of its original intention. Thus, adult motives are not necessarily related to the earlier experiences in which the motive or activity initially appeared; they are contemporaneous with the behaviors themselves.

For example, let us imagine that young Johnny's father was a baseball fan. During his spare time and on Saturdays he played baseball with his son. Originally, Johnny played baseball with his Dad to gain his attention and to please him. During his school years, Johnny also played baseball with the other children in his neighborhood and was an active member of Little League. He discovered that he was competent in the game and, what is more, he enjoyed it. In high school and college, he played in the intramural sports program. Later, he was recruited to play with a major league. Today, as he is standing at bat for the Yankees or Dodgers, does it make sense to insist that his motive for playing baseball continues to be that of pleasing his father? Does it not seem more reasonable to suggest that he plays because he enjoys the game and the financial rewards that it brings? His present motives are entirely different and free from his original motives. There may be a historical tie, but there is no functional tie. His motive is functionally autonomous.

Allport refers to two levels of functional autonomy: perseverative functional autonomy and propriate functional autonomy.

Perseverative functional autonomy refers to acts or behaviors that are repeated even though they may have lost their original function; they are not controlled by the proprium and have no genuine connection with it. A teenage girl may, in a spirit of rebellion against her parents, begin to smoke cigarettes, which she knows will annoy them. As an adult, she may continue to smoke cigarettes, long after her period of teenage rebellion. Perseverative functional autonomy refers to repetitive activities such as compulsions, addictions to drugs or alcohol, ritualistic or routine behaviors.

Propriate functional autonomy refers to those acquired interests, values, attitudes, intentions, and life-style that are directed from the proprium. Abilities frequently convert into interests. The person selects those motives that are important and organizes them in a fashion that is consistent with his or her self-image and life-style.

Allport acknowledged that not all behaviors are functionally autonomous. Among the processes that are not are: drives, reflexes, constitutionally determined capacities such as physique and intellect, habits, primary reinforcements, infantilisms and fixations, some neuroses, and sublimations. At times it is difficult to determine whether or not a motive is functionally autonomous. Further, certain motives may be autonomous only to a certain degree. Nevertheless, Allport believed that many of the motives of the healthy, mature adult may be considered to be governed by propriate functional autonomy. Allport's rationale for developing the concept of propriate functional autonomy is the desire to underscore the concept that we live in the present, not in the past.

A Definition of Maturity

As we have seen, Allport believed that there is a radical discontinuity between the neurotic and healthy personality. Allport concurred with Carl Jung that too many personality theorists center their discussion of personality on the characteristics of the neurotic and view health simply as the absence of neurotic symptoms. In his discussion (1961), Allport posited six criteria of maturity.

Extension of the Sense of Self   Mature adults genuinely participate in important realms of human achievement. They are interested in others and consider the welfare of others as important as their own. Their sense of self is not limited to their own selves but embraces many interests.

Warm Relating of Self to Others   Mature adults are able to relate intimately to other persons in appropriate situations. They are compassionate and able to tolerate many differences in human beings. In their relationships, they neither impose themselves on others nor hinder their own freedom of self-identity.

Emotional Security (Self-Acceptance)   Mature people are able to accept themselves and their emotional states. Their emotions, even though they are not always pleasant, do not lead them into impulsive acts or actions that hurt others. They are sufficiently secure in who they are to accept themselves and not wish to be somebody else.

Realistic Perception, Skills, and Assignments   Mature adults do not need to create a fantasy world but live in "the real world." They are problem solvers and have developed the appropriate skills to complete their assigned tasks and work. Moreover, their work is not a burden to them, it is a responsibility whose challenge can be accepted without self-pity.

Self-Objectification (Insight and Humor)   Self-insight is difficult to acquire. Mature people know what they can do, what they cannot do, and what they ought to do. They have no need to deceive either themselves or other people. An important corollary of insight is a sense of humor. Mature individuals are able to laugh at themselves rather than feel threatened by their human weaknesses. Such humor is to be distinguished from the ordinary sense of the comic. The sense of humor to which Allport referred entails recognizing the ludicrous behaviors we share with others because of our common humanity.

Unifying Philosophy of Life   Maturity entails a clear understanding of life's goals and purposes. In the mature person, this philosophy is clearly marked and outwardly focused. It is strongly informed by a set of values that may but does not necessarily include religious sentiments. Further, a unifying philosophy of life is governed by a generic conscience. The *must* conscience of childhood is replaced by the *ought* conscience of the adult. Whereas the child's values are introjected from others, the adult's values arise from a chosen style of being and are based on propriate judgments.

Essentially, maturity for Allport is summed up by expression of the propriate functions to a high degree and freedom from one's past. Allport indicated that human beings are always in the process of *becoming* (1955). The urge to grow and fulfill oneself is present from birth. We have the ability to develop and follow a creative life-style. Further, with maturity we can consciously design and effect our plans without being hindered by unconscious forces of the past. His theory holds echoes of Jung's concept of self-realization and Adler's construct of the creative self and points toward the concepts of Rogers and Maslow. Maslow explicitly acknowledged Allport's influence on his interest in the study of self-actualized persons.

Assessment and Research in Allport's Theory

Allport wrote extensively on methods of inquiry and investigation that are useful for the study of personality, and some of his own research in the area is considered classic. Allport pointed out that personality is so complex that every legitimate method of study should be included in its pursuit. He was critical of those who limit their research and do not encourage or permit the study of personality concepts that are not easily submitted to empirical test. At the same time, he was also critical of applying methods appropriate to the study of neurotic individuals to the normal individual.

Allport's view of personality as open and discontinuous does not lend itself very well to study by the traditional methods in academic psychology, which seek to discover general laws that apply to all individual cases. The emphasis, particularly in American psychology, has been on a **nomothetic** (from the Greek *nomos,* law, and *thetēs,* one who establishes) approach, studying large groups of individuals to determine the frequency with which certain events occur and from this to infer common traits, general variables, or universal principles. Normalcy is often conceived as that behavior that occurs most regularly. Thus, the behavior that is considered normal for a two-year-old is the behavior that is shared in common by most two-year-olds. Allport encouraged an **idiographic** (from the Greek *idios,* one's own, and *graphein,* to write) approach that centers on the individual, employing techniques and variables that are appropriate to understanding the uniqueness of each person and uncovering personal dispositions. Although such methods are difficult, time consuming, and often expensive to evolve, their aim is to account for the unique event that is theoretically just as open to lawful explanation as the frequent event.

In the 1940s, over three hundred letters written to a young married couple by a woman (Jenny Masterson) between her fifty-ninth and seventieth years came to Allport's attention. He and his students analyzed these letters to determine Jenny's central dispositions. In studying these documents, Allport tried to note the frequency with which certain themes or ideas appeared. He asked other people to read the letters and assess Jenny in terms of her traits. He also discussed Jenny's personality in terms of different personality theories. Allport believed that the study of personal documents, such as diaries, autobiographies, and letters, could be a potentially valuable idiographic approach.

In his analysis of Jenny's correspondence (1965), Allport looked for recurring patterns and was able to identify eight unmistakable central dispositions that he believed were significant for understanding her personality: quarrelsome-suspicious, self-centered, independent, dramatic, aesthetic-artistic, aggressive, cynical-morbid, and sentimental. Allport then conducted a formal *content analysis* of the letters. The research technique of content analysis provides a systematic, objective, and quantitative way of describing written or spoken communications. Jenny's comments in the letters were classified into different categories (e.g., independence, hostility, affective, love of art, cynicism) and a frequency count was taken. The data were then subjected to a study by factor analysis (a complex statistical analysis). The findings of factor analysis were quite similar to Allport's own.

In his preface to *Letters from Jenny,* Allport wrote: "To me the principle fascination of the letters lies in their challenge to the reader (whether psychologist or layman) to 'explain' Jenny if he can. Why does an intelligent lady behave so persistently in a self-defeating manner?"

With Philip Vernon and Gardner Lindzey, Allport developed a Study of Values Scale, a dimensional measurement designed to examine individuality. The scale measures six common traits originally delineated by Spranger (1928): the theoretical, aesthetic, social, political, religious, and economic. Because the test reflects the relative strengths of these six values within one's own personality, one individual's score cannot be compared with anyone else's. The test has been widely used in counseling and vocational guidance and has proved to be a significant research tool in studies of selective perception.

Allport and Philip Vernon also initiated research into expressive behavior during the early 1930s. **Expressive behavior** refers to an individual's manner of performing. Every behavior has a coping and an expressive aspect. The *coping aspect* refers to what the act does to deal with or adapt to the task at hand. The *expressive aspect* refers to how the act is done.

Ordinarily we pay more attention to coping behavior than to expressive behavior. But expressive behavior, because it is more spontaneous, can be highly revelatory of basic personality aspects. Allport and others conducted considerable research on several expressive features of personality: the face, voice, posture, gesture, gait, and handwriting. They discovered that there is a marked consistency in a person's expressive behavior. In some instances, Allport was able to deduce certain traits and make accurate judgments about an individual's personality. Allport suggested that further research in this area is highly desirable because a person's expressive manner and style may be the most important factor in understanding the personality.

THINKING CRITICALLY

Traits Due to Victimization

Can you think of other examples with reference to women or other minority groups in which people are first compelled to behave in a specific way, they learn specific traits in order to adapt, and these same traits are employed as confirmation that the group is inferior? See if you can come up with several different examples for several different groups. What are some steps that we might take to help improve relationships among people of diverse cultures?

Another outgrowth of Allport's personality theory has been his interest in religion as a healthy, productive aspect of human life. Allport has contributed to research on understanding the relation between religion and prejudice and has become very important to research in the psychology of religion.

In his authoritative study on prejudice (1954), Allport centered on race and religious prejudice. However, identical forces occur with reference to women or any other minority. Allport suggests that first a group is compelled to respond in a specific way; then they learn specific traits in order to adapt and those same traits are employed as confirmation that the group is inferior. Thus, for example, women are often seen as weak when they communicate their need for relationships. The same need, however, could be seen as healthy and constructive for improving human relations among people of diverse cultures (Symonds, 1991).

Allport's Theory: Philosophy, Science, and Art

Allport's personality theory is a highly creative one. Although many of his ideas are reminiscent of other theories, he combined others' insights with his own to develop a truly unique approach. His original concepts, like personal dispositions, the proprium, and functional autonomy, are highly controversial and extremely stimulating. In his emphasis on the uniqueness of the individual and the contemporaneity of motives Allport foreshadowed the humanist theories of Rogers and Maslow. Indeed, the emphasis in his theory is not on the past but on forward movement.

Allport maintained that because personality is so complex, every legitimate method of study should be included in our efforts to comprehend it. He used rigorous scientific methods to establish common traits. At the same time, he pointed out that we need to develop alternative methods that help us understand the uniqueness of each individual. In his own research, Allport recognized the value of other methodologies and used information drawn from literature, philosophy, art, and religion, as well as from science. Allport believed that an open system of personality encourages the invention of new methods of research; these methods aim at rigor but do not forfeit the study of certain aspects of personality because present scientific methodologies cannot embrace such study.

Allport realized that to understand the whole human being, it is necessary to comprehend the individual philosophically as well as scientifically. "The philosophy of the person is inseparable from the psychology of the person" (1961). Indeed, any psychological stance, Allport pointed out, is implicitly linked to basic philosophical assumptions.

Allport's concept of functional autonomy has been the subject of a great deal of controversy and criticism. In presenting his theories to the public, Allport's concern was to teach and provoke interest rather than to make statements that are above reproach. Thus, it is often very difficult to differentiate between what he assumed and what he established through empirical procedures. The concept of functional autonomy is not a construct that lends itself to operational definition, predictions, or empirical tests. The phenomena that Allport explained as functionally autonomous can also be explained by rival constructs. Further, Allport did not clearly describe the developmental processes that underlie functional autonomy. He failed to explain how or why it occurs (Hall & Lindzey, 1978).

Still, Allport's concepts are highly congruent with recent developments in personality theory. His emphasis on discontinuity is picked up by humanist and cognitive theorists. His concepts of functional autonomy and propriate functions harmonize with recent expansions in psychoanalysis. The goal of psychoanalysis is to strengthen the functioning of the ego. The intent of the reconstruction of the past in psychoanalysis is to permit the patient to work through the past so that it loses its grip. By becoming aware of one's unconscious motivations, one is free to behave differently in the future if one so wishes. Thus, the intent of psychoanalysis is congruent, if not synonymous, with the development of propriate functional autonomy.

Allport was not a practicing psychotherapist and did not develop a specific therapeutic technique. Nevertheless, many of his ideas, like functional autonomy, propriate functions, and the radical discontinuity between normal and neurotic adults, have been useful to clinicians.

Allport did not develop a school of followers, but his theory has had considerable impact, as attested to by the frequent references to Allport in psychological literature. Indeed, when a group of clinicians were asked which personality theorist was most influential for them in their everyday work, the name of Gordon Allport ranked second only to that of Freud. His work offers a bridge between traditional academic psychology, which emphasizes psychometrics and nomothetic studies, and clinical psychology, which concentrates on a more idiographic approach to the understanding of personality.

There has been a resurgence of interest in idiographic approaches to the study of personality. The *Journal of Personality* published a special edition exploring nomothetic and idiographic approaches to personality and prediction (West, 1983). Because of the emphasis on personal and unique determinants of behavior, an idiographic approach should provide greater accuracy in explanation and prediction. Lamielle (1981) argues "against continued adherence to the long dominant 'nomothetic' paradigm for personality research" because from it we cannot make any legitimate interpretations at the level of the individual. Thus nomothetic research is not very helpful to a theory of personality that seeks to comprehend the uniqueness of individuals (Lamielle & Trierweiler, 1986; see also Howard & Myers, 1990; Pelham, 1993). DeCarvalho (1990) has argued that Allport's complex and unifying suggestion in the late 1960s for a humanistic psychology was an exceptional happening in Western psychology that illuminates the conflict between an experimental as compared to an experiential approach to psychological exploration.

Henry Murray, like Gordon Allport, emphasized the complexity of personality and the need for interdisciplinary research in personality.

Henry A. Murray

Henry A. Murray: Biographical Background

Henry A. Murray was born in New York City on May 13, 1893. His parents were well-to-do and Murray grew up as a privileged American boy in a time before automobiles, motorboats, or movies. Winters were spent in the city in a brownstone on what is now the site of Rockefeller Center. Summers were spent on Long Island, where he enjoyed outdoor physical activity, animals, and the woods in back of his home.

Murray did not believe that he qualified as a typical Freudian child. It was difficult for him to recognize the presence of an Oedipal complex in his life. His training analysis did not uncover any indications of hidden resentment toward his father. On the other hand, his childhood evokes several Adlerian themes. Murray recalled an incident at about four years of age when his mother suggested that the queen and her son pictured in a fairy-tale book were sad because of the prospect of death. Later he suggested that memory embodied feelings of having been abandoned (left to die) by his mother in favor of his siblings because he was difficult to care for. This led to an early development of self-reliance as well as tender feelings of pity toward his mother and others with emotional problems.

Unlike Allport, Murray received little formal training in psychology. After six years in two private schools in New York City, he went to Groton, a private preparatory school in Massachusetts. He obtained his B.A. from Harvard, where he majored in history but received only below-average grades. It appears he was more interested in going out for the crew team. Yet he went on to medical school at Columbia University and graduated at the top of his class. Later he received an M.A. in biology from Columbia and a Ph.D. in biochemistry from Cambridge University.

In contrast to Allport, whose meeting with Freud left him somewhat skeptical about unconscious processes, Murray spent three weeks with Carl Jung in Zurich during an Easter vacation from Cambridge and emerged a "reborn man." He had "experienced the unconscious" and thereafter devoted himself exclusively to psychology and to probing the deepest recesses of personality.

A new biography (Robinson, 1992) suggests Murray had a number of troubling intellectual and emotional shortcomings and, while he kept a traditional marriage, he was also involved in a torrid affair with Christiana Morgan, a talented married woman who was also interested in the work of Carl Jung. Morgan made important contributions to the early development of psychoanalysis, especially in the area of feminism and also to Murray's theory of personality, for which she was never given proper recognition (Douglas, 1993). Nevertheless, Murray was a highly regarded professor of psychology at Harvard University from the 1920s to the 1960s, where he set up the Harvard Psychological Clinic expressly to study personality.

Murray gathered around him a group of capable young and mature scholars, many of whom are notable psychologists in their own right. He was awarded the Distinguished Scientific Contribution Award of the American Psychological Association and the Gold Medal Award of the American Psychological Foundation for his contributions to psychology. Murray died in 1988.

The Study of Personology

Murray suggested that the concept of personality is a hypothesis, a construct that helps us account for an individual's behavior. As opposed to Allport who saw personality as a real entity, Murray did not believe that the concept of personality refers to any real physical substance. An individual's personality is dependent upon brain processes, and hence the anatomical center of personality is the brain. There is an intimate relationship between cerebral physiology and personality. Neurophysiological processes are the source of human behavior.

In his study of personology, which is Murray's term for the study of individual "human lives and the factors that influence their course" (1938), Murray emphasized the understanding of normal individuals in natural settings. He believed that psychologists should primarily concern themselves with the detailed and careful study of individual lives.

In studying the individual, Murray believed that it is useful to separate the total behavior of a person into identifiable and manageable units. His basic unit is a **proceeding**, a short, significant behavior pattern that has a clear beginning and ending. Proceedings are interactions between the subject and another person or object in the environment, for example, picking up a book, writing a letter, or holding a conversation. Proceedings may be internal (imagined) or external (real). A succession of proceedings constitutes a *serial.* Thus, a friendship or a marriage consists of a serial of proceedings that needs to be studied as a whole. A planned series of proceedings is a *serial program,* which leads toward a goal such as becoming a lawyer. Serial programs may stretch into the future for months or even years. Each proceeding in the series may be seen as having a subgoal that brings the individual closer to the final goal. Serial programs are governed by a mental process known as *ordination.* This enables us, once we understand our world, to develop a strategy for coping with it. Ordination also permits us to develop *schedules* or plans for resolving conflicting proceedings. A schedule, like a family budget, tries to accommodate all of the competing needs and goals by permitting them to be expressed at different times.

Some aspects of Murray's theory of personology were drawn from Freud's theory. However, Murray did not hesitate to redefine terms or to elaborate and enrich Freud's concepts. Thus, he used the terms id, ego, and superego in describing the basic divisions of personality but added his own meaning.

Murray agreed with Freud that the id is the source of basic drives and needs, but he emphasized that the id contains positive impulses as well as negative ones. The superego is an internalized representation of the social environment, indicating when, where, how, and what needs can be expressed. The ego is the "organized, discriminating, time-binding, reasoning, resolving, and more self-conscious part of the personality" (1938). Its role is to facilitate the id in meeting its impulses; its effectiveness in doing so affects an individual's adjustment. Murray assumed a more active role for the ego, in line with the ego psychoanalysts discussed in Chapter 7.

Human Needs

Murray's most significant contribution to the study of personality was probably his extensive research on human needs. He constructed what is undoubtedly the most careful and thorough list of human needs found in psychology.

Murray (1938) defined a **need** as a construct representing a force in the brain that organizes our perception, understanding, and behavior in such a way as to change an unsatisfying situation and increase our satisfaction. A need may be aroused by an internal state, such as hunger, or by an external stimulus, such as food.

An observer can infer a need from the following signs: a typical behavior effect or pattern, the search for and avoidance of certain kinds of press (discussed on page 275), the expression of a specific emotion, and signs of satisfaction or dissatisfaction with the effects of one's behavior. In addition, a subject can usually confirm the presence of a need through subjective reports.

From his intensive study of individuals at Harvard (1938), Murray constructed a list of twenty basic needs, which are listed and briefly defined in Table 10.1. Although this list has been revised and modified since that time, it remains highly representative of a comprehensive overview of human needs.

Not all of the needs are present in everyone and the needs vary in their strength and intensity. Murray believed that there is a hierarchy of needs, a concept later elaborated on by Maslow (Chapter 13). Where two or more needs conflict, the most insistent need will be met first. Some needs are *prepotent*, which means they become very urgent if they are not satisfied, such as the need for food or to eliminate waste. Other needs may be met together. An actor may be able to meet achievement and exhibition needs in one and the same performance.

Table 10.1   *Murray's List of Needs*

Dominance	To control one's human environment
Deference	To admire and support a superior other
Autonomy	To resist influence or coercion
Aggression	To overcome opposition forcefully
Abasement	To submit passively to external force
Achievement	To accomplish something difficult
Sex	To form and further an erotic relationship
Sentience	To seek and enjoy sensuous impressions
Exhibition	To make an impression
Play	To relax, amuse oneself, seek diversion and entertainment
Affiliation	To form friendships and associations
Rejection	To snub, ignore, or exclude another
Succorance	To seek aid, protection, or sympathy
Nurturance	To nourish, aid, or protect a helpless other
Infavoidance	To avoid humiliation
Defendance	To defend the self against assault, criticism, and blame
Counteraction	To master or make up for a failure by restriving
Harmavoidance	To avoid pain, physical injury, illness, and death
Order	To put things in order
Understand	The tendency to ask or to answer general questions

SOURCE: From *Explorations in Personality*; edited by Henry A. Murray. Copyright 1938 by Oxford University Press, Inc.; renewed 1966 by Henry A. Murray. Reprinted by permission of the publisher.

THINKING CRITICALLY

Evaluating Needs

Look over Murray's list of twenty needs and study their definitions. Think of instances in which the needs have applied to your life and make a list of the needs that seem to be important to you. When you have finished your list, select the five most important needs and rank them, with 1 indicating the strongest need and 5 indicating the weakest. In evaluating your own hierarchy of needs, it will be helpful if you consider specific events in your life when the needs were apparent.

It will also be helpful for you to consider the way in which diverse cultures and eras foster and encourage the development of different needs. Can you think of needs that you have in the 1990s that may not be characteristic of people in another place and culture? Do you think that Murray's list of needs is itself culture bound? Are you aware of other human needs that are not on Murray's list?

To characterize an individual's behavior simply on the basis of needs is to give a one-sided portrait. This is why Murray introduced the concept of **press**, forces from objects or persons within the environment that help or hinder an individual in reaching goals. Stimuli that arouse needs motivate us to look for or avoid certain kinds of press. Examples of press are cultural discord, family discord, poverty, accident, loss of possessions, presence of siblings, maltreatment by contemporaries, religious training, encouragement, friendship, sexual abuse, and illness. It is important to distinguish between *alpha press,* actual properties or attributes of the environment, and *beta press,* the individual's subjective perception of the environment. The beta presses are the determinants of behavior.

Assessment and Research in Murray's Theory

Henry Murray was a pioneer in the area of assessment, an aspect of personality theory that is increasingly the focus of attention and concern. Like Allport, Murray emphasized an idiographic approach to personality, which focuses on the individual, rather than the usual nomothetic approach, which deals with groups. The basic principle of Murray's concept of assessment was that multiple indicators are required to adequately assess an individual's performance. In other words, one single test could not adequately describe an individual. It is preferable to use multiple instruments administered by multiple assessors from

*Sometimes multiple needs — play, senti-
ence, and nurturance, for example — can
be satisfied by a single activity.*

different areas of specialization. Murray also believed that if feedback were provided to the individual, improved performance could be achieved.

In a unique interdisciplinary effort at Harvard, Murray led a staff of twenty-
eight different specialists in studying fifty-two male undergraduates for a period
of six months. Together they amassed a great deal of data through interviews,
tests, questionnaires, and observations, using an array of clinical, psychoanalytic, experimental, physiological, and life history methods. By having several
trained researchers observe the same individual, Murray believed he could can-
cel out personal errors in assessment. A diagnostic council permitted several
observers to study the same subject and then integrate their findings into a final
diagnosis. This type of interdisciplinary approach was unprecedented at the
time.

Murray's concept of assessment has been generalized to programs and institutions; for example, multiple indicators of assessment have been used to
accurately reflect their performance. Douglas Bray pioneered the use of assessment for personnel selection and the evaluation of performance at AT&T. The

assessment center approach is widely used today for the selection of executives and leaders in industry and government.

Murray himself developed several techniques for assessing personality. The best known is the **Thematic Apperception Test (TAT)**, developed by Murray and C. D. Morgan, which is widely used as a projective device. The TAT consists of a series of thirty ambiguous pictures (for example, see Figure 10.1). The subject is asked to make up stories for the pictures, telling what led up to the event, what is happening, what the characters in the picture are thinking and feeling, and how the event will turn out. The responses to the TAT suggest how the subject thinks in relation to the physical and social environment. Responses are noted in terms of predominant themes and special attention is paid to those forces that emanate from the "hero" in the picture or from the environment.

Figure 10.1   *Thematic Apperception Test Picture*
This is a sample of the pictures in the Thematic Apperception Test. What story does the picture tell? What led up to the events in the picture? What is happening? How are things going to work out?

THINKING CRITICALLY

The Thematic Apperception Test

Look at the picture in Figure 10.1 and describe what the picture means to
you by making up a story for it. When you have finished, read the material
in the text on the TAT and see if you can identify the needs and press that
characterized your story, as well as any thema that emerged.

PHILOSOPHICAL ASSUMPTIONS

Examining Allport and Murray

How would you rate Allport and Murray on each of the basic philosophical assumptions described in Chapter 1? Each basic issue was presented as a bipolar dimension
along which a person's view can be placed according to the degree of agreement
with one or the other extreme. Rate Allport's and Murray's views on these issues.

When you have determined where you think the theorists stand, compare your
responses with those of your classmates and your instructor. You should be willing
to defend your ratings, but also be prepared to change them in light of others' compelling arguments. Afterward, compare your ratings of Allport and Murray with your
own position on each issue and with those of other theorists. Does this comparison
help you to understand why their theories do or do not appeal to you?

Would strongly agree	Would agree	Is neutral or believes in synthesis of both views	Would agree	Would strongly agree
1	2	3	4	5

freedom

People basically have control over
their own behavior and
understand the motives behind
their behavior.

determinism

The behavior of people is
basically determined by internal
or external forces over which they
have little, if any, control.

Through the data, the examiner can infer how the subject relates to other people and molds the environment to meet personal needs. There are special scoring guides, but many clinicians also develop their own system of analysis.

Because the stimuli are ambiguous and the subject is free to respond in any way, it is believed that any meaning the subject gives to the story must come from within. It is said that the subject projects meaning into the story, and thus the TAT is called a projective test. In the TAT we are dealing with imaginative projection rather than a Freudian defense mechanism of projection. Subjects unwittingly project their own attitudes and feelings onto the pictures and thereby reveal themselves.

TAT stories are interpreted in terms of *needs* and *press*. The interaction of

1	2	3	4	5

hereditary
Inherited and inborn characteristics have the most important influence on a person's behavior.

environmental
Factors in the environment have the most important influence on a person's behavior.

1	2	3	4	5

uniqueness
Each individual is unique and cannot be compared with others.

universality
People are basically very similar in nature.

1	2	3	4	5

proactive
Human beings primarily act on their own initiative.

reactive
Human beings primarily react to stimuli from the outside world.

1	2	3	4	5

optimistic
Significant changes in personality and behavior can occur throughout the course of a lifetime.

pessimistic
A person's personality and behavior are essentially stable and unchanging.

need and press together with the outcome of a story make up a *simple thema*. Simple themas that run through several stories become *complex themas,* which help to characterize an individual's mode of functioning. Themas are merely symbolic; they are not considered literal translations of actual subject behavior. Their inference is a hypothetical construct that guides the clinician in evaluating an individual's personality dynamics.

The TAT has proven to be a valuable personality assessment device. It and the Rorschach Ink Blot Test are the most widely used projective techniques. A Children's Apperception Test (CAT) has also been developed by Percival Symonds. The TAT, along with Murray's system of needs, has influenced the development of other assessment techniques, such as the Edwards Personal Preference Schedule and the Jackson Personality Research Form. Moreover, the TAT is frequently used as a research tool for further study of Murray's needs, especially achievement and affiliation.

Murray's Theory: Philosophy, Science, and Art

Murray's pioneering studies helped to shape the growth of personality theory in this country. He was largely responsible for bringing Freud to the attention of academic psychologists and stimulating a great deal of scientific research on Freudian concepts. Although Murray tried to provide operational definitions and specific data, he recognized that he did not have sufficient data to justify calling his theory a scientific construct. The proceedings of his diagnostic council also fall short of today's typical standards in scientific research. Nevertheless, Murray was a forerunner in fostering scientific research in personality theorizing and a pioneer in the area of assessment.

Murray advocated an interdisciplinary approach to the study of personality, which was unprecedented. He was equally at home studying the literature of Herman Melville, the writings of Freud, and the latest empirical data as possible sources of knowledge about human nature. At the Harvard Psychological Clinic, he generated an atmosphere in which lively and creative minds could work together, exchanging ideas and developing syntheses. He spoke of the virtues of bringing different approaches and specialities together to shed light on human nature, and of the need to expand our scope beyond that of a narrow, limited model.

Recent essays on personology, such as McAdams (1992), stress that the "person can be said to be a history—a subjectively composed and construed life story that integrates one's past, present, and future." In addition, people develop their own scripts, most of which are both innate and learned (Tompkins, 1992).

Murray was uniquely successful in avoiding a one-sided picture of personality. He tried to strike a careful balance between constitutional elements and environmental factors. He recognized the importance of both past and future events. His theory embraces both behavioral and experiential aspects. Although he is not explicit about his philosophical position, his efforts are clearly rooted in a humanistic philosophy that encourages a comprehensive and holistic view of human nature. His concepts were "organismic when the rest of psychology was atomistic" (White, 1992).

His classification of needs is considered more useful than any other classification of its type. His emphasis on the brain's physiological processes foreshadows contemporary appreciation of the importance of biological and chemical forces in the human organism. Finally, Murray's Thematic Apperception Test, widely used as a diagnostic tool, represents his major contribution to the art of personality theory.

Conclusions

Together, Gordon Allport and Henry Murray stimulated a great deal of interest and research in personality in American psychology. Each emphasized the uniqueness of the individual. Allport's theory emphasized the contemporaneity of motives and a holistic view of the person. His concept of the proprium emphasized the difference between the child and the healthy adult. Murray explicitly discussed motivation; his careful construction of the list of twenty needs and his work in the area of assessment has contributed significantly to ongoing personality research. Both Allport and Murray emphasized that personality is very complex and urged that its study be both interdisciplinary and idiographic. With the contemporary resurgence of interest in idiographic techniques, their pioneering efforts are even more appreciated.

Summary

1. Allport described and classified over fifty definitions of personality before finalizing his own definition: "Personality is the dynamic organization within the individual of those psychophysical systems that determine his characteristic behavior and thought."
2. Allport distinguished between **continuity** theories of personality that are closed and admit little change and **discontinuity** theories that are open and provide for extensive growth.
3. Allport distinguished between **common traits**, hypothetical constructs that permit us to make comparisons between individuals, and **personal dispositions,** which are unique to each person. Common traits and personal dispositions are studied by different research methods.
4. There are three levels of personal dispositions: **cardinal, central,** and **secondary.**

5. Allport coined the term **proprium** to refer to the central experience of self-awareness that a person has in growing and moving forward. Allport described seven **propriate functions:** sense of **bodily self, self-identity, self-esteem, self-extension, self-image, self as rational coper,** and **propriate striving.**

6. The concept of **functional autonomy** implies that adult motivation is not necessarily tied to the past. There are two levels of functional autonomy: **perseverative** and **propriate.**

7. Allport was one of the first theorists to discuss the healthy personality. He posited six criteria of maturity.

8. The **nomothetic** approach to the study of personality studies large groups of individuals in order to infer general variables or universal principles. The **idiographic** approach centers on the individual, using techniques that are appropriate to understanding the uniqueness of each person.

9. Allport respected and used the methods of rigorous science in establishing common traits, but he also recognized the value of other methods and the need to understand the individual philosophically as well as scientifically.

10. Murray's term **personology** refers to his unique interdisciplinary study of the individual, which employs a wide array of clinical, psychoanalytic, and experimental methods.

11. Murray separated a person's behavior into identifiable units. The basic unit is a **proceeding,** a succession of proceedings is a *serial,* a planned series is a *serial program,* and a plan for resolving conflicting proceedings is a *schedule.*

12. A **need** is a construct representing a force in the brain that organizes our perception, understanding, and behavior in such a way as to lead us to change an unsatisfying situation. Needs can be inferred from behavioral signs and confirmed through subjective reports. The twenty basic needs that Murray identified are: dominance, deference, autonomy, aggression, abasement, achievement, sex, sentience, exhibition, play, affiliation, rejection, succorance, nurturance, infavoidance, defendance, counteraction, harmavoidance, order, and understanding.

13. A **press** is a force from the environment that helps or hinders an individual in reaching goals. Murray distinguishes between *alpha press* and *beta press.* Examples of press are poverty, illness, and encouragement.

14. Murray urged an interdisciplinary and idiographic approach to the study of personology. He set up a diagnostic council in which several different specialists would study an individual and integrate their findings. The **Thematic Apperception Test (TAT)** is a projective device in which a subject makes up a story for ambiguous pictures. These stories may be interpreted in terms of needs, press, and thema.

15. Murray's interdisciplinary approach was unprecedented. It helps to underscore the values of an interdisciplinary approach to understanding personality and the limitations of a narrow model.

Suggestions for Further Reading

Allport was a prolific author whose many writings have a clear teaching intent. He sought to describe and illustrate his concepts vividly. His writings are enjoyable to read and of great interest to the student of personality.

Allport's pioneer effort in personality theory was *Personality: A Psychological Interpretation* (Holt, 1937). This work constitutes the initial presentation of his theory, distinguishing between common and individual traits and introducing the concept of functional autonomy. A revised and updated statement of his position is given in *Pattern and Growth in Personality* (Holt, Rinehart, and Winston, 1961). In this work, Allport introduced the concept of personal disposition and emphasized the uniqueness of each individual. The book is highly readable and strongly recommended as an introduction to Allport's thought. *Becoming: Basic Considerations for a Psychology of Personality* (Yale University Press, 1955) underscores Allport's humanistic and futuristic approach. In it he discussed the criteria for maturity. Also recommended are *The Person in Psychology: Selected Essays* (Beacon Press, 1968), which contains a group of Allport's important articles; and *The Nature of Prejudice* (Beacon Press, 1954), Allport's classic study. Special tribute was extended to Gordon Allport in the work edited by Craik, K. H.; Hogan, R. and Wolfe, R. N. *Fifty years of personality psychology. Perspectives on individual differences.* (Plenum Press, 1993).

Considering the extensive amount of research that Murray did, he wrote very little. He studied Melville intensively for twenty-five years and is widely respected as a Melville scholar through his valuable articles on that author. Unfortunately, his writing tends to be stiff and formal and he had a penchant for coining new words that makes him difficult to read. The student who is interested in his work is encouraged to read *Explorations in Personality* (Oxford University Press, 1938), his major work, written in collaboration with colleagues at the Harvard Psychological Clinic, which describes the findings of his monumental study undertaken there. Also useful is "Outline of a Conception of Personality," written with C. Kluckholn and included in C. Kluckholn, H. A. Murray, and D. M. Schneider (Eds.), *Personality in Nature, Society, and Culture* (Knopf, 1953). A most delightful read is his autobiography, in E. G. Boring and G. Lindzey, *A History of Psychology in Autobiography,* Vol. 5 (Appleton-Century-Crofts, 1967). Robinson's biography is *Love's Story Told* (Harvard University Press, 1992).

CHAPTER 11

Trait and Temperament Theories

YOUR GOALS FOR THIS CHAPTER

1. Distinguish between *typologies* and *traits*.
2. Cite Cattell's definition of *personality* and compare his interest in personality theorizing with that of other theorists.
3. Distinguish between *source* and *surface* traits and give examples of each.
4. Explain how Cattell identifies traits through *factor analysis*.
5. Describe two fundamental personality dimensions that Eysenck has identified.
6. Describe Eysenck's methods of assessment and research.
7. Identify the hypothesized causal agents of *extraversion-introversion* and *emotional stability-neuroticism* in Eysenck's theory.
8. Distinguish between the *genotype* and the *phenotype*.
9. Discuss research on Eysenck's theory.
10. Discuss the salient features of Buss and Plomin's theory.
11. Describe other biological and genetic research.
12. Discuss the Big Five personality traits and support for this model.
13. Evaluate trait and temperament theories in terms of their function as philosophy, science, and art.

A central issue in personality theorizing has been the importance of genetic and environmental factors in shaping personality. In the lay person's mind, differences in behavior have often been thought to result in part from general physical characteristics that are inherited. Thus we have common stereotypes such as "Fat people are jolly" or "Redheads are hot-tempered." Similarly, it has been thought that an individual's potential is clearly limited by inherited factors. Thus, although a better diet may help us grow taller or act more intelligently, limitations may have been imposed by our genetic makeup.

For many years, personality theorists debated over whether personality is influenced by inner biological patterns or by the experiences an individual has had. This dispute, variously known as the issue of *heredity versus environment* or the *nurture versus nature* controversy, was frequently conducted in a way that suggested that one or the other had to be the primary factor. Today, most theorists recognize that the answer is both. The term *interaction* means that *each affects the other.* Trait and temperament views recognize that the contributions of heredity and the environment are not merely additive but rather complex combinations.

This chapter highlights salient features of theories that have wrestled with these issues. The theorists discussed in this chapter do not deny the influence of environmental forces on personality — they take a biosocial view and seek to clarify the role that biological and genetic factors play. Several of the theories are complex and somewhat difficult for the lay person to understand. It is not the intent of this text to summarize the whole of these theories, but rather to provide an overview.

Some Historical Background

One of the earliest efforts to describe personality in terms of dispositions was made by the Greek physician Hippocrates (460?–377?B.C.), who suggested that personalities could be classified according to a predominance of certain body fluids, or *humors.* A predominance of blood led to a *sanguine* character marked by sturdiness, high color, and cheerfulness. A predominance of mucus led to the slow, solid, and apathetic *phlegmatic* personality. A predominance of black bile led to the *melancholic* or depressed personality, whereas yellow bile infused the irascible and violent *choleric* personality.

Although the theories on which Hippocrates' concepts were based may strike us as quaint and outdated, they presage many concepts in modern psychology and continue to influence some personality theorists. In addition, contemporary research suggests a relationship between hormones (chemicals released into the blood stream by the endocrine glands), emotions, and behavior, and depression is thought to be attributable to a chemical reaction in the brain.

Ernest Kretschmer, a German psychiatrist (1888–1964), suggested that people could be classified on the basis of their body measurements. *Asthenics* were thin, long limbed, and narrow chested; they tended to be aloof, withdrawn, shy, and sensitive. *Pyknics* were short, fat, and barrel chested; they were inclined to fluctuations in mood — being either jovial and outgoing or deeply depressed. *Athletics* were balanced in physique and muscular development and they tended to be energetic, aggressive, and sanguine. Although Kretschmer's work was very influential, it was criticized because it was difficult to fit everyone into a proper category.

The early dispositional theorists, such as Kretschmer, described people in terms of types or **typologies,** which imply distinct, discrete, and separate categories into which an individual can be placed. To avoid these problems, William Sheldon (1899–1977) described individuals in terms of traits based on physiques and temperaments (see Table 11.1). **Traits** refer to continuous dimensions that individuals possess to varying degrees. Modern **trait theories** recognize that individuals vary considerably with regard to the same characteristic. For instance, we can speak of two types of stature — tall or short. Within any given population, however, we find a continuous gradation of statures from tall to short. Most of the population, moreover, tends to fall in the middle, being neither extremely tall nor extremely short. For modern typologists, types customarily refer to *clusters* of traits or being extreme in a particular trait. Sheldon's theory was important because it marked the transition from earlier typologies to a much more sophisticated approach to understanding personality. He laid the groundwork for and helped to create a significant movement in contemporary personality theory — psychometric trait theory.

Raymond Cattell: Biographical Background

Raymond Cattell was born in Staffordshire, England, in 1905. His childhood was happy. England became involved in World War I when Cattell was nine. He later acknowledged that the war had a significant impact on him.

Cattell received his B.S.C. from the University of London in 1924 at the age of nineteen. He majored in chemistry and physics, but his interest in social concerns led him to pursue psychology, in which he earned a Ph.D. in 1929. His graduate work was also undertaken at the University of London, where he studied under Spearman, a distinguished psychologist who developed the procedure of factor analysis that Cattell would later employ.

The following years were difficult. Employment was hard to come by for a psychologist, so Cattell worked at several part-time jobs. Meanwhile, he continued his own research. The depressed economy and his own poor health led to several lean years, during which he was haunted by poverty and his marriage broke up. Nevertheless, he remained steadfast in his dedication to his work.

In 1937, the University of London awarded Cattell an honorary doctorate of science for his contributions to research in personality. That same year he served as a research associate to E. L. Thorndike at Columbia University in New York. Subsequently, he became a professor of psychology at Clark University

Table 11.1 *Sheldon's Relationships among Components of Physique and Temperament*

Physique		Temperament	
Component	*Description*	*Component*	*Description*
Endomorphy	Predominance of soft roundness	Visceratonia	General love of comfort, relaxation, sociability, people, and food
Mesomorphy	Predominance of muscle, bone, and connective tissue	Somatotonia	Tendency to seek action and power through bodily assertiveness
Ectomorphy	Predominance of linearity and fragility	Cerebrotonia	Predominance of restraint, inhibition, and concealment

Raymond Cattell

and later at Harvard, the University of Illinois, and the University of Hawaii at Manoa. As of this writing, Cattell is still on the faculty of Forrest Institute of Professional Psychology in Honolulu, Hawaii, where he supervises graduate student theses.

Cattell has received several honors and made significant contributions to the study of personality. Although his primary emphasis has been on the study of personality through the techniques of factor analysis, he does not lack interest in or concern with other areas of psychology.

Cattell's Definition of Personality

Cattell begins with a tentative definition of **personality.** "Personality is that which permits a prediction of what a person will do in a given situation" (1950). He believes that a full definition of personality must await further investigation into the types of concepts that are included in the study of behavior. His general statement may be expressed in the formula $R = f(P, S)$, which reads: A response (R) is a function (f) of the person (P) and the stimuli (S). Cattell observes that the response and the stimuli can be precisely determined in an experiment in which the experimenter carefully structures the situation. However, the person is a less well known factor that needs further exploration.

Cattell's definition of personality provides a striking and important contrast between his approach to personality research and that of other theorists, such as the Freudians. Freud developed psychoanalysis as a means of understanding one's self and developing a comprehensive theory of human nature. He was particularly concerned not with the efficacy of psychoanalysis as a predictive tool but with the compelling character of the vision of one's self or humanity that it provided. Cattell, on the other hand, is concerned with the power of a construct to predict future events. His stance is that of the empirical scientist who derives from his or her theory propositions that are subject to empirical test. In a sense, prediction is more difficult than explanation, as it is easier to account for events that have happened than to predict them. Prediction is also useful in that it enables us to anticipate what will happen in certain situations. On the other hand, a theory may have considerable predictive power and garner an impressive array of validating evidence, but still fail to provide a comprehensive or compelling explanation. In his theorizing, Cattell provides an exemplary instance of a scientist who is concerned with validating evidence.

Cattell believes that the exploration of traits will assist us in understanding the structure and function of personality. Knowledge of underlying traits will allow us to make predictions about our own behavior and that of others. Although Cattell is interested in the physical and neurological components that influence behavior, unlike Allport, he does not maintain that the traits he is exploring necessarily have any real physical or neural status.

Surface Traits versus Source Traits

Cattell reminds us that if a trait theory is to be useful, the traits postulated need to go beyond the overt behaviors that an individual shows. Just as any successful hypothesis in science refers to future experiences that might occur if the hypothesis turns out to be useful, a successful trait construct goes beyond simply asserting that a particular behavior pattern exists. To argue that Dale is lazy because of a lazy disposition is to argue in a circle and not provide genuinely useful information. To argue that Pat is honest, thoughtful, and disciplined because of an underlying source variable or trait of ego strength is a much more useful way to proceed. The underlying trait of ego strength accounts for the surface manifestation and also permits us to speculate about other related characteristics, such as assertiveness or confidence, that Dale or Pat will display.

Thus, Cattell distinguishes between surface traits and source traits (1950). **Surface traits** are clusters of overt behavior responses that appear to go together, such as integrity, honesty, self-discipline, and thoughtfulness. **Source traits** refer to the underlying variables that seem to determine the surface manifestation, in this case, ego strength.

Table 11.2 *Cattell's Sixteen Basic Source Traits*

Raymond Cattell identified sixteen basic source traits that represent the building blocks of personality. Certain traits are indicative of an outgoing temperament, while others indicate a more reserved disposition.

outgoing	—	reserved
more intelligent	—	less intelligent
emotionally stable	—	emotionally unstable
assertive	—	humble
happy-go-lucky	—	sober
strong conscience	—	lack of internal standards
adventuresome	—	shy
tough-minded	—	tender-minded
trusting	—	suspicious
imaginative	—	practical
shrewd	—	forthright
apprehensive	—	self-assured
experimental	—	conservative
group-dependent	—	self-sufficient
casual	—	controlled
relaxed	—	tense

The study of source traits is valuable for several reasons. Because they are probably few in number, source traits permit economy in describing an individual. Second, source traits presumably have a genuine structural influence on personality and thus determine the way we behave. Thus, knowledge of a particular source trait may permit us to go beyond mere description and make predictions about additional behaviors that we might observe further.

Source traits may have their origin in heredity or environment. From extensive research, utilizing factor analysis techniques, Cattell has identified sixteen basic temperament and ability source traits that he suggests represent the "building blocks" of personality (1966). The traits are presented in Table 11.2 as bipolar dimensions.

Assessment and Research in Cattell's Theory

Cattell's personality theory made its major impact through his methods and techniques of researching and identifying traits. Cattell's primary tool has been factor analysis.

Cattell begins by gathering large masses of data from a great many individuals in a variety of ways, such as life records, self-report questionnaires, or projective tests. All of the data garnered from these sources are subjected to the complex, sophisticated statistical technique of **factor analysis.** Factor analysis is essentially a correlational procedure, but it interrelates many correlations at one time. Hundreds, or even thousands, of variables may be considered in a single study. Factor analysis is based on the assumption that if several variables correlate highly with one another, it is possible that a common dimension underlies them.

Factor analysis enables researchers to draw conclusions such as: similar scores in reading, vocabulary, and spelling tests are due to a common underlying factor of verbal ability, whereas performance in addition, subtraction, and multiplication depends on mathematical ability. Many of the studies undertaken involve a great deal of mathematical computation. The advent of the computer made factor analysis a feasible technique for personality research.

Thus, beginning with hundreds of surface personality traits, Cattell has discovered through factor analysis which of the traits cluster and occur together with the greatest frequency. These traits are then placed together under a common source trait, thereby reducing the number of traits to be dealt with and making them easier to handle.

In the end Cattell hopes that he can use the information garnered to facilitate the prediction of behavior. Given the ability to describe an individual in terms of various traits and the understanding of how these traits enter into certain behavior response patterns, we would be able to apply this information to a particular instance. Eventually, we will be able to predict how a particular individual might respond in a given situation. Cattell (1965) suggests that this may someday be done by means of a **specification equation:**

$$R = s_1 T_1 + s_2 T_2 + s_3 T_3 + \ldots + s_n T_n$$

This equation simply means the following: The response (R) equals the sum of the characteristics of the person ($T_1, T_2, T_3 \ldots T_n$). Each trait is weighted according to its relevance to the particular situation; that rating constitutes the situational index ($s_1, s_2, s_3 \ldots$). If a particular trait is highly relevant to the response, its corresponding situational index would be high. If a particular trait is irrelevant to a response, the situational index would be zero. If the trait inhibits or detracts from the response, the situational index would be negative. The model is basically a very simple one.

For example, suppose R were to stand for the classroom performance of a professor. The factor of intelligence would be very important because an instructor needs to understand the subject and know how to communicate it to others. Thus, the characteristic of intelligence would be assigned a high situational index. The characteristic of assertiveness might also be important, but less so than intelligence. Therefore, it would be assigned a lower number. Each trait that is relevant to classroom performance would be included until all the elements in the equation were filled in. We would then be able to predict how an instructor might behave in the classroom. Cattell has applied some of his methods to the area of personnel selection, where he has had considerable success in predicting job satisfaction and worker effectiveness.

Cattell's formula is based on addition and thus it has been criticized for not providing for possible interrelations or interactions among traits. Cattell acknowledges that we may eventually need more sophisticated formulas, but suggests that his specification equation is a useful starting point. Cattell's rigorous methodology and approach, as well as Eysenck's theory, highlights of which follow, are characteristic of the scientific enterprise at its best.

Hans J. Eysenck: Biographical Background

Berlin, Germany, was the birthplace of Hans Eysenck, who was born on March 4, 1916. Germany was losing World War I, and many suffered from the mass unemployment, high inflation, and political turmoil that followed that loss. Thus the war had a significant impact on Eysenck as it had on Cattell. His parents, well-known actors, divorced when he was two. He was raised by his maternal grandmother. Eysenck's father encouraged him to become an actor, but his mother dissuaded him and he followed her "more sensible" advice.

In school, Eysenck, a Lutheran, had been taunted with the label "white Jew" because he sympathized with the plight of the Jews. Eysenck left Germany at the age of eighteen. His hatred of the Nazi regime led him to study politics and become a socialist. Later he developed serious reservations about socialism and left the party.

After traveling around Europe, Eysenck settled in England and prepared to attend the University of London. Someone suggested he study the newly emerging science of psychology, to which Eysenck replied, "What on earth is psychology?" (1982). When assured, "You'll like it," he embarked on his distinguished career as a psychologist. Psychometrically oriented, the University of London was an exciting place to study psychology, and in 1940 Eysenck received the Ph.D.

Eysenck was hired as a research psychologist at Mill Hill Emergency Hospital. There, he independently conducted a study on the reliability of psychiatric diagnoses and prescribed treatments at the hospital. Eysenck's undercover research demonstrated that there was very little agreement among psychiatrists concerning diagnoses and treatment. Later, using factor analysis, Eysenck concluded that disorders could be embraced under two major personality factors: neuroticism and extraversion/introversion. His findings led him to publish *Dimensions of Personality* (1947).

When World War II ended, Eysenck became director of the psychology department at Maudsley Hospital, the most prestigious teaching psychiatric hospital in England. There he established a program of behavior therapy as well as a program of study that was scientifically oriented and relied on the interdependence of clinical and experimental research. He also organized a behavior

Hans Eysenck

THINKING CRITICALLY

Should We Selectively Breed Humans?

Cattell (1972) suggests that we consider selective breeding as a means of cultivating desired traits in human beings. Eysenck posits a clear biological and genetic basis to personality and behavior, including undesirable behaviors such as criminality and substance abuse. Buss and Plomin's twin studies show that heredity plays a large part in determining personality. Selective breeding has long been accepted as a way of developing superior animals, fruits, and vegetables. Ancient people used plants, such as queen anne's lace and rue, to deliberately limit their populations (Kolata, 1994). Actually, many people selectively breed by choosing their mate on the basis of appearance, intellect, and so forth. The couple who decide to limit family size or abort a ''defective'' fetus are also engaging in their own form of selective breeding. These informal efforts at selective breeding have led to significant, but not necessarily optimal, changes in the distribution of the human population. Arguing that the goal is not to create an ideal type of person or master race, but rather a diversity that would maximize evolutionary progress and the survival of humanity, Cattell suggests that governments extend their concern to the genetic quality of their populations.

In time, psychology and medicine will permit us to directly determine those mental and physical traits that are most desirable. In the meantime, Cattell suggests that a reasonably efficient criterion can be developed based on economics: birth rate proportional to income. Since earnings are not always fairly related to social worth and contribution, some adjustments would be needed to important social occupations (such as teaching, religion, and research) where supply and demand in the market does not provide an adequate evaluation. But, on the whole, Cattell believes that relating family size to earnings would result in a positive eugenic trend. By this measure, parents who have demonstrated their ability to contribute to society would be encouraged to have more children while others who have not demonstrated that ability and cannot afford to raise children would be discouraged through government taxation and other forms of manipulation.

What do you think? Should we consider selectively breeding humans on a more deliberate basis? Is Cattell's assumption, that an individual's worth to society can in most cases be measured by his or her income, appropriate? What other considerations do you think need to be taken into account besides economic ones? Should decisions continue to be made individually or socially, at a national or even international level? The Clinton administration has made population control a main key in its foreign policy of ''sustainable development'' in the Third World (Rowan, 1993). These are issues that deserve serious thought by anyone who is interested in the future of the human race. What difficulties do you envision might arise in trying to be fair to all people?

genetics division. In 1955, he was awarded a chair of psychology at the University of London. In 1988, he was awarded the Distinguished Scientist Award of the American Psychological Association. At present he is a member of the Board of Scientific Affairs of the American Psychological Association.

A prolific writer whose output exceeds even that of Cattell, Eysenck has written for both technical and lay audiences. He has not hesitated to criticize psychoanalysis, psychotherapy, and nonempirical theories of behavior. In turn, his theory has been both praised and denounced. In 1985 Eysenck retired, but he continues to lecture, conduct research, and write on coronary heart disease and cancer, IQ, and the psychophysiology of the brain.

The Identification of Superfactors

Hans Eysenck has marshaled all of the forces of biology, historical typologies, learning theory, and factor analysis in order to understand personality. Eysenck uses factor analysis in his work but his use of it is more deductive than that of Cattell. In Cattell's research, conclusions were drawn from the clusters that appeared in the process of factoring. Eysenck begins with a clear hypothesis about possible underlying variables and then uses statistical analysis to test his hypothesis. Moreover, Eysenck considers factor analysis at best a preliminary tool that paves the way for subsequent laboratory and experimental research to gain a causal understanding of the factors that have been posited. As he stated to Richard Evans,

> I think probably of all of the factor analysts you may know, I'm the one who thinks the least of it. I regard it as a valuable adjunct, a technique that was invaluable under certain circumstances, but one which we must leave behind as soon as possible in order to get a proper causal type of understanding of the factors and to know just what they mean (Evans, 1976).

Eysenck is extraordinarily rigorous in his adherence to a scientific method and outspokenly critical of nonscientific or prescientific theories of personality.

Eysenck defines personality as "a more or less stable and enduring organization of a person's character, temperament, intellect, and physique which determines his unique adjustment to the environment" (1970). Eysenck views personality as a hierarchy (see Figure 11.1). At the bottom of the hierarchy are *specific responses,* behaviors that we can actually observe, such as someone answering a phone. The next level is that of *habitual responses,* clusters of specific behaviors that characteristically recur in similar circumstances, such as buying groceries or giving parties. Above this are more generalized traits, clusters of related habitual responses such as the source traits that Cattell identified. At the top of the hierarchy, related clusters of traits make up broad general dimensions or basic types, such as extraversion or introversion. Eysenck's research has focused on the identification of these superfactors. Moreover, he has sought not

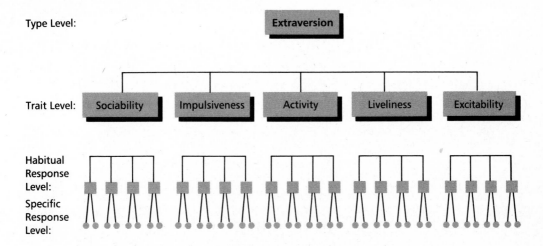

Type Level: Extraversion

Trait Level: Sociability | Impulsiveness | Activity | Liveliness | Excitability

Habitual Response Level:

Specific Response Level:

Figure 11.1 *Eysenck's Hierarchical Model of Personality Development*

From H.J. Eysenck, *The Biological Basis of Personality,* 1967, Courtesy of Charles C Thomas, Publisher, Springfield, Illinois.

only to describe behavior in terms of basic typologies but also to understand the causal factors behind the behavior.

When Eysenck conducted a review of temperament theories, he observed that there were distinct patterns in the various typologies that had been used throughout history to describe personality. He sought to test the hypothesis that the behavior included in Hippocrates' ancient typology could be accounted for by two fundamental personality dimensions or superfactors: introversion versus extraversion and emotionality versus stability.

The **extraversion versus introversion** dimension reflects the degree to which a person is outgoing and participative in relating to other people. Extraversion-introversion is a continuous dimension that varies among individuals. Some people tend to be friendly, impulsive, and talkative whereas others tend to be reserved, quiet, and shy. These dimensions are similar to Jung's two basic attitudes.

The **emotionality versus stability** dimension refers to an individual's adjustment to the environment and the stability of his or her behavior over time. Some people tend to be well integrated and emotionally stable, while others tend to be poorly integrated, emotionally unpredictable, and neurotic. In Eysenck and Rachman's (1965) words: "At the one end we have people whose emotions are labile, strong and easily aroused; they are moody, touchy, anxious, restless, and so forth. At the other extreme we have the people whose emotions are stable, less easily aroused, people who are calm, even-tempered, carefree, and reliable." In both dimensions, most people fall somewhere in the middle of the two extremes. Eysenck suggests that these basic dimensions of personality may be

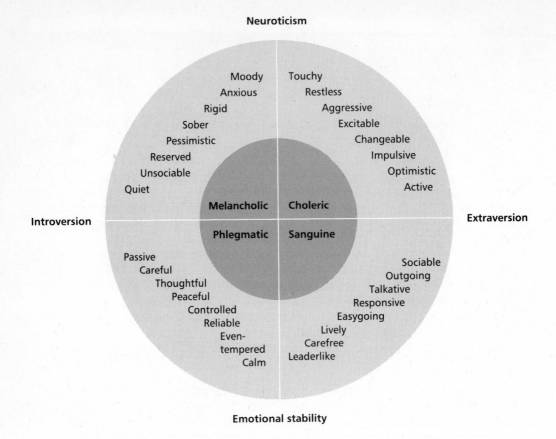

Figure 11.2 *The Intercorrelation of Traits*
The inner circle shows Hippocrates' four temperaments. The outer ring shows the results of factor analysis studies of the intercorrelations between traits done by Eysenck and others.

summarized as shown in Figure 11.2. The inner circle shows Hippocrates' four temperaments. The outer ring shows the results of factor analysis studies of the intercorrelations among traits. The traits, which are on a continuum, clearly reflect the two fundamental dimensions of emotional security versus neuroticism and introversion versus extraversion.

Following his research in the first two superfactors, Eysenck investigated a third one: **psychoticism.** Psychoticism is usually characterized by the loss or distortion of reality and the inability to distinguish between reality and fantasy. The person may have disturbances in thought, emotion, and motor behavior, as well as hallucinations or delusions. The psychoticism factor also includes some degree of psychopathy: disorders characterized by asocial and impulsive behavior, egocentricity, and an absence of guilt (1975). Unlike the dimensions of extraversion/introversion and emotionality/stability, psychoticism is not a dimension with an opposite pole; rather it is an ingredient present in varying degrees in individuals. Eysenck (1975) lists eleven characteristics of individuals who score high in tests of psychoticism:

1. solitary, not caring for people
2. troublesome, not fitting in
3. cruel, inhumane
4. lack feeling, insensitive
5. sensation seeking, underaroused
6. hostile to others, aggressive
7. like odd, unusual things
8. disregard danger, foolhardy
9. like to make fools of other people, upsetting them
10. opposed to accepted social customs
11. engage in little personal interaction; prefer "impersonal" sex

Eysenck's studies have suggested that psychotic disorders are very different from neurotic disorders. There are different routes to psychoticism and neuroticism. Thus, a person may become more and more neurotic without becoming psychotic.

A final superfactor that Eysenck believes plays a major role in personality is *intelligence*. "If we were reduced to describing a person in just three figures, then I have no doubt that we would get the closest approximation to his real nature by using these figures for an assessment of his intelligence, his extroversion, and his neuroticism" (1965). Eysenck has conducted a considerable amount of research on intelligence, relying strongly on the pioneering work of L. L. Thurstone and J. P. Guilford, who used factor analysis to identify components of intelligence. Eysenck has been particularly interested in the use and abuse of intelligence tests and the role of heredity in intelligence. He believes that in the future, experimental methods will be used to study intelligence in cases where ordinary IQ tests are inappropriate (1985).

Assessment and Research in Eysenck's Theory

Personality inventory questionnaires became very popular during the first part of this century. A number of them were developed to measure characteristics such as intelligence, emotional instability, and extraversion/introversion. Eysenck (1957) was critical of early ratings and inventories used in personality assessment. He observed that inventory constructors have mistakenly assumed that individuals answer questions truthfully. In some cases, people deliberately answer a question falsely to avoid being judged in a negative way. Moreover, people do not always know the truth about themselves. In one experiment, 98 percent of the subjects "claimed to have a better than average sense of humor"

(1957). The fact is that in a normal bell-shaped curve, about 50 percent of the population score in the average range.

The problem with personality inventories stems from the fact that there is no objective outside criterion against which to make measurements. Eysenck (1957) notes that psychologists were able to overcome some of the difficulties involved in questionnaires when they gave up the notion of *interpreting* the answers and simply dealt "with the objective fact that a person puts a mark on one part of the paper rather than in another."

Eysenck constructed improved personality inventory questionnaires using a method that he calls **criterion analysis**. He begins with a hypothesis concerning a possible underlying variable, for instance, emotional stability versus neuroticism. He then identifies two criterion groups: a group of people who have been clearly identified as emotionally stable and another group who have been identified as neurotic. He gives each group a questionnaire and observes how many yes and no answers there are in each group to each question. If it is clear that there is a greater tendency for one group to answer a particular question in the affirmative or negative, then that question may be a good item for distinguishing between the two groups.

Eysenck makes it clear that he is not concerned with the *reasons* for the answers, but simply the fact that there are significant differences in the two groups' answers. By studying the differences in answers to multiple questions, it is possible to determine probabilities and develop a questionnaire that will distinguish between the two groups and rank each individual along a continuum. The use of criterion groups helps to show how sensitive a question is to a particular variable, such as emotional stability versus neuroticism. The approach is strictly empirical and makes use of complex statistical analysis.

Contemporary questionnaires and rating procedures are much more sophisticated and more carefully constructed than earlier ones. Tested by complex statistical studies and experimentation, and with careful procedures for establishing reliability and validity, the resulting instruments can be useful tools for the psychologist who wishes to measure personality. Eysenck has constructed a number of paper and pencil self-report inventories to measure the dimension of introversion/extraversion. Among them are the Maudsley Personality Inventory, the Eysenck Personality Inventory, and the Eysenck Personality Questionnaire. These inventories have been used in an extraordinarily large number of research projects.

Looking for Causal Agents of Behavior

In his discussion of personality, Eysenck has gone beyond a descriptive analysis to a *causal* analysis that hypothesizes the agents that may cause certain behavior patterns.

In his early descriptive research, Eysenck (1957) pointed out that individuals differ in the reactivity of their brains and central nervous systems and in the speed with which they develop conditioned responses. These differences correlate with the dimensions of emotional stability/neuroticism and introversion/extraversion. Influenced by the work of Pavlov and Hull, Eysenck developed a theory of excitation inhibition and was successful in making predictions that were supported by experimental results. Later (1967), he hypothesized that specific biological functions were responsible for excitation inhibition and detailed a number of testable deductions that could be made from the theory (1965).

Eysenck (1967) suggests that introversion/extraversion is related to arousal thresholds in the ascending reticular activating system (RAS) of the brain and emotional stability/neuroticism is related to differences in visceral brain (VB) activation (see Figure 11.3). The primary function of the RAS is to regulate levels of arousal ranging from sleep to states of high alertness. Destruction of these tissues causes an animal to sleep almost continuously, whereas stimulation will cause it to become more aroused. Thus, the RAS controls the brain's level of excitability and its responsiveness to stimuli.

Eysenck believes that introverts may have higher levels of RAS reactivity than extraverts. Thus, given identical stimulating conditions, the state of arousal would be higher in introverts than in extraverts. The high level of arousal may create a constraint on their behavior and contribute to the specific traits, such as reserved and careful, that generally characterize introverts. In the same way, the low levels of arousal experienced by extraverts may lead to an absence of constraints and a predominance of impulsive and outgoing behavior normally associated with extraversion.

Eysenck hypothesizes that emotional stability versus neuroticism is due to differences in visceral brain activity. The visceral brain includes the limbic

Figure 11.3 *The Reticular Activating System and the Visceral Brain*
The anatomical structures that Eysenck hypothesizes may be responsible for inherited differences in Introversion/Extraversion and Emotional Stability/Neurosis.

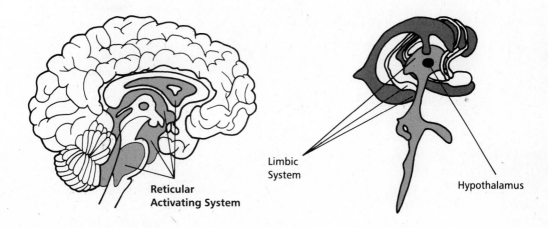

Reticular
Activating System

Limbic
System

Hypothalamus

Visceral Brain

system and the hypothalamus, which are both involved in motivation and emotional behavior. They exert their influence through the autonomic or involuntary nervous system. Eysenck theorizes that individuals who have a low threshold of visceral brain activation may be very emotional in their behavior and more susceptible to neurotic disorders. In short, Eysenck suggests that there is a causal connection between biological functions of the brain and the basic personality dimensions of emotional stability/neuroticism and introversion/extraversion.

Behavior itself is not inherited; certain structures of the nervous system are. Eysenck distinguished between the **genotype**, the genetic makeup of an individual, and the **phenotype**, the individual's observable appearance and behav-

Figure 11.4 *The Personality Phenotype*
A diagram of the interplay between genotype and environment, which leads to the phenotype of extraverted/introverted personality.

From H.J. Eysenck, *The Structure of Human Personality,* London: Methuen & Co. Ltd., 1970, p. 456. Copyright H.J. Eysenck 1970.

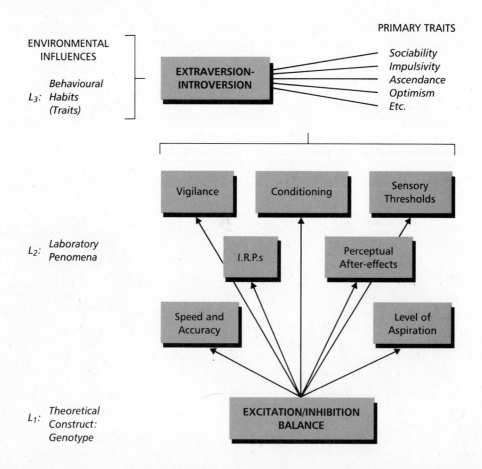

ior that arise out of the genotype's interaction with the environment. Figure 11.4 diagrams the hypothesized chain of events that leads from the genotype to the phenotype. The genotype evolves into inherited anatomical structures, which include the cortex, the autonomic nervous system, the ascending reticular activating system, and the visceral brain. Individuals differ widely in the particulars of these structures (Williams, 1986). These differences lead to the development of different habitual levels of arousal and thresholds for emotional response, which can be seen in laboratory experiments. Through interactions with a particular environment, these tendencies lead to the various emotionally stable or unstable, introverted or extraverted phenotypic patterns of behavior and primary traits that have been identified through factor analysis (1970). Expressed in a formula, $P_B = P_C \times E$, "Behavioral personality equals the constitutional personality times environment."

The distinction between the genotype and the phenotype is an important one. Eysenck is not suggesting that genes determine the outcome for any given individual. Genes are not certain predictors for specific patterns of behavior or development. Many genes express themselves only under certain conditions. Our genetic predispositions are affected by the specific experiences we have from conception onward.

Thus, even though people differ in the extent to which they are genetically predisposed to neurosis, Eysenck believes that neurotic behaviors themselves are learned. In this respect he shares similar views with the behavior and learning theorists on the origin and treatment of neurotic disorders and is a staunch advocate of behavior therapy. However, his recognition of the biological basis of personality is also consistent with biological therapies: physical or chemical interventions, such as drugs, may affect the brain or other body functions and thus provoke or inhibit certain behaviors.

Research on Eysenck's Theory

One of the strengths of Eysenck's theory is that it allows for specific prediction and test. For example, if introverts have strong excitatory brain processes and relatively weak inhibitory effects, they should and do react more quickly in certain structured laboratory situations such as eye-blink conditioning (Eysenck & Rachman, 1965). Electrocardiogram studies and other electrophysiological studies also lend some support to Eysenck's theory (1970). It has even been possible to indicate introversion or extraversion by comparing the amount of salivation produced when lemon juice is applied to someone's tongue with the amount created without lemon juice. Introverts produce considerably more salivation than extraverts (Corcoran, 1964). This suggests that the same physiological functions control both salivation characteristics and introversion/extraversion characteristics. Research has also shown that introverts are more sensitive to stimulant drugs while extraverts are more sensitive to depressant drugs (1970).

Eysenck (1990) is optimistic that biological factors have a significant role in "the genesis of personality differences on P. E. and N. [psychoticism, extraversion and neuroticism]." He points out that "identical factors have been found cross culturally in over 35 different countries covering most of the globe, from Uganda and Nigeria to Japan and mainland China, from the Capitalist countries of the West and the American continent to Eastern-bloc countries such as the Soviet Union, Hungary, Czechoslovakia, Bulgaria, and Yugoslavia" (Barrett & Eysenck, 1984). "Such cross cultural unanimity would be unlikely if biological factors did not play a predominant part (1990)."

Cross-cultural studies continue to be conducted on Eysenck's personality dimensions. Most of these use the Eysenck Personality Questionnaire to make comparisons. Some of the findings of these studies have been significant, others have not. What is important is that these cross-cultural studies are being done and in the future we may have a better idea of how heredity, learning experiences, and cultural expectations contribute to individual differences in personality.

Eysenck (1990) believes it is plain that while there are interesting and enlightening findings about the association between personality and psychobiology, there are also several exceptions, inabilities to repeat, and areas with inadequate information. The association between some type of excitement and the dimension of extraversion appears to be best confirmed. In general, the data is adequate to imply that the theory is headed in the right direction. However, more labor needs to be completed to remove the exceptions that remain. Moreover, it appears hard to question the fact that human beings are "biosocial" animals (1991).

It is important to remember, however, that Eysenck's theory is speculative. He does not describe the actual workings of the brain. He acknowledged that his hypothesis "must stand and fall by empirical confirmation" (1965). In the past twenty-five years there has been enormous growth in research on the biochemistry of the brain and its functions. It is possible that some major personality dimensions have biochemical roots and may someday be explained in those terms. Levels of the neurotransmitter dopamine, for example, as well as "subtle abnormalities in brain structure" have been associated with schizophrenia (Goleman, 1990).

Arnold Buss and Robert Plomin's Temperament Theory

Arnold Buss and Robert Plomin introduced their theory in 1975. Arnold Buss is professor of psychology at the University of Texas in Austin and Robert Plomin is Distinguished Professor of Human Development at Pennsylvania State University at University Park, Pennsylvania. Their theory is an interaction-temperament model of personality that also combines biological, learning, and trait concepts.

Buss and Plomin suggest that a number of inborn or inherited dispositions are influenced by interactions with the environment. The interaction between temperament and environment in structuring personality is particularly important in early childhood, although there are limits to how much the environment can modify basic disposition.

Through factor analysis, Buss and Plomin (1975) identified four temperament dimensions that can be remembered by the acronym EASI:

Emotional versus impassive: The emotional person is easily aroused and responds more intensely than the impassive person.

Active versus lethargic: The active person is usually busy and in a hurry compared with the slower-paced lethargic individual.

Sociable versus detached: The sociable person is affiliative, seeking others out and responding to them. The detached person tends to prefer being alone.

Impulsive versus deliberate: Impulsive people respond quickly, whereas deliberate people inhibit their responses and plan them.

In determining which personality dispositions should appropriately be termed temperaments, Buss and Plomin (1975) employed five criteria. The most important criterion is that a temperament has a genetic component. Because it is *inherited,* we can expect that the temperament will show signs of *stability during childhood* and *retention into maturity.* In addition, the trait should have or have had an *adaptive value* in the evolution of the human race and be *present in our animal forebears.* Subsequent research failed to show clear evidence for a genetic component in impulsivity, leading Buss and Plomin to reduce their list of temperaments to the first three (1984) and refer to them by the acronym EAS. Buss (1991a) suggested that temperaments be seen as a subset of personality traits delineated by manifestation in the initial year of life, perseverance afterward, and genetic transmission. Emotionality, activity, and sociability are three personality traits that fulfill those measures.

What is inherited is a tendency to fall into a particular range on each dimension of the temperaments. The initial range could be somewhat broad, but it is narrowed by life experiences during development. Buss and Plomin assume that an interaction between the child and environmental forces shapes personality. For example, "children affect the behavior of their parents. A highly active child may require more parental supervision or control than a lethargic child, and a sociable child may elicit (and reward) more attention and affection than an unsociable child" (1975). The child is not passive but initiates, reinforces, and responds, thereby modifying the impact of the environment on personality.

Buss and Plomin (1975) used twin studies to demonstrate empirically the existence of the temperaments. Identical twins develop from the same fertilized ovum and thus share the same genotype. Fraternal twins, on the other hand, develop from two separate fertilized ova and are thus no more alike in genetic structure than any other brothers and sisters. Comparisons show that identical twins are significantly more alike in temperament than fraternal twins. Indeed, identical twins separated at birth and brought up in very different environments are often more alike than identical twins brought up together (Bouchard

Robert Plomin

et al., 1990). This may be because the need to establish themselves as distinct individuals is not present. In addition, Buss and Plomin (1975) developed a twenty-item questionnaire, the EASI Temperament Survey, by which parents could rate their children, and a self-report inventory, the EAS Temperament Survey for Adults (1984). Plomin, Scheier, Bergeman, and Pedersen (1992) reported on a twin adoption analysis that yielded significant heritability estimates for both optimism and pessimism.

Plomin and Nesselroade (1990) suggest that behavioral genetic studies of long-term changes in development indicate that there is little genetic involvement in the personality of adults. However, personality changes during childhood are determined largely by genetic factors. Plomin and Rende (1991) are impressed with the progress that has been made in the twentieth century toward understanding the genetic and environmental contributions to behavior and feel that new powerful research tools make behavioral genetics an exciting field.

Buss and Plomin's temperament theory of personality development is based on empirical findings, quantitative analysis, and rigorous experimental research. Its emphasis on heredity is helping to compensate for the neglect of genetic factors that characterized American psychology for many years.

THINKING CRITICALLY

Personality Traits That Have Appeared in Families Throughout the Generations

Interview your parents, grandparents, and even great-grandparents (if you have them) to see what personality traits have appeared in the family throughout various generations. Many times, older family members can remember traits such as shyness, creativity, depressive disorder, alcoholism, or high intelligence that seem to run in families.

You might also wish to interview identical twins (or even just one of the twins) to see what traits they share with each other. As an identical twin, I can affirm that while my twin sister and I are not completely alike, we are still very similar to one another.

Such activities might help you to appreciate that genes also have an impact on our personalities.

Other Biological and Genetic Research

Recent breakthroughs and discoveries in medicine, neurobiology, artificial intelligence, and cognitive science (the latter focuses on how we come to know things) are providing us with a great deal of information on how the brain functions. New brain-scanning techniques, neural network computer models, neurophysical and behavioral students of animals and people are leading to an emerging field of cognitive neuroscience that concentrates on how mental activities occur in the brain. Post and Ketter employed positron emission imaging, (PET scans) to measure comparative blood flow in the brain, and found that when people said they were depressed, some areas of the limbic system showed less activity. However, when a drug procane caused a euphoric state, like mania . . . limbic activity grew (Angier, 1993). This is the first piece of empirical data that *may* some day establish that Eysenck's fundamental dimensions of personality are tied to specific structures or functions of the brain. Most of the research on the brain to date has been in areas such as growing neurons in the laboratory (Angier, 1990), reading and language (Blakeslee, 1991), memory (Hilts, 1991), genetic instructions (Angier, 1992), "emergenic" traits — genetic traits that "tend not to run in families" (Lykken, et al 1992), visual perception and cognition (Blakeslee, 1993, and Brody, 1993), movement (Seitz, 1993), and genetic engineering (Liebmann-Smith, 1993). It is anticipated that within ten years all of us will be able to know our personal genetic risks (Kolata, 1993), which raises serious ethical issues as to how the information will be used (Fisher, 1994). We need to begin to address these issues. Moreover, it is just a matter of time before research in cognitive neuroscience turns to the topic of personality (Mulder, 1992, and Kramer, 1993) and begins to illumine this area for us.

Edward O. Wilson, an evolutionary biologist, suggests that human beings have an intense need to belong to the rest of the living world (Wilson & Kellert, 1993). This need has been called *the biophilia hypothesis* and some people believe that it may be as significant for human well-being as is the need to have intimate personal relations (Stevens, 1993).

The Big Five Personality Traits

A consensus has been emerging as it has become clear that five primary factors typically surface from personality questionnaires and self-report inventories. These factors are so strong and dependable that they have become popularly known as the "Big Five" (Goldberg, 1990; Digman & Inouye, 1986; McCrae & Costa, 1987; John, 1990). Norman (1963) was the first to identify factors similar

Table 11.3 *The "Big Five" Personality Factors*

Factor	*Description of Traits*
Neuroticism	anxious vs. calm insecure vs. secure high-strung vs. content self-pitying vs. content
Extraversion	sociable vs. withdrawn fun-loving vs. sober affectionate vs. reserved friendly vs. aloof
Openness	original vs. conventional imaginative vs. down-to-earth broad interests vs. narrow interests curious vs. incurious
Agreeableness	good-natured vs. irritable soft-hearted vs. ruthless forgiving vs. vengeful courteous vs. rude
Conscientiousness	conscientious vs. negligent well-organized vs. disorganized reliable vs. undependable careful vs. careless

SOURCE: Kassin, Saul M., PSYCHOLOGY, First Edition. Copyright © 1995 by Houghton Mifflin Company. Used with permission.

to the big five, and it was Goldberg (1981) who reviewed research on them and argued for their power and consistency. Investigators of personality have become persuaded that the most fruitful manner of characterizing people at the present time is to find out where they fall on the following factors: extraversion, agreeableness, conscientiousness, emotional stability, and openness to experience (Loehlin, 1992). An acronym for remembering these factors can be formed by rearranging the first letters to form the word *OCEAN* (John, 1990, p. 96). Table 11.3 summarizes the description of traits that fall under each factor.

Initial support for the five-factor model comes from the analysis of language: terms that have been used to describe personality traits. Sophisticated factor analysis procedures are used to see which traits cluster together. Goldberg (1990) points out that Sir Francis Galton (1822–1911), an English scientist, may have been one of the first to see clearly the basic lexical hypothesis that suggests that in some or all languages of the world, the most significant specific differences in interpersonal interactions are converted into single words. Over time, Goldberg believes people zero in on those characteristics that are crucial for interpersonal interaction and develop terms for them. Digman (1990) and John (1990) have reviewed studies in diverse languages (such as Japanese, Chinese,

Extraversion vs. introversion is one of the
"Big Five" personality factors.

and German) from different cultures and found support for this hypothesis and for the Big Five model.

Another major source of support for the Big Five model comes from the study of questionnaires and ratings. Costa and McCrae (1985, 1989) developed an objective assessment device, the NEO-Personality Inventory (NEO-PI), and then revised it to form the Neuroticism Extraversion Openness Personality Inventory, Revised (NEO-PI-R). This test is precisely developed to assess the "Big Five" (Costa and McCrae 1992). There are thirty scales with ten items each. Subjects are asked to indicate, on a 5-point scale (strongly agree to strongly disagree) whether or not certain descriptions apply to them. This mode of assessment incorporates self and peer observations, and this instrument may be useful in the diagnosis of personality disorders (McCrae and Costa 1989; Widiger, 1993) as well as implying modalities of treatment. For example, an extravert might do better in group therapy while an introvert might be more comfortable in a one-on-one situation. This wider approach to assessment incorporating peer observations appears to be a coming trend (Funder & Sneed, 1993).

The NEO-PI-R correlates well with other personality inventories such as the Cattell 16 PF and Eysenck Personality Inventory, as well as assessment devices developed from other theoretical orientations such as Rogers's (Q-sort ratings) and Murray's.

Finally, evidence concerning the inheritability of traits (Bouchard et al., 1990; Plomin, Chipuer, & Loehlin, 1990) also support the Big Five theory. Twin and other sibling studies are beginning to show that siblings resemble each other primarily due to common genes rather than shared environment. It is clear that each child in a singular family (even identical twins) experiences a unique and different environment because of the child's particular place and role within the family (Plomin et al., 1990). Moreover, how parents and other significant others react to children is deeply influenced by the child's early emerging personality temperament (Plomin & Bergeman, 1991; Plomin et al., 1990).

Nevertheless it is difficult to know exactly to what extent genetic influence is involved in the development of the Big Five. For example, consider the factor of neuroticism. Do genes place broad parameters within which personal experiences decide which individuals end up as anxious, insecure, or high-strung, or do the genes actually decide which way of responding to misfortune will occur? Considerable research has been done in this area, but we have no definitive answers. There has to be some mixture of environmental effects singular to the individual as well as genotype-environment interaction (Loehlin, 1992). Moreover, we need to be careful not to move from a simplistic emphasis on the environment that characterized much of psychology in the twentieth century to an equally simplistic emphasis on biology (Plomin et al., 1990). There is a complex interaction among many factors.

Buss (1991) believes that personality psychology needs evolutionary theory as a framework and that the Big Five may be seen as significant features of human "adaptive landscape," giving some individuals a selective advantage.

Trait and Temperament Theories: Philosophy, Science, and Art

Trait and temperament theories of personality are excellent examples of scientific theories of personality. Some critics suggest they are based on highly objective and precise scientific techniques. Others consider factor analysis a weak and highly misleading technique. The theories are generating an enormous amount of significant empirical research.

At the same time, Cattell's theory arises out of his philosophical commitment to an empirical approach. He views the world as lawful, consistent, and controllable. Moreover, Cattell suggests that a system of ethical values, which he calls *beyondism,* may be developed on the foundation of science. Beyondism is based on the view that humanity is in the process of a physical and biological advance. Moral laws that will foster and ensure this evolutionary process need to be developed. Such ethics will enable us to adapt to a wider range of circumstances and will give us a better chance of survival. Strictly speaking, Cattell's new morality cannot be said to arise from science. Scientists may have discovered the process of evolution, but the judgment that such evolution is good and should be fostered is a value judgment that takes us outside the realm of validating evidence and into the realm of philosophy. The moral issues that Cattell raises, like the advisability of selective breeding as a means of cultivating certain traits, deserve serious consideration. Herein lies the value of science for Cattell and others who cherish the importance of validating evidence: our intuition is subsequently checked by explicit logic and experimentation.

Cattell's theory is not as popular as other theories among psychologists and it is almost totally unknown among the general public. In part this lack of popularity is due to its complexity, but it is also because factor analysis creates an artifact or a para-person that has no real relationship to a real person. As we have seen, it is difficult for the conclusions of a scientific method to command the same degree of compellingness as a philosophical vision.

Eysenck's theory is also a superb model of a scientific approach to personality. There is considerable support for his "type" approach. It is in his recent ideas regarding brain function that there is disagreement. It is important to reiterate that Eysenck's speculation is a hypothesis, not a factual description of how the brain works. Research has not yet provided direct empirical data to fully support it. Eysenck's concept of scientific activity is, however, somewhat narrow. There are alternative ways of gathering empirical data and operationally defining terms, which Eysenck disallows even though other scientists would permit them. Moreover, Eysenck's own procedures are not as objective or purely scientific as he contends. For example, the data of factor analysis may be interpreted in various ways. Also, the conclusions of factor analysis studies are only as good as the original data. The average individual has undoubtedly been more directly influenced by the trait approach to personality than by any other approach. Most people have been assessed by some device based on the trait approach, for instance, an intelligence test, an achievement test, or an aptitude test. Such psychometric measuring devices and techniques have not been used without criticism. Most of the constructs supposedly indicated by these tests cannot be measured directly. Often the validity of the tests is assumed rather than demonstrated.

On the other hand, the judicious use of appropriate assessment techniques can be invaluable in developing individual and group potential. Accurate understanding of one's limitations and abilities is important for developing one's potential.

Trait and temperament theories are controversial because, among other things, they imply that some personality differences are genetically based.

PHILOSOPHICAL ASSUMPTIONS

Examining Trait and Temperament Theories

How would you rate the various trait and temperament theorists on each of the basic philosophical assumptions described in Chapter 1? Each basic issue was presented as a bipolar dimension along which a person's view can be placed according to the degree of agreement with one or the other extreme. Rate the views of Cattell, Eysenck, Buss and Plomin, and the "Big Five" theorists on these issues.

When you have determined where you think the theorists stand, compare your responses with those of your classmates and your instructor. You should be willing to defend your ratings, but also be prepared to change them in light of others' compelling arguments. Afterward, compare your ratings of these theorists with your own position on each issue and with those of other theorists. Does this comparison help you to understand why these theories do or do not appeal to you?

Would strongly agree	Would agree	Is neutral or believes in synthesis of both views	Would agree	Would strongly agree
1	2	3	4	5

freedom

People basically have control over their own behavior and understand the motives behind their behavior.

determinism

The behavior of people is basically determined by internal or external forces over which they have little, if any, control.

Eysenck has said that people "are created equal in the sight of God and as regards the judicial system, but they are not created equal as far as beauty is concerned, or strength, or intelligence or a great many other things" (as quoted in Evans, 1976). This is not to say, however, that heredity is the sole determinant of personality. All of the theorists discussed in this chapter emphasize the interaction of biology and society. Heredity may place limits on an individual's potential, but environment probably determines where within that range his or her actual behavior will fall.

The research on trait and temperament in personality needs to be supplemented by research on how culture affects personality. We need to look at not only the similarities and variations between peoples who are widely separated

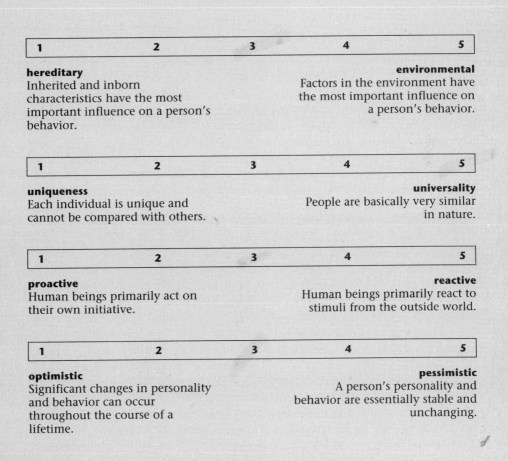

| 1 | 2 | 3 | 4 | 5 |

hereditary
Inherited and inborn characteristics have the most important influence on a person's behavior.

environmental
Factors in the environment have the most important influence on a person's behavior.

| 1 | 2 | 3 | 4 | 5 |

uniqueness
Each individual is unique and cannot be compared with others.

universality
People are basically very similar in nature.

| 1 | 2 | 3 | 4 | 5 |

proactive
Human beings primarily act on their own initiative.

reactive
Human beings primarily react to stimuli from the outside world.

| 1 | 2 | 3 | 4 | 5 |

optimistic
Significant changes in personality and behavior can occur throughout the course of a lifetime.

pessimistic
A person's personality and behavior are essentially stable and unchanging.

physically (such as Australia and Canada) but also at various subcultures within the same country, in order to find out whether primary factors such as the "Big Five" are universal and found in all cultures or whether they are culture specific or somewhere in the middle of that continuum (Paunonen et al., 1992; Yang & Bond, 1990).

As research in behavioral genetics continues, questions will be answered and others asked about the genetic components of traits and temperaments, their stability, and cultural components (Woodall & Matthews, 1993). Moreover, an evolutionary view will look at the adaptive nature of temperament and traits (Buss, 1991b).

The recognition of similarities and differences among all people enables the effective development and application of a social philosophy that intends to provide equal opportunity for all people in our global community to achieve their potential. Such a recognition underscores the desirability of a reciprocal relationship between the philosophy, science, and art of a personality theory. Scientists should be aware of the ways in which philosophical assumptions inform their work and, in turn, of the ways in which their findings influence ethical and social decisions.

Summary

1. **Typologies** tend to separate people into distinct categories whereas **trait** theories conceive of dimensions that individuals possess to varying degrees.

2. Cattell defines **personality** as that which will permit prediction of what a person will do in a given situation. His interest in personality theorizing is clearly heuristic.

3. **Surface traits** are clusters of overt behavior responses that appear to go together. **Source traits** are the underlying variables, which may have their origin in heredity or in influences of the environment. Cattell has identified sixteen basic **temperament** and **ability traits.**

4. Cattell uses **factor analysis** to identify traits. Factor analysis is a correlational procedure that interrelates many correlations at one time and identifies common dimensions that underlie them. Cattell hopes he can use his findings to facilitate the prediction of behavior by means of a specification equation.

5. Eysenck identifies two fundamental dimensions of personality: *emotional stability/neuroticism* and *extraversion/introversion.*

6. Eysenck rigorously employs scientific methods in assessment. He has criticized the shortcomings of early versions of ratings and inventories, developed a way of constructing more accurate questionnaires, and developed a number of self-report inventories to measure the dimensions he has identified.

7. Eysenck suggests that extraversion/introversion is related to arousal thresholds in the *ascending reticular activating system* of the brain and emotional stability/neuroticism is related to differences in *visceral brain* activity.

8. The **genotype** refers to the genetic makeup of an individual and the **phenotype** refers to the individual's observable appearance and behavior that arise out of the interaction of the genotype with the environment.

9. Eysenck's theory allows for specific prediction and test. Research has been conducted on differences between introverts and extraverts and cross-cultural studies have been conducted on his personality dimensions.

10. Buss and Plomin have developed an interaction-temperament model of personality that combines biological, learning, and trait concepts and emphasizes genetic factors.

11. Other biological and genetic research has focused on cognitive neuroscience, which studies how the brain functions.

12. A consensus is emerging on the Big Five personality traits, which can be remembered by the acronym OCEAN: openness to experience, conscientiousness, extraversion, agreeableness, and neuroticism. Support for this model comes from analysis of language, the study of questionnaires and ratings, and studies concerning the inheritability of traits.

13. Trait and temperament theories of personality are excellent examples of scientific theories of personality, although in Eysenck's case his definition of science is narrow.

Suggestions for Further Reading

Cattell has been prolific, writing over thirty books and three hundred articles. His work is technical and difficult to digest. However, an introductory primer to his theory is provided in *The Scientific Analysis of Personality* (Aldine, 1965), which is not too technical and is aimed at a lay public. Also readable and exciting because of the ethical issues that it raises is *A New Morality from Science: Beyondism* (Pergamon, 1972). Beyond that the interested reader has a vast array of primary sources to choose from. A broad critical review of Cattell's work is found in an article by S. B. Sells, "Structured measurement of personality and motivation: A review of contributions of Raymond B. Cattell," *Journal of Clinical Psychology,* 1959, *15,* 3–21.

Even more prolific, Eysenck has written seventy-five books and one thousand articles. The level of readability varies widely. A work that is relatively easy for the lay person to understand is *Psychology Is about People* (Open Court, 1972). The definitive statement of his cortical hypothesis of arousal is found in *The Biological Basis of Personality* (Charles C Thomas, 1967). A three-volume collection of research essays related to his theory has been published under the title

Readings in Extroversion–Introversion (Staples, 1970–1971). His autobiography, *Rebel with a Cause,* was published in London by W. H. Allen in 1990.

Buss and Plomin formally introduced their theory in 1975 with *A Temperament Theory of Personality Development,* published by John Wiley & Sons. For McCrae and Costa's work, I recommend *Personality in Adulthood* (Guilford, 1990). However, research in the area of trait and temperament is growing at such an incredible speed that to keep up with it one really needs to read recent journal articles.

PART 6

Humanist and Existential Theories

The humanist theories of Carl Rogers and Abraham Maslow emerged in the 1950s in an effort to correct the limited concepts of human nature of both classical psychoanalysis and radical behaviorism. Rogers and Maslow disagreed with the dark, pessimistic, and largely negative picture of personality presented by Freudian psychoanalysis. They also disagreed with the picture of the person as a machine or robot that characterized the early behavior and learning approach.

Rogers and Maslow emphasized a view of the person as an active, creative, experiencing human being who lives in the present and subjectively responds to current perceptions, relationships, and encounters. The humanist view of personality is a positive, optimistic one that stresses the tendency of the human personality toward growth and self-actualization.

Rollo May's existential theory also began to appear in the 1950s. It represents a singular effort to bring together the psychoanalytic tradition in psychology and the existential movement in philosophy. May is deeply aware that the technology that we have developed has yet to provide satisfactory answers to the most fundamental questions of human existence. In today's postmodern society our social security numbers have become more important than our names. In the midst of our abundant technological advance, the person appears to have been lost. In combining the insights of psychoanalysis and existentialism, May has developed a theory that is clearly expressive of our concerns in the final decade of the twentieth century.

CHAPTER 12

Carl Rogers

1. Explain the following concepts in Rogers's theory: *phenomenal field*, self-actualization, organism, *self*. Explain how emotions affect the process of self-actualization.
2. Explain what Rogers means by *congruence* and *incongruence* and identify denial and distortion as two processes that may lead to incongruence.
3. Discuss what is meant by *unconditional* and *conditional positive regard* and recognize their roles in influencing personality development.
4. Describe Rogers's concept of a *fully functioning person*.
5. Describe three therapist attitudes that lead to change.
6. Distinguish among five different responses to emotional communications.
7. Discuss *person-centered psychotherapy*, describing its supportive character, changes in Rogers's conception of it, and efforts at empirical validation.
8. Evaluate Rogers's theory in terms of its function as philosophy, science, and art.
9. Discuss criticism of Rogers position.

For Carl Rogers, a person's behavior is completely dependent on how he or she perceives the world and its events. Rogers's theory of personality describes the **self** as an important element of experience; it is largely due to Rogers's efforts that the self has re-emerged as a useful construct for understanding personality. In much of behaviorist thought the concept of the self had been ignored as a remnant of earlier religious or philosophical views. Rogers presented the self as a scientific construct that helps to account for what we observe. The self is Rogers's term for those psychological processes that govern our behavior. At the same time, his theory emphasizes the organism or the total person.

Biographical Background

Carl Rogers was born in 1902 in Oak Park, Illinois, a suburb of Chicago. He was the fourth of six children. Rogers's parents, educated and conservative middle-class Protestants, instilled in their children high ethical standards of behavior and emphasized the importance of hard work.

Rogers had little social life outside of his large family, but this did not bother him. He was an avid reader and developed a certain level of independence early in life. When he was twelve, the family moved to a farm. Farm life spurred his interest in science and increased his ability to work independently. He was fascinated with the literature on scientific agriculture that his father brought home. Rogers worked hard at his chores on the farm; he raised lambs, pigs, and calves. He also collected, studied, and bred moths. A superior student, Rogers entered the University of Wisconsin, a family alma mater, with the full intent of studying agriculture. However, in his second year, he decided to prepare for the ministry. After his graduation in 1924, he married Helen Elliot and moved to New York City to begin preparation for the ministry at Union Theological Seminary.

Rogers's fate, however, was not to become a minister. During his final years at college, Rogers found himself departing from his parents' fundamentalist ways of thinking (see Thorne, 1990). The liberal philosophical approach toward religion fostered at Union Theological Seminary and the insights Rogers gained from participation in several YMCA conferences led him to feel that he could not work in a field that would require him to profess a specific set of beliefs. This was a difficult period for both Rogers and his parents but it nurtured Rogers's growing conviction that one must ultimately rely on personal experiences for developing a philosophy of life. His interests were turning toward psychology; therefore, he transferred to Columbia University Teachers College, where he was introduced to the philosophy of John Dewey and began his training in clinical psychology.

In 1931, Rogers received the Ph.D. and joined the staff of the Rochester Guidance Center, where he helped develop a highly successful child study department. Here, Rogers first met what was to be many years of opposition from members of the psychiatric profession who felt that psychologists and counselors should not be permitted to practice or have any administrative responsibility over psychotherapy. In 1939, when Rogers was made the director of the center, a vigorous campaign was waged to unseat him. No one criticized his work, but the general opinion was that a psychologist simply could not do this kind of work. Fortunately, the board of trustees decided in Rogers's favor.

In 1940, Rogers accepted an appointment as professor of psychology at Ohio State University. He worked with intellectually adept graduate students and began to clearly articulate his views on psychotherapy using college students as his primary data base. In 1945, he moved to the University of Chicago where, as professor of psychology and executive secretary of the counseling center, he again championed his view that psychologists and counselors could effectively conduct therapy. Rogers's efforts, along with others, led to the reconciliation of psychiatry and psychology as two professions in search of a common goal. Throughout his life, Rogers referred to himself as a counselor. This reconciliation and challenge were reflected in Rogers's appointment as professor of psychology and psychiatry at the University of Wisconsin in 1957. In 1963, Rogers became a fellow at the Center for Studies of the Person in La Jolla, California.

In his final years, Rogers sought to bring together in encounter groups people from conflicting political factions, such as Protestants and Roman Catholics in Belfast, Ireland. As his son David observed, "Over his career, he moved from one-on-one psychotherapy, to small groups, to nations" (Goleman, 1987). He was planning to return to South Africa to lead a second encounter session with blacks and whites when he died in 1987 of a heart attack following surgery for a broken hip.

Carl Rogers

Rogers's Theory of Personality

Rogers (1959) maintained that each individual exists in the center of a phenomenal field. Rogers was influenced by a philosophical movement called **phenomenology.** The word *phenomenon* comes from the Greek *phainomenon,* which means "that which appears or shows itself." In philosophy, phenomenology seeks to describe the data, or the "given," of immediate experience. In psychology, phenomenology has come to mean the study of human awareness and perception. Phenomenologists stress that what is important is not the object or the event in itself but how it is perceived and understood by the individual. The **phenomenal field** refers to the total sum of experiences. It consists of everything that is potentially available to consciousness at any given moment. As you read you may not be aware of the pressure of the chair on your buttocks, but when attention is drawn to this fact you become conscious of it.

The organism, or person as a whole, responds to the phenomenal field. Roger's emphasis here is on the individual's perception of reality. In this respect he was consistent with the recent emphasis on cognition in psychology. For social purposes, we agree that the perceptions commonly shared by others in our culture are the correct perceptions. However, reality is essentially a very personal matter. Two individuals walking along at night may see an object by the road and respond very differently. "One . . . sees a large boulder and reacts with fright. The other, a native of the country sees a tumbleweed and reacts with nonchalance" (1951, p. 484). The individual's perception rather than the reality itself is most important. Suppose a young boy were to complain that his father was dogmatic, authoritarian, and dictatorial. In fact, an impartial observer might conclude that the father was open and democratic. Rogers would point out that what the father is really like is meaningless; what is important is how the boy perceives his father.

It follows that the best vantage point for understanding an individual is that of the individual. Rogers pointed out that the individual is the only one who can fully know her or his field of experience. Rogers acknowledged that it is not always easy to understand behavior from the internal frame of reference of another person. We are limited to the individual's conscious perception and communication of experiences. Nevertheless, such an empathic understanding of the experiences of another is useful in understanding a person and therefore useful in understanding personality processes.

Actualization

The primary tendency of the organism is to maintain, actualize, and enhance itself. This actualizing tendency follows lines laid down by genetics and may also be influenced by temperament (Ford, 1991). The particular type of seed that is planted determines whether or not the flower will be a chrysanthemum or snapdragon, but the environment can greatly influence the resulting bloom.

The process of actualization is neither automatic nor effortless; it involves struggle and even pain. The young child may struggle with the first step but it is a natural struggle. Thus, each organism, or living being, moves in the direction of maturation as it is defined for each species.

Behavior is the "goal-directed attempt" of the organism to meet its needs as it perceives them (1951). Rogers's definition is very different from that of the learning theorists, who see behavior largely as a response to stimuli, or that of the psychoanalysts, who stress unconscious determinants of behavior. Behavior is a response to one's perception of one's needs.

This goal-directed behavior is accompanied by emotions that usually facilitate the process of actualization. Pleasant emotions accompany the attainment of a goal. Even emotions that we generally think of as unpleasant, such as fear or anger, may have a positive effect of integrating and concentrating our behavior on a goal. The intensity of the emotion varies according to the perceived significance of the behavior toward achieving the goal. Emotions assist the organism in evaluating its life experiences in terms of how well they serve the actualizing tendency. Jumping out of the path of an oncoming truck is accompanied by very strong emotions, particularly if this behavior is seen as crucial to life or death. Unless they are excessive or inappropriate, emotions facilitate goal-oriented behavior.

Rogers's view of emotions is a very positive one. Fully experiencing one's emotions facilitates growth, whereas the denial or distortion of emotions may permit them to raise havoc in our lives. In the psychoanalytic point of view the impulses of the id are savage, ignoble, and in need of civilization. Rogers had a more optimistic view of our basic motivational strivings and urges. He suggested that actualization occurs most freely when the person is open and aware of all experiences, be they sensory, visceral, or emotional.

The Self

Out of the interaction of the organism and the environment, and in particular the interaction with significant others, there gradually emerges a structure of self, or a concept of "who I am" (1951). As young children interact with their environment in the process of actualization, they acquire ideas about themselves, their world, and their relationship to that world. They experience things that they like or dislike and things that they can or cannot control. Those experiences that appear to enhance one's self are valued and incorporated into one's self-image; those experiences that appear to threaten the self are denied and rendered foreign to the self.

The **self-concept** is a portion of the phenomenal field that has gradually become differentiated. It is composed of those conscious perceptions and values of "me" or "I," some of which are a result of the organism's own valuing of its experiences and some of which have been introjected or taken over from important others. Because the self-concept comes in part through others the potential for dissociation or estrangement exists (and usually occurs to some degree). As a result, the actualizing tendency may be perverted into behaviors that do not lead to actualization. The self-concept, then, is an object of perception. It is the person as she or he perceives herself or himself. Thus we have a distinction between the organism or real self in the process of actualization, and the self as perceived, or object. The "self" that one forms may be at variance with the real experience of one's organism because it includes values that are taken over from other people rather than the actual experiences of the organism.

For example, a young boy quickly learns that his parents withdraw their affection when he hits his baby brother. Even though hitting his brother is a satisfying act, the boy forfeits his satisfaction in order to conceive of himself as lovable to his parents. He denies that he wants to hit his brother. When children deny or distort their experiences, they are no longer aware of them. They begin to experience the attitudes of others, such as their parents, as if these were the direct experiences of their own organisms. Through such distortion, an individual may come to experience any expression of anger as bad and therefore may no longer accurately perceive that at times its expression is satisfying. In such cases the experiences of the self and that of the organism do not coincide.

Rogers did not believe that the self-structure must be formed on the basis of denial and distortion. The child values experiences as positive or negative. If a parent is able to accept the child's feeling of satisfaction and also accept her or his *own* feelings that certain actions are inappropriate, the parent can help the child curb actions without threatening the integrity of the child's self-concept. The parent can make it clear that the action of hitting the baby is wrong. Nevertheless, the feelings of satisfaction from the aggression and the child's desire are recognized and accepted. Such recognition provides the child an accurate symbolization of experience. The child can weigh the satisfaction obtained from hitting the baby with the satisfaction gained from pleasing the parent and then act accordingly. The child would not need to deny personal satisfaction that would have been gained by expressing aggression, nor would he need to introject parental attitudes or identify his own reaction with that of the parent.

The experiences that occur in our lives are either symbolized, ignored, denied, or distorted. If an experience is *symbolized,* it is accepted into consciousness, perceived, and organized into a relationship with the self. Generally, such experiences are related to the needs of the self. Thus, we select from our many sensory experiences those that fit in with our concept of self. We permit those experiences conscious acknowledgment and symbolization. If we cannot perceive any relationship between an experience and our self, we simply fail to pay attention to irrelevant experiences.

Experiences are denied or distorted if they appear to be inconsistent with the self-structure. Young women who are brought up to believe that aggression is unfeminine may deny or distort their natural feelings of anger and find it difficult to be assertive because they seek to behave in ways that are feminine. Likewise, men frequently deny or distort natural feelings of being nurturing because they find them inconsistent with being masculine. In short, the individual's awareness is highly dependent on the self-concept. One tends to regard such perceptions as alien. The experiences occur in reality and the organism reacts to them but they are not symbolized or recognized by the conscious self.

Congruence and Incongruence

There is a need for the self as perceived and the real self, the organism, to be congruent. A state of **congruence** exists when a person's symbolized experiences reflect all of the actual experiences of the organism. When one's symbolized experiences do not represent all of the actual experiences, or if they deny or distort them, there is a lack of correspondence between the self as perceived and the real self. In such a situation, there is incongruence and possible maladjustment. Diagrammatically, we can show this with overlapping circles, much as we depicted Horney's distinction between the real self and the ideal self (Figure 12.1).

When an individual denies or distorts significant sensory and visceral experiences, certain basic tensions arise. The self as perceived, which primarily governs behavior, is not an adequate representative of the true experiences of the organism. It becomes increasingly difficult for the self to satisfy the organism's needs. Tension develops and is felt as anxiety or uncertainty.

Rogers (1951) offered the following example. A young mother conceives of herself as a "good and loving mother." She cannot recognize her negative, rejecting attitudes toward her child because they do not coincide with her self-image. Nevertheless, these negative attitudes exist, and her organism seeks aggressive acts that would express these attitudes. She is limited to expressing herself only through channels that are consistent with her self-image of being

Figure 12.1   *The Total Personality*
Diagram *a* depicts a personality in a state of psychic tension. Diagram *b* shows a personality in a state of relative congruence, wherein more elements of experience have been integrated into the self.

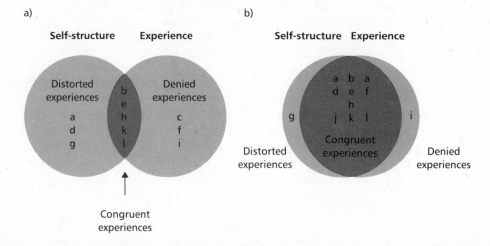

a good mother. Since it is appropriate for a good mother to behave aggressively toward her child when the child's behavior is bad, she perceives a great deal of the child's behavior as bad and punishes the child accordingly. In this manner, she can express her negative attitudes but retain her self-image of being a good mother.

When the self-concept is congruent with the experiences of the organism, the person is free from inner tension and psychologically adjusted. Rogers made it clear that he did not advocate the free and unrestrained expression of all our impulses and emotions. Part of the reality of the organism's experience is that certain social and cultural values require suppression of certain activities. Nevertheless, one's self-concept can include both the desire to behave one way and the desire to behave in other, more socially accepted ways. If parents can accept their feelings of rejection for their children as well as their feelings of affection, they can relate to their children more honestly.

When people become aware of and accept their impulses and perceptions, they increase the possibility of conscious control over their expression. The driver who is adept on icy roads knows the importance of steering "with the skid" in order to gain control over the car. In the same manner, by accepting all experiences, a person acquires better self-control.

Development of Personality

Rogers did not posit any specific stages of personality development from infancy to adulthood. He concentrated on the way in which the evaluations of others impede or facilitate self-actualization. Although the tendency to actualize follows genetic determinants, Rogers noted that it is subject to strong environmental influences.

The young child has two basic needs: the need for positive regard by others and the need for positive self-regard. **Positive regard** refers to being loved and accepted for who one is. Young children behave in such a way as to show their strong need for the acceptance and love of those who care for them. They will undergo significant changes in their behavior in order to attain positive regard.

In an ideal situation, positive regard is unconditional. It is given freely to children for who they are regardless of what they do. **Unconditional positive regard** is not contingent on any specific behaviors. A parent can limit or curb certain undesirable behaviors by objecting only to the behaviors and not disapproving of the child or the child's feelings. A parent who sees a child scribble on the wall may say, "Writing on the wall destroys it. Use this blackboard instead." Here, the parent limits remarks to the behavior itself. But the parent who says, "You are a bad boy (girl) for writing on the wall," has shifted from disapproval of the behavior to disapproval of the child. Such regard is no longer unconditional.

Conditional positive regard is given only under certain circumstances. Children are led to understand that their parents will not love them unless they think, feel, and act as their parents want them to. In such cases, the child perceives the parent as imposing **conditions of worth**, specifying the provisions

*The young child has two basic needs: the
need for positive regard by others and the
need for positive self-regard.*

under which the child will be accepted. Such conditions of worth may lead the child to introject values of others rather than of the self and lead to a discrepancy between the self-concept and the experiences of the organism.

Positive self-regard follows automatically if one has received unconditional positive regard. Children who are accepted for who they are come to view themselves favorably and with acceptance. It is very difficult, however, to view oneself positively if one is continually the target of criticism and belittlement. Inadequate self-concepts such as feelings of inferiority or stupidity frequently arise because a person has not received adequate positive regard from others.

In the course of development, any experience that is at variance with the emerging self-concept is denied entrance into the self because it is threatening and evokes anxiety. If children are taught that it is wrong to feel angry, they may begin to perceive the emotion of anger itself rather than certain *expressions* of anger as dangerous or incorrect.

Rogers's primary distinction is between feelings and actions. Feelings simply *are*. They have an important value in that they help us to understand our experience. Actions may or may not be appropriate. Some of them have to be curbed or prevented if we are going to live together in society.

When an experience is denied entrance into the self, it is not simply ignored; rather, it is falsified either by the pretense that it does not exist or by distortion. In psychoanalytic terms, the experience is repressed. As Rogers (1951) explained it, an object or event may be **subceived** or unconsciously perceived as a threat. Although it produces visceral reactions in the organism, it is not consciously identified; instead, the mechanisms of denial or distortion prevent the threatening experience from becoming conscious. Rogers pointed out that some people will adamantly insist on a self-concept that is clearly at odds with the reality of their experience. A young woman who believes that she is inferior and receives a raise may believe that the boss felt sorry for her, rather than take credit where credit is due. The person who has achieved a significant goal may enter into a deep depression, believing the goal was undeserved.

Research on social cognition concurs with Rogers's belief that self-perception is important in personality development and that congruence is needed for psychological health. Moreover, research has shown that people try to verify their self-concept even if the self-concept is negative. Thus people who have a negative self-concept often choose partners who think unfavorably about them. Perhaps disapproving judgments increase their perception that their world is predictable. In this view, people "may go to great lengths to maintain the perception that they are in touch with social reality, however harsh that reality may be" (Swann, Stein-Seroussi, & Giesler, 1992).

It is clear that for Rogers psychological adjustment is a function of the congruence of the self with reality. The individual who has an accurate perception of self and environment is free to be open to new experiences and to fulfill his or her potential.

Rogers believed that supportive parents and a creative environment can facilitate psychological adjustment (1951). Longitudinal studies have suggested a positive correlation between Rogers's prescribed child-rearing practices and a composite index of creative potential in early adolescence (Harrington, Block, & Block, 1987). Individuals who have experienced a positive development are more likely to become fully functioning people.

The Fully Functioning Person

The individual who is functioning at an optimal level, as a result either of personal development or of psychological treatment, is a fully functioning person. Rogers described five characteristics of the fully functioning person (1959).

1. *Openness to Experience* Fully functioning persons are aware of all of their experiences: they are not defensive and do not need to deny or distort experiences. They can recognize a feeling even if it is inappropriate to act on it. During a lecture, a young man may experience the desire to have sexual relations with the young woman sitting next to him. He refrains from acting at the moment because he recognizes that such action would be imprudent, but the feeling does not threaten him.

2. *Existential Living* Fully functioning persons are able to live fully and richly each moment of existence. Each experience is potentially fresh and new. They do not need preconceived structures to interpret each happening. They are flexible and spontaneous.

3. *Organismic Trust* Fully functioning persons trust the experiences of their own organism. They may take other people's opinions and the consensus of their society into account, but they are not bound by them.

4. *Experiential Freedom* Fully functioning persons operate as free choice agents. They assume responsibility for their decisions and behavior. Obviously, they are subject to the laws of causality. They know that their behavior is largely determined by genetic makeup, past experiences, and social forces. Nevertheless, fully functioning people subjectively feel free to be aware of their needs and to respond appropriately.

5. *Creativity* Fully functioning persons live constructively and effectively in their environment. The spontaneity and flexibility characteristic of fully functioning people enable them to adjust adequately to changes in their surroundings and to seek new experiences and challenges. Free from constraints, they move confidently forward in the process of self-actualization.

Rogers emphasized that his is not a "pollyanna," or naively optimistic, point of view. Terms such as "happy," "blissful," or "contented" do not necessarily describe fully functioning people; rather, such people are challenged and find life meaningful. Their experiences are exciting, enriching, and rewarding. Self-actualization requires the "courage to be" and the willingness to launch oneself into the process of life.

Psychotherapy

Carl Rogers is best known for the method of psychotherapy that he developed, known originally as **client-centered** or **nondirective therapy** and more recently as person-centered. Rogers not only originated this type of therapy but also carefully studied it to determine what makes it work. As a scientist, he tried to define operationally the conditions that underlie successful therapy to generate hypotheses that can be empirically tested. Rogers's leadership in demanding empirical validation of psychotherapy was a significant contribution, particularly considering his phenomenological and idiographic orientation.

Conditions for Therapeutic Change

Rogers's studies suggested that there are three necessary and sufficient therapeutic attitudes for change. By *necessary,* Rogers meant that these three therapist attitudes are essential and must be present. By *sufficient,* he meant that if the client is uncomfortable with his or her present self and perceives these attitudes, change will occur. No other conditions are required. Not only did Rogers maintain that these three attitudes underlie his method of therapy, he also suggested that they underlie any good relationship and successful therapeutic technique, and lead to the development of the same attitudes in the client (1961).

The first attitude is **empathy**, the ability to experience another person's feelings as if they were one's own, but never lose sight of the "as if." Through empathy, the therapist is able to put him- or herself in the client's shoes without trying to wear those shoes or lose his or her own shoes. The therapist understands the client's internal frame of reference and communicates this understanding, largely through statements that reflect the client's feelings.

The second attitude is one of **acceptance**, in which the therapist does not posit any conditions of worth. Acceptance essentially means a nonjudgmental recognition of oneself and the other person. Through acceptance the therapist lets the other person be.

The final attitude is **genuineness**. The effective therapist is genuine, integrated, free, and deeply aware of experiences within the relationship. The therapist need not be a model of perfect mental health in all aspects of his or her own life and may have shortcomings and difficulties in other situations. But within the relationship of therapy, the therapist needs to be congruent.

Given these conditions, Rogers believed that positive, constructive personality changes will occur. In a climate of acceptance or unconditional positive regard, the client will be able to explore those feelings and experiences that were previously denied or distorted and can drop earlier conditions of worth and defenses to be open to organismic experiencing. In doing so, the client's self-concept will gradually become more congruent with the actual experiences of the organism.

Responses to Emotional Communications

Rogers did not use any special techniques, such as free association or dream analysis, in his therapy. The direction of the therapy is determined by the client. In Rogerian therapy, if there were any instructions, they would be, "Talk about whatever you would like to talk about." The client determines what will be discussed, when, and to what extent. This is why Rogers's form of therapy has been labeled "client-centered." The client who does not want to talk about a particular subject is not pressed to do so. The client does not even have to talk at all. Rogers felt strongly that his clients had the ability to understand and to explore their problems and that given the appropriate therapeutic relationship, that is, an attitude of acceptance, they would move toward further self-actualization.

In Rogerian therapy, the therapist communicates the attitude of acceptance largely through statements that reflect the client's feelings. We can understand this better by distinguishing among different kinds of responses to emotional communications. Rogers developed a number of studies in which he explored how people communicate in face-to-face situations in everyday life as well as in therapy (Rogers & Roethlisberger, 1952). Consider the following hypothetical communication: "The doctor keeps telling me not to worry, but I'm frightened of this operation." There are many different ways in which one could respond to such a statement. Rogers discovered that most responses fall into one of five categories used in the following order of frequency in everyday life: (1) evaluative, (2) interpretative, (3) reassuring, (4) probing, and (5) reflective. Each of these responses tends to lead toward a different consequence.

An **evaluative response** places a value judgment on the person's thoughts, feelings, wishes, or behavior. One might say, "You shouldn't be afraid of the operation." Evaluative responses may have their place when the listener is specifically asked to give an opinion or to disclose values or attitudes. However, because evaluative responses are judgmental, they tend to detract from an attitude of basic acceptance of the other individual. Our natural tendency to approve, disapprove, judge, or evaluate another person's comments is a primary barrier to understanding in communication, often leading to a defensive reaction in the speaker and to a situation in which each party simply looks at the problem from her or his own point of view. A person who is defensive is no longer open to further exploration of anxiety.

An **interpretative response** is an effort on the listener's part to tell the original speaker what the problem really is or how the speaker really feels about the situation. One might say, "That's because you're afraid of being unconscious during the operation." Interpretation is a technique that is frequently employed in intensive therapy. In the hands of a trained and skilled technician, it can be a valuable adjunct to assist in developing insight. But in the hands of an amateur, interpretation can be a dangerous tool. In the first place, the interpretation may be wrong. Second, if it is correct, it must be properly timed. If an interpretation is ill timed, it may be rejected because the speaker was not ready for it and may further make the speaker feel misunderstood and reluctant to discuss the issue further. For these reasons any interpretation should be presented only tentatively and left open for further confirmation. Further, an interpretation should be timed so that it is not given until just before the speaker is about to make the same discovery. When properly used and given with skill, empathy, and integrity, interpretations can be potent catalysts for growth.

A **reassuring response** attempts to soothe the original speaker's feelings. It implies that the speaker need not feel that way. One might reply, "Many others have come through the same operation well." Reassuring responses may be helpful in conveying acceptance to the speaker or in encouraging a person to try out new behaviors that might help to resolve a problem. However, an individual frequently perceives reassurance as an attempt to minimize the problem. The individual is concerned with his or her own dilemma, not other people. Introducing other people's problems or one's own in an effort to pacify may suggest that the listener is not taking the speaker's problem seriously or wants to dismiss it.

A **probing response** seeks further information. One might ask, "What is it about the operation that frightens you?" Additional information can be very helpful in assisting the listener to understand the problem. All too frequently, however, a probing response is taken to be an infringement of privacy. The individual may inwardly react, "That's none of your business." Rogers would recommend that a probing response be avoided or presented in such a way that the speaker is free to drop the subject. One might simply ask, "Would you like to talk about it?" in which case the speaker is free to say, "No, I'd rather not," if the subject is too painful.

The **reflective response** seeks to capture the underlying feelings that are expressed in the original communication. One might say, "You're very scared." An effective reflective statement does not simply echo the original words or thoughts of the speaker, it tries to zero in on the underlying emotion that was expressed. It is most effective if the listener uses her or his own words and responds in a manner that matches the depth of the original communication.

A distinction should be made between a reflective response and mere restatement. A *restatement* repeats the *thought* of the original comment, whereas a reflective comment seeks to express the underlying *emotion*. Reflective responses are useful because they tell the speaker that the listener is interested and understands what he or she is trying to say. A reflective response is most likely to encourage the speaker to elaborate and explore the problem further. In addition, it assists the listener to understand the other person's internal frame of reference. For these reasons, it is probably the most fruitful response to employ, particularly for a lay person and even for a skilled therapist in the initial phases of a relationship.

Rogers believed that meaningful therapy is not confined to the professional therapist's or counselor's office. Any relation can be therapeutic when it has the necessary and sufficient conditions. Most people could use practice in cultivating the reflective response inasmuch as it is the most fruitful but least used response. Rogers's theory strongly pertains to the development of effective interpersonal and communication skills.

Supportive versus Reconstructive Psychotherapy

Different methods of psychotherapy vary in their ambitions. Some therapies aim at strengthening adaptive behaviors and others seek to reorganize the basic personality structure. At one end of the spectrum, psychoanalysis stands as an example of **reconstructive psychotherapy**. Through analysis of the resistances and transference the analyst seeks to remove defenses so that the analysand can communicate true feelings and integrate his or her personality. On the other hand, many psychotherapeutic techniques are best characterized as **supportive**, since they seek to strengthen adaptive instincts and defenses without necessarily tampering with the underlying personality structure. Clearly, reconstructive psychotherapy is a much more intensive undertaking, which accounts for the long duration of psychoanalysis. Although he was not averse to providing insight when the occasion merits it, Rogers's approach tends to be supportive rather than reconstructive.

One technique is not better than the other; rather, we need to recognize that for different people, in different circumstances, and perhaps even at different times in their lives, one approach may be more suitable than another. Such variation may also help to explain why Rogers's therapeutic technique has been particularly successful with college-age students, many of whom are not seriously impaired but are undergoing a difficult period of identity during which supportive therapy may be very helpful. Rogers pointed out that we all can benefit from counseling. Although we may not be suffering from overt problems that seriously affect our lives, we may not be functioning as well as we would like. Rogers acknowledged that at one particularly stressful period of his life he was treated by a colleague. He was thankful that he was able to develop a method of therapy and train therapists and counselors who were not only independent but also able to offer him the kind of help that he needed. After he himself received therapy, Rogers felt that his own work with clients was increasingly free and more spontaneous.

Changes in Rogers's View of Therapy

Rogers's earlier writings on therapeutic techniques stressed the idea that the potential for better health lies in the client. The counselor's role was essentially that of making the kinds of reflective responses that would enable the client's potential to flower. Later, Rogers shifted from his emphasis on technique to therapist genuineness and use of self in therapy (Bozarth, 1990).

In later years, Rogers was less interested in individual counseling and more interested in group counseling, as well as broader social concerns. He was a leader in the field of encounter groups and sponsored some interracial and intercultural groups. He challenged some of the concepts on which our society is based, such as that power is power over other people or that strength is the strength to control. Instead he suggested that influence is gained only when power is shared and that control is constructive when it is self-control. He wrote about education, particularly higher education, describing a plan for radical change in teacher education and researching the effects of teachers' attitudes on students' learning. He emphasized the importance of combining experiential with cognitive learning. He also explored various forms of partnership unions or alternatives to marriage as well as other interpersonal relationships in contemporary society.

Assessment and Research in Rogers's Theory

Rogers was exceptionally open to the empirical test of his theories. The private, confidential character of clinical treatment has made it very difficult to study in its natural setting. With the permission of his clients, however, Rogers introduced the tape recorder and film camera into the treatment room. He did not believe that they detract from the therapy. Within a short time, both client and counselor forget about the recording equipment and act naturally and spontaneously.

The recordings Rogers made have provided a group of actual transcriptions of therapeutic sessions that can be observed and studied. The sessions have been

THINKING CRITICALLY

Assessment with the Q-Sort Test

You may explore the Q-sort technique by making and sorting a set of cards. Copy the list of twenty-five different ways in which you might perceive yourself in Table 12.1 onto individual index cards. First, sort the cards into seven different piles, ranging from "least like me" to "most like me." In order to have your piles follow a normal curve of distribution, you will need to place most of the cards in the middle piles, indicating that the characteristic is somewhat like you but not the most or least like you. Your final distribution should be like this:

	(least like me)				(most like me)		
pile #	1	2	3	4	5	6	7
no. of cards	1	2	5	9	5	2	1

After you have sorted the cards to describe your self-concept as you perceive it, you may wish to re-sort the cards to describe your ideal self — the person that you would most like to be. A comparison of these two sortings will give you a rough idea of the discrepancy between your self-concept and your self-ideal. You might also wish to ask some friends to sort the cards as they perceive you, to gain an idea of the image you project to others in comparison with your own self-perception.

analyzed in various ways. A classification system permits us to note the kinds of statements made by both the client and the counselor. Rating scales monitor the progress and change that occur during therapy from the viewpoints of both the client and the counselor.

One method that Rogers used for studying changes in a person's self-concept is the **Q-sort technique,** developed by William Stephenson. The Q-sort test uses a packet of one hundred cards containing descriptive statements or words that can be used to describe the self. The person is given the cards and asked to sort them according to his or her self-perception into a prearranged order, which resembles a normal curve of distribution. The Q-sort technique has been used to measure changes that occur throughout therapy. In short, Rogers provided an impetus to developing means for ongoing empirical research on the processes of therapy and the self.

From his studies, Rogers concluded that there is a clear predictability to the therapeutic process. Given certain conditions, such as the three therapist atti-

Table 12.1   *Suggested Ways of Perceiving the Self*

I make strong demands on myself.
I often feel humiliated.
I often get down on myself for the things I do.
I doubt my sexual powers.
I have a warm emotional relationship with others.
It is difficult to control my aggression.
I am responsible for my troubles.
I tend to be on my guard with friendly people.
I am a responsible person.
I usually feel driven to work hard.
Self-control is no problem for me.
I am disorganized.
I express my emotions freely.
I feel apathetic.
I am optimistic.
I try not to think about my problems.
I am sexually attractive.
I am shy.
I am liked by most people who know me.
I am afraid of a full-fledged disagreement with a person.
I can usually make up my mind and stick to it.
I can't seem to make up my mind one way or another.
I am impulsive.
I am afraid of sex.
I am ambitious.

tudes outlined earlier, certain predictable outcomes may be expected. The client will express deep motivational attitudes and begin to explore and become more aware of attitudes and reactions. The client will begin to accept him- or herself more fully and will discover and choose more satisfying goals. Finally, the client will begin to behave in a manner that indicates greater psychological growth and maturity.

Research by others with troubled individuals and in education has supported the view that when facilitating conditions are present, changes in personality and behavior will occur (see Aspy, 1972; Aspy and Roebuck, 1976; Tausch, 1978).

Rogers's Theory: Philosophy, Science, and Art

Rogers did a great deal to bring the human being back as the primary focus of psychological study. In doing so, he clearly reasserted the philosophical character of personality theorizing. At the same time, he was very careful to distinguish between his philosophical assumptions and his scientific hypotheses. For instance, in Rogers's theory the self is not a philosophical concept but a name for a group of processes, which can be studied scientifically. The issue of the usefulness of the concepts of self and self-actualization continue to attract discussion and debate (see Geller, 1984; Ginsburg, 1984).

Still, Rogers's emphasis on subjectivity and the individual's internal frame of reference made scientific research difficult. Researchers have traditionally stressed the role of the external observer because, as we have seen, introspective reports are much more difficult to validate than extrospective reports. Rogers was criticized for using self-reports in his research, and many scientific psychologists have rejected Rogers's notion of the self because of his methods.

However, Roger encourages us to invite the person as a co-investigator in personality research. The concept of self, which he revitalized, is increasingly described as a complex psychological construct stemming from interpretations of cognitive, affective-motive, and attitudinal facets. Within individuals, there is one self with varied interrelated aspects as compared to a multiplicity of selves. The existence of a harmony between the pattern and typology of the personality and the self provides a framework for explaining both realities (Zlate, 1989).

Tendencies to suppress data or to supply socially acceptable data instead of the truth do exist in subjective reporting. However, if we are aware of these tendencies toward error, we can take steps to avoid them. In this sense, introspection is no different from any other scientific method. Extrospection is also open to a great deal of error: sense organs may be defective or deluded. Psychologists have known for a long time that there is hardly a perfect correspondence between the stimulus, or the evidence of the world that reaches our senses, and our perception of the world. Introspection does not involve the sense organs to the same extent as extrospection and so in some respects may be more trustworthy. Thus, Rogers's emphasis on introspection was a useful correction of the emphasis on extrospection that characterized American psychology. Introspective self-reports have gained wider acceptance with social and cognitive behavior theorists with the present emphasis on cognition.

Nevertheless, a major criticism of Rogers's position is that it is based on a simplistic concept of phenomenology and does not reflect a sophisticated understanding of the complexity of the processes underlying human awareness. It also does not take into account a child's immature cognitive structures and inability to make clear distinctions between feelings and actions. To say that the best vantage point for understanding an individual is that of the individual minimizes how frequently human beings deny or distort the truth about themselves to themselves. Many of us seem bent on self-deception rather than on self-understanding. Although Rogers acknowledged that there are experiences of which a person may be unaware through the processes of denial and distortion, he did not believe that repression is inevitable and held that an atmosphere of acceptance is sufficient to lift repression. Critics suggest that this belief is naive and that Rogers failed to recognize the power and intensity of unconscious forces.

Rogers's own example of the two men, one of whom saw a boulder and the other a tumbleweed, depicts the limitations of his approach. In spite of how an object is perceived, or even if it is not perceived, its reality has an impact. After all, "contact with a boulder will hurt no matter how it is perceived." "Reality is not wholly determined internally" (Lerman, 1992). Research in feminist psychology shows that individuals' personalities are intimately related to the world

PHILOSOPHICAL ASSUMPTIONS

Examining Rogers

How would you rate Rogers on each of the basic philosophical assumptions described in Chapter 1? Each basic issue was presented as a bipolar dimension along which a person's view can be placed according to the degree of agreement with one or the other extreme. Rate Rogers's views on these issues.

When you have determined where you think Rogers stands, compare your responses with those of your classmates and your instructor. You should be willing to defend your ratings, but also be prepared to change them in light of others' compelling arguments. Afterward, compare your rating of Rogers with your own position on each issue and with those of other theorists. Does this comparison help you to understand why his theory does or does not appeal to you?

Would strongly agree	Would agree	Is neutral or believes in synthesis of both views	Would agree	Would strongly agree
1	2	3	4	5

freedom	**determinism**
People basically have control over their own behavior and understand the motives behind their behavior.	The behavior of people is basically determined by internal or external forces over which they have little, if any, control.

they live in and the conditions of worth that are imposed upon them. The reality of women's subjugation (and I might add that of other oppressed groups) influences what they can be, how they conceive of themselves, and their personality development (Miller, 1976). Thus, Rogers and other humanists "failed to recognize that no person constructs their own reality without external influences." The fact is "patriarchal institutions limit and severely constrict the possibilities for women, regardless of whether the women involved believe themselves to be oppressed or not. . . . To imply that . . . all a woman has to do is to change her perception of herself . . . [and] such . . . change would eliminate all cultural, economic, legal and interpersonal obstacles . . . is absurd. . . . Believing that one has the legal right to leave a battering relationship does not, in and of itself, guarantee that any particular woman can succeed in leaving, that she will

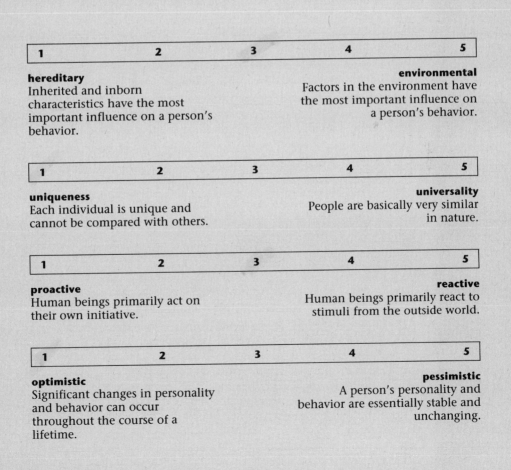

| 1 | 2 | 3 | 4 | 5 |

hereditary
Inherited and inborn characteristics have the most important influence on a person's behavior.

environmental
Factors in the environment have the most important influence on a person's behavior.

| 1 | 2 | 3 | 4 | 5 |

uniqueness
Each individual is unique and cannot be compared with others.

universality
People are basically very similar in nature.

| 1 | 2 | 3 | 4 | 5 |

proactive
Human beings primarily act on their own initiative.

reactive
Human beings primarily react to stimuli from the outside world.

| 1 | 2 | 3 | 4 | 5 |

optimistic
Significant changes in personality and behavior can occur throughout the course of a lifetime.

pessimistic
A person's personality and behavior are essentially stable and unchanging.

be safe after she does leave, or that she has the economic wherewithal to support herself and her children if she does" (Lerman, 1992).

However, Rogers's view of the development and actualization of self may be highly culture bound. He has been accused of encouraging selfishness (Marin, 1975; Wallach & Wallach, 1983) and making interpersonal relations "instrumental" and "competitive" (Geller, 1982). His portrait of the healthy self as an actualizing being, differentiated from others and dependent on achievement, may not be relevant to non-Western cultures where the self is delineated in terms of relation to others, particularly within the family (Markus & Kitayama, 1991). This may be strange, because Rogers (1963) indicated that one of the outcomes of self actualization is harmonious and deep social relations. Das (1989) argues that Rogers's view can be seen as complementary to the concept of self-realization in Vedandic Hinduism and the two major schools of Buddhism—Thervada and Mahayana.

At the same time, a phenomenological view gives balance to psychology by providing a human voice in an expanding electronic world of computerization and reminds us that psychology is principally a human science (Mruk, 1989).

Rogers's careful empirical study of the therapeutic process has shed considerable light on the phenomenon and practice of therapy. Scientific research has helped to clarify the types of situations and relationships that are conducive to change. Rogers's discussion of the therapist's attitude of acceptance is a helpful correction of Freud's overemphasis on transference. It is the real, personal relationship between therapist and client that fosters personality change. Rogers's most lasting contribution may be the therapeutic impact of the art of listening (Cain, 1990): An attitude of openness and readiness to hear, that is generally taken for granted and sounds so easy, but in fact is exceedingly difficult to do. Rogers, in encouraging empirical validation of his theories, has facilitated the development of person-centered therapeutic techniques.

THINKING CRITICALLY

External Influences on One's Construction of Reality

Can you think of other examples of how external realities and conditions of worth influence the way in which individuals construct their reality? A woman may be raped even though she believes she is safe in her home, or has faith in her date or spouse. What other examples can you think of for women and other oppressed minorities in various cultures? Can you give examples of people who go to extremes to keep the belief that they are in touch with reality even though that reality may be very cruel?

Rogers (1961) criticized the social and philosophical implications of a rigid behavioral science, like that proposed by B. F. Skinner, who advocated the development of a technology to control human behavior (see Chapter 8). Rogers believed that kind of society would destroy our personhood. He acknowledged that science brought us the power to manipulate; if we value the ability to control other people, our scientific technology can tell how to achieve this goal. On the other hand, if we value individual freedom and creativity, our scientific technology can facilitate these ends as well. In either case, the goal that directs the scientific enterprise lies outside of the scientific enterprise. The basic difference between a behavioristic approach and a humanistic approach is a philosophical choice (1980). Each choice leads to different topics of research and different methods of validation (see also Harari, 1989; DeCarvalho, 1989).

Rogers suggested that we need to be explicit about the goals we want our scientific endeavor to serve. Rogers, in his role as scientist, studied the predictability of the therapeutic process, not to control his client's behavior but to help his client be less predictable and more free, responsible, and spontaneous.

Psychologists have welcomed Rogers's reintroduction of the importance of subjectivity and perception in determining behavior, a theme consistent with the current cognitive emphasis. His therapeutic techniques have been widely applauded and adopted in education, industry, and social programs. Moreover, Rogers's theory prompted a great deal of further study and research, particularly concerning his concept of the self and the process of psychotherapy. His emphasis on human potentiality and freedom provides an attractive alternative to theories that emphasize the idea that we are largely controlled by external or unconscious forces. His theory has tremendous appeal for those who share his humanistic and optimistic philosophy of the human being.

Tena (1993) argues that Rogers's theory of an "emerging new person" can best be conceived in the framework of a "World evolutionary-revolutionary process not limited by any one specific culture." In Latin America, where people are actively involved in transpersonal psychology, these ideas are seen as relevant. In this connection, Smith (1990) reminds us that humanistic psychology originated as a social movement as well as a perspective on human nature.

Summary

1.   Rogers's humanist theory is influenced by **phenomenology**, which emphasized that what is important is not an object or event in itself but how it is perceived. In psychology this means an emphasis on human awareness and the conviction that the best vantage point for understanding an individual is that of the individual him- or herself. The **phenomenal field** refers to the total sum of experiences an organism has, the organism is the individual as a process, and the **self** is a concept of who one is. Self-actualization is the dynamic within the organism leading it to actualize, fulfill, and enhance its

potentials. Emotions accompany and facilitate the process of self-actualization. Fully experiencing emotions facilitates growth and repression is unnecessary.

2. A state of **congruence** exists when a person's symbolized experiences reflect actual experiences. When denial or distortion is present in the symbolization, there is a state of **incongruence**.

3. The young child has a strong need for **positive regard.** Ideally, positive regard is **unconditional.** If it is contingent upon specific behaviors it becomes **conditional positive regard** and posits **conditions of worth** that may lead the child to introject values of others and become incongruent.

4. According to Rogers, a **fully functioning person** is characterized by openness to experience, existential living, organismic trust, experiential freedom, and creativity.

5. Rogers is best known for his method of person-centered therapy. He believed that there are three necessary and sufficient therapeutic attitudes for change: **empathy, acceptance,** and **genuineness.**

6. Rogers distinguished among five different **responses** to emotional communications: **evaluative, interpretative, reassuring, probing,** and **reflective.** Each of them has different effects. Rogers encouraged the cultivation of the reflective response.

7. **Person-centered therapy** tends to be **supportive** rather than **reconstructive.** In his later writings, Rogers stressed the need for the therapist to be present as a person in the relationship and showed more interest in group therapy and social change. He has encouraged the empirical test of his theories and developed methods of assessing and predicting therapeutic change.

8. Rogers was very careful to distinguish between his philosophical assumptions and his scientific hypotheses. He criticized Skinner's view of science and his goal of controlling human nature rather than increasing human freedom, responsibility, and spontaneity. He pointed out that our technology may be used to foster many different goals. His own position has been criticized for its reliance on a simplistic phenomenology and for being highly culture bound, and praised for increasing our understanding of interpersonal relationships. Rogers's careful empirical study of the therapeutic process has shed considerable light on the phenomenon of therapy and counseling.

Suggestions for Further Reading

Carl Rogers was a lucid writer whose works are relatively easy for the lay person to understand. In *Counseling and Psychotherapy* (Houghton Mifflin, 1942), Rogers first introduced his therapy technique, gave examples, and compared it with other therapeutic methods. *Client-Centered Therapy* (Houghton Mifflin, 1951) reflects the change in name Rogers gave his technique in order to focus attention on the client as the center of the therapeutic process. This book discusses the practice and implications of client-centered therapy and also describes his theory of personality and behavior. With Rosalind Dymond, Carl Rogers edited *Psychotherapy and Personality Change* (University of Chicago Press, 1954), which presents thirteen empirical studies investigating hypotheses that arose out of the client-centered approach. In a group of significant articles organized into the book *On Becoming a Person* (Houghton Mifflin, 1961), Rogers described his own experiences as a counselor, his view of the fully functioning person, the place of research in psychotherapy, and its implications for education, family life, and group functions. Also included is Rogers's critique of B. F. Skinner. *Freedom to Learn* (Charles E. Merrill, 1969) discusses ways of making classroom learning more relevant and meaningful to students. Rogers explained how the atmosphere that makes learning effective is similar to those attitudes that are conducive to personality change in therapy. *A Way of Being* (Houghton Mifflin, 1980) describes the changes that occurred in Rogers's life and thought during the 1970s. Rogers felt that the best and most rigorous presentation of his theory is his article in Koch, *Psychology: A Study of a Science* (McGraw-Hill, 1959).

Summaries of Rogers's own research may be found in a book edited by him, *The Therapeutic Relationship and Its Impact* (University of Wisconsin Press, 1967) and the Rogers and Dymond book mentioned above. For a discussion of the research generated by self-theory, the reader is referred to R. Wylie's chapter on "The Present Status of Self-Theory" in E. F. Borgotta and W. W. Lambert, *Handbook of Personality and Research* (Rand McNally, 1968) and his book *The Self-Concept* (University of Nebraska Press, 1974, 1978), as well as D. N. Aspy, *Toward a Technology for Humanizing Education* (Research Press, 1972), and R. Tausch's article "Facilitating dimensions in interpersonal relations: Verifying the theoretical assumptions of Carl Rogers," *College Student Journal,* 1978, *12* (1).

CHAPTER 13

Abraham Maslow

YOUR GOALS FOR THIS CHAPTER

1. Explain why Maslow has been critical of psychoanalysis and radical behaviorism.
2. Distinguish among *motivation, metamotivation, D-needs,* and *B-needs* and indicate the importance of these distinctions.
3. Describe Maslow's *hierarchy of human needs.* Cite studies that show that the needs are essential for optimal human life and development.
4. Describe how Maslow identified and studied *self-actualized persons.*
5. Identify four key dimensions of self-actualized persons and describe the characteristics of each dimension.
6. Explain what is meant by a *peak experience* and give examples of experiences that might be recognized as peaks.
7. Describe some of the criticisms of Maslow's portrait of the self-actualized person.
8. Distinguish between *basic needs therapy* and *insight therapy* and indicate the criteria that Maslow believed were necessary for effective and expanded therapy.
9. Evaluate Maslow's theory in terms of its function as philosophy, science, and art.

Even though historical analysis reveals that humanistic psychology had no single founder (De Carvalho, 1991a), Abraham Maslow has been described as its spiritual father. An articulate, persuasive writer, he described humanist psychology as a "third force" in American psychology. He criticized both psychoanalysis and radical behaviorism for their limited conceptions of human nature. "The study of crippled, stunted, immature, and unhealthy specimens," he wrote, "can only lead to a crippled psychology" (1970).

The study of human nature as a machine, typical of radical behaviorism, cannot comprehend the whole person. Maslow offered his view as a complement rather than an alternative to these two other forces. He did not reject the contributions that psychoanalysis and behaviorism have made, but he believed that the picture of human nature needs to be rounded out. In particular, Maslow sought to emphasize the positive rather than the negative side of human nature. The brighter side of humanity is emphasized in his concept of the self-actualized person.

Biographical Background

Abraham Maslow was born in 1908 in a poor Jewish district of Brooklyn, New York, the first of seven children. His parents were Russian immigrants. As his father's business as a cooper (one who makes or repairs wooden casks and tubs) improved, Maslow's family moved out of the slums and into lower-middle-class neighborhoods. As a result, the young Maslow found himself the only Jewish boy in the neighborhood and a target of anti-Semitism. Embarrassed by his physical appearance and taunted, isolated, friendless, and lonely, he spent a great deal of his early years cloistered in the library in the companionship of books.

His father was an ambitious man who instilled in his children a desire to succeed. At an early age, Maslow delivered newspapers. Later he spent several summers working for the family company. Maslow was not close to either of his parents. He was fond of his father but afraid of him. He described his mother as schizophrenic and later wondered how he had turned out so well in spite of his unhappy childhood. His mother clearly favored his younger brothers and sister and mercilessly punished her eldest son at the least provocation. Recalling a painful memory, Maslow told how his mother once killed two stray cats he had brought home by smashing their heads against the wall. Later, Maslow admitted that he hated his mother and all that she stood for (Hoffman, 1988). They were never reconciled and he did not attend her funeral. His mother's brother, however, was a kind and devoted uncle who spent a great deal of time with him and may have been responsible for Maslow's mental stability.

Maslow attended New York City schools through the eighth grade and then the Brooklyn Borough High School, where he had an excellent record. At the age of eighteen he entered the City College of New York, where the tuition was

Abraham Maslow

free. His father wanted him to study law, a subject that he was not interested in, and his grades fell. Undecided about his studies and in love with a girl of whom his parents disapproved, he floundered, spending time at Cornell, returning to New York City, and trying to escape by going to the University of Wisconsin.

Within a few months of his arrival at Wisconsin, he announced his intention of marrying his sweetheart. Later, he suggested that life didn't begin for him until he married and began studying at Wisconsin. His wife encouraged his academic work. Further, he had discovered John Watson and was totally absorbed in behaviorism, which he saw as a very practical way of improving society. During his college and graduate years, Maslow received a solid grounding in empirical laboratory research. He worked as an assistant to William H. Sheldon, although he was not personally impressed by Sheldon's theory of the varieties of temperament. He also studied animal behavior, working with Harry Harlow, a well-known psychologist who conducted extensive research with rhesus monkeys. Maslow's own doctoral research concerned the sexual and dominance characteristics of monkeys.

After receiving the Ph.D. from Wisconsin in 1934, Maslow returned to New York. He worked as a research assistant to Edwin L. Thorndike and then began to teach at Brooklyn College. New York was a vibrant place for a young psychologist during the 1930s. Many European psychologists, psychiatrists, and others of the intelligentsia who had come to America to escape the Nazis were in New York. Maslow eagerly met and learned from them. He was influenced by

Max Wertheimer (a founder of the Gestalt school), Erich Fromm, Karen Horney, and Alfred Adler. He was also impressed by the anthropologist Ruth Benedict, who inspired him with her optimism about the potentialities of society.

Within such an eclectic climate, it was probably inevitable that Maslow's interest in behaviorism would diminish. The birth of his first daughter was the "thunderclap that settled things" once and for all. All of his experimentation with rats and primates did not prepare him for the mystery of the child. Behaviorist theory might explain what was observed in the laboratory, but it could not account for human experiences. The advent of World War II also profoundly affected Maslow. His attention turned more fully to research on the human personality in an effort to improve it, "to show that human beings are capable of something grander than war and prejudice and hatred" (Hall, 1968).

Maslow remained at Brooklyn for fourteen years. In 1951, he moved to Brandeis University where he stayed until one year before his death in 1970. These later years at Brandeis were again marked by a feeling of isolation, in spite of the fact that Maslow had become a very popular figure in the field of psychology. He clarified and refined his theories and shortly before his death had embarked on a fellowship that would have enabled him to undertake a large-scale study developing a philosophy of economics, politics, and ethics informed by humanistic psychology.

Human Motivation: A Hierarchical Theory

Maslow believed that human beings are interested in growing rather than simply restoring balance or avoiding frustration. He described the human being as a "wanting animal" who is almost always desiring something. Indeed, as one human desire is satisfied, another arises to take its place. In the drive to self-actualize, the individual moves forward toward growth, happiness, and satisfaction.

Maslow (1970) distinguished between motivation and metamotivation. **Motivation** refers to reducing tension by satisfying deficit states or lacks. It entails **D-needs** or deficiency needs, which arise out of the organism's requirements for physiological survival or safety, such as the need for food or rest, and motivate the individual to engage in activities that will reduce these drives. Motivation and the D-needs are powerful determinants of behavior. **Metamotivation** refers to growth tendencies. It entails **B-needs** or being needs, which arise out of the organism's drive to self-actualize and fulfill its inherent potential. B-needs do not stem from a lack or deficiency; rather, they push forward to self-fulfillment. Their goal is to enhance life by enriching it. Rather than reduce tension, they frequently heighten it in their quest for ever-increasing stimuli that will bring a life lived to the fullest.

Motivation and the D-needs take precedence over metamotivation and the B-needs. The deficiency needs must be satisfied first. An individual who is wondering where the next mouthful of food is going to come from can hardly be concerned with spiritual goals like truth or beauty. Thus, the needs may be

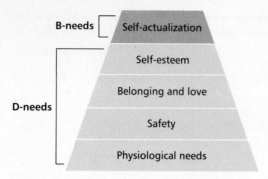

Figure 13.1 *Maslow's Hierarchy of Needs*
Maslow suggests that human needs may be conceived of as a hierarchy in which the needs that stand at the bottom must be satisfied before those at the top can be fulfilled.

conceived as arranged in a hierarchy, in that the needs at the bottom must be satisfied before those at the top can be fulfilled (Figure 13.1).

In his **hierarchy of needs**, Maslow (1970) described five basic needs. In order of their strength they are: physiological needs, safety needs, belonging and love needs, self-esteem needs, and self-actualization needs. Each lower need must be satisfied before an individual can become aware of or develop the capacity to fulfill the needs above it. As each need is satisfied, the next higher order need attains importance. Some individuals, because of their circumstances, find it very difficult to satisfy even the lowest needs. The higher one is able to go, however, the greater psychological health and self-actualization one will demonstrate.

1. *Physiological needs* The strongest needs of all are the physiological ones that pertain to the physical survival and biological maintenance of the organism. They include the need for food, drink, sleep, oxygen, shelter, and sex. For many Americans, physiological needs are satisfied almost automatically. However, if biological needs are not met for a protracted period of time, an individual will not be motivated to fulfill any other needs. The person who is really starving has no other interest than obtaining food. Several experiments and real-life experiences have demonstrated the overwhelming behavioral effects produced by a lack of food, sleep, or other life-sustaining needs. Gratification of these needs renders them less important and permits other needs to appear (1970).

2. *Safety needs* Safety needs refer to the organism's requirements for an orderly, stable, and predictable world. These can be seen clearly in young children, neurotics, or individuals who live in unsafe environments. The young child, who is helpless and dependent, prefers a certain amount of structured routine and discipline. The absence of these elements makes the child anxious and insecure. The neurotic frequently behaves like the insecure child,

If physiological needs are not met, an individual will not be motivated to fulfill other needs.

compulsively organizing the world and avoiding strange or different experiences. Individuals who live in unsafe environments or suffer from job insecurity may need to spend a great deal of time and energy trying to protect themselves and their possessions.

3. *Belonging and love needs* Once the physiological and safety needs are met, needs for love and belonging arise. The individual seeks affectionate and intimate relationships with other people, needing to feel part of various reference groups, such as the family, neighborhood, gang, or a professional association. Maslow noted that such needs are increasingly more difficult to meet in our technological, fluid, and mobile society. Such problems may account for new styles of living together. Love, rather than being physiological or simply sexual, involves a healthy, mutual relationship of trust, in which each person is deeply understood and accepted.

4. *Self-esteem needs* Maslow described two kinds of esteem needs — the need for respect from others and the need for self-respect. Self-esteem entails competence, confidence, mastery, achievement, independence, and freedom. Respect from others entails recognition, acceptance, status, and appreciation. When these needs are not met an individual feels discouraged, weak, and inferior. Healthy self-esteem is a realistic appraisal of one's capacities and has its roots in deserved respect from others. For most people,

the need for regard from others diminishes with age because it has been fulfilled and the need for self-regard becomes more important.

5. *Self-actualization needs* If the foregoing needs have been met, the needs for **self-actualization** may emerge *if* the individual has the courage to choose them. These needs are difficult to describe because they are unique and vary from person to person. In general, self-actualization refers to the desire to fulfill one's highest potential. The individual on this level who does not fully exploit his or her talents and capacities is discontented and restless. In Maslow's words, "A musician must make music, an artist must paint, a poet must write, if he is to be at peace with himself" (1970).

Self-actualization is possible only if the lower needs have been sufficiently met so that they do not detract from or engross a person's basic energies. Rather than organize their behavior toward tension reduction, individuals whose deficiency needs are satisfied may, in fact, seek states of increased optimal tension in order to enhance their opportunities for self-actualization. Higher needs may become as compelling as food to the hungry. In short, those who are living on a B-level have a radically different motivation from those who are still striving to satisfy deficit states.

A number of prerequisites are necessary for a person to be motivated on the B-level. Cultural, economic, and social conditions must be such that the individual does not need to be preoccupied with physiological or safety needs. Employment settings must consider the growth needs of employees. Emotional needs for interpersonal relationships and self-esteem must be met. This may be very difficult in periods of economic recession or in a climate that emphasizes productivity over human relations.

The decade of the 1990s is an era of intense downsizing, where management rather than leadership is encouraged and employees receive their layoff notices through the fax machine. While Maslow's theory could yield many fruitful applications in a highly technological society leading to both increased productivity and the fulfillment of human needs, unfortunately it is not being given much consideration in today's business world.

In addition to the hierarchy just outlined, Maslow posited the important human needs to *know* and *understand* (1970). These form a small but powerful hierarchy of their own, in which the need to know is more potent than and prior to the need to understand. Children, by nature, are curious; when their cognitive impulses are satisfied, they seek further comprehension and understanding. Clinical studies also convinced Maslow that in some individuals aesthetic needs are very important: "They get sick [in special ways] from ugliness, and are cured by beautiful surroundings; they *crave* actively, and their cravings can be satisfied *only* by beauty" (1970). Some people actually become ill when they are confronted by ugliness. These needs are not sharply delineated from the needs of the earlier hierarchy; they overlap with them and are interrelated.

Maslow described all human needs as *instinctoid,* or inherent in human nature (1970). He recognized that human beings cannot be said to have instincts in the same sense that animals do because whatever "instincts" humans possess are heavily overlaid with learning. Still, humans have tendencies that need to be nourished and cultivated. They are instinctoid or basic in that unless the needs are met, illness develops, just as a lack of vitamin C leads to illness. Xu (1985) has reviewed genetic and psychological research that directly or indirectly supports the concept of instinctoid needs.

A number of clinical experiments have demonstrated that the needs that Maslow described are essential for optimal human life and development. Studies of children in institutions who do not receive adequate love and attention show that these children do not develop normally, although all of their physical needs are met (Spitz, 1951). Maslow's own clinical experience showed that individuals who satisfy their basic needs are happier, healthier, and more effective, whereas those whose needs are frustrated display neurotic symptoms (1970). Furthermore, other clinicians, such as Karen Horney and Carl Rogers, have pointed out that given the appropriate conditions, the individual chooses to move forward and grow. From where does such a choice or impulse come, unless it is inherent in the individual? Psychologists speak of **species-specific behavior,** that is, an inborn tendency for members of a biological subgroup to behave in a certain way. Chickens tend to scratch for their food, whereas pigs root for it. Maslow suggests that the species-specific characteristics of human beings include the hierarchical needs and a drive toward self-actualization. Kristiansen (1989) suggests that there may be gender differences and that Maslow's hierarchy reflects a male paradigm; Ma (1989) has pointed out cultural differences. Of course, for an adequate test of Maslow's theory we would have to conduct extensive cross-cultural and longitudinal studies. Such studies have not yet been conducted.

Some tools have been developed to measure Maslow's hierarchy of needs, such as Williams and Page's (1989) Maslowian Assessment Survey and Haymes and Green's (1982) Needsort. The Needsort also draws upon Kagan's (1972) formulation of motivation that describes a group of secondary motives that come from particular cultural forces, for example, in the West, the need for achievement. Preliminary analysis with the Needsort supports the idea that deliberately imparting healthy dependency needs might help to prevent aggressive behaviors in populations at high risk for those disorders.

The Study of Self-Actualized Persons

Maslow has been described as preoccupied with healthy persons rather than with neurotics. He conducted an extensive, although informal, study of a group of persons whom he considered to be self-actualized. His study was initially private and motivated by his own curiosity rather than by the normal demands of scientific laboratory research. Thus, it lacked the rigor and distinct methodology of strict empirical study. Nevertheless, the study generated such interest among other psychologists that Maslow felt it was wise to publish his findings

(1970). He admitted that his findings represented only an initial, tentative attempt to study optimum health, but they may serve as a focal point for further empirical research.

Maslow defined *self-actualizing persons* as those who are "fulfilling themselves and doing the best that they are capable of doing" (1970). His subjects consisted of friends and personal acquaintances, public figures living and dead, and selected college students. Some of the figures included in his study are well known (see the list on p. 355). Others are not as well known and several of them were never identified publicly. In his initial study of three thousand college students, Maslow found only one individual who could be termed self-actualized. He hypothesized that self-actualizing tendencies probably increase with age. Thereafter, he limited his studies of the college population to the most well-adjusted 1 percent of the Brandeis College population. Not all of his subjects were deemed fully actualized. Studying these individuals, their personalities, characteristics, habits, and abilities enabled Maslow to develop his definition of optimal mental health.

Techniques of Assessment and Research

In his study of self-actualized individuals, Maslow used whatever techniques appeared to be most appropriate to the particular situation. In dealing with historical figures, he analyzed biographical material and written records. With living persons, he also utilized in-depth interviews and psychological tests, such as the Rorschach Ink Blot Test and the Thematic Apperception Test. He obtained global impressions from the subject's friends and acquaintances. In some cases, he found that he had to be rather careful because a number of his subjects were suspicious of the intrusions on their privacy that his research constituted.

By ordinary standards of laboratory research, what Maslow did in his study was not true research. He was quick to acknowledge that his investigation was not conducted along strict scientific lines. His descriptions were not based on standardized tests nor were his conclusions obtained from controlled experimental situations. Moreover, his definition of a self-actualized person tended to be a subjective one: the self-actualized person was one whom Maslow deemed to be self-actualized. Nevertheless, Maslow pointed out that the canons of rigorous scientific procedures would not have encompassed or permitted research into the areas that he was studying. Further, he presented his data as only an initial observation and effort to study health as opposed to neurosis. Maslow hoped that future studies would yield more information as to the nature of self-actualization and confirm or disprove his own expectations.

For some years research on Maslow's concept of self-actualization was slow, since an adequate assessment device for measuring the variables of self-actualization was lacking. The development of the Personal Orientation Inventory (POI) by Shostrom (1965), considered to be a reliable, valid measure of self-actualization, has led to increased empirical research related to Maslow's constructs (Kelly & Chovan, 1985; Rychman et al., 1985; Gray, 1986; Bordages, 1989; Alexander, Rainforth, & Gelderloos, 1991; Leitschuh & Rawlins, 1991). However, it has also led to the conclusion that Maslow's concept may reflect a primarily male bias (Faulkender, 1991).

Characteristics of Self-Actualizers

Maslow listed several characteristics of self-actualized persons that emerged from his study (1970). For simplicity, these characteristics may be grouped under four key dimensions: awareness, honesty, freedom, and trust (1969).

Awareness   Self-actualizers are characterized by awareness. They are aware of the inner rightness of themselves, of nature, and of the peak experiences of life. This awareness emerges in an *efficient perception of reality.* Self-actualizers are accurate in their perception of the world and comfortable in it. They can see through phoniness and assess the real motives of other people. They have a clearer perception of reality and realism in areas such as politics and religion, which permits them to cut through extraneous issues and recognize true ones. They have a higher acuity or sharpness of perception. Colors appear brighter and more vibrant to them than to the average person. They have a more efficient sense of smell. Their hearing is more precise.

Self-actualizers display a continued *freshness of appreciation.* Each sunrise and sunset refreshes them anew, and each new flower is an event that never loses its miraculous quality. Self-actualizers have no preconceptions of what things ought to be. They are open to experience and let each experience speak for itself.

The self-actualized person frequently experiences what Maslow called a peak experience. A **peak experience** is an intensification of any experience to the degree that there is a loss or transcendence of self. These kinds of experiences are often termed mystical or religious, but Maslow emphasized that they do not necessarily entail traditional religious labels or interpretations. A peak experience may be provoked by a secular event as well. Events that may be mundane and ordinary to others, such as viewing a work of art or reaching a sexual climax, may be the sparks that trigger a peak experience.

During a peak experience, the individual experiences not only an expansion of self but also a sense of unity and meaningfulness in life. For that moment, the world appears to be complete and the person is at one with it. After the experience is over, and the person has returned to the routine of everyday living, the experience lingers on. It has an illuminating quality that transforms one's understanding so that things do not seem to be quite the same afterwards. Research using a questionnaire about peak experiences has confirmed the characteristics Maslow described (Privette, 1986). Maslow believed that *all* human beings, not only self-actualizers, are potential peakers. People at any stage can have peak experiences, though they are what Maslow considered a moment

*Intense concentration on an activity may
provoke a peak experience.*

of self-actualization. Maslow distinguished between "transcenders" and the "merely healthy": Transcenders are inclined to have peaks; the merely healthy tend not to. Some people have peak experiences but they suppress them and therefore do not recognize them when they occur. In other cases, one may inhibit a peak experience, thereby preventing its occurrence.

Stimulated by Maslow's concept, Mihaly Csikszentmihalyi (1975, 1990) talked with people from many different cultures, backgrounds, vocations, and avocations and discovered that they describe a comparable experience that he terms "flow" and "optimal experience" in which they become so totally involved in what they are doing that they forget all sense of time and awareness of self. In this condition, people are very focused and concentrated on what they are doing. Csikszentmihalyi believes that flow occurs when people are doing something that they are good at but are also being appropriately challenged. Their goals are clear and they are being given immediate feedback. Flow has also been characterized by play and the significance of other people (Privette & Bundrick, 1991).

Self-actualizers show a high degree of *ethical awareness*. They are clear about the distinction between good and evil. Self-actualizers have definite ethical standards, although their standards are not necessarily the conventional ones; rather, they know what for them is right and do it.

Self-actualizers are able to distinguish between the goal that they are striving for and the means by which they are accomplishing it. For the most part, they are focused on ends rather than means. At the same time, they often consider as ends activities that are simply means for other people. They can enjoy and appreciate the journey as well as the destination.

Honesty   Self-actualizers are characterized by honesty, which permits them to know their feelings and to trust them. They can trust the wide range of feelings — love, anger, and humor — present in interpersonal relations.

Self-actualizers have a *philosophical sense of humor* rather than an ordinary one. Most common jokes and wisecracks express hostility, superiority, or rebellion against authority. The self-actualizer's humor is more closely allied to philosophy. It is essentially an ability to laugh at the ridiculousness of the human situation and to poke fun at our shared human pretensions. Such humor was characteristic of Abraham Lincoln, whose jokes were not at other peoples' expense. Such humor is spontaneous rather than planned. Often it cannot be repeated or retold. Maslow suggests that he once felt this humor in a room full of kinetic art, sculptures having mechanical parts that can be set into motion. It seemed to him to be a "humorous parody of human life, with the noise, movement, turmoil, hurry and bustle, all of it going no place" (1970).

Self-actualizers experience *social interest* or a deep feeling of kinship with humanity. Maslow borrowed Adler's term *Gemeinschaftsgefuhl,* which means "community feeling," to describe the identification with humanity that is experienced. Although on occasions they may experience feelings of anger, impatience, or disgust, self-actualizers have a general sense of identification, sympathy, and affection for the human race and all its members.

Self-actualizers form deep *interpersonal relations.* However, they are highly selective and therefore have a small but close circle of friends. They have no need for admirers or large groups of disciples although at times they may attract such followers, creating a situation that they try to handle with tact. Their love of others involves the *being* of the other person rather than having the love of a person who cares for them. This love stems from a fullness of being rather than a state of deprivation and need.

Their love is not indiscriminate. At times they are quick to anger; they can speak harshly to others and express righteous indignation where a situation calls for it; yet their attitude is one of pity rather than attack. They react to the behavior rather than to the person.

Self-actualizers display a *democratic character structure.* They are free of prejudice, tolerant, and accepting of all people regardless of their background. They listen and they learn from those who are able to teach them.

Freedom   Self-actualizers experience a high degree of freedom, which permits them to withdraw from the chaos that surrounds others. They are free to be independent, creative, and spontaneous.

Self-actualizers show a high degree of *detachment* and a *need for privacy.* Many of us avoid being alone and compulsively seek the company of other people. Self-actualizers relish and require times when they can be by themselves. They are not secretive but they often stand apart from other people. Maslow discovered that many of them did not particularly welcome his questions because they considered such activities a violation of their privacy.

This ability to be detached extends to other areas as well. It permits the self-actualizer to concentrate to a greater degree than the average person. Whereas others may become excited and involved in the storm of things around them, self-actualizers remain above the battle, calm and unruffled.

Free to be themselves, self-actualizers are also free to let other people be. As parents, this means they have the ability to refrain from meddling with a child, because they like the way the child is growing. They can permit the child to experience the consequences of behavior without overprotecting.

Self-actualizers are *autonomous and independent* of their physical and social environment. Motivated by growth rather than by deficiency, they do not need to depend on the world or others for their real satisfaction. Their basic needs and gratifications have been met; therefore, they are free to depend on their own development.

Autonomy also entails the ability to choose freely and to govern oneself. Many people let other people such as advertisers make up their minds, but self-actualizers come to their own decisions and assume responsibility for them.

Maslow found that without exception all of his self-actualizers demonstrated *creativity,* originality, or inventiveness. This is not to say that they possess a special talent akin to that of a Mozart or a Picasso, but that they have a drive and a capacity to be creative. They do not necessarily write books, compose music, or produce art; instead, their creativeness is projected onto and touches whatever activity they undertake. The carpenter or clerk works creatively, adding a personalized touch to whatever she or he does. Self-actualizers even perceive the world creatively, as a child does, envisioning new and different possibilities.

Self-actualizers are *spontaneous,* simple, and natural. They are free to be what they are at any given moment. Although their behavior is often conventional, they do not allow conventionality to hamper or prevent them from doing the things that they deem important. They are acutely aware of their feelings, thoughts, and impulses and do not hide them unless their expression would hurt others. Their codes of ethics are autonomous and individual, based on fundamentally accepted principles rather than on social prescriptions.

Trust   Self-actualizers demonstrate a high degree of trust. They trust themselves, their mission in life, others, and nature.

Self-actualizers are generally *problem centered* rather than focused on themselves. They have a high sense of mission in life. They are task oriented and commit themselves to important tasks that must be done. They live and work within a wide frame of reference that does not permit them to get bogged down in what is petty or trivial. Problems outside themselves enlist most of their attention.

Self actualizers demonstrate *acceptance of self, others, and nature.* They accept themselves without disappointment or regret. This is not to say that they are smug or self-satisfied but rather that they accept their weaknesses and frailties as given. They are not embarrassed about the bodily processes that humans share with animals. The needs to eat, defecate, and express their sexuality do not distress them. They feel guilty about characteristics that they could and should improve on, but they are not overrun with neurotic guilt. As Maslow pointed out, they are not disturbed by the shortcomings of human nature but accept them in the way that one accepts other natural things, such as the fact that water is wet, rocks are hard, and grass is green. Healthy people do not feel bad about what is per se but about differences between what is and what might realistically be.

Self-actualizers are not well adjusted in the normal sense of the term, which entails conformity with one's culture: they show *resistance to enculturation.* Essentially, they live in harmony with their culture, yet they remain somewhat detached from it. Often they are labeled "oddball," as they do not always react in the expected fashion. They generally conform in matters of dress, speech, and food, and other matters that are not of primary concern to them. But where an issue is important they are independent in their thought and behavior. This resistance to enculturation leads to their transcendence of any one particular culture. Thus their identification is with humanity as a whole rather than any one particular group.

Maslow acknowledged that the picture he drew of the self-actualized person is a composite. No one person that he studied possessed all of the above qualities. Each of them demonstrated the characteristics to varying degrees. Furthermore, Maslow emphasized that self-actualizers are not perfect. They show many lesser human failings. They frequently have silly, wasteful, or thoughtless habits. At times they are vain and take too much pride in their achievements. They may sometimes lose their tempers. Because of their concentration on their work, they may appear absent minded, humorless, or impolite. At times their kindness toward others leads them to permit others to take undue advantage of them. At other times they may appear to be ruthless and inconsiderate in their relations with other people. Sometimes they are boring, even irritating. In short, they are not perfect; yet, Maslow's definition of self-actualization did not imply perfection but a higher level of functioning.

The principles and values of self-actualizers differ from those of the average person. Perceiving the world in an essentially different manner, they are not threatened by it and do not need to adopt a morality of self-protection. Maslow suggests that a great deal of that which passes for moral and ethical standards may simply be "by-products of the pervasive pathology of the average" (1970). Maintenance at the level of self-actualization requires meeting the previous needs continuously, but self-actualizers are able to satisfy them routinely so that they can devote themselves to the values that concur with the B-needs. Thus, at one and the same time, their values are universal and reflect shared humanity but are also distinct, individual, and unique.

Maslow concluded that self-actualization entails the ability to transcend and resolve dichotomies. The usual oppositions between heart and head, reason and emotion, body and mind, work and play that fragment most of us do not exist as antagonists, because they are seen as functioning together simultaneously. For example, the distinction between being selfish and unselfish is no longer bothersome. Self-actualizers can recognize that every act is at one and the same time selfish and unselfish. That which is done for the benefit of others is frequently that which benefits the self. Maslow suggested that in the self-actualized individual the id, ego, and superego work cooperatively together.

Maslow suggested that the number of people who achieve self-actualization is relatively small, less than 1 percent of the entire population. Concepts such as "the self-actualized person" may apply to only a select few. Obviously, the possibility of self-actualization is limited or even closed to large numbers of the human population, whose environment and life-style have yet to meet the lesser needs depicted in Maslow's hierarchy, let alone the higher needs. This is not to say, however, that some groups of people are by nature unable to self-actualize. Maslow did point out that some people can be healthier than their environment. He concluded that they have some kind of inner freedom but did not specify how or why.

Contemporary research on competent children from high-risk environments is seeking to clarify why children are more or less vulnerable to the effects of their environment. Heylighen (1992) has constructed a cognitive systemic reconstruction of Maslow's theory redefining self-actualization as perceived competence that one is able to meet one's needs. Childhood poverty or ineptitude may cause feelings of incompetence that inhibit the development of self-actualization.

Some critics suggest that Maslow's view of the self-actualized individual is based on American values of individual achievement. Because of cultural training, many people in Western societies tend to believe that personality is best rooted on a high sense of positive self-esteem. Thus parents in middle-class America are encouraged to take steps to develop positive self-esteem in their children, especially their sons (Markus & Katayama, 1991; Josephs, Markus, & Tafarodi, 1992), and psychological disorders such as anxiety and depression are often seen as a failure to develop such autonomy, achievement, and feeling of self-worth. However, people in many non-Western cultures cultivate very dissimilar personalities. In Japan and China, an autonomous self is not stressed and children are taught to cooperate and not to demonstrate their superiority so as to avoid diminishing other people. The expression *tiqau* in Japanese denotes both "different" and "wrong" (Markus & Kitayama, 1991, and Kitayama & Marcus, 1992). Japanese children are encouraged to be extremely modest about any personal accomplishment so that they will adapt to the more important social and group environment. Thus activities that American children are more apt to engage in individually, such as painting, in Japan are more likely to be group projects (Kitayama & Marcus, 1992). As a result, people perceive themselves to be part of a whole and define themselves in terms of the group.

When Kitayama and his coworkers compared the responses of Japanese and American university students asked to indicate the frequency and origin of certain emotions, Japanese students associated positive feelings with good interpersonal relations rather than personal achievements, whereas the opposite was true of the Americans (Kitayama & Marcus, 1992).

Likewise, even within the same culture gender differences may apply. Thus in North America a woman's self-esteem tends to be based on interpersonal

THINKING CRITICALLY

Who's Among the Self-Actualized?

Look at the following list of persons whom Maslow identified as self-actualized: Jane Addams, Sholom Aleichem, Robert Benchley, Martin Buber, George Washington Carver, Pablo Casals, Eugene V. Debs, Albert Einstein, Ralph Waldo Emerson, Benjamin Franklin, William James, Thomas Jefferson, Abraham Lincoln, Camille Pissarro, Eleanor Roosevelt, Albert Schweitzer, Baruch Spinoza, Adlai Stevenson, Harriet Tubman. If you do not recognize some of these names, look them up in the **Biographical Names** section of a collegiate dictionary. While Maslow indicated that self-actualization is a potential for everyone, would a review of his list indicate that it is most likely to include American presidents or politicians or great creative figures or scientists in the West? How many women do you find as compared with men?

Not everyone agrees with Maslow's choice of examples of self-actualized persons. Eleanor Roosevelt, a very controversial figure, had to overcome crippling roots of being born into a privileged family destroyed by alcoholism (Cook, 1992). Abraham Lincoln suffered from serious bouts of depression. Others point out that as currently delineated, Maslow's concept would not include many genuinely creative persons such as Wolfgang Mozart, Karen Horney (whose lower needs were by no means fully satisfied), or Martin Luther King. Perhaps his choice reflects his subjective preference and bias. Can you think of any modifications of Maslow's criteria for self-actualization that would need to be made before his goal of self-actualization truly could be said to be a potential for everyone? Can you think of individuals from non-Western cultures whom you would consider self-actualized, such as Mother Teresa and Gandhi?

relations whereas a man's tends to be based on personal accomplishments (Josephs et al., 1992). Lerman (1992) reminds us that Maslow did not demonstrate how the environment frequently fails to permit the gratification of basic needs of women and other subjugated groups. She believes, however, that there is a place in his and other humanist theories for contributions from a feminist examination of the environment and its potential impact on the well-being of humanity. Such an inquiry would require the elimination of sexism and careful examination of blind spots.

However, others (such as Chang & Page, 1991) believe that cross-cultural comparisons between Rogers, Malsow, Lao Tzu, and Zen Buddhism point more toward a universality of human experience in that they all share the assumption that people have an actualizing tendency that fosters positive growth. Miller (1991) suggests that placing self-actualization in the context of transpersonal psychology removes its elitism and fosters cross-cultural comparisons with Eastern concepts. Rather than emphasize one concept of an ideal, Coan (1991) suggests we look at the diverse ways in which people can realize their potential.

It is to Maslow's credit that he has turned the attention of psychologists to those qualities that constitute optimal human health and functioning rather than represent human life gone awry. The example of the self-actualized individual suggests and inspires us to improve our human condition.

Therapeutic Relationships

Abraham Maslow was not a practicing therapist. He did not develop any new theory or method of therapy. However, he made several comments about therapy (1970) that are worth attention. Maslow made a distinction between basic needs therapy and insight therapy. **Basic needs therapy** refers to therapeutic procedures that meet the primary needs of people: safety, belonging, love, and respect. **Insight therapy** refers to the deeper, more protracted effort of self-understanding that leads to profound motivational changes.

The first and primary criterion for both forms of therapy is a relationship between human beings. On this point Maslow concurred with Rogers. Both Maslow and Rogers point out that the kind of relationship that satisfies our basic needs is not a unique relationship but one that shares the fundamental qualities found in all good human relationships. The relationship of therapy is not at its base unique, because it shares the primary characteristics of all good human relationships.

What is needed, Maslow suggests, is a more careful study of all relationships that foster and fulfill the satisfaction of our needs of safety, belongingness, love, respect, and, ultimately, self-actualization. A constructive marriage, close friendship, or healthy parent-child relationship permits these satisfactions to occur. Thus, every human relationship is potentially a therapeutic one. New studies show good relations may "protect the human immune system from stress" (Goleman, 1992). One task of psychology is to try to identify those qualities that make for good human relations as opposed to poor ones. We can then foster those relationships that enable us to grow.

Maslow criticized Freud for limiting his discussion of the relationship that emerges in analysis to the elements of transference. By failing to recognize the underlying relationship between analyst and patient and by focusing almost entirely on the elements of transference, Freud failed to perceive the healthy character of the relationship. In effect, Freud suggested that the only feelings a patient could have toward the analyst were those of a positive or negative transference. In return, the only emotions an analyst could have toward the patient were those of countertransference. Thus, in Freud's discussion of analysis, the only feelings that emerge in the relationship are neurotic ones. Freud failed to articulate the fact that it is only because a basic healthy relationship underlies the process of analysis in the first place that elements of transference can arise and be sustained, analyzed, and worked through.

If the qualities of relationship that emerge in psychotherapy are the qualities that are found in any good, healthy relationship, we should look more closely at those everyday therapeutic happenings that occur in good marriages, good friendships, and good jobs. We ought to try to expose ourselves and others

THINKING CRITICALLY

Do We Need a New Concept of Maturity?

Many theorists have grappled with the concept of "the mature person." You can increase your understanding of their concepts and identify your own perception of maturity by comparing and contrasting them. Review Allport's six criteria of maturity, Rogers's image of the fully functioning person, and Maslow's concept of the self-actualized person. List the criteria for maturity that all of them would agree on. Take note of criteria that are unique to any of the theorists. Are there any points of noticeable disagreement among them?

Carol Gilligan (1982) and Jean Baker Miller (1984) have suggested that most definitions of maturity are based on a male paradigm and values of separation, autonomy, mastery, and power. "Because they are male oriented, women do not measure up" (Symonds, 1991). Along with her colleagues, Baker suggests a fresh theory based on the "self-in-relation," emphasizing relationships and sensitivity to others rather than individuality. Betcher and Pollack (1993) remind us that it is time to stop thinking of women as inadequate men or men as deficient women. "It is time to stop arguing about which is the better half and to look for what is good in both." What do you think? Would a new concept of maturity also facilitate living in a global world of cultural diversity?

to these kinds of situations. It also follows that each human being is potentially a therapist who can function in a therapeutic way by entering into these kinds of relationships that are based on love and respect. We should approve of, encourage, and teach these fundamentals of sound human relationships and foster the development of lay psychotherapy.

There are times when the constructive therapeutic processes of life fail and insight therapy is called for. A person who is severely ill may not be able to benefit from basic needs therapy, having given up trying to satisfy those needs in favor of satisfying neurotic ones.

Insight therapy is not only valuable for those neurotics for whom basic needs therapy is no longer helpful; it is also a valuable method by which relatively

PHILOSOPHICAL ASSUMPTIONS

Examining Maslow

How would you rate Maslow on each of the basic philosophical assumptions described in Chapter 1? Each basic issue was presented as a bipolar dimension along which a person's view can be placed according to the degree of agreement with one or the other extreme. Rate Maslow's views on these issues.

When you have determined where you think Maslow stands, compare your responses with those of your classmates and your instructor. You should be willing to defend your ratings, but also be prepared to change them in light of others' compelling arguments. Afterward, compare your rating of Maslow with your own position on each issue and with those of other theorists. Does this comparison help you to understand why his theory does or does not appeal to you?

Would strongly agree	Would agree	Is neutral or believes in synthesis of both views	Would agree	Would strongly agree
1	2	3	4	5

freedom
People basically have control over their own behavior and understand the motives behind their behavior.

determinism
The behavior of people is basically determined by internal or external forces over which they have little, if any, control.

healthy persons can acquire insight and facilitate their own self-actualization. Unfortunately, psychoanalysis and psychotherapy have not become as effective or active forces of individual and cultural self-understanding as they have the potential to be. The emphasis, particularly in America, on therapy as a medical method of treatment has prevented its entrance into other fields. Interestingly, Freud did not originally conceive of analysis as simply a method for treating neurotics. That, he wrote, "is only one of its applications, the future will perhaps show that it is not the most important one" (1926b). Freud also recommended that since it would be impossible to analyze each and every parent, teachers might undergo analysis in order to avoid passing on unconscious conflicts to children. Maslow picked up this suggestion, pointing out that if

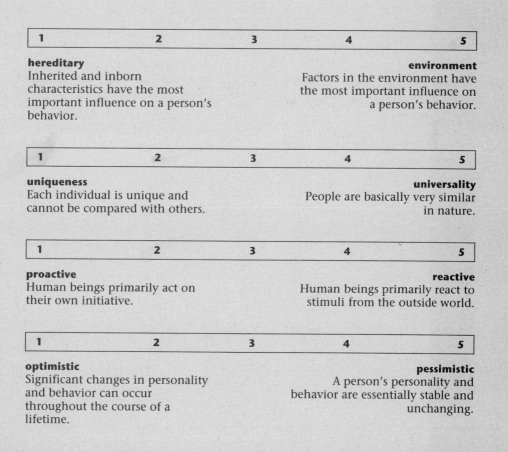

1	2	3	4	5

hereditary
Inherited and inborn characteristics have the most important influence on a person's behavior.

environment
Factors in the environment have the most important influence on a person's behavior.

1	2	3	4	5

uniqueness
Each individual is unique and cannot be compared with others.

universality
People are basically very similar in nature.

1	2	3	4	5

proactive
Human beings primarily act on their own initiative.

reactive
Human beings primarily react to stimuli from the outside world.

1	2	3	4	5

optimistic
Significant changes in personality and behavior can occur throughout the course of a lifetime.

pessimistic
A person's personality and behavior are essentially stable and unchanging.

relatively healthy people are deeply touched by therapy, it is all the more important to invest our energies in them, particularly if they happen to be in key therapeutic positions, as teachers, social workers, and physicians.

Maslow's Theory: Philosophy, Science, and Art

Maslow's theory clearly points away from pure science toward the broader outlines of philosophy. Maslow acknowledged that his portrait of self-actualization is part of a larger, evolving philosophy of human nature, greatly influenced by Aristotle (Ivie, 1986). He reminded us that all too frequently we conceive of science as an autonomous method that exists in and of itself, governed by its own distinct rules and totally divorced from human beings or human values. We forget that human beings create science, establish its goals, and use its technology for their own purposes. Maslow believed that it is misleading to think science is value free, since its procedures are employed for human purposes. We may use science to create mechanistic robots out of human nature or we may use it to increase human freedom and potential. Maslow suggested that we conceive of science as a problem-solving activity rather than a specific technology. Only the goals of science can dignify or validate its methods.

Theories that entail self-actualization deal primarily with issues of moral philosophy rather than psychological science (Daniels, 1988). This is a fact that we have wanted to ignore because in our postmodern individualistic society, we have no logically recognized way of agreeing on morals and ethics. Instead, value judgments are commonly seen as simply personal preferences. This moral relativism stems from the loss of a teleological point of view (MacIntyre, 1984). Daniels (1988) suggests that we develop a myth (or "mode of being in the world," Eliade, 1983) of actualization in which life "becomes a shared quest for the human good" as we move beyond ego to community.

Maslow's study of self-actualized persons lacks the rigor and distinct methodology characteristic of strict empirical science. Nevertheless, his work underscores the fact that the canons of rigorous scientific procedures do not necessarily encompass or permit research into important human questions. The tension between the demands of the subject matter of psychology and the requirements of good science continues to concern psychologists.

Maslow suggested the need for a broader definition of science and the development of methodologies appropriate for the human subject. His "third force" became a very powerful force in psychology and its impact was reflected in the creation of a new division of the American Psychological Association, called Humanistic Psychology. A separate Association for Humanistic Psychology was also formed; it publishes the *Journal of Humanistic Psychology*. Centers for personal growth have sprung up across the United States, Canada, Mexico, and Europe. Two of the best known are the Esalen Institute in Big Sur, California, and the Center for the Study of the Person in La Jolla, California. These centers encourage the development of ways in which individuals can further their growth and self-actualization.

Maslow's portrayal of the self-actualized person is similar to that of Carl Rogers — optimistic, generating much confidence in human potential. Yet some critics suggest that his picture may be simplistic, neglecting the hard work and pain that is involved in growth and development and ignoring the phenomenon of tragedy (Daniels, 1988). It is important to note that Maslow's research originated in an era of growth and prosperity accompanied by a seemingly limitless view of human potential. But is this picture realistic? In fact, the likelihood of self-actualization may be more remote than Maslow indicated. Perhaps it is naive to hope to reduce all conflict and more justified to assume that we can merely strengthen the ego, enabling it to be more effective in its executive functions. Freud, we recall, was pessimistic about reducing human conflict.

More attention needs to be given to the processes within the individual and various cultures and societies that permit self-actualization and creativity to flower. In Maslow's words, "How good a human being does society permit?" (1970). In what instances can an individual overcome and compensate for needs that have not been met in life? As it stands, Maslow's discussion of self-actualization is descriptive rather than functional. He describes the characteristics of the self-actualizer but does not tell how these characteristics may be concretely acquired.

Near the end of his life, Maslow urged the promotion of a "fourth force" to deal with spiritual and religious issues. By articulating the concept of peak experiences, Maslow believed that he had brought all major religions under the rubric of the natural science of psychology. He felt that a study of positive forces that foster self-actualization and an improved culture should be a primary focus of psychology.

Summary

1. Abraham Maslow has been called the spiritual father of humanistic psychology. He criticized psychoanalysis for being pessimistic and negative, and behavior and learning theories for being mechanistic.

2. Maslow distinguished between **motivation** and **metamotivation**, which entail **D-needs** and **B-needs** respectively. Motivation and the D-needs take precedence over metamotivation and the B-needs.

3. Maslow's **hierarchy of human needs** includes physiological, safety, belonging and love, self-esteem, and **self-actualization**. A number of studies have demonstrated that the needs that Maslow described are essential for

optimal human life and development and some tools have been developed to measure them.

4. **Self-actualized persons** fulfill themselves and do the best that they are capable of doing. The subjects of Maslow's study included friends, personal acquaintances, public and historical figures, and selected college students, and he used a variety of research techniques. His investigations were not conducted along strict scientific lines, as he felt that those limitations would not be suitable for his research.

5. Maslow described several characteristics of self-actualizers. These may be grouped under four key dimensions: awareness, honesty, freedom, and trust.

6. A self-actualized person often experiences a **peak experience**, which can be provoked by both religious and secular events.

7. Some critics suggest that Maslow's picture of self-actualized persons is simplistic and neglects the hard work that is involved in growth and development. Others suggest it is based on American values and a Western male paradigm of individual achievement.

8. Maslow distinguished between **basic needs therapy** and **insight therapy** and called for more effective and expanded therapy.

9. Maslow's theory points in a direction away from pure science. His work underscores the fact that rigorous scientific procedures may not encompass or permit research into important human questions.

Suggestions for Further Reading

Maslow's best-known work is *Motivation and Personality* (Harper & Row, 1970), which presents his theory of personality and describes in full his concepts of the hierarchy of needs and self-actualization. Originally published in 1954, it was completely revised shortly before his death. *Religions, Values, and Peak Experiences* (Viking, 1964) presents Maslow's argument that religion should be viewed as a normal, potentially healthy phenomenon and studied scientifically. In this work he outlined his concept of peak experiences, although he did not limit them to religious experiences. Nevertheless, Maslow pointed out the need of human beings for spiritual expression and he suggested that science can assist us in understanding this need and its expressions. *Toward a Psychology of Being* (Van Nostrand, 1968) is a collection of papers in which Maslow discussed his theory of B-values as well as peak experiences and self-actualization; the book also makes clear Maslow's humanistic stance as opposed to those who present a mechanistic or negative picture of human nature. Maslow's last work, *The Farther Reaches of Human Nature* (Viking, 1971), is a cumulative effort to integrate his theory with the latest developments in science. It covers topics such as biology, creativity, cognition, and synergy.

   Two readable secondary sources on Maslow's thought are Frank Goble, *The Third Force: The Psychology of Abraham Maslow* (Grossman, 1970) and Colin Wilson, *New Pathways in Psychology: Maslow and the Post-Freudian Revolution* (Taplinger, 1972). A biography of Maslow, based on diaries, interviews with friends and associates, and his published works is Edward Hoffman, *The Right to be Human* (Tarcher, 1988).

CHAPTER 14

Rollo May

1. Identify two major traditions that Rollo May combines.
2. Describe the philosophy of *existentialism.*
3. Explain the existentialist approach to scientific methodology.
4. Describe the central problem May believes we face at the end of the twentieth century.
5. Explain how May conceives of *anxiety* and tell how it is intensified in contemporary culture.
6. Discuss the source of the human dilemma according to May.
7. Identify four ontological assumptions May makes concerning human beings and explain how they can give us a structural basis for a science of personality.
8. Discuss what is involved in rediscovering selfhood.
9. Show how May confronts the *paradoxes* involved in each of the following goals of integration: love, *intentionality,* the *daimonic,* courage and creativity, power, freedom and destiny.
10. Explain how May defines *myth* and why he believes we need new myths.
11. Describe the existentialist approach to psychotherapy.
12. Describe May's methods of assessment and research.
13. Evaluate May's theory in terms of its function as philosophy, science, and art.

Existentialism and psychoanalysis grew out of the same cultural situation. Both seek to understand anxiety, despair, and the alienation that people feel from themselves and society. During the last half of the nineteenth century, there was a strong tendency to make the person over into a machine, thinking of people in terms of the industrial system for which they worked. This segmentation of culture had a psychological counterpart in extreme repression within the individual. It was Freud's genius to speak to, and help cure, the problem of repression (May, Angel, & Ellenberger, 1958). However, the problem went deeper than neurotic repression in the individual. Kierkegaard, Nietzsche, and other forerunners of the existentialist position foresaw that the forces of disintegration were gradually destroying the inner emotional and spiritual life of the person and leading to ultimate despair and alienation from self and society.

Rollo May's work brings together the psychoanalytic tradition in psychology and the existentialist movement in philosophy. As we have seen, Freud's writings, though transcending his own era, nevertheless clearly reflect tendencies of nineteenth-century philosophy that are considered inappropriate today. In combining the insights of psychoanalysis and existentialism, May has not only clarified the continued relevance of many of Freud's contributions but he has also developed his own original stance. In doing so, he has helped to underscore the importance of philosophy and the understanding of values for the psychologist and the theory of personality.

Biographical Background

Rollo May was born on April 21, 1909, in Ada, Ohio, and grew up in Marine City, Michigan, where a middle-American anti-intellectual attitude prevailed. His father commented several times that a psychotic breakdown experienced by Rollo's older sister was due to "too much education." May felt that the comment was "inhumane and destructive" and came to hate the disease of anti-intellectualism. However, he indicates that in other respects his father was a very sympathetic man (1983).

May graduated from Oberlin College in Ohio where he completed the A.B. in 1930. There, he marveled at the simple yet beautiful lines of an antique Greek vase displayed on a table in one of the classrooms and resolved to go to Greece, which he did immediately after his graduation. He worked in Greece for three years, teaching at Anatolia College in Salonika and traveling during the summer. He spent two summers with a group of modern artists, painting and studying peasant art. The impact of Greek philosophy and mythology is clear in his writings. He also went to Vienna and studied briefly with Alfred Adler, whose approach influenced him considerably.

Europe's tragic view of human nature prevented May from ever accepting a mechanistic concept of the person. Upon his return, American psychology seemed "naive and simplistic." So he enrolled at Union Theological Seminary in New York — not with the intent of becoming a preacher, but with the intent to ask questions. There he could raise penetrating inquiries into the meaning of despair, suicide, and anxiety, issues largely ignored by psychologists. He also hoped that in doing so he might learn about their counterparts: courage, joy, and the intensity of living (1983). At Union, he began a lifetime friendship with the eminent Protestant theologian Paul Tillich, an association that enriched the lives, work, and writings of both of them.

May's parents were divorced while he was at Union, so he interrupted his studies and returned to East Lansing, Michigan, to take care of what remained of his family, his mother, a younger sister, and a brother. During that time, he served as an advisor to students at Michigan State College. He was able to return to New York and complete the B.D. in 1938. During his senior year at Union, his first book, *The Art of Counseling,* was written.

Thereafter, May served briefly as a parish minister in Montclair, New Jersey, before going back to New York to study psychoanalysis at the William Alanson White Institute for Psychiatry, Psychoanalysis, and Psychology. He enrolled at Columbia University and eventually received its first Ph.D. in clinical psychology.

Rollo May

May's life was sharply interrupted when he came down with tuberculosis in his early thirties. At that time there was no medication for the disease. May spent three years at the Saranac TB Sanatorium in upstate New York, not knowing whether he would live or die. During his illness, he read, among other works, *The Problem of Anxiety* by Freud and *The Concept of Dread* by Sören Kierkegaard, the founder of the existential movement in philosophy. He appreciated Freud's careful formulations but felt that Kierkegaard "portrayed what is immediately experienced by human beings in crisis" (1969). May's illness helped him to appreciate the importance of an existential point of view. His own book *The Meaning of Anxiety* (1977) has been widely recognized as the first in America to encourage a genuine union between psychology and philosophy and to demonstrate the importance of values for psychology.

May's professional life has been busy and productive. He served as a counselor to college students at City College of New York, developed a private practice in psychoanalysis, and became a member of the White Institute. He has taught at The New School for Social Research, New York University, Harvard, Yale, and Princeton. He has numerous publications and has been honored with several awards. At present, May lives in Tiburon, California.

The Existential Attitude

Existentialism is a movement in contemporary philosophy and psychology that sprang up spontaneously in different parts of Europe and among different schools of thought. It has its roots in the resistance movements during World War II and in the philosophies of Sören Kierkegaard (1813–1855), Martin Heidegger (1889–1976), and Jean Paul Sartre (1905–1980). The name existentialism comes from the Latin *exsistere,* which means "to stand out" or "to emerge," and the existential approach focuses upon the human being as he or she is emerging and becoming.

In the past, Western philosophy has traditionally looked for the **essence** of being, the unchangeable principles and laws that are believed to govern existence. Mathematics is the purest form of this approach. In psychology, the essentialist attitude expresses itself in the effort to understand human beings in terms of forces, drives, and conditioned reflexes. Existentialists point out that a law can be true and still not be real. "Two unicorns plus two unicorns equals four unicorns" is a logically true statement but it does not talk about anything that is real. Existentialism seeks to bridge the gap between what is abstractly true and what is existentially real (May et al., 1958).

The existential attitude can be a bewildering one that defies simple definition. We can illustrate it, however, by comparing two possible postures that a person might have at a football game. The first is that of the spectator up in the stands; the second is that of the player on the field. Both spectator and player are involved in the football game, but there is a considerable difference in their involvement. The spectator may get very agitated and excited as the game proceeds, urging and cheering on a favorite team. But this involvement is very different from that of the player. The outcome of the game does not depend on the activity of the spectator, who remains outside the game as an observer. The outcome does depend very much on how the player behaves and performs on the field. What the player does is not indifferent to the game. The player cannot stand back and observe the game while involved in it.

The posture of existentialism is that of the player, and the game of existentialism is the game of life. In life, existentialists point out, we cannot play the role of a detached or uninvolved spectator because we are already participants in the game.

Existentialists suggest that there is no truth or reality for us as human beings except as we participate in it, are conscious of it, and have some relation to it. Knowledge is not an act of thinking but an act of doing. Existentialists do not necessarily rule out essences, but "existence precedes essence." May, for example, does not deny the validity of concepts such as conditioning or drives; he simply points out that we cannot adequately explain a person on that basis because when we try to, we end up talking about abstractions rather than the living person. It is all right to have concepts, but we must recognize that they are only tools and not substitutes for the living person. Thus, when we use concepts, we must make it clear that we are abstracting them from the living person and we are not talking about the real person.

Psychologists have generally tended to study those phenomena that lend themselves to control and analysis and permit one to formulate abstract laws. They are not particularly concerned with whether or not the phenomena are real or even close to everyday life. Indeed, in some laboratory experiments, the phenomenon under consideration is far removed from real life. Existentialists believe that psychologists' preoccupation with lawfulness and predictability stands in the way of understanding the real person. May points out that the behavior of a neurotic is quite predictable because it is compulsive, whereas the healthy person is "predictable" in that behavior is integrated and unified, but at the same time can be flexible and spontaneous. The existentialist approach has been criticized for rendering the individual unlawful and unpredictable. It is true that existentialists do not see the human being in terms of our traditional conceptual theories, looking instead at the structure of a particular person's existence and its own lawfulness.

The existentialist approach is not antiscientific. It arose out of a desire to be not *less* but *more* empirical, but it does urge a greater breadth to our scientific methodology. Contrary to the conventional approach of the scientist in which the more complex is explained by the simpler, existentialists believe that a reductionistic approach misleads and that the "simpler can be understood and explained only in terms of the more complex" (May, 1969). When a new level of complexity emerges, it becomes crucial for understanding the forms that have preceded it. What makes a horse a horse is not what it shares with the organisms it evolved from but what constitutes its distinctive "horseness"

(1983). Science, therefore, must look for the distinguishing characteristic of what it is trying to understand, namely, the human being.

The existentialist view takes the inquiry to a deeper level to look at the structure in which those concepts are rooted. It seeks to develop an empirical science that deals with the whole of our knowledge of what it means to be human. As such, it looks at the unity of the person prior to any split into subject versus object, body versus mind, nature versus nurture, or any other conceptual "either-or" dimensions. It asks what it means to be and to exist under these particular psychological, cultural, and historical conditions.

In studying the structure of human existence, the very nature of the subject shapes the science that investigates it. Existentialists have made clear the limits of objectivity in our understanding and the need to broaden the scope of our methodology. Objectivity is a goal that many psychologists have prized and sought to achieve. They believe that unless we are objective, our emotions and prejudices will come between us and the facts, clouding our reasoning processes. Students of psychology are encouraged to take a detached, objective stance. At times, however, objectivity prevents understanding. Some truths, such as understanding what it means to be, are discovered not by objectivity but by intense personal involvement. The existentialist attitude strongly resists the tendency to treat a person as an object.

In their insistence that human knowledge is ultimately interpersonal, May and other existentialists are indebted to the thought of Martin Buber (1878–1965), whose book *I and Thou* made a classic distinction between knowing that is transpersonal (I-Thou) and knowing that is objective or subjective (I-it). In his book, Buber describes an entirely different way in which the world, particularly the world of persons, reveals itself to us. Knowledge is not simply objective (of an external object) or subjective (of the self) but also interpersonal, arising out of the encounter of human beings with one another. Understanding through encounter is just as real as understanding through objectification.

Existentialism begins with personal existence. It asks, "What does it mean to be a self?" It questions the purpose and nature of existence. It views individuals as agents with free choices who are responsible for their actions. Each one of us carves out his or her own destiny. We are literally what we do. The existentialist posture leads to an emphasis on choice and responsibility and to the view that a worthwhile life is one that is authentic, honest, and genuine.

Our Predicament

May points out (1967) that in the second half of the twentieth century, the central problem that we face is a feeling of *powerlessness,* a "pervasive conviction that the individual cannot do anything effective in the face of enormous cultural, social, and economic problems." Our feelings of powerlessness are compounded by anxiety and the loss of traditional values.

Powerlessness

The problem of powerlessness goes much deeper than the fact that this is an age of uncertainty and social upheavals. The unwanted war in Vietnam and the continued unrest in the Middle East illustrate how we can become caught in a historical situation in which no one person or group of persons feels capable of exercising significant power. We are told that the cold war is over, but the world seems no safer. Rather, the "developed world" often acts as if there were no real problems in the "developing world" in spite of its massive poverty and suffering (Sloan, 1990). With our increased technology, power has become impersonal, an autonomous force acting on its own behalf (1967).

In the early 1950s, May observed that many of the patients who came to see him were suffering from inner feelings of emptiness (1953). He noted that the neurotic frequently acts out what others are temporarily unaware of. May anticipated that the experience of emptiness and powerlessness he was seeing in his patients would in time become epidemic, and of course it has. The 1970s saw considerable talk about human potentialities, yet very little confidence on the part of individuals about their power to make a significant difference (1975). This feeling of paralysis has accompanied us throughout the 1980s and into the 1990s.

The most striking example of the individual's sense of insignificance and powerlessness is the impotence many of us feel concerning the threat of nuclear war or accident. The potentiality for such disaster rapidly increases along with

Feelings of impotence may breed violence and hostility.

a recognition that it could begin through a simple incident such as a computer malfunction. The threat of nuclear war and other unsettling social conditions are but symptoms of the deeper problem. Contemporary men and women feel helpless and insignificant. Our impotence leads to anxiety and repression, leading in turn to apathy, which is a form of protection. Impotence and apathy, however, also breed violence and hostility that further alienate us from one another and only serve to increase our isolation (1972).

Anxiety

It has become commonplace to describe our age as an age of anxiety. However, prior to 1950, only two books had been written that concerned themselves specifically with presenting an objective picture of anxiety and suggesting constructive ways of dealing with it: Freud's *The Problem of Anxiety* and Kierkegaard's *The Concept of Dread.* After May wrote *The Meaning of Anxiety,* which was first published in 1950, hundreds of works followed on the same topic. May's efforts helped to spur research into this area. *The Meaning of Anxiety* was revised in 1977 and at that time May pointed out that the tremendous interest in anxiety that attended its initial publication had indicated the need for an integrated theory of anxiety. May's work is distinguished by its efforts to synthesize the insights of both psychology and philosophy. Since that time, he has applied his analytic synthesis to the dilemmas of love and will, power and innocence, creativity, and freedom and destiny.

Some psychologists prefer to use the term "stress" in place of anxiety. May believes that this tendency is unfortunate and inaccurate. The word *stress* has become popular because it comes from engineering and physics; it can be defined easily and measured accurately. The problem with the concept of stress is that it does not adequately describe the apprehension we ordinarily refer to as anxiety. Moreover, it puts the emphasis on what happens *to* a person, whereas anxiety is distinctly bound up with consciousness and subjectivity (1977).

May proposes the following definition of **anxiety:** "Anxiety is the apprehension cued off by a threat to some value that the individual holds essential to his or her existence as a person" (1977). Anxiety is an inevitable characteristic of being human (1983), a given. Anxiety is objectless, "because it strikes at that basis of the psychological structure on which the perception of one's self as distinct from the world of objects occurs" (1977). Thus, in anxiety, the distinction between self and object breaks down.

The potential for anxiety is innate, although the particular events that may become threatening are learned. Fear is the expression of anxiety in a specific objectified form. May suggests that anxiety is intensified in our contemporary competitive culture by the interpersonal isolation and alienation that have emerged out of a particular pattern in which one's self is viewed as an object and self-validation depends upon winning over others (1977). Anxiety, therefore, is another symptom of the deeper problem.

Our current stepped-up efforts to dispel anxiety actually end up increasing it. May reminds us that we cannot live in an empty condition for a sustained period of time (1953). We need something to fill the gap, be it a destructive authority, drugs, or alcohol. Earlier in this century, the emotional vacuum in Europe permitted fascist dictators to seize power. Today, many young people "waste" themselves on alcohol and drugs. The problem is that human consciousness, responsibility, and intentions have not been able to keep up with all of the rapid changes in contemporary society. If we were able to recognize our historical situation and its psychological implications, we might be able to move from self-defeating activities to constructive ones.

The Loss of Values

The source of our problem lies in the loss of the center of values in our society (1967). Ever since the Renaissance, the dominant value in Western society has been competitive prestige measured in terms of work and financial success. Such values are no longer effective in the postmodern world in which we have to learn to work with other people in order to survive. Individual competition no longer brings the greatest good to one's self or to the community. Instead, it creates problems where previously it did not.

Our ability to stand outside of ourselves and relate to ourselves permits us to create values that help to shape our lives (1967). For several centuries, we were able to validate ourselves by our power over nature. Then we began to supply the methods that had been so successful in understanding and controlling nature to ourselves. In so doing, we rendered ourselves impersonal objects that could be exploited. Along with the loss of the dominant value of individualism, we lost a sense of the worth and dignity of the human being. We became estranged from nature and from one another. Today, many people are more comfortable conversing with a computer than with another human being. The loneliness and isolation that were potential in Western society have become widely apparent in our time.

The answer to our dilemma is to discover and affirm a new set of values. There are those who would suggest that we need to reaffirm the traditional values, embodied in earlier philosophies and religion, that we have permitted to go by the wayside. Here, May's existential stance becomes apparent. Because we have no "essence," there are no given or pre-established values to which we can turn. Our values are established in the course of our existence and our destiny now includes the historical situation in which we have placed ourselves (1981). There can be no simple reaffirmation of our human "essence," because there is none; the human being is forever in the process of becoming. We have to choose our values in the process of living.

The choice is ours, and so is the responsibility. We can withdraw in anxiety, giving up our distinctive human capacity to influence our own development through our awareness; we can surrender to the power of the technology that we created; or we can muster the courage that we need to preserve our sensitivity and responsibility and consciously work together in developing a new society (1975).

Rediscovering Selfhood

May (1953) believes that *consciousness of self* is the unique mark of the human person. Self-consciousness enables us to distinguish between ourselves and the world, to learn from the past and to plan for the future, to see ourselves as others do, and to have empathy with others. However, such self-consciousness comes at the risk of anxiety and inward crisis. It means that we must stand on our own and develop an identity apart from that of our parents and forebears. We can even stand against them, if necessary.

Unlike the acorn that grows automatically into an oak tree, the human being, in self-actualizing, must do so consciously through choice and affirmation. Selfhood is not automatic but is born in a social context and grows in interpersonal relations. However, May's emphasis is not on the extent to which we are created by others, but rather on our capacity to create and experience our own selves.

Some psychologists avoid the concept of self because it separates humans from animals and complicates scientific experimentation. May, along with Rogers and Maslow, believes that in doing so psychologists miss an important feature of the human experience. Our capacity for self-relatedness is prior to, not established by, our science. It is presupposed in the fact that one can be a scientist. May would like to see us develop a science to illuminate the concept of self.

Ontological Assumptions Concerning the Person

Many psychologists emphasize the study of behavior, but May believes that they need to ask questions on a deeper *ontological* level, the level of being. They need to ask what is the nature of the person as a person and how can we best describe human existence?

As a clinician, May frankly admits that he makes certain ontological and philosophical assumptions about what it means to be a human being (1967). First, he assumes that all living organisms are potentially centered in themselves and seek to preserve that center. In psychotherapy, a patient is engaged in the process of such preservation. Second, human beings have the need and the possibility of going out from their centeredness to participate with other people. This entails risk and is illustrated in psychotherapy in the encounter with the therapist. Third, May suggests that sickness is a method whereby an individual seeks to preserve his or her being, a strategy for survival, even though that method may be limiting and block off potentials for knowledge and action. Finally, May asserts that human beings can participate in a level of self-consciousness that permits them to transcend the immediate situation and to consider and actualize a wider range of possibilities. These ontological assumptions can give us a structural basis for a science of personality. They precede analytic activity and make it possible. In turn, our analytic activity can help to illumine them.

Psychological concepts need to be oriented within an ontological framework. Thus, May suggests that the concept of *unconscious experience* can be understood in terms of self-deception and experiences that an individual cannot actualize. May interprets the Oedipal myth and conflict as indicative of the problems involved in a person's relation to the world through the emergence and development of consciousness (1967). The main question in the drama does not concern murder and incest but is "Shall Oedipus recognize what he has done?" It is significant that Oedipus plucks out his eyes and thereby blinds himself, rather than, for example, attacking his genitals. What is at issue is seeing reality and the truth about oneself.

May believes that the theme of exile in the story is very important. Oedipus was exiled as a baby and at the end of the drama he exiles himself. Being aware that one is responsible for one's life, a person can confront life and death. This is why the symbol of suicide is centrally placed in the existentialist approach.

Rediscovering Feelings

In rediscovering selfhood, most people have to start back at the beginning and rediscover their feelings (1953). Many of us have only a vague idea of what we are feeling at any given time. We react to our bodies as if they were separate and distinct. While denying our own emotions, we ascribe feelings to machines, describing them as "friendly," "affectionate," and so forth. We need to recognize that we play an active role in creating our bodies and feelings. Awareness of one's body and feelings lays the groundwork for knowing what one wants. Surprisingly few people are actually clear on what they want. Being aware of one's desires does not imply that one must act on them. But we cannot have any basis for judging what we will and will not do unless we first know what we want to do.

Becoming a person requires not only getting in touch with one's feelings and desires but also fighting against those things that prevent us from feeling and wanting (1953). The development of a human being is a process of differentiation from an original unity with the mother toward freedom as an individual. The physical umbilical cord is cut at birth, but the infant is still dependent on its mother. Unless the psychological cord is severed in due time, the individual's growth is stunted. In order to advance and be oneself, a person has to become free of domineering and authoritarian powers even if that requires taking a stand against one's parents or other authorities. It is our infantile ties of dependency that keep us from being clear as to our feelings and wants. The early struggle against authority is external; as we grow, the problem becomes internal. Thus, as adults many of us continue to act as if we still have to fight the original forces that enslaved us when in fact we are now enslaving ourselves.

Four States of Consciousness of Self

May (1953) suggests that there are four stages of consciousness of self. The first is the *stage of innocence* before consciousness of self is born. This stage is characteristic of the infant. The second is the *stage of rebellion* in which the individual seeks to establish some inner strength. The toddler and the adolescent illustrate this stage, which may involve defiance and hostility. The third stage is *ordinary consciousness of self.* This is the stage most people refer to when they speak of a healthy personality. It involves being able to learn from one's mistakes and live responsibly. May refers to the last stage as *creative consciousness of self.* It involves the ability to see something outside one's usual limited viewpoint and gain a glimpse of ultimate truth as it exists in reality. This level cuts through the dichotomy between subjectivity and objectivity. Not everyone achieves each level of consciousness. As we have seen, part of our predicament is the lessening of human consciousness. The fourth stage, achieved only rarely, is somewhat analogous to Maslow's peak experience. Nevertheless it is the level that gives meaning to our actions and experiences on the lesser levels.

The Goals of Integration

May conceives of the human being as conscious of self, capable of intentionality, and needing to make choices. In his existential analysis of personality, May seeks to undercut the traditional dualism of subject and object that has haunted Western self-understanding ever since Descartes, who said that we are conscious of ourselves either as a subject or as an object. May considers the self as a unity. In his discussion of the goals of integration, May further reveals an intent to discuss key issues in personality in such a way as to avoid the tendency to abstract the real person and life itself into artificial dualisms and constructs. Instead of abstract conceptualizations, we need to recognize and confront the paradoxes of our own lives (1981). In a **paradox** two opposing things are posited against and seem to negate each other yet they cannot exist without each other. Thus, good and evil, life and death, beauty and ugliness appear to be at odds with each other but the very confrontation with the one breathes life and meaning into the other. "Harmony," as Heraclitus reminded us, "consists of opposing tension, like that of the bow and the lyre" (May, 1981). The goals of integration include confronting one's potentialities for the daimonic, power, love, intentionality, freedom and destiny, and courage and creativity.

The Daimonic

In a world that vaunts rationality, May (1969) reintroduces the concept of the daimonic and insists that we come to terms with it. The **daimonic** is "any natural function which has the power to take over the whole person." Sex, anger, a craving for power, all of these may become evil when they take over the self without regard for the integration of the self. We can repress the daimonic but we cannot avoid its consequences. In repressing it, we become its pawns.

The daimonic is potentially creative and destructive at the same time. By becoming aware of it, we can integrate it into ourselves. We can learn to cherish our internal demons and permit them to give us the salt of life. The daimonic begins as impersonal; by bringing it into consciousness, one makes the daimonic urges personal. With a more sensitive understanding of these forces in one's body and life, the daimonic pushes one toward the universal structure of reality. The movement is from impersonal to personal to a transpersonal dimension of consciousness (1969).

Power

As we have seen, a basic factor in our contemporary crisis is the feeling of insignificance and powerlessness. Human life can be seen as a conflict between achieving a sense of the significance of one's self on the one hand and the feeling of powerlessness on the other. We tend to avoid both sides, the former because of evil connotations associated with being too powerful and the latter because our powerlessness is too painful to bear.

Violence has its breeding ground in impotence and apathy. As we make people powerless, we encourage their violence rather than control it. Violent deeds such as the taking of hostages are done by those who seek to enhance their self-esteem. Powerless people sometimes invite exploitation in order to feel significant or seek revenge in passive-aggressive ways, such as the use of drugs and alcohol.

May points out that the argument against violence on television would be stronger if it were made against the passive character of television viewing rather than the emulation of aggressive models. Televised entertainment cultivates the spectator role rather than active participation; as such, its greatest danger may lie in the cultivation of feelings of impotence that contribute to violent behavior.

"The culture admittedly has powerful effects upon us. But it could not have these effects were these tendencies not already present in us, for, . . . we constitute the culture" (1983). Power is an ontological state of being. The potentiality to experience and to express power is present in all of us. No one can escape experiencing power in desire or in action. Our goal is to learn how to use our power in ways that are appropriate for the situation, to be assertive rather than aggressive. We must find social ways of sharing and distributing power so that every person can feel significant.

Love and Sex

Love used to be seen as the answer to human problems. Now love itself has become the problem (1969). The real problem is being able to love. Our world is schizoid, out of touch, unable to feel or to enter into a close relationship. Affectlessness and apathy are predominant attitudes toward life, forms of protection against the tremendous overstimulation of modern society.

Our highly vaunted sexual freedom has turned out to be a new form of puritanism in which emotion is separated from reason and the body is used as a machine. Commercialization of sex destroys true feelings as badly as traditional taboos once did. We have set sex against *eros,* the drive to relate to another person and create new forms of life. It is now socially sanctioned to repress eros, and we rush to the sensation of sex in order to avoid the passion and responsibility that eros commands. The sexual freedom established during the past few decades has not led to the increase in happiness that many thought would follow a freeing of sexual mores. The premature awakening of sex so prevalent in our time can lead us to dodge awakening at other levels (1991). In the midst of wide availability of information and birth control, unwanted pregnancies are on the rise. Why? The real issue is not on the level of conscious rational intentions but in the deeper realm of intentionality, where a deep defiance mocks our withdrawal of feeling.

May (1969) suggests that only the experience and rediscovery of *care,* the opposite of apathy, will enable us to stand against the cynicism that characterizes our day. The mythos of care points to the need to develop a new morality of authenticity in human relations.

Intentionality

May believes that we must put decision and will back into the center of our picture of personality. His intent is not to rule out deterministic influences but to place the problem of determinism and freedom on a deeper level. May does this by introducing the concept of **intentionality** (1969), which underlies will and decision.

By intentionality, May means "the structure which gives meaning to experience." A distinctly human capacity, intentionality is an imaginative attention that underlies our intentions and informs our actions. It is the capacity to participate in knowing. How a piece of paper is perceived will differ depending on whether one intends to write on it or to make a paper airplane. It is the same piece of paper that provides the stimulus and the same person responding to it but the paper and experience will have a different meaning.

Intentionality bridges the gap between subject and object because it is the structure of meaning that permits a subject to understand the world as object. Perception is directed by intentionality. Contrary to the popular belief that truth is perceived through a detached objective stance, May holds that we cannot know the truth until we have taken a stand on it. Both the detached type and the asocial personality avoid confronting their intentionality. When you face your intentionality, then you can decide whether or not to act it out in your behavior.

Freedom and Destiny

The existentialist attitude is sometimes mistakenly criticized for portraying the individual as absolutely free with no restraints whatsoever. May, however, reminds us that freedom can be considered only together with destiny (1981). Freedom means "openness, readiness to grow, flexibility, and changing in pursuit of greater human values" (1953). It entails our capacity to take a hand in our own development. Freedom is basic to the existentialist understanding of human nature because it underlies our ability to choose and to value. However, freedom can be experienced only in juxtaposition with human destiny.

Another existentialist, Victor Frankl, developed a theory called *logotherapy,* which suggests that people realized freedom because of the change from a vertical society (where ethics and values are dictated from above) to a horizontal society (where we follow the mandates of our own conscience). However, we have not necessarily taken responsibility for our freedom. Logotherapy proposes a view of life that encourages looking for meaning (Fabry, 1988).

May (1981) defines *destiny* as the vital design of the universe expressed in each one of us. In its extreme form, our destiny is death, but it also expresses itself in our individual talents, our personal and collective histories, and the culture and society into which we were born. Destiny sets limits for us but it also equips us to perform certain tasks. Confronting these limits yields constructive values.

Freedom is in crisis today because we have viewed it without its necessary opposite. We have become irresponsible with our laissez-faire free enterprise system and culture of narcissism. We have lost sight of the fact that we can exist only as a community. The tendency to believe that nothing is fixed and that we can change everything we wish is not only a misperception of life but also a desecration of it. When people cannot or will not accept their destiny, it is repressed and often projected onto others such as the perception of one's enemy as totally bad (1981).

May points out that "freedom and determinism give birth to each other. Every advance in freedom gives birth to a new determinism, and every advance in determinism gives birth to a new freedom" (1981). Freud's and Darwin's theories, deterministic as they were, opened the door to new possibilities. However, the word **determinism**, borrowed from physics, is not very adequate for the rich nuances of human experience. To the extent to which one is unaware of one's responses, the term *determinism* may be appropriate, yet May suggests that we reserve it for inanimate objects, such as billiard balls, and use the term *destiny* for human beings. Determinism is merely one aspect of destiny. The shift from determinism to destiny occurs when a person is self-conscious about what is happening to him or her (1981).

Are we responsible for our destiny? May reminds us that responsibility is inseparable from freedom. To acknowledge one's destiny is to accept personal responsibility. In the terms of our psychology, freedom is the capacity to pause between a stimulus and a response. The key word here is *pause.* The significance of the pause is that it breaks the rigid chain of cause and effect. In the debate between situational and dispositional factors, May reminds us that there is a third alternative. Human beings can choose when and whether they are to be acted upon or do the acting. In moving between being controlled and controlling, one moves on a deeper level of freedom, the freedom of being (1981).

The past and future live in the psychological present. On the deepest level, the question of which age we live in is irrelevant. Instead the question is how, in our awareness of self and the period we live in, we are able through our choices to attain inner freedom and live according to our own inner integrity (1953). One reason we are reluctant to confront our destiny is that we are afraid it will lead us to despair. But despair may be a prelude to better things. Indeed, authentic despair is the emotion that forces us to come to terms with our destiny and permits us to let go of false hopes (1981).

Courage and Creativity

Courage is the capacity to move ahead in spite of despair. In human beings, courage is necessary in order to make being and becoming possible. Courage is not a virtue but a foundation that underlies and gives reality to all other values. The paradox of courage is that we must be fully committed but we must also be aware at the same time that we might be wrong. Creative courage is the discovery of new forms, symbols, and patterns on which a new society can be built. The creative person must fight the actual order so as to bring about what is new. Thus, creativity brings upon us the wrath of the gods, the anger of the authority of the past. Psychologists frequently ignore creativity because, as an act of encounter between two poles, it is very difficult to study. Yet our contemporary crisis requires creativity if we are to deal with it effectively (1975).

A Cry for Myth

In his most recent book, *The Cry for Myth* (1991), May argues passionately that many of the problems we confront, such as increases in suicide, anxiety, depression, substance abuse, and the growth of cults, stem from the absence of myths that would help us to make meaning in what has become a "senseless world." May defines **myths** as "narrative patterns that give significance to our existence" and deems them essential for psychological health. Our current myths no longer play that role; rather they increase our frustrations.

We do not generate the necessity for myths. That necessity comes from our destiny as humans, our language, and a mode of knowing one another. May describes the pseudomyths that are filling the vacuum created by the lack of genuine myths for people living today in the West. Our denial of myth in the West reflects our overemphasis on left-brain activities, rationalistic speech, and "our refusal to confront our own reality and that of our society."

THINKING CRITICALLY

Experiencing Freedom

May points out that freedom is not to be confused with rebellion, although rebellion is a necessary step in the evolution of consciousness and freedom. People earn their right to be free through an inner act of rebellion. Destiny structures the shape that struggle will take and also the effect of any outward expression of it. In the Western world, we experience freedom as individual self-expression. In the East, freedom is experienced as participation in a group. These are two very different situations, yet both permit the experience of freedom. Our need is not to imitate but to develop a form of community and means of experiencing freedom in the West that is compatible with our own history and nature (1981).

Can you think of other ways that destiny (the culture and society into which we are born) shapes the human struggles that we face and our outward expression of them? For example, Sigmund Freud and Rollo May lived in very different cultures and societies. Both wrote their theories for the society in which they lived. Can you see how each theory was appropriate for the society from which it emerged? How can we develop a form of community and means of experiencing freedom in the West that is compatible with our own history and nature?

The myths that we create are both conscious and unconscious, personal and collective. Thus each of us develops our own unique narrative in which we play the primary role, and by which we model our lives. That myth may follow infinite patterns, but generally also reflects a primary motif of classical myths, such as that of Satan, who appears over and over again under many different names in our literature. This is because "myths are archetypal patterns in human consciousness": being born, dying, making choices, and so forth.

The need for myth is also the need to belong to a community and to have heroes who act as role models as compared to celebrities who are simply well known. Martin Luther King, Alex Haley, and Mother Teresa are heroes whom we can identify with as compared to celebrities Donald Trump and Madonna.

"Myth leads to fact rather than the reverse." The American myth of the frontier permitted many people to make a new, more constructive, beginning of their lives. But there was also the myth of the Lone Ranger, which eventually became the myth of lonely individualism that characterizes the narcissistic personality and expresses itself in our loneliness and violence.

The most influential myth in America during the twentieth century has been that of Horatio Alger, which couples individualism with success and leads

THINKING CRITICALLY

The Myth That Surrounds Our Birth

We have noted that "myths are archetypal patterns in human consciousness" surrounding the existential crises of life. Birth is the first of these crises. Even though we are not aware of it at the time, a lot of fuss (or lack of it) is made over our birth. You may recall that Freud was born in a caul, a sign that his mother took to mean he was destined for greatness. Our parents may or may not have told us stories about it. In any event, in time each of us gives our birth a special meaning accompanied by strong feelings. We may be proud of it, perplexed by it, or wish that it had never occurred. Such response constitutes our personal myth.

What is the myth that surrounds your birth? Do you recall any stories your parents told concerning your birth? What narrative can you tell? How do you believe your parents reacted to your particular gender? Were they happy or would they have preferred a child of the opposite sex? Even though you may never have thought about these questions before, taking the time to do so now and writing down your narrative can help you to become more aware of the myth that surrounds your birth.

people to be driven, competitive, tense, and predisposed to stress and depression. Meanwhile anxiety disorders and depression have soared and we must rediscover myths that can help us combat them. If not, our gambling (which defrauds primarily the poor) and use of drugs will continue to skyrocket.

Dante's *The Divine Comedy* tells us we must go through hell before we can love and live "life as community." May reminds us that "a person's hell may consist of confronting the fact that his mother never loved him; or it may consist of fantasies of destroying those a person loves most, like Medea destroying her children; or undergoing the hideous cruelty released in wartime when it becomes patriotic to hate and to kill." What is important is not the particulars of one's own hell but the journey itself.

In the nineteenth century, Ibsen anticipated the twentieth and tolled the death of hyperindividualism. Counterposing humans and subhuman trolls, his *Peer Gynt* describes the conflicting life of a man who wished to be honored and taken care of by one woman. The struggle rendered him passive, dependent, and powerless.

Goethe's *Faust* is the myth of patriarchal society and power that has dominated the West. Much as we would like to believe that our tremendous technology is leading to progress, the tale of Faust reveals that, in a patriarchal society, men have a serious problem with the feminine dimension of life.

Washington politics, some say, demands a Faustian pact from even its finest people. Vince Foster, Jr., President Clinton's boyhood chum and later his aide, is said to have commented before he committed suicide, "Before we came here, we thought of ourselves as good people" (Farmer, 1993). Faust steered Gretchen into condemnation. In the twentieth century, May suggests, Germany itself became Faust and tumbled to its death in Nazism, a guilt that is shared by all in the West. One does not have to commit the specific evil to be guilty. We are guilty because we are human and the only way we can save ourselves is to assume responsibility.

Myths motivate us because they imply new potentialities and interpretations. Our current distress with parental sexual abuse of children is a new form of the Oedipal myth. May is amazed that Sophocles' sequel to *Oedipus Rex, Oedipus in Colonus,* is neglected in American psychoanalytic circles because in that drama the blind Oedipus comes to terms with what he has done. Oedipus knows that he is not guilty because he was unaware that the man he murdered was his father, but he must assume responsibility for his action.

Finally, May asks if we can construct a new myth for our survival. The Peer Gynt and Faust myths teach us that we must develop a myth of equality between men and women to undermine the primarily male, left-brain concepts of reason and hyperindividualism that have misled us. We need myths that give meaning to a woman's life other than just in the context of her relationship to men. The Navaho have a myth in which women, by their power of creativity, save the world from chaos, much as Ma Joad in Steinbeck's *The Grapes of Wrath* holds a migrant family together.

May believes we can develop a new myth out of our explorations of the heavens. On Christmas Eve 1968, three astronauts circled the moon and read from the Bible making that experience sacred. Those astronauts could become heroes in a myth in which they look back in space upon the earth and recognize that the borders over which people kill each other are not really there and were a terrible, demented mistake. Pictures of the earth from space tell us that we must develop a new myth that fosters world community and learn to live in one global family (see also Kaplan, 1994).

Psychotherapy

The existential approach to psychotherapy maintains that the central goal of therapy is to help promote understanding of the self and one's mode of being in the world. Psychological constructs for understanding human beings are, therefore, placed on an ontological basis and take their meaning from the present situation. Drives, dynamisms, or behavior patterns are understood only in the context of the structure of the existence of the particular person.

May points out that *being* in the human sense is not given once and for all. As humans we have to be aware of ourselves, be responsible for ourselves, become ourselves. "To be *and* not to be" (May's rephrasing of Hamlet) is a choice we make at every moment. An "I am" experience is a precondition for solving specific problems (1983). Otherwise, we merely trade one set of defenses for another.

Becoming aware of one's own being is not to be explained in social terms. The acceptance of the therapist may facilitate the "I am" experience but it does not automatically lead to it. "The crucial question is what the individual himself, in his own awareness of and responsibility for his existence, does with the fact that he can be accepted" (1983). Nor is the emergence of an "I am" experience identical to the development of the ego. It occurs on a more basic level, an ontological one, and is a precondition for subsequent ego development.

In order to grasp what it means to exist, one also needs to grasp the option of nonbeing. Death is an obvious form of the threat of nonbeing, but conformity is an alternative mode that May finds very prevalent in our day. People give up their own identity in order to be accepted by others and avoid being ostracized or lonely, but in doing so they lose their power and uniqueness. Whereas repression and inhibition were common neurotic patterns in Freud's day, today *conformism* is a more prevalent pattern. Such denial of one's potentialities leads to the experience of guilt. Ontological guilt does not come from cultural prohibition but arises from the fact of self-awareness and the recognition that one has not fulfilled one's potentialities. Facing such guilt in the process of therapy leads to constructive effects.

Thus, the central task of the therapist is to seek to understand the patient's mode of being and nonbeing in the world. It is the context that distinguishes the existential approach rather than any specific techniques. The human being is not an object to be managed or analyzed. Technique follows understanding. Various psychotherapeutic devices may be used, depending on which method will best reveal the existence of a particular patient at any given time.

May believes that free association is particularly useful in revealing intentionality. The relationship between the therapist and patient is seen as a real one. When transference occurs, May points out that it distorts the therapeutic encounter. The therapist seeks to help the patient experience existence as real. This does not imply simply adjusting to one's culture or relieving anxiety but rather experiencing one's existence or mode of being in the world.

May warns against the use of drugs in psychotherapy. For the most part, he believes they have a negative effect because, in removing the patient's anxiety, they may remove the motivation for change and thereby deny an opportunity for learning and destroy vital resources. Occasionally, May employs techniques developed by *gestalt therapists* such as Fritz Perls. An emphasis might be placed on nonverbal behaviors to show the inconsistency between a verbal and nonverbal statement. If a patient states that she is frightened but has a smile on her face, May might point out that a frightened person does not smile and seek to explore the meaning of the smile. A patient might be asked to fantasize that a significant other was sitting in an opposite chair, to have a conversation with that person, and then to reverse roles. Such techniques are designed to help the patient confront and experience actual present feelings. Finally, May's approach emphasizes commitment, believing that patients cannot receive any insight until they are ready to decide and take a decisive orientation to life.

Assessment and Research in May's Theory

May believes that in their efforts to be "scientific" many psychologists lose sight of the real person that they seek to understand. However, while May is critical of some of the so-called scientific forms of psychology, he is by no means antiscientific. His aim is to speak out against concepts of personality that dogmatically foreclose avenues of research.

In the 1950s, May criticized psychologists for having singled out for study those aspects of human behavior that overlap with animal behavior and can ultimately be described in physiological or stimulus-response terms. In doing so, May pointed out that psychologists neglected the problem of symbols, even though the use of symbols is part of the distinct human condition (1958). Although cognitive psychology studies symbols and other events that occur in the mind, May does not look to cognitive psychology for answers because its conceptions are also too limited for the psychological problems of our time (1981).

May criticizes contemporary psychological research for being impressed with data and numbers at the expense of theory. Psychologists tend to be contemptuous of imagination and speculation, yet the most important scientific discoveries (Copernicus's concept of the universe, Darwin's theory of evolution, Freud's construct of unconscious forces, Einstein's theory of relativity) were made not by accumulating facts but by perceiving the relationship among them (1983). Human nature can be understood only within a theoretical framework.

The existential approach suggests three basic changes in psychological methods of research on personality. First, "we must cut through the tendency in the West to believe we understand things only if we know their causes, and to find out and describe instead what the thing is as a phenomenon — the experience, as it is given to us, in its 'givenness.' First, that is, we must know what we are talking about. This is not to rule out causation and genetic development, but rather to say that the question of *why* one is what one is does not have meaning until we know *what* one is" (1967). This phenomenological approach is very similar to the view maintained by Rogers.

Second, psychologists must recognize that all ways of understanding what it means to be a human being are based on philosophical assumptions and myths. We need to examine these presuppositions continually, for it is one's philosophical concept of human being that guides one's empirical research. Here May also reminds us of Rogers's and Maslow's emphasis on science serving previously chosen goals.

Finally, we must ask the question of the nature of person as person, the ontological question of what it means to be. Understanding the being of another person occurs on a very different level from knowing specific things about the person. This is the classical distinction between *knowing* and *knowing about.* Our culture tends to believe that something is not real unless we can reduce it to a mathematical abstraction. But according to May, this denies the reality of our own experience. May suggests that it would be more scientific to first try to see clearly what we are talking about and then try to find symbols to describe what we see with a minimum of distortion (1983).

At this time, much of our research is governed by the myth of the technological man, which May describes as "a set of assumptions postulating that the human being is governed by what he can rationally understand, that his emotions will follow this understanding, and that his anxiety and dread will thus be cured" (1969). May is trying to help us develop a new form, a new myth that will be more adequate for our day. After all, he reminds us, "Anyone can do the research. . . . The original contribution lies in seeing a new *form* for the problem" (1967). May believes that new forms of symbols and myths for understanding human nature are more likely to come from our art, literature, humanities, and religion than from our present psychology (1983; also see DeCarvalho, 1992).

Two particular areas that May has researched are anxiety and dreams. May undertook a study of unmarried mothers in order to illuminate the meaning of anxiety (1969). Because he believed that there might be damaging effects in inducing anxiety experimentally, he took what was an anxiety-creating situation at that time in our society and studied it to reveal a pattern that would be characteristic of other anxiety-creating situations as well. May believes that the more intensely we study the individual, the more we arrive at data that lie below individual differences and are applicable to human beings in general.

His study led to some rich observations concerning the meaning of anxiety itself, the origin of neurotic anxiety in a particular parent-child relationship in which rejection is covered over with pretenses of love so that it cannot be appraised realistically, and the greater prevalence of neurotic anxiety among women of the middle class.

May believes that dreams reflect how we perceive, cope, and give meaning to our world. Our dream life reflects our intentionality and deepest concerns. It permits the person to experience rather than merely explain important symbols and myths. In analyzing dreams, May takes them phenomenologically as self-revealing givens, patterns of data within themselves. He looks for consistency over a period of time and notices that latent meanings in earlier dreams often become manifest in the later dreams. The latent meaning of dreams is thus reconceived by May as a dimension of communication that the patient is unwilling or unable as yet to actualize.

Each dream has a theme and a motif. The *theme* is the unity and inner consistency that is a part of the dreamer. It is characteristic of all dreams and reflects the unity of a person's character. The *motif* is the central thread running through the various dreams and the goal one is moving toward. The purpose of interpreting a dream is not to tell the individual what it means but to expand the individual's consciousness so that what is going on can be more fully and deeply experienced. In dreams we successfully resist the temptation to intellectualize and, instead, wrestle with our real problems.

After May had painted a portrait of one patient from her dreams, he compared his picture with that which had emerged in the course of her three-year analysis with Dr. Leopold Caligor by comparing his findings with the doctor's case notes. He found a remarkable consistency between the two accounts, con-

PHILOSOPHICAL ASSUMPTIONS

Examining May

How would you rate May on each of the basic philosophical assumptions described in Chapter 1? Each basic issue was presented as a bipolar dimension along which a person's view can be placed according to the degree of agreement with one or the other extreme. Rate May's views on these issues.

When you have determined where you think May stands, compare your responses with those of your classmates and your instructor. You should be willing to defend your ratings, but also be prepared to change them in light of others' compelling arguments. Afterward, compare your rating of May with your own position on each issue and with those of other theorists. Does this comparison help you to understand why his theory does or does not appeal to you?

Would strongly agree	Would agree	Is neutral or believes in synthesis of both views	Would agree	Would strongly agree
1	2	3	4	5

freedom	determinism
People basically have control over their own behavior and understand the motives behind their behavior.	The behavior of people is basically determined by internal or external forces over which they have little, if any, control.

firming his hypothesis that one can get an accurate and meaningful picture of a person from the symbols and myths created in dreams.

May's Theory: Philosophy, Science, and Art

May clearly recognizes that science derives from prior philosophical forms and is fundamentally dependent upon them. He believes the reason we don't understand the truth about ourselves is not that we haven't amassed enough data,

1	2	3	4	5

hereditary
Inherited and inborn characteristics have the most important influence on a person's behavior.

environment
Factors in the environment have the most important influence on a person's behavior.

1	2	3	4	5

uniqueness
Each individual is unique and cannot be compared with others.

universality
People are basically very similar in nature.

1	2	3	4	5

proactive
Human beings primarily act on their own initiative.

reactive
Human beings primarily react to stimuli from the outside world.

1	2	3	4	5

optimistic
Significant changes in personality and behavior can occur throughout the course of a lifetime.

pessimistic
A person's personality and behavior are essentially stable and unchanging.

conducted the right experiments, or read enough books, but because we "do not have enough courage." Scientific facts and technical proofs rarely help us answer the questions that really matter. We have to "venture" (1953).

In psychotherapy May is "the implacable friend," insisting that his patients "grapple with the disabling forces inside of them and fight their way back into life" (Harris, 1969). He has not been afraid to risk re-introducing concepts vehemently rejected by mainstream psychologists — intentionality, the will, the daimonic. He re-introduced these concepts because he believes that they are vital to an understanding of what it means to be human today. There is a prophetic note to his writing, reminiscent of Erich Fromm, and his thinking frequently has a theological quality. Indeed, there are those who suggest that May has taken up where Paul Tillich, the theological giant of our century, left off (Harris, 1969). May acknowledges that for him the great periods in history were not those when psychological concerns were dominant but those when philosophical and religious concerns were uppermost (1983).

May does not give us a series of hypotheses that may be tested by empirical procedures. Instead, he gives us a philosophical picture of what it means to be a person in today's world. Reasons are offered in support of his affirmations, but they do not serve as proof; they cooperate as pieces of evidence in favor of a certain picture of reality. To reduce our understanding of personality to scientific, causative, and abstract terms means that we will lose some significant content and fail to understand the full reality of a human being. May encourages us to examine the philosophical assumptions of our scientific endeavor so that we can maintain a creative dialogue between our science and our philosophy.

May's philosophical picture of human nature is coherent, relevant, comprehensive, and compelling. He successfully avoids dualisms that have troubled us since the philosophy of Descartes. The existential framework that informs his theory is more compatible with our world than the philosophical assumptions of nineteenth-century science that informed Freud's work. An existential philosophy provides a helpful background for discussing what Freud meant to say about the nature of psychic functioning. Although Freud was not an existentialist, existentialism provides categories that clarify Freudian thought and intent. Thus, May fruitfully reconceives many Freudian concepts.

Whereas Freud's philosophy was an extension of the assumptions inherent in the scientific community of his time, May begins as a philosopher. His image of human nature provides a welcome antidote to the technological view of the person that permeates radical behavior and learning theories as well as the naive optimism of the humanists. May differs from traditional learning and behavior theories in his open examination of his philosophical assumptions. He differs from the humanists in his insistence that we directly confront our own evil.

For the most part, psychologists tend to ignore May's theory because they cannot treat it as a scientific hypothesis. Concepts like intentionality and the daimonic are virtually impossible to define operationally and test empirically, but the findings of an empirical test do not establish a philosophical assumption; they may not even significantly relate to it. Nevertheless, the very strength of May's theory, the fact that it has its roots in a new philosophical conception of human life, may also be its greatest liability. May runs a strong risk of being given short shrift by the psychological establishment and having little impact on personality theorizing. This is ironic because in many ways the humility and openness to change characteristic of May's theory are more in keeping with the nature of the scientific enterprise than the attitude of those who seek to limit and confine research. By ignoring May, psychologists deprive themselves of the challenge of re-examining their own philosophical assumptions and, perhaps, reconceiving the goals and methods of their science.

Summary

1. Rollo May's work brings together the psychoanalytic tradition in psychology and the existentialist movement in philosophy.

2. **Existentialism** emphasizes *existence* rather than **essence**. It suggests that there is no truth or reality except as we participate in it. Knowledge is an act of doing.

3. Existentialists believe that the psychologist's preoccupation with lawfulness and predictability stands in the way of understanding the real person and they urge a greater breadth to our scientific methodology. They seek to study the structure of human existence and to look at the unity of the person prior to any split into subject and object.

4. The central problem we face in the second half of the twentieth century, according to May, is a feeling of *powerlessness* in the face of nuclear war.

5. May defines **anxiety** as the apprehension cued off by a threat to an essential value. It is intensified in contemporary culture by the interpersonal isolation and alienation that have come out of the way in which we view ourselves. Many of our present efforts to dispel anxiety actually end up increasing it.

6. The source of the human dilemma lies in the loss of the center of values in our society. A distinguishing mark of the human animal is that of creating values. The need today is to discover and affirm a new set of values.

7. May assumes (a) that all living organisms are centered on themselves and seek to preserve that center; (b) they can go out from their centeredness to participate with other people; (c) sickness is a means of preserving one's being; (d) human beings can engage in a level of self-consciousness that permits them to transcend the present and consider alternatives. These *ontological assumptions* precede our scientific activity and make it possible, but our analytic activity may in turn illumine them.

8. *Rediscovering selfhood* involves rediscovering our own feelings and desires and fighting against those things that prevent us from feeling and wanting. There are *four stages of consciousness* of self: innocence, rebellion, ordinary consciousness of self, and creative consciousness of self.

9. May discusses key issues in personality in ways that avoid abstraction and facilitate the confronting of **paradoxes**. *Love,* which used to be seen as the answer to human problems, has now become the problem. We are unable to love. We need to experience and rediscover *care.* May introduces the concept of **intentionality** to bridge the gap between subject and object and to place the problem of determinism and freedom on a deeper level. He re-introduces the concept of the **daimonic** and insists that we must come to terms with it. He emphasizes our need to be *courageous and creative.* We also need to rediscover our *power* and express it in constructive ways. May points out how our *freedom* needs to be considered in light of our *destiny.*

10. May defines **myth** as "narrative patterns that give significance to our existence." He believes pseudomyths, such as that of Horatio Alger, are filling the vacuum created by the lack of genuine myths of people living today in the West. We need new myths to give our lives meaning, provide heroes, suggest new possibilities. Two possible new myths that we need are equality between women and men, and a global community with no boundaries.

11. In psychotherapy the existentialist seeks to understand the patient's mode of being in the world. It is the context that distinguishes the existential approach rather than any specific technique. Use has been made of the psychotherapeutic devices of both Freud and gestalt psychotherapists.

12. May criticizes contemporary psychological research for being impressed with data and uninterested in theory. We need continually to re-examine our presuppositions and raise ontological questions. Two specific research activities that May engaged in were a study of unmarried mothers and the study of a dream sequence.

13. May's theory is not a scientific theory of personality giving us a series of hypotheses that may be tested by an empirical procedure. Instead he suggests a philosophical picture of human nature that is coherent, relevant, comprehensive, and compelling.

Suggestions for Further Reading

Rollo May's books are extremely readable and enlightening for the lay person. His theory of personality was initially outlined in *Man's Search for Himself* (Norton, 1953) and *Psychology and the Human Dilemma* (Van Nostrand Reinhold, 1967). *The Meaning of Anxiety* (Norton, 1950; revised, 1977) is now considered a classic. In it May encouraged a genuine union between psychology and philosophy and demonstrated the importance of values for psychology. *Love and Will* (Norton, 1969) explores the experience of sex and love in contemporary society.

It was hailed by the *New York Times* as the "most important book of the year." May's most recent works are *Freedom and Destiny* (Norton, 1981), which rethinks the problem of determinism and personal freedom, *The Discovery of Being* (Norton, 1983), which describes the human search for being and nonbeing in an age of anxiety, *My Quest for Beauty* (Saybrook, 1985), which describes the creative and therapeutic role of art, and *The Cry for Myth* (Norton, 1991), a passionate plea for a new myth to guide our lives.

PART 7

Cognitive Theories

Cognitive theories of personality, exemplified here by George Kelly and the cognitive behavioral theories of Albert Ellis, Aaron Beck, and Arnold Lazarus, emphasize the processes by which an individual becomes aware of the world and makes judgments about it. Cognitive theories stress that behavior is determined not simply by the environment but also, and primarily, by an individual's attitudes, expectations, and beliefs.

Other theories have recognized the importance of cognition, but they did not make it the mainstay of their theory. Freud emphasized emotional processes of the heart rather than intellectual processes of the mind. The behavior and learning tradition, until recently, was concerned with the analysis of environmental stimuli and the individual's final overt response to the environment rather than with the intermediate subjective processes that led to the behavior.

CHAPTER 15

George Kelly

1. Explain why Kelly suggested that we view ourselves as scientists.
2. Describe the philosophical position of *constructive alternativism*.
3. Discuss Kelly's fundamental postulate and identify eleven corollaries that support it.
4. Explain how Kelly reconceived traditional concepts in personality theorizing.
5. Describe the Rep Test.
6. Discuss Kelly's view of and contributions to psychotherapy.
7. Identify some of the criticisms of Kelly's theory.
8. Evaluate Kelly's theory in terms of its function as philosophy, science, and art.

Reading Kelly is like entering a new terrain, as he avoided many of the concepts traditionally present in personality theorizing. Kelly was forthright in describing the differences between his approach and that of others. "It is only fair," he wrote, "to warn the reader about what may be in store for him. In the first place, he is likely to find missing most of the familiar landmarks. . . . For example, the term *learning,* so honorably embedded in most psychological texts, scarcely appears at all. That is wholly intentional; we are for throwing it overboard all together. There is no *ego,* no *emotion,* no *reinforcement,* no *drive,* no *unconscious,* no *need"* (1955). It is not that these concepts are entirely omitted from Kelly's work; rather, they are given new meanings and incorporated into his philosophy of constructive alternativism.

Biographical Background

George Kelly was born on a farm in Perth, Kansas, in 1905. His father was a Presbyterian minister, but ill health prevented him from actively leading a church congregation. Kelly's parents were devout fundamentalists who practiced their faith, prescribed hard work, and rigorously shunned the evils of dancing, drinking, and card playing. As an only child, Kelly received extensive attention and love. His mother, in particular, was devoted to him.

Kelly's early education was somewhat sporadic. He attended a one-room country school and was taught by his parents at home. He was sent to Wichita, Kansas, for high school, where he attended four different schools. He studied for three years at Friends University and received the B.A. degree one year later (1926) from Park College. Kelly had majored in physics and mathematics and planned a career in mechanical engineering. However, his interests were turning to social problems. While holding a number of different jobs related to engineering and education, he pursued the M.A. degree in educational sociology at the University of Kansas.

In 1929, Kelly was awarded a fellowship for study at the University of Edinburgh in Scotland. He earned the B.Ed. degree there based on his previous academic experience and his year of residency in Scotland. Kelly wrote his dissertation on the problem of predicting teaching success and discovered that his interests were turning to psychology. On his return to the United States, he enrolled as a doctoral student in psychology at the State University of Iowa. He received the Ph.D. in 1931 with a dissertation on speech and reading disabilities.

Kelly began his career as an academic psychologist in the middle of the Depression of the 1930s. Opportunities for work in physiological psychology, his specialty, were scarce, so he turned his attention to clinical psychology, a growing field. During the next twelve years, Kelly taught at Fort Hays Kansas State College and developed a program of traveling psychological clinics that sought to identify and treat emotional and behavioral problems in students in the state's public school system. His experience with the clinics was crucial to his later development and theorizing. Not committed to any one theoretical

George Kelly

approach, Kelly experimented with several different methods in his work with students referred for counseling. His position gave him a unique opportunity to try out innovative as well as traditional clinical approaches. His work with the clinics sparked several ideas that later found application in his own theory of personality and therapy.

World War II briefly interrupted Kelly's academic career. He enrolled in the navy as an aviation psychologist, headed a training program of local civilian pilots, and worked for the bureau of medicine and surgery, gaining recognition for his clinical services. After the war, a significant demand for clinical psychologists appeared as returning servicemen required help with personal problems. Clinical psychology came to be seen as an essential part of health services. Kelly played a leading role in fostering the development and integration of clinical psychology into the mainstream of American psychology. After teaching one year at the University of Maryland, he joined the faculty of Ohio State University as professor and director of clinical psychology. During the next twenty years at Ohio State, Kelly built a distinguished program of clinical psychology and refined and published his theory of personality.

In 1965, Kelly received a prestigious appointment to the Riklis Chair of Behavioral Science at Brandeis University. This appointment would have given him great freedom to pursue his research, but he died in 1967.

Kelly did not publish a great deal but he lectured extensively in the United States and abroad and he exerted a significant influence on psychology through his personal impact on his students and friends. In his later years, he spent considerable time suggesting how personal construct theory could be applied to help resolve social and international problems. He held several important positions, such as president of both the Clinical and Counseling Divisions of the American Psychological Association. He assisted in developing and also served as president of the American Board of Examiners in Professional Psychology.

The Person as Scientist

George Kelly invited us to look at ourselves and other people as scientists, an image that he noted psychologists are quick to ascribe to themselves but perhaps not as readily to other people. Kelly suggested that the posture we take as we attempt to predict and control the events in our world is similar to that of the scientist who develops and tests hypotheses. In our efforts to understand the world, we develop constructs that act as hypotheses that make the world meaningful to us. If these patterns appear to fit our subsequent experience, we find them useful and hold onto them. Thus, if we construe the world or certain events as hostile, we will act in certain ways to protect ourselves. If our protective behaviors appear to be useful ways to cope with the events, we will continue to hold onto the hostile interpretation. If the pattern or construct does not lead to behaviors that help us adjust to events in our world, we will seek to alter or change the construct in order to develop a better one. Just as the scientist employs hypotheses to make predictions about certain consequences, people employ their constructs to predict what is going to happen to them in the future. Subsequent events are then used to indicate whether the predictions and underlying constructs were correct or were misleading.

Because of the emphasis he placed on the ways in which people construe the world, Kelly is often perceived as a cognitive theorist who stressed the process of knowing as the primary factor in personality development (see also Warren, 1990). One could also easily defend labeling Kelly a humanist (Epting and Leitner, 1992) or a phenomenologist. Kelly repeatedly protested that his was not a cognitive theory: "I have been so puzzled over the early labeling of personal construct theory as 'cognitive' that several years ago I set out to write another short book to make it clear that I wanted no part of cognitive theory" (Mahler, 1969, p. 216). He felt that his theory belied any such classification and should be considered independently. However, interest in Kelly's approach has grown in recent years in that it has been seen as compatible with the growing interest in cognition that characterizes contemporary psychology.

The cognitive movement in contemporary psychology rejects the behaviorist view that people react passively to stimuli. It explores the various ways in which we respond to the environment by actively processing the information we receive into new forms, categories, and "mental representations of the world'' (Klatzky, 1980) and thereby actively construe reality (Soffer, 1993). Kelly's theory is cognitive because he stressed that an individual's behavior is determined not simply by the environment or heredity but also, and primarily, by attitudes, expectations, and beliefs.

Constructive Alternativism

Kelly's theory of personality is based on his philosophical position of **constructive alternativism:** the assumption that any one event is open to a variety of interpretations. The world, in and of itself, does not automatically make sense to us. We have to create our own ways of understanding the events that happen. In effect, there is no reality outside our interpretations of it. Take, for example, the situation of a boy who is late for school. His father may think that it is because the boy is lazy. His mother may suggest that her son is forgetful and daydreams on the way to school. His teacher may view the pupil's tardiness as an expression of his distaste and hostility toward academic work. His best friend might see it as an accident. The boy himself could construe his lateness as an indication of his inferiority. The event itself is merely a given datum but it gives rise to many different alternative constructions that may lead to different actions. For Kelly, the individual's complex constructions are the appropriate object of study. The objective truth of a person's interpretations are unimportant because they are unknowable. What is important is their implications for behavior and life.

In our efforts to understand the world, we develop constructs or patterns that make the world meaningful to us. We look at the world "through transparent patterns or templates" of our own creation. It is as if each person can view the world only through sunglasses of his or her own choosing. No one construct or pattern is final and a perfect reflection of the world. There is always an alternative construct that might do a better job of accounting for the facts that we perceive. Thus, our position in the world is one of constructive alternativism, as we change or revise our constructs in order to understand it more accurately.

For example, at the beginning of a semester, students develop certain constructs or ideas about the subjects that they are studying. Usually, these constructs are based on a very limited sample of the actual course or the instructor's behavior. One student may conclude that a particular course will be a snap, requiring a minimum of time and preparation. Another student may conclude that the same course will be a challenge, requiring considerable effort. As the semester progresses, each student acts on and gradually tests the preliminary hypothesis for its accuracy. The lectures, reading assignments, written papers, and tests are all subsequent events that serve to confirm or disprove the initial assumptions. By the middle of the semester, a student has a much clearer idea of the accuracy of the original construct concerning the course.

A student's behavior in a college course is simply an example in miniature of what happens to us all throughout our lives. As was pointed out earlier, the

THINKING CRITICALLY

How We Behave as Scientists

Kelly (1955) suggested that each one of us behaves as a scientist in our efforts to understand the world. You can gain a deeper appreciation of your own attempts to understand other people by analyzing a recent situation and your effort to understand it in terms of the scientific method. Suppose one night, when you arrive home, you observe that there are tears in your roommate's eyes. You might conclude that your roommate was upset about something. However, when you inquire what the problem is your roommate says, "Nothing is the matter" and points to a pile of onions recently chopped for tonight's stew.

Analyze this situation, or another one, in terms of the scientific method. What was the problem? What hypothesis did you develop? What prediction did you make about possible experiences you could have if the hypothesis were useful? How did you test your hypothesis and what conclusions did you draw?

Anderson and Kirkland (1990) suggest that in his metaphor of the personal scientist, Kelly provides a constructive alternative to the mechanistic metaphor of the machine. What do you think?

world is not a fixed given that can be immediately comprehended and understood. In order to understand the world, we have to develop constructs or ways of perceiving it. During the course of our lives, we develop many different constructs. Further, we continually test, revise, and modify them. As none of our constructs is ultimate, alternative constructs that we could choose from are always available. Thus, a person is free to change constructs in an effort to make sense out of, predict, and control the world. This validation process is central to the psychology of personal constructs (Landfield, 1988).

Fundamental Postulate and Corollaries

In order to present and explain his theory, Kelly (1955) set forth one basic assumption, or fundamental postulate, and then elaborated on it with eleven corollaries.

The *fundamental postulate* reads:

A person's processes are psychologically channelized by the ways in which he anticipates events.

Probably the most important word in Kelly's primary assumption is *anticipates*. Essentially, Kelly suggested that the way in which an individual predicts future happenings is crucial to behavior. As scientists, people seek to forecast what is going to happen. They orient their behaviors and ideas about the world toward the goal of accurate, useful predictions. According to Kelly, the future, rather than the past, is the primary impetus of behavior.

Each of the eleven corollaries that Kelly presented to elaborate his fundamental postulate focuses on a primary word that sums up the essence of these supportive statements and his theory.

1. *Construction* "A person anticipates events by construing their replications" (Kelly, 1955). The term **construe** means to place an interpretation on an event. As we have seen, the universe is not an automatically knowable given. We must create constructs or ways in which to understand it.

2. *Individuality* "Persons differ from each other in their construction of events" (Kelly, 1955). No two people interpret events in the same way. Each of us experiences an event from our own subjective point of view. This corollary underscores Kelly's belief that it is the subjective interpretation of an event, rather than the event itself, that is most important.

3. *Organization* "Each person characteristically evolves, for his convenience in anticipating events, a construction system embracing ordinal relationships between constructs" (Kelly, 1955). Our interpretation of events in the world is neither haphazard nor arbitrary. Each one of us organizes constructs in a series of ordinal relationships in which some constructs are more important and others are less important. The fact that our constructs fall into an organized pattern means that we develop a system of constructs rather than simply a number of isolated ones.

4. *Dichotomy* "A person's construction system is composed of a finite number of dichotomous constructs" (Kelly, 1955). In making an interpretation about an event, we not only make an assertion about it, but we also indicate that the opposite quality is not characteristic of it. A dichotomy is an opposition; Kelly suggested that all of our constructs are of a bipolar form. When we construe that a person is strong, we also imply that the person is not weak. The dichotomous form of our constructs provides the basis for constructive alternativism. Riemann (1990), however, suggests that bipolarity is an important but not necessary aspect of personal constructs.

5. *Choice* "A person chooses for himself that alternative in a dichotomized construct through which he anticipates the greater possibility for extension and definition of his system" (Kelly, 1955). The choice corollary is a very important one. It underlines Kelly's belief that a person is free and able to choose from among the various alternatives the construct that will be most useful.

6. *Range* "A construct is convenient for the anticipation of a finite range of events only" (Kelly, 1955). Each construct has a certain range or focus. The construct of *tall versus short* is useful for describing people, trees, or horses, but virtually useless for understanding the weather. Some people apply their constructs broadly and others limit their constructs to a narrow focus.

7. *Experience* "A person's construction system varies as he successively construes the replication of events" (Kelly, 1955). People change their interpretation of events in the light of later experience. Such reconstruction forms the basis for learning.

8. *Modulation* "The variation in a person's construction system is limited by the permeability of the constructs within whose range of convenience the variants lie" (Kelly, 1955). The extent to which a person's constructs may be adjusted or modulated depends on the existing framework and organization of the constructural system. Constructs are *permeable,* that is, they are open to change and alteration.

   Some constructs are more permeable than others. Concrete constructs are rather difficult to change because of their specificity in definition and range. The construct *good versus evil* might be narrowly conceived by one individual so as to contain relatively few experiences. In that case it would be very difficult for the individual to change the construct. For another individual, the same construct might be much more permeable and easily penetrated by new experiences.

9. *Fragmentation* "A person may successfully employ a variety of construction subsystems which are inferentially incompatible with each other" (Kelly, 1955). There are times when people employ constructs that appear to be incompatible with each other. Because of this, we are often surprised by other people's behavior and we cannot always infer what people are going to do tomorrow from the way they behave today. Such fragmentation is particularly apt to occur either when a person's constructs are impermeable and concrete or when they are undergoing change.

10. *Communality* "To the extent that one person employs a construction of experience which is similar to that employed by another, his psychological processes are similar to the other person" (Kelly, 1955). This does not mean that their experiences are identical, but our ability to share and communicate with other people is based on the fact that we share similar personal constructs with them.

11. *Sociability* "To the extent that one person construes the construction processes of another, he may play a role in a social process involving the other person" (Kelly, 1955). Our ability to interact socially with other people entails understanding a broad range of their constructs and behaviors. Thus other people are also important for testing one's construing system (Walker, 1990).

The Reconstruction of Old Concepts

Kelly avoided many of the concepts traditionally associated with personality theorizing. He gave familiar landmarks and terms new meanings and subordinated them to his theory of personal constructs.

Some of Kelly's constructs refer to self-identity or the identity of others. The **self-construct** is based primarily on what we perceive as consistencies in our own behavior. For example, we believe that we are honest, sincere, friendly, and so forth. The self-construct is developed out of our relationships with other people. When we construe other people, we also construe ourselves. When we think of another person as "hostile" or "aggressive," we are making those qualities and their opposites a dimension of our own experience. Our self-interpretation is linked to our role relationships with other people.

A **role** is a process or behavior that people engage in based on their understanding of the behavior and constructs of others. We do not have to be accurate in our constructions to enter into a role. A student may play a certain role with a professor believed to be unduly demanding and unfair when in fact the professor is not. Nor does a role have to be reciprocated by the other person. The professor may remain fair in spite of the student's misconstruction. What is needed in order to play a role is simply some construct of the other person's behavior.

Kelly's use of the term "role" should not be confused with its use in social psychology. In social psychology, "role" usually refers to a set of behavioral expectations such as mother, teacher, physician, ruler, and so on, set forth by a particular society and fulfilled by its members. In Kelly's theory, the role is defined by the individual in an effort to understand the behavior of other people and relate to them. One's self-construct may be seen as a core or basic role structure by which one conceives of oneself as an integral individual in relation to other people.

For Kelly, the person is a process, an organism in continual activity, whose behavior is governed by a system of personal constructs. *Learning* and *motivation* are built into the very structure of the system. Kelly believed that no special inner forces, such as drives, needs, instincts, or motives, are needed to account for human motivation. Human nature in and of itself implies motivation because it is alive and in process. Nor need behavior be accounted for in terms of external forces, such as stimuli and reinforcements. Learning is synonymous with all of the psychological processes themselves. It is simply inappropriate to conceive of an individual as motivated by other internal or external forces. Kelly (1958) declared that "there are pitchfork theories on the one hand and the carrot theories on the other. But our theory is neither of these. Since we prefer to look at the nature of the animal itself, ours is probably best called a jackass theory."

Not all constructs are verbalized; therefore, conscious and unconscious processes may be accounted for by our capacity to form constructs that are not put into words. *Emotions* are also subsumed under the general framework of personal constructs. Although some critics (Bruner and Rogers, 1965) suggest that Kelly's theory is too intellectual and mentalistic, Kelly refused to divide the person into cognitive and emotional states. Feelings and emotions refer to inner states that need to be construed. They arise when constructs are in a state of change.

Traditional psychological concepts such as anxiety, guilt, and aggression were also reconceived by Kelly in accordance with his personal construct theory. *Anxiety* is "the recognition that the events with which one is confronted lies outside the range of one's construct system" (1955). In other words, we feel anxious when we can no longer understand ourselves and the events of our lives in terms of our past experiences. Such discrepancy can lead to construct change. If a change is merely incidental, the individual may experience some fear, but if the change is comprehensive, the individual will feel deeply threatened.

Guilt is a "perception of one's apparent dislodgement from his core role structure" (1955). In our relationships with significant others, we develop a *core role* in which we construe ourselves in certain ways, such as loving or responsible. If we behave, either intentionally or unintentionally, in a way that violates the core role structure, we will experience guilt.

Aggression entails "the active elaboration of one's perceptual field" (1955). Aggression involves action: the deliberate placement of oneself into situations that call for decisions. Such aggression is distinguished from hostility, in which an individual forces other people or events to fit into the current personal construct system. In Kelly's theory, *hostility,* the "continued effort to extort validational evidence in favor of a type of social prediction which has already proven itself a failure," (1955) is the opposite of aggression. Kelly uses the term aggression in the way most of us would use the term assertiveness.

Assessment and Research in Kelly's Theory

Clinical experience with public school and college students provided the basis for Kelly's theory of personal constructs. Although these students may have had problems, they were essentially functioning normally in the academic setting. In assessing the students who came to him, therefore, Kelly primarily used the interview. "If you don't know what is going on in a person's mind," Kelly wrote, "ask him; he may tell you!" (1958). Kelly might have asked his client to respond to questions such as, "What kind of child were you?" "What kind of a person do you expect to become?" and "What do you expect from therapy?" Such questions, and their answers, were useful in elaborating the construct system.

At other times, Kelly would ask his clients to write a character sketch of themselves as if they were the primary character in a play. Written in the third person and beginning "The client's name is . . .", the character sketch was to be written as if by an intimate and sympathetic friend who knew the individual better than anyone else. Such character sketches were also helpful in determining the individual's constructs and relations with others.

In order to understand further how a person interprets the world, Kelly developed the Role Construct Repertory Test, known more simply as the **Rep Test** (see Figure 15.1). Essentially, the Rep Test permits a person to reveal constructs by comparing and contrasting a number of significant persons in her or

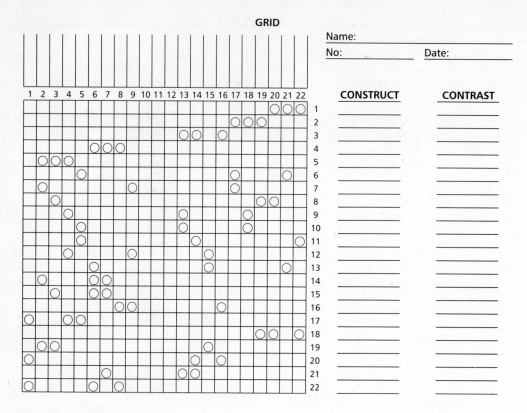

Figure 15.1 *Rep Test Grid*

his life. You will have an opportunity to learn about the Rep Test and to explore your own constructs in the *Thinking Critically* exercise that follows.

The philosophical aspect of Kelly's theory may help to account for the fact that his work initially generated little research. Most of the empirical studies based on his work concern the Rep Test (Bannister & Mair, 1968). Other studies like Bannister and Fransella (1966) and Bannister and Salmon (1966) suggest that the Rep Test and Kelly's constructs can help us understand the disturbance of thought in schizophrenia. They conclude that the thought constructs of a schizophrenic are less interrelated and more inconsistent than other people's, particularly regarding interpersonal constructs.

The Rep Test has also been used to explore the complexity of an individual's construct system and changes in the construct system throughout the lifespan (Crockett, 1982). Such research has focused on **cognitive complexity**, the ability to perceive differences in the way in which one construes other people. Individuals who are high in cognitive complexity are better able to predict what others will do and to relate with them.

As psychologists pay increased attention to the role of cognitive factors in personality, personal construct theory has generated more and more research

(Chambers & Epting, 1985; Chambers & Graves, 1985; Chambers & Stonerock, 1985; Tobacyk & Downs, 1986). Recent research has used the Rep grid to assess values and beliefs (Horley, 1991), and computer-based methods of analysis have been developed (Bringmann, 1992; see also Ford & Adams-Webber, 1991).

Psychotherapy

According to Kelly (1955), psychological disorders arise when a person clings to and continues to use personal constructs in spite of the fact that subsequent experience fails to validate them. Such a person has difficulty anticipating and predicting events and is unable to learn from experiences. The neurotic flounders in an effort to develop new ways to interpret the world or rigidly holds onto constructs that are useless. Instead of developing more successful constructs and solving problems, the neurotic develops symptoms.

Kelly conceived of his therapeutic methods as "reconstruction" rather than psychotherapy. He sought to help his patient reconstrue the world in a manner that would foster better predictions and control. The first step in his therapy is usually that of "elaborating the complaint." In this step, the therapist seeks to identify the problem, discover when and under what conditions it first arose, indicate what changes have occurred in the problem, discover any corrective measures that the client may have already taken, and find out under what conditions the problem is most and least noticeable. Elaboration of the complaint usually reveals many aspects of the person's construct system, but Kelly conceived of a second step as that of elaborating the construct system itself. Such elaboration gives a fuller picture of the elements encompassed in the complaint, allows more alternatives to arise, broadens the base of the relationship between therapist and client, and reveals the conceptual framework that created and sustained the symptoms.

Many of the techniques that Kelly employed to effect psychotherapeutic change are similar to those used by other therapists. However, in part through exposure to the psychodrama of J. Moreno (Stewart & Barry, 1991), Kelly made a unique contribution to therapeutic methodology by developing and fostering the use of **role playing.** In the course of therapy, if a client mentioned difficulty with a particular interpersonal relationship, such as an overly demanding boss or unsympathetic professor, Kelly would suggest that they pretend they were in the boss's or the professor's office and re-enact the troublesome scene. Afterward, alternative methods of handling the scene would be explored and the scene itself re-enacted and changed in the light of alternative ways in which the client might deal with it in the future. Kelly encouraged the use of role reversal, having the client play the role of the significant figures while he played the client. Role reversal allows the client to understand his or her own participation more fully and also to understand the framework of the other person.

Kelly also used fixed-role therapy, in which he had the client enact the role of someone else for a more protracted period of time. Beginning with the

THINKING CRITICALLY

Assessing Personal Constructs: The Rep Test*

The following activity will help you become acquainted with the Rep Test and also tell you about some of your own personal constructs.

Make up a list of representative persons in your life by choosing from among people you know the individual who most suits each description below. Using the form provided (Figure 15.1 on page 404), write the name of the person in the grid space above the column with the number corresponding to the description.

List of Representative Persons

1. Write your own name in the first blank.

2. Write your mother's first name. If you grew up with a stepmother, write her name instead.

3. Write your father's first name. If you grew up with a stepfather, write his name instead.

4. Write the name of your brother who is nearest your own age. If you had no brother, write the name of a boy near your own age who was most like a brother to you during your early teens.

5. Write the name of your sister who is nearest your own age. If you had no sister, write the name of a girl near your own age who was most like a sister to you during your early teens.

    From this point on do not repeat any names. If a person has already been listed, simply make a second choice.

6. Your wife (or husband) or, if you are not married, your closest present girl (boy) friend.

7. Your closest girl (boy) friend immediately preceding the person mentioned above.

8. Your closest present friend of the same sex as yourself.

9. A person of the same sex as yourself whom you once thought was a close friend but in whom you were badly disappointed later.

10. The minister, priest, or rabbi with whom you would be most willing to talk over your personal feelings about religion.

11. Your physician.

12. The present neighbor whom you know best.

13. A person with whom you have been associated who, for some unexplained reason, appeared to dislike you.

*Reprinted from THE PSYCHOLOGY OF PERSONAL CONSTRUCTS, Volume One, by George A. Kelly, Ph.D., by permission of W. W. Norton & Company, Inc. Copyright 1955 by George A. Kelly.

14. A person whom you would most like to help or for whom you feel sorry.

15. A person with whom you usually feel most uncomfortable.

16. A person whom you have recently met and would like to know better.

17. The teacher who influenced you most when you were in your teens.

18. The teacher whose point of view you found most objectionable.

19. An employer, supervisor, or officer under whom you served during a period of great stress.

20. The most successful person whom you know personally.

21. The happiest person whom you know personally.

22. The person known to you personally who appears to meet the highest ethical standards.

After you have written the names in the space above the columns, look at the first row. There are circles under three persons' names (20, 21, 22). Decide how two of them are alike in an important way and how they differ from the third person. Put an X in each of the two circles under the names of the persons who are alike. Then write on the line under the column headed "Construct" a word or phrase that identifies the likeness. Write the opposite of this characteristic under the heading "Contrast." Now go back and consider all the other people you listed on your grid. If any of them also share the same characteristic, put a check mark under their name. Repeat this procedure until you have completed every row on the form.

When you have completed the form, take a close look at your results. First consider the nature of the constructs you listed. How many different constructs did you list? What kind of constructs were they? Did you tend to make comparisons on the basis of appearance (skinny versus fat) or personality characteristics (thoughtful versus unthoughtful; honest versus dishonest)? Do any of the constructs overlap? You can discover this by examining the pattern of checks and X's in the various rows. If the pattern for one construct (such as honest versus dishonest) is identical to that of another construct (such as sincere versus insincere), you can suspect that these two constructs may really be one and the same for you. To how many different people did you apply each of the constructs? A construct that is applied to a large number of people may be more permeable than one that is restricted to only one person. Are the constructs divided in terms of their application to persons of the same age or sex? This may give you some idea of the limits on the range of your constructs. Now take a look at your list of contrasting constructs. Are there any constructs that you list only as a difference and never as a similarity? If so, you may be reluctant to use that construct. If you list a contrasting pole for one person only, perhaps that construct is impermeable and limited to that person. Are any names associated only with contrasting poles? If so, your relationship to those persons may be rigid and unchanging even though you get along with them. Finally, compare your own column with those of the other people on the list. Which of the other people are you most like?

This analysis will not give you definitive answers; it will simply provide a starting point for further questions. Rather than consider the results on the grid as final, you should use your findings as the basis for additional study of yourself. For example, if you discover identical patterns for two constructs, such as honest versus dishonest and sincere versus insincere, you might ask yourself, "Do I believe that all honest people are sincere?" In other words, use your findings for further questions. Numerous possibilities for self-exploration are initiated by the Rep Test.

client's own character sketch, developed during the phase of elaborating the construct system, the therapist creates a fictitious role for the client to play that is different from the normal role and is designed to help the client explore possible ways of reconstruing experiences. The client is introduced to the fictitious role and asked to try to think, talk, and behave like that other person for a period of a few days or weeks. Obviously, the role must be carefully contrived ahead of time. It must be realistic and not too threatening for the client. Eventually the client may discover that the construct system of the character played is more effective and adopt some of those constructs. More importantly, the client learns that change is a real possibility. Fixed role therapy has proved to be a very creative way to reconstrue the self under professional guidance. Mair (1988) believes that Kelly was reaching toward a new conception of inquiry in which the narrative form becomes very important and psychology is seen as a story-telling discipline.

Kelly believed that his theory had wide implications for social and interpersonal relationships. By actively considering alternative constructions, Kelly suggested, it is possible for us individually and collectively to envision new, more creative ways of dealing with a problematic situation. Take the problem that arises when a teacher observes an inattentive student who does not listen, turns in work late, and appears to put forth very little effort. The teacher might conclude that the pupil is lazy. Kelly would ask us to pose the question: Is this the most fruitful interpretation that the teacher can make, or is it simply a cop-out? Perhaps a different construction would give the teacher more latitude in creatively dealing with the problem. At the same time, the student may have a construction of the classroom situation that is hindering rather than facilitating learning. The student may, for instance, perceive that teachers are out to prove the stupidity of their pupils and play an obliging role.

Kelly acknowledged the integral relation of values and theory. Indeed, his metaphor of the scientist may be seen as a proscription instead of a description of human nature (Walker, 1992). Kalekin-Fishman (1993) believes that Kelly's theory escapes the limitation of radical individualism and enriches our understanding of sociocultural processes by emphasizing shared social construction of reality. As such, it may help us to build a bridge to the social constructionists and deal with the problem of alienation.

Kelly also encouraged the use of group therapy to help solve individual and common problems. The technique of role playing is particularly well adapted to groups, where several people may assist an individual in acting out a scene. By the end of his life, Kelly was suggesting ways in which his theory could be applied to help solve social and international problems. Much of our difficulty as Americans in international relations has been our problem as a nation in understanding how different events are construed or interpreted variously by people in other countries. An enrichment of Kelly's theory, termed *perspectivism,*

THINKING CRITICALLY

Role Playing

Kelly's method of role playing can be fruitfully employed as a way of understanding one's own interpersonal relationships. Ask a close friend to help as you play the role of an important figure in your life. You might wish to play the role of your mother, father, instructor, boss, or boy or girl friend. Ask your friend to play yourself. Identify a problem situation or a potential problem. First consider how your parent, or whoever, would handle the situation. Then act it out, with your friend playing yourself. It is important that you try to look at the situation and behave as you believe your mother, or the other figure, would. Afterward, discuss with your friend what happened and consider alternative ways of handling the scene. Seeing yourself through your friend's eyes may help you to a closer understanding of how you come across to other people. Playing the role of other important people in your life can help you construe their interpretation of the way in which you behave.

It is also possible for the reader to obtain some of the benefits of fixed-role therapy by employing it in a limited scope. Choose one aspect of your personality that you would like to work on. It is important that you choose only one aspect at a time and one with which you feel you can deal relatively comfortably. If you believe that you are generally too passive, you might try to become more assertive. Ask yourself, "How does an assertive person think, respond, or behave in certain situations?" Then for a period of one day, try to pretend that you are an assertive person. You might even give yourself a new name. Of course, all of your friends will call you by the same old name and assume that you are your same old passive self. However, unknown to them, the passive you is taking a day off and the new you is going to respond to them and other events as an assertive person would. When the day is over, take time to consider how you performed in your new role. How did other people react to you? You may find yourself quite surprised by the impact that your new role has had on other people.

conceives of other people as equal partners and promotes tolerance of multiple perspectives (Warren, 1992).

Kelly's Theory: Philosophy, Science, and Art

Although Kelly encouraged us to think of the person as a scientist, his discussion of the way we validate personal constructs involved the compelling character of philosophical insights as well. Kelly's theory suggests that a construct is validated if the anticipations it gives rise to occur. Validation refers to the compatibility between one's predictions and one's observation of the outcome, both of

PHILOSOPHICAL ASSUMPTIONS

Examining Kelly

How would you rate Kelly on each of the basic philosophical assumptions described in Chapter 1? Each basic issue was presented as a bipolar dimension along which a person's view can be placed according to the degree of agreement with one or the other extreme. Rate Kelly's views on these issues.

When you have determined where you think Kelly stands, compare your responses with those of your classmates and your instructor. You should be willing to defend your ratings, but also be prepared to change them in light of others' compelling arguments. Afterward, compare your rating of Kelly with your own position on each issue and with those of other theorists. Does this comparison help you to understand why his theory does or does not appeal to you?

Would strongly agree	Would agree	Is neutral or believes in synthesis of both views	Would agree	Would strongly agree
1	2	3	4	5

freedom	**determinism**
People basically have control over their own behavior and understand the motives behind their behavior.	The behavior of people is basically determined by internal or external forces over which they have little, if any, control.

which are subjectively construed. This form of everyday validation does not precisely parallel the controlled procedures of science. A scientist testing hypotheses does not look for events that will verify the hypotheses but rather sets up conditions that might falsify them. In a well-designed experiment one's anticipations are of little consequence to the outcome of the hypothesis (Rychlak, 1973, 1990). In Kelly's theory people are philosophers as well as scientists, or, at least, the scientific activities in which they engage are predicated on a philosophical stance. Kelly candidly acknowledged that his view of the person as a scientist was based on the philosophical position of constructive alternativism.

Kelly's theory is better known in England and Europe than in the United States (see also Feixas, 1989). There, industrial-organizational psychologists, management development specialists, and occupational counselors have computerized the

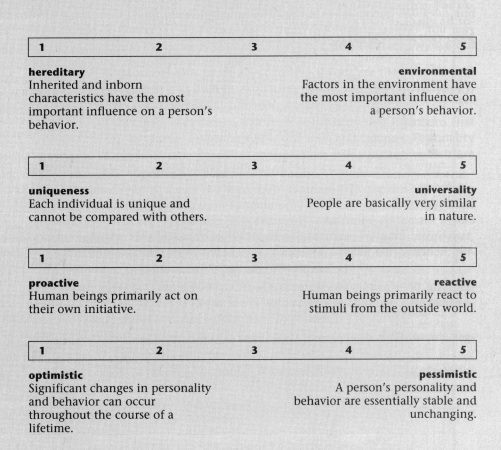

| 1 | 2 | 3 | 4 | 5 |

hereditary
Inherited and inborn characteristics have the most important influence on a person's behavior.

environmental
Factors in the environment have the most important influence on a person's behavior.

| 1 | 2 | 3 | 4 | 5 |

uniqueness
Each individual is unique and cannot be compared with others.

universality
People are basically very similar in nature.

| 1 | 2 | 3 | 4 | 5 |

proactive
Human beings primarily act on their own initiative.

reactive
Human beings primarily react to stimuli from the outside world.

| 1 | 2 | 3 | 4 | 5 |

optimistic
Significant changes in personality and behavior can occur throughout the course of a lifetime.

pessimistic
A person's personality and behavior are essentially stable and unchanging.

Rep Test and grid and have seen enormous potential for the instrument as an assessment device in industry. In spite of the fact that Kelly's own writings were scholarly and academic in tone, replete with their own technical vocabulary, his personal construct theory lends itself well to industrial-organizational psychology, in which there is a need for the psychologist to speak the language of the employee rather than that of the psychologist (Jankowicz, 1987). Translated into lay terms and concretely applied to the everyday lives of individuals, Kelly's theory is particularly relevant in the workplace.

Kelly emphasized the rationality of the human being. He believed that as the scientific world becomes increasingly sophisticated, the constructs we form are increasingly more successful approximations of reality. Nevertheless, he did not believe that the world or the person is ultimately knowable through a scientific methodology. Science is simply a construct system that helps us explain events. It is one system of constructs among many alternatives. Since we cannot posit any objective reality apart from our understanding of it, we cannot assert that science can ever comprehend the real person. It can, however, provide useful constructions that assist us in making predictions. This point of view characterized Kelly's attitude toward his own philosophizing and theorizing as well, since he readily acknowledged and expected that his own theory would ultimately be succeeded by an alternative construction (1970). "At best," he wrote, "it is an ad interim theory" (1955).

In spite of the "ad interim" character of Kelly's theory, it has attracted considerable attention and controversy. Kelly has been brought to task for his overly intellectual view of the individual and therapy, his neglect of developmental antecedents, his failure to deal adequately with human emotions, and his insistence on dichotomous concepts. The biggest criticism of Kelly's work has been that he ignored the full range of the human personality in his effort to do justice to the human intellect (Bruner & Rogers, 1956).

Although Kelly insisted that his theory was not a cognitive one, his work foreshadowed the contemporary interest in cognitive factors in personality. As such, some critics suggest that Kelly's theory is a "classic that was ahead of its time" (Rorer & Widiger, 1983, p. 426). At the same time, psychologists who are influenced by information processing models (discussed in Chapter 9) often conceive of Kelly's constructs as schemas, scripts, or neural networks when in fact Kelly's personal constructs are structures of the phenomenal field.

By viewing personal constructions as the primary factor governing personality, Kelly developed a theory that encompasses cognitive, emotional, behavioral, perceptual, and motivational aspects of personality. Perhaps this is why Kelly was entertained by various efforts to classify his theory. After he gave a lecture at Harvard, Kelly noted that "Professor Gordon Allport explained to the students that my theory was not a 'cognitive' theory but an 'emotional' theory. Later the same afternoon, Dr. Henry Murray called me aside and said, 'You know, don't you, that you are really an existentialist'" (in Mahler, 1969, p. 216; see also Soffer, 1993).

However one wishes to classify Kelly's theory, his emphasis on construction is compatible with recent trends in cognitive psychology, and, thus, his theory is likely to continue to attract attention. Moreover, his techniques of assessment and role playing have proved to be very useful tools in psychotherapy, education, and industry.

Summary

1. Kelly suggested that we view ourselves as scientists because, in our efforts to understand the world, we develop constructs that act as hypotheses.

2. His theory is based on the philosophical position of **constructive alternativism,** the assumption that any one event is open to a number of interpretations.

3. Kelly's fundamental postulate is "A person's processes are psychologically channelized by the ways in which he anticipates events." He elaborates on his fundamental postulate with eleven corollaries: construction, individuality, organization, dichotomy, choice, range, experience, modulation, fragmentation, communality, and sociality.

4. Kelly gave new meanings to many traditional concepts in personality theorizing, such as the **self-construct,** role, learning, motivation, and emotion.

5. Kelly developed the Rep Test, which permits a person to reveal his or her constructs by comparing and contrasting a number of different persons in his or her life.

6. In his psychotherapy Kelly sought to help his patient reconstrue the world by first elaborating the complaint and then elaborating the construct system. His unique contribution was the technique of role playing.

7. Kelly has been criticized for being too intellectual and for failing to deal with the whole of personality or the emotions.

8. The way in which we validate personal constructs involves philosophical insights as well as scientific methods.

Suggestions for Further Reading

George Kelly was not a prolific writer. Two books and about a dozen articles constitute the sum of his publications. His basic theory was published in a two-volume work called *The Psychology of Personal Constructs* (Norton, 1955). The first three chapters of those volumes were published separately as *A Theory of Personality: A Psychology of Personal Constructs* (Norton, 1963). Kelly's writing is rather academic and difficult reading for the lay person, who might be better advised to begin with a good secondary source such as D. Bannister and F. Fransella, *Inquiring Man: The Theory of Personal Constructs* (Penguin, 1966) or D. Bannister, *New Perspectives in Personal Construct Theory* (Academic Press, 1985). Donald Bannister, an Englishman, is Kelly's most fervent disciple.

CHAPTER 16

Cognitive-Behavioral Theorists: Albert Ellis, Aaron Beck, and Arnold Lazarus

YOUR GOALS FOR THIS CHAPTER

1. Discuss the philosophical origins of Ellis's *rational-emotive therapy*.
2. Explain the theory behind Ellis's rational-emotive therapy.
3. Discuss the *A-B-C theory of personality* and tell how people develop irrational and *mustabatory* belief systems.
4. Explain how people get their belief systems.
5. Explain the goal of rational-emotive therapy and tell how it is achieved.
6. Compare the contrast Ellis's theory with other theorists.
7. Discuss the philosophical origins of Beck's cognitive theory.
8. Discuss the theory of personality behind *cognitive therapy*.
9. Explain what is meant by *cognitions, schemas,* and *cognitive distortions.*
10. Discuss the dimensions of *sociotrophy* and *autonomy*.
11. Describe the *cognitive triad.*
12. Give an overview of Beck's cognitive therapy.
13. Describe some cognitive and behavioral techniques used in cognitive therapy.
14. Discuss assessment and research in Beck's theory and compare him with other theorists.
15. Discuss the development of Lazarus's theory and the *BASIC-ID.*
16. Describe the personality theory behind *multimodal therapy*.
17. Describe *multimodal therapy.*
18. Evaluate behavioral cognitive therapies and theories in terms of their function as philosophy, science, and art.

In recent years, behavioral cognitive therapies have revolutionized the fields of psychotherapy and counseling. Albert Ellis, Aaron Beck, and Arnold Lazarus are primarily clinicians who have developed techniques and strategies for helping people cope better with their problems. These theorists became disgusted with the relatively long (and to them inefficient) process of psychoanalysis and created counseling methods that are often very brief, client-centered, and to the point. Rather than take a long time to bring out issues that are related to events in the distant past, they deal directly with elements of the client's immediate present and attempt to change existing thoughts or client values. In their writing, they primarily talk about the type of therapy that they do. Nevertheless, their counseling and therapy strategies are based on underlying theories (although they are not necessarily clearly articulated or a primary concern of these thinkers, who emphasize practical advantages over theoretical orientations). While these theories are a little difficult to extract from their writings, we can try to examine them as theories of personality. The significance of these clinicians is apparent when we note that a survey of clinical and counseling psychologists on the "Ten Most Influential Psychotherapists" (D. Smith, 1982) placed Ellis second. Beck seventh, and Lazarus fifth.

Albert Ellis: Biographical Background

Albert Ellis (1991) does not believe that his childhood experiences shaped his becoming a psychotherapist. Born September 27, 1913, in Pittsburgh and raised "on the streets of the Bronx," Ellis says that he was a "semiorphan" because his father (before his parents were divorced) did a great deal of traveling and spent little time with him and his younger brother and sister. He believes that his mother was totally unprepared to raise children. As a result, Ellis suggests, "I was almost as instrumental in raising my mother (and, to an even greater degree my younger brother and sister) as she was in raising me."

Neglected by his parents, he was also ill (with nephritis, chronic inflammation of the kidney, which led to severe headaches), frequently hospitalized, and not permitted to engage in active childhood play. Shy and introverted, he was readily exceeded by his brave extraverted brother. To top things off, during the Great Depression, the family just barely managed without having to go on welfare.

With an incompetent mother, a brother who "acted out" and a sister who "whined," you might think that the stage was set for a pretty miserable childhood. Nevertheless, Ellis "refused to be miserable." In his immediate family, only his sister suffered from depression and anxiety, leading him to speculate that emotional disorders are due to genetics rather than environmental factors. Fortunately, when they became adults, Ellis's rational-emotive therapy (RET) was able to help her.

He went to the High School of Commerce in New York with the intent to quickly become a millionaire, but upon graduation the Great Depression shattered that dream. He enrolled in City College, where he ended up majoring in

Albert Ellis

English. He did a great deal of writing, supporting himself with odd jobs. When he could not get any of his six novels published, he decided to focus on nonfiction.

It was sex that launched him into clinical psychology. Wanting to write about promiscuity, he did a great deal of reading in erotic fiction and nonfiction. Friends began to ask him to assist them in solving some of their problems. He found that he was good at helping and enjoyed doing it, and decided to begin graduate training. At Teachers College of Columbia University he received his M.A. degree and matriculated for the Ph.D. Ellis wanted to write his dissertation on love, but two prudish members of the department censored the topic, leading him to deliberately choose and successfully defend a dull and harmless topic. *A Comparison of the Use of Direct and Indirect Phrasing with Personality Questionnaires.* He thereby became very knowledgeable about personality inventories.

Returning to his love of research on sex, Ellis wrote a great many articles and books that became very popular. He spent six years in analysis and was trained at the Horney Institute for Psychoanalysis. He found he was an effective analyst but gave it up in 1953 because he was looking for a more "efficient" method. Ellis had rapidly risen to a position of high authority in the state of

New Jersey, but "prudes" in the state system objected to his research in sex, so he left New Jersey in 1952, became a well-known practicing psychologist in New York, and continued to write.

In 1955, Ellis began to do rational-emotive therapy. Rational-emotive therapy is the first primary cognitive-behavioral therapy and Ellis is proud to have been its founder. His career soared in the 1960s due to the popularity of his books and therapy method and he founded the Institute for Rational-Emotive Therapy in New York.

In the late 1960s and early 1970s, Ellis began to remake RET, "making it both simpler and more complex" (1991). In the 1990s this incredibly busy, productive, and controversial man continues to actively practice, write, and conduct workshops.

Philosophical Origins

The philosophic origins of rational-emotive therapy go back to the Stoic philosophers, particularly Epictetus (60–120) and Marcus Aurelius (121–180). Although most early Stoic writings have been lost, Epictetus wrote in the first century of the common era in his work the *Encheiridion* (or Handbook), "People are disturbed not by things, but by the view which they take of them." Emotions, the stoics believed, are an ethical disease that obstructs the reason from making sound choices.

The modern precursor of rational-emotive theory was Alfred Adler. In his first book on individual psychology, Adler's motto was "Everything depends on opinion." It would be hard to state one of the essential tenets of rational-emotive theory more accurately.

The Theory of Rational-Emotive Therapy (RET)

Ellis (1978) points out that from the beginning rational-emotive therapy has denoted a theory of personality that arises from its theory of personality change.

Ellis (1958) suggests that human beings are "sign-, symbol-, and language-creating" animals who have four fundamental processes: perception, movement, thinking, and emotion. These are all necessarily interrelated. Thus thinking not only entails brain activity (such as remembering, learning, and problem solving); it also entails perception, emotion, and movement. Therefore it would be more accurate to say that a person "perceives-moves-feels-THINKS about" a problem than to simply say he or she "thinks" about it. Likewise emotion is not one thing but a combination of related phenomena. Thus cognitions, emotions, and behavior are consistently interactional and transactional. The theory behind rational-emotive therapy is a comprehensive cognitive-affective behavioral one viewing cognition and emotion integratively and seeing thought as normally included and being triggered by some degree of desire or feeling and seeing feeling as significantly including cognition (Ellis, 1962).

Since thoughts and emotions frequently overlap, much of what we consider emotion is a type of evaluative thinking. Perhaps it is somewhat less dispassionate than that which we usually label thinking, but nevertheless it may be seen as a type of thought. Since humans are raised in a social culture in which thinking and emoting are highly interrelated, thinking and emotion tend to develop into a cause and effect relationship, "so that one's thinking *becomes* one's emotion and emoting *becomes* one's thought." These processes tend to assume a type of "self-talk" in which our "internalized sentences" determine our thoughts and emotions. While it is conceivably possible to have a momentary outburst of emotion without thought, in order to sustain the emotion it has to be backed up by some form of thought (1958). Thus, the basic personality theory of rational-emotive theory suggests that human beings largely create their own emotional consequences.

Ellis believes that people have strong innate inclinations to live and be happy, to seek pleasure and to avoid pain. They are goal-oriented active and changing creatures with a strong compulsion to fulfill their potential.

Nevertheless, people of all ages engage in numerous unrational throughts, unsuitable feelings, and dysfunctional behaviors that are inclined to undermine their potential. People are born with a distinct proneness to engage in self-destructive behavior and learn, through social conditioning, to exacerbate rather than to minimize that proneness. They, nonetheless, have considerable ability to understand that what they are foolishly believing may be causing their distress, and to train themselves to change their self-sabotaging beliefs, emotions, and behavior.

Most of these human self-sabotaging tendencies may be summarized by stating that humans are born with an exceptionally strong tendency to want, to "need," and to condemn first themselves, others, and then the world when they do not immediately get what they supposedly "need." They consequently think "childishly" or "humanly" all their lives and are able only with enormous difficulty to achieve and maintain "mature" or realistic behavior (1976).

People grow up in social groups and spend much of their energy trying to impress, live up to the expectations of, and outdo the performances of other people. On the surface they are "ego-oriented," "identity seeking" or "self-centered." Even more importantly, however, they usually define them selves as "good" or "worthwhile" when they believe that others accept and approve of them. Ellis says that it is realistic and sane for people to find or fulfill "themselves" in their interpersonal relations and to have a considerable amount of what Adler called social interest.

However, what we call emotional disturbance is frequently associated with people's caring too much about what others think and stems from their believing they can accept themselves only if others think well of them. When disturbed, people escalate their desire for others' approval and the practical advantages that normally go with such approval into an absolute *dire need* to be liked, and they can hardly avoid becoming anxious and prone to depression (Bernard 1986; Ellis 1962, 1987, 1988; Ellis & Dryden, 1987; Ellis & Harper, 1975).

Given that we are beings in the world, it is quite important that others to some degree value us: but it is not *all* important that they regard us very highly, and it is our tendency to exaggerate the importance of others' acceptance that often causes our inappropriate emotions (Ellis 1985a, 1985b; Ellis & Becker, 1982, Ellis & Dryden 1987).

The **A-B-C theory of personality** behind rational-emotive therapy holds that when a highly charged *emotional consequence* (C) (such as an anxiety attack) follows a significant *activation event* (A) (such as being chased by a large dog), A may seem to but actually does not cause C. Instead, emotional consequences are largely created by (B), the individual's *belief system* (Oh, dear, all dogs are dangerous and that is horrible). "If two people get labeled 'stupid,' and one laughs at the statement and the other feels depressed, we cannot explain these radically different Consequences by A (the Activating Event) but rather by B (the Belief System) *about* A" (1978).

When an undesirable emotional consequence occurs, such as severe anxiety, it can usually be traced to the person's irrational beliefs. When these beliefs are effectively challenged (at point D) by *disputing* them rationally and behaviorally (Some, but not all, dogs are dangerous, thus while it pays to be prudent, you don't have to be afraid of and avoid all dogs), the disturbed consequences are minimized and greatly decreased (see Figure 16.1).

According to the theory behind rational-emotive therapy, people become psychologically disordered by needlessly upsetting themselves. When individuals feel upset at point C, after experiencing an obnoxious occurrence at point A, they almost always convince themselves of highly inappropriate, irrational beliefs (B's) such as: "I can't stand this activating event! It is awful that it exists! It shouldn't exist! I am a worthless person for not being able to ward it off or immediately get rid of it. You are a louse for inflicting it on me!"

This set of beliefs is irrational because people *can* stand the noxious activating event, even though they may never like it, and it is hardly *awful* because awful is an essentially undefinable term, with surplus meaning and no empirical referent. By calling the noxious activation event *awful*, the disturbed individual means it is highly inconvenient, disadvantageous, and unbeneficial. However, what noxious stimulus can be, in point of fact, more than highly inconvenient? By contending that they are worthless persons because they have not been able to ward off an unfortunate activating event, people think that they should be able to control the universe, and that because they are not succeeding in doing what they cannot do, they are obviously worthless. This makes two unprovable premises.

The basic tenet of the theory behind rational-emotive therapy is that emotional upsets, as distinguished from feelings of sorrow, regret, annoyance, and

A. Activation Event

B. Belief System

Oh dear, all dogs are dangerous and that is horrible.

C. Emotional Consequence

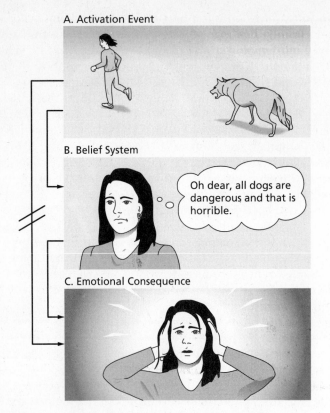

A does *not* cause C; rather, B does.

Figure 16.1 *Ellis's A-B-C Theory*
The A-B-C theory of personality holds that when a highly charged emotional consequent (C) follows a significant activation event (A), A may seem to, but actually does not, cause C. Instead, emotional consequences are largely created by B — the individual's belief system.

frustration, are caused by irrational beliefs. These beliefs are irrational because they magically insist that something in the universe should, ought, or must be different from the way it really is. Although these irrational beliefs are thought to be connected with reality, they are actually magical ideas beyond the realm of science.

Once people upset themselves there is a tendency to escalate and to become even more upset. These inappropriate feelings usually interfere with people doing something constructive about the noxious activating events, and people tend to condemn themselves for their unconstructiveness and to experience more feelings of shame, inferiority, and hopelessness. A vicious circle develops.

It doesn't matter to Ellis what the original activating event that you are damning is about, because the activating event A is not really that important. People eventually tend to end up with a chain of disturbed reactions that is only obliquely related to the original "traumatic event" of life. That is why Ellis finds psychoanalytic theories quite misleading—they strongly emphasize early events rather than a person's self-condemnatory attitudes *about* these events—and that is why their therapies are virtually powerless to help with any secondary disturbance, such as fear of fear. Most major personality theories also concentrate either on A, the activating events in a person's life, or on C, the emotional consequences experienced subsequent to the occurrence of these events, and rarely consider B, the belief system, which is the vital factor in the creation of the disturbance.

According to Ellis, there is not too much we can do by concentrating attention on life events that belong to the past. There is nothing that anyone can do to change those prior happenings. As for clients' present feelings, the more we focus on them, the worse they are likely to feel. If we keep talking about their anxiety, they can easily become more anxious. The most logical way to interrupt the process is to get people to focus on and dispute their anxiety-creating belief system.

If people think and work hard at understanding and contradicting what Ellis calls **mustabatory belief systems** in which they escalate probabilistic statements into absolutes (1978), they can make amazing curative and preventive changes in their disturbance-creating tendencies. Instead of thinking "I must always have the approval of other people," they can think "I like to have the approval of other people, but I know I am not always going to get it." Thus the personality theory behind rational-emotive therapy "may at first sound grim and pessimistic" (1987), but it is actually very realistic. It is also highly optimistic and pragmatic.

How do people get their belief systems? Ellis believes that heredity has a large influence in that as human beings we inherit a great many biological hedonistic predispositions and a high degree of "teachability." Ellis believes that "probably 80 percent of the variance of human behavior rests on biological bases and about 20 percent on environmental training" (1978). We inherit a tendency to raise cultural *preferences* into *musts* and social *norms* into absolute *shoulds*.

There are so many variables (both internal and external, conscious and unconscious) that lead to the origin and maintenance of personality that Ellis believes there are no simple answers concerning the existence of traits or explanations of certain behavior. While behavior is somewhat determined by internal and external forces, Ellis believes people do have *some,* albeit limited, free will and capability of changing their behavior patterns. While he recognizes that we can make some general statements about what people have in common, he also believes that each individual is unique and must assume responsibility for his or her behavior. In spite of his strong emphasis on heredity, Ellis would place himself firmly in the proactive camp.

Rational-Emotive Psychotherapy

Albert Ellis takes a very directive approach in his rational therapy and argues strongly for the view that people must judge their behavior not in terms of what others may believe, but in terms of what they sense is right for them. The goal of therapy for Ellis is to enable clients to commit themselves to actions that correspond to their true value system. The goal of therapy should not be to understand the causes or to remove the symptoms of pathological behavior, but rather to free individuals to develop a constructive and confident image of their self-worth. Clients should be led to appreciate their "true identity" and encouraged to venture forth to test their personal tastes and values.

If clients are helped to focus on their irrational thinking and inappropriate emoting and behaving by a highly active, directive, didactic, philosophic, homework-assigning therapist, they are more likely to change their symptom-creating beliefs than if they mainly work with a dynamically oriented, client-centered, existentialist, or classical behavior-modification therapist (Ellis 1978, 1985a, 1987; Ellis & Dryden 1987).

Three main therapeutic processes are used in rational-emotive theory: (1) cognitive, (2) emotive-evocative, and (3) behavioral.

Rational-emotive **cognitive therapy** attempts to show clients how to recognize their should and must thoughts, how to separate rational from irrational beliefs, and how to accept reality. It assumes that clients can think, can think about their thinking, and can even think about thinking about their thinking. In one-to-one sessions, the therapists not only listens but also gives information and seeks to stimulate clients to explore their own philosophy of life. In group therapy or workshops, members are encouraged to discuss, explain, and reason with one another.

Emotive-evocative therapy employs role-playing, psychodrama, humor, and other ideas such as unconditional acceptance to reduce disturbance-creating ideas to absurdity; to convince clients that others can accept them with their failings; and to get in touch with their "shameful" feelings so they can zero in on the exact things they are telling themselves to create these feelings.

Behavior therapy is employed in rational-emotive theory not only to help clients change maladaptive patterns of behavior but also to help change their cognition. Thus, clients can be told to deliberately fail at a small task in order to survive a failure and thus learn that it is not dangerous. Clients may be persuaded to momentarily stay in a difficult situation, such as an uncomfortable job or marriage, in order to work on the problem. RET therapists give specific active homework assignments and may suggest that clients develop penalties for failure to do their assignments.

Ellis's first paper on RET (1958) pointed out how cognitions, emotions, and behaviors are consistently interactional and transactional. Early RET papers advocated **in vitro desensitization**, a process whereby anxieties and fears are reduced by repeated imagined exposure to the noxious stimuli paired with re-

THINKING CRITICALLY

A Self-Help Form

The Institute for Rational-Emotive Therapy has developed a Self-Help Form that can be useful for individuals trying to identify irrational beliefs that lead to emotional disturbance or self-defeating behavior.

First you are asked to identify an activating event which precipitates a negative consequence or condition that you would like to change. For example, the prospect of having to drive on a high-speed highway makes me very anxious and leads me to avoid such trips.

Then you identify those irrational beliefs that lead to your self-defeating feelings and behavior. For example:

1. I <u>must</u> do things perfectly.
2. I am a <u>worthless person</u> if I become anxious.
3. I <u>must</u> be approved and accepted by other people.
4. People <u>must</u> live up to my expectations, and if they don't it is terrible.
5. It is <u>awful</u> or <u>horrible</u> when major things don't go my way.

Next you develop a dispute for each of your irrational beliefs.
For example:

1. Why <u>must</u> I do things perfectly?
2. Where is it written that I am a worthless person if I become anxious?
3. Why do people <u>have to</u> approve or accept everything I do?
4. Many people do not live up to my expectations. It's disappointing, but not terrible.
5. Is it really <u>awful</u> or <u>horrible</u> when major things don't go my way? Or only a hassle or inconvenience.

Finally, work on coming up with an effective rational belief to replace your irrational beliefs. For example:

1. I'd <u>prefer</u> to do very well, but I don't always <u>have</u> to.
2. I can be a worthwhile person and still feel a little anxious.
3. While it is nice to be approved and accepted by everybody, it isn't absolutely necessary. I won't die of rejection.
4. It's disappointing when people don't live up to my expectations but it is not the end of the world.
5. It's pretty inconvenient when major things don't go my way; and I don't <u>like</u> it, but I can stand it.

After you have come up with some effective rational beliefs for some of the activating events which used to create problems for you, notice the different types of feelings and behaviors that you experience. By thinking rationally when negative events occur, you will be more likely to feel _appropriate_ feelings, such as disappointment or frustration—rather than _disturbed_ feelings such as rage, anxiety, or depression.

Continue to regularly practice and repeat these rational beliefs to yourself—out loud—in order to help yourself feel better and behave more rationally.

This exercise is based on the RET Self-Help Form published by the Institute for Rational-Emotive Therapy, 45 E. 65th Street, New York, NY 10021.

laxation, skill training, and other behavioral techniques. Thus individuals who were anxious about driving on major high-speed highways might first be taught how to deeply relax (a skill that can be learned, but takes practice) and then to imagine themselves driving on a highway as a safe, competent driver. If there was any question about their driving ability, they might be encouraged to take a driving class. Other goal-oriented steps might be encouraged as well to help them maintain a reasonable speed, and so forth. Some RET therapists favor **implosive** (or sudden, instead of gradual in vitro) confrontation of phobic situations, depending on the circumstances. Later RET embraced experiential-encounter techniques, and Ellis invented some of his own, such as his well-known "shame-attacking exercises" (Ellis, 1969, 1971a).

The rational-emotive theory of psychotherapy asserts that there are many kinds of psychological treatment and that most of them work to some degree. An efficient system of therapy includes (a) economy of time and effort, (b) rapid symptom reduction, (c) effectiveness with a large cross-section of clients, (d) solution-oriented discussions, and (e) long-term results that last. Ellis (1987a) says that rational-emotive theory is realistic and unindulgent. It gets to the core of and ruthlessly persists at undermining childish demandingness, the main element of serious emotional disturbance.

Unlike many other systems of psychotherapy, Ellis emphasizes the biological aspects of human personality. Although Ellis holds that people have vast untapped resources for growth and that they are in many important ways able to change their social and personal destinies, he also holds that they have exceptionally powerful innate tendencies to think irrationally and to harm themselves (Ellis, 1976).

The rational therapist assumes that people somehow imbibe illogical ideas or irrational modes of thinking and that, without doing so, they could hardly be as disturbed as they are. It is the therapist's function not merely to show clients their irrational ideas or thinking processes but to persuade them to change and substitute for them more rational ideas and thought processes. Rational-emotive therapy employs many techniques such as role-playing, or free association and other expressive emotive techniques, but the therapist does not isolate her- or himself but rather acts "as his or her own person" (1987) so that these relationship-building techniques really get to the core of illogical thinking and induce clients to think in a more rational manner.

The rational-emotive therapist will keep pounding away, time and again, at the illogical ideas that underlie the client's fears. This means showing the client that it is not fear of father but fear of being blamed, of being disapproved, of being unloved, of being imperfect, of being a failure.

Ellis (1987) points out that eclecticism is "hardly new to RET." His willingness to draw creatively from many areas of effective psychotherapy is impressive.

Comparisons and Contrasts with Other Theorists

Ellis largely agrees with Freud that the pleasure principle tends to run most people's lives. He agrees with Karen Horney and Erich Fromm that cultural influences as well as early family influence tend to play a significant part in building up people's irrational thinking; with Alfred Adler that fictitious goals tend to order and run human lives; with Gordon Allport that once individuals begin to think and act in a certain manner, they find it very difficult to think or act differently, even when they really want to. He also agrees that Ivan Pavlov that humans' large cerebral cavities provide them with a secondary signaling system through which they often become cognitively conditioned; with Jerome Frank that people are especially prone to the influence of suggestion; and with Jean Piaget that active teaching is much more effective than passive learning. Moreover, he agrees with Sigmund and Anna Freud that people frequently refuse to acknowledge their mistakes and resort to defenses and rationalizations that cover up underlying feelings of shame and self-deprecation; and with Abraham Maslow and Carl Rogers that humans, however disturbed they may be, have great potential for continued growth and development.

On the other hand, Ellis has serious objections to certain aspects of many popular personality theories. He opposes the Freudian concept that people have clear-cut libidinous instincts, which if unduly satisfied or thwarted must lead to emotional disturbance. He thinks in terms of human senses, which become needs only when people foolishly define them as such.

Ellis places the Oedipus complex as a relatively minor subheading under people's major irrational belief that they absolutely have to receive the approval of their parents. Virtually all so-called sexual problems partly result from peoples' irrational beliefs that they need approval.

Ellis holds that parenting and early childhood environment do not create irrational belief systems. He does admit that people quite generally add their own rigid commands and musts to the sayings and values handed down by parents.

Ellis looks skeptically at anything mystical, devout, transpersonal, or magical. He believes that reason itself is limited, ungodlike, and not absolute (Ellis, 1962, 1985c, 1991). He holds that people may in some way transcend themselves in altered states of consciousness, they can become more competent but they remain human. Ellis's favorite saying, which he often wears on his T-shirt, is, "I am a fallible human being, and make mistakes." He believes that people have thoughts and feelings that are just below the level of consciousness. These unconscious thoughts and feelings can be brought to consciousness by some brief directive questioning (Dryden, 1984; 1988; Ellis & Bernard, 1983, 1985; Ellis & Dryden, 1987; Ellis, McInerney, DiGiuseppe, & Yaeger, 1988).

Aaron T. Beck: Biographical Background

Aaron T. Beck was born in Providence, Rhode Island, on July 18, 1921. He has not written about his childhood. He graduated from Brown University magna cum laude in 1943 and was elected to Phi Beta Kappa. The Yale School of Medicine granted him the M.D. in 1946. During the next two years, he was at the Rhode Island Hospital as a rotating intern and did his residency in pathology. The following two years, he was at the Cushing Veterans Administration Hospital in Framingham, Massachusetts, as a resident in neurology and also psychiatry. The next two years he served as a fellow in psychiatry at the Austen Riggs Center, in Stockbridge, Massachusetts. The American Board of Psychiatry and Neurology certified him in psychiatry in 1953. The following year, he joined the faculty of the Department of Psychiatry of the University of Pennsylvania Medical School where he has been ever since. In his early years at the university, he received training in psychoanalysis from the Philadelphia Psychoanalytic Institute, where he graduated in 1958.

Following his education, Beck set out "to prove to the world that analytic theory was correct." But he was unable to get that proof in a study of depressed people's dreams. Beck had hypothesized on the basis of Freud's theory that their dreams "would contain more hostility than those of nondepressed people. . . . Instead their dreams reflected three common themes: defeat, deprivation, and loss." This failure led him eventually to develop cognitive therapy as a way of understanding and treating depression. He began to believe that "depressed people did not seek failure; rather they distorted reality to the point where they could not recognize success when it happened" (Greenburg, 1981).

In addition to his teaching duties at the University of Pennsylvania, Beck has administered research of issues such as depression, suicide, anxiety and panic disorders, substance abuse, marital problems, and personality disorders. He has received a number of honors for his contributions to the comprehension and therapy of depression, anxiety, and suicidal behaviors. His alma mater, Brown, gave him an honorary Doctor of Medical Science in 1982 and the Distinguished Alumnus Award in 1990. In 1987, he was elected a fellow of the Royal College of Psychiatrists. Beck has written or coauthored over 250 articles and eight books. He has also developed a number of assessment instruments.

Aaron Beck

Philosophical Origins

Cognitive therapy's theoretical foundation is derived from three main sources: the phenomenological approach to psychology, structural theory and depth psychology, and cognitive psychology. The phenomenological approach holds that an individual's view of self and the personal world are central to behavior. This approach is demonstrated in the writings of Adler (1936), Alexander (1950), Horney (1950), Sullivan (1953), and Rogers (1959).

The second major influence is the structural theory and depth psychology of Kant (1798) and Freud, particularly Freud's concept of the hierarchical structuring of cognition into primary and secondary processes.

Finally, more modern developments in cognitive psychology have had an impact. George Kelly (1955) is credited with being the first among contemporaries to derive the cognitive model through his use of "personal constructs" and his emphasis on the role of beliefs in behavior change even though he did not like being called a cognitivist. Cognitive theories of emotion, such as those of Magda Arnold (1960) and Richard Lazarus (1984), which stress the importance of cognition in emotional and behavioral change, have also contributed to cognitive theory.

The Theory Behind Cognitive Therapy

Cognitive therapy is based on a theory of personality that maintains that how one thinks largely determines how one feels and behaves. Similar in many ways to rational-emotive theory and therapy, which preceded but developed parallel to Beck's cognitive theory and therapy, Beck's system has acquired strong empirical support for its theoretical foundations. Both Ellis and Beck believe that people can consciously adapt reason, and both view the client's underlying assumptions as targets of intervention. While Ellis confounded and persuaded clients that the philosophies they lived by were irrational, Beck "turned the client into a colleague who researches verifiable reality" (Wessler, 1986, p. 5).

While one might wish to argue that Beck's cognitive therapy is just a therapy and *not* a theory of personality, nevertheless there is an underlying concept of personality. Beck views personality as reflecting the individual's cognitive organization and structure, which are both biologically and socially influenced. Within the constraints of one's neuroanatomy and biochemistry, personal learning experiences help determine how one develops and responds. Beck further views personality as shaped by central values, or superordinate schemas, and sees psychological distress as "caused" by a number of factors. People may have biochemical predispositions to illness. Childhood depression may foreshadow depression later in life (Goleman, 1994). However, people respond to specific stressors because of their learning. Thus Beck has said, "People are missing the boat if they say that because it can be treated by drugs, depression is primarily biological in nature. . . . People who receive psychotherapy learn something; people on drugs don't." "Biochemical changes probably do occur in the brain during depression, he adds, but those come back into balance once the person recovers through therapy" (Greenberg, 1981). Psychopathology is on a continuum with normal emotional reactions. Sometimes emotions are exaggerated. In depression, sadness and loss of interest are intensified and prolonged, in mania there is grandiosity, and in anxiety there is fear of fear.

The concepts involved in Beck's cognitive theory include cognitions, schemas, and cognitive distortions or errors in logic (1979). **Cognitions** refer to a person's awareness. They are rather changeable and brought about by stimuli. An example of a negative cognition is the feeling "I'm a total failure."

Cognitive Schemas

Schemas are cognitive structures that consist of an individual's fundamental core beliefs and assumptions about how the world operates. These schemas develop early in life from personal experiences and identification with significant others. People form concepts about themselves, others, and the world. These schemas shape personality. Schemas may be adaptive or maladaptive. They may be general or specific in nature. The behavioral and emotional patterns that make up personality, therefore, are derived from individual rules about life and beliefs about the self. Examples of schemas are "Unless other people approve of me, I am worthless" or "Unless I can do something perfectly, I should not do it at all." Schemas are much more stable than cognitions but they are somewhat dependent on a person's moods.

Cognitive Distortions

Systematic errors in reasoning called **cognitive distortions** are evident during psychological distress (Beck, 1967). Distortions in cognitions arise when stressful events trigger an unrealistic schemata. Each individual has a set of idiosyncratic vulnerabilities that predispose the person to psychological distress in a unique way. These vulnerabilities appear related to personality structure and cognitive schema.

There a number of these cognitive distortions. *Arbitrary interference* entails drawing a specific conclusion without supporting evidence, even in the face of contradictory evidence (for example, after getting a C rather than an A on the first test, a student might erroneously conclude that she would not be able to pass the course). *Selective abstraction* refers to conceptualizing a situation on the basis of a detail taken out of context and ignoring all other possible explanations (for example, an individual who is nervous about getting into an accident while driving will zero in on all the reports about traffic accidents on the morning news, reconfirming the belief that driving is a dangerous activity). *Overgeneralization* involves abstracting a general rule from one or two isolated incidents and applying it too broadly (for example, hearing about a robbery in the city may lead one to conclude that everyone is being robbed). *Magnification and minimization* entail seeing an event as more significant or less significant than it actually is (for example, thinking that if one is not asked to go to the senior prom, one's life is over). *Personalization* consists of attributing external events to oneself without evidence of connection (for example, parents assuming that they are to blame every time their children misbehave). *Dichotomous thinking* refers to categorizing situations in extremes (for example, seeing one's performance on a task as a complete success or total failure). Frequently people express their cognitive distortions in terms of *conditional assumptions,* beliefs that are dependent on certain conditions. Such assumptions frequently begin with an *if.* A depression-prone patient may say: "If I don't succeed, nobody will respect me," or "If that one person doesn't like me I must be unlovable." Such persons may function rather well until they experience a series of failures or rejections. Such *errors in logic* frequently entail a systematic negative style of thinking.

Dimensions of Sociotropy and Autonomy

Beck further describes personality in terms of two dimensions. The **sociotropic dimension** is characterized by dependence on interpersonal relationships and needs for closeness and nurturance. This dimension is organized around closeness, nurturance, and dependency. The **autonomous dimension** is characterized by independence and organized around goal setting, self-determination, and self-imposed obligations (Beck, Epstein, & Harrison 1983).

While "pure" cases of sociotropy and autonomy do exist, most people display features of each, depending on the situation. Thus, sociotropy and autonomy are modes of behavior, not fixed personality structures. This position stands in marked contrast with psychodynamic theories of personality that hold to fixed personality dimensions.

Beck's research shows that dependent individuals become depressed when their relationships are disrupted. Autonomous people become depressed when they fail to achieve a certain goal.

Cognitive Triad

According to Beck (1967), the depressed individual has a negative view of the self, the world, and the future. These three perceptions are known as the **cognitive triad.** The world seems to devoid of pleasure or gratification. The depressed person's view of the future is pessimistic or nonexistent. The increased dependency often observed in depressed patients reflects the view of self as incompetent, an overestimation of the difficulty of normal life tasks, the expectation of failure, and the desire for someone more capable to take over. Indecisiveness similarly reflects the belief that one is incapable of making correct decisions. The physical symptoms of depression—low energy, fatigue, and inertia—are also related to negative expectations.

THINKING CRITICALLY

Cognitive Distortions

Can you think of ways in which you make the errors in logic that Beck describes as cognitive distortions? Are you more prone to make certain types of distortions as opposed to other ones? Do you believe that any of these types of errors could underlie your own depressive mood changes? Being aware of the tendency to make cognitive distortions can be helpful, because if we are aware of our tendencies we can take steps to control them.

Cognitive Psychotherapy

Borrowing some of its concepts from psychodynamic therapy and a number of techniques from behavior therapy and client-oriented psychotherapy, **cognitive therapy** consists of a broad theoretical structure of personality and psychopathology, a set of well-defined therapeutic techniques. The ultimate goal of cognitive therapy is to remove systematic biases in thinking by correcting faulty information processing, thus helping clients to modify assumptions that maintain maladaptive behaviors and emotions. Cognitive and behavioral methods are used to challenge dysfunctional beliefs and to promote more realistic thinking.

Cognitive therapy fosters change in clients' beliefs by conceiving of beliefs as testable hypotheses to be examined through behavioral experiments jointly agreed upon by client and counselor. The cognitive therapist does not tell the client that the beliefs are irrational or wrong. Instead, the therapist asks questions that elicit the meaning, function, usefulness, and consequences of the client's beliefs. It is up to the individual client to decide which beliefs to keep and which ones to eliminate.

Cognitive therapy is not as simple as replacing negative thoughts with positive self statements. Change can occur only if the client experiences **affective arousal.** In the language of cognitive therapy, **hot cognitions** happen when a person experiences arousing emotions and reality testing at the same time. For example, a hot cognition is the actual phrase, fear, or critical self-blaming thought, such as "Oh, what a klutz I am." An examination of personal experience and logic at the same time allows the client to change the inner attitude or belief.

Cognitive therapy is present centered, directive, active, problem oriented, and best suited for cases in which problems can be delineated and cognitive distortions are apparent. It is not designed for personal growth or developmental work. Cognitive therapy is widely recognized as an effective treatment for unipolar depression. Sometimes cognitive therapy is used in combination with medication (Beck, Rush, Shaw, & Emery, 1979).

Cognitive therapy consists of highly specific learning experiences designed to teach clients to do five things: (1) to monitor their negative, automatic thoughts or cognitions; (2) to recognize the connections between cognition, affect, and behavior; (3) to examine the evidence for and against distorted automatic thoughts; (4) to substitute more reality-oriented interpretations for these biased cognitions; and (5) to learn to identify and alter the beliefs that predispose them to distort their experiences (Beck, Rush et al., 1979).

Cognitive Techniques

Decatastrophizing, also known as the "what if" technique (Beck & Emery, 1979), helps clients prepare for anticipated consequences. Anxious clients commonly "catastrophize" and anticipate the worst possible outcome of a situation. Specifically asking a client, "What if the worst possible thing did happen?" can be helpful in decreasing phobic avoidance, particularly when combined with exposure plans (Beck & Emery, 1985). *Retribution* techniques test automatic thought and assumptions by using reality testing in the present situation of therapy. *Redefining* a problem is used to mobilize clients who believe themselves to be out of control. *Decentering* is used for clients who focus on their own discomfort to the extreme. *Imagery* encourages clients to use their imagination. Some clients report images more easily than thoughts and thus provide useful data before and during episodes of anxiety.

Behavioral Techniques

Clients are given *homework* assignments focusing on self-observation and self-monitoring. In *hypothesis testing,* specific criteria are listed for monitoring so that the client sets up a framework for feedback during actual life experience. During *exposure therapy,* self-reported levels of tension are examined during specific practice sessions according to the individual client's needs. Clients are asked to **role-play** or rehearse situations that will later happen in real life. Their performance is jointly evaluated by the client and the therapist. In *diversion,* self-rating of tension levels provides structure while fluctuation of moods are tracked during normal everyday activities. Giving *graduated task assignments* that gradually become more difficult enables the client to begin assignments at a low level of tension.

These various cognitive and behavioral techniques enable the client and therapist or counselor to work together to effect genuine changes.

Assessment, Research, and Comparison with Other Theorists

Aaron Beck developed an instrument to measure depression called the **Beck Depression Inventory,** which is widely seen as the finest psychometric instrument for this objective. Equally important have been his longitudinal studies on suicide and its deterrence. Other assessment devices that Beck has published include Beck Anxiety Scale, Beck Hopelessness Scale, Beck Scale for Suicide Ideation, and Beck Self-concept Test.

Ninety percent of the two hundred studies testing the cognitive model have supported it. More than thirty outcome studies have corroborated the power of the cognitive theory of depression. Other studies show cognitive therapy is helpful in panic disorders, obsessive-compulsive disorder, substance abuse, personality disorders, marital problems, and sex offenses (Beck, 1991). In addition, Beck's theory helps to account for mood regulation (Catanzaro, 1993) and for the fact that individuals who are prone to anxiety tend to prefer threatening interpretations of ambiguous situations (MacLeod & Cohen, 1993). There is growing evidence that the technique really works.

In contrast with other behaviorists, who seek to modify behavior without caring about the roots of emotions, Beck believes it is essential that people "understand" that their unrealistic view of the world and life is responsible for their depression (Greenberg, 1981).

Beck's cognitive therapy disagrees with Ellis's rational-emotive therapy in several ways: (1) it does not dispute the client's cognitive distortions as actively and directly; (2) it never uses the word "irrational" and would never, never interrupt a client in midsentence; (3) it does not hold that major cognitive distortions stem from "shoulds" and "musts"; (4) it does not believe that appropriate negative feelings are responsible for depression; (5) it does not generally think of self-talk as provoking emotions, albeit in some situations self-talk may. However, it does favor and employ in vivo (in actual life) desensitization: cognitive therapy does not. Also, rational-emotive therapy recognized the usefulness of penalties in behavioral work.

At present, more than thirty-five books have been published on cognitive therapy and two scholarly journals focus on the topic. Most big cities in North America and numerous cities in other nations have centers for instruction in cognitive therapy.

Because of his work in controversial domains, Aaron Beck is often seen as a "maverick." His "approach is so straightforward in shunning traditional complexities that Dr. Beck says it befuddles many psychiatrists. 'Analysts view me as a behaviorist and behaviorists view me as an analyst.'. . . He says simply, 'I am a researcher'" (Greenberg, 1981).

Arnold A. Lazarus: Biographical Background

Johannesburg, South Africa, was the birthplace of Arnold Lazarus on January 27, 1932. When he was born, his older sisters were seventeen and fourteen and his brother was almost nine. "'A skinny kid, who was bullied a lot,'" Lazarus took to lifting weights, and at seventeen he left school thinking he would open a health and training center. Two years later, he was convinced it would be smarter to return and finish his education (Dryden, 1991).

All of his degrees are from the University of Witwatersrand in Johannesburg: a B.A. in psychology and sociology in 1955, a B.A. with honours in psychology in 1956, an M.A. in experimental psychology in 1957, and a Ph.D. in clinical psychology in 1960. At first he thought he would major in English, but he was fascinated by psychology.

In the 1950s, while Lazarus was a student at the University of Witwatersrand, the psychotherapeutic climate was predominantly Freudian and Rogerian. Visiting lectures by Joseph Wolpe, a general medical practitioner who was applying "conditioning methods" with his patients, led to the formation of a

Arnold Lazarus

small group of "neobehaviorists." The members of this group knew that performance-based methods were usually better in clinical practice than purely verbal and cognitive approaches. Whereas the psychotherapeutic establishment viewed behavior as the outward manifestation of more fundamental psychic processes, the neobehaviorists stressed that behavior per se is often clinically significant. People can acquire insight and change significant beliefs and still use maladaptive coping behavior and self-destructive behavior.

To legitimize behavioral intervention as an essential part of clinical practice, Lazarus in 1958 introduced the terms "behavior therapy" and "behavior therapist" in an article published by the *South African Medical Journal* (Lazarus, 1958). In an earlier publication, Lazarus stated, "The emphasis in psychological rehabilitation must be on a synthesis which would embrace a diverse range of effective therapeutics techniques, as well as innumerable adjunctive measures, to form part of a wide and all-embracing re-educative program" (1956).

Joseph Wolpe became his dissertation chairperson. His thesis, "New Group Techniques in the Treatment of Phobic Conditions," was "the first study to employ systematic desensitization in groups, and it was also perhaps the first time that anyone had devised objective scales for assessing phobic avoidance. For example, acrophobics [people who are afraid of heights] were required to see how high up they would climb a metal fire escape." Pre- and posttreatment assessments were developed to measure improvement (Dryden, 1991).

In 1959, Lazarus began private practice. He began to use hypnosis and was elected to the presidency of the South African Society for Clinical and Experimental Hypnosis. Then a paper informed by his doctoral dissertation was published in the *Journal of Abnormal and Social Psychology* in 1961 and captured the attention of Albert Bandura, who asked him to come to California and teach for a year at Stanford.

For a long time, Lazarus had been upset with the political circumstances in South Africa, so he was pleased to take the chance to see "'how the other half lived'" (Dryden, 1991).

The work of Ellis (1962) influenced Lazarus, convincing him of the crucial significance of emotional freedom and rational thinking.

However, growing distress with apartheid led the Lazaruses to return to the United States, and in 1967 he began working with Joseph Wolpe as a professor in the Department of Behavioral Science at Temple University Medical School in Philadelphia. However, it quickly became apparent that Wolpe's and Lazarus's interests and thinking were headed in different directions. After teaching briefly at Yale University in 1970 and publishing *Behavior Therapy and Beyond* (1971), Lazarus assumed the rank of Distinguished Professor at Rutgers in 1972.

Lazarus has received several honors and been president of many professional organizations. He has written fourteen books and over 180 journal articles. He has lectured widely and is often cited as "one of the most influential psychotherapists of the twentieth century" (Dryden, 1991). In 1992 he received the Distinguished Psychologist Award, Division of Psychotherapy, from the American Psychological Association.

The Development of His Theory and the BASIC-ID

In 1966 Lazarus published an article that challenged narrow stimulus-response formulations of the early 1960s and focused on dyadic transactions, or significant interpersonal relationships, as a significant part of the maintenance of maladaptive behavior. This was the first step in a significant movement in contemporary behavior theory and therapy, away from the radical behaviorism of an earlier period. Contemporary behavior theory and therapy has moved from the individual to the group and to society at large.

No one exemplifies these developments more than Lazarus (Franks, 1976). Spurning psychoanalytic methods in favor of the apparently more favorable pattern of early stimulus-response conditioning therapy, Lazarus soon became disillusioned with the then current behavioral strategies. Slowly and carefully, he developed a new set of clinical strategies that has come to be known as **multimodal behavior therapy**.

The importance of overt behavior is well documented in the writings and practices of behavior theorists and therapists, but Lazarus felt that they gloss over crucial interpersonal factors. A comprehensive appraisal based on the observation that clients are usually troubled by a multitude of specific problems called for an examination of behavior, affect, sensation, imagery, cognition, and interpersonal relationships. The first letter of each word forms the acronym BASIC-I.

Behavior entails overt behaviors. *Affect* refers to the emotions. *Sensation* entails the wide realm of sensory stimuli. *Imagery* may entail a memory or the deliberate imaging of a relaxing image or scene. *Cognition* includes the intuition, ideology, concepts, and judgments that make up our basic attitudes, values, and beliefs (1976). *D* was added to the acronym to stand for *drugs* (neurological and biochemical factors that influence behavior). Lazarus is aware that some clients may require medication, but *D* has also come to stand for all aspects of physical well-being. With the addition of drugs, the acronym became **BASIC-ID.**

Theory of Personality

Lazarus believes that the seven modalities—behavior, affect, sensation, imagery, cognition, interpersonal processes, and drugs—may be said to make up human personality. The BASIC-ID is presumed to comprise human temperament and personality, and it is assumed that everything from anger, disappointment, greed, fear, grief, awe, contempt, and boredom to love, hope, faith, and joy can be accounted for by examining components and interactions within a person's BASIC-ID.

Lazarus holds that each person is a product of genetic history, environment, and learning. He gives great importance to the concept of individual physical **thresholds.** People have different thresholds, or tolerance levels, for pain, frustration, or stress. These thresholds are unique and individual. Psychological interventions can bolster physical thresholds but genetics, which also influences thresholds, cannot be overcome.

People tend to favor some BASIC-ID modality; thus, we may speak of a "sensory reactor" or an "imagery reactor" or a "cognitive reactor." This does not imply that a person will always react in a certain way, but over time, a tendency to value certain response patterns can be noted. As Bandler and Grinder (1976) say, visualizers tend to "make pictures" out of what they hear. In terms of split-brain research (Galin, 1974; Kimura, 1979), imagery reactors are probably right-hemispheric dominant, whereas cognitive reactors are frequently left-hemispheric dominant.

The totality of habits that make up a personality are acquired through genetics, but also through association and conditioning. A good bit of human thoughts, feelings, and behaviors are due to the simple conditioning of family life. Many aversions appear to result from an association of one stimulus with another. Bandura (1969, 1977) speaks of limitation, observational learning, modeling, and vicarious processes as means of acquiring life-styles and habits that make up our personalities. As Bandura's (1978) principle of reciprocal determination underscores, people do not react automatically to external stimuli. Their thoughts about those stimuli will determine which stimuli are noticed, how much they are valued, and how long they are remembered. Lazarus's view of the role for the unconscious is related to the recognition that different people have different levels of self-awareness and also that nonawareness (subliminal) or nonrecognition of thoughts and feeling does not prevent these nonconscious processes from influencing a person's attitudes and behaviors. Lazarus simply does not deal with traditional psychoanalytic notions and concepts in his writing.

In the multimodal orientation, it is acknowledged that people are capable of denial, displacement, and projection of thought and feelings. Impulses and aggressions are recognized and displaced. When accounting for these important human reactions, multimodal theory adds the concept of **metacommunication,** which is to say that people not only communicate, they also can think and communicate about their communications. The use of **paradox**, or contradictions, in therapy, in which the therapist or counselor exaggerates the client's irrationality, so popular nowadays, draws its energy from the process of metacommunication (e.g., Foa 1990, Fay, 1978, Frankl 1960, 1978; Zeig, 1982).

Fay (1976) gives the following example of the effectiveness of paradox:

> A twelve-year-old boy, whose over-protective mother constantly peppered him with solicitous questions about his health, vociferously protested but to no avail. However, he virtually extinguished the undesired behavior when on several occasions, in response to her frantic "Are you alright?" he clutched his abdomen and said, "No, I'm not all right. I'm dreadfully ill and I don't think I can last much longer!"

Mental and emotional disorders arise due to the genetic inheritance of certain vulnerabilities combined with the learning of faulty cognition, exposure to inadequate or abusive role models, and the collection of a variety of inhibitions and needless defenses. Emotional problems and disorders also arise from inadequate attention to learning. People with inadequate social learning cannot cope with the demands of everyday life and society's demands. "Adaptive living among the Hottentots or the Nilotes of Africa calls for different behavioral repertoires than those demanded by Western society" (Lazarus, 1976).

Multimodal Therapy

Multimodal therapy rests primarily on the theoretical base of social learning theory (Bandura, 1969, 1977, 1986) while also drawing from general systems theory (Bertalanffy, 1974; Buckley, 1967) and group communications theory (Watzlawick, Weakland, & Fisch, 1974).

Lazarus's search for systematic therapies led him to the awareness that changing a client's cognitive modality often called for more than the correction of misconceptions. Lazarus needed to help clients change the messages conjured up by their imaginations. He added *goal rehearsal,* imagining yourself fulfilling your goal, *time projection,* imagining yourself projected into the future, and other coping imageries to his repertoire (see Lazarus, 1978, 1982).

Lazarus takes a holistic approach to his clients. Initially (Lazarus, 1973, 1976) the term "multimodal behavior therapy" was used to describe BASIC-ID assessment and treatment, but because emphasis in on comprehensive coverage of all the modalities, it is misleading to single out any one dimension over another. In a critical review of multimodal therapy, Kwee (1981) underscores its historical development from a narrow band of stimulus-response conditioning therapy by way of broad-spectrum behavior therapy to its present multimodal therapy and concludes that "whether or not multimodal therapy can be classified as behavior therapy is less important than the method itself" (p. 65).

Detailed accounts of multimodal assessment and therapy have been presented in several textbooks (for example Dryden & Golden, 1986; Jacobson, 1987; Norcross, 1986). Books, articles, and chapters on multimodal therapy have been written or translated into German, Italian, Portuguese, Spanish, and Dutch. Multimodal therapy has been proven effective beyond the traditional therapeutic settings and can be found in day hospitals, nursing homes, and self-help support programs (Brunell & Young, 1982; O'Keefe & Castaldo, 1981; Roberts, Jackson, & Phelps, 1980). Training in multimodal therapy has been a formal aspect of the clinical doctoral program at Rutgers University since 1972.

Another fundamental multimodal therapy assumption is that without new experiences there can be no change. The multimodal therapy methods, therefore, are *performance based.* Woody puts it very clearly when he says that an effective therapist "must be more than a 'nice guy' who can exude prescribed interpersonal conditions—he must have an armamentarium of scientifically derived skills and techniques to supplement this effective interpersonal relations" (1971).

Multimodal therapy is predicated on the assumption that the more disturbed the client is, the greater the specific excesses and deficits there will be throughout the BASIC-ID. Lazarus bases his model on actualization and self-determination rather than on pathology. His theory places primary emphasis on the uniqueness of each person. Maximum flexibility is demanded of the therapist in selecting and matching therapeutic interventions to each client. The fundamental question is always "what is best for this particular client?"

While multimodal therapy draws heavily from several systems (both rational-emotive and cognitive), there are distinctive features that set multimodal therapy apart: (1) its holistic approach of giving attention to the full BASIC-ID; (2) the use of **modality profiles,** or a specific list of problems and proposed treatments across the client's BASIC-ID; (3) the use of a **structural profile,** or a quantitative assessment of the relative involvement of each of the elements of the BASIC-ID; (4) the use of **bridging,** a multimodal technique used by counselors to deliberately begin work in terms of their client's preferred modality. With a feeling-sensory client it can be detrimental to insist on cognitive restructuring right at the onset of treatment. Multimodal therapy starts where the client is and bridges into more challenging areas as the therapeutic relationship develops; (5) the use of **tracking,** paying careful attention to the "firing order" of the different modalities. The "firing order" refers to "how the modalities interact to cause the client's problems" (Lazarus, 1985) or the order in which the modalities appear. Most people report a reasonably stable range of firing order much of the time. Recognition of these patterns permits intervention at any point in the firing sequence. Tracking also enables one to select the most appropriate intervention techniques.

Multimodal therapy offers a precise and disciplined behavioral retraining process. Behaviorists are sometimes insensitive to the individual's interpersonal needs and affective reactions. Multimodal therapy helps them to meet this challenge (Lazarus, 1989).

THINKING CRITICALLY

Using the BASIC-ID

The following are sample questions that are used to rate BASIC-ID. Use a scale from six to zero. High scores characterize you. A zero means that the tendency does not describe you at all. How would you rate yourself on the following questions?

1. *Behavior:* Are you active, a doer, always busy?
2. *Affect:* How emotional are you?
3. *Sensation:* How intently do you monitor your bodily sensations?
4. *Imagery:* Do you think in pictures, fantasy?
5. *Cognition:* Do you like to make plans, anticipate?
6. *Interpersonal:* Are you gregarious, intimate?
7. *Drugs/Biology:* Are you healthy? Do you abuse drugs or alcohol?

It takes a considerable amount of skill for a therapist or a counselor to diagnose a client's BASIC-ID, but these questions may give you an idea of the type of questions that would be asked.

Technical Eclecticism

Lazarus is also very well known for advocating **technical eclecticism.** He maintains that good treatment methods may be derived from many sources without necessarily agreeing with the theories that generated them. He further believes that if therapists or counselors use only the methods included in their favored theoretical view, they will invariably neglect effective techniques that are used by therapists or counselors of other persuasions. Thus Lazarus may borrow techniques that were generated in Gestalt therapy, Transactional Analysis, or existential therapy without embracing the theory held by their founders and disci-

PHILOSOPHICAL ASSUMPTIONS

Examining Cognitive-Behavioral Therapists

How would you rate the cognitive-behavioral therapists on each of the basic philosophical assumptions described in Chapter 1? Each basic issue was presented as a bipolar dimension along which a person's view can be placed according to the degree of agreement with one or the other extreme. Rate Ellis's, Beck's, and Lazarus's views on these issues.

When you have determined where you think Ellis, Beck, and Lazarus stand, compare your responses with those of your classmates and your instructor. You should be willing to defend your ratings, but also be prepared to change them in light of others' compelling arguments. Afterward, compare your ratings of these theorists with your own position on each issue and with those of other theorists. Does this comparison help you to understand why their theories do or do not appeal to you?

Would strongly agree	Would agree	Is neutral or believes in synthesis of both views	Would agree	Would strongly agree
1	2	3	4	5

freedom

People basically have control over their own behavior and understand the motives behind their behavior.

determinism

The behavior of people is basically determined by internal or external forces over which they have little, if any, control.

ples. Lazarus says he prefers to operate out of social and cognitive learning theory as "its tenets are grounded in research and are open to verification and disproof. . . . [moreover] I have yet to find any effective procedure that cannot be readily explained in terms of social and cognitive learning theory" (Dryden, 1991).

Lazarus further maintains that the greater number of coping skills clients develop, the less likely they will backslide. Thus Lazarus's method is performance based. He starts by observing behavior and develops a re-education plan custom-made for each client.

Lazarus's eclectic multimodal theory and therapy, performance based and tailor-made for each client, is demonstrably effective.

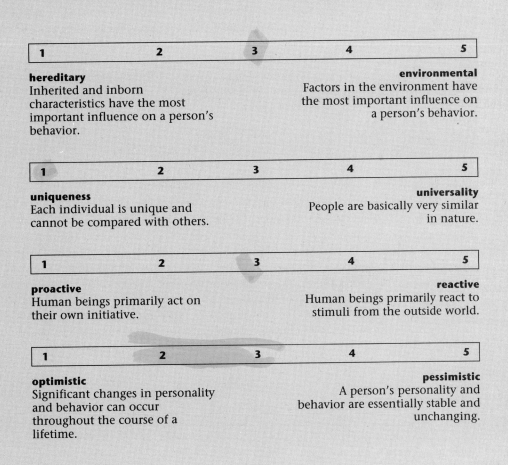

| 1 | 2 | 3 | 4 | 5 |

hereditary
Inherited and inborn characteristics have the most important influence on a person's behavior.

environmental
Factors in the environment have the most important influence on a person's behavior.

| 1 | 2 | 3 | 4 | 5 |

uniqueness
Each individual is unique and cannot be compared with others.

universality
People are basically very similar in nature.

| 1 | 2 | 3 | 4 | 5 |

proactive
Human beings primarily act on their own initiative.

reactive
Human beings primarily react to stimuli from the outside world.

| 1 | 2 | 3 | 4 | 5 |

optimistic
Significant changes in personality and behavior can occur throughout the course of a lifetime.

pessimistic
A person's personality and behavior are essentially stable and unchanging.

Cognitive-Behavioral Therapies and Theories: Philosophy, Science, and Art

While cognitive-behavioral therapies and theories clearly emphasize the art of psychotherapy and counseling, one can find some key underlying philosophical assumptions. Ellis's roots in Stoic philosophy and his realistic attitude of both pessimism and optimism concerning human nature (that human beings have a strong tendency to sabotage themselves but at the same time have enormous potential for change and self-actualization) are important philosophical assumptions. Beck's strong roots in phenomenology, the structural theory and depth psychology of Kant and Freud, and more modern developments in cognitive psychology lead him also to concur that people have great potential to change. Lazarus further agrees with the crucial significance of emotional freedom and rational thinking. These theorists recognize that behavior is both determined and free, that both hereditary and environmental factors influence behavior, and that while there are similarities among people, each one of us develops a unique way of coping with life's problems. While learning is important in shaping our behaviors, people can also act primarily on their own initiative.

At the same time these methods of therapy and counseling have received considerable empirical and scientific support. In particular, Ellis's research at the Institute for Rational-Emotive Therapy confirm his approach to counseling; Beck's research studies into many areas of maladaptive behaviors and his development of assessment inventories demonstrate the effectiveness of his cognitive therapy; and Lazarus's development of objective scales for assessing phobic avoidance, pre- and posttreatment assessments, and research on the BASIC-ID demonstrates the effectiveness of multimodal therapy.

Nevertheless, it is in the application and art of psychotherapy and counseling that these behavioral cognitive therapies and theories really shine. Extremely practical, down to earth, directive, and eclectic, these theorists are determined to help people change and to improve their life-style. And they are effective! Moreover, much of the work that they do can be done in groups—a cost-saving factor that is important in this climate of economic concerns. While Ellis, Beck, and Lazarus are criticized for being simple, incomplete, and one-sided as philosophers of human nature, there is little reason to doubt that they will continue to have an enormous impact in the areas of therapy and counseling.

Summary

1. The philosophical origins of Ellis's **rational-emotive therapy** go back to the Stoics. The most important modern precursor was Alfred Adler.

2. Ellis suggests that human beings are "sign-, symbol-, and language-creating" animals who have four fundamental processes: perception, movement, thinking, and emotion. These are all necessarily interrelated and tend to assume a type of "self-talk" in which our "internalized sentences" determine our thoughts and emotions. Ellis believes that people have a strong tendency to engage in dysfunctional behaviors but that they also have potential to change and self-actualize. Emotional disturbance usually arises when people care too much about what others think of them.

3. The **A-B-C theory of personality** suggests that people develop irrational and **mustabatory** belief systems when a highly charged emotional consequence (C) follows a significant *activation event* (A). A may seem to but does not actually cause C. Instead, emotional consequences are large created by inappropriate *irrational beliefs* (B's).

4. As human beings we inherit a tendency to raise cultural *preferences* into *musts* and social *norms* into absolute *shoulds*.

5. The goal of rational-emotive therapy is for people to commit themselves to actions that correspond to their true value system. The three main therapeutic processes are **cognitive, emotive-evocative,** and **behavioral.**

6. Ellis's theory has many points of comparison with other theorists. For example, in comparison to Freud's theory, Ellis believes that virtually all so-called sexual problems result from people's irrational beliefs that they need approval.

7. The philosophical origins of Beck's cognitive theory are the phenomenological approach to psychology, structural theory and depth psychology, and cognitive psychology.

8. **Cognitive therapy** is based on a theory of personality that maintains that how one thinks largely determines how one feels and behaves. Personality reflects the individual's cognitive organization and structure, which are both biologically and socially influenced.

9. **Cognitions** refer to a person's awareness. **Schemas** are cognitive structures that consist of an individual's fundamental core beliefs and assumptions about how the world operates. **Cognitive distortions** are systematic errors in reasoning. Examples of cognitive distortions are: *arbitrary interference, selective abstraction, overgeneralization, magnification and minimization, personalization, dichotomous thinking,* and *conditional assumptions.*

10. The **sociotropic dimension** is characterized by dependence no interpersonal relationships and needs for closeness and nurturance. The **autonomous dimension** is characterized by independence.

11. The **cognitive triad** refers to the fact that depressed individuals have a negative view of the self, the world, and the future.

12. Beck's **cognitive therapy** consists of a broad theoretical structure of personality and psychopathology and a set of well-defined therapeutic techniques designed to help the client experience **affective arousal.**

13. Some cognitive and behavioral techniques are *decatastrophizing, retribution, redefining, decentering, imagery, homework, hypothesis testing, exposure therapy, role-playing, diversion,* and *graduated task assignments.*

14. Beck developed several assessment instruments, among them the *Beck Depression Inventory,* widely seen as the finest psychometric instrument for this objective. Unlike other behaviorists, Beck believes it is essential that people understand that their unrealistic view of the world and life is responsible for their depression.

15. Lazarus's theory developed out of an emphasis on *dyadic transactions.* He developed a comprehensive appraisal of personality called the **BASIC-ID.** These letters stand for the following words: *behavior, affect, sensation, imagery, cognition, interpersonal relations,* and *drugs.*

16. Lazarus says people have different physical **thresholds** and tend to favor some BASIC-ID. The habits that make up a personality are acquired through genetics, association, and conditioning. Multimodal theory also talks about **metacommunication** and the use of **paradox.**

17. **Multimodal therapy** methods are *performance based.* Lazarus added *goal rehearsal* and *time projection* as therapeutic methods. Some other features that set it apart from other therapies are the use of **modality profiles, structural profiles, bridging, tracking,** and Lazarus's emphasis on **technical eclecticism.**

18. While behavioral cognitive therapies and theories function as philosophy, science, and art, it is in the application and art of psychotherapy and counseling that they really shine.

Suggestions for Further Reading

Albert Ellis is witty, humorous, pragmatic, and highly readable. Most recommended are *The Handbook of Rational-Emotive Therapy* (Springer, 1986); *How to Live with a Neurotic* (Crown, 1957); *The Art and Science of Love* (Lyle Stuart, 1966); *How to Stubbornly Refuse to Make Yourself Miserable about Anything—Yes Anything* (Lyle Stuart, 1988); *How to Live With—and—Without Anger* (Reader's Digest Press, 1977); with R. Harper, *A New Guide to Rational Living* (Wilshire Books, 1975); and with W. Dryden, *The Practice of Rational Emotive Therapy* (Springer, 1987). The titles are all self-explanatory.

Good secondary sources include W. Dryden's *Rational Emotive Therapy: Fundamentals and Innovations,* published in Beckenham, England, by Croom-Helm, 1984; and M. E. Bernard's *Staying Alive in an Irrational World: The Psychology of Albert Ellis,* published in South Melbourne, Australia, by Carlton and Macmillan in 1986.

A little bit more technical but still very readable are Aaron T. Beck's works. Most recommended are *Depression: Causes and Treatment* (University of Pennsylvania Press, 1967); *Cognitive Therapy and the Emotional Disorders* (International Universities Press, 1976); *Cognitive Therapy of Depression* (Guilford, 1987); and with G. Emery, *Cognitive Therapy of Anxiety and Phobic Disorders* (Center for Cognitive Therapy, 1979). A biography about Aaron Beck written by Marge Weishaar is *Dr. Beck Biography* (Sage, 1993).

Again, a wee bit more technical yet still readable by the lay person are Arnold Lazarus's works. Most recommended are *Behavior Therapy and Beyond* (McGraw-Hill, 1971); *Multimodal Behavior Therapy* (Springer, 1976); *In the Mind's Eye: The Power of Imagery for Personal Enrichment* (Rawson, 1978); and *The Practice of Multimodal Therapy* (McGraw-Hill, 1981).

A Non-Western Approach

During the past century, we have made enormous progress in gathering together a significant amount of information about human nature and personality. However, although we have learned a great deal about ourselves, we are still far from an adequate understanding of what it means to be a human being. Our modern technology and culture have given rise to practices that may relieve many forms of human illness and suffering, but they have yet to provide satisfactory answers of the most fundamental questions of human existence. Those questions about the ultimate meaning, purpose, and goal of our lives continue to haunt us and to demand answers. There has been a growing feeling that the dominant concerns of Western science and psychology have ignored the inner nature of the person. Many people have turned to the East in the hope of finding something that could temper or humanize the thrust of modern technology that threatens to destroy the very civilization that developed it.

CHAPTER 17

Zen Buddhism

As Westerners, we are frequently unaware of or tend to depreciate other psychologies, such as those that come from the Oriental traditions. Many movements of Eastern thought raise questions about the ultimate meaning and purpose of human life and have developed psychologies insofar as they have investigated what it means to be a human being. The assumptions that constitute the consensus about reality in the twentieth-century Western world are not necessarily universal and shared by other cultures. From the viewpoint of many of these movements, several of our contemporary Western ideas about personality are very alien. No wonder we often have difficulty communicating, as long as we tacitly assume that our comprehension of human behavior is universally shared.

There are many varieties of Eastern thought: Hinduism, Buddhism, Confucianism, Taoism, and Sufism, among others. In many respects these thought systems do not resemble philosophy or religion as much as they resemble the art of psychology and psychotherapy (Watts, 1961). Their basic concern is with the human situation: the suffering and frustrations of people. They emphasize the importance of techniques to accomplish change. Eastern thought aims at transformations in consciousness, feelings, emotions, and one's relation to other people and the world. In describing the whole person, Eastern thought qualifies as a theory of personality, providing a different way of looking at the data.

Ponder this story before reading this chapter: A professor once asked a Zen master to teach him about Zen. The master agreed, and offered him a cup of tea. He accepted. The master prepared the tea and filled his guest's cup, continuing to pour tea until it was overflowing. The professor exclaimed, "What are you doing? Can't you see that the cup is already full?" "Ah," replied the master, "it is just like your mind, which is full with your ideas and misconceptions. How can I teach you something about Zen? Before you can receive more fresh tea, you must first empty your cup." Only if you empty your cup and approach the material in this chapter with an open mind will you be able to appreciate and understand it.

General Characteristics of Eastern Psychology

Although there are many differences among them, almost all Eastern movements of thought have certain characteristics in common. Jacob Needleman (1970) singled out two features that distinguish Eastern movements from the general pattern of thought in the West: an emphasis on the self and an emphasis on the practical. To these can be added a third: an emphasis on experiential knowledge.

An Emphasis on the Self

For the most part, Eastern religions are centered on the self. But the self that they focus on is not the conscious ego or individual mind of Western psychology. The East conceives of the true self as a deeper, inner consciousness that identifies the individual with the universe or cosmos. Eastern thinkers point out that many of us confuse ourselves with the social role or social identity that others assign to us (Jung's *persona*). This identification is **maya**,[1] or an illusion. Our ego is simply a social convention. When we speak of "I," "you," "him," an "individual," and so forth, we are conforming to the conventions of this world. However, the truth is that there is no "I" or "individual" in ultimate reality, and the "I" should not be confused with reality. Once we can see through the illusion of individual existence, we can recognize ourselves for who we are, both unique and universal. I am universal because my organism is inseparable from the universe at large. I am unique in that I am I, not who others say or expect me to be.

An Emphasis on the Practical

Eastern psychology is very practical. The writings of Eastern thinkers do not concentrate on telling their readers "how" to do it; they present anecdotes about a methodology that, if followed, may enable readers to do it. Eastern thinkers believe the truth that we seek is not found in books. It emerges only in the course of living; to permit it to emerge, we need to undergo a process. The process is not undertaken by following a recipe but through the guidance of a master, or teacher, who is indispensable.

The practice of Eastern psychology entails a systematic training of body and mind that lets one perceive the truth that lies within the inner being. The follower of Eastern thought is introduced to a variety of techniques and is taught to meditate and to engage in physical and psychological exercises. Such techniques have not been totally absent in the West. However, for many westerners the rituals and practices that are available today seem empty and meaningless. They may go to church or temple and enjoy the beautiful service, obtaining some emotional release from various practices and rituals that momentarily allay their discontents. But these practices no longer initiate them into a process that transforms them; it is as if they tried to cure an illness by hearing about a new method of treatment but never went to the doctor for the treatment (Needleman, 1970).

An Emphasis on Experiential Knowledge

Most Eastern psychologies, and especially **Zen Buddhism**, emphasize direct, experiential knowledge, as opposed to book or academic knowledge. To read about something is not enough to provide this immediate, intimate knowledge. No matter how many films on swimming one has watched, how many books about

---

1. As a rule of thumb to help you approximate the pronunciation of Sanskrit, Pali, Chinese, or Japanese terms appearing in Buddhist literature, vowels should be pronounced as they are in Spanish, Italian, or German. The *a* tends to sound as it does in the word *father, e* as in *let, i* as the *ee* in *meet. o* as the last letter in *tomato*, and *u* as the *oo* in *boot*. This is only an approximation, for there are long as well as short vowels, but you should come close enough if you follow this rule.

it one has read, or how vast one's knowledge is concerning swimming, unless one actually gets in the water and swims, one does not really *know* what swimming is like, The weakness of most education is that it is primarily theoretical and academic, and has no direct relationship to real life. "Academic study is like a stage sword—sharp in appearance, but unable to cut. Hence, in the battlefield of human life, it is useless. Zen practice, on the other hand, is the continuous training of body and mind. Through this practice our being becomes a real sword" (Gempo Yamamoto in Shimano, 1984).

In order to understand the psychology of Zen it is not enough to read about it; it is essential to actually practice and experience Zen training directly. Thus one of the goals for this chapter is to actually practice and experience Zen meditation, instead of being satisfied with merely explaining or describing it.

Of the many forms of Eastern thought, Zen Buddhism in particular has caught the interest of the West. Thus we will focus on it as an introduction to the kinds of personality theorizing characteristic of the East, rather than give an overview of several viewpoints.

The Introduction of Zen to the West

Daisetz Teitaro Suzuki (1870–1966) is often credited with singlehandedly introducing Zen Buddhism to the West. A follower of the Rinzai school of Zen, Suzuki seldom mentioned the Soto school, although it was and is the main form of Zen in Japan. Alan Watts (1915–1973) later popularized the ideas of Suzuki in America. As a result, Rinzai Zen became well known in the West and Soto Zen remained virtually unknown. Paradoxically, the Zen of D. T. Suzuki, although stressing satori, or enlightenment, as the goal of Zen, never provided a practice method or any practical guidance to experience it.

In the 1960s and 1970s, due to the efforts of several masters such as Shunryu Suzuki and Dainin Katagiri in America and Taisen Deshimaru in Europe, Zen spread. These masters, among others, deserve credit for being the true introducers of Zen in the West.

The Origins of Zen

Zen is a school of Buddhism that claims to represent the purest essence of Buddhist teachings. The origins of Zen trace back to the story of Siddhartha Gautama, born about 563 B.C. in northern India, the son of a king. Upon his birth, the story goes, a local sage prophesied that the child would become either a great sage or a conquering monarch. His father, preferring the latter, decided to accustom the child to a life of luxury and comfort, as befitted a future king. Siddhartha grew up a virtual prisoner in the palaces his father built for him, married a princess from a neighboring kingdom, and had a son.

*The joy and radiance of an enlightened
master is evident in this photograph of
Dainin Katagiri-roshi (1928–1990), who
brought Zen to the American Midwest.*

Wanting to know the kingdom he was to rule one day, he finally got his father's permission to leave the palaces and see the country, but he was greatly disturbed by seeing on successive occasions a very old man, a severely ill person, and a funeral procession. These were his first encounters with old age, sickness, and death, since information about such aspects of the human condition had been withheld from him. Recognizing impermanence and suffering, he was so moved that he vowed to forsake his kingdom and to dedicate his life to finding a solution to the problem of suffering. He left in the middle of the night, leaving behind his wealth as well as his family, knowing that they would be cared for. He was twenty-nine years old.

For six years, Siddhartha sought out and trained under the greatest Yoga teachers of northern India. He learned and practiced their meditation techniques and achieved the most advanced states of altered consciousness his teachers had accomplished. But he was dissatisfied, for he realized that regardless of the nature of the mental trance he experienced, it provided only a temporary escape—not a permanent cure for human suffering. He tried all the methods and studied under all available teachers, even engaging in intense ascetic practices and self-mortification designed to liberate the mind from the demands of the body, but to no avail.

In desperation, leaving the ascetic practices that brought him near to death from starvation, he accepted food, regaining his strength, and sat down under a great peepul tree (an Indian fig tree, which would become known as the *bodhi tree* of enlightenment). He determined not to rise again until he found the answer to the problem of suffering. After seven days of intense concentration, he reached a profound flash of awakening, and the nature of reality as well as the solution to the problem that had tormented him were clear. From that moment on, he was known as the *Buddha,* the Awakened One. He was then thirty-five years old, and spent the following forty-five years of his life traveling, teaching others, and sharing his great discovery. He made no claims of divine origin or of having received a divine revelation. When asked whether he was a god, or a supernatural being, he always replied no. When asked what he was, he said "I am Awake" ("I am Buddha"). Radiant, peaceful, compassionate, and charismatic, he continued his work until he died at the age of eighty, in about 483 B.C.

The Buddha's teachings, preserved initially through an oral tradition, were eventually written down in the form of three collections or "baskets," known as the **Tripitaka.** The oldest version of these is believed to have been written in Pali, an ancient Indic language; it constitutes the scriptures of one of the two main branches of Buddhism, sometimes called the **Hinayana,** or "small vehicle," and represented today by the **Theravada** school. Theravada Buddhism is dominant today in parts of Southeast Asia. The second major branch, the **Mahayana,** uses primarily the Sanskrit version of the *Tripitaka,* in addition to which it recognizes a large number of additional scriptures not in the Pali Canon, some attributed to the historical Buddha and others to diverse authors. The total number of scriptures in Buddhism surpasses 85,000, a massive body of literature. The Mahayana (or "great vehicle") branch of Buddhism is dominant in East Asia. Zen belongs to the Mahayana tradition, developing from roots in India through the filter of Taoism in China, passing from there to Korea and to Japan, and to the rest of the world. A primary difference between Theravada and Mahayana Buddhism lies in their ideals of personal development. The former stresses renunciation of worldly life and a monastic life-style, seeking to develop the practitioner into an *arhat,* a sage who through practice and discipline is liberated from suffering. The latter accepts that enlightenment is possible also for lay practitioners. Its ideal is the **bodhisattva,** a person who vows to dedicate life to the salvation of all sentient beings, not accepting full liberation until all others are free from suffering. Of the two key virtues in Buddhism, wisdom and compassion, Theravada stresses the former, while Mahayana emphasizes the latter. As we will see below, this does not necessarily represent a contradiction.

The Teachings of the Buddha

What the Buddha discovered at the time of his awakening is very profound, complicated, and difficult to understand, and yet amazingly simple, direct, and self-evident. To appreciate his great insight, it is helpful first to reflect on the philosophical background in India two and a half millenia ago.

There were then more philosophical schools and positions in India than ever developed in ancient Greece. These ranged from a form of Vedic mysticism that postulated a universal creator, or *Brahma,* and individual souls (**atman**) who transmigrated through many lives in order to become purified and rejoin the universal *Brahma,* to those who believed that all that existed was the material substance evident to the senses, and that at death the individual was totally extinguished. One extreme was the eternalist position, where a person's soul or atman continues eternally, and the other the annihilationist position, postulating that a human being is completely destroyed at death. The Buddha discovered a position between these extremes. He called this position **dependent origination.** He also advocated a life-style that avoided the extremes of self-indulgence and self-mortification. His position became known as "the Middle Way."

The teaching of dependent origination is at the core of the Buddha's **Dharma** (meaning "Doctrine," "Truth," or "Law"). Simply stated, dependent origination is a law of causality that says "this is, because that is; this is not, because that is not; when this arises, that arises; when this ceases, that ceases." Despite the apparent simplicity of this law, it is a far-reaching truth that leaves nothing untouched and causally connects everything in the universe, for it implies that all phenomena, whether they be external or internal events, come into existence depending on causes and conditions without which they could not be. These causes and conditions can themselves be either internal or external.

As Hanh (1988) suggests, consider the page of the book you are reading. This piece of paper can be, because a tree was, since the tree had to be in order to be cut down to make the paper. This same piece of paper is also because there was rain and sunshine; without them the tree could not have grown. The same is true for the seed and the fertile soil, and the logger who cut the tree down. Without them, the tree would not have been there for the paper to be. But for the logger to be, his parents had to be, and the food they consumed, and all the conditions that made their lives possible, and those lives upon which theirs depended, and on, and on. There is no end to this causal interconnectedness. Everything in the universe is connected to this piece of paper. If the component conditions are seen as elements, we can say that this piece of paper is composed of non-paper elements: conditions other than the paper itself are necessary for the paper to exist. The paper cannot exist by itself. Neither can you or anything else in the universe. The same is true of cognitive or mental states. For every emotion, every perception, every thought, there are necessary causal conditions without which they would not have come into being. Everything is dependently arisen, everything exists only if the necessary conditions are there. This means nothing is ever truly independent or separate from everything else. Dependent origination is not simply A causing B, but simultaneously A being a necessary condition for B to occur, and B being necessary for A to arise. Thus the best label is that used by Katagiri (1988), "interdependent co-origination," or Hanh's (1988) "interbeing," where things and mental states "inter-are." Modern general systems theory, derived from our relatively recent awareness of the interconnectedness of ecological factors, approximates this, although the theory lacks the generality and universality of the Buddha's position (Macy, 1991).

The concept of dependent origination results in an understanding of existence as a process of change, the result of an infinite web of causal conditions, with birth and death marking neither the start nor the end. The conditions that result in our present existence represent a beginningless chain; the consequences of our actions become causal conditions whose effects will continue after we die. While there is no separate, immutable self or soul that can continue forever, the process of which we are a part continues forever (Katagiri, 1988). The Buddha talked about "rebirth." By this expression he did not mean reincarnation in the Vedic sense, where a soul (atman) inhabits a succession of bodies, but continuation in the sense in which a wave is "reborn" in the ocean after apparently "dying" on the seashore. All the water is still there, and the process continues endlessly, but no "soul" travels from one wave to the other. There are no transmigrating souls, only a continuing karmic process. Who we are lives on in the effects we have on others and on our world.

The Three Characteristics of Existence

The Buddha realized that there are three characteristics of existence: anicca, dukkha, and anatta. **Anicca** or impermanence means that everything is always changing. Nothing is immutable or permanent. Children grow, people age, things break down, spring follows winter, rivers flow, subatomic particles fluctuate, galaxies spin, everything is in a state of flux. Impermanence is not good or bad, it's just the way things are. Understanding and accepting impermanence leads to the avoidance of unrealistic expectations. Ultimately there is nothing we can hold onto or keep forever. Attachment and aversion will not change this.

Dukkha, usually translated as suffering, refers to the dissatisfaction and distress that results from attachment and aversion. The Buddha's solution to the problem of suffering, which has been called "the most important psychological discovery of all time" (Mosig, 1989), represents an application of the far-reaching principle of dependent origination. If suffering is, it must have come into being as the result of causal conditions, and if suffering is to cease, those conditions must cease. His solution was expressed in the form of the **Four Noble Truths.**

The *first noble truth* describes the problem of suffering, the universal dissatisfaction that characterizes human existence: our perception of pain, illness, old age, and death; not getting what we want and being exposed to what we don't want; not being able to keep forever what we love and not being able to eliminate what we hate.

The *second noble truth* begins the application of dependent origination to the problem, identifying the causal conditions on which suffering depends. Suffering and dissatisfaction, the "dis-ease" of human existence, cannot be by themselves, but arise due to our craving, our "thirsting" and desiring for things to be other than what they are. Old age is not suffering, it is just old age. Suffering arises because we do not want to be old. This thirsting for things not to be as they are comes in two "flavors," attachment (which includes greed and possessive love) and aversion (including anger, resentment, and hate).

The *third noble truth* derives a solution through the application of the same principle. Since human suffering arose out of craving, to bring our "dis-ease" to an end we must cease the self-defeating liking and disliking that causes it, we must stop the "picking and choosing" that is "the sickness of the mind" (Seng T'san in Sheng-Yen, 1987). While we cannot get rid of illness, physical pain, aging, and death, we can eliminate the anxiety we cause ourselves with our cognitive processing. In doing so, we can achieve freedom from unnecessary psychological pain (Kalupahana, 1982). To eliminate suffering, we must get rid of craving.

The answer to how we can do this is contained in the Buddha's *fourth noble truth,* known as the **Eightfold Path.** It consists of *Right Understanding* (understanding the interconnectedness and impermanence of everything, and specifically the Four Noble Truths); *Right Thinking* (cultivating thoughts of selfless detachment, compassion, and non-harming, and extending these to all sentient beings); *Right Speech* (abstaining from lying, slander, gossip, and injurious speech, speaking only that which is positive and constructive, otherwise maintaining a "noble silence"); *Right Action* (acting in ways that will benefit and not cause suffering to others or oneself); *Right Livelihood* (avoiding ways of making a living that are based on the exploitation of the suffering of animals or people); *Right Effort* (cutting off unwholesome thoughts before they can be transformed into actions and nurturing wholesome ones); *Right Mindfulness* (maintaining full awareness of our actions and experiences in the present moment, and their likely consequences); *Right Concentration* (the disciplining, concentration, and one-pointedness of mind) resulting from the practice of meditation) (Piyadassi, 1974; Rahula, 1974).

The first two components of the Eightfold Path are related to wisdom; the following three, to moral conduct; and the last three, to mental discipline. The different aspects of the Path are themselves interdependent. Without wisdom one would not see the necessity of undertaking the Path, without moral development one would not be ready to undertake it, and without mental discipline one would not be able to do it! The moral conduct aspects of the path relate also to the concept of karma. **Karma** means volitional action, whether of word, deed, or thought. Every action has effects or consequences, which "rebound." One could hardly expect to free oneself from suffering while inflicting it on others.

The third characteristic of existence, **anatta** or non-self, is the one that sets Buddhism apart from practically all other religious, philosophical, and psychological theories and positions.

> Buddhism stands unique . . . in denying the existence of a soul, self, or *atman.* According to the teaching of the Buddha, the idea of a [personal] self is an imaginary, false belief which has no corresponding reality, and it produces harmful thoughts of "me" and "mine," selfish desire, craving, attachment, hatred, ill-will, conceit, pride, egoism, and other defilements, impurities and problems. It is the source of all the troubles in the world, from personal conflicts to wars between nations . . . to this false view can be traced all the evil in the world. (Rahula, 1974)

Craving is one of the links in the chain of dependent origination, and suffering the end product. The doctrine of *anatta* links craving to the false idea of a separate ego or self. It is important to realize what is meant by the "self" that the Buddha rejected as illusory. Not only are human beings said to lack a soul or self, so is everything else: rivers, mountains, this book, and your pencil. This means they cannot have any reality except in terms of the interconnected net of causal conditions that made their existence possible. All things (including human beings) are composites; they are composed of parts and have no real existence other than as temporary collections of parts. There is no separate essence, self, or soul, that could exist by itself, apart from the component parts and conditions.

What we call a "person" is the composite of five groups of elements or **skandhas.** The skandhas are form, feelings, perceptions, impulses, and consciousness. Just as an automobile is a temporary collection of car parts, a person is a temporary arrangement of these five skandhas. There is no separate, independent self or soul that would be left if we removed form (which includes the body), feelings, perceptions, impulses, and consciousness. While these aggregates are together, the functioning gestalt we call a person exists; if they are removed, the gestalt ceases to be. For this reason, the self can be said to be "empty": a view of the self radically different from Western perspectives (Page & Berkow, 1991).

Close your hand into a fist and look at it. What do you see? A fist. Is it real? It certainly seems to be. Now open your fingers. What happened to the "real" thing called "fist" that was there a moment ago? Where did it go? Consider your self, your ego. Is it real? Certainly. Or is it? What would remain of it if you removed form, feelings, perceptions, impulses, and consciousness? Just as the term "fist" is a convenient label to designate a transient arrangement of the fingers, the term "self" or "I" is nothing but a label for an impermanent arrangement of the skandhas. There is no little person inside the head, no inner ego or self, other than the temporary gestalt formed by the skandhas. This is the Buddha's concept of anatta, and why the self is an illusion.

The concept of anatta does not negate the person, nor does it diminish it. Rather, it empowers the individual by erasing the boundaries of separateness that limit the personal ego or self. The person becomes transformed from an isolated and powerless individual struggling against the rest of the world, into an interconnected integral part of the universe. The person's boundaries dissolve, and the person *becomes* the universe. This is the realization known as enlightenment, the emergence of the big self, the Self with capital *S,* which is boundless.

Consider a wave in the ocean. It has no reality apart from the water. Although its form seems to last as it continues to move on the surface of the ocean, it is composed each moment of different water particles. It seems so real, and yet we can see that there is no thing called "wave" there at all; there is only the movement of the water. The wave has no separate "self," no reality apart from the water. The separation is just an illusion created by our perceptions and by the words we use to describe them. Now assume that the collection of elements forming the wave had resulted in the phenomenon of consciousness. As long as the wave was unaware of the nature of the ocean, believing itself to be separate and independent of it, it might develop attachments and aversions, fears, jealousies, and worries about its size, its purpose, its importance, or its destination. Any such concerns would vanish instantly upon realizing the water-nature of the ocean, and its oneness with it. In the same way, all human problems disappear when the illusion of a separate self is eliminated.

The transcendent wisdom of realizing the universal oneness generates compassion and caring for everyone as oneself. To hurt or help another is to hurt or help oneself. True wisdom is automatically manifested as universal compassion, and true compassion manifests itself as wisdom. Wisdom and compassion "inter-are" In the final analysis, wisdom is compassion, and compassion is wisdom (Mosig, 1989).

The ultimate state of mind in Buddhism is **nirvana**, not a place like heaven, but a mental state, where all cravings, desires, and dualistic ideas have been completely extinguished, through the complete realization of *anicca* and *anatta.* The Buddha taught that liberation is within the grasp of everyone. Just as he said that there had been many fully enlightened beings or buddhas before him, he indicated that there would be countless buddhas after him.

Vasubandhu and the Eight Consciousnesses

One of the most important commentators who explicated the insights of the Buddha was Vasubandhu, who said that all that can be experienced to exist is "mind only," the mental processes of knowing. There is experience, but there is no subject having the experience. **Vijnana,** or "consciousness," the last of the five skandhas, is a multilayered concept, including both conscious and unconscious aspects.

There are eight consciousnesses, not just one. The first five correspond to the five basic sense fields, and share the same level of depth. They are the consciousnesses of seeing, hearing, smelling, tasting, and touching. Below is the **manovijnana,** the integrating basis of the five sense consciousnesses, which has functions such as knowing, evaluating, imagining, conceiving, and judging. Next comes **manas** ("mind"), which is where the illusion of a subjective "I" or "ego" arises. Finally comes the vast **alayavijnana,** or "storehouse consciousness," the ground of knowledge and the repository of all previous impressions, which exist in the form of "seeds" (Hanh, 1974). The "seeds" produce all sorts of mental phenomena and affect each other in various ways. The "seeds" are "watered" by conscious activities, so that, for example, engaging in kind or compassionate thoughts makes the seeds of compassion ripen, grow, and become more powerful so that it will be easier to think compassionately next time. Allowing oneself to indulge in anger or hatred waters the corresponding seeds, so that it becomes easier to grow angry and to experience hate. This is why mindfulness of thoughts is so important, and why the "right effort" aspect of the Eightfold Path deals with cutting off negative or destructive thoughts as soon as they appear, while nurturing positive ones. This develops positive mental habits rooted in the seeds of the alayavijnana, and has far-reaching effects on the life and well-being of an individual. The alayavijnana is a vast unconscious realm, often compared to a stream, constantly flowing and renewing itself. If the individual is likened to a wave in the ocean, the alayavijnana is the unconsciousness (or subconsciousness) of the ocean, providing the continuity of the karmic process.

The eight consciousnesses should not be conceived as discrete and separate, but as eight aspects of the same consciousness, or as eight forms of awareness. At the level of the *sense consciousnesses,* awareness is of sights, sounds, smells, tastes, and the sensation of the body; the *manovijnana* involves awareness of thoughts; *manas* is awareness of being aware, the "self-consciousness" out of which emerges the delusion of being a separate self having the awareness; at the level of the *alayavijnana,* awareness is of the potentialities of human nature, or rather of the Buddha-nature that we all are.

Bodhidharma and the Transmission of Zen to China

Zen Buddhism was introduced to China around 520 A.D. by the Buddhist monk Bodhidharma. Upon his arrival in China, Bodhidharma met with the emperor, a devout but superficial Buddhist who asked, "I have built temples, support the monks, and have had the scriptures translated, tell me, what will all of this bring me?" "It will bring you nothing," replied Bodhidharma. "Then tell me, what are the sacred things in Buddhism?" "There is no sacred things—only vast emptiness." Irritated, the emperor asked, "And who are you to stand in front of me and talk to me like this?" "I do not know," said Bodhidharma, and he left. The emperor was functioning at the relative plane, while Bodhidharma made repeated references to the absolute one, where there are no "things," nothing can be sacred or profane, and there is no "I" or "self" to know.

Bodhidharma is said to have practiced sitting meditation for nine years at the Shaolin Temple, teaching the monks with his example. He is also said to have summarized his teaching as "a special transmission outside the scriptures; no reliance upon words and letters; direct pointing to the heart of man, and the realization of enlightenment" (Hoover, 1980). This statement emphasizes that the scriptures must be practiced and not just read, for words by themselves are as useless as a picture of a cake is to satisfy hunger. Only an enlightened teacher can verify the awakening of a disciple, which is thus transmitted "from mind to mind" (or "from heart to heart").

As Zen Buddhism passed into China, it adopted expressions from **Taoism,** which helped to convey Buddhist ideas. The philosophy of Taoism, attributed to the Chinese philosopher Lao-tse (approximately 4th century B.C.), the author of the *Tao Te Ching* ("The Way and its Power"), is essentially compatible with that of Buddhism. Lao-tse referred to the absolute as the **Tao,** or the "Way" of Nature, which is inexpressible in words, and stressed the desirability of harmonizing with nature. Many references to the "Way" (Tao) appear in Chinese Zen literature, usually to express the Buddha-nature.

In China, the Tao was thought to manifest itself in the form of two forces: **yin** and **yang.** Yin stands for the feminine, receptive, internal, negative aspect of nature, while yang represents the masculine, active, external, positive aspect. As shown by the well-known diagram (Figure 17.1), yin and yang are not merely opposites, but exist in a state of dynamic complementation, expressing the unity of the Tao. In Buddhist terms, we can say that yin and yang are dependently arisen, so that yin is yin because of yang, and yang is yang because of yin. The yin and yang symbol thus becomes a convenient expression of the principle of dependent origination, its dynamic quality corresponding to the impermanence and constant change the Buddha saw in the universe. The white dot in the black yin signifies that there is yang in the yin, while the black dot on the white field reflects the yin in the yang.

Figure 17.1   *The Classic Diagram of Yin and Yang*

The Practice of Zen

We need to distinguish between Zen as a school of the Mahayana division of Buddhism, and Zen as an experience. To speak of the latter is immediately to distort and misrepresent it. Zen masters have often said that those who say what Zen is do not know what it is, while those who know what it is, do not talk about it, but teach the practice of Zen, so that others will be able to experience it.

The practice of Zen entails a systematic training of the mind designed to create in the disciple a state of mind that will permit the realization of enlightenment. The indispensable form of Zen practice is **zazen**, which is traditionally practiced sitting cross-legged on a firm, round cushion or *zafu*, maintaining a precise physical posture for a period of time. Eastern psychologies, and especially Zen, do not regard the mind and the body as separate, but as intimately

In the practice of zazen, the correct body position creates the right state of mind. The main positions used are the full lotus (below) and the half-lotus.

interconnected, to the point that one could more properly refer to a "body-mind" than to a body *and* a mind. The posture of the body in zazen is extremely important, and is expressed in the mental state that accompanies it.

The main position recommended for zazen is the full lotus, with the right foot placed on the left thigh, and the left foot on the right thigh. This position expresses the oneness of duality. Even though we have two legs, in this posture they have become one. The head, neck, and spine are kept in a straight vertical line, which is the hallmark of all proper zazen postures. When one sits correctly, the body is held in perfect balance. Everything exists in the right place and in the right way. In such a position, a person can maintain physical and mental balance and can breathe naturally and deeply. The state of consciousness that exists when one sits in the correct posture is, itself, enlightenment.

The harmonization of the mind with the posture of zazen is usually accomplished through awareness of one's breathing. The mind tends to act like a monkey or a misbehaving child, constantly engaging in discursive thought. As the practitioner notices that the mind is climbing the treetops, he or she returns awareness to the breath, and continues to repeat this process.

Any thoughts, ideas, visions, or unusual experiences that may occur while one is practicing zazen are to be dismissed as *makyo*, delusions or hallucinations. The student is to attach no significance to them. Zazen is not the pursuit of mystical experiences. Zazen done properly is just sitting, body and mind together, right here and now—*just sitting*. While some recommend that beginners count their breaths, follow a mental sound or mantra, use some sort of visualizations, or ponder a paradoxical riddle during zazen, these are "unnecessary training wheels" (Kosko, 1993).

Zazen is not a means to reach enlightenment, thus it is not a tool to be discarded once the mind has become awakened. At that point, zazen becomes a manifestation of this realization. "The reason why you have to practice zazen is that if you do not practice zazen, things stick to you, and you cannot let go of them" (Katagiri, 1988). In the same way that showering allows us to wash away dust and dirt, practicing zazen allows us to let go of past regrets and future worries. Just as it would not occur to us to discontinue showering because the body is now clean, we should not regard any mental state as an indication that zazen is no longer necessary.

In the **Rinzai** school of Zen, **koans** are often used as themes for Zen meditation. The term "koan" literally means a "public document." It consists of an apparently paradoxical anecdote, statement, or question that has no logical, rational, or intellectual solution, as long as the student continues functioning at the level of the *relative*, the realm of duality. The koan statement is perfectly clear to an enlightened individual able to experience the *absolute* realm of nonduality. Since language is a tool developed to express dualistic concepts, it is totally inadequate to convey a nondualistic experience or understanding. For this reason, any attempt to provide an answer based on language or discursive Aristotelian-style logic is futile.

The koan usually describes actions or words by an enlightened teacher attempting to jolt a student out of discursive thinking into an intuitive realization. The use of such incidents as meditation aids is relatively recent in the long history of Zen Buddhism. Examples of koans are "What was your face before your parents were born?" and "What is the sound of one hand clapping?"

Students using a koan typically have individual daily interviews (called *sanzen*) with the master, to express their current understanding of the koan. Students' answers are almost invariably rejected, and they are sent back to meditate on the koan until they become one with it and arrive at a breakthrough, transcending dualistic thinking. Once they have broken through the koan, they are assigned another one, and the process is repeated. It may take weeks, months, or years for a student to work through a particular koan.

Teachers of the **Soto** school of Zen also use koans, but not as meditation themes. Zazen in Soto Zen is essentially **shikantaza**, themeless, just sitting. Shikantaza is not based on trying to realize anything. It is a pure practice that allows any effects to take place without being sought after. A Soto Zen teacher may use a koan as a focal point for a *teisho,* a "dharma talk" offered by a master to his students to enhance their understanding. A koan can be seen as a miniature exaggeration of the problem of life. Just as the koan seems to defy logical comprehension and resolution, so life itself cannot be held or contained within the categories constructed by dualistic thinking.

A number of studies have examined the physiological responses that occur during the practice of Zen meditation (Murphy & Donovan, 1988) and a considerable body of literature supports the notion that zazen as well as other Eastern meditative disciplines can lead to better health and an increased ability to deal with stress and tension (e.g., Hirai, 1989; Kabat-Zinn, 1990; the Dalai Lama et al., 1991). The efficacy of such practices is gaining recognition from contemporary Western medicine.

Zen practice has many other forms, which serve to extend the mindfulness of zazen to daily life. **Kinhin** is a slow walk performed between consecutive periods of zazen, while maintaining concentration and mindfulness. The kinhin walk allows for rest and normalization of circulation in the legs when one is doing several sittings. As during zazen one just sits, when walking in kinhin one just walks. In a more informal form of walking meditation, a person, alone or in a group, just walks (in the park, around the block, or wherever), maintaining awareness of the breath and of everything experienced during the walk, but without labeling or discussing what is being experienced. In order to maintain mindfulness when walking in this manner, it is recommended that the person notice the number of steps taken while inhaling, and also the number while exhaling (Hanh, 1985). Counting the steps and maintaining awareness of the breathing keeps the individual focused on the present, and this mindfulness is extended to everything encountered. If you try this exercise, you may be amazed at how many things you notice during your walk that you had never noticed before.

Gathas, short verses to help focus attention on the task at hand, by mentally dedicating the activity to the benefit of all sentient beings, may also be used.

This practice makes every activity into something sacred and clarifies that no activity is more or less valuable than any other activity—as we engage in it, it is our life at that moment.

Another form of Zen practice is the **gassho**, the putting together of the hands, palm to palm. The gassho position is a symbol of nonduality. It reminds us that the mind and body are one. One hand stands for you, the other for the person you are greeting, or for the entire universe, and you become aware that you and the other are one. When you put the hands together in gassho, just do gassho. Zen teaches to do each action completely and for its own sake.

Chanting sutras is Zen, too; here the important thing is to just chant, expecting nothing out of it, as an **autotelic** activity, in other words, an activity that contains its own goal. Chanting is not a form of prayer. It is not aimed at a superior power, nor does it petition anything. When chanting, just experience the sound.

A practice that many Westerners find difficult at first because of their cultural upbringing is bowing. In Zen, bowing is not an act of worship but an action expressing respect and gratitude. You may put your hands in gassho and bow to give thanks or to show appreciation for another, or merely as a greeting. Bowing in front of an altar, whether it be a standing bow or a full prostration, is an exercise that helps to subdue the ego and expresses gratitude. All the statues found in a Zen temple are symbolic of mental states and abilities, and do not represent external deities. In Zen you can bow to anything, people, statues, animals, your meditation cushion, a cup of tea. The important thing when bowing is to just bow, expecting nothing out of it.

Eating can also be a form of Zen practice, whether it be with the traditional *oryoki* bowls often used in Zen centers and monasteries, or in the everyday setting of the Western dining room. The key element in this is the maintenance of mindfulness. When you eat, just eat. Give your food your undivided attention—you can take care of other matters when their turn arrives.

Many aspects of Japanese culture show the imprint of Zen. This is true of the tea ceremony, the Noh theatre, the art of calligraphy, ink brush painting, haiku poetry, flower arranging, the *shakuhachi* flute, as well as the martial arts, such as karate, aikido swordsmanship, and archery. These are meditative arts based on the discipline of zazen. These and other forms of Zen practice are no substitutes for zazen, but serve to extend the mindfulness of zazen to everyday life (Mosig, 1988, 1990, 1991). The martial arts in particular necessitate the development of two mental states associated with Zen: "no-mindedness," the ability to react without conscious thought, and the "immovable mind," the ability to remain calm and undisturbed regardless of the circumstances (Mosig, 1988).

But you do not need to bow, chant, play the shakuhachi, write haikus, recite gathas, learn calligraphy, or engage in a martial art in order to practice Zen. All those manners of Zen expression, however helpful they may be, are ultimately superfluous and can be dispensed with. The only Zen practice that is completely indispensable is zazen.

It is important to find a master or a teacher to learn the correct way to practice Zen. The most important thing to look for in a teacher is not the depth

THINKING CRITICALLY

Meditation

Unlike Western personality theories, Zen cannot be grasped by thinking, critically or otherwise—it must be experienced. For this reason, you cannot expect to begin to understand Zen unless you actually practice zazen. The following are instructions on how to do it.

Wear loose-fitting clothes. Find a quiet, temperate, and neat place where you are not likely to be disturbed. Put a mat or folded blanket on the floor close to a wall, and place a thick cushion above it. Facing the wall, you should sit on the edge of the cushion, which should support the base of your spine, elevating it 6–8 inches from the floor. The cushion should allow you to sit straight and be stable, with your spine and your two knees forming three points of a tripod. The knees must be on the mat, not elevated from it.

Place your legs in one of the following positions (in descending order of stability and desirability): *full lotus* (right foot on left thigh and left foot on right thigh), *half lotus* (one foot on the opposite thigh, the other tucked underneath), *quarter lotus* (one foot on the opposite calf, the other tucked underneath), *burmese* (both legs flat on the mat), or *seiza* (kneeling, with the cushion on edge between your legs). If none of these are possible for you, sit on a cushion at the edge of a chair (keep your back straight, do not lean on the backrest). Put your hands on your knees, palms up. Breathing deeply, slowly arch your body back and then forward, and then sway from side to side in *decreasing* arcs, until you are perfectly centered. Then put your right hand on your lap (resting on your left foot, if you are in a lotus position), palm up, and the left hand on top of it, with the thumbs slightly touching over your middle fingers. Your hands should now be forming an oval, with the blades touching the stomach a few inches below the navel. The arms are relaxed and extend slightly forward, without touching the sides of your body.

Push your lower back slightly forward, then straighten your back, pushing upward with the top of your head. Keep your neck straight and tuck your chin slightly in. There should be a straight line now from the bottom of your spine to the top of your head. Your nose and navel should be in a vertical line, and your ears and shoulders on a horizontal line. Your eyes should remain slightly open, with your gaze cast downward at a 45-degree angle. Don't look at a specific spot—just let your eyes rest; don't try to see or visualize anything. Your mouth should be closed, with lips and teeth touching. Rest the tongue against the roof of the palate. Swallow any saliva, creating a vacuum inside your mouth. Breathe in and out through your nose and let the air go down to your lower abdomen so that you are breathing with the diaphragm. Breathe naturally, don't force the breath.

Keep your mind with your breath. When you inhale, be aware of your lower abdomen going out. When you exhale, notice your lower abdomen going in. Maintain this awareness. If you become distracted, don't get upset. If thoughts arise, notice them and let them go, gently returning to your breath. Keep repeating this. Just sit there, doing nothing, just being present in the reality of your life, beyond likes and dislikes. Sit firmly and immovable, like a mountain. At the end of your sitting period, release the posture of your hands, and put them on your knees, palms up. Gently sway from side to side in *increasing* arcs, exhaling each time as you sway to one side and then the other; then undo the position of your legs and stretch them out. Stand up slowly and carefully.

The traditional length of a zazen "sitting" is 40 minutes, but you may start with shorter periods. It is better to sit 5, 10, or 20 minutes every day than to do one 40-minute sitting once a week. Early in the morning and late at night are the best times of the day to practice. Sit every day, expecting nothing from your practice.

of his or her enlightenment—that is secondary. The most important point is how much the truth the teacher has experienced has been "digested" and manifests itself in the teacher's life (Katagiri, 1988). Only a teacher who has received "Dharma transmission," in other words, whose experience has been verified and authenticated by an enlightened master, is in a position to verify and authenticate the awakening of others.

Enlightenment

The reflective illumination or awakening of Zen is known as **satori.** Satori, or enlightenment, cannot be communicated with words, any more than words could communicate the experience of color to someone who is blind. In the Rinzai school, satori is regarded as the goal of Zen practice, and zazen as a method to achieve it. Practitioners sit in meditation, attempting to circumvent linear, rational thought through the use of a koan.

The Soto school, in comparison, stresses that satori is not a goal to be attained but is identical with the practice of zazen, which must be engaged in with no gaining idea in mind. Dogen Zenji (1200–1253), the founder of the Soto school in Japan, interpreted the Buddha's statement that everyone has the Buddha-nature as *everyone is the Buddha nature.* This is because the Buddha-nature is not something outside or inside of the individual, but the absolute universal reality. Each and every one of us is the universe, whether we realize it or not. Satori means to wake up to this fact, to the way things are and have always been, a transformative experience that entails the realization of the universal Self.

To clarify satori, Loori (1988) tells the story of the ugly duckling who felt terrible because he was so different from the other ducks who made fun of him.

One day, as he was looking at his reflection in the water, he noticed the reflection of another ugly duckling just like him. As he looked up, he discovered a group of swans, and *in that moment* he realized that he himself was a swan. He instantly became a perfect and complete swan. Suddenly everything was right and he was free from all his psychological suffering. He was enlightened, and yet, nothing had changed, for he had always been a perfect swan. The difference, though, was transformative, for he was liberated from the delusion of his imperfection.

Okumura (1985) wrote, "satori is nothing but being aware of, or being alert in whatever activity you are doing right now, right here. Any activity is not a step, means, or preparation for other things, but rather should be done for its own sake, being accomplished in each moment." This description is a far cry from the mystical misconceptions often connected with the subject of enlightenment.

The activities of an enlightened individual are autotelic. Such enlightened functioning is similar to Csikszentmihalyi's "flow," mentioned in Chapter 13 (1975, 1990). When we become totally immersed in an activity, we can "flow" with it to the point that we lose awareness of ourselves as separate from the activity.

When an enlightened person eats, that person just eats, when resting, just rests, in the same manner that one just sits when practicing zazen. The awakened one does not discriminate between activities, knowing that no task is intrinsically better or worse than any other. Whatever is being done, painting a landscape or cleaning the toilet bowl, is one's life at that moment. Giving the activity full attention is to be able to flow with it, without attempting to get it out of the way to do something else that may be more enjoyable. One is thus fully living one's life. Zen is the art of losing the self (the ego) in the everyday flow of autotelic activities.

The awakening of Zen can be precipitated by any stimulus or event occurring at the right time in the life of a person who is ready to experience it. Recorded instances provide the subject matter for numerous Zen stories. The manner in which a given incident manages to trigger the awakening of a specific individual cannot be understood intellectually, and any attempt to imitate another's realization experience is futile.

Satori must be personally experienced. A master can point the way but cannot experience it for the student. If we are hungry or thirsty, another person's eating or drinking will not fill our stomach or moisten our throat. This is why Zen masters insist that they have nothing to teach or impart. All they can do is show how Zen is practiced and exemplify it in their lives.

Enlightenment is not the end of Zen practice. If it were, it would represent the outcome of a selfish interest if one's own happiness and fulfillment. Practitioners seek enlightenment not for themselves but for the benefit of all sentient beings. Zen teaches that in the enlightenment of one person, all sentient beings are enlightened, for all boundaries are illusions. It has been said that Zen training is like climbing a mountain. Satori is being on top of the mountain. But

The performance of work, when done with mindfulness, is a meditative experience in the Zen tradition.

after reaching the top, coming down the other side of the mountain and return-ing to the "marketplace" to help everyone else is the bodhisattva spirit, exem-plified in the enlightened master.

Eastern Thought and Psychotherapy

Alan Watts (1961) has compared the modes of liberation or psychotherapeutic change developed by the East and the West. Both Western psychotherapy and Eastern ways of life aim at change. However, whereas Western psychotherapy has emphasized change for neurotic or disturbed individuals, Eastern disciplines are concerned with change in the consciousness of normal or healthy people. Eastern psychotherapies recognized long ago that the culture in which one lives not only defines what is normal and abnormal in that particular society but also provides the context for and fosters a more pervasive form of neurosis that is endured by all of its members.

In the West, Sigmund Freud drew our attention to the offenses committed against the human being by social repression. In large measure, the task of the psychoanalyst is to liberate the patient from stressful social conditioning to facilitate more effective functioning. Eastern psychotherapy, however, goes further than classical Freudian psychoanalysis and other Western psychotherapies. It seeks not just to restore the disturbed individual to normal, healthy social functioning but points out that the distress of the normal person, as well as the abnormal, is caused by maya or illusion. The neurosis of all humanity lies in the fact that we take the world picture of our culture too literally and identify with our social role.

The construct of the self as an "individual" is a social process created in the history of our relations with others that gives us our categories of subjective identity but cannot be identified with anything ultimate or real. We need to recognize the relative and impermanent nature of the self, while being aware of the absolute interconnected reality. When crossing the street, it is not enough to contemplate an approaching car and to realize that we are one with it. True, the car, the road, our body, and everything else are nothing more than temporary collections of energy and particles and have no more reality than the transient shape of a wave on the surface of the ocean. Nevertheless, unless we act in the relative plane, and get out of the way of the car, the collection of skandhas that allows this awareness to occur will be promptly dissolved. What is needed is appropriate action in the relative world, while maintaining awareness of the big picture.

The Eastern disciplines provide a path of liberation from unnecessary psychological suffering and its aggravation into mental illness. Western psychotherapy, as Watts points out, falls short of being a way of liberation because it fails to deal with the bigger problem of rectifying the breach between the individual and the world. It is content to limit itself to the individual's adjustment to society. Frequently its aim is to fortify the ego rather than to dissolve it. Such an approach cannot heal the alienation experienced by the ego as the result of the delusion of separation.

There may be another way in which Western psychotherapy has failed, and that is in terms of the development of a method to enhance and protect the mental health of the practicing clinician. Western psychotherapists have rightly stated that it is not possible to bring someone to a higher level of mental health than one has accomplished oneself, but Western psychotherapy has failed to develop the equivalent of zazen as a method to dissolve the delusion of the ego in therapists and patients alike. Therapists need to heal themselves before they are in a position to help others. They need to develop inner peace, and the capacity for compassionate action, to be able to be islands of refuge for those immersed in psychological pain. This is the mental characteristic known as the "immovable mind" of Zen, the natural outcome of the practice of zazen. Echoing Zen master Katagiri's words: if we don't practice zazen, painful events stick to our consciousness and we cannot let go of them.

With the current meeting of East and West, more Western psychotherapists are discovering the value of adopting a meditative discipline as part of their own training, and of meditation as a powerful therapeutic tool (e.g., Hirai, 1989; Kabat-Zinn, 1990; Fickling, 1991; Fuld, 1991; Miller, 1991).

Perhaps one of the most significant developments in the field of psychotherapy over the past couple of decades has been the introduction in the West of several Eastern systems of treatment. Reynolds (1980) identified several Japanese forms of psychotherapy, which he called the "quiet therapies" because their main therapeutic tool is some form of silent meditation, in contrast with the "talking cures" so prevalent in the West. **Morita therapy** was developed by Japanese psychiatrist Shoma Morita in the early 1900s and is founded on the theoretical concepts and practice of Zen, as shown by Rhyner (1988). The method consists of isolated bedrest (to force patients to come in touch with themselves), followed by periods of light and then heavier manual work, and a period of retraining to help patients rejoin normal life. During part of the treatment patients keep a diary that is annotated by the therapist. Standard hospitalization lasts usually from 40 to 60 days (Reynolds, 1976).

The Moritist method requires that patients acknowledge their feelings and take full responsibility for their actions, being trained to behave appropriately despite any feelings that might arise. In other words, they learn to gradually develop a degree of "immovable mind," realizing that if they do not react to their feelings, these feelings have no power over them. This is similar to a person sitting in zazen learning that whatever thoughts, stimuli, or feelings pop up in consciousness and are noticed but not reacted to will pass away, demonstrating their impermanent character. Instead of attempting to remove symptoms, Morita therapy regards patients as students and teaches them to live constructively despite any symptoms or feelings that may be present.

Morita therapy seems to be most effective with neuroses grouped under the name **shinkeishitsu**, which overlap primarily with anxiety disorders in the standard DSM-IV classification. The rates of success of Morita therapy, as reported by Rhyner (1988), are very high, over 90 percent when significant improvement and cures are combined.

Naikan introspective therapy emphasizes the development of a sense of responsibility and obligation in the patient, consonant with the Buddhist principle of interconnectedness or dependent origination, as well as with the sense of societal and familial duty that characterizes Confucian ethics. For instance, one may be instructed to sit in introspective meditation, considering specific things one's mother has done for one, the things one has done for one's mother, and the troubles caused her. Reflection continues with respect to father, siblings, teachers, and others in one's life. What emerges is a deep insight into the imbalance of the relationships and a desire to repay others for their care and support (Reynolds, 1980). Morita and Naikan therapies have been successfully combined by Reynolds into the "constructive living" approach that is rapidly growing in popularity here and abroad.

The value of Zen meditation as therapy and as an adjunct to other forms of psychotherapy has been documented by Hirai (1989) and others. A more general application of mindfulness therapy is advocated by Hanh (1991, 1992), where awareness of emotions (such as anger) is used to transform the energy of the emotion into constructive channels. Kabat-Zinn (1990) has also developed a program based on mindfulness meditation for stress reduction and is currently helping develop similar programs across the country. We are likely to continue to see the increasing impact of Zen and other Eastern disciplines on Western psychotherapy in the future.

THINKING CRITICALLY

Mindfulness and the Search for a Higher Synthesis

At this point you would normally be asked to rate Zen Buddhism on each of the philosophical assumptions described in Chapter 1. However, such an activity would be contrary to the spirit of Zen, which aims at a higher synthesis and asks that we experience rather than analyze. Can you see how the experience of Zen undercuts traditional dualisms such as freedom versus determination, uniqueness versus universality, proactive versus reactive? Can you suggest ways in which thinking in terms of these dualisms may stand in the way of our experiencing ourselves? Can you further suggest ways in which people in the West can benefit from the teachings of the East?

As an additional experiential exercise to appreciate the power of mindfulness, try the following. Select a task you normally dislike or avoid. For example, let's say that you hate to wash dishes. The next time the opportunity presents itself, approach this task as something to be done as a meditative experience. Do the job with full concentration, without rushing through it to get it out of the way to do something else that you regard as more interesting or enjoyable. While you are washing dishes, this is your life at the moment. No activity is intrinsically better or worse than any other activity; it is merely the content of your life at the moment. Pick up each dish, each cup, each glass, each utensil, and carefully wash it, one by one, as if you were polishing a precious jewel. Look at each item in your hands and actually see it. Don't allow your attention to wander. Don't think of anything else. Be there, in the present moment. Maintain awareness of your breath, of your inhalations and exhalations while you do the washing—it will help you to stay in the present moment. Don't look at the clock. Don't talk with someone else while doing this. Just wash the dishes, one at a time, carefully, mindfully, with your whole being. Afterward you may wish to reflect on this experience. Was the task distasteful? Was it enjoyable? What would your life be like, if you did everything with mindfulness? What is keeping you from it? You will find other mindfulness exercises in Hanh (1975, 1993) and Kabat-Zinn (1990).

Eastern Theories: Philosophy, Science, and Art

An extensive literature on Buddhist psychology exists, including diagnosis and psychotherapy. Allport (1975) acknowledged that Eastern psychological theories were more extensive and complete than any Western theories and highly recommended that they be investigated by Western psychologists. In the East, the emphasis is relational rather than individual; the person is not considered in isolation but in relation to the self, to others, and to the larger cosmos.

Most certainly, Eastern concepts of personality do not qualify, nor do they aspire to qualify, as science. The very need to evaluate and demonstrate a personality theory's usefulness constitutes a bias that is foreign to Eastern thought. While Eastern theories are sometimes considered a philosophy or a religion, they do not entail the same logic or speculation that characterizes Western religion and philosophy. Zen and Eastern personality theories in general are in many ways closer to science than to philosophy or religion, but since they do not utilize the scientific method of investigation, it is perhaps most accurate to describe them as art.

Eastern theories are highly practical. They offer a variety of techniques for cultivating a deeper understanding of the self. These practices move the individual away from intellectual, rational consciousness and cultivate a deeper awareness that transcends everyday consciousness. Systematically training the body and the mind, Eastern disciplines aim at enabling the individual to perceive the truth that lies within the inner being.

There has been a steady growth of interest in the ideas and practices of the East. The influence of Eastern concepts is apparent in the work of several personality theorists included in this book: Jung explicitly incorporated Eastern concepts into his theory; Fromm and Horney turned to the East to enrich their theories and practices, and the same is true to some extent of Rogers, Maslow, and many others, particularly in the emerging field of transpersonal psychology. By looking for the commonalities between Buddhism and Western thought, especially existentialism, we may be taken to even greater insights. Exciting new holistic metatheories of personality integrate Western psychology's obsession with early development and self-esteem with Eastern traditions concerned with self-transcendence and enlightenment. Today, with increasing opportunities for cooperation, it is vitally important that East and West appreciate each other's attempts to understand the self. To do so can only enrich both.

Summary

1. Eastern psychology is characterized by an emphasis on the self, on practical techniques, and on experiential knowledge.

2. Siddhartha Gautama, the **Buddha,** renounced everything he had and left home in search of a solution to the problem of human suffering. After six years he attained enlightenment. Theravada and Mahayana Buddhism grew out of his teachings. **Zen Buddhism,** a branch of the Mahayana, adopted **Taoist** language in China and spread from there to Japan and the rest of the world.

3. The principle of **dependent origination** says "this is, because that is; this is not, because that is not; when this arises, that arises; when this ceases, that ceases."

4. The three characteristics of existence are **anicca** (impermanence), **dukkha** (suffering), and **anatta** (non-self). The Buddha's solution to the problem of suffering was expressed in the form of the **Four Noble Truths.**

5. The experience of enlightenment, or **satori,** is an awakening to the reality of the universe that cannot be grasped through intellectual analysis, but must be experienced personally.

6. The five **skandhas** are form, feelings, perceptions, impulses, and consciousness. A person is a temporary arrangement of these aggregates or skandhas and has no reality separated from them.

7. Of the eight consciousnesses, the first five correspond to the basic sense fields: seeing, hearing, smelling, tasting, and touching. Below that are the **manovijnana,** the integrating basis of the five sensory consciousnesses; **manas** ("mind"), where the illusion of a separate "I" or "ego" arises; and the **alayavijnana** ("storehouse consciousness"), the ground of knowledge and impressions that exist in the form of "seeds" affecting each other in various ways.

8. The practice of Zen entails a systematic training of the mind through the practice of **zazen,** sitting meditation, and the extension of the mindfulness and concentration of zazen to daily life. The two main schools of Zen are **Soto,** which stresses the practice of zazen as "just sitting," or **shikantaza,** and **Rinzai,** which employs the **koan** (an apparently paradoxical statement, question, or anecdote) as a focus of concentration during zazen. Furthermore, the Rinzai school sees zazen as a method to reach enlightenment, while the Soto school stresses that practice and enlightenment are one and the same.

9. It is necessary to actually practice zazen in order to understand it. Detailed instructions are given on pages 465–466.

10. Whereas Western psychotherapy has emphasized change for neurotic or disturbed individuals, Eastern disciplines are concerned with change in the consciousness of normal or healthy people, pointing out that the distress of both is caused by **maya,** or illusion.

11. Eastern theories do not entail the speculation or the kind of logic characteristic of Western theories. For our purposes, it is most accurate to characterize them as art.

Suggestions for Further Reading

It is often said that the best Zen books are those that make you put them down and head for the meditation cushion. S. Suzuki's *Zen Mind, Beginner's Mind* (Weatherhill, 1970), Katagiri's *Returning to Silence* (Shambhala, 1988), and Uchiyama's *Opening the Hand of Thought* (Penguin, 1993) do an excellent job of explaining and encouraging the practice and application of Zen in daily life. The best manual of Zen meditation, clearly illustrated and including a number of classic and modern texts, is Okumura's *Shikantaza* (Kyoto, 1985). A lot of common questions about Zen are answered in Deshimaru's *Questions to a Zen Master* (Dutton, 1985).

For an introduction to the basic teachings of Buddhism, the best is Rahula's *What the Buddha Taught* (Grove, 1974). Three worthwhile biographies of the Buddha from different perspectives are Kalupahana's novelized *The Way of Siddhartha* (Shambhala, 1982), Nanamoli's *The Life of the Buddha* (B.P.S., 1978), based on the Pali Canon, and Carrither's historical *The Buddha* (Oxford, 1983).

A fair historical outline of the development of Zen can be found in Hoover's *The Zen Experience* (New American Library, 1980), while the history of the coming of Buddhism to America is extensively treated in Field's *How the Swans Came to the Lake* (Shambhala, 1992). Goldberg's *Long Quiet Highway* (Bantam, 1993) is a writer's delightful account of her relationship with her Zen teacher.

To begin an exploration of the works of that deepest of Zen masters, Eihei Dogen, the student is referred to Cleary's *Rational Zen* (Shambhala, 1992), the Dogen & Uchiyama volume *Refining Your Life* (Weatherhill, 1983), and Abe's challenging *A Study of Dogen* (S.U.N.Y., 1992). For the practice of mindfulness and an understanding of "dependent origination" in everyday life, the various books by Thich Nhat Hanh are without peer. Especially recommended are *Being Peace* (Parallax, 1987), *Touching Peace* (Parallax, 1992), *Peace is Every Step* (Bantam, 1991), and *The Heart of Understanding* (Parallax, 1988). Another extremely worthwhile volume is Kabat-Zinn's *Wherever You Go, There You Are* (Hyperion, 1994).

Those interested in feminist issues will find of value several volumes on the contributions of women teaching Zen Buddhism in America, such as Boucher's *Turning the Wheel* (Harper & Row, 1988) and Friedman's *Meetings with Remarkable Women* (Shambhala, 1987). Also worthwhile are several excellent books on Zen practice written by Western women, such as Beck's *Everyday Zen* (Harper & Row, 1989) and *Nothing Special: Living Zen* (Harper Collins, 1993), Mountains's *The Zen Environment* (Morrow, 1982) and Packer's *The Work of This Moment* (Shambhala, 1990), as well as the collection of essays by the Japanese Zen nun Shundo Aoyama, *Zen Seeds* (Kosei, 1990).

For applications of Zen in the field of psychotherapy, you may wish to start with Wellwood's *Awakening the Heart* (Shambhala, 1983) and Claxton's *Beyond Therapy* (Wisdom, 1986). Further reading on the Zen-based Morita therapy can be found in the many excellent books on the subject by David K. Reynolds, especially *Morita Psychotherapy* (U.C., 1976), *Playing Ball on Running Water* (Morrow, 1984), and *Plunging Through the Clouds* (S.U.N.Y., 1993).

A general application of Buddhist meditation in the area of stress management is Kabat-Zinn's *Full Catastrophe Living* (Delacorte, 1990), while for the stresses of college life Gibbs's *Dancing with Your Books* (Penguin, 1990) is highly recommended. An excellent discussion of the convergence of psychoanalysis and Zen Buddhism can be found in Suler's *Contemporary Psychoanalysis and Eastern Thought* (S.U.N.Y., 1993).

Finally, Kosko's *Fuzzy Thinking* (Hyperion, 1993) is an exploration of the impact of Zen ideas at the cutting edge of modern science—a thoroughly enjoyable and informative volume.

Beyond reading, you may wish to practice zazen. A traditional meditation cushion (*zafu*) and mat (*zabuton*) will make this a lot easier. One source is the Minnesota Zen Meditation Center (3343 East Calhoun Parkway, Minneapolis, MN 55408-3313). A set costs about $75, including postage ($35 for the *zafu* alone). The same source can also supply the otherwise hard to find meditation manual by Shohaku Okumura, *Shikantaza,* published in Japan. You may also like to locate a Zen center to try practicing Zen under the guidance of a qualified teacher. If you cannot find one in your area, a handy reference is Morreale's *Buddhist America* (John Muir, 1988), which in addition to giving addresses and descriptions of numerous centers contains many interesting articles. You may also wish to check the directory of meditation groups in *Tricycle: The Buddhist Review,* a nationally distributed magazine.

CONCLUSION

Personality Theory in Perspective

YOUR GOALS FOR THIS CHAPTER

1. Compare different personality theories in terms of their emphasis on philosophy, science, and art.
2. Compare different personality theories in terms of their stand on some basic philosophical issues.
3. Discuss the history of the terms *psyche* and *psychology* from their origins in Greek thought to their present-day use.
4. Indicate how Western psychology has narrowed the definition of *empirical*. Explain how the scientific method may separate us from experience rather than illuminate it.
5. Describe some signs of change on the horizon.
6. Explain why it is important to conceive of personality theories as philosophy and art as well as science.

This final chapter seeks to place the personality theories we have studied into perspective by making some comparisons and contrasts among them and by pointing to a problem in contemporary personality theorizing, suggesting a view toward the future.

Personality Theories: Philosophy, Science, and Art

Although personality theories are a branch of academic scientific psychology, they also entail philosophy and art. As scientists, personality theorists seek to develop workable hypotheses that enable us to understand human behavior. As philosophers, personality theorists seek to give us insight into what it means to be a person. As artists, personality theorists seek to apply what is known about people and behavior to foster a better life. Some critics evaluate theories simply in terms of their efficacy as science. Yet, as we have seen, few of the theories described in this text demonstrate purely scientific concerns. This text has described a variety of theories ranging from Freud's emphasis on the ego to Eastern psychology's denial of it. Most theories reflect a great variety of concerns and need to be evaluated in terms of the criteria that suit their goals.

Some of the theories we have considered clearly reflect philosophical concerns. The psychoanalytic tradition, for instance, tends to be philosophical, rather than scientific, in its approach. Psychoanalytic theorists, by and large, are clinicians who develop their theoretical structures within the context of therapy. Although their methods and results are frequently empirical, that is, based on observation, they could not be described as rigorous or precise scientific techniques. Psychoanalytic theorists tend to consider proof as arising from the internal consistency of a theory and the ability of the theory to illumine the human condition. Their work is ultimately evaluated in terms of its coherence, relevance, comprehensiveness, and compellingness. The theories of Sigmund Freud, Carl Jung, Alfred Adler, Erich Fromm, and Rollo May represent a deep commitment to an underlying philosophy of life. More recent psychoanalytic theorists appreciate the need to validate their constructs and are thus open to scientific test. But psychoanalytic theory remains largely philosophical. This is best seen in the work of Erik Erikson who did not insist on a scientific pretense for his work but tried to make his philosophical assumptions explicit.

Other theories make a greater effort to be successful scientific theories. Behavior and learning theories are expressly scientific in their approach. Committed to a rigorous methodology, behavior and learning theories shun theoretical speculation in favor of careful observation and experimentation. Thus, John Dollard and Neal Miller emphasized empirical research in their efforts to combine psychoanalytic theory with the behaviorist tradition. B. F. Skinner's view also evolved from experimental laboratory investigations. This emphasis has continued in the work of cognitive and social learning theorists, like Albert Bandura and Julian Rotter, whose theories are superb examples of a rigorous scientific approach to personality. Their methodologies have produced precise and economical theories and have given strong empirical support to their constructs. Psychometric trait theories also demonstrate a deep commitment to scientific methodologies and validating evidence; Raymond Cattell's theories are excellent examples of an effort to comprehend personality through a scientific model.

Some theorists deliberately seek an interdisciplinary approach. Henry A. Murray was one of the first to recognize the value of an interdisciplinary methodology; the diagnostic council that he established at Harvard was unprecedented in its vision and scope. Jung, Fromm, Gordon Allport, and Abraham Maslow all drew upon several areas of research—art, literature, history, philosophy, and science—in their efforts to understand human nature. Carl Rogers very carefully distinguished between his philosophical assumptions and his scientific hypotheses, emphasizing the need for a balanced view.

Other theories are primarily concerned with the art of personality theory, or the practical applications. We saw how Eastern thinkers do not seek to demonstrate the validity of their constructs or engage in philosophical speculation; rather, they are concerned with offering a variety of practices for cultivating a deeper understanding of the self. Likewise, Ellis, Beck, and Lazarus are best known for their contributions in the area of counseling. Freud, Horney, Adler, Rogers, and Kelly also made substantial contributions to the understanding and practice of psychotherapy.

None of the personality theories that we have studied can be appropriately labeled as simply philosophy, science, or art. For instance, although behavior and learning theories largely seek to present a scientific conception of personality, they also reflect basic philosophical assumptions that influence their scientific hypotheses and their practical applications.

Initially, behavior and learning theorists were unable to recognize the philosophical roots of their approach. In recent years, however, they have acknowledged the philosophical assumptions that undergird their work. It is now widely recognized that even the most scientific approach to understanding personality addresses philosophical questions and suggests philosophical answers. Indeed, the basic difference among personality theories appears to be one of philosophical stance.

Philosophical Issues

Personality theories, then, can be compared in terms of where they stand on each of the basic philosophical issues outlined in Chapter 1.

For example, theorists differ as to whether they believe people are basically free to control their own behavior or whether they believe that behavior is essentially determined by forces over which people have little, if any, control. Both Freud and Skinner saw the individual as determined but for very different reasons. For Freud, the individual is motivated by internal unconscious forces. For Skinner, the individual is shaped by forces within the environment. Theorists also differ in the extent to which they would like their theories to be used to cultivate freedom in human nature or to exercise greater control over it. Skinner sought to develop a technology to control human behavior, whereas Rogers tried to increase a client's sense of freedom and responsibility.

As we have seen, another of the most puzzling questions in personality theorizing has been the dichotomy between hereditary and environmental determinants of behavior. Theorists differ over whether they believe that inborn characteristics or factors in the environment have the more important influence on a person's behavior. Dispositional theorists stress the importance of long-term personality traits in understanding behavior; behaviorists emphasize situational factors. These philosophical differences also lead to different recommendations for action. An emphasis on inborn factors sometimes leads to the support of selective breeding; an emphasis on situational factors may lead to efforts to change the environment. Thus, Cattell urged consideration of *eugenics,* the study of improving hereditary qualities by genetic control, and Bandura encouraged *euthenics,* the study of advancing human life by improving living conditions. The most recent theories stress an interactionist and biosocial view.

A third major issue is that of uniqueness versus universality. Allport clearly grappled with this issue. On one hand he recognized that common traits permit us to make generalizations and comparisons among individuals, but in the final analysis he held that each individual is particular and unique. Eastern theories point out that we need to see through the illusion of individual existence, called maya. Jung described a twofold process of individuation and transcendence.

Proaction versus reaction is a fourth dimension that influences personality theories. Allport discovered in a study of psychological terms with the prefixes *re-* and *pro-* that most theories tend to be reactive. Concepts such as "repression" and "regression" in psychoanalysis and "reflex" and "reinforcement" in stimulus-response theory suggest an emphasis on the past and a preoccupation with homeostasis. Humanist theories, on the other hand, suggest that the human being is motivated toward heterostasis, that is, growth and self-actualization. Cognitive theories also emphasize the present and the future rather than the past, viewing the individual as purposeful and active rather than passive.

Finally, personality theories can be compared according to whether they are optimistic or pessimistic about the possibility of change. Freud is generally seen as a pessimist because he believed that adult behavior is deeply structured by early childhood. Dispositional theorists believe that some constitutional factors place firm limits on personality change. Behavior and learning, cognitive, and humanist theorists, on the other hand, are usually very optimistic concerning the possibility of change.

These basic issues are typically presented as bipolar dimensions. However, Rollo May reminds us that they are actually paradoxes of human existence that

seek resolution in a creative synthesis. An either/or position is generally misleading. Personality theorists must avoid being impaled on either horn of the
dilemma as they try to reflect the truth of human existence.

In any event, a response to a theorist can take one of three forms. We can
agree with the theorist and adopt his or her philosophical categories as part of
our scientific activity. We can object to a theorist's own philosophical grounds
and maintain that another view is more compelling. Or, we can maintain that
none of these views is adequate. If we adopt the third position, we are then faced
with the responsibility of suggesting an alternative philosophical framework
that provides a more convincing model for understanding personality.

The Challenge of Contemporary Personality Theorizing

Although psychology is a young science, it represents the oldest of human concerns. Our Western tradition initially fostered a mystical view of the self, emphasizing the spiritual side of the person. The effort to comprehend the human
personality within the framework of a scientific methodology is largely the recent product of the twentieth century.

The term *psychology* comes from the ancient Greek word *psyche,* first introduced by the poet Homer to express the essence of a human being, or "the self."
During the early Christian era, as philosophy and rhetoric replaced poetry and
mythology, the term *psyche* came to be identified with *pneuma,* or "spirit." It
later became identified with the more rationalistic and intellectual concept of
nous, or "mind." By the time of the Enlightenment, "psyche" had become synonymous with consciousness or mental processes. As we have seen, John Watson, the founder of behaviorism, subsequently pointed out that states of consciousness are not objectively verifiable. He deemed them unfit as data for
science and encouraged psychologists simply to study behavior. Under Watson's
leadership, psychology was transformed from the largely introspective study of
consciousness into the study of overt or observable behaviors. Thus, in the typical American university a strange situation prevailed throughout most of the
twentieth century. Students of psychology discovered that, for the most part,
they were not engaged in the study of the psyche; they were engaged in the
study of behavior.

Behaviorism came to be the dominant position of psychology in American
universities. Psychologists sought to pursue psychology as an experimental science that emulated the natural science of physics. The mainstream of American
psychology still tends to emphasize extrospective observation and a rigorous
scientific methodology. This emphasis is found in the cognitive approach,
which has superseded behaviorism as the dominant trend.

Not all of the personality theorists that we have considered agree that a
rigorous scientific method is the best way to understand personality. Indeed,
some (Allport, Maslow, Rogers, and May, for example) have been very critical of

the narrow view of psychology as an experimental science. Their critiques have fostered trends toward a more humanistic approach and an interest in alternative means of studying the person.

Unfortunately, however, humanistic psychology became a "divisive force." Psychologists tend to be divided as to whether they belong to a "humanistic" or a "scientific" camp. Thus, "the early promise of this approach, as emphasized by Abraham Maslow and Carl Rogers, was never realized in the mainstream of psychology" (Ornstein, 1977; see also Boneau, 1992). Humanistic psychology and mainstream psychology share the same problem: How do we overcome the tension between the demands of good science and the demands of the subject matter? (Giorgi, 1987).

The behaviorist and cognitive positions, with their emphasis on extrospective observation and experimental research, continue to represent the strongest and most predominant modes of psychological study in the American academy today. Those theorists who choose not to imitate the mainstream run the risk of being considered less respectable because of their lack of allegiance to a purely scientific approach and methodology. They are tolerated, particularly when they are willing to subject their findings to scientific scrutiny, but their theories are not fully recognized as sound.

We have seen that the keynote of science is observation. Scientific theories rest on empirical data, that which is based on experience. In Western psychology, however, the term *empirical* has been rendered practically synonymous with "relying on or derived from extrospective observation." Empirical data have been largely limited to objective findings. Other data of experience or observation, such as subjective introspection, have been discouraged or depreciated, largely because it is so difficult to test these findings experimentally.

Historical, philosophical, and mythological data, because they invariably entail subjective as well as objective elements, are often viewed as incompatible with science. According to this conception, a competent scientist generally does not permit subjective assumptions to interfere with his or her work. The scientist remains detached, objective, and value free, which Maslow and Fromm said is an error. As a result, Western psychology has tended to isolate itself. It has divorced itself from other possible modes of investigation on the grounds that their findings, because they are difficult to test experimentally, are not objective and are therefore incompatible with science.

David Bakan has pointed out that the rigorous scientific methodology of the Western experimental psychologist may, at times, actually stand in the way of the empirical and divorce us from experience rather than illuminate it (1969). In a well-developed experiment the experimenter does not deal with the everyday world; instead, she or he creates a **paraworld** of quantified, logico-mathematical imaginary constructs. In this paraworld, events are carefully chosen and precisely controlled in order to avoid the haphazard occurrences of the everyday world that might jeopardize the results. Further, in a well-designed experiment all the possible alternatives and outcomes are anticipated in advance. The experimenter can predict within limits what is going to happen as a result of the manipulation of the variables in the experiment. And so the more carefully designed an experiment is, the more separate it becomes from the world of experience that it seeks to clarify. The Western psychologist's reliance on a rigid experimental method may, therefore, interfere with the possibility of learning from experience.

The emphasis on extrospection and rigorous scientific methodology also limits the findings of psychology to those that can be demonstrated within the experimental laboratory. It circumscribes the study of personality to merely those aspects about the person that can be comprehended in specifically scientific terms. Because of this, many questions about the ultimate meaning, purpose, and goal of human living, questions that traditionally have been and could be included in the study of personality, and are addressed by some theorists, are ruled out of inquiry.

Few theories of personality resemble an ideal scientific theory. Their assumptions lack explicitness, making it difficult for us to derive empirical statements that would permit us to move from abstract theory to empirical observation. Many personalty theories, although provocative, have failed to generate a significant amount of research, thus depriving us of some of the "most important evaluative comparison" that can be made among theories (Hall & Lindzey, 1978). And yet, those personality theories that successfully emulate a scientific model can be criticized as gaining their precision, accuracy, and predictive power at the price of evoking little depth of insight or new understanding.

In part, the problem results from the fact that theories of personality explore phenomena that by their very nature elude a narrow definition of science. At the heart of the experimental method is the search for cause and effect. Theories that emphasize motivation or free will make it difficult to look for underlying causes and limit the possibility of prediction and control. Moreover, they call into question the value of experimentation as a primary means of gaining insight into the human condition.

We need to recall that American psychology struggled valiantly to become a respectable science. This struggle entailed severing its early ties with philosophy and modeling itself along the lines of the natural sciences. Sound training in experimental design and statistical methods characterize the curriculum of academic psychology. Because of the earlier struggle to gain recognition as a science, many psychologists, particularly those with a behaviorist orientation, are suspicious of recent efforts by personality theorists to defy strict scientific methodology and reassert the philosophical character of psychology.

As a result, much of the current research in personality is fragmented (cf. Sarason, 1989; Magnusson & Törestad, 1993), limited to a special domain that can be precisely defined, articulated, measured, and tested. Feshbach (1984) suggested that "the study of personality has not moved in the direction of actualization; rather it appears to have become constricted, dissociated, and overly defensive." A particular variable, such as locus of control, need to achieve, or cognitive style, is isolated for study, leading to a multiplicity of interesting and reliable empirical findings.

Many current texts in personality, after providing a brief introduction to theories, concentrate on major research issues such as intelligence, anxiety and stress, perceived control, aggression, altruism, sex roles, and gender differences. But as May reminds us, contemporary psychological research is preoccupied with data and numbers at the expense of theory. The most important scientific discoveries were not made by accumulating facts but by perceiving relationships among the facts (1983). Retief (1986) points out that "data and methods, no matter how profuse and sophisticated they may be, can lead nowhere on their own: it is obvious that good theories are needed to guide them. . . . Psychology has made a firm commitment to method: the time for an equal commitment to theory is overdue." Human nature can be understood only within a theoretical framework. The real contribution lies in seeing a new *form* that avoids the misconceptions of an existing mythology (see also Noble, 1993).

The reluctance to reassert the philosophical character of psychology to some extent reflects a realistic fear that our present disillusionment with science may foster a tendency to disregard the substantial contributions that it has made to our understanding. We developed the experimental method as a tool because we discovered that we could increase our understanding and act more efficiently if our activities were guided by information about the determined aspects of our everyday world. Although it may be true that the experimental method cannot establish truth, it has provided a very pragmatic means of testing some of our assumptions.

Still, we should recognize that a purely experimental approach is not the only option available to the personality theorist and we should be aware of the effects of a narrow scientific conception of psychology. Moreover, we must not allow the popularity of the experimental approach in the American academy to close our eyes to the importance of other methods or to the reality of the phenomena that other methods draw to our attention. We should seek a higher perspective in which science and philosophy are no longer in opposition to one another but complement each other.

Many contemporary personality theorists urge us to be *more,* not less, empirical—that is, *more* empirical in the original sense of the term, "based on experience." They point out that our traditional scientific methods may not only fail to do justice to the experiental data but may also camouflage it. They suggest that when we limit our analysis to those phenomena that can be comprehended in terms of current experimental methodology, we prejudice our results. By becoming "less scientistic," psychology could become "more scientific" (Bakan, 1969).

Although psychology represents the oldest of human concerns, the science of psychology and the effort to comprehend the human personality within the framework of a scientific methodology is largely a product of the twentieth century. We have seen (in Chapter 1) that Wilhelm Wundt conceived of psychology as an experimental science that ought to emulate the natural science of physics. Psychology may have failed as a scientific enterprise because it did not develop its own methodology but borrowed it from the physical sciences

(Kruger, 1986). Many psychologists have been moving away from the social sciences toward the biological sciences and clinical practice. This has led to an increased isolation of scientific psychology from the insights and problems of other social sciences (Harzem, 1987). In contemporary sciences from biology to physics, the concept of *pattern* has replaced earlier concepts, such as cause and effect, as the key principle of explanation. Psychology has yet to incorporate that view (Rychlak, 1986).

There are signs of change on the horizon. Rychlak (1981) and Valentine (1988) argue for a teleological (goal-oriented) perspective. The renewed interest in idiographic methods of research is heartening. In 1988, the *Journal of Personality* devoted an entire issue to psychobiography and life narratives. These are contemporary forms of case histories and studies of the unique life stories of individuals such as those explored by Freud, Erikson, Murray, and Allport. Alasdair MacIntyre (1984) has suggested that narrative history may be "the basic and essential genre for the characterization of human actions." Larry Davidson (1987) suggests that if psychology reconceives itself as based on an analysis of motivational/intentional relations, it will place itself in a closer and more appropriate relationship to the sociocultural sciences than to the physical sciences.

The narrative form is increasingly being seen as the most appropriate form for understanding the construction of self in a postmodern era (Miller, Potts, Fung, & Hoogstra, 1990; Atkinson, 1990; Freeman, 1992). "Instances of cultural diversity take on a different hue when viewed from a narrative perspective (Howard, 1991)." A study of Japanese children's personal narratives may help us to understand how those children are trained in empathy (Minami & McCabe, 1991). Gardner (1992) suggests that psychology turn toward literature and other artistic studies in an effort to help understand issues such as self, will, consciousness, and personality. His suggestion has stirred considerable discussion (see Markova, 1992; Oatley, 1992; Potter & Wetherell, 1992; Sternberg, 1992; and Woodward, 1992). Students of personality would do well to emulate van Krogten's interpretive-theoretical research method modeled in his *Proustian Love* (1992), in which he presents a complex theory on the psychology of love built on principles originating from a study of Proust's *Remembrance of Things Past.* "The stories we live by" (McAdams, 1993) and the scientific method itself (Suchecki, 1989) are being seen as mythical texts.

Maher (1991) has argued that the meager real increase in our understanding of the psychology of personality in recent years may be due to methodological procedures and our underlying notion of human behavior. These notions and procedures induced us to "invent artificial problems to solve" instead of focusing on real ones, "namely the identification of the processes that govern" human behavior "in the natural habitat" (1991). As psychologists increasingly argue that psychology needs to be relevant, to "adequately explain the immediate causes influencing people's lives" (Retief, 1989), and to take a proactive role in helping us to understand our values and moral development in a postmodern society (Neufeldt, 1989; Packer, 1992), narrative thought is being seen as a major form of cognition and an important part of moral education (Vitz, 1990).

No more can we assume that science considers facts and ethics considers values living in different domains. Ethics are the result of social life and need to be studied "in their own right." "When we do this, the outlines of a different kind of ethical justification becomes apparent, one that legitimatizes multiple objective moralities rather than a universal moral system" (Packer, 1992).

As we focus on cultural diversity, we also must recognize that ideas such as actualization, individuation, and autonomy, and the psychotherapies rooted in them are not apt to be immediately germane to other portions of U.S. society or to people who relate to diverse other societies which do not cultivate or prize these notions. Many theories of personality "imply that their stance is apolitical, while in actuality, they serve a highly political function—in service of the continued acceptance of the specifically patriarchal status quo of present society in the United States" (Lerman, 1992). Sexism and racism as ideologies that try to justify white male supremacy need to be challenged (Andersen, 1991). We need to specifically ask of personality theories whether they embrace the diversity and complexity of women and other minorities and insist that they begin to address those issues (Espin & Gawelek, 1992). As technologies are increasing our communication with people of diverse cultures and values, we need to recognize that "there is no distinct American identity. America exists as it does because of the relationships of which it is a part" (Gergen, 1992).

Burkitt (1991) suggests that we try to understand people as social selves rather than self-contained individuals. It may be desirable to develop indigenous psychologies more appropriate to various cultures (Naidu, 1991; Puhan & Sahoo, 1991) or at least a pluralistic psychology aiming to transform dehumanizing social contexts (O'Hara, 1992).

Concentration on the biological basis of personality will also increase. As we turn to genetics and neurobiology we will be looking at temperament or traits that are innate and explore how these are changed by social and developmental events (Woodall & Matthews, 1993). An evolutionary perspective will also be apparent, looking at how personality traits adapt and have helped to ensure the survival of the human race (Buss, 1991).

The spirit of the new physics combats the estrangement and segmentation of life in the twentieth century and supplants it with a view of reality in which the human consciousness is just one form of consciousness within a wider cosmic consciousness. Such a quantum world view goes beyond the two poles of individual and relationship by demonstrating that human beings can only be the persons they are within a framework. "The quantum self thus mediates between the extreme isolation of Western individualism and the extreme collectivism of Marxism or Western mysticism" (Zohar, 1991). A therapeutic universal narrative is now coming into consciousness from many diverse fields of science and telling us that it is futile to be disconnected. The cosmos is "one system of which we're one part integrated into the totality. . . . The fate of the earth is our fate as we're part of the same totality" (Coelho, 1993).

Boneau (1992) predicts students and faculty will be leaving psychology "to become interdisciplinary cognitive scientists and neuroscientists." However, he adds, these subjects are only concerned with parts of a larger picture. We "need to have a science of humanity, a discipline concerned with understanding and explaining the human individual coping in a social-cultural-environmental context? . . . That is not what psychology is now, but perhaps it should be."

It is not wise for a field of investigation that claims to explore the human condition to refuse to deal with a wide variety of concepts and data simply because they are difficult to state in narrow, preconceived scientific terms. The crises in living that we face today mandate that we marshal whatever means are available to assist us in self-understanding. A true portrait of personality must come to terms with all the experiences that are central to being a person, even though they may be difficult to conceptualize, test, or express. Lopsided theories err not simply because they present us incomplete portraits that are often biased or stereotyped but because they fail to develop concepts that adequately represent human potential. In doing so, lopsided theories deprive us of important aspects of our own consciousness.

This book has suggested that personality theorizing invariably entails more than science; it also involves philosophy and art. Every activity that we engage in rests on certain philosophical assumptions. Contemporary personality theorizing is tied to and limited by certain assumptions that characterize our view

Figure C.1 *Dymaxion Map*
Here is a map that seeks to portray more accurately the world that we all share.

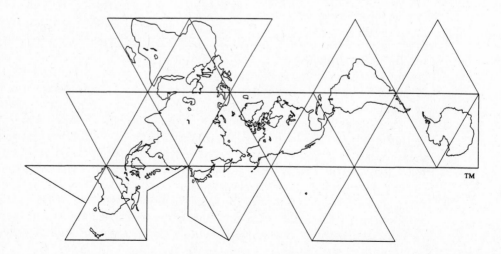

of the world. Frequently, these assumptions are implicit rather than explicit; that is, they are not clearly recognized. Nevertheless, they profoundly influence our concept of the world and its inhabitants. Only by making our assumptions explicit and continually re-examining them can we place ourselves in a better position to understand ourselves. Herein lies the value of the scientific method: it has provided us with a means of testing and consensually validating our theoretical speculations. What we need to do is twofold. We need to evaluate our philosophical assumptions in the light of contemporary scientific information and to judge our scientific findings in the light of their adequacy as philosophy. In the final analysis, however, neither the speculations of science nor the speculations of philosophy can express the ultimate meaning of personality. The ultimate expression of personality does not lie in the constructs of science or philosophy. It lies in the art of living.

Summary

1. Personality theories can be compared in terms of their emphasis on philosophy, science, and art. For example, psychoanalytic theories tend to emphasize philosophy, whereas behavior and learning theories emphasize science.

2. They can also be compared in terms of where they stand on basic philosophical issues, like freedom versus determinism, heredity versus environment, uniqueness versus universality, proactive versus reactive emphases, and optimism versus pessimism. For instance, humanist theories stress an individual's responsibility and free will; psychoanalytic and behaviorist theories see the individual as determined.

3. Although psychology is a young science, it represents one of the oldest human concerns. The term *psyche* is an ancient Greek term that originally referred to "the self." Later it came to mean "spirit" and, finally, "mind." Through the influence of the behaviorist movement, *psychology* came to be the study of behavior, emphasizing a rigorous scientific method based on extrospective observation.

4. In Western psychology the term *empirical* has been rendered synonymous with "relying on or derived from extrospective observation." The rigorous scientific methodology of the Western experimental psychologist may at times tend to divorce us from experience, rather than illumine it, by separating us from the everyday world.

5. Some signs of change are the emphasis on the narrative form, the introduction of values, an emphasis on cultural diversity, and a possible reconceptualization of psychology.

6. Personality theories need to be seen as philosophy, science, and art in order to do justice to the full range of human existence and potentiality.

Suggestions for Further Reading

For additional information on problems in current psychological research, see David Bakan, *On Method: Toward a Reconstruction of Psychological Investigation* (Jossey-Bass, 1969). Bakan points out that our enormous expenditures on psychological research are not yielding much new information. He suggests ways in which psychology might become "more scientific" and "less scientistic."

The following three books were previously recommended in conjunction with the Introduction; they are again suggested as invaluable for the student who is interested in pursuing personality theory in greater depth: Joseph Rychlak, *A Philosophy of Science for Personality Theory* (Houghton Mifflin, 1968); T. S. Kuhn, *The Structure of Scientific Revolutions,* 2nd ed. (University of Chicago Press, 1970); and I. Chein, *The Science of Behavior and the Image of Man* (Basic Books, 1972).

More recent books include Danah Zohar in collaboration with I. N. Marshall, *The Quantum Self: Human Nature and Consciousness Defined by the New Physics* (Morrow, 1990) and Ian Burkitt, *Social Selves: Theories of the Social Formation of Personality* (Sage, 1991). Igor van Krogten's interpretive-theoretical research method is described in *Proustian Love* (Swets & Zeitlinger, B.V. Amsterdam/Lisse, 1992).

GLOSSARY

A-B-C theory of personality In Ellis's rational-emotive therapy, the theory that a highly charged *emotional consequence* (C) is caused not by a significant *activation event* (A), but by the individual's *belief system* (B).

acceptance A nonjudgmental recognition of oneself, others, and the world.

active imagination In Jung's psychotherapy, a method for getting in touch with the archetypes.

affective arousal The arousal of emotions in conjunction with cognitions.

alayavijnana Sanskrit for the storehouse consciousness, the last of the eight consciousnesses.

alienation In Horney's theory, a state in which the real self and the idealized self are disjunct.

amplification In Jungian therapy, an analytical method whereby one focuses repeatedly on an element and gives multiple associations to it.

anal stage One of Freud's psychosexual stages, in which the major source of pleasure and conflict is the anus.

analytical psychology The school of psychology founded by Carl Jung.

anatta Pali for non-selfness, the lack of a permanent separate self, one of the three characteristics of existence in Buddhism.

androgyny The presence of both masculine and feminine qualities in an individual and the ability to realize both potentials.

anicca Pali for impermanence and transiency, one of the three characteristics of existence according to the Buddha.

anima In Jung's theory, an archetype representing the feminine side of the male personality.

animus In Jung's theory, an archetype representing the masculine side of the female personality.

anxiety An emotional state characterized by a vague fear or premonition that something undesirable may happen. In May's theory, the apprehension cued off by a threat to some value that the individual holds as essential to his or her existence as a person.

archetype In Jung's theory, a universal thought form or predisposition to perceive the world in certain ways.

assessment Evaluation or measurement.

atman Sanskrit for soul, self, or ego.

attitude A positive or negative feeling toward an object. a) In Jung's theory, a basic psychotype. b) In Cattell's theory, a surface dynamic trait.

authoritarian ethics In Fromm's theory, a value system whose source lies outside the individual.

authoritarianism In Fromm's theory, a way of escaping from freedom by adhering to a new form of submission or domination.

autoeroticism Self-love. In Freud's theory, the child's sexual activity.

automaton conformity In Fromm's theory, a way of escaping from freedom by adopting the personality proffered by one's culture.

autonomous dimension In Beck's theory, a personality dimension characterized by independence.

autonomous self In Kohut's theory, an ideal self with qualities of self-esteem and self-confidence.

autonomy versus shame and doubt Erikson's psychosocial stage, corresponding to Freud's anal stage, in which the child faces the task of developing control over his or her body and bodily activities.

autotelic Containing its own goal, an activity done for its own sake.

avoiding type In Adler's theory, people who try to escape life's problems and who engage in little socially constructive activity.

basic anxiety In Horney's theory, feelings of insecurity in which the environment as a whole is dreaded because it is seen as unrealistic, dangerous, unappreciative, and unfair.

BASIC-ID In Lazarus's theory, an examination of the seven modalities, behavior, affect, sensation, imagery, cognition, interpersonal relationships, and drugs, that make up human personality.

basic needs therapy Therapeutic procedures that seek to meet the primary needs of people.

basic orientations In Horney's theory, fundamental modes of interaction with the world.

Beck Depression Inventory An instrument developed by Beck to measure depression.

behavior The activity of an organism. a) In learning theory, a response to stimuli. b) In Rogers's theory, the goal-directed attempt of the organism to meet its needs as it perceives them.

behavior modification A form of therapy that applies the principles of learning to achieve changes in behavior.

behavior potential In Rotter's theory, a variable that refers to the likelihood that a particular behavior will occur.

behavior therapy a) A form of therapy that aims to eliminate symptoms of illness through learning new responses. b) In Ellis's theory, helping clients change maladaptive patterns of behavior and their cognition.

behaviorism A movement in psychology founded by John Watson, who suggested that psychologists should focus their attention on the study of overt behavior.

being mode In Fromm's theory, a way of life that depends solely on the fact of existence.

Big Five Five primary factors that typically surface from personality questionnaires and inventories: extraversion, agreeableness, conscientiousness, emotional stability, and openness to experience.

biophilia hypothesis In Wilson's theory, an intense need to belong to the rest of the living world.

biophilous character In Fromm's theory, a character orientation that is synonymous with the productive orientation.

B-needs A term used by Maslow to refer to being needs that arise from the organism's drive to self-actualize and fulfill its potential.

bodhisattva Sanskrit for "enlightenment being," a person who has vowed not to accept final liberation from suffering until all sentient beings are liberated; the ideal of the Mahayana tradition.

bodily self In Allport's theory, a propriate function that entails coming to know one's body limits.

borderline patients In Kernberg's theory, patients with oral tendencies but also powerful aggressive tendencies.

bridging A multimodal technique used by counselors to deliberately begin work in terms of their client's preferred modality.

Buddha "Awake" or "enlightened one." One who has fully awakened to the Truth.

cardinal disposition In Allport's theory, a personal disposition so pervasive that almost every behavior of an individual appears to be influenced by it.

castration anxiety In Freud's theory, the child's fear of losing the penis.

catharsis An emotional release that occurs when an idea is brought to consciousness and allowed expression.

central disposition In Allport's theory, a highly characteristic tendency of an individual.

cerebrotonia In Sheldon's theory, a component of temperament characterized by a predominance of restraint, inhibition, and the desire for concealment.

choleric One of Hippocrates' temperaments, referring to an individual who tends to be irascible and violent.

classical conditioning A form of learning in which a response becomes associated with a previously neutral stimulus.

client-centered psychotherapy A therapeutic technique developed by Rogers that focuses attention on the person seeking help.

closed system A concept of personality that admits little or nothing new from outside the organism to influence or change it in any significant way.

cognition   The process of knowing.

cognitions   In Beck's theory, a person's awareness.

cognitive complexity   The ability to perceive differences in the way in which one construes other people.

cognitive distortions   In Beck's theory, systematic errors in reasoning.

cognitive neuroscience   A field that concentrates on how mental activities occur in the brain.

cognitive theories   Theories of personality that emphasize cognitive processes such as thinking and judging.

cognitive therapy   Beck's method of psychotherapy.

cognitive therapy   In Ellis's theory, showing clients how to recognize their should and must thoughts, how to separate rational from irrational beliefs, and how to accept reality.

cognitive triad   In Beck's theory, the depressed individual has a negative view of the self, the world, and the future.

coherence   One of the criteria for judging philosophical statements: the quality or state of logical consistency.

collective unconscious   In Jung's theory, a shared, transpersonal unconscious consisting of potential ways of being human.

common traits   In Allport's theory, hypothetical traits that permit us to compare individuals according to certain shared dimensions.

compatibility   A criterion for evaluating rival hypotheses: the agreement of the hypothesis with other previously well-established information.

compellingness   One of the criteria for evaluating philosophical statements: the quality of appealing to someone with a driving force.

compensation   Making up for or overcoming a weakness.

compensatory function   In Jung's theory, an effort to complement one's conscious side and speak for the unconscious.

compensatory mechanisms   In Adler's theory, safeguarding tendencies that ward off feelings of inferiority.

complex   In Jung's theory, an organized group of thoughts, feelings, and memories about a particular concept.

comprehensiveness   One of the criteria for evaluating philosophical statements: the quality of having a broad scope or range and depth of coverage.

conditional positive regard   In Rogers's theory, positive regard that is given only under certain circumstances.

conditioned response   A response that becomes associated with a stimulus through learning.

conditioned stimulus   A previously neutral stimulus that becomes associated with a response.

conditions of worth   In Rogers's theory, stipulations imposed by other people indicating when an individual will be given positive regard.

conflict   a) In Freud's theory, the basic incompatibility that exists among the id, ego, superego, and the external world. b) In Dollard and Miller's theory, frustration that arises from a situation in which incompatible responses occur at the same time.

congruence   In Rogers's theory, the state of harmony that exists when a person's symbolized experiences reflect the actual experiences of his or her organism.

conscience   In Freud's theory, a subsystem of the superego that refers to the capacity for self-evaluation, criticism, and reproach.

conscious   In Freud's theory, the thoughts, feelings, and wishes that a person is aware of at any given moment.

consensual validation   Agreement among observers about phenomena.

constellating power   In Jung's theory, the power of a complex to admit new ideas into itself.

constellatory construct   In Kelly's theory, a construct that sets clear limits to the range of its elements but also permits them to belong to other realms.

constitutional traits   In Cattell's theory, traits that have their origin in heredity or the physiological condition of the organism.

constructive alternativism   In Kelly's theory, the assumption that any one event is open to a variety of interpretations.

construe   To place an interpretation on events.

continuity theory   A theory that suggests that the development of personality is essentially an accumulation of skills, habits, and discriminations without anything really new appearing in the make-up of the person.

continuous reinforcement   A schedule of reinforcement in which the desired behavior is reinforced every time it occurs.

control group   In an experiment, a group

control group (cont.)
equally matched to the experimental group and used for comparison.

conversion disorder A reaction to anxiety or stress expressed through physical symptoms; the modern term for hysteria.

correlation A statistical tool for making comparisons by expressing the extent to which two events covary.

covert behavior A behavior that can be observed directly only by the individual actually experiencing it.

creative self In Adler's theory, that aspect of the person that interprets and makes meaningful the experiences of the organism and establishes the life-style.

criterion analysis A method of analysis employed by Eysenck that begins with a hypothesis about possible variables and conducts statistical analyses in order to test the hypothesis.

critical periods Periods during which an organism is highly responsive to certain influences that may enhance or disrupt its development.

cue In Dollard and Miller's theory, a specific stimulus that tells the organism when, where, and how to respond.

daimonic In May's theory, any natural function that has the power to take over a person.

defense mechanism In Freud's theory, a procedure that wards off anxiety and prevents its conscious perception.

definition A statement that is true because of the way in which we have agreed to use words.

delayed reinforcement Reinforcement that is delayed after a response.

denial In Freud's theory, a defense mechanism that entails refusing to believe a reality or a fact of life.

dependent origination The Buddhist concept of interconnected causality.

dependent variable In an experiment, the behavior under study.

destructiveness In Fromm's theory, a way of escaping from freedom by eliminating others and/or the outside world.

determinism The philosophical view that behavior is controlled by external or internal forces and pressures.

developmental line In A. Freud's theory, a series of id-ego interactions in which children increase ego mastery of themselves and their world.

Dharma Sanskrit for the truth or law of the universe discovered by the Buddha; the Buddha's teaching.

diagnostic profile A formal assessment procedure developed by Anna Freud that reflects developmental issues.

dichotomy An opposite or bipolar construct.

directive A term used to describe therapies whose course is primarily structured by the therapist.

discontinuity theory A theory of personality that suggests that in the course of development an organism experiences genuine transformations or changes so that it reaches successively higher levels of organization.

discrimination The learned ability to distinguish among different stimuli.

displacement In Freud's theory, a defense mechanism in which one object of an impulse is substituted for another.

D-needs A term used by Maslow to refer to deficiency needs that arise out of a lack.

dream analysis A technique used by Freud and other analysts to uncover unconscious processes.

dream work In Freud's theory, the process that disguises unconscious wishes and converts them into a manifest dream.

drive The psychological correlate of a need or stimulus that impels an organism into action. a) In Freud's theory, a psychological representation of an inner bodily source of excitement characterized by its source, impetus, aim, and object. b) In Dollard and Miller's theory, the primary motivation for behavior.

drive reduction A concept formulated by Hull that suggests that learning occurs only if an organism's response is followed by the reduction of some need or drive.

dukkha Pali for suffering, dissatisfaction, imperfection, incompleteness; one of the three characteristics of existence according to the Buddha.

dynamic traits In Cattell's theory, traits that motivate an individual toward some goal.

eclectic Selecting the best from a variety of different theories or concepts.

ego The self. a) In Freud's theory, a function of the personality that follows the reality principles and operates according to secondary processes and reality testing. b) In Jung's theory, one's conscious perception of self.

ego-ideal In Freud's theory, a subsystem of the superego consisting of an ideal self-image.

ego identity versus role confusion Erikson's psychosocial stage of adolescence in which one faces the task of developing a self-image.

ego integrity versus despair Erikson's psychosocial stage of maturity that entails the task of being able to reflect on one's life with satisfaction.

ego-psychoanalytic theory Psychoanalytic theory that emphasizes the role of the ego in personality development.

Eightfold Path The Buddha's prescription for living constituting the fourth Noble Truth; the "Middle Way" leading to nirvana.

Electra complex A term that some critics have used to express the feminine counterpart to the male Oedipus complex.

emotionality versus stability One of Eysenck's personality dimensions, involving an individual's adjustment to the environment and the stability of his or her behavior over time.

emotive-evocative therapy In Ellis's theory, helping clients to get in touch with their feelings.

empathy The ability to recognize and understand another's feelings.

empirical Based on experience and observation.

empiricism The philosophical view that human knowledge arises slowly in the course of experience through observation and experiment.

environmental-mold traits In Cattell's theory, traits that originate from the influences of physical and social surroundings.

epiphany A usually sudden manifestation of the essential nature of something.

equilibrium Balance or harmony.

Eros In Freud's theory, life impulses or drives—forces that maintain life processes and ensure reproduction of the species.

erg In Cattell's theory, a constitutional dynamic trait.

erogenous zones Areas of the body that provide pleasure.

essence In philosophy, the unchangeable principles and laws that govern being.

evaluative response In Rogers's theory, a response that places a value judgment on thoughts, feelings, wishes, or behavior.

expressive psychoanalytically oriented psychotherapy Kernberg's method of treatment.

existential dichotomy In Fromm's theory, a dilemma or problem that arises simply from the fact of existence.

existentialism A philosophical movement that studies the meaning of existence.

expectancy In Rotter's theory, the individual's subjective expectation about the outcome of his or her behavior.

experimental method A scientific method involving a careful study of cause and effect by manipulating variables and observing their effects.

exploitative orientation In Fromm's theory, a character type in which a person exploits others and the world.

expressive behavior In Allport's theory, an individual's manner of performing.

extinction The tendency of a response to disappear when it is not reinforced.

extrinsic A quest that serves other purposes outside the original goal.

extraversion An attitude of expansion in which the psyche is oriented toward the external world.

extraversion versus introversion One of Eysenck's personality dimensions, involving the degree to which a person is outgoing and participative in relating to other people.

factor analysis Employed by Cattell, a procedure that interrelates many correlations at one time.

falsification The act of disproving.

family atmosphere In Adler's theory, the quality of emotional relationships among members of a family.

family constellation In Adler's theory, one's position within the family in terms of birth order among siblings and the presence or absence of parents and other caregivers.

feeling One of Jung's functions, involving valuing and judging the world.

fictional finalism In Adler's theory, a basic concept or philosophical assumption that cannot be tested against reality.

finalism In Adler's theory, a principle that reflects the concept of goal orientation.

fixation In Freud's theory, a concept in which there is an arrest of growth, and excessive needs characteristic of an earlier stage are created by overindulgence or undue frustration.

fixed schedule of reinforcement A schedule of reinforcement in which the time period or number of responses before reinforcement is identical.

Four Noble Truths The essence of the practical teaching of the Buddha, specifying the nature of suffering, its cause, its cessation, and the path to accomplish liberation from suffering.

frame of orientation and object of devotion In Fromm's thought, the need for a stable thought system by which to organize perceptions and make sense out of the environment.

free association In Freud's psychoanalysis, a technique in which a person verbalizes whatever comes to mind.

freedom of movement In Rotter's theory, the degree of expectation a person has that a particular set of responses will lead to a desired reinforcement.

frustration In Dollard and Miller's theory, an emotion that occurs when one is unable to satisfy a drive because the response that would satisfy it has been blocked.

fully functioning person A term used by Rogers to indicate an individual who is functioning at an optimum level.

functional autonomy In Allport's theory, a concept that present motives are not necessarily tied to the past but may be free of earlier motivations.

functions In Jung's theory, ways of perceiving the environment and orienting experiences.

gassho Japanese for "palms of the hands pressed together," expressing the unity of the person and the universe, a gesture commonly used for greeting in many cultures in the East.

generalization A statement that may be made, when a number of different instances coincide, that something is true about many or all of the members of a certain class.

generalized conditioned reinforcers In Skinner's theory, learned reinforcers that have the power to reinforce a great number of different behaviors.

generativity versus stagnation Erikson's psychosocial stage of the middle years, in which one faces the dilemma of being productive and creative in life.

genital stage Freud's final psychosexual stage, in which an individual reaches sexual maturity.

genotype The genetic makeup of an individual.

genuineness A therapist's attitude characterized by congruence and awareness in the therapeutic relationship.

gestalt Configuration or pattern that forms a whole.

gestalt principle The notion that the whole is more than the sum of its parts.

gestalt psychology A branch of psychology that studies how organisms perceive objects and events.

getting type In Adler's theory, dependent people who take rather than give.

goal of superiority In Adler's theory, the ultimate fictional finalism, entailing the desire to be competent and effective in whatever one strives to do and to actualize one's potential.

gradient The changing strength of a force, which may be plotted on a graph.

habit In Dollard and Miller's theory, the basic structure of personality: a learned association between a stimulus and response.

habitual responses In Eysenck's theory, clusters of specific behaviors that characteristically recur in similar circumstances, such as buying groceries or giving parties.

having mode In Fromm's theory, a way of existence that relies on possessions.

heterostasis The desire not to reduce tension, but to seek new stimuli and challenges that will further growth.

heuristic value The ability of a construct to predict future events.

hierarchy of needs Maslow's theory of five basic needs ranked in order of strength: physiological, safety, belonging and love, self-esteem, and self-actualization.

hierarchy of response In Dollard and Miller's theory, a tendency for certain responses to occur before other responses.

Hinayana Sanskrit for "small vehicle," a designation for the southern schools of Buddhism concerned with personal liberation. One of the two major divisions of Buddhism.

historical dichotomy In Fromm's theory, a dilemma or problem that arises out of human history because of various societies and cultures.

hoarding orientation In Fromm's theory, a character type in which the person seeks to save or hoard and protects him- or herself from the world by a wall.

homeostasis Balance or harmony.

homosexuality Primary attraction to the same sex.

hormones Chemicals released into the blood stream by the endocrine glands.

hot cognitions In Beck's therapy, experiencing arousing emotions and reality testing at the same time.

humanist theories Theories of personality that emphasize human potential.

Humanistic Communitarian Socialism The name of Fromm's ideal society.

humanistic ethics In Fromm's theory, a value system that has its source in the individual acting in accord with the law of his or her human nature and assuming full responsibility for his or her existence.

humors In earlier psychology, bodily fluids thought to enter into the constitution of a body and determine, by their proportion, a person's constitution and temperament.

hypercompetitiveness In Horney's theory, American society's sweeping desire to compete and win.

hypothesis A preliminary assumption that guides further inquiry.

hysteria An earlier term for an illness in which there are physical symptoms, such as paralysis, but no organic or physiological basis for the problem.

id In Freud's theory, the oldest and original function of the personality, which includes genetic inheritance, reflex capacities, instincts, and drives.

idealization In Kohut's theory, the tendency children have to idealize their parents.

idealized self In Horney's theory, that which a person thinks he or she should be.

identification In Freud's theory, (a) a defense mechanism in which a person reduces anxiety by modeling his or her behavior after that of someone else, and (b) the process whereby the child resolves the Oedipus complex by incorporating the parents into the self.

identity crisis In Erikson's theory, transitory failure to develop a self-image or identity.

idiographic In Allport's theory, an approach to studying personality that centers on understanding the uniqueness of the individual.

I-E Scale A questionnaire developed by Rotter to measure internal versus external locus of control.

immediate reinforcement Reinforcement that immediately follows a response.

implosive A sudden, instead of gradual, confrontation of a phobic situation.

imprinting A bond of attraction that develops among members of a species shortly after birth.

incongruence In Rogers's theory, the lack of harmony that results when a person's symbolized experiences do not represent the actual experiences.

independent variable In an experiment, the factor that is manipulated by the experimenter.

individual psychology The school of psychology developed by Adler.

individuation In Jung's theory of self-realization, a process whereby the systems of the individual psyche achieve their fullest degree of differentiation, expression, and development.

industry versus inferiority Erikson's psychosocial stage, corresponding to Freud's latency period, in which children face the task of learning and mastering the technology of their culture.

inferiority complex In Adler's theory, a neurotic pattern in which an individual feels highly inadequate.

inferiority feelings In Adler's theory, feelings of being inadequate that arise out of childhood experiences.

infrahuman species Species lower than human organisms.

inhibition The prevention of a response from occurring because it is in conflict with other strong unconscious responses.

initiative versus guilt Erikson's psychosexual stage, corresponding to Freud's phallic stage, in which children face the task of directing their curiosity and activity toward specific goals and achievements.

inner space In Erikson's theory, tendency on the part of girls to emphasize qualities of openness versus closedness in space.

insight A form of therapeutic knowing that combines intellectual and emotional elements and culminates in profound personality change.

insight therapy Therapeutic procedures that seek to increase self-understanding and lead to deep motivational changes.

intentionality In May's theory, a dimension that undercuts conscious and unconscious, and underlies will and decision.

interpretative response In Rogers's theory, a response that seeks to interpret a speaker's problem or tell how the speaker feels about it.

interpsychic Between psyches or persons.

interval reinforcement A schedule of reinforcement in which the organism is reinforced after a certain time period has elapsed.

intimacy versus isolation Erikson's psychosocial stage of young adulthood in which one faces the task of establishing a close, deep, and meaningful genital relationship with another person.

intrapsychic Within the psyche or individual self.

introversion An attitude of withdrawal in which personality is oriented inward toward the subjective world.

intuition One of Jung's functions, entailing perception via the unconscious.

in vitro desensitization A process whereby anxieties and fears are reduced by repeated imagined exposures to the noxious stimuli paired with relaxation, skill training, and other behavioral techniques.

IQ Intelligence quotient: a number used to express the relative intelligence of a person.

karma Sanskrit for volitional action.

kinhin Japanese for the meditational walking performed between periods of zazen.

koan Japanese for "public document," an apparently paradoxical story, anecdote, or statement expressing the realization of a Zen master.

latency period A period in Freud's psychosexual stages of development in which the sexual drive was thought to go underground.

latent dream In Freud's theory, the real meaning or motive that underlies the dream that we remember.

law of effect A law formulated by Thorndike that states that when a behavior or a performance is accompanied by satisfaction it tends to increase; if accompanied by frustration, it tends to decrease.

L-data In Cattell's theory, observations made of a person's behavior in society or everyday life.

learning dilemma In Dollard and Miller's theory, the situation an individual is placed in if present responses are not reinforced.

libido a) In Freud's theory, an emotional and psychic energy derived from the biological drive of sexuality. b) In Jung's theory, an undifferentiated life and psychic energy.

life crisis In Erikson's theory, a crucial period in which the individual cannot avoid a decisive turn one way or the other.

logotherapy Frankl's theory that suggests people have realized freedom but we have not necessarily taken responsibility for our freedom.

love In Fromm's theory, the productive relationship to others and the self, entailing care, responsibility, respect, and knowledge.

Mahayana Sanskrit for "great vehicle," one of the two major divisions of Buddhism, concerned with the liberation of all sentient beings.

manas Sanskrit for "mind," the seventh of the eight consciousnesses, where the illusion of the ego arises.

mandala A concentrically arranged figure often found as a symbol in the East that denotes wholeness and unity. In Jung's theory, a symbol for the emerging self.

manifest dream In Freud's theory, the dream as it is remembered the next morning.

manovijnana Sanskrit for "mental consciousness," the sixth of the eight consciousnesses and the basis for the five sensory consciousnesses.

marketing orientation In Fromm's theory, a character type in which the person experiences him- or herself as a commodity in the marketplace.

masculine protest In Adler's early theory, the compensation for one's inferiorities.

masochism A disorder in which a person obtains pleasure by receiving pain.

maya Sanskrit for deception, delusion, or illusion.

melancholic One of Hippocrates' temperaments, referring to an individual characterized by depression.

mergers In Orlofsky's theory, individuals who commit themselves to a relationship at the price of their own independence.

metacommunication In Lazarus's theory, the fact that people not only communicate but also think and communicate about their communications.

metamotivation A term used by Maslow to refer to growth tendencies within the organism.

metapsychological A term used by Freud to indicate the fullest possible description of psychic processes.

minimum goal level In Rotter's theory, the lowest level of potential reinforcement that is perceived as satisfactory in a particular situation.

mirrored In Kohut's theory, the need for children to have their talk and their accomplishments acknowledged, accepted, and praised.

mistaken style of life In Adler's theory, a style of life that belies one's actual capabilities and strengths.

modality profiles In Lazarus's therapy, a specific list of problems and proposed treatments across the client's BASIC-ID.

moral anxiety In Freud's theory, fear of the retribution of one's own conscience.

Morita therapy A system of psychotherapy developed in Japan early in the twentieth century by Shoma Morita, combining elements of Zen Buddhism and psychoanalysis.

motivation Maslow's term for the reduction of tension by satisfying deficit states or lacks.

moving against One of Horney's three primary modes of relating to other people, in which one seeks to protect him- or herself by revenge or controlling others.

moving away One of Horney's three primary ways of relating to other people, in which one isolates him- or herself and keeps apart.

moving toward One of Horney's three primary modes of relating to other people, in which one accepts his or her own helplessness and becomes compliant in order to depend on others.

multimodal behavior therapy Lazarus's method of therapy.

mustabatory belief systems In Ellis's theory, escalating probalistic statements into absolutes.

myths In May's theory, narrative patterns that give significance to our existence.

Naikan therapy A system of psychotherapy based on the Pure Land (Jodo) school of Buddhism and on Confucian ethics. One of the "quiet therapies."

narcissism A form of self-encapsulation in which an individual experiences as real only that which exists within him- or herself.

necrophilous character In Fromm's theory, a character orientation in which an individual is attracted to that which is dead and decaying and seeks to destroy living things.

need a) In Murray's theory, a force in the brain that organizes perception, understanding, and behavior in such a way as to change an unsatisfying situation and increase satis-

faction. b) In Rotter's theory, a behavior that leads to a reinforcement.

need potential In Rotter's theory, the likelihood that a set of behaviors directed toward the same goal will be used in a given situation.

need value In Rotter's theory, the importance placed on a goal.

negative identity In Erikson's theory, an identity opposed to the dominant values of one's culture.

negative reinforcement Unpleasant or aversive stimuli that can be changed or avoided by certain behavior.

NEO-PI The Neuroticism Extraversion Openness Personality Inventory developed by Costa and McCrae.

NEO-PIR The Neuroticism Extraversion Openness Personality Inventory, Revised, developed by McCrae and Costa.

neopsychoanalytic theories Psychoanalytic theories that revise or modify Freud's original theories.

neurotic anxiety In Freud's theory, the fear that one's inner impulses cannot be controlled.

neurotic needs or trends In Horney's theory, exaggerated defense strategies that permit an individual to cope with the world.

nirvana Sanskrit for a mental state where craving and suffering have been completely extinguished.

nomothetic In Allport's theory, an approach to studying personality that considers large groups of individuals in order to infer general variables or universal principles.

nondirective A term used by Rogers to describe therapies whose course is primarily determined by the patient.

normal curve of distribution A bell-shaped curve representing many events in nature in which most events cluster around the mean.

nuclear self In Kohut's theory, a well-developed self that ideally emerges in the second year.

objective data Data acquired through extrospection, the act of looking outward on the world as object.

objectivism The philosophical view that valid knowledge arises gradually in the course of experience through observation and experimentation.

objectivity The quality of recognizing or expressing reality without distortion by per-

objectivity (cont.)
sonal feeling. In test construction, construction of a test in such a way that it can be given and scored in a way that avoids the scorer's subjective bias.

observational learning In Bandura's theory, learning that occurs through observation without any direct reinforcement.

Oedipus complex In Freud's theory, an unconscious psychological conflict in which the child loves the parent of the opposite sex.

open system A concept of personality that conceives of it as having a dynamic potential for growth, reconstitution, and change through extensive transactions within itself and the environment.

operant behavior In Skinner's theory, a response that acts on the environment and is emitted without a stimulus necessarily being present.

operant conditioning In Skinner's theory, the process by which an operant response becomes associated with a reinforcement through learning.

operational definition A definition that specifies those behaviors that are included in the concept.

oral stage One of Freud's psychosexual stages, in which the major source of pleasure and potential conflict is the mouth.

outer space In Erikson's theory, tendency on the part of boys to emphasize qualities of highness or lowness in space.

overcompensation In Adler's theory, an exaggerated effort to cover up a weakness that entails a denial rather than an acceptance of the real situation.

overt behavior Behavior that can be observed by an external observer.

paradigm A pattern or model.

paradox Two opposites that seem to negate each other but cannot exist without each other.

paradox In Lazarus's therapy, the use of contradictions.

paraworld A world of quantified, logical, and mathematical imaginary constructs used by the scientist to draw conclusions about the everyday world.

peak experience In Maslow's theory, an intensified experience in which there is a loss of self or transcendence of self.

penis envy In Freud's theory, the concept that women view themselves as castrated males and envy the penis.

performance phase In Dollard and Miller's therapy, a phase in which the patient acquires new, more adaptive responses and habits.

perseverative functional autonomy In Allport's theory, acts or behaviors that are repeated even though they may have lost their original function.

persona In Jung's theory, an archetype referring to one's social role and understanding of it.

personal dispositions In Allport's theory, traits that are unique to an individual.

personal unconscious In Jung's theory, experiences of an individual's life that have been repressed or temporarily forgotten.

personality a) In social speech, one's public image. b) In Fromm's theory, the totality of an individual's psychic qualities. c) In Cattell's theory, that which permits prediction of what a person will do in a given situation.

personology Murray's term for his study of individual persons.

phallic stage One of Freud's psychosexual stages, in which pleasurable and conflicting feelings are associated with the genital organs.

phenomenal field In Rogers's theory, the total sum of experiences an organism has.

phenomenology The study of phenomena or appearances.

phenotype An individual's observable appearance and behavior.

philosophical assumption An underlying view of the world that influences a person's thinking.

philosophy The systematic love and pursuit of wisdom.

phlegmatic One of Hippocrates temperaments, referring to an individual who is slow, solid, and apathetic.

pleasure principle In Freud's theory, the seeking of tension reduction followed by the id.

polymorphous perverse A phrase used by Freud to emphasize the point that children deviate in many ways from what is thought to be normal reproductive sexual activity.

positive regard In Rogers's theory, being loved and accepted for who one is.

positive reinforcement Anything that serves to increase the frequency of a response.

positive self-regard In Rogers's theory, viewing the self favorably and with acceptance.

predictive power A criterion for evaluating rival hypotheses: the range or scope of the hypothesis.

pre-emptive construct In Kelly's theory, a construct that limits its elements to one range only.

press In Murray's theory, a force coming from the environment that helps or hinders an individual in reaching goals.

primary drive A drive associated with a physiological process that is necessary for the organism's survival.

primary process In Freud's theory, a psychological activity of the id characterized by immediate wish fulfillment and the disregard of realistic concerns.

primary reinforcer A reinforcer that is inherently rewarding as it satisfies a primary drive.

proactive Referring to theories of personality that view the human being as acting on his or her own initiative rather than simply reacting.

probing response In Rogers's theory, a response that seeks further information.

proceeding In Murray's theory, a short, significant behavior pattern that has a clear beginning and ending.

productive orientation In Fromm's theory, the character type that represents the ideal of humanistic development.

projection In Freud's theory, a defense mechanism that refers to the unconscious attribution of an impulse, attitude, or behavior to someone else or some element in the environment.

projective techniques Personality tests in which an ambiguous stimulus is presented to the subject who is expected to project aspects of his or her personality into the response.

propositional construct In Kelly's theory, a construct that leaves its elements open to other constructions.

propriate functional autonomy In Allport's theory, acquired interests, values, attitudes, intentions, and lifestyle that are directed from the proprium and are genuinely free of earlier motivations.

propriate functions In Allport's theory, the functions of the proprium.

propriate striving In Allport's theory, a propriate function that entails projection of long-term purposes and goals and development of a plan to attain them.

proprium In Allport's theory, a term that refers to the central experiences of self-awareness that a person has as he or she grows and moves forward.

psyche From the Greek term meaning "breath" or "principle of life," often translated as "soul" or "self." a) In Freud's theory, the id, ego, and superego. b) In Jung's theory, the total personality encompassing all psychological processes: thoughts, feelings, sensations, wishes, and so on.

psychoanalysis A method of therapy developed by Freud that concentrates on cultivating a transference relationship and analyzing resistances to the therapeutic process.

psychohistory The combined use of psychoanalysis and history to study individuals and groups.

psychological situation The psychological context within which an organism responds.

psychometrics The quantitative measurement of psychological characteristics through statistical techniques.

psychophysical Entailing components of both the mind and the body.

psychosexual stages In Freud's theory, a series of developmental stages through which all people pass as they move from infancy to adulthood.

psychosis An abnormal personality disturbance characterized by loss or distortion of reality testing and the inability to distinguish between reality and fantasy.

psychosocial stages A series of developmental stages proposed by Erikson to emphasize the social dimension of personality.

psychotherapy Treatment of emotional disorders by psychological means.

psychoticism One of Eysenck's personality dimensions, involving the loss or distortion of reality and the inability to distinguish between reality and fantasy.

punishment An undesirable consequence that follows a behavior and is designed to stop or change it.

Q-sort technique A card-sorting technique employed by Rogers for studying the self-concept.

radical behaviorism A label that has been given to B. F. Skinner's point of view.

random assignment In an experiment, insuring that every subject has an equal chance of being assigned to any of the treatment groups.

ratio reinforcement   A schedule of reinforcement in which the organism is reinforced after a number of appropriate responses.

rational-emotive therapy   Ellis's method of psychotherapy.

rationalism   The philosophical view that the mind can, in and of its own accord, formulate ideas and determine their truth.

rationalization   In Freud's theory, a defense mechanism that entails dealing with an emotion or impulse analytically and intellectually, thereby not involving the emotions.

reaction formation   In Freud's theory, a defense mechanism in which an impulse is expressed by its opposite.

reactive   Referring to theories of personality that view the human being as primarily responding to external stimuli.

real self   In Horney's theory, that which a person actually is.

reality anxiety   In Freud's theory, the fear of a real danger in the external world.

reality principle   In Freud's theory, the way in which the ego satisfies the impulses of the id in an appropriate manner in the external world.

reassuring response   In Rogers's theory, a response that attempts to soothe feelings.

receptive orientation   In Fromm's theory, a character type in which the individual reacts to the world passively.

reciprocal determinism   In Bandura's theory, the regulation of behavior by an interplay of behavioral, cognitive, and environmental factors.

reconstructive (or intensive) psychotherapy   Therapeutic methods that seek to remove defenses and reorganize the basic personality structure.

reflective response   In Rogers's theory, a response that seeks to capture the underlying feeling expressed.

reflexes   Inborn automatic responses.

regression   In Freud's theory, a defense mechanism that entails reverting to earlier forms of behavior.

reinforcement   The process of increasing or decreasing the likelihood of a particular response.

reinforcement value   In Rotter's theory, a variable that indicates the importance or preference of a particular reinforcement for an individual.

reinforcer   Any event that increases or decreases the likelihood of a particular response.

relatedness   In Fromm's theory, the basic need to relate to and love other people.

relevance   One of the criteria for evaluating philosophical statements, the quality of having some bearing or being pertinent to one's view of reality.

reliability   The quality of consistently yielding the same results over time.

reproduction of mothering   Chodorow's belief that women's mothering reproduces itself cyclically.

Rep Test   Role Construct Repertory Test: a device developed by Kelly to reveal personal constructs.

repression   a) In Freud's theory, the key defense mechanism, which entails blocking a wish or desire from expression so that it cannot be experienced consciously or directly expressed in behavior. b) In Dollard and Miller's theory, a learned process of avoiding certain thoughts and thereby losing verbal control.

resignation solution   One of Horney's three basic orientations, representing the desire to be free of others.

respondent behavior   In Skinner's theory, reflexes or automatic responses elicited by a stimulus.

response   A behavior that results from a stimulus. In Dollard and Miller's theory, one's reaction to a cue or stimulus.

Rinzai   One of the two major schools of Zen Buddhism in Japan, stressing the use of koans and zazen to reach enlightenment.

role   a) In social psychology, a set of behavioral expectations set forth by a particular society and fulfilled by its members. b) In Kelly's theory, a process or behavior that a person plays based on his or her understanding of the behavior and constructs of other people.

role confusion   In Erikson's theory, an inability to conceive of oneself as a productive member in one's society.

role-playing   A therapeutic technique in Kelly and Beck's therapy, in which clients are asked to rehearse situations that will later happen in real life.

rootedness   In Fromm's theory, the basic need to feel that one belongs in the world.

ruling type   In Adler's theory, aggressive, dominating people who have little social interest or cultural perception.

sadism A disorder in which a person obtains pleasure by inflicting pain.

safeguarding tendencies In Adler's theory, compensatory mechanisms that ward off feelings of insecurity.

sanguine One of Hippocrates' temperaments, referring to a personality marked by sturdiness, high color, and cheerfulness.

sanzen Individual consultations between a Zen Buddhist monk and his master.

satiation Engaging in a behavior until one tires of it.

satori Japanese for "enlightenment," the goal of Zen practice.

schemas In Beck's theory, cognitive structures that consist of an individual's fundamental core beliefs and assumptions about how the world operates.

science A system or method of acquiring knowledge based on specific principles of observation and reasoning.

scientific construct An imaginary or hypothetical construct used to explain what is observed in science.

scientific (or empirical) generalization An inductive conclusion based on a number of different instances of observation.

scientific method A method of inquiry that consists of five steps: recognizing a problem, developing a hypothesis, making a prediction, testing the hypothesis, and drawing a conclusion.

scientific statement A statement about the world based on observations arising from a currently held paradigm.

scientism Exclusive reliance on a narrow conception of science.

secondary dispositions In Allport's theory, more specific, focused tendencies of an individual that tend to be situational in character.

secondary drive A drive that is learned or acquired on the basis of a primary drive.

secondary processes In Freud's theory, higher intellectual functions that enable the ego to establish suitable courses of action and test them for their effectiveness.

secondary reinforcer A reinforcer that is originally neutral but that acquires reward value on the basis of association with a primary reinforcer.

self a) In Jung's theory, a central archetype representing the striving for unity of all parts of the personality. b) In Rogers's theory, the psychological processes that govern a person's behavior.

self-actualization In the theories of Rogers and Maslow, a dynamic within the organism leading it to actualize, fulfill, and enhance its inherent potentialities.

self-analysis In Horney's theory, a systematic effort at self-understanding conducted without the aid of a professional.

self-as-rational coper In Allport's theory, a propriate function that entails the perception of oneself as an active problem-solving agent.

self-concept In Rogers's theory, a portion of the phenomenal field that has become differentiated and is composed of perceptions and values of "I" or "me."

self-construct In Kelly's theory, perception of similarities in one's behavior based on role relationships with other people.

self-effacing solution One of Horney's three basic orientations toward life, which represents an appeal to be loved by others.

self-efficacy In Bandura's theory, a person's perception of his or her effectiveness.

self-esteem In Allport's theory, a propriate function that entails feelings of pride as one develops the ability to do things.

self-expansive solution One of Horney's three basic orientations toward life, which represents a striving for mastery.

self-extension In Allport's theory, a propriate function that entails a sense of possession.

self-identity In Allport's theory, a propriate function that entails an awareness of inner sameness and continuity.

self-image In Allport's theory, a propriate function that entails a sense of the expectations of others and its comparison with one's own behavior.

self-love In Fromm's theory, love of self that is a prerequisite for love of others.

self-realization In Jung's theory, a drive within the self to realize, fulfill, and enhance one's maximum human potentialities.

self-sentiment In Cattell's theory, an environmental-mold dynamic source trait composing a person's self-image.

self-system In Bandura's theory, cognitive structures that underlie the perception, evaluation, and regulation of behavior.

sensation One of Jung's functions, referring to sense perception of the world.

sense of identity In Fromm's theory, the need to be aware of oneself as an individual.

sentiment In Cattell's theory, an environmental-mold dynamic source trait.

separation-individuation process A sequence of stages posited by Mahler through which the ego passes in the process of becoming an individual.

shadow In Jung's theory, an archetype that encompasses one's animalistic and unsocial side.

shaping In Skinner's theory, a process by which an organism's behavior is gradually molded until it approximates the desired behavior.

shikantaza Japanese for "just sitting," the form of zazen practice stressed particularly in the Soto Zen tradition.

shinkeishitsu A Japanese label for a group of neuroses overlapping with the anxiety disorders in the DSM-IV classification.

simplicity A criterion for evaluating rival hypotheses: the quality of being simple and avoiding complicated explanations.

skandha Sanskrit for "aggregate" or "heap." The five *skandhas* are form, feelings, perceptions, impulses, and consciousness.

slips In Freud's theory, bungled acts, such as a slip of the tongue, a slip of the pen, or a memory lapse.

social interest In Adler's theory, an urge in human nature to adapt oneself to the conditions of one's environment and society.

social learning theories Theories that attempt to explain personality in terms of learned behavior within a social context.

social psychoanalytic theories Psychoanalytic theories that emphasize the role of social forces in shaping personality.

socially useful type In Adler's theory, people who have a great deal of social interest and activity.

sociotropic dimension In Beck's theory, a personality dimension characterized by dependence on interpersonal relationships and needs for closeness and nurturance.

somatotonia In Sheldon's theory, a component of temperament characterized by a predominance of muscular activity and vigorous bodily assertiveness.

somatotype Sheldon's term for the expression of body type through three numbers that indicate the degree of each physical component.

Soto One of the two major schools of Zen Buddhism in Japan, stressing the practice of zazen as shikantaza and the identity of practice and enlightenment.

source traits In Cattell's theory, underlying variables that determine surface manifestations.

species-specific behavior Complex automatic behaviors that occur in all members of a species.

specific responses In Eysenck's theory, behaviors that we can actually observe, such as someone answering a phone.

specification equation An equation by which Cattell suggests we may eventually be able to predict human behavior.

splitting In Kernberg's theory, failing to consolidate positive and negative experiences between oneself and other people.

spontaneous recovery Following extinction, the return of a learned behavior.

standardization Pre-testing of a large and representative sample in order to determine test norms.

statement An utterance that makes an assertion or a denial.

statistics The application of mathematical principles to the description and analysis of measurements.

stereotype Prejudgment that we make about people on the basis of their membership in certain groups.

stimulus An agent that rouses or excites a response.

structural profile In Lazarus's therapy, a quantitative assessment of the relative involvement of each of the elements of the BASIC-ID in a client.

structuralism Early school of psychology that suggested that psychology study conscious experience.

stupidity-misery syndrome Dollard and Miller's term for a neurosis.

style of life In Adler's theory, the specific ways in which an individual seeks to attain the goal of superiority.

subception In Rogers's theory, a discriminative evaluative response of the organism that precedes conscious perception.

subjective data Data acquired through introspection, the act of looking inward on the self as subject.

subjectivism A philosophical view that constructs of knowledge are creations of the self.

sublimation In Freud's theory, a defense mechanism that refers to translating a wish, the direct expression of which is socially unacceptable, into socially acceptable behavior.

subsidiation In Cattell's theory, the principle that certain traits are secondary to other traits.

successive approximations In Dollard and Miller's therapy, the interpretations of the therapist that provide increasingly more accurate labels for the patient's responses.

superego In Freud's theory, a function of the personality that represents introjected and internalized values, ideals, and moral standards.

superiority complex In Adler's theory, a neurotic pattern in which an individual exaggerates his or her importance.

supportive psychotherapy Therapeutic measures that seek to strengthen adaptive instincts and defenses.

surface traits In Cattell's theory, clusters of over behavior responses that appear to go together.

sutra Sanskrit for a sermon or discourse, usually of the Buddha.

symbiotic relationship In Fromm's theory, a relationship in which one or the other of two persons loses or never attains his or her independence.

symbol An element in a dream that stands for something else.

syntality In Cattell's theory, the behavior of a group as a whole or its "group personality."

talking phase In Dollard and Miller's therapy, a phase in which neurotic habits are studied, examined, and identified so that the patient may unlearn them.

Tao A Chinese term for "Way" or "Path"; the absolute and ineffable nature of ultimate reality.

Taoism A Chinese philosophy and way of life based on the teachings of Lao-tse (ca. 4th century B.C.), stressing harmony with the Tao.

TAT Thematic Apperception Test: a projective test consisting of ambiguous pictures to which a subject is asked to respond.

T-data In Cattell's theory, objective tests.

technical eclecticism In Lazarus's therapy, deriving treatment methods from many sources without necessarily agreeing with the theories that generated them.

telos A purpose or goal.

temperament traits In Cattell's theory, traits that determine how a person behaves in order to obtain his or her goal.

Thanatos In Freud's theory, the death impulse or drive, the source of aggression, the ultimate resolution of all of life's tension in death.

theory A set of abstract concepts made about a group of facts or events to explain them.

therapy The practical application of psychology in ways that will assist individuals.

Theravada Pali for "the teaching of the Elders," the form of Buddhism dominant in Sri Lanka, Burma, Thailand, Laos, and Cambodia. Sometimes referred to as the Hinayana.

thinking One of Jung's functions, referring to giving meaning and understanding to the world.

thresholds In Lazarus's theory, tolerance levels for pain, frustration, or stress.

token economy A community based on Skinnerian principles in which individuals are rewarded for appropriate behavior with tokens that can be exchanged for various privileges.

tracking In Lazarus's therapy, paying careful attention to the "firing order" of the different modalities.

trait Continuous dimension that an individual can be seen to possess to a certain degree. a) In Allport's theory, a determining tendency to respond that represents the ultimate reality of psychological organization. b) In Cattell's theory, an imaginary construct or inference from overt behavior that helps to explain it.

trait theories Theories that conceive of personality as being composed primarily of traits.

transcendence a) In Jung's theory of self-realization, a process of integrating the diverse systems of the self toward the goal of wholeness and identification with all humanity. b) In Fromm's theory, the basic human need to rise above the accidental and passive creatureliness of animal existence and become an active creator.

transference In Freudian psychoanalysis, a process in which the patient projects onto the analyst emotional attitudes felt as a child toward important persons.

Tripitaka Sanskrit for the "three baskets" or collections of Buddhist scriptures.

trust versus mistrust Erikson's psychosocial stage, corresponding to Freud's oral stage, in which infants face the task of trusting the world.

typology Division of human beings into distinct, separate categories.

tyranny of the should In Horney's theory, creating false needs instead of meeting genuine ones.

unconditional positive regard In Rogers's theory, positive regard that is not contingent on any specific behaviors.

unconditioned response A reflex or automatic response to a stimulus.

unconditioned stimulus A stimulus that normally elicits a particular reflex or automatic response.

unconscious process a) In Freud's theory, processes of which a person is unaware because they have been repressed or never permitted to become conscious. b) In Dollard and Miller's theory, drives or cues of which we are unaware because they are unlabeled or repressed.

usefulness a) In scientific theorizing, the ability of a hypothesis to generate predictions about experiences that we might observe. b) In Adler's theory, the ability of a goal to foster productive living and enhance one's life.

validating evidence Observable consequences that follow an experiment designed to test a hypothesis and are used to support a construct or theory.

validity The quality of measuring what a construct is supposed to measure.

variable A characteristic that can be measured or controlled.

variable schedule of reinforcement A schedule of reinforcement in which the time period or number of responses prior to reinforcement varies.

vijnana Sanskrit for "consciousness."

virtues In Erikson's theory, ego strengths that develop out of each psychosocial stage.

Walden II Skinner's name for his utopian community.

wish fulfillment In Freud's theory, a primary-process activity that seeks to reduce tension by forming an image of the object that would satisfy needs.

wishes In Freud's theory, desires that may be rendered unconscious if they go against a person's ego-ideal.

withdrawal-destructiveness relationship In Fromm's theory, a relationship characterized by distance, apathy, or aggression.

womb envy In Horney's theory, the concept that men and boys experience jealousy over women's ability to bear and nurse children.

yang Chinese Taoist term for the positive, masculine, active, external aspect of the complementary yin and yang polarity.

yin Chinese Taoist term for the negative, feminine, passive, internal aspect of the complementary yin and yang polarity.

zazen Japanese for "sitting meditation," the most important and indispensable aspect of Zen practice. The typical length of a period of *zazen* in Japan is 40 minutes.

Zen Japanese rendering of the Chinese *ch'an*, meaning absorption or meditation. It can refer to a school of Buddhism or to the ineffable experience of oneness with reality.

REFERENCES

Abelson, R. P. (1981). Psychological status of the script concept. *American Psychologist, 36,* 715–729.

Adler, A. (1917). *Study of organ inferiority and its psychical compensation.* New York: Nervous and Mental Diseases Publishing Co.

Adler, A. (1927). *The practice and theory of individual psychology.* New York: Harcourt, Brace, & World.

Adler, A. (1929a). *The science of living.* New York: Greenberg.

Adler, A. (1929b). *Problems of neurosis.* London: Kegan Paul.

Adler, A. (1930). Individual psychology. In C. Murchison (Ed.), *Psychologies of 1930.* Worcester, MA: Clark University Press.

Adler, A. (1931). *What life should mean to you.* Boston: Little, Brown.

Adler, A. (1936). The neurotic's picture of the world. *International Journal of Individual Psychology, 2,* 3–10.

Adler, A. (1939). *Social interest.* New York: Putnam.

Adler, A. (1954). *Understanding human nature.* New York: Fawcett.

Adler, A. (1964). *Superiority and social interest: A collection of later writings.* H. L. & R. R. Ansbacher (Eds.). Evanston, IL: Northwestern University Press.

Agarwal, R., & Misra, G. (1986, January). Locus of control and attribution for achievement outcomes. *Psychological Studies, 31*(1), 15–20.

Alexander, C. N., Rainforth, M. V., & Gelderloos, P. (1991). Transcendental Meditation, self-actualization, and psychological health: A conceptual overview and statistical meta-analysis. Special Issue: Handbook of self-actualization. *Journal of Social Behavior & Personality, 6*(5), 189–248.

Alexander, F. (1950). *Psychosomatic medicine: Its principles and applications.* New York: Norton.

Allport, G. W. (1937). *Personality: A psychological interpretation.* New York: Holt.

Allport, G. W. (1954). *The nature of prejudice.* Boston: Beacon Press.

Allport, G. W. (1955). *Becoming: Basic considerations for a psychology of personality.* New Haven: Yale University Press.

Allport, G. W. (1961). *Pattern and growth in personality.* New York: Holt, Rinehart, and Winston.

Allport, G. W. (1965). *Letters from Jenny.* New York: Harcourt Brace and World.

Anderson, M. (1991). *Thinking about women: Sociological perspectives on sex and gender* (3rd ed.). New York: Macmillan.

Anderson, R., & Kirkland, J. (1990). Constructs in context. *International Journal of Personal Construct Psychology, 3*(1), 21–29.

Angier, N. (1990, May 4). Researchers succeed in growing brain cells. *The New York Times.*

Angier, N. (1992, October 6). Blueprint for a human. *The New York Times.*

Angier, N. (1993, August 10). Drawing big lessons from fly embryology. *The New York Times,* p. C1.

Angier, N. (1993, October 12). An old idea about genius wins new scientific support. *The New York Times,* pp. C1, C8.

Ansbacher, H. L. (1990). Alfred Adler's influence on the three leading co-founders of humanistic psychology. *Journal of Humanistic Psychology, 30*(4), 45–53.

Ansbacher, H. L., & Ansbacher, R. R. (1956). *The individual psychology of Alfred Adler.* New York: Basic Books.

Archer, S. L. (1989). Gender differences in identity development: Issues of process, domain, and timing. *Journal of Adolescence, 12,* 117–138.

Aries, E., & Moorehead, K. (1989). The importance of ethnicity in the development of identity of Black adolescents. *Psychological Reports, 65*(1), 75–82.

Arnold, M. (1960). *Emotion and personality* (Vol. 1). New York: Columbia University Press.

Aspy, D. (1972). *Toward a technology for humanizing education.* Champaign, IL: Research Press.

Aspy, D., & Roebuck, F. (1976). *A lever long enough.* Washington, DC: National Consortium for Humanizing Education.

Atkins, R. C. (1990). *Dr. Atkins' health revolution: How complementary medicine can extend your life.* New York: Bantam.

Atkinson, R. (1990). Life stories and personal mythmaking. *Humanistic Psychologist, 18*(2), 199–207.

Badcock, C. (1992). *Essential Freud* (2nd ed.). Oxford, England: Blackwell Publishers.

Bakan, D. (1969). *On method: Toward a reconstruction of psychological investigation.* San Francisco: Jossey-Bass.

Balter, L., & Spencer, J. H. (1991). Observation and theory in psychoanalysis: The self psychology of Heinz Kohut. *Psychoanalytic Quarterly, 60*(3), 361–395.

Bandler, R., & Grinder, J. (1976). *The structure of magic: A book about communication and change* (Vol. 2). Palo Alto, CA: Science and Behavior Books.

Bandura, A. (1969). *Principles of behavior modification.* New York: Holt, Rinehart & Winston.

Bandura, A. (1973). *Aggression: A social learning analysis.* Englewood Cliffs, NJ: Prentice-Hall.

Bandura, A. (1974). A behavior theory and the models of man. *American Psychologist, 29,* 859–869.

Bandura, A. (1977). *Social learning theory.* Englewood Cliffs, NJ: Prentice-Hall.

Bandura, A. (1978). The self system in reciprocal determinism. *American Psychologist, 33,* 344–358.

Bandura, A. (1986). *Social foundations of thought and action: A social cognitive theory.* Englewood Cliffs, NJ: Prentice-Hall.

Bandura, A. (1986). The explanatory and predictive scope of self-efficacy theory. *Journal of Social and Clinical Psychology, 4*(3), 359–373.

Bandura, A. (1989). Human agency in social cognitive theory. *American Psychologist, 44*(9), 1175–1184.

Bandura, A. (1990). Some reflections on reflections. *Psychological Inquiry, 1,* 101–105.

Bandura, A. (1991a). The changing icons in personality psychology. In J. Cantor (Ed.), *Psychology at Iowa: Centennial Essays.* Hillsdale, NJ: Lawrence Erlbaum.

Bandura, A. (1991b). Self-efficacy. In R. Schwarzer & R. Wicklund (Eds.), *Anxiety and self-focused attention.* New York: Harwood Academic.

Bandura, A. (1991c). Social cognitive theory of moral thought and action. In W. Kurtines & J. Gewirtz (Eds.), *Handbook of Moral Behavior and Development* (pp. 45–103). Hillsdale, NJ: Lawrence Erlbaum.

Bandura, A. (1991d). Social cognitive theory of self-regulation. *Organizational Behavior & Human Decision Processes, 50*(2), 248–287.

Bandura, A. (1992). Social cognitive theory. In R. Vasta (Ed.), *Six theories of child development: Revised formulations and current issues* (pp. 1–60). England: Jessica Kingsley.

Bandura, A., & Mischel, W. (1965). Modifications of self-imposed delay of reward through exposure to live and symbolic models. *Journal of Personality and Social Psychology, 2,* 698–705.

Bandura, A., & Walters, R. (1963). *Social learning and personality development.* New York: Holt, Rinehart, & Winston.

Bandura, A., Adams, N. E., Hardy, A. B., & Howells, G. N. (1980). Tests of the generality of self-efficacy theory. *Cognitive Therapy and Research, 4,* 39–66.

Banks, W., Ward, W., McQuater, G., & DeBritto, A. (1991). Are blacks external: On the status of locus of control in black populations. In J. Reginald (Ed.), *Black psychology* (pp. 181–192). Berkeley, CA: Cobb & Henry.

Bannister, D., & Fransella, F. (1966). A grid test of schizophrenic thought disorder. *British Journal of Social and Clinical Psychology, 5,* 95–102.

Bannister, D., & Mair, J. M. M. (1968). *The evaluation of personal constructs.* New York: Academic Press.

Bannister, D., & Salmon, P. (1966). Schizophrenic thought disorder: Specific or diffuse? *British Journal of Medical Psychology, 39,* 215–219.

Barrett, P., & Eysenck, S. (1994). The assessment of personality factors across 25 countries. *Personality and Individual Differences, 5,* 615–632.

Baumrind, D. (1972). Socialization and instrumental competence in young children. In W. W. Hartup (Ed.), *The young child: Reviews of research* (Vol. 2), 202–224. Washington, DC: National Association for the Education of Young Children.

Beck, A. (1991). *Biological sketch.* Unpublished manuscript.

Beck, A., & Freeman, A. (1990). *Cognitive therapy of personality disorders.* New York: Guilford Press.

Beck, A. T. (1967). *Depression: Clinical, experimental, and theoretical aspects.* New York: Hoeber. (Republished as *Depression: Causes and treatment.* Philadelphia: University of Pennsylvania Press, 1972.)

Beck, A. T. (1972). *Depression: Causes and treatments.* Philadelphia: University of Pennsylvania Press.

Beck, A. T., & Emory, G. (1979). *Cognitive therapy of anxiety and phobic disorders.* Philadelphia: Center for Cognitive Therapy.

Beck, A. T., & Emory, G. (1985). *Anxiety disorders and phobias: A cognitive perspective.* New York: Basic Books.

Beck, A. T., Epstein, N., & Harrison, R. (1983). Cognitions, attitudes, and personality dimensions in depression. *British Journal of Cognitive Psychotherapy, 1*(1), 1–16.

Beck, A. T., Rush, A. J., Shaw, B. F., & Emery, G. (1979). *Cognitive therapy of depression.* New York: Guilford.

Benjamin, J. (1988). *The bands of love.* New York: Pantheon Books.

Berkowitz, L., & Powers, P. (1979). Effects of timing and justification of witnessed aggression on observers' punitiveness. *Journal of Research in Personality, 13,* 71–80.

Bernal, M. E., Knight, G. P., Garza, C. A., Ocampo, K. A. et al. (1990). The development of ethnic identity in Mexican-American children. *Hispanic Journal of Behavioral Sciences, 12*(1), 3–24.

Bernard, M. E. (1986). *Staying alive in an irrational world: The psychology of Albert Ellis.* South Melbourne, Australia: Carlton & Macmillan.

Bernstein, D. (1991). The female oedipal complex. In P. Hartocollis & I. D. Graham (Eds.), *The personal myth in psychoanalytic theory.* Madison, CT: International Universities Press.

Bertalanffy, L. von. (1974). General systems theory and psychiatry. In S. Arieti (Ed.), *American handbook of psychiatry* (Vol. 1), 1095–1117. New York: Basic Books.

Betcher, R. W., & Pollack, W. (1993). *In a time of fallen heroes: The re-creation of masculinity.* New York: Atheneum.

Bettelheim, B. (1977). *The uses of enchantment.* New York: Knopf.

Bettelheim, B. (1982). *Freud and man's soul.* New York: Knopf.

Bezjak, J., & Lee, W. (1990). Relationship of self-efficacy and locus of control constructs in predicting college students' physical fitness behaviors. *Perceptual & Motor Skills, 71*(2), 499–508.

Bitter, J. R. (1991). Conscious motivations: An enhancement to Dreikurs' goals of children's misbehavior. *Individual Psychology: Journal of Adlerian Theory, Research & Practice, 47*(2), 210–221.

Blackman, D. (1991). B. F. Skinner and G. H. Mead: On biological science and social science. *Journal of the Experimental Analysis of Behavior, 55*(2), 251–265.

Blakeslee, S. (1991, September 10). Brain yields new clues on its organization for language. *The New York Times,* p. C1.

Blakeslee, S. (1993, August 31). Seeing and imaging: Clues to the workings of the mind's eye. *The New York Times.*

Boneau, C. A. (1992). Observations on psychology's past and future. *American Psychologist, 47*(12), 1586–1596.

Bordages, J. W. (1989). Self-actualization and personal autonomy. *Psychological Reports, 64*(3, Pt. 2), 1263–1266.

Boring, E. G. (1929). *A history of experimental psychology.* New York: Appleton-Century-Crofts.

Bouchard, T. J., Jr., Lykken, D. T., McGue, M., Segal, N. L., & Tellegen, A. (1990). Sources of human psychological differences: The Minnesota study of twins reared apart. *Science, 250,* 223–250.

Bozarth, J. D. (1990). The evolution of Carl Rogers as a therapist. Special Issue:

Fiftieth anniversary of the person-centered approach. *Person-Centered Review, 5*(4), 387–393.

Breger, L., Hunter, I., & Lane, R. W. (1971). The effect of stress on dreams. *Psychological Issues, 7* (3, Monograph 27), 1–213.

Bringmann, M. W. (1992). Computer-based methods for the analysis and interpretation of personal construct systems. In R. A. Neimeyer & G. J. Neimeyer (Eds.), *Advances in personal construct psychology, 2,* 57–90. Greenwich, CT: JAI Press.

Brody, J. (1993, March 23). Brain yields clues to its visual maps. *The New York Times,* p. C-1.

Brooke, R. W. (1991). Psychic complexity and human existence: A phenomenological approach. *Journal of Analytical Psychology, 36,* 505–518.

Brunell, L. J., & Young, W. T. (Eds.). (1982). *Multimodal handbook for a mental hospital.* New York: Springer.

Bruner, J. S. (1965). A cognitive theory of personality. And Rogers, C. R., Intellectualizing psychotherapy. [Reviews of G. A. Kelly. *Psychology of personal constructs.*] *Contemporary Psychology, 1,* 355–358.

Brunner, J. (1991). The (ir)relevance of Freud's Jewish identity to the origins of psychoanalysis. *Psychoanalysis & Contemporary Thought, 14*(4), 655–684.

Bryant, B. L. (1987, March). Birth order as a factor in the development of vocational preferences. *Individual Psychology: Journal of Adlerian Theory, Research and Practice, 43*(1), 36–41.

Buckley, W. (1967). *Modern systems research for the behavioral scientist.* Chicago: Aldine.

Burkitt, I. (1991). *Social selves: Theories of the social formation of personality.* Newbury Park, CA: Sage.

Burlingham, M. J. (1990). The relationship of Anna Freud and Dorothy Burlingham. *Journal of the American Academy of Psychoanalysis, 19*(4), 612–619.

Busick, B. S. (1989). Grieving as a hero's journey. Special issue:

Bereavement care: A new look at hospice and community based services. *Hospice Journal, 5,* 89–105.

Buss, A. (1989). Personality as trait. *American Psychologist, 44,* 1378–1388.

Buss, A. (1991). The EAS theory of temperament. In J. Stelau & A. Angleitner (Eds.), *Exploration in temperament: International perspectives on theory and measurement* (p. 43). New York: Plenum Press.

Buss, A. H., & Plomin, R. A. (1975). *A temperament theory of personality development.* New York: John Wiley & Sons.

Buss, A. H., & Plomin, R. A. (1984). *Temperament: Early developing personality traits.* Hillsdale, NJ: Erlbaum.

Buss, D. (1990). Biological foundations of personality. *Journal of Personality, 58,* 1–345.

Buss, D. (1991). Evolutionary personality psychology. *Annual Review of Psychology, 42,* 459–491.

Buss, D. (1991). Evolutionary personality psychology. *Annual Review of Psychology, 42,* 161–190.

Buss, D., & Cantor, N. (Eds.). (1989). *Personality psychology: Recent trends and emerging directions.* New York: Springer-Verlag.

Cain, D. J. (1990). Celebration, reflection, and renewal: 50 years of client-centered therapy and beyond. Special Issue: Fiftieth anniversary of the person-centered approach. *Person-Centered Review, 5*(4), 357–363.

Cantor, N. & Kihlstrom, J. F. (1982). Cognitive and social processes in personality. In G. T. Wilson & C. M. Franks (Eds.), *Contemporary behavior therapy.* New York: Guilford.

Cantor, N. (1990). From thought to behavior: "Having" and "doing" in the study of personality and cognition. *American Psychologist, 45*(6), 735–750.

Cantor, N., & Kihlstrom, E. (1987). *Personality and social intelligence.* Englewood Cliffs, NJ: Prentice-Hall.

Carson, R. (1989). Personality. *Annual Review of Psychology, 40,* 227–248.

Cartwright, D. S. (1979). *Theories and models of personality.* Dubuque, IA: W. C. Brown Co.

Cassel, R. N. (1990). Transpersonal psychology as the basis for health care. *Psychology: A Journal of Human Behavior, 27*(1), 33–38.

Catanzaro, S. (1993). Mood regulation expectancies, anxiety sensitivity, and emotional distress. *Journal of Abnormal Psychology, 102*(2), 327–330.

Cattell, R. B. (1950). *Personality: A systematic, theoretical and factual study.* New York: McGraw-Hill.

Cattell, R. B. (1965). *The scientific analysis of personality.* Chicago: Aldine.

Cattell, R. B. (Ed.), (1966). *Handbook of multivariate experimental psychology.* Chicago: Rand McNally.

Cattell, R. B. (1972). *A new morality from science: Beyondism.* New York: Pergamon.

Cattell, R. (1990). Advances in Cattellian personality theory. In L. Pervin (Ed.), *Handbook of personality: Theory and research.* New York: Guilford Press.

Cavell, M. (1991). The subject of mind. *International Journal of Psycho-Analysis, 72*(1), 141–154.

Chambers, W. V. (1987, Feb.). Personality and personal construct constriction: A secondary analysis. *Journal of Social Behavior and Personality, 2*(1), 153–160.

Chambers, W. V., & Epting, F. R. (1985, Dec.). Personality and personal construct: Logical consistency. *Psychological Reports, 57*(3), 1120.

Chambers, W. V., & Graves, P. (1985, Dec.). A technique for eliciting personal construct change. *Psychological Reports, 57*(3), 1041–1042.

Chambers, W. V., & Stonerock, B. (1985, Dec.). Truth and logical consistency of personal constructs. *Psychological Reports, 57*(3), 1178.

Chang, R., & Page, R. C. (1991). Characteristics of the self-actualized person: Visions from the East and West. *Counseling & Values, 36*(1), 2–10.

Cheshire, N., & Thoma, H. (1991). Metaphor, neologism, and "open texture": Implications for translating Freud's scientific thought. *International Review of Psycho-Analysis, 18*(3), 429–455.

Chodorow, N. (1985). Gender, relation, and difference in psychoanalytic perspective. In H. Eisenstein & A. Jardine (Eds.), *The future of difference.* New Brunswick, NJ: Rutgers State University.

Chodorow, N. J. (1978). *The reproduction of mothering.* Berkeley: University of California Press.

Chodorow, N. J. (1989). *Feminism and psychoanalytic theory.* New Haven, CT: Yale University Press.

Chodorow, N. J. (1991). "Freud on women" in J. Neu (editor) *The Cambridge companion to Freud.* New York: Cambridge University Press.

Chomsky, N. (1959). Review of Skinner's *Verbal behavior. Language, 35,* 26–58; 234; 246–249.

Clarke, J. J. (1992). *In search of Jung: Historical & philosophical enquiries.* London, England: Routledge.

Coan, R. W. (1991). Self-actualization and the quest for the ideal human. Special Issue: Handbook of self-actualization. *Journal of Social Behavior & Personality, 6*(5), 127–136.

Coelho, M. C. (1993). *The universe story.* Unpublished manuscript.

Coles, R. (1970). *Erik H. Erikson: The growth of his work.* Boston: Little, Brown.

Coles, R. (1974). Karen Horney's flight from orthodoxy. In J. Strouse (Ed.), *Women and analysis.* New York: Grossman.

Comstock, G., & Strasburger, V. (1990). Deceptive appearances: Television violence and aggressive behavior. *Journal of Adolescent Health Care, 11*(1), 31–44.

Conant, J. B. (1947). *On understanding science.* New Haven: Yale University Press.

Cook, B. W. (1992). *Eleanor Roosevelt.* New York: Penguin.

Cooper, J., & Mackie, D. (1986). Video games and aggression in children. *Journal of Applied Social Psychology, 16*(8), 726–744.

Cooper, S. H. (1989). Recent contributions to the theory of defense mechanisms: A comparative view. *Journal of the American Psychoanalytic Association, 37,* 865–891.

Corcoran, D. W. J. (1964). The relation between introversion and salivation. *American Journal of Psychology, 77,* 298–300.

Corcoran, K. (1991). Efficacy, "skills," reinforcement, and choice behavior. *American Psychologist, 46*(2), 155–157.

Costa, P., & McCrae, R. (1992). Revised NEO Personality Inventory: NEO PI and NEO Five-Factor Inventory (NEO FFI) professional manual. Odessa, FL: Psychological Assessment Resources.

Costa, P. T., Jr., & McCrae, R. R. (1985). *The NEO Personality Inventory manual.* Odessa, FL: Psychology Assessment Resources.

Cousins, N. (1989). *Head 1st: The biology of hope.* New York: Dutton.

Coward, H. (1989). Jung's conception of the role of religion in psychological transformation. *Humanistic Psychologist, 17*(3), 265–273.

Crandall, J. E. (1981). *Theory and measurement of social interest: Empirical tests of Alfred Adler's concept.* New York: Columbia University Press.

Crockett, W. H. (1982). The organization of construct systems: The organization corollary. In J. C. Mancuso & R. Adams-Webber (Eds.), *The construing person.* New York: Praeger.

Csikszentmihalyi, M. (1975). *Beyond boredom and anxiety.* San Fransisco, CA: Jossey-Bass.

Csikszentmihalyi, M. (1990). *Flow: The psychology of optimal experience.* New York: Harper & Row.

Dalai Lama et al. (1991). *Mind science: An East-West dialogue.* Boston: Wisdom.

Daniels, M. (1988). The myth of self-actualization. *Journal of Humanistic Psychology, 28*(1), 7–38.

Das, A. K. (1989). Beyond self-actualization. *International Journal for the Advancement of Counseling, 12,* 13–27.

Davidson, L. (1987, Fall). What is the appropriate source for psychological explanation?

Humanistic Psychologist, 15(3), 150–166.

Davis, P. J. (1987, September). Repression and the inaccessibility of affective memories. *Journal of Personality and Social Psychology, 53*(3), 585–593.

de Brabander, B., & Boone, C. (1990). Sex differences in perceived locus of control. *Journal of Social Psychology, 130*(2), 271–272.

de Courcy-Hinds, M. (1993, October 19). Not like the movie: A dare leads to death. *The New York Times*, p. C-1.

de Mann, A., Leduc, C., & Labreche-Gauthier, L. (1992). Parental control in child rearing and multidimensional locus of control. *Psychological Reports, 70*(1), 320–322.

DeCarvalho, R. J. (1989). Contributions to the history of psychology: LXII. Carl Rogers' naturalistic system of ethics. *Psychological Reports, 65*(3, Pt. 2), 1155–1162.

DeCarvalho, R. J. (1990). Contributions to the history of psychology: LXIX. Gordon Allport on the problem of method in psychology. *Psychological Reports, 67*(1), 267–275.

DeCarvalho, R. J. (1991). *The founders of humanistic psychology.* New York: Praeger.

DeCarvalho, R. J. (1992). The humanistic ethics of Rollo May. *Journal of Humanistic Psychology, 32,* 7–18.

DeMartino, R. J. (1991). Karen Horney, Daisetz T. Suzuki, and Zen Buddhism. *American Journal of Psychoanalysis, 51*(3), 267–283.

Demont, W. C., & Wolper, E. A. (1958). The relationship of eye movements, body motility, and external stimuli to dream content. *Journal of Experimental Psychology, 55,* 543–553.

Derlega, V., Winstead, B., & Jones, W. (Eds.). (1991). *Personality: Contemporary theory and research.* Chicago, IL: Welson-Hall.

Digman, J. M. (1990). Personality structure: Emergence of the five-factor model. *Annual Review of Psychology, 41,* 417–440.

Digman, J. M., & Inouye, J. (1986). Further specification of the five robust factors of personality. *Journal of Personality and Social Psychology, 50,* 116–123.

Diller, J. V. (1991). *Freud's Jewish identity: A case study in the impact of ethnicity.* Rutherford, England: Fairleigh Dickinson University Press/Associated University Press.

Dinkmeyer, D. (1989). Adlerian psychology. *A Journal of Human Behavior, 26*(1).

Dixon, P. N., & Strano, D. A. (1989). The measurement of inferiority: A review and directions for scale development. *Individual Psychology, 45,* Austin: University of Texas Press.

Doherty, W. J., & Baldwin, C. (1985, April). Shifts and stability in locus of control during the 1970s: Divergence of the sexes. *Journal of Personality and Social Psychology, 48*(4), 1048–1053.

Dollard, J., & Miller, N. (1950). *Personality and psychotherapy: An analysis in terms of learning, thinking, and culture.* New York: McGraw-Hill.

Dominick, J. R. (1984, Spring). Videogames, television violence, and aggression in teenagers. *Journal of Communication, 34*(2), 136–147.

Dornbusch, S., Gross, R., Duncan, P., & Ritter, P. (1987). Stanford studies of adolescence using the national health examination survey. In R. Lerner & T. Fuch (Eds.), *Biological-psychosocial interactions in early adolescence* (pp. 189–206). Hillsdale, NJ: Erlbaum.

Douglas, C. (1993). *Translate this darkness: The life of Christiana Morgan.* New York: Simon & Schuster.

Downing, C. (Ed.). (1991). *Mirrors of the self: Archetypal images that shape your life.* Los Angeles: Jeremy P. Tarcher.

Dreifurs, R. (1952–1953). Adler's contribution to medicine, psychology, education. *American Journal of Individual Psychology, 10,* 83–86.

Drwal, R. L., & Wiechnik, R. (1984). The effect of locus of control and self-esteem on attributions and expectancies after success and failure. *Polish Psychological Bulletin, 15*(4), 257–266.

Dryden, W. (1984). *Rational-emotive therapy: Fundamentals and innovations.* Beckenham, England: Croom-Helm.

Dryden, W. (1991). *A dialogue with Arnold Lazarus: "It depends."* Philadelphia: Open University Press.

Dryden, W., & Golden, W. (Eds.). (1986). *Cognitive behavioral approaches to psychotherapy.* London: Harper & Row.

Ducat, S. (1985). Science and psychoanalysis: The implications of recent findings in psychopathology research and neurophysiology for the Freudian theory of the mind. *International Journal of Biosocial Research, 7*(2), 94–107.

Duhs, L., & Gunton, R. (1988). TV violence and childhood aggression: A curmudgeon's guide. *Australian Psychologist, 23*(2), 183–195.

Duke, M. P. (1986, February). Personality science: A proposal. *Journal of Personality and Social Psychology, 50*(2), 382–385.

Dyer, R. (1983). *Her father's daughter: The work of Anna Freud.* New York: Jason Aronson.

Eagle, M. N. (1984). *Recent developments in psychoanalysis: A critical evaluation.* New York: McGraw-Hill.

Eckardt, M. H. (1991). Feminine psychology revisited: A historical perspective. *American Journal of Psychoanalysis, 51*(3), 235–243.

Edelson, M. (1986, October). The convergence of psychoanalysis and neuroscience: Illusion and reality. *Contemporary Psychoanalysis, 22*(4), 479–519.

Eisenman, R. (1992). Birth order, development, and personality. Acta Paedopsychiatrica: *International Journal of Child & Adolescent Psychiatry, 55,* 25–27.

Eliade, M. (1983). *The sacred and the profane: The nature of religion.* Magnolia, MA: Peter Smith.

Ellenberger, H. F. (1970). *The discovery of the unconscious.* New York: Basic Books.

Elliot, B. A. (1992). Birth order and health: Major issues. *Social Science & Medicine, 35*(4), 443–452.

Ellis A., & Bernard, M. E. (Eds.). (1985). *Clinical applications of rational-emotive therapy.* New York: Plenum.

Ellis A., & Dryden, W. (1987). *The practice of rational emotive therapy.* New York: Springer.

Ellis, A. (1955). New approaches to psychotherapy techniques. *Journal of Clinical Psychology Monograph Supplement.* Brandon, VT.

Ellis, A. (1958). Rational psychotherapy. *Journal of General Psychology, 59,* 35–49.

Ellis, A. (1962). *Reason and emotion in psychotherapy.* New York: Lyle & Stuart.

Ellis, A. (1969). A weekend of rational encounter. *Rational Living, 4* (2), 1–8.

Ellis, A. (1973). *Humanistic psychotherapy.* New York: Julian Press.

Ellis, A. (1976). The biological basis of human irrationality. *Journal of Individual Psychology, 32,* 145–168.

Ellis, A. (1978). Toward a theory of personality. In R. J. Corsini, (Ed.), *Readings in current personality theories.* Itasca, IL: Reacock.

Ellis, A. (1985a). *Overcoming resistance: Rational-emotive therapy with difficult clients.* New York: Springer.

Ellis, A. (1985b). Expanding the ABC's of rational emotive therapy. In M. Mahoney & A. Freemany (Eds.), *Cognition and psychotherapy* (pp. 313–323). New York: Plenum.

Ellis, A. (1985c). Two forms of humanistic psychology: Rational-emotive therapy vs. transpersonal psychology. *Free Inquiry, 15*(4), 14–21.

Ellis, A. (1987a). How rational-emotive therapy (RET) helps to actualize the human potential. *New Jersey Journal of Professional Counseling, 50,* 2.

Ellis, A. (1987b). A sadly neglected cognitive element in depression. *Cognitive Therapy and Research, 11,* 121–146.

Ellis, A. (1988). *How to stubbornly refuse to make yourself miserable about anything—yes anything.* Secaucus, NJ: Lyle & Stuart.

Ellis, A. (1991). My life in clinical psychology. In C. E. Walker (Ed.), *The history of clinical psychology in autobiography* (Vol. 1, pp. 1–37). Pacific Grove, CA: Brooks/Cole.

Ellis, A., & Becker, I. (1982). *A guide to personal happiness.* North Hollywood, CA: Wilshire.

Ellis, A., & Bernard, M. E. (Eds.) (1983). *Rational-emotive approaches to the problems of childhood.* New York: Plenum.

Ellis, A., & Harper, R. A. (1975). *A new guide to rational living.* North Hollywood, CA: Wilshire.

Ellis, A., McInerney, J., DiGiuseppe, R. A., & Yaeger, R. (1988). *Rational-emotive treatment of alcoholism and substance abuse.* New York: Pergamon.

Epting, F. R., & Leitner, L. M. (1992). Humanistic psychology and personal construct theory. Special Issue: The humanistic movement in psychology: History, celebration, and prospectus. *Humanistic Psychologist, 20*(2–3), 243–259.

Erdelyi, M. H. (1985). *Psychoanalysis: Freud's cognitive psychology.* New York: W. H. Freeman.

Erikson, E. H. (1958). *Young man Luther.* New York: Norton.

Erikson, E. H. (1963). *Childhood and society* (2nd ed.). New York: Norton.

Erikson, E. H. (1964). *Insight and responsibility.* New York: Norton.

Erikson, E. H. (1968). *Identity, youth and crisis.* New York: Norton.

Erikson, E. H. (1969). *Gandhi's Truth.* New York: Norton.

Erikson, E. H. (1974). *Dimensions of a new identity.* New York: Norton.

Erikson, E. H. (1975). *Life history and the historical moment.* New York: Norton.

Espin, O., & Gawelek, M. (1992). Women's diversity: Ethnicity, race, class, and gender in theories of feminist psychology. In L. Brown & M. Ballou (Eds.), *Personality and psychopathology: Feminist reappraisals.* New York: Guilford Press.

Evans, R. I. (1967). *Dialogue with Erik Erikson.* New York: Harper & Row.

Evans, R. J. (1976). *The making of psychology: Discussions with creative contributors.* New York: Knopf.

Evans, T. D., & Meredith, D. W. (1991). How far can you go and still be Adlerian? Special Issue: "On beyond Adler." *Individual Psychology: Journal of Adlerian Theory, Research & Practice, 47*(4), 541–547.

Eyer, D. (1993, February 21). Infant bonding and guilty mothers. *The New York Times,* p. 25.

Eysenck, H. (1990). Biological dimensions of personality. In L. A. Pervin (Ed.), *Handbook of personality: Theory and research.* New York: Guilford Press.

Eysenck, H. (1990). Genetic and environmental contributions to individual differences: The 3 major dimensions of personality. *Journal of Personality, 58,* 245–261.

Eysenck, H. (1991). Dimensions of personality: The biosocial approach to personality. In J. Strelau & A. Angleitner (Eds.), *Exploration in temperament: International perspectives on theory and measurement* (p. 365). New York: Plenum Press.

Eysenck, H. J. (1947). *Dimensions of personality.* London: Routledge & Kegan Paul.

Eysenck, H. J. (1965). *Fact and fiction in psychology.* Baltimore: Penguin.

Eysenck, H. J. (1970). *The structure of human personality* (3rd ed.). New York: Methuen.

Eysenck, H. J. (1952). The effects of psychotherapy: An evaluation. *Journal of Consulting Psychology, 16,* 319–324.

Eysenck, H. J. (1957). *The dynamics of anxiety and hysteria.* London: Routledge & Kegan Paul.

Eysenck, H. J. (1967). *The biological basis of personality.* Springfield, IL: Charles C. Thomas.

Eysenck, H. J. (1982). *Personality, genetics, and behavior: Selected papers.* New York: Praeger.

Eysenck, H. J. (1985). Revolution in the theory and measurement of intelligence. *Evaluación Psicológica, 1*(1–2), 99–158.

Eysenck, H. J. (Ed.). (1961). *Handbook of abnormal psychology: An experimental approach.* New York: Basic Books.

Eysenck, H. J., & Rachman, S. (1965). *The causes and cures of neurosis*. San Diego, CA: Knapp.

Fairbairn, W. R. D. (1952). *Psychoanalytic studies of the personality*. London: Tavistock; Routledge & Kegan Paul.

Farmer, J. J. (1993, July 29). Vince Foster's reasons may never be known. *Newark Star Ledger*.

Farran, D., Haskins, R., & Galligher, J. (1980). Poverty and mental retardation: A search for explanations. *New Directions for Exceptional Children, 1*, 47–66.

Faulkender, P. J. (1991). Does gender schema mediate between sex-role identity and self-actualization? *Psychological Reports, 68*(3, Pt. 1), 1019–1029.

Fay, A. (1976). Clinical notes on paradoxical therapy. In A. A. Lazarus, *Multimodal behavior therapy*. New York: Springer.

Fay, A. (1978). *Making things better by making them worse*. New York: Hawthorne.

Feixas, G. (1989). Personal construct psychology in Spain: A promising perspective. *International Journal of Personal Construct Psychology, 2*(4), 433–442.

Feshbach, S. (1984, September). The "personality" of personality theory and research. *Personality and Social Psychology Bulletin, 10*(3), 446–456.

Fickling, W. (1991, Fall/Winter). Zen as therapy. *The Ten Directions*, pp. 38–40.

Fingarette, H. (1963). *The self in transformation: Psychoanalysis, philosophy, and the life of the spirit*. New York: Basic Books.

Fisher, L. M. (1994, January 30). Profits and ethics clash in research on genetic coding. *The New York Times*, p. 3-10.

Fisher, S., & Greenberg, R. P. (1977). *Scientific credibility of Freud's theory and therapy*. New York: Basic Books.

Fiske, S., & Taylor, S. (1991). *Social cognition*. New York: McGraw-Hill.

Foa, E. B. (1990). Continuous exposure and complete response prevention of obsessive compulsive neuroses. *Behavior Therapy 32*, 821–829.

Ford, J. G. (1991). Inherent potentialities of actualization: An initial exploration. *Journal of Humanistic Psychology, 31*(3), 65–88.

Ford, K. M., & Adams-Webber, J. R. (1991). The structure of personal construct systems and the logic of confirmation. *International Journal of Personal Construct Psychology, 4*(1), 15–41.

Fordham, F. (1953) *An introduction to Jung's psychology*. Baltimore: Penguin.

Forisha-Kovach, B. (1983). *The experience of adolescence: Development in context*. New York: Scott, Foresman & Co.

Frankl, V. E. (1960). Paradoxical intention: A logo-therapeutic technique. *American Journal of Psychotherapy, 14*, 520–535.

Frankl, V. E. (1978). *The unheard cry for meaning*. New York: Simon & Schuster.

Franks, C. M. (1976). Foreword. In A. A. Lazarus, *Multimodal behavior therapy*. New York: Springer.

Freeman, M. (1991). Rewriting the self: Development as moral practice. In M. B. Tappan & M. J. Packer (Eds.), *Narrative and storytelling: Implications for understanding moral development. New directions for child development*. San Francisco, CA: Jossey-Bass.

Freeman, M. (1992). Self as narrative: The place of life history in studying the life span. In T. Brinthaupt & R. Lipka (Eds.), *The self: Definitional and method-ological issues*. New York: State University of New York.

Freud, A. (1946). *The ego and the mechanisms of defense*. New York: International Univer-sities Press.

Freud, A. (1965–). *The Writings of Anna Freud*. New York: International Universities Press.

Freud, S. (1953–). *The complete psychological works: Standard edition* (24 vols.). J. Strachey (Ed.). London: Hogarth Press. (Hereafter referred to as *SE* with year of original publication.)

Freud, S. (1895). Studies in hysteria. *SE* (Vol. 2).

Freud, S. (1900). The interpretation of dreams. *SE* (Vols. 4 & 5).

Freud, S. (1901). The psychopathology of everyday life. *SE* (Vol. 6).

Freud, S. (1905). Three essays on sexuality. *SE* (Vol. 7).

Freud, S. (1910). Five lectures on psychoanalysis. *SE* (Vol. 11).

Freud, S. (1917). Introductory lectures on psychoanalysis. *SE* (Vols. 15 & 16).

Freud, S. (1923). The ego and the id. *SE* (Vol. 19).

Freud, S. (1926b). The question of lay analysis. *SE* (Vol. 20).

Freud, S. (1933). New introductory lectures on psychoanalysis. *SE* (Vol. 22).

Freud, S. (1940). An outline of psychoanalysis. *SE* (Vol. 23).

Fromm, E. (1941). *Escape from freedom*. New York: Rinehart.

Fromm, E. (1947). *Man for himself*. New York: Rinehart.

Fromm, E. (1955). *The sane society*. New York: Rinehart.

Fromm, E. (1956). *The art of loving*. New York: Harper & Row.

Fromm, E. (1964). *The heart of man*. New York: Harper & Row.

Fromm, E. (1973). *The anatomy of human destructiveness*. New York: Rinehart.

Fromm, E. (1976). *To have or to be*. New York: Harper & Row.

Fromm, E., & Maccoby, M. (1970). *Social character in a Mexican village*. Englewood Cliffs, NJ: Prentice-Hall.

Fuld, P. J. (1991, Fall/Winter). Zen and the work of a psychotherapist. *The Ten Directions*, pp. 40–41.

Fullerton, C. S., Ursano, R. J., Harry, P., & Slusarcick, A. (1989). Birth order, psychol-ogical well-being, and social supports in young adults. *Journal of Nervous & Mental Disease, 177*(9), 556–559.

Funder, D., & Sneed, C. (1993). Behavioral manifestations of personality: An ecological approach to judgmental accuracy. *Journal of Personality and Social Psychology, 64*, 479–490.

Furedy, J. J. (1990). A realist perspective. *Canadian Psychology, 31*, 254–261.

Furnham, A. (1990). Can people accurately estimate their own personality test scores? *European Journal of Personality, 4*(4), 319–327.

Galin, D. (1974). Implications for psychiatry of left and right cerebral specialization. *Archives of General Psychiatry, 31,* 572–583.

Gardner, H. (1992). Scientific psychology: Should we bury it or praise it? *New Ideas in Psychology, 10*(2), 179–190.

Garrison, D. (1981). Karen Horney and feminism. *Signs: Journal of Women in Culture and Society, 6,* 4.

Geisler, C. (1985). Repression: A psychoanalytic perspective revisited. *Psychoanalysis and Contemporary Thought, 8*(2), 253–298.

Geller, L. (1982). The failure of self-actualization theory. *Journal of Humanistic Psychology, 22,* 56–73.

Geller, L. (1984, Spring). Another look at self-actualization. *Journal of Humanistic Psychology, 24*(2), 93–106.

Gergen, K. (1992, November/December). The decline and fall of personality. *Psychology Today,* pp. 59–60.

Gergen, K. J. (1990). Toward a postmodern psychology. Special Issue: Psychology and postmodernity. *Humanistic Psychologist, 18,* 23–34.

Gilligan, C. (1982). *In a different voice.* Cambridge, MA: Harvard University Press.

Ginsberg, C. (1984, Spring). Toward a somatic under-standing of self: A reply to Leonard Geller. *Journal of Humanistic Psychology, 24*(2), 66–92.

Giora, Z. (1991). *The unconscious and its narratives.* Budapest, Hungary: Twins Publishing House.

Giorgi, A. (1987, Spring). The crisis of humanistic psychology. *Humanistic Psychologist, 15*(1), 5–20.

Gist, M., & Mitchell, T. (1992). Self-efficacy: A theoretical analysis of its determinants and malleability. *Academy of Management Review, 17*(2), 183–211.

Glucksberg, S., & King, I. (1967, October 27). Motivated forgetting mediated by implicit verbal chaining: A laboratory analog of repression. *Science,* 517–519.

Glymour, C. (1991). Freud's androids. *The Cambridge companion to Freud. Cambridge companions to philosophy.* New York: Cambridge University Press.

Goldberg, L. R. (1981). Language and individual differences: The search for universals in personality lexicons. In L. Wheeler (Ed.), *Review of personality and social psychology* (Vol. 2, pp. 141–165). Beverly Hills, CA: Sage.

Goldberg, L. R. (1990). An alternative "description of personality": The big-five factor structure. *Journal of Personality and Social Psychology, 59,* 1216–1229.

Goleman, D. (1985). *Vital lies, simple truths.* New York: Simon & Schuster.

Goleman, D. (1987, February 6). Carl R. Rogers, 85, leader in psychotherapy, dies. *The New York Times,* pp. D16.

Goleman, D. (1990, March 22). Brain structure differences linked to schizophrenia in study of twins. *The New York Times,* p. C-1.

Goleman, D. (1991, September 29) Fluid identities. *The New York Times Book Review.*

Goleman, D. (1992). New light on how stress erodes health. *New York Times,* p. C-1.

Goleman, D. (1993a, May 4). Some patients arouse hatred, therapists find. *New York Times,* p. C-1.

Goleman, D. (1993b, April 6). Studying the secrets of childhood memory. *New York Times,* p. C-1.

Goleman, D. (1994, January 11). Childhood depression may herald adult ills. *The New York Times,* p. C-1.

Goleman, D. (1994, March 22). The "wrong" sex: a new definition of childhood pain. *The New York Times.*

Gray, S. W. (1986). The relationship between self-actualization and leisure satisfaction. *Psychology: A Quarterly Journal of Human Behavior, 23*(1), 6–12.

Green, C. D. (1992). Of immortal mythological beasts: Option-ism in psychology. *Theory & Psychology, 2*(3), 291–320.

Greenberg, J. (1981, August 11). A psychiatrist who wouldn't take no for an answer. *The New York Times,* pp. C1–C2.

Greever, K., Tseng, M., & Friedland, B. (1973). Development of the social interest index. *Journal of Consulting and Clinical Psychology, 41,* 454–458.

Greisers, C., Greenberg, R., & Harrison, R. H. (1972). The adaptive function of sleep: The differential effects of sleep and dreaming on recall. *Journal of Abnormal Psychology, 80,* 280–286.

Griffith, C. E. (1987). Teaching old dogmatists new tricks: Contributions from child development literature to Freud's Oedipal theory. *Contributions to Human Development, 18,* 1–35.

Grotstein, J. S. (1991). An American view of the British psychoanalytic experience: Psychoanalysis in counter-point: The contributions of the British Object Relations School. *Melanie Klein & Object Relations, 9*(2), 34–62.

Grünbaum, A. (1979). Is Freudian psychoanalytic theory pseudo-scientific by Karl Popper's criterion of demarcation? *American Philosophical Quarterly, 16,* 131–141.

Grünbaum, A. (1980). Episte-ological liabilities of the clinical appraisal of psychoanalytic theory. *Nous, 14,* 307–385.

Grünbaum, A. (1984). *The foundations of psychoanalysis: A philosophical critique.* Berkeley, CA: University of California Press.

Guest, H. (1989). The origins of transpersonal psychology. *British Journal of Psycho-herapy, 6*(1), 62–69.

Gupta, M. D. (1987, January). Role of age and birth order in Machiavellianism. *Psycho-logical Studies, 32*(1), 47–50.

Hall, C. S., & Lindzey, G. (1978). *Theories of personality* (3rd ed.). New York: Wiley.

Hall, C. S., & Van de Castle, R. (1965). An empirical inves-igation of the castration complex in dreams. *Journal of Personality, 33,* 20–29.

Hall, M. (1968, July). A conversation with Abraham H. Maslow. *Psychology Today,* 34–37; 54–57.

Hamacheck, D. (1990). Evaluating self-concept and ego status in Erickson's last three psychosocial stages. *Journal of Counseling & Development, 68*(6), 677–683.

Hammer, J. (1970). Preference

for gender of child as a function of sex of adult respondents. *Journal of Individual Psychology, 33,* 20–29.

Hamon, S. A. (1987, Summer). Some contributions of Horneyan theory of enhancement of the Type A behavior construct. *American Journal of Psychoanalysis, 47*(2), 105–115.

Hanh, T. N. (1974). *Zen keys.* Garden City, NY: Anchor/Doubleday.

Hanh, T. N. (1975). *The miracle of mindfulness! A manual on meditation.* Boston: Beacon.

Hanh, T. N. (1985). *A guide to walking meditation.* Nyack, NY: Fellowship.

Hanh, T. N. (1988). *The heart of understanding.* Berkeley, CA: Parallax.

Hanh, T. N. (1991). *Peace is every step: The path of mindfulness in everyday life.* New York: Bantam.

Hanh, T. N. (1992). *Touching peace.* Berkeley, CA: Parallax.

Hanh, T. N. (1993). *The blooming of a lotus: Guided meditation exercises for healing and transformation.* Boston: Beacon.

Harari, C. (1989). Humanistic and transpersonal psychology: Values in psychotherapy. *Psychotherapy in Private Practice, 7*(4), 49–56.

Harrington, D. M., Block, J. H., & Block, J. (1987, April). Testing aspects of Carl Rogers's theory of creative environments: Child-rearing antecedents of creative potential in young adolescents. *Journal of Personality and Social Psychology, 52*(4), 851–856.

Harris, K. A., & Morrow, J. B. (1992). Differential effects of birth order and gender on perceptions of responsibility and dominance. *Individual Psychology: Journal of Adlerian Theory, Research & Practice, 48*(1), 109–118.

Harris, T. (1969). *I'm O.K. — You're OK.* New York: Harper & Row.

Harrison, W., Lewis, G., & Straka, T. (1984, September). Locus of control, choice, and satisfaction with an assigned task. *Journal of Research in Personality, 18*(3), 342–351.

Hartmann, H. (1958). *Ego psychology and the problem of adaption.* New York: International Universities Press.

Hartmann, H. (1964). *Essays in ego psychology: Selected problems on psychoanalytic theory.* New York: International Universities Press.

Harzem, P. (1987, Fall). On the virtues of being a psychologist. *Behavior Analyst, 10*(2), 175–181.

Hayes, S., & Hayes, L. (1988). Inadequacies not just obstacles. *Counselling Psychology Quarterly, 1*(2–3), 291–294.

Heaven, P. (1991). Venturesomeness, impulsiveness, and Eysenck's personality dimensions: A study among Australian adolescents. *Journal of Genetic Psychology, 152*(1), 91–99.

Heaven, P., & Connors, J. (1988). Personality, gender, and "just world" beliefs. *Australian Journal of Psychology, 40*(3), 261–266.

Henwood, K. L., & Pidgeon, N. F. (1992). Qualitative research and psychological theorizing. *British Journal of Psychology, 83*(1), 97–111.

Hermans, J. J., Kempen, H. J., & Van Loon, R. J. (1992). The dialogical self: Beyond individualism and rationalism. *American Psychologist, 47*(1), 23–33.

Heylighen, R. (1992). A cognitive-systemic reconstruction of Maslow's theory of self-actualization. *Behavioral Science, 37*(1), 39–58.

Hilts, P. (1991, September 24). A brain unit seen as index for recalling memories. *The New York Times,* p. C-1.

Hinds, M. (1993, October 19). Not like the movie: a dare leads to death. *The New York Times,* p. C-1.

Hirai, T. (1989). *Zen meditation and psychotherapy.* Tokyo: Japan Publications.

Hjelle, L. A. (1991). Relationship of social interest to internal-external control and self-actualization in young women. Special Issue: Social interest. *Individual Psychology: Journal of Adlerian Theory, Research & Practice, 47*(1), 101–105.

Hoffman, E. (1988). *The right to be human: A biography of Abraham Maslow.* Los Angeles: Tarcher.

Hogan, R. (1982). A socioanalytic theory of personality. In M. Page (Ed.), *Nebraska symposium on motivation.* Lincoln: University of Nebraska Press.

Hogan, R. J. (1976). *Personality theory: The personological tradition.* Englewood Cliffs, NJ: Prentice-Hall.

Holden, G. (1991). The relationship of self-efficacy appraisals to subsequent health outcomes: A meta-analysis. *Social Work in Health Care, 16*(1), 53–93.

Hollon, S. D., & Kriss, M. (1984). Cognitive factors in clinical research and practice. *Clinical Psychology Review, 4,* 355–376.

Hoover, T. (1980). *The Zen experience.* New York: New American Library.

Horley, J. (1991). Values and beliefs as personal constructs. *International Journal of Personal Construct Psychology, 4*(1), 1–14.

Horney, K. (1937). *The neurotic personality of our time.* New York: Norton.

Horney, K. (1939). *New ways in psychoanalysis.* New York: Norton.

Horney, K. (1942). *Self-Analysis.* New York: Norton.

Horney, K. (1945). *Our inner conflicts.* New York: Norton.

Horney, K. (1950). *Neurosis and human growth.* New York: Norton.

Horney, K. (1967). *Feminine psychology.* New York: Norton.

Howard, G. (1991). Culture tales: A narrative approach to thinking, cross-cultural psychology, and psychotherapy. *American Psychologist, 46*(3), 187–197.

Howard, G. S., & Myers, P. R. (1990). Predicting human behavior: Comparing idiographic, nomothetic, and agentic methodologies. *Journal of Counseling Psychology, 37*(2), 227–233.

Huot, B., Makarec, K., & Persinger, M. A. (1989). Temporal lobes signs and Jungian dimensions of personality. *Perceptual & Motor Skills, 69*(3, Pt. 1), 841–842.

Ingram, D. H., & Lerner, J. A. (1992). Horney theory: An object relations theory. *American Journal of Psychoanalysis, 52*(1), 37–44.

Ishiyama, F. I., Munson, P. A., & Chabassol, D. J. (1990). Birth order and fear of success among midadolescents. *Psychological Reports, 66*(1), 17–18.

Ivie, S. D. (1986, Winter). Was Maslow an Aristotelian? *Psychological Record, 36*(1), 19–26.

Jackson, D. J. (1991). Contributions to the history of psychology: LXXXI. The friendship of Anna Freud and Dorothy Burlingham. *Psychological Reports, 68*(3, Pt. 2), 1176–1178.

Jacobson, N. S. (1987). *Psychotherapists in clinical practice: Cognitive and behavioral perspectives.* New York: Guilford Press.

Jager, B. (1989). Language and human science: The vocabularies of academic psychology and psycho-analysis. *Humanistic Psychologist, 17,*(2), 112–130.

Jankowicz, A. D. (1987, May). Whatever became of George Kelly? Applications and implications. *American Psychologist, 42*(5), 481–487.

John, O. P. (1990). The "Big Five" factor taxonomy: Dimensions of personality in the natural language and in questionnaires. In L. A. Pervin (Ed.), *Handbook of personality: Theory and research* (pp. 66–100). New York: Guilford Press.

Johnson, R. A. (1991). *Understanding the dark side of the psyche.* San Francisco, CA: Harper San Francisco.

Jones, E. (1953–1957). *The life and work of Sigmund Freud* (3 vols.). New York: Basic Books.

Josephs, R., Markus, R., & Tafarodi, R. (1992). Gender and self-esteem. *Journal of Personality and Social Psychology, 63,* 391.

Juda, D. P. (1991). Freud versus Freud: Healing the divided field of victimization. *Psychoanalysis & Psychotherapy, 9*(1), 3–17.

Jung, C. G. (1953–). *Collected works.* H. Read, M. Fordham, &

G. Adler (Eds.). Princeton: Princeton University Press. (Hereafter referred to as *CW* with year of original publication.)

Jung, C. G. (1916). Symbols of transformation. *CW* (Vol. 5).

Jung, C. G. (1933a). *Psychological types.* New York: Harcourt, Brace.

Jung, C. G. (1934). A review of complex theory. *CW* (Vol. 8).

Jung, C. G. (1936). The archetypes and the collective unconscious. *CW* (Vol. 9).

Jung, C. G. (1938). Psychology and religion. *CW* (Vol. 11).

Jung, C. G. (1939). The integration of the personality. *CW* (Vol. 17).

Jung, C. G. (1951). Two Essays on Analytical Psychology. *CW* (Vol. 7).

Jung, C. G. (1954). Psychological aspects of the mother archetype. *CW* (Vol. 9).

Jung, C. G. (1955). Mandalas. *CW* (Vol. 9).

Jung, C. G. (1961). *Memories, dreams, and reflections.* New York: Random House.

Jung, C. G. (1964). *Man and his symbols.* New York: Doubleday.

Kabat-Zinn, J. (1990). *Full catastrophe living: Using the wisdom of your body and mind to face stress, pain, and illness.* New York: Delacorte.

Kaczor, L. M., Ryckman, R. M., Thornton, B., & Kuelnel, R. H. (1991). Observer hyper-competitiveness and victim precipitation of rape. *Journal of Social Psychology, 131,* 131–134.

Kagan, J. (1972). Motives and development. *Journal of Personality and Social Psychology, 22,* 51–66.

Kagan, J. (1991). The theoretical utility of constructs for self. Special Issue: The devel-opment of self: The first three years. *Developmental Review, 11*(3), 244–250.

Kalekin-Fishman, D. (1993). The two faces of hostility: The implications of personal construct theory for understanding alienation. *International Journal of Personal Construct Psychology, 6*(1), 27–40.

Kalupahana, D. J., & Kalupahana, I. (1982). *The way of*

Siddhartha: A life of the Buddha. Boulder, CO: Shambhala.

Kant, I. (1798). *Anthropology from a pragmatic point of view.* ts. by V. L. Dowdel. Carbondale and Edwardsville, IL.: Southern University Press. A new translation published in 1978.

Kaplan, R. D. (1994, February 20). There is no "Middle East." *The New York Times Magazine,* p. 14.

Katagiri, D. (1988). *Returning to silence: Zen practice in daily life.* Boston: Shambhala.

Keirsey, D., & Bates, M. (1984). *Please understand me: Character and temperament types.* Del Mar, CA: Prometheus Nemesis.

Kelly, G. A. (1955). *The psychology of personal constructs* (2 vols.). New York: Norton.

Kelly, G. A. (1958). Man's construction of his alternatives. In G. Lindzey (Ed.), *Assessment of human motives.* New York: Rinehart & Winston.

Kelly, G. A. (1970). A brief introduction to personal construct theory. In D. Bannister (Ed.), *Perspectives in personality construct theory.* New York: Academic Press.

Kelly, R. B., & Chovan, W. (1985, February). Yet another empirical test of the relationship between self-actualization and moral judge-ment. *Psychological Reports, 56*(1), 201–202.

Kelly, W. L. (1991). *Psychology of the unconscious.* Buffalo, NY: Prometheus Books.

Kernberg, O. F. (1975). *Borderline conditions and pathological narcissism.* New York: Jason Aronson.

Kernberg, O. F. (1990). Sexual excitement and rage: Building blocks of the drives. *Sigmund Freud House Bulletin, 15*(1), 3–38.

Kernberg, O. F. (1992). *Aggression in personality disorders and perversions.* New Haven and London: Yale University Press.

Kernberg, O. F., Selzer, M. A., Koenigsberg, H. W., Carr, A. C., & Appelbaum, A. H. (1989). *Psychodynamic psychotherapy of borderline patients.* New York: Basic Books.

Kidwell, J. (1982). The neglected

birthorder: Middleborns. *Journal of Marriage and the Family, 44,* 225–235.

Kimura, D. (1979). The asymmetry of the human brain. *Scientific American, 2128,* 70–78.

Kinkead, G. (1994, April 10). Spock, Brazelton, and now Penelope Leach. *The New York Times Magazine,* p. 32.

Kiracofe, N. M., & Kiracofe, H. N. (1990). Child-perceived parental favoritism and birth order. *Individual Psychology: Journal of Adlerian Theory, Research & Practice, 46*(1), 74–81.

Kitayama, S., & Markus, H. R. (1992, May). *Construal of self as cultural frame: Implications for internationalizing psychology.* Paper presented to Symposium on Internationalization and Higher Education, Ann Arbor, MI.

Klatzky, R. L. (1980). *Human memory: Structures and processes* (2nd ed.). San Francisco: Freeman.

Klein, M. (1932). *The psychoanalysis of children.* London: Hogarth.

Klein, M. (1975). The writings of Melanie Klein, vol. 3. London: Hogarth.

Kline, P. (1972). *Fact and fantasy in Freudian theory.* London: Methuen.

Kline, P. (1987, September). The experiential study of the psychoanalytic unconscious. *Personality and Social Psychology Bulletin, 13*(3), 363–378.

Koch, E. (1991). Nature-nurture issues in Freud's writings: The complemental series. *International Review of Psycho-Analysis, 18,* 473–487.

Kohut, H. (1971). *The analysis of the self.* New York: International Universities Press.

Kohut, H. (1977). *The restoration of the self.* New York: International Universities Press.

Kohut, H. (1984). *How does analysis cure?* In A. Goldberg and P. Stepansky (Eds.), *Contributions to the psychology of the self.* Chicago, IL: University of Chicago Press.

Kolata, G. (1993, November 30). Unlocking the secrets of the genome. *The New York Times,* p. C-1.

Kolata, G. (1994, March 8). In ancient times, flowers and fennel for family planning. *The New York Times,* p. C-1.

Kosko, B. (1993). *Fuzzy thinking: The new science of fuzzy logic.* New York: Hyperion.

Kramer, P. (1993, July/August). The transformation of personality. *Psychology Today.*

Kreitler, H., & Kreitler, S. (1982). The theory of cognitive orientation. In B. Mahler (Ed.), *Experimental personality research.* New York: Springer-Verlag.

Kristiansen, C. M. (1989). Gender differences in the meaning of "health." *Social Behavior, 4*(3), 185–188.

Kruger, D. (1986, December). Phenomenology and the fundamentals of psychology. *South African Journal of Psychology, 16*(4), 109–116.

Krystal, H. (1990). An information processing view of object-relations. *Psychoanalytic Inquiry, 10*(2), 221–251.

Kuhn, T. S. (1970). *The structure of scientific revolutions.* Chicago: University of Chicago Press.

Kvale, S. (1990). Postmodern psychology: A contradictio in adjecto? Special Issue: Psychology and post-modernity. *Humanistic Psychologist, 18*(1), 35–54.

Kwee, M. G. T. Towards the clinical art and science of multimodal psychotherapy. *Current Psychological Reviews, 1,* 55–68.

Lambert, M. (1988). Beyond psychology as the science of behavior. *Counselling Psychology Quarterly, 1*(2–3), 313–315.

Lamielle, J. T. (1981). Toward an idiothetic psychology of personality. *American Psychologist, 36,* 276–289.

Lamielle, J. T., & Trierweiler, S. J. (1986, June). Interactive measurement, idiothetic inquiry, and the challenge to conventional nomotheticism. *Journal of Personality, 54*(2), 460–469.

Landfield, A. W. (1988). Personal science and the concept of validation. *International Journal of Personal Construct Psychology, 1*(3), 237–249.

Landman, J. T., & Dawes, R. M. (1982). Psychotherapy outcomes. *American Psychologist, 37*(5), 504–516.

Landrine, H. (1992). Clinical implications of cultural differences: The referential versus the indexical self. *Clinical Psychology,* (11)42.

Landrine, H., & Klonoff, E. (1992). Culture and health-related schemas: A review and proposal for interdisciplinary integration. *Health Psychology, 11,* 267–276.

Lasch, C. (1978). *The culture of narcissism.* New York: W. W. Norton.

Lawton, H. W. (1990). The field of psychohistory. *Journal of Psychohistory, 17*(4), 353–364.

Lazarsfeld, S. (1991). The courage for imperfection. Special Issue: Social interest. *Individual Psychology: Journal of Adlerian Theory, Research & Practice, 47*(1), 93–96.

Lazarus, A. A. (1956). A psychological approach to alcoholism. *South African Medical Journal, 30,* 707–710.

Lazarus, A. A. (1958). New methods in psychotherapy: A case study. *South African Medical Journal, 32,* 660–664.

Lazarus, A. A. (1966). Broad spectrum behavior therapy and the treatment of agoraphobia. *Behavior Research and Therapy, 4,* 95–97.

Lazarus, A. A. (1971). *Behavior therapy and beyond.* New York: McGraw-Hill.

Lazarus, A. A. (1973). Multimodal behavior therapy: Treating the BASIC-ID. *Journal of Nervous and Mental Disorders, 156,* 404–411.

Lazarus, A. A. (1976). *Multimodal behavior therapy.* New York: Springer.

Lazarus, A. A. (1978). *In the mind's eye: The power of imagery for personal enrichment.* New York: Rawson.

Lazarus, A. A. (1982). Personal enrichment through imagery. New York: BMA Audio Cassettes.

Lazarus, A. A. (1985). *Casebook of multimodal therapy.* New York: Guilford Press.

Leak, G. K., Gardner, L. E., & Pounds, B. (1992). A comparison of Eastern religion, Christianity, and social interest. *Individual Psychology: Journal of Adlerian Theory, Research & Practice, 48,* 53–64.

Lefcourt, H. (1976). *Locus of control: Current trends in theory and research.* Hillsdale, NJ: Erlbaum.

Lefcourt, H. (1992). Durability and impact of the locus of control construct. *Psychological Bulletin, 112*(3), 411–414.

Lefcourt, H. M., Martin, R. A., & Saleh, W. E. (1984, August). Locus of control and social support: Interactive moderators of stress. *Journal of Personality and Social Psychology, 47*(2), 378–389.

Leitschuh, G. A., & Rawlins, M. E. (1991). Personal orientation inventory correlated with physical health. *Psychological Reports, 69*(2), 68.

Lerman, H. (1986). *A mote in Freud's eye: From psychoanalysis to the psychology of women.* New York: Springer.

Lerman, H. (1992). The limits of phenomenology: A feminist critique of the humanistic personality theories. In L. S. Brown & M. Ballou (Eds.), *Personality and psychopathology.* New York and London: Guilford Press.

Lester, D. (1992). Cooperative/competitive strategies and locus of control. *Psychological Reports, 71*(2), 594.

Lester, D., Eleftheriou, L., & Peterson, C. A. (1992). Birth order and psychological health: A sex difference. *Personality & Individual Differences, 13,* 379–380.

Levin, D. M. (1991). Psychology as a discursive formation: The post-modern crisis. *Humanistic Psychologist, 19*(3), 250–276.

Levitz-Jones, E. M., & Orlofsky, J. L. (1985). Separation-individualization and intimacy capacity in college women. *Journal of Personality and Social Psychology, 49,* 156–169.

Lewis, A. (1991). Developing social feeling in the young child through his play life. *Individual Psychology: Journal of Adlerian Theory, Research & Practice, 47*(1), 72–75.

Lewis, H. B. (1988, Winter). Freudian theory and new information in modern psychology. *Psychoanalytic Psychology, 5*(1), 7–22.

Lieberman, L., Shaffer, T. G., & Reynolds, L. T. (1985, September). Scientific revolutions and birth order. *Individual Psychology: Journal of Adlerian Theory, Research and Practice, 41*(3), 328–335.

Liebmann-Smith, R. (1993, February). It's a boy: Welcome to the multiple-choice world of genetics. *The New York Times Magazine,* p. 21.

Likierman, M. (1990). "Translation in transition": Some issues surrounding the Strachey translation of Freud's works. *International Review of Psycho-Analysis, 17,* 115–120.

Loehlin, J. (1992). *Genes and environment in personality development.* New York: Sage.

Loomis, M. E. (1991). *Dancing the wheel of psychological types.* Wilmette, IL: Chiron Publications.

Loori, J. D. (1988). *Mountain record of Zen talks.* Boston: Shambhala.

Lovaas, O. T., et al. (1966). Acquisition of imitative speech in schizophrenic children. *Science, 151,* 705–707.

Lykken, D., Mcgue, M., Tellegen, A., & Bouchard, T. (1992). Emergeneses: Genetic traits that may not run in families. *American Psychologist, 47*(12), 1565.

Ma, H. K. (1989). Moral orientation and moral judgement in adolescents in Hong Kong, mainland China, and England. *Journal of Cross-Cultural Psychology, 20*(2), 152–177.

Maccoby, E. E., & Martin, J. A. (1983). Socialization in the context of the family: Parent-child interaction. In E. M. Hetherington (Ed.), *Handbook of child psychology: Socialization, personality, and social development* (Vol. 4), 1–102. New York: Wiley.

Maccoby, M. (1976). *The gamesman.* New York: Simon & Schuster.

Maccoby, M. (1981). *The leader.* New York: Simon & Schuster.

MacIntyre, A. (1958). *The unconscious: A conceptual analysis.* London: Routledge & Kegan Paul.

MacIntyre, A. (1984). *After virtue* (2nd ed.). Notre Dame, IN: University of Notre Dame Press.

MacLeod, C., & Cohen, I. (1993). Anxiety and the interpretation of ambiguity: A text comprehension study. *Journal of Abnormal Psychology, 102*(20), 238–247.

Macy, J. (1991). *Mutual causality in Buddhism and general systems theory.* Albany: State University of New York.

Magnusson, D., & Torestad, B. (1993). A holistic view of personality: A model revisited. *Annual Review of Psychology, 44,* 427–452.

Mahers, B. A. (1991). Deception rational man and other rocks on the road to a personality psychology of real people. In P. E. Meehl (Ed.), *Matters of public interest: Vol. 2, Personality and psychopathology.* Minneapolis: University of Minnesota Press.

Mahler, B. (Ed.). (1969). *Clinical psychology and personality: The selected papers of George Kelly.* New York: John Wiley.

Mahler, M. (1975). *The psychological birth of the human infant.* New York: Basic Books.

Mair, M. (1988). Psychology as storytelling. *International Journal of Personal Construct Psychology, 1*(2), 125–137.

Mansfield, V., & Spiegelman, J. M. (1991). The opposites in quantum physics and Jungian psychology: I. Theoretical foundations. *Journal of Analytical Psychology, 36*(3), 267–287.

Maqsud, M. (1992). Psychoticism, extraversion, and neuroticism among Batswann adolescents. *Journal of Social Psychology, 192*(2), 275–276.

Marcia, J. E. (1966). Development and validation of ego-identity status. *Journal of Personality and Social Psychology, 49,* 156–169.

Marcia, J. E. (1980). Identity in adolescence. In J. Adelson

(Ed.), *Handbook of adolescent psychology.* New York: Wiley.

Margolis, D. P. (1989). Freud and his mother. *Modern Psychoanalysis, 14,* 37–56.

Marin, P. (1975). The new narcissism. *Harper's,* 45–56.

Markova, I. (1992). On solos, duets, quartets, and quintets: A response to Gardner. *New Ideas in Psychology, 10*(2), 215–221.

Markstrom-Adams, C. (1992). A consideration of intervening factors in adolescent identity formation. In G. R. Adams, T. P. Gullotta, & R. Montemayor (Eds.), *Adolescent identity formation. Advances in adolescent development, 4,* 173–192. Newbury Park, CA: Sage.

Markus, H. R., & Kitayama, S. (1991). Culture and the self: Implications for cognition, emotion, and motivation. *Psychological Review, 98,* 224–253.

Masling, J. M., Rabie, L., & Blondheim, S. H. (1967). Obesity, level of aspiration, and Rorschach and TAT measures of oral dependence. *Journal of Consulting Psychology, 31,* 233–239.

Maslow, A. (1969). *Maslow and self-actualization* [Film]. Orange, CA: Psychological Films.

Maslow, A. (1970). *Motivation and personality* (2nd ed.). New York: Harper & Row.

Masson, J. M. (1983). *The assault on the truth: Freud's suppression of the seduction theory.* New York: Farrar, Straus, & Giroux.

May, R. (1953). *Man's search for himself.* New York: Norton.

May, R. (1967). *Psychology and the human dilemma.* New York: Van Nostrand Reinhold.

May, R. (1969). *Love and will.* New York: Norton.

May, R. (1972). *Power and innocence.* New York: Norton.

May, R. (1975). *The courage to create.* New York: Norton.

May, R. (1977). *The meaning of anxiety.* New York: Norton.

May, R. (1981). *Freedom and destiny.* New York: Norton.

May, R. (1983). *The discovery of being.* New York: Norton.

May, R. (1991). *The cry for myth.* New York: Norton.

May, R., Angel, E., & Ellenberger, H. F. (Eds.). (1958). *Existence: A new dimension in psychiatry and psychology.* New York: Basic Books.

McAdams, D. (1993). *The stories we live by: Personal myths and the making of the self.* New York; William Morrow.

McAdams, D. P. (1992). Unity and purpose in human lives: The emergence of identity as a life story. In R. A. Zucker, A. I. Rabin, J. Aronoff, & S. J. Frank (Eds.), *Personality structure in the life course: Essays on personology in the Murray tradition,* 323–375. New York: Springer.

McAdams, D. P., & Ochberg, R. C. (Eds.). (1988, March). Special Issue: Psychobiography and Life Narratives. *Journal of Personality, 56*(1).

McCrae, R. R., & Costa, P. T. (1989). Validation of the five-factor model of personality across instruments and observers. *Journal of Personality and Social Psychology, 52,* 81–90.

McCrae, R. R., & Costa, P. T. (1990). *Personality in adulthood.* New York: Guilford Press.

McCrae, R. R., & Costa, P. T., Jr. (1987). Validation of the five-factor model of personality across instruments and observers. *Journal of Personality and Social Psychology, 52,* 81–90.

McGuire, W. J. (1984). Search for the self. In R. A. Zucker (Ed.), *Personality and the prediction of behavior.* New York: Academic.

McKay, J., Pyke, S. W., & Goranson, R. (1984, November–December). Whatever happened to "inner-space": A failure to replicate. *International Journal of Women's Studies, 7*(5), 387–396.

Miller, C. (1991). Self-actualization and the consciousness revolution. Special Issue: Handbook of self-actualization. *Journal of Social Behavior & Personality, 6*(5), 109–126.

Miller, J. (1976). *Toward a new psychology of women.* Boston, MA: Beacon Press.

Miller, J. B. (1984). *The development of women's sense of self.* Work in Progress Series. The Stone Center for Development Studies, Wellesley College, MA.

Miller, N. E. (1944). Experimental studies of conflict. In J. McV. Hunt (Ed.), *Personality and the behavior disorders* (Vol. 1). New York: Ronald Press.

Miller, N. E. (1951). Comments on theoretical models: Illustrated by the development of a theory of conflict behavior. *Journal of Personality, 20,* 82–100.

Miller, N. E. (1959). Liberalization of basic S-R concepts: Extensions to conflict behavior, motivation, and social learning. In S. Koch (Ed.), *Psychology: A study of a science* (Vol. 2). New York: McGraw-Hill.

Miller, N. J. (1991, Fall/Winter). To study the self. *The Ten Directions,* pp. 35–37.

Miller, N. S., & Katz, J. L. (1989). The neurological legacy of psychoanalysis: Freud as a neurologist. *Comprehensive Psychiatry, 30,* 128–134.

Miller, P., Potts, R., Fung, H., & Hoogstra, L. (1990). Narrative practices and the social construction of self in childhood. *American Psychologist, 17*(2), 292–311.

Minami, M., & McCabe, A. (1991). Haiku as a discourse regulation device: A stanza analysis of Japanese children's personal narratives. *Language in Society, 20*(4), 577–599.

Mischel, W. (1968). *Personality and assessment.* New York: Wiley.

Mitchell, J. (1974). *Psychoanalysis and feminism: Freud, Reich, Laing and women.* New York: Vintage.

Mitchell, J. (1991). "Deconstructing difference: Gender, splitting and transitional space": Commentary. *Psychoanalytic Dialogues, 1*(3), 353–357.

Mogenson, G. (1990). The resurrection of the dead: A Jungian approach to the mourning process. *Journal of Analytical Psychology, 35*(3), 317–333.

Moore, J. (1992). On private events and theoretical terms. *Journal of Mind and Behavior, 13*(4), 329–345.

Mosig, Y. D. (1988). Karate-do and the actualization of enlightenment. *Udumbara: Journal of Zen Practice, 4*(2)/5(1), 45–50.

Mosig, Y. D. (1989). Wisdom and compassion: What the Buddha taught. *Theoretical and Philosophical Psychology, 9*(2), 27–36.

Mosig, Y. D. (1990). Zen meditation and the art of kobudo. *U.S.K.A. Forum, 1*(1), 2–3.

Mosig, Y. D. (1991). A guide to Zen practice. *U.S.K.A. Forum, 2*(1), 2–3.

Mruk, C. J. (1989). Phenomenological psychology and the computer revolution: Friend, foe, or opportunity? *Journal of Phenomenological Psychology, 20*(1), 20–39.

Mueller, E., & Tingley, E. (1990). The Bears' Picnic: Children's representations of themselves and their families. *New Directions for Child Development, 48,* 47–65.

Mulder, R. (1992). The biology of personality. *Australian and New Zealand Journal of Psychiatry, 26*(3), 364–376.

Murk, D., & Addleman, J. (1992). Relations among moral reasoning, locus of control, and demographic variables among college students. *Psychological Reports, 70*(2), 467–476.

Murphy, M., & Donovan, S. (1988). *The physical and psychological effects of meditation.* San Rafael, CA: Esalen Institute.

Murray, H. A. (1938). *Explorations in personality.* New York: Oxford University Press.

Mwamwenda, T. (1991). Africans and Canadians: Cross-cultural personality similarity in extraversion. *Psychological Reports, 69*(3, Pt. 2), 1213–1214.

Mwamwanda, T. (1992). Black South Africans and Canadians on neuroticism as a dimension of personality. *Psychological Reports, 7*(1), 332–334.

Myers, I. B., & McCaulley, M. H. (1985). *A guide to the development and use of the Myers-Briggs Type Indicator.* Palo Alto, CA: Consulting Psychologists Press.

Myyra, J. (1992). The great mother. In K. Bjorkqvist & P. Niemela (Eds.), *Of mice and women: Aspects of female aggression* (pp. 263–271). San Diego, CA: Academic Press.

Naidu, R. (1991). Etic principles in psychology: An evaluation of the myth in support of indigenous psychologies. *Indian Journal of Current Psychological Research, 5*(2), 93–100.

Narayan, C. (1990). Birth order and narcissism. *Psychological Reports, 67*(3, Pt. 2), 1184–1186.

Neubauer, P., & Neubauer, A. (1990). *Nature's thumbprint: The new genetics of personality.* Reading, MA: Addison-Wesley.

Neufeldt, A. (1989). Applying psychology: Some real world possibilities for scientists and practitioners. *Canadian Psychology, 30*(4), 681–691.

Nisbett, R., & Ross, L. (1980). *Human inference: Strategies and shortcomings of social judgment.* Englewood Cliffs, NJ: Prentice-Hall.

Nisbett, R., & Ross, L. (1991). *The person and the situation.* New York: McGraw-Hill.

Noble, B. P. (1993, February 21). Infant bonding and guilty mothers. *The New York Times,* p. 25.

Noel, D. C. (1991). Traveling with Jung toward an archetypal ecology. *Quadrant, 24*(1), 83–91.

Norcross, J. C. (1986). *Handbook of eclectic psychotherapy.* New York: Brunner/Mazel.

Norman, W. T. (1963). Toward an adequate taxonomy of personality attributes. *Journal of Abnormal and Social Psychology, 66,* 574–583.

Oatley, K. (1992). Not psychologists but psychology: A response to Gardner. *New Ideas in Psychology, 10*(2), 207–214.

O'Hara, M. (1992). Relational humanism: A psychology for a pluralistic world. *Humanistic Psychologist, 20*(2–3), 439–446.

O'Keefe, E. J., & Castaldo, C. (1981). Multimodal management: A systematic and holistic approach for the 80's. *Proceedings of the Marist College Symposium on Local Government Productivity.* Poughkeepsie, NY.

Okumura, S. (Ed.). (1985). *Shikantaza.* Kyoto, Japan: Kyoto Soto-Zen Center.

Orlofsky, J. L. (1976). Intimacy status: Relationship of interpersonal perception. *Journal of Youth and Adolescence, 5,* 73–88.

Ornstein, A. (1993). Little Hans. In B. Magid (Ed.), *Freud's case studies.* Hillsdale, NJ: Analytic Press.

Ornstein, R. E. (1977). *The psychology of consciousness.* New York: Harcourt Brace Jovanovich.

Packer, M. (1992). Toward a postmodern psychology of moral action and moral development. In W. Kurtines, M. Azmitia, & J. Gewirtz (Eds.), *The role of values in psychology and human development* (pp. 30–59). New York: John Wiley.

Packer, M. J. (1991). Interpreting stories, interpreting lives: Narrative and action in moral development research. In M. B. Tappan & M. J. Packer (Eds.), *Narrative and storytelling: Implications for understanding moral development. New directions for child development.* San Francisco, CA: Jossey-Bass.

Page, R. C., & Berkow, D. N. (1991). Concepts of the self: Western and Eastern perspectives. *Journal of Multicultural Counseling and Development, 19,* 83–93.

Papini, D. R., Micka, J. C., & Barnett, J. K. (1989). Perceptions of intrapsychic and extrapsychic functioning as basis of adolescent ego identity statuses. *Journal of Adolescent Research, 4*(4), 462–482.

Parkes, C., Stevenson-Hinde, J., & Marris, P. (Eds.). (1991). *Attachment across the life cycle.* London, England: Tavistock/Routledge.

Patterson, S. J., Sochting, I., & Marcia, J. E. (1992). The inner space and beyond: Women and identity. In G. R. Adams, T. P. Gullotta, & R. Montemayor (Eds.), *Adolescent identity formation: Advances in adolescent development, 4,* 9–24. Newbury Park, CA: Sage.

Paul, R. A. (1985, Summer). Freud and the seduction theory: A critical examination of Masson's *The Assault on Truth. Journal of Psychoanalytic Anthropology, 8*(3), 161–187.

Paul, R. A. (1989). Psychoanalytic anthropology. *Annual Review of Anthropology, 18,* 177–202.

Paul, R. A. (1992). Bettelheim's contribution to anthropology. *Educating the emotions: Bruno Bettelheim and psychoanalytic development.* New York: Plenum.

Paunonen, S., Jackson, D., Trzebinski, J., & Forsterling, F. (1992). Personality structure across cultures: A multimethod evaluation. *Journal of Personality and Social Psychology, 62,* 447–456.

Pelham, B. W. (1993). The idiographic nature of human personality: Examples of the idiographic self-concept. *Journal of Personality & Social Psychology, 64*(4), 665–677.

Perrez, M. (1991). The difference between everyday knowledge, ideology, and scientific knowledge. *New Ideas in Psychology, 9,* 227–231.

Pervin, L. A. (1978). *Current controversies and issues in personality.* New York: John Wiley.

Pervin, L. A. (1985). Personality: Current controversies, issues, and directions. *Annual Review of Psychology, 36,* 83–114.

Piyadassi, T. (1974). *The Buddha's ancient path.* Kandy, Sri Lanka: Buddhist Publication Society.

Place, U. (1988). What went wrong? *Counselling Psychology Quarterly, 1*(2–3), 307–309.

Plomin, R. (1989). Environment and genes. *American Psychologist, 44,* 105–111.

Plomin, R., & Bergeman, C. S. (1991). The nature of nurture: Genetic influence on "environmental" measures. *Behavioral and Brain Science, 14,* 373–385.

Plomin, R., Chipuer, H. M., & Loehlin, J. C. (1990). Behavioral genetics and personality. In L. A. Pervin (Ed.), *Handbook of personality: Theory and research* (pp. 225–243). New York: Guilford Press.

Plomin, R., & Dunn, J. (Eds.), 1986. *The study of temperament.* Hillsdale, NJ: Erlbaum.

Plomin, R., & Nesselrode, R. (1990). Behavioral genetics and personality change. *Journal of Personality, 58*(1), 191–220.

Plomin, R., & Rende, R. (1991). Human behavioral genetics. *Annual Review of Psychology, 42,* 161–190.

Plomin, R., Scheier, M., Bergeman, C., & Pedersen, N. (1992). Optimism, pessimism and mental health: A twin/adoption analysis. *Personality and Individual Differences, 13*(8), 921–930.

Potter, J., & Wetherell, M. (1992). On the literary solution: A response to Gardner. *New Ideas in Psychology, 10*(2), 223–227.

Powell, L. (1992). The cognitive underpinnings of coronary-prone behaviors. *Cognitive Therapy & Research, 16*(2), 123–142.

Power, M. (1988). Seven sins of behaviourism. *Counselling Psychology Quarterly, 1*(2–3), 279–286.

Power, M. J., & Brewin, C. R., (1991). From Freud to cognitive science: A contemporary account of the unconscious. *British Journal of Clinical Psychology, 30*(4), 289–310.

Power, T., & Chapleski, M. (1986). Childrearing and impulse control in toddlers: A naturalistic investigation. *Developmental Psychology, 22,* 271–275.

Privette, G. (1986, April). From peak performance and peak experience to failure and misery. *Journal of Social Behavior and Personality, 1*(2), 233–243.

Privette, G., & Bundrick, C. M. (1991). Peak experience, peak performance, and flow: Correspondence of personal descriptions and theoretical constructs. Special Issue: Handbook of self-actualization. *Journal of Social Behavior & Personality, 6*(5), 169–188.

Puhan, B. N., & Sahoo, F. M. (1991, October). Indigenization of psychological studies: Research agenda. *Indian Journal of Current Psychological Research, 6*(2), 101–107.

Rahula, W. (1974). *What the Buddha taught.* New York: Grove.

Rapaport, D. (1953). A critique of Dollard and Miller's *Personality and psychotherapy. American Journal of Orthopsychiatry, 23,* 204–208.

Rattner, J. (1983). *Alfred Adler.* New York: Ungar.

Reichlin, R. E., & Niederehe, G. (1980). Early memories: a comprehensive bibliography. *Journal of Individual Psychology, 36*(2), 209–218.

Reik, T. (1956). *The search within.* New York: Farrar, Straus, & Cudahy.

Retief, A. (1986, September). The need for theory development in psychology: Some care studies. *South African Journal of Psychology, 16*(3), 71–78.

Retief, A. (1989). The debate about the relevance of South African psychology: A metatheoretical imperative. *South African Journal of Psychology, 19*(2), 75–83.

Reynolds, D. K. (1976). *Morita psychotherapy.* Berkeley: University of California.

Reynolds, D. K. (1980). *The quiet therapies: Japanese pathways to personal growth.* Honolulu: University of Hawaii.

Rhymer, B. (1988). *Morita-Psychotherapie und Zen-Buddhismus.* Zurich, Switzerland: Volkerkundemuseum der Universitat Zurich.

Richards, A. D. (1990). The future of psychoanalysis: The past, present, and future of psychoanalytic theory. *Psychoanalytic Quarterly, 59,* 347–369.

Riemann, R. (1990). The bipolarity of personal constructs. *International Journal of Personal Construct Psychology, 3*(2), 149–165.

Roberts, T. K., Jackson, L. J., & Phelps, R. (1980). Lazarus' multimodal therapy model applied to an institutional setting. *Professional Psychology, 11,* 150–156.

Robinson, F. G. (1992). *Love's story told: A life of Henry A. Murray.* Cambridge, MA: Harvard University Press.

Rogers, C. R. (1951). *Client-centered therapy: Its current practice, implications, and theory.* Boston: Houghton Mifflin.

Rogers, C. R. (1959). A theory of therapy, personality, and interpersonal relationships as developed in the client-centered framework. In S. Koch (Ed.), *Psychology: A study of a science* (Vol. 3). New York: McGraw-Hill.

Rogers, C. R. (1961). *On becoming a person.* Boston: Houghton Mifflin.

Rogers, C. R. (1963). The concept of a fully functioning person. *Psychotherapy: Theory, Research, and Practice, 1*(1), 17–26.

Rogers, C. R. (1980). *A way of being.* Boston: Houghton Mifflin.

Rogers, C. R., & Roethlisberger, F. J. (1952, July–August). Barriers and gateways to communication. *Harvard Business Review,* 28–35.

Romaniello, J. (1992). Beyond archetypes: A feminist perspective on Jungian theory. In L. S. Brown & Mary Ballou (Eds.), *Personality and psychopathology: Feminist reappraisals.* New York: Guilford Press.

Rorer, L. G., & Widiger, T. A. (1983). Personality structure and assessment. *Annual Review of Psychology, 34,* 401–430.

Rosolack, T., & Hampson, S. (1991). A new typology of health behaviours for personality–health predictions: The case of locus of control. *European Journal of Personality, 5*(2), 151–168.

Rotter, J. B. (1954). *Social learning and clinical psychology.* Englewood Cliffs, NJ: Prentice-Hall.

Rotter, J. B. (1966). Generalized expectancies for internal versus external control of reinforcement. *Psychological Monographs, 80* (whole no. 609).

Rotter, J. B. (1982). *The development and application of social learning theory: Selected papers.* New York: Praeger.

Rotter, J. B., Chance, J. E., & Phares, E. J. (1972). *Applications of a social learning theory of personality.* New York: Holt, Rinehart & Winston.

Rotter, J. B., & Hochreich, D. J. (1975). *Personality.* Glenview, IL: Scott, Foresman.

Rottschaefer, W. (1991). Some philosophical implications of Bandura's social cognitive theory of human agency. *American Psychologist, 46*(2), 153–155.

Rousselle, R. (1990). On the nature of psychohistorical evidence. *Journal of Psychohistory, 17*(4), 425–434.

Rowan, C. (1993, December 8). The tide has turned on family planning. *The Star Ledger.*

Runco, M. A., & Bahleda, M. D. (1987, March). Birth-order and divergent thinking. *Journal of Genetic Psychology, 148*(1), 119–125.

Russell, G. (1992). Response of the macho male to viewing a combatant sport. *Journal of Social Behavior & Personality, 7*(4), 631–638.

Rychlak, J. (1968). *A philosophy of science for personality theory.* Boston: Houghton Mifflin.

Rychlak, J. F. (1973). *Introduction to personality and psychotherapy.* Boston: Houghton Mifflin.

Rychlak, J. F. (1981). Logical learning theory: Propositions, corollaries, and research evidence. *Journal of Personality and Social Psychology, 40*(4), 731–749.

Rychlak, J. F. (1986, December). Logical learning theory: A teleological alternative in the field of personality. *Journal of Personality, 54*(4), 734–762.

Rychlak, J. F. (1990). George Kelly and the concept of construction. *International Journal of Personal Construct Psychology, 3*(1), 7–19.

Rychman, R. M., et al. (1985, September). Physical self-efficacy and actualization. *Journal of Research in Personality, 19*(3), 288–298.

Ryckman, R. M., & Malikiosi, M. X. (1975). Relationship between locus of control and chronological age. *Psychological Reports, 36,* 655–658.

Ryckman, R. M., Hammer, M., Kaczor, L. M., & Gold, A. (1990). Construction of a hypercompetitive attitude scale. *Journal of Personality Assessment, 55,* 630–639.

Saeeduzzafar, R., & Sharma, R. (1991). A study of independence-proneness among Hindu and Muslim youths in relation to locus of control. *Journal of Personality & Clinical Studies, 7*(2), 199–202.

Sampson, E. E. (1991). The democraticization of psychology. *Theory & Psychology, 1*(3), 275–298.

Sampson, H. (1990). The problem of adaptation to reality in psychoanalytic theory. *Contemporary Psychoanalysis, 26*(4), 677–691.

Samuels, A. (1992). National psychology, national socialism, and analytical psychology: Reflections on Jung and anti-Semitism: II. *Journal of Analytical Psychology, 37*(2), 127–147.

Sarason, S. (1989). The lack of an overarching conception in psychology. *Journal of Mind and Behavior, 10*(3), 263–279.

Sarbin, T. (Ed.). (1986). *Narrative psychology: The storied nature of human conduct.* New York: Praeger.

Sarbin, T. R. (1986). The narrative as root metaphor for psychology. In T. R. Sarbin (Ed.), *Narrative psychology: The storied nature of human conduct* (pp. 3–21). New York: Praeger.

Sass, L. (1982, August 22). The borderline personality. *New York Times Magazine.*

Sayers, J. (1987). Freud revisited: On gender, moral development, and androgyny. *New Ideas in Psychology, 5*(2), 197–206.

Schibuk, M., Bond, M., & Bouffard, R. (1989). The development of defenses in childhood. *Canadian Journal of Psychiatry, 34*(6), 581–588.

Schimek, J. G. (1987). Fact and fantasy in the seduction theory: A historical review. *Journal of the American Psychoanalytic Association, 35*(4), 937–965.

Schultz, D. (1990). *Theories of personality* (4th ed.). Pacific Grove, CA: Brooks/Cole.

Schwarzer, R. (Ed.). (1992). *Self-efficacy: Thought control of action.* Washington, DC: Hemisphere.

Sears, R. R. (1943). Survey of objective studies of psychoanalytic concepts. *Social Science Research Council Bulletin, 51.*

Seitz, J. (1993, March/April). I move, therefore I am. *Psychology Today.*

Seligman, M. (1992). *Helplessness* (2nd ed.). San Francisco: CA: Freeman.

Shell, W. E., Hargrove, L., & Falbo, T. (1986, September). Birth order and achievement motivation configurations in women and men. *Individual*

Psychology: Journal of Adlerian Theory, Research and Practice, 42(3), 428–438.

Sheng-Yen (1987). *The advantages one may derive from Zen meditation.* Elmhurst, NY: Dharma Drum.

Shevrin, H. (1992). The Freudian unconscious and the cognitive unconscious: Identical or fraternal twins? In J. W. Barron, M. N. Eagle, & D. L. Wolitzly (Eds.), *Interface of psychoanalysis and psychology.* Washington, DC: American Psychological Association.

Shimano, E. T. (1984). Yamamoto Gempo Roshi. *Journal of the Zen Studies Society,* Patriarch Series: 2.

Shostrom, E. (1965). An inventory for the measurement of self-actualization. *Educational and Psychological Measurement, 24,* 207–218.

Shotter, J. (1990). Getting in touch: The metamethodology of a postmodern science of mental life. Special Issue: Psychology and postmodernity. *Humanistic Psychologist, 18*(1), 7–22.

Shur, M. (1972). *Freud: Living and dying.* New York: International Universities Press.

Shurcliff, J. (1968). Judged humor, arousal, and the relief theory. *Journal of Personality and Social Psychology, 8,* 360–363.

Silverman, L. H. (1976). Psychoanalytic theory: The reports of my death are greatly exaggerated. *American Psychologist, 31,* 621–637.

Silvern, S. B., & Williamson, P. A. (1987, October–December). The effects of video game play on young children's aggression, fantasy, and prosocial behavior. *Journal of Applied Developmental Psychology, 8*(4), 453–462.

Simon, H. A. (1979). Information processing models of cognition. *Annual Review of Psychology, 30,* 363–396.

Singer, J. (1991). Closeness and androgyny. In H. A. Wilmer (Ed.), *Closeness in personal and professional relationships.* Boston, MA: Shambhala Publications.

Singer, J. L., & Kolligian, J. (1987). Personality: Developments in the study of private experience. *American Review of Psychology, 38,* 533–574.

Singh, K. (1990). Tough-mindedness in relation to birth order, family size, and sex. *Individual Psychology: Journal of Adlerian Theory, Research & Practice, 46*(1), 82–87.

Singh, R. P. (1984, January). Experimental verification of locus of control as related to conformity behavior. *Psychological Studies, 29*(1), 64–67.

Skinner, B. (1988). Whatever happened to psychology as the science of behavior? *Counselling Psychology Quarterly, 1*(1), 111–122.

Skinner, B. (1990). To know the future. *Behavior Analyst, 13*(2), 103–106.

Skinner, B. F. (1938). *The behavior of organisms.* New York: Appleton-Century-Crofts.

Skinner, B. F. (1948). *Walden II.* New York: Macmillan.

Skinner, B. F. (1953). *Science and human behavior.* New York: Macmillan.

Skinner, B. F. (1969). *Contingencies of reinforcement: A theoretical analysis.* New York: Appleton-Century-Crofts.

Skinner, B. F. (1971). *Beyond freedom and dignity.* New York: Knopf.

Skinner, B. F. (1972, November). Will success spoil B. F. Skinner? (Interview). *Psychology Today, 6,* 66–72, 130.

Skinner, B. F. (1981). Why are we not acting to save the world? Paper prepared for the annual meeting of the American Psychological Association.

Skinner, B. F. (1984, December). Selection by consequences. *Behavior and Brain Sciences, 7*(4), 477–510.

Skinner, B. F. (1986, January). The evolution of verbal behavior. *Journal of the Experimental Analysis of Behavior, 45*(1), 115–122.

Skinner, B. F. (1987, August). Whatever happened to psychology as the science of behavior? *American Psychologist, 42*(8), 780–786.

Sliker, G. (1992). *Multiple mind: Healing the split in psyche and world.* Boston, MA: Shambhala Publications.

Sloan, T. S. (1990). Psychology for the Third World? *Journal of Social Issues, 46*(3), 1–20.

Small, F. E. (1989). The psychology of women: A psychoanalytic review. *Canadian Journal of Psychiatry, 34*(9), 872–878.

Smith, D. (1982). Trends in counseling and psychotherapy. *American Psychologist, 37*(7), 802–809.

Smith, L. (1992). On prediction and control: B. F. Skinner and the technological ideal of science. *American Psychologist, 47*(2), 216–223.

Smith, M. B. (1990). Humanistic psychology. *Journal of Humanistic Psychology, 30*(4), 6–21.

Smith, M., & Glass, J. (1977, September). Metaanalysis of psychotherapy outcome studies. *American Psychologist,* 752–760.

Smith, T. L. (1983, Fall). Skinner's environmentalism: The analogy with natural selection. *Behaviorism, 11*(2), 133–153.

Soffer, J. (1993). Jean Piaget & George Kelly: Toward a stronger constructivism. *International Journal of Personal Construct Psychology, 6*(1), 59–77.

Spieker, S. J., & Booth, C. L. (1988). Maternal antecedents of attachment quality. In J. Belsky & T. Nezworski (Eds.), *Clinical implications of attachment* (pp. 95–135). Hillsdale, NJ: Erlbaum.

Spitz, R. A. (1951). The psychogenic diseases in infancy: An attempt at the etiologic classification. *Psychoanalytic Study of the Child, 6,* 255–275.

Spranger, E. (1928). *Types of men.* New York: Stechert.

Steelman, L. C. (1985). A tale of two variables: A review of the intellectual consequences of sibship size and birth order. *Review of Educational Research, 55,* 353–386.

Steelman, L. C. (1986). The tale retold: A response to Zajonc. *Review of Educational Research, 56,* 373–377.

Stein, D. J. (1992). Psychoanalysis and cognitive science: Contrasting models of the mind. *Journal of the American Academy of Psychoanalysis, 20*(4), 543–559.

Stern, D. (1985). *The interpersonal world of the infant: A view from psychoanalysis and development psychology.* New York: Basic Books.

Sternberg, R. (1992). Too young to die—Let's not bury psychology alive: A response to Gardner. *New Ideas in Psychology, 10*(2), 195–205.

Stewart, A. E., & Barry, J. R. (1991). Origins of George Kelly's constructivism in the work of Korzybski and Moreno. *International Journal of Personal Construct Psychology, 4*(2), 121–136.

Stolorow, R. D., & Atwood, G. E. (1989). The unconscious and unconscious fantasy: An intersubjective-developmental perspective. *Psychoanalytic Inquiry, 9*(3), 364–374.

Stone, I. (1971). *Passions of the mind.* New York: Doubleday.

Strecher, V. J., DeVellis, B. M., Becker, M. H., & Rosenstock, I. M. (1986, Spring). The role of self-efficacy in achieving health behavior change. *Health Education Quarterly, 13*(1), 73–92.

Strickland, B. R. (1978). I-E expectations and health-related behaviors. *Journal of Consulting and Clinical Psychology, 46,* 1192–1211.

Strickland, B. R. (1979). I-E expectations and cardio-vascular functioning. In L. C. Perlmuller & R. A. Monty (Eds.), *Choice and perceived control.* Hillsdale, NJ: Erlbaum.

Suchecki, J. (1989). Can scientific method be perceived as mythical text? *Polish Psychological Bulletin, 20*(2), 83–93.

Sullivan, H. S. (1953). *The interpersonal theory of psychiatry.* New York: Norton.

Sullivan, H. S. (1954). *The psychiatric interview.* New York: Norton.

Swann, W. B., Stein-Seroussi, A., & Giesler, R. B. (1992). Why people self-verify. *Journal of Personality and Social Psychology.* Austin: University of Texas.

Symonds, A. (1991). Gender issues and Horney theory. *The American Journal of Psychoanalysis, 51*(3).

Tappan, M. B. (1991). Narrative, authorship, and the development of moral authority. In M. B. Tappan & M. J. Packer (Eds.), *Narrative and storytelling: Implications for understanding moral development. New directions for child development.* San Francisco, CA: Jossey-Bass.

Tart, C. T. (Ed.). (1975). *Transpersonal psychologies.* New York: Harper & Row.

Tassi, N. (1993). *Urgency addiction: How to slow down without sacrificing success.* N.Y.: NAL-Dutton.

Tausch, R. (1978). Facilitating dimensions in interpersonal relations: Verifying the theoretical assumptions of Carl Rogers. *College Student Journal, 12*(1).

Tena, C. (1993). Impact of the theories of Carl Rogers and Teihard De Chardin in Mexico. In G. M. Gonzalez, I. Alvarado, & A. S. Segrera (Eds.), *Challenges of cultural and racial diversity to counseling, 2,* (p. 105).

Thompson, S., & Spacapan, S. (1991). Perceptions of control in vulnerable populations. *Journal of Social Issues, 47*(4).

Thorne, B. (1990). Carl Rogers and the doctrine of original sin. Special Issue: Fiftieth anniversary of the person-centered approach. *Person-Centered Review, 5*(4), 394–405.

Thrasher, P. (1991). A Jungian view of postmodernism: A response to "Psychology and postmodernity." *Humanistic Psychologist, 19*(2), 242–245.

Tobacyk, J. J., & Downs, A. (1986, Oct.). Personal construct threat and irrational beliefs as cognitive predictors of increases in musical performance anxiety. *Journal of Personality and Social Psychology, 51*(4), 779–782.

Tolpin, M. (1993). The unmirrored self, compensatory structure, and cure. In B. Magid (Ed.). *Self-Psychological Perspectives.* Hillsdale, NJ: Analytic Press.

Tompkins, S. S. (1992). Script theory. In R. A. Zucker, A. I. Rabin, J. Aronoff, & S. J. Frank (Eds.), *Personality structure in the life course: Essays on personology in the Murray tradition.* New York: Springer.

Toronto, E. L. (1991). The feminine unconscious and psychoanalytic theory. *Psychoanalytic Psychology, 8*(4), 415–438.

Torrey, E. F. (1992). *Freudian fraud: The malignant effect of Freud's theory on American thought and culture.* New York: HarperCollins.

Treurniet, N. (1989). On having and giving value. *Sigmund Freud House Bulletin, 13*(1), 1–14.

Tribich, D., & Messer, S. (1974). Psychoanalytic character type and states of authority as determiners of suggestibility. *Journal of Consulting and Clinical Psychology, 42,* 842–848.

Ugwu-Oju, D. (1993, November 14). Hers: Pursuit of happiness. *The New York Times Magazine.*

Vaillant, G. E. (1992). *Ego mechanisms of defense: A guide for clinicians and researchers.* Washington, DC: American Psychiatric Press.

Vaillant, G. E. (1992). The historical origins and future potential of Sigmund Freud's concept of the mechanisms of defense. *International Review of Psycho-Analysis, 19*(1), 35–50.

Valentine, E. (1988). Teleological explanations and their relation to causal explanations in psychology. *Philosophical Psychology, 1*(1), 61–68.

Van de Water, D. A., & McAdams, D. P. (1989). Generativity and Erikson's "Belief in the species." *Journal of Research in Personality, 23,* 435–449.

Van den Daele, L. (1987, Summer). Research in Horney's psychoanalytic theory. *American Journal of Psychoanalysis, 47*(2), 99–104.

Van Eenwyk, J. R. (1991). Archetypes: The strange attractors of the psyche. *Journal of Analytical Psychology, 36,* 1–25.

van Krogten, I. (1992). *Proustian love.* B. V. Amsterdam/Lisse: Swets & Zeitlinger.

Visher, S. (1986, May). The relationship of locus of control and contraception use in the adolescent population. *Journal of Adolescent Health Care, 7*(3), 183–186.

Vitz, P. (1990). The use of stories in moral development: New psychological reasons for an old education method. *American Psychologist, 45*(6), 709–720.

Wakefield, J. C. (1992). Freud and cognitive psychology: The conceptual interface. In J. W. Barron, M. N. Eagle, & D. L. Wolitzly (Eds.), *Interface of psychoanalysis and psychology.* Washington, DC: American Psychological Association.

Walker, A. & Parmar, P. (1993). *Warrior marks: Female genital mutilation and the sexual blinding of women.* New York: Harcourt Brace.

Walker, B. M. (1990). Construing George Kelly's construing of the person-in-relation. *International Journal of Personal Construct Psychology, 3*(1), 41–50.

Walker, B. M. (1992). Values and Kelly's theory: Becoming a good scientist. Special Issue: Papers from the Eighth International Congress on Personal Construct Psychology. *International Journal of Personal Construct Psychology, 5*(3), 259–269.

Walker, K., & Bates, R. (1992). Health locus of control and self-efficacy beliefs in a healthy elderly sample. *American Journal of Health Promotion, 6*(4), 302–309.

Wallach, M. A., & Wallach, L. (1983). *Psychology: Sanction for selfishness.* San Francisco, CA: Freeman.

Wallwork, E. (1991). *Psychoanalysis and ethics.* New Haven, CT: Yale University Press.

Warner, S. L. (1991). Freud and the mighty warrior. *Journal of the American Academy of Psychoanalysis, 19*(2), 282–293.

Warren, W. G. (1990). Is personal construct psychology a cognitive psychology? *International Journal of Personal Construct Psychology, 3*(4), 393–414.

Warren, W. G. (1992). Personal construct theory and mental health. Special Issue: Papers from the Eighth International Congress of Personal Construct Psychology. *International Journal of Personal Construct Psychology, 5*(3), 223–237.

Waterman, A. S. (1982). Identity development from adolescence to adulthood: An extension of theory and a review of research. *Developmental Psychology, 18,* 341–358.

Watson, P. J., Little, T., & Biderman, M. D. (1992). Narcissism and parenting styles. *Psychoanalytic Psychology, 9*(2), 231–244.

Watzlawick, P., Weakland, J., & Fisch, R. (1974). *Change: Principles of problem formation and problem resolution.* New York: Norton.

Weingberg, L. (1991). Infant development and the sense of self: Stern vs. Mahler. *Clinical Social Work Journal, 19*(1), 9–22.

Weinraub, W. (1993, December 28). Despite Clinton, Hollywood is still trading in violence. *The New York Times,* A1.

Weiss-Rosmarin, T. (1990). Adler's psychology and the Jewish tradition. *Individual Psychology: Journal of Adlerian Theory, Research & Practice, 46,* 108–118.

Wertsch, J. V. (1990). A meeting of paradigms: Vygotsky and psychoanalysis. *Contemporary Psychoanalysis, 26*(1), 53–73.

Wessler, R. L. (1986). Conceptualizing cognitions in the cognitive-behavioral therapies. In W. Dryden & W. Golden (Eds.), *Cognitive-behavioral approaches to psychotherapy* (pp. 1–30). London: Harper & Row.

West, S. G. (Ed.). (1983, September). Personality and prediction: Nomothetic and idiographic approaches. *Journal of Personality, Special Issue, 51*(3).

West, S. G. (Ed.). (1986, March). Methodological developments in personality research. *Journal of Personality, Special Issue, 54*(1).

Westen, D. (1992). The cognitive self and the psychoanalytic self: Can we put our selves together? *Psychological Inquiry, 3*(1), 1–13.

Whitbourne, S. K., Zuschlag, M. K., Elliot, L. B., & Waterman, A. S. (1992). Psychosocial development in adulthood: A 22-year sequential study. *Journal of Personality & Social Psychology, 63*(2), 260–271.

White, R. W. (1992). Exploring personality the long way: The study of lives. In R. A. Zucker, A. I. Rabin, J. Aronoff, & S. J. Frank (Eds.), *Personality structure in the life course: Essays on personology in the Murray tradition* (pp. 3–21). New York: Springer.

Widiger, T. A. (1993). The DSM-III-R categorical personality disorder diagnoses: A critique and an alternative. *Psychological Inquiry,* in press.

Williams, D. E., & Page, M. M. (1989). A multi-dimensional measure of Maslow's hierarchy of needs. *Journal of Research in Personality, 23,* 192–213.

Wilson, E., & Kellert, S. (Eds.), (1993). *The biophilia hypothesis.* Washington, DC: Island Press.

Wolberg, A. (1989). Pilgrim's progress through the psychoanalytic maze. *Psychoanalysis & Psychotherapy, 7*(1), 18–26.

Woodall, K., & Matthews, K. (1993). Changes in and stability of hostile characteristics: Results from a 4-year longitudinal study of children. *Journal of Personality and Social Psychology, 64,* 491–499.

Woodward, W. (1992). On opening the psychology of personality to philosophy and literature in our time: A response to Gardner. *New Ideas in Psychology, 10*(2), 191–194.

Woody, R. H. (1971). *Psychobehavioral counseling and therapy: Integrating behavioral and insight techniques.* New York: Appleton-Century Crofts.

Xu, J. A. (1985). A key concept in Maslow's theory of need. *Acta Psychologica Sinica, 17*(1), 31–37.

Yang, K., & Bond, M. (1990). Exploring implicit personality theories with indigenous or imported constructs: The Chinese case. *Journal of Personality and Social Psychology, 58,* 1087–1095.

Young, T. W., & Shorr, D. N. (1986, November). Factors affecting locus of control in school children. *Genetic, Social and General Psychology Monographs, 112*(4), 405–417.

Young-Eisendrath, P., & Hall, J. A. (1991). *Jung's self psychology: A constructivist perspective.* New York: Guilford Press.

Zajonc, R. B. (1986). Family factors and intellectual test performance: A reply to Steelman. *Review of* *Educational Research, 56,* 365–371.

Zajonc, R. B., & Markus, G. B. (1975). Birth order and intellectual development. *Psychological Review, 82,* 74–88.

Zeig, J. K. (Ed). (1982). *Eriksonian approaches to hypnosis and psychotherapy.* New York: Brunner/Mazel.

Zlate, M. (1989). The place and role of the self in the pattern of personality: Controversial questions. *Revue Roumaine des Sciences Sociales—Serie de Psychologie, 33*(1), 3–15.

Zohar, D., & Marshall, I. (1990). *The quantum self: Human nature and consciousness defined by the new physics.* New York: William Morrow.

NAME INDEX

SUBJECT INDEX